Molecular Biology of
DNA Repair

Molecular Biology of DNA Repair

Proceedings of the
joint meeting of the DNA Repair Information Network
and the British Society for Photobiology
Manchester, April 1986

Organized and edited by

Andrew Collins

(Department of Biochemistry, University of Aberdeen)

Robert T. Johnson

(Department of Zoology, University of Cambridge)

and

John M. Boyle

(Paterson Laboratories, Manchester)

SUPPLEMENT 6   1987
JOURNAL OF CELL SCIENCE
Published by THE COMPANY OF BIOLOGISTS LIMITED, Cambridge

Typeset, Printed and Published by
THE COMPANY OF BIOLOGISTS LIMITED
Department of Zoology, University of Cambridge, Downing Street,
Cambridge CB2 3EJ

© The Company of Biologists Limited 1987

ISBN: 0 948601 06 X

JOURNAL OF CELL SCIENCE SUPPLEMENTS

All supplements are available free to subscribers to *Journal of Cell Science* or may be purchased separately from The Biochemical Society Book Depot, PO Box 32, Commerce Way, Colchester CO2 8HP, UK

PREFACE

DNA repair is a subject which avoids being pigeon-holed. Researchers may call themselves radiobiologists, biochemists, cell biologists, geneticists, photobiologists, chemists . . . fortunately, there is no such term as 'DNA repairologist'. Recently, the topic has become even more interdisciplinary with an influx of molecular biologists, and recombinant DNA technology and the molecular genetic approach are the order of the day. In many areas of biology, the application of these new techniques holds great promise. But perhaps this is especially so for DNA repair, since conventional biochemistry is hampered by the fact that repair, though vital, usually goes unnoticed among more celebrated activities of the cell; it is hard to get sufficient quantities of repair enzymes for normal enzymology. Devious strategies have been adopted: interfering with repair pathways using metabolic inhibitors is one, producing mutants defective in specific steps of repair is another. Currently, the most desirable route is seen to be through DNA transfection and the cloning of repair genes. Much progress has been made in prokaryotic systems towards the reconstitution of fully functional DNA repair complexes using proteins made *in vitro* from cloned genes. In eukaryotes, such investigations are at a more preliminary stage; one early impression is that there is a surprising and encouraging overlap at the molecular level between prokaryotic and eukaryotic systems. In addition, prokaryotic organisms introduced into eukaryotic cells (e.g. as plasmid shuttle vectors) promise to be of great value as probes for DNA repair and mutagenesis.

An international symposium was held in Manchester in the spring of 1986 with the theme 'The Molecular Biology of DNA Repair'. This book is based on the main presentations at the symposium. The title does not imply a definitive account, but more of a prospectus for the next few years. We are aware that we have stretched the term 'molecular biology' to cover investigations whose claim to be included rests only on the fact that DNA is a biological molecule. We do not apologize for this; it is important to be conscious all the time of the relations between phenomena occurring at molecular and cellular levels (and, indeed, at the level of whole organisms).

If there are no DNA repairologists there is at least a DNA Repair Information Network, which, together with the British Photobiology Society, organized the Manchester symposium. We could not have achieved such a successful meeting without the support of the following sponsors, to whom we express our sincere thanks: The Company of Biologists Limited; Cancer Research Campaign; International Agency for Research on Cancer; Beckman; Wellcome Trust; British Petroleum Company; Smith Kline and French Research; Amersham International; Gibco; Anachem; Packard; Scientific and Medical Products; Leec.

We also thank the contributors to this volume for their prompt delivery of manuscripts of uniformly high quality, which has enabled us to produce what we believe is an up-to-date review of the molecular biology of DNA repair.

Andrew Collins
Bob Johnson
John Boyle

MOLECULAR BIOLOGY OF DNA REPAIR

CONTENTS

Continued overleaf

Contents

MUTAGENESIS AS A CONSEQUENCE OF DNA DAMAGE AND REPAIR

J. Cell Sci. Suppl. 6, 1–23 (1987)
Printed in Great Britain © The Company of Biologists Limited 1987

THE MOLECULAR BIOLOGY OF NUCLEOTIDE EXCISION REPAIR OF DNA: RECENT PROGRESS

ERROL C. FRIEDBERG

Department of Pathology, Stanford University School of Medicine, Stanford, CA 94305, USA

SUMMARY

Recent years have witnessed significant progress towards understanding the molecular mechanism of nucleotide excision repair in living cells. Biochemical studies in *Escherichia coli*, and genetic and molecular studies in lower and higher eukaryotes have revealed an unexpected complexity suggesting interesting protein–protein and protein–DNA interactions. This review considers selected aspects of nucleotide excision repair in *E. coli*, *Saccharomyces cerevisiae* and mammalian cells, with a particular emphasis on new observations and on models that may provide explanations for the complexity evident from genetic and biochemical studies.

INTRODUCTION

The concept of excision repair of DNA evolved during the mid-1960s (see Friedberg, 1985, for a review) following the demonstration that when *Escherichia coli* cells are ultraviolet (u.v.)-irradiated and then incubated, pyrimidine dimers are lost from acid-precipitable (high molecular weight) DNA and can be recovered as acid-soluble material. The additional demonstration of repair synthesis of DNA at about the same time led to a general model for a multistep process in *E. coli* consisting of the following sequential events:

(1) DNA incision 5′ to sites of base damage

(2) Concomitant 5′→3′ excision-resynthesis catalysed by DNA polymerase I

(3) DNA ligation.

Mutants of *E. coli* defective in the excision of pyrimidine dimers are also abnormally sensitive to killing by a variety of chemicals known to damage DNA. This suggested that the model presented above was distinguished by its generality, i.e. that living cells probably excise all forms of base damage by a single molecular mechanism. Progress during the past 15 years has proven this concept to be simplistic. The discovery by Tomas Lindahl and his colleagues in the early 1970s of a repair-specific class of enzymes called DNA glycosylases (see Friedberg, 1985, for a review), was of fundamental importance, for it provided definitive evidence for a distinct and novel mechanism for the excision of damaged and inappropriate (e.g. uracil) bases, involving their excision as free bases. Hence, the phrase *base excision repair* was coined to distinguish this mode of excision repair of DNA from so-called *nucleotide excision repair* in which damaged bases are excised as part of a nucleotide structure. Since then, at least one other distinct mode of excision repair has been discovered. In *E. coli* the process of post-replicative mismatch correction involves the recognition of hemimethylated GATC sequences and of mismatched bases in newly replicated DNA (see Friedberg, 1985, for a review). A cell-free system for mismatch correction has been established (Lu *et al.* 1983) and although the detailed mechanism of this process has not been elucidated, it is evident that it requires a number of gene products not utilized in either base excision or nucleotide excision repair. Finally, in at least two biological systems, elements of both base and nucleotide excision repair are represented in a 'hybrid' biochemical mechanism specific for the removal of pyrimidine dimers from DNA. Thus, in phage T4-infected *E. coli* and in *Microccus luteus*, pyrimidine dimers are excised as part of an oligonucleotide, as is true of nucleotide excision repair (see Friedberg, 1985, for a review). However, the mechanism of DNA incision involves a specific DNA glycosylase and in this respect resembles other examples of base excision repair. It is of ironic historical interest that for many years the enzyme in T4-infected *E. coli* and *M. luteus* served as a general model for the study of nucleotide excision repair before it was appreciated that the mechanism of excision repair involving this enzyme is specific for pyrimidine dimers and is apparently limited to these two organisms.

It is now apparent that the general term *excision repair of DNA* is an oversimplification that embraces multiple diverse biochemical mechanisms. Living cells utilize discrete processes of base excision repair, nucleotide excision repair or mismatch correction, depending on the type of damage present in DNA, and manifest other cellular responses to DNA damage depending on the proximity of damaged bases to sites of active DNA replication. Both excision repair and other cellular responses to DNA damage have been subjects of a number of recent reviews (see Friedberg, 1985, and references therein; Walker, 1985; Walker *et al.* 1985; Cleaver, 1986; Sedgwick, 1986; Weiss & Grossman, 1986). This review deals exclusively with the process of nucleotide excision repair, with particular emphasis on recent advances in *E. coli*, the yeast *Saccharomyces cerevisiae*, and mammalian cells.

ESCHERICHIA COLI: A GENERAL MODEL FOR NUCLEOTIDE EXCISION REPAIR?

The demonstration that mutants in the *uvr*A, *uvr*B or *uvr*C genes of *E. coli* are defective in the excision of pyrimidine dimers during post-ultraviolet incubation led to a search for the proteins encoded by these genes. These were first partially purified by Seeberg and his colleagues using an assay in which ATP-dependent incision of ultraviolet (u.v.)-irradiated DNA was complemented in extracts of a particular *uvr* mutant by fractions from *uvr*$^+$ cells or from different *uvr* mutants (Seeberg, 1978, 1981; Seeberg *et al.* 1978). This was an arduous task since constitutive untransformed *E. coli* cells contain very small amounts of UvrA, UvrB and UvrC proteins (Sancar *et al.* 1981*a*,*b*; Yoakum & Grossman, 1981). Subsequent isolation of the relevant *uvr* genes by molecular cloning facilitated studies on the genes themselves, as well as their overexpression to yield large amounts of proteins for biochemical studies.

The uvr *genes of* E. coli

Regulation. While the isolation and overexpression of the *uvrA*, *uvrB*, *uvrC* and *uvrD* genes from recombinant plasmids have greatly facilitated inroads into the biochemical mechanism of nucleotide excision repair in *E. coli* (see below), much remains to be learned about the expression of the chromosomal genes, particularly those that are controlled by other regulatory loci. The expression of the *uvrA* and *uvrB* genes of *E. coli* is enhanced fivefold following exposure of cells to DNA-damaging agents, and there is good evidence that the induced expression of these genes is part of the general SOS phenomenon regulated by the *recA/lexA* system (see Friedberg, 1985, for a review). The *uvrA* gene contains a single typical prokaryotic promoter with a Pribnow box and a '-35 sequence' appropriately located with respect to a single transcriptional start-site. This promoter is overlapped at its 5' end by a consensus SOS box and binding of LexA protein to this operator region has been demonstrated *in vitro* (Sancar *et al.* 1982*b*).

Regulation of the *uvrB* gene is less straightforward. Sequence analysis has identified three distinct promoter regions and three transcriptional start-sites have been mapped by studies *in vitro* (Sancar *et al.* 1982*a*). Two of these promoters (P1 and P2) are located relatively close to each other and to the presumed translation start-site; the third (P3) is located about 300 base-pairs (bp) upstream from them. A typical SOS box overlaps P2 (the more distal of the two closely spaced promoters), and in the presence of LexA protein *in vitro* transcription from this promoter is blocked while that from the more proximal promoter P1 is unaffected (Sancar *et al.* 1982*a*). This suggests that constitutive expression of *uvrB* is from P1, and that induced expression is from P2 and is regulated by the *recA/lexA* system. On the other hand, studies in living cells show that both promoters are active in the constitutive and induced states, but P1 is the stronger of the two (van den Berg *et al.* 1983). Thus, it is possible that all transcription of *uvrB* is controlled by P1 and that LexA protein regulates expression from P1 by binding to P2. The role, if any, of the most upstream promoter P3 is unknown; however, there are indications that this promoter may be regulated by *E. coli* DnaA protein (see below).

The situation with respect to the *uvrC* gene is even more complicated. This gene was not among the many *E. coli din* (*damage in*ducible) genes isolated by the operon fusion strategy that used the Mud (Ap^R *lac*) system (Kenyon & Walker, 1980). Using *uvrC-galK* fusion plasmids, *recA/lexA*-dependent induction of galactokinase has been demonstrated (van Sluis *et al.* 1983). However, in contrast to other SOS genes, induction of *uvrC* under these experimental conditions is very slow and is not effected by treatment of cells with nalidixic acid, characteristically a strong inducer of SOS genes. The *uvrC* gene has been cloned and studied in a number of laboratories; however, the promoter(s) for constitutive expression has not been unambiguously identified. Current evidence suggests the presence of multiple promoters of different strength, and of transcriptional regulation by attenuation (Forster & Strike, 1985). In a recent study two different *uvrC* fusions to the *E. coli cat* gene (one of which contains as much as 1200 bp of *uvrC* upstream sequence) were tested for inducible expression of chloramphenicol acetyl-transferase (CAT). No enhanced expression of CAT was observed in response to treatment with either u.v. radiation or mitomycin C, and the levels of CAT expression were unaffected by mutations in *recA* or *lexA* known to prevent induction or to result in constitutive induction of SOS genes (Forster & Strike, 1985). Thus, it would appear that the *uvrC* gene is not induced by DNA-damaging agents.

There is compelling evidence from cellular-biological studies for involvement of the *uvrD* gene in nucleotide excision repair in *E. coli*. Unlike *uvrA*, *uvrB* and *uvrC* strains in *uvrD* mutants, excision of pyrimidine dimers is not completely abolished. However, such mutants show a reduced rate and extent of loss of thymine-containing pyrimidine dimers during post-irradiation incubation (see Friedberg, 1985, for a review). In addition, the extent (but not the initial rate) of ATP-dependent DNA *incision* in semipermeabilized u.v.-irradiated cells is reduced in *uvrD* mutants relative to uvr^+ cells (Ben-Ishai & Sharon, 1981). There is also good evidence that the *uvrD* gene is inducible and under SOS regulation. *uvrD*::Mud (Ap^R *lac*) insertion mutants have been identified and yield enhanced β-galactosidase activity following treatments known to induce SOS genes. Furthermore, the genetics of this response is consistent with *recA/lexA* regulation (Maples & Kushner, 1982; Siegel, 1983; Kumura & Sekiguchi, 1984). In addition, sequence analysis of the *uvrD* gene revealed a typical LexA binding box, which functions as an operator for purified LexA protein *in vitro* and is situated downstream from a single promoter (Easton & Kushner, 1983). In the absence of LexA protein a significant fraction of the mRNA transcribed from this promoter *in vitro* terminates after about 60 nucleotides at a sequence that resembles a rho-independent terminator (Easton & Kushner, 1983). Hence, like the *uvrC* gene, expression of *uvrD* may be subject to regulation by transcriptional attenuation.

Structural features. The *uvr* and *polA* genes have been sequenced (Joyce *et al.* 1982; Finch & Emmerson, 1984; Sancar *et al.* 1984; Arikan *et al.* 1986; Backendorf *et al.* 1986; Husain *et al.* 1986) and examination of the predicted amino acid sequences of the proteins has revealed a number of interesting homologies. For example, a number of nucleotide binding proteins have regions of amino acid sequence homology that include the tripeptide GKS(T) (single-letter code for amino acids) (Walker *et al.* 1982). (The third position of the tripeptide is sometimes G, which has a hydropathic index very similar to that of S and T (Kyte & Doolittle, 1982).) Some of the proteins that contain the GKS (T or G) sequence are also purine nucleoside triphosphatases and include the *E. coli* RecA, UvrD (Finch & Emmerson, 1984) and UvrA (Husain *et al.* 1986) proteins. A related sequence is also present in UvrB protein (Arikan *et al.* 1986; Backendorf *et al.* 1986) as well as in UvrC and DNA polymerase I (Fig. 1). Since the latter protein binds deoxynucleoside triphosphates it can be considered a nucleotide binding protein. Neither triphosphatase nor nucleotide binding activities have been associated with UvrB or UvrC protein; however, a mixture of UvrA and UvrB protein has more ATPase activity than UvrA protein alone (see below), suggesting the possible activation of such an activity in UvrB protein. The sequence of UvrA protein shows two GKS (T or G)

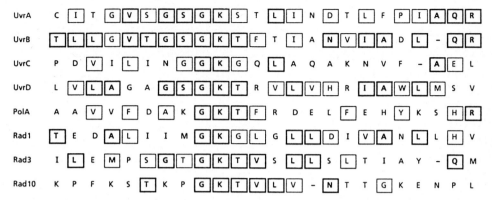

Fig. 1. Sequence homology between the predicted amino acid sequences of regions of *E. coli* and yeast nucleotide excision repair genes. The single-letter amino acid code is used throughout. Boxes denote identical amino acids or amino acids with similar hydropathic values.

regions and examination of their predicted secondary structure shows a striking similarity between them and to other known ATPases, suggesting the presence of two nucleotide binding sites in the protein (Husain *et al.* 1986).

A comparison of the amino acid sequences of the predicted UvrB and UvrC polypeptides shows two other regions of homology (Backendorf *et al.* 1986; Husain *et al.* 1986) and it is perhaps relevant in this regard that antisera to UvrB and to UvrC proteins crossreact with both proteins (Backendorf *et al.* 1986). A region near the amino-terminal end of UvrB protein also shows homology with a region of the predicted amino acid sequence of the *alkA* gene product, a DNA glycosylase called 3-methyladenine-DNA glycosylase II.

Are uvr *genes involved in other DNA transactions?*

The study of the *E. coli uvr* genes has perhaps led to the implicit (if not explicit) assumption that the process of nucleotide excision repair defines their exclusive role in DNA metabolism. This section examines evidence that some of these genes may be involved in other DNA transactions. I particularly wish to address the possibility that in *E. coli* DNA repair may be linked to processes such as DNA replication, through one or more gene products common to both events. If such linked functions do indeed exist for particular *uvr* genes, they could have interesting and important regulatory potential. Thus, for example, the sequestration of Uvr proteins by an excision repair complex could limit the amount of these proteins available for a replication complex, hence providing a mechanism for regulating the initiation and/or progression of semi-conservative DNA synthesis during nucleotide excision repair.

Several provocative examples of the possible involvement of *uvr* genes in DNA replication have been documented. Early studies demonstrated that *uvrD* mutants that are also defective in the *polA* gene are inviable (Horiuchi & Nagata, 1973; Siegel, 1973; Smirnov *et al.* 1973), implicating the *uvrD* gene in DNA replication. More recently, it has been shown that the *uvrD* gene encodes an ATP-dependent DNA helicase called DNA helicase II (Arthur *et al.* 1982; Maples & Kushner, 1982; Kumura & Sekiguchi, 1984). Antiserum raised against purified DNA helicase II inhibits the replication of phage λ or ColE1 DNA in subcellular systems (Klinkert *et al.* 1980); and the addition of DNA helicase II to a cell-free system stimulates the replication of artificially forked λ DNA (Kuhn & Abdel-Monem, 1982). Mutants defective in just the *uvrD* gene are viable; hence DNA helicase II is apparently not absolutely required for DNA replication. Nonetheless, the results just summarized are consistent with an involvement of UvrD protein in normal DNA replication in *E. coli.*

The double mutant *uvrB polA* is also inviable; an observation that dates back to the early 1970s (Shizuya & Dykhuizen, 1972; Morimyo & Shimazu, 1976). More recently, evidence has emerged for the possible regulation of the *uvrB* gene by *E. coli* DnaA protein. DnaA protein is a polypeptide of $M_r \approx 48 \times 10^3$ required for the initiation of bidirectional replication at *oriC*, the *E. coli* origin of replication (Kornberg, 1980). Studies on the specific cooperative binding of DnaA protein to oriC have defined a minimal binding sequence with the consensus 5′ TTAT^C_ACA^C_AA 3′ (Fuller *et al.* 1984). This sequence is highly conserved in the chromosomal replication origin of other prokaryotes, in the replication origin of a number of plasmids, and in the upstream regulatory region of a number of *E. coli* genes, including the *dnaA* gene itself, *pyrB1*, *argF*, *polA*, *dam* and *uvrB* (Fuller *et al.* 1984). In the case of the *dnaA* gene, DnaA protein appears to act as a negative auto-regulator of expression. Thus, in cells transformed with *dnaA-lacZ* fusion plasmids, the expression of β-galactosidase correlates inversely with levels of DnaA protein (Fuller *et al.* 1984).

In the *uvrB* gene two putative DnaA protein binding sites are located in inverted orientation in a region with potential stem–loop structure that includes part of P3, the most 5′ of the three functional promoters identified in this gene (see above) (van den Berg *et al.* 1985). The possible interaction of DnaA protein with the *uvrB* gene represents another potential mechanism for coupling *uvrB* expression to DNA replication. Fuller *et al.* (1984) have suggested that the replication of *oriC* during initiation of DNA synthesis could generate sequences that may act as a sink for high-affinity binding of DnaA protein, resulting in the derepression of genes negatively regulated by this protein. The *uvrB* gene (and perhaps other genes that are regulated by *dnaA*) might encode products that play a role in replication initiation. Thus, in the case of UvrB protein, we have a possible example of a gene product involved in both nucleotide excision repair and DNA replication, the enhanced expression of which is independently regulated for both functions by using distinct operator/ promoter sites. In cells containing damaged DNA the amount of available UvrB protein may limit replication initiation during excision repair or *vice versa*, depending on the relative affinity of UvrB protein for the excision repair and replication complexes.

Finally, it is interesting to consider another gene involved in DNA replication in *E. coli*, mutations in which can result in an abnormal excision-repair phenotype. The *dnaB* gene of *E. coli* encodes a protein of molecular weight $\approx 50 \times 10^3$ essential for replication of the *E. coli* chromosome (Kornberg, 1980). A strain designated CM1031 carries a temperature-sensitive mutation in the *dnaB* gene (Bridges, 1975). At permissive temperatures, this strain has normal resistance to u.v. radiation but is deficient in host-cell reactivation of bacteriophage λ. Bridges *et al.* (1976) observed that this mutant loses sites sensitive to a dimer-specific enzyme probe at a reduced rate relative to the parental strain, suggesting a partial defect in excision repair. The possible involvement of DnaB protein in nucleotide excision repair represents a third potential component of the *E. coli* replication complex, which may be limited in cells exposed to DNA damage (Fig. 2).

The UvrA, UvrB and UvrC proteins

Isolation of the *uvrA*, *uvrB* and *uvrC* genes and their overexpression in *E. coli* has greatly facilitated the purification of the proteins they encode and their use in biochemical studies. The measured molecular weights of the UvrA, UvrB and UvrC proteins are $\approx 114 \times 10^3$, $\approx 84 \times 10^3$ and $\approx 67 \times 10^3$, respectively (Thomas *et al.* 1985), and agree well with values calculated from the coding regions of the cloned genes (103 749, 76 118 and 66 038) (Sancar *et al.* 1984; A. Sancar, personal communication).

Purified UvrA protein is a DNA-independent ATPase (Seeberg & Steinum, 1982). Neither of the other two Uvr proteins has demonstrable catalytic activity of any kind. However, as indicated above, a mixture of UvrA and UvrB proteins shows more ATPase activity than UvrA protein alone (Thomas *et al.* 1985). It is not known

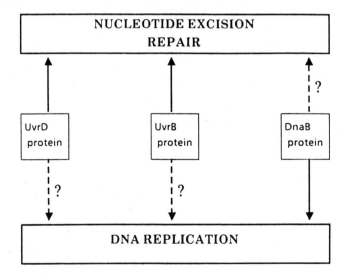

Fig. 2. The UvrD and UvrB proteins are known to be involved in nucleotide excision repair in *E. coli*, and may also be involved in DNA replication. DnaB protein is required for DNA replication, and may also be involved in nucleotide excision repair.

whether this reflects stimulation of the activity associated with UvrA protein or the unmasking of an activity in the UvrB protein that is dependent on binding to UvrA protein. None of the Uvr proteins in isolation or in any pairwise combinations catalyses the incision of damaged DNA. But when u.v.-irradiated DNA is incubated with a mixture of all three Uvr proteins incision is observed and is strictly dependent on the presence of Mg^{2+} and ATP (Seeberg, 1978; Sancar & Rupp, 1983; Yeung *et al.* 1983). On the basis of the long-standing preconception of the molecular mechanism of nucleotide excision repair in *E. coli* discussed in the Introduction, it was anticipated that this reaction would generate incisions exclusively 5' to sites of base damage, thus setting the stage *in vivo* for coordinated excision/resynthesis mediated by DNA polymerase I. Surprisingly, incision occurs on both sides of each lesion of a given DNA strand (Sancar & Rupp, 1983; Yeung *et al.* 1983). With respect to cyclobutyl pyrimidine dimers as well as so-called (6-4) or Py-C products (the two major photoproducts in DNA) the UvrABC catalytic activity hydrolyses the eighth phosphodiester bond 5' and the fourth or fifth phosphodiester bond 3' to the lesions (Sancar & Rupp, 1983). A fundamentally similar mode of incision *in vitro* has been observed with DNA containing monoadduct base damage caused by photo-activated psoralen or N-acetoxy-acetylaminofluorene (Sancar *et al.* 1985). The only difference is that with these substrates incisions 3' to sites of base damage are exclusively at the fifth phosphodiester bond. The pattern of DNA incision is insensitive to the ratio of psoralen monoadducts and psoralen crosslinks and hence it has been suggested that DNA containing interstrand crosslinks is cut in the same way as DNA containing monoadduct or dipyrimidine base damage (Sancar *et al.* 1985). Incision of DNA by the purified UvrABC activity has been observed with a variety of other chemicals that produce bulky base adducts in DNA (Fuchs & Seeberg, 1984; Kacinski & Rupp, 1984; Husain *et al.* 1985) and, while not specifically demonstrated, it is a reasonable assumption that in all cases a bilateral incision mechanism operates.

The demonstration *in vitro* of bilateral DNA incision that is strictly dependent on all three Uvr proteins raises a number of interesting questions concerning its mechanism. How do the Uvr proteins interact with DNA and with one another? How is a catalytically active endonuclease constituted? How is incision apparently confined to the DNA strand containing sites of base damage? How are the bilateral incisions placed at precise locations with respect to sites of base damage? How does bilateral incision facilitate *excision* of base damage? Answers to these questions are beginning to emerge. There are no indications that the Uvr proteins constitute a preformed complex prior to incision of damaged DNA. On the contrary, the available evidence suggests that individual proteins bind to damaged DNA in a sequential fashion and that a catalytically active UvrABC complex is generated on the substrate (Weiss & Grossman, 1986; Yeung *et al.* 1986). UvrA protein binds preferentially to double-stranded u.v.-irradiated DNA relative to unirradiated DNA, and this binding is stimulated in the presence of ATP and inhibited by ADP (Weiss & Grossman, 1986; Yeung *et al.* 1986). Binding of ATP to UvrA protein results in conformational alterations of the protein that may be important for the constitution of a catalytically active UvrABC complex (Weiss & Grossman, 1986). Thus, in the presence of ATP or non-hydrolysable ATP analogues such as ATP[γS] UvrA protein is more readily iodinated at tyrosine residues. Furthermore, in the absence of ATP UvrA protein forms dimers that exist in an equilibrium state with monomers, whereas in the presence of ATP[γS] the protein exists almost exclusively in the dimerized form. The combination of UvrA protein with UvrC protein does not increase its binding affinity for u.v.-irradiated DNA, and UvrB protein alone does not bind to u.v.-irradiated DNA. However, when UvrA and UvrB proteins are mixed both proteins bind to u.v.-irradiated DNA to form a DNA–protein complex with a half-life significantly longer than that of the UvrA–DNA complex (Weiss & Grossman, 1986; Yeung *et al.* 1986). Once UvrA and UvrB proteins bind to u.v.-irradiated DNA the addition of UvrC protein results in incision. Evidence suggests that UvrC protein binds directly to the UvrAB–DNA complex without first binding to DNA and that the formation of a stable UvrAB–DNA complex is the rate-limiting step in the incision reaction catalysed by the UvrABC endonuclease (Weiss & Grossman, 1986; Yeung *et al.* 1986).

Following incision of u.v.-irradiated DNA by the UvrABC endonuclease *in vitro* the DNA–protein complex persists, thus limiting the turnover of Uvr proteins. However, the addition of UvrD protein and DNA polymerase I alters the stability of this complex and also has a significant effect on the incision reaction itself (Caron *et al.* 1985; Husain *et al.* 1985; Kumura *et al.* 1985). When the amount of UvrC protein is rate-limiting for the UvrABC endonuclease-catalysed incision reaction the addition of UvrD protein stimulates the incision of u.v.-irradiated DNA, suggesting that this protein causes UvrC protein in the complex to turn over (Caron *et al.* 1985). However, the complete turnover of UvrA, UvrB and UvrC proteins requires the addition of both UvrD protein and DNA polymerase I (Husain *et al.* 1985). The role of DNA polymerase I is at least partially dependent on concurrent DNA polymerization (i.e. repair synthesis), since less stimulation of nicking of u.v.-irradiated DNA is observed in the absence of deoxyribonucleoside triphosphates (Husain *et al.* 1985). T4 DNA polymerase or the Klenow fragment of DNA polymerase I can replace intact *E. coli* DNA polymerase I; however, *E. coli* Rep protein cannot substitute for UvrD protein (Husain *et al.* 1985). The complete reaction involving the four Uvr proteins and DNA polymerase I is not associated with an increase in the initial *rate* of DNA incision (Husain *et al.* 1985). Thus, UvrD protein and DNA polymerase I apparently do not influence the kinetics of formation of the UvrABC complex on damaged DNA, or its intrinsic endonucleolytic activity.

The precise mechanism of the release (excision) of the oligonucleotide created by bilateral incision of u.v.-irradiated DNA is not yet established. Studies by Caron *et al.* (1985) have shown that under non-denaturing conditions the oligonucleotide fragment is not released *in vitro* and is dependent on the addition of both DNA helicase II and DNA polymerase I. On the other hand, Husain *et al.* (1985) observed some removal of cisplatin adducts from DNA in the absence of the latter two proteins, but, as is true for the incision reaction, the extent of damage excision was stimulated by their addition.

Collectively the data summarized above suggest the following model for the molecular mechanism of nucleotide excision repair in *E. coli* (Husain *et al.* 1985; Weiss & Grossman, 1986; Yeung *et al.* 1986). UvrA protein binds ATP and undergoes a conformational change that favours the formation of protein dimers. In this state UvrA protein has a high affinity for sites in duplex DNA with conformational alterations in secondary structure. UvrB protein binds specifically to UvrA–DNA complexes and these complexes are recognized by UvrC protein, the binding of which generates a catalytically active endonuclease that nicks the DNA at precise locations relative to DNA adducts. The events that determine strand specificity for DNA incision and the locations of these incisions relative to each lesion are uncertain at present. However, it is presumably not pure coincidence that the distance separating the two incisions flanking each lesion approximates one helical turn of *B*-DNA. It is also likely that the conformational distortion generated by bulky base adducts is asymmetrical with respect to the helical axis of DNA and this may facilitate preferential binding of UvrA protein to the damaged strand. The structure of the UvrABC complex subsequently assembled on the DNA may provide for contact of catalytic sites separated by a distance that is close to a single helical turn. Alternatively, the binding of the UvrABC complex to DNA may unwind the DNA helix, generating regions of local denaturation precisely 12 (and in the case of pyrimidine dimers sometimes 13) nucleotides long. The enzyme may then cleave the DNA strand to which it is preferentially bound at the boundaries of the denaturation bubble. Following DNA incision UvrD protein alone (or in combination with DNA polymerase I) promotes turnover of UvrC protein, which is freed to interact with other UvrAB–DNA complexes. A complex consisting of UvrA and UvrB proteins bound to a potential oligonucleotide 12 (or 13) nucleotides long remains relatively stable until both UvrD protein and DNA polymerase I (or DNA polymerase II or III) effect its displacement from the DNA duplex with concurrent repair synthesis and DNA ligation.

This model is consistent with the phenotype of mutants defective in the *uvr* or *polA* genes. *uvrA*, *uvrB* and *uvrC* strains are completely defective in DNA incision. Mutants defective in the *uvrD* or *polA* genes should not manifest a defect in the initial rate of DNA incision. However, because these genes are required for turnover of UvrA, UvrB and UvrC proteins, one would expect mutations in these genes to reduce the extent of DNA incision relative to wild-type strains. As indicated above, a reduced efficiency of DNA incision in a *uvrD* mutant was demonstrated some years ago by Ben-Ishai & Sharon (1981), and both *uvrD* and *polA* mutants have been shown to be deficient in the loss of thymine-containing pyrimidine dimers (excision) from DNA during post-irradiation incubation *in vivo* (see Friedberg, 1985).

The model presented above predicts that DNA incision, damage excision, repair synthesis (and presumably DNA ligation) are highly coordinated events possibly effected by a multiprotein complex (*repairosome*) that acts in a strictly processive fashion (Weiss & Grossman, 1986). Assuming stoichiometric interactions of Uvr proteins and DNA polymerase, and in the absence of competing reactions such as DNA replication, the rate of nucleotide excision repair in *E. coli* is presumably limited by the amount of UvrA, UvrB and UvrC protein, all of which are present at levels of <100 molecules per cell (Husain *et al.* 1985). DNA polymerase I and UvrD protein are present in larger amounts and are not expected to be rate-limiting for nucleotide excision repair in the presence of semiconservative DNA synthesis. However, if, as suggested earlier, UvrB is also involved in DNA replication and DnaB protein is involved in excision repair, these proteins could limit the rate of replication during nucleotide excision repair.

NUCLEOTIDE EXCISION REPAIR IN EUKARYOTES

At the present time, *E. coli* is the only organism for which any detailed information exists on the biochemistry of nucleotide excision repair. However, recent years have witnessed interesting developments in at least two eukaryotic systems that offer the potential for exploring the generality of this process as we know it in *E. coli*.

The yeast S. cerevisiae

Close to 100 yeast mutants (some of which may represent alleles of the same gene) have been isolated with the phenotype of abnormal sensitivity to killing by DNA-damaging agents (see Haynes & Kunz, 1981, for a review). Using u.v. radiation as a source of DNA damage the sensitivity of some mutants known to be defective in different single genes was compared with that of mutants defective in more than one of these genes. If mutations in both genes impart no more u.v. sensitivity than mutations in either gene alone the genes are said to be epistatic, and the most obvious interpretation of an epistatic interaction is that the two genes function in the same biochemical pathway (see Haynes & Kunz, 1981, for a review). Such experiments, when combined with the results of studies that directly measure parameters of nucleotide excision repair in u.v.-irradiated yeast cells (e.g. loss of thymine-containing pyrimidine dimers or introduction of strand breaks during post-u.v.-incubation) have identified 10 loci unique to the nucleotide excision repair (so-called *RAD3*) epistasis group. Two other mutant loci also behave epistatically with mutants in this group, but are also epistatic with mutant loci in other groups, suggesting an involvement in more than one type of cellular response to DNA damage. One of these was originally designated r_3^s, but has been renamed *RAD24* (F. Eckhardt-Schump, W. Siede & J. C. Game, personal communication). The *rad24*-1 mutant is epistatic to other mutants in the *RAD3* epistasis group with respect to u.v. radiation sensitivity and is epistatic to mutants in the *RAD52* group with respect to sensitivity to X- or γ-radiation (F. Eckhardt-Schump, W. Siede & J. C. Game, personal communication). Similarly, a strain mutated in the *CDC8* gene that encodes thymidylate kinase is u.v.-sensitive and epistatic to a *rad1* mutant (belonging to the *RAD3* epistasis group) (Prakash *et al.* 1979). In addition, this mutant shows reduced u.v. mutability, and in this regard is epistatic to *rad6* from the *RAD6* epistasis group (Prakash *et al.* 1979). Thus, at least 12 genetic loci may be involved in nucleotide excision repair in yeast (Fig. 3).

GENETIC COMPLEXITY OF EXCISION REPAIR IN YEAST

RAD3 Epistasis Group

RAD1

RAD2

RAD3

RAD4

RAD7

RAD10

RAD14

RAD16

RAD23

(RAD24)

MMS19

(CDC8)

Fig. 3. Genes in the *RAD3* epistasis group are thought to be involved in nucleotide excision repair in yeast. The involvement of the two genes marked in parenthesis has not been firmly established.

Mutations in five of these loci (*RAD1*, *RAD2*, *RAD3*, *RAD4*, *RAD10*) confer marked sensitivity to killing by u.v. radiation and a complete defect in phenotypes associated with nucleotide excision repair. Mutations in five others (*RAD7*, *RAD14*, *RAD16*, *RAD23*, *MMS19*) result in less sensitivity to u.v. radiation and retain a significant residual capacity for repair, though at levels less than those in wild-type cells (see Friedberg, 1986; Friedberg *et al.* 1986). (The nucleotide excision repair capacity of the *rad24* and *cdc8* mutants has not been reported.) This segregation of gene functions into those absolutely required for nucleotide excision repair and those that apparently are not resembles that which distinguishes the *uvrA*, *uvrB* and *uvrC* genes from the *uvrD* and *polA* genes of *E. coli*, and suggests the possibility that the Rad1, Rad2, Rad3, Rad4 and Rad10 proteins are involved in the incision of DNA while the second group of gene products are involved in post-incision events. This comparison is *not* intended to suggest that the Rad1, Rad2, Rad3, Rad4 and Rad10 proteins function as a specific homologue of the UvrABC complex of *E. coli* or that the Rad7, Rad14, Rad16, Rad23 and Mms19 proteins are strictly analogous to *E. coli* UvrD protein and DNA polymerase I.

The RAD *genes and Rad proteins.* The *RAD1*, *RAD2*, *RAD3* and *RAD10* genes have been cloned by screening yeast genomic libraries for multicopy plasmids containing sequences that complement the u.v. sensitivity of appropriate mutants (see Friedberg, 1986; Friedberg *et al.* 1986). Such screening failed to reveal recombinant plasmids containing the *RAD4* gene. Recent studies in my laboratory (R. Fleer, C. Nicolet, G. Pure & E. C. Friedberg, unpublished) have shown that *RAD4* is located very close to a gene called *SPT2*, and that a recombinant plasmid previously isolated by Roeder *et al.* (1985) contains the entire *RAD4* gene. However, in this plasmid, as well as in other plasmids propagated in *E. coli*, the gene is mutationally inactivated. Deletion of defined regions of the mutant plasmid-borne gene and repair of the resultant gaps by gene transfer from yeast genomic sequences reconstitutes circular plasmids with a functional *RAD4* gene that complements the u.v. sensitivity of all *rad4* mutants tested (R. Fleer, C. Nicolet, G. Pure & E. C. Friedberg, unpublished data). However, propagating such plasmids in *E. coli* again results in inactivation of the gene. These results suggest that Rad4 protein is toxic to *E. coli* and explain the failure to isolate the functional gene on a plasmid from a yeast library cloned in this bacterium. The confines of the *RAD4* gene have been established by insertional mutagenesis at defined sites and by mapping the transcriptional start-sites, and indicate that the gene is $\approx 2 \cdot 3 \times 10^3$ bp in size, thus yielding a calculated molecular weight of $\approx 90 \times 10^3$ for Rad4 protein.

The nucleotide sequences and predicted amino acid sequences of the *RAD1*, *RAD2*, *RAD3* and *RAD10* genes and the proteins they encode have been determined (Yang & Friedberg, 1984; Naumovski *et al.* 1985; Reynolds *et al.* 1985*a,b*; Nicolet *et al.* 1985; Weiss & Friedberg, 1985; Madura & Prakash, 1986) and have revealed several points of interest. (1) The four genes can encode proteins of calculated molecular weight $\approx 110 \times 10^3$, $\approx 118 \times 10^3$, $\approx 89 \times 10^3$ and $\approx 24 \times 10^3$, respectively. Hence, if the products of all 10 genes known to be involved in nucleotide excision repair assemble as a single multiprotein complex at sites of base damage in yeast chromatin, the size of such a complex is at least $500 \times 10^3 M_r$ and could be as large as $10^6 M_r$. (2) Intervening sequences have not been detected in any of these genes and all are present in the yeast genome in single copy. (3) Hydropathicity profiles of the predicted polypeptides show a balanced distribution of hydrophobic and hydrophilic domains in the Rad1, Rad3 and Rad10 polypeptides. Rad2 protein appears to be unusually hydrophilic (Fig. 4). (4) We have not detected extensive nucleotide sequence homology between any of these genes, or with other genes evaluated by computer search. Furthermore, using the cloned *RAD* genes as probes we have not observed hybridization to total human, rodent, *Drosophila* or *E. coli* DNA. Several limited regions of amino acid sequence homology have been noted between the Rad proteins themselves and between one or more Rad proteins and other proteins. The most interesting of these are the following: (a) the tripeptide GKS (T or G) observed in the amino acid sequence of the *E. coli* Uvr proteins and DNA polymerase I (see *Structural features*, p. 4) is also common to the Rad3 (Reynolds *et al.* 1985*a*; Naumovski & Friedberg, 1986), Rad1 and Rad10 proteins of *S. cerevisiae* (Fig. 1), suggesting a convergent evolutionary relationship between these three yeast proteins and the excision repair proteins of *E. coli*. The homology between the yeast Rad3 protein and the *E. coli* UvrA, UvrB and UvrD proteins is particularly impressive. Over a stretch of 22 amino acids, 19 are common to two or more of these four proteins and the pentapeptide GS(T)GKT(S) is common to all of them. This has focused attention on the possibility that Rad3 protein may possess ATPase, GTPase and/or nucleotide binding activity (see below). (b) There is significant homology between the carboxy-terminal half of the Rad10 polypeptide and a region of a protein designated Ercc1, which is believed to be involved in nucleotide excision repair of

E. C. Friedberg

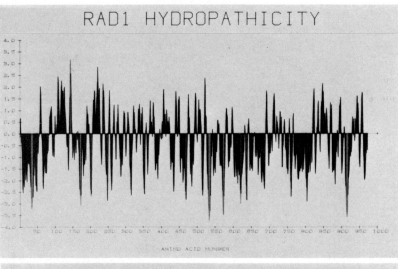

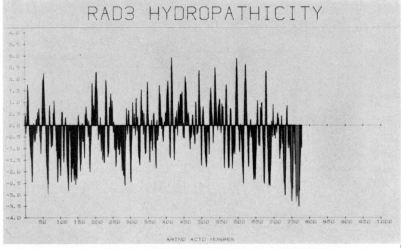

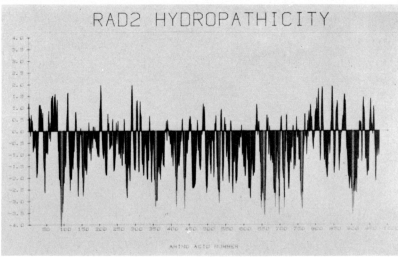

Fig. 4

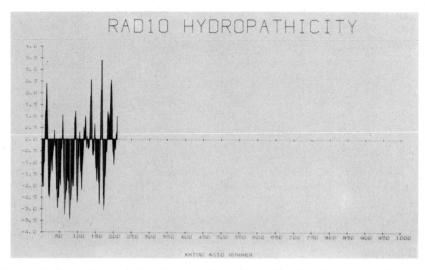

Fig. 4. Hydropathicity profiles of the Rad1, Rad2, Rad3 and Rad10 proteins. The light areas highlight peaks with values greater than +2·5 or −2·5.

DNA in human cells (van Duin *et al.* 1986) (see below). Over a stretch of ≈100 consecutive amino acids, 39 are common to both proteins and a further 37 are closely related (van Duin *et al.* 1986). (c) A number of prokaryotic specific DNA binding proteins share a consensus amino acid sequence consistent with the α-helix–turn–α-helix secondary structure that is characteristic of their DNA binding domain. Among the lower eukaryotes many of the proteins with so-called homeo boxes match this consensus rather well, as do regions in the yeast DNA binding proteins Matα1 and Matα2. Comparison of a number of these proteins with Rad10 and Rad3 suggests that these two proteins may interact with DNA through a α-helix–turn–α-helix motif (van Duin *et al.* 1986; Naumovski & Friedberg, 1986).

   In summary, these amino acid sequence comparisons suggest that the *E. coli* and some of the yeast nucleotide excision repair proteins share a common domain, which may be important functionally in nucleotide binding and/or nucleotide triphosphatase activity. In addition, Rad3 and Rad10 proteins may bind to DNA, perhaps in a sequence-specific fashion.

   The functional relationships suggested by these homologies can be explored in a number of ways. One is to determine whether any of the Rad proteins can complement phenotypes related to excision repair defects in *E. coli* and mammalian cells. To the extent that such experiments have been completed no interspecies complementation has been reported. The *RAD3* and *RAD10* genes have been expressed in *E. coli* and yield proteins of the expected size, yet these proteins do not complement the u.v. sensitivity of *uvrA*, *uvrB*, *uvrC* or *uvrD* mutants (L. Naumovski, W. A. Weiss & E. C. Friedberg, unpublished observations). Similarly, the *uvrA* and *uvrB* genes have been expressed in *rad1*, *rad2*, *rad3* and *rad10* strains without detectable phenotypic complementation of these mutants (Planque *et al.* 1984). The *RAD3* and *RAD10* genes have also been tailored into mammalian cell expression vectors (L.

Couto, G. Chu, R. Schultz, P. Berg & E. C. Friedberg, unpublished observations). At the time of writing, it has not been definitively established that the respective Rad proteins are actually expressed in mammalian cells transfected with these recombinant plasmids. Nonetheless, no enhancement of the u.v. resistance of xeroderma pigmentosum (XP) group A cells (by *RAD3*) or of a Chinese hamster ovary (CHO) cell line designated UV20 (see below) (by *RAD10*) has been observed.

A second way of exploring structural relationships between proteins from different organisms is by using specific antibodies. We have recently raised rabbit antisera that react specifically with yeast Rad2 and Rad3 proteins (L. Naumovski, C. Nicolet & E. C. Friedberg, unpublished observations). The antiserum containing rabbit anti-Rad3 antibodies does not react with purified UvrA, UvrB or UvrC proteins by immunoblotting (C. Backendorf, L. Naumovski & E. C. Friedberg, unpublished observations). Reactions of both antisera against extracts of mammalian cells and of anti-Rad2 antiserum against Uvr proteins, are in progress.

Finally, it is important to determine whether any of the Rad proteins catalyse reactions suggested by sequence homology with other proteins. Rad3 protein has been extensively purified, but no ATPase or GTPase activity has been detected (L. Naumovski & E. C. Friedberg, unpublished observations). However, we have not yet excluded the possibility that such activity is dependent on the association of Rad3 with other Rad protein(s), or on some other specific mechanism of activation. Studies on nucleotide and DNA binding by Rad3 protein and on DNA helicase activity in this protein are in progress.

RAD3 is an essential gene in S. cerevisiae. Disruption (as opposed to point mutagenesis) of the *RAD3* gene is lethal to haploid cells, indicating that this gene is essential for viability. None of the other *RAD* genes under study has this property. The nature of the essential function is not known. However, the observation that *rad3* alleles carrying point mutations are viable, but defective in nucleotide excision repair, suggests that Rad3 protein may have two distinct activities. In an effort to gain insight into the nature of these activities and their localization at the level of the primary structure of Rad3 protein, we mutagenized a number of sites in the cloned *RAD3* gene and examined their effect on the phenotypes of u.v. sensitivity and viability (Naumovski & Friedberg, 1986). Single point mutations in the putative nucleotide or DNA binding domains had no effect on the essential function of Rad3; indeed, the essential function of Rad3 protein is very resistant to inactivation by single point mutations and the only such mutant isolated to date contains a temperature-sensitive point mutation at codon position 73. A site of tandem point mutations affecting two adjacent codons in the putative DNA binding domain also inactivates the essential function, but the site specificity of these mutations is uncertain, pending study of the effect of tandem mutations in other regions of the protein. The excision repair function of Rad3 protein is inactivated by single point mutations at many sites (including both the putative nucleotide binding and DNA binding domains), an observation that explains the facile isolation of viable, excision repair-defective mutants. Collectively, these results suggest that whatever the nature of the nucleotide excision repair function of the Rad3 protein, it is highly sensitive to conformational changes, whereas the essential function of the protein is not. Hence, it is likely that the type of protein–protein and/or protein–DNA interactions that characterize the two Rad3 functions are different.

The essentiality of the *RAD3* gene may constitute an example in yeast of the suggestion made earlier with respect to *E. coli*, i.e. that some proteins involved in nucleotide excision repair are also involved in other DNA transactions such as replication. As indicated above, we have isolated a temperature-sensitive *rad3* mutant that is defective for growth at non-permissive temperatures. Studies on DNA replication in this mutant at permissive and restrictive temperatures may be illuminating.

The RAD2 *gene is inducible by DNA damage.* As indicated earlier, the *E. coli* UvrA, UvrB and UvrC proteins are constitutively expressed in very small amounts ($\approx$10–20 copies per cell). In the case of the first two proteins this level is amplified $\approx$fivefold in cells exposed to DNA damage or other treatments that interfere with normal semiconservative DNA synthesis. At least some of the yeast *RAD* genes are also weakly expressed. Accurate quantitative measurements of transcriptional activity are difficult to obtain; however, qualitative observations from DNA–RNA hybridization experiments indicate the presence of very small amounts of *RAD1*, *RAD2*, *RAD3* and *RAD10* transcripts (L. Naumovski, C. Nicolet, E. Yang & E. C. Friedberg, unpublished observations). In addition, fusions of the promoter and 5′ coding region of these genes to the *E. coli lacZ* coding region results in very limited expression of *E. coli* β-galactosidase relative to fusions with highly expressed yeast genes (Robinson *et al.* 1986).

When yeast cells containing a single integrated copy of a *RAD2-lacZ* fusion plasmid (or an autonomously replicating multicopy fusion plasmid) are exposed to treatments known to induce *E. coli* SOS genes, fivefold enhanced expression of β-galactosidase is observed (Robinson *et al.* 1986). Cells transformed with *RAD1*-, *RAD3*- or *RAD10-lacZ* fusions do not show this result. Consistent with the notion of enhanced gene expression, untransformed cells exposed to 4-nitroquinoline-1-oxide (4NQO) show increased levels of *RAD2* mRNA. The levels of *RAD10* messenger are unaffected by treatment of cells with 4NQO, while *RAD3* and *RAD4* transcripts actually decrease in amount (Robinson *et al.* 1986).

The regulation of this inducible response to DNA damage is currently under investigation. Investigators have shown that other yeast genes are induced by DNA damage. These include the *CDC9* gene, which encodes DNA ligase (Barker *et al.* 1985; Peterson *et al.* 1985) the *RAD51* and *RAD54* genes (D. Schild & R. K. Mortimer, personal communication), which are involved in genetic recombination and which confer sensitivity to ionizing radiation when mutated, and a group of unidentified genes referred to as damage-inducible (*DIN*) (Ruby & Szostak, 1985) or DNA damage-responsive (*DDR*) genes (McClanahan & McEntee, 1984, 1986). Whether or not some or all of these genes belong to the *RAD2* regulon remains to be determined.

Nucleotide excision repair in mammalian cells

Information on the molecular biology of nucleotide excision repair in mammalian cells is very limited. Genetic analyses in human and in rodent cells support the notion of biochemical complexity evident from studies in yeast. Somatic cell hybridization using fibroblasts from patients with the human disease xeroderma pigmentosum (XP) has revealed nine complementation groups, suggesting that at least nine distinct genes are involved in nucleotide excision repair in humans (see Friedberg, 1985). Similar analyses with u.v.-sensitive and excision repair-defective CHO cells has demonstrated five complementation groups to date (Thompson *et al.* 1985*a*). Systematic hybridization between human and CHO cells representative of all these complementation groups has not been completed. However, the hybrids tested to date show enhanced levels of u.v. resistance (Thompson *et al.* 1985*a*), suggesting that the human and CHO mutations examined are in different loci. It seems improbable to me that the molecular mechanism of nucleotide excision repair in these two mammals is completely distinct. Hence, the observation that related human and hamster genes have not been identified raises the interesting and awesome possibility that the spectrum of excision repair genes is larger than that revealed by either of the existing complementation groups alone. Since a case has been made for the involvement of at least 12 genes in nucleotide excision repair in yeast, the operational definition of 14 nucleotide excision repair genes in mammalian cells (9 by analysis of XP cells and 5 by analysis of CHO cells) is perhaps not unreasonable. In this regard, it is important to bear in mind that the CHO mutants were selected in the laboratory by screening mutagenized immortalized cells for enhanced u.v. sensitivity, whereas the XP cell lines are derived from human diploid strains established from biopsy of human patients. The human cell lines may therefore reflect a bias against mutations incompatible with normal human embryogenesis and development, while the CHO lines may (for reasons that are not clear) represent a bias against mutations in genes that in human cells characterize the disease XP.

Human excision repair genes and proteins

Attempts to isolate human genes by phenotypic complementation of XP cells in culture have not been successful (see Schultz *et al.* 1985). On the other hand, complementation of u.v.-sensitive CHO mutants by transfection with human DNA has been observed in several studies (Rubin *et al.* 1983, 1985; Westerveld *et al.* 1984) and has facilitated the isolation of a DNA fragment containing a gene called *ERCC-1* (*e*xcision *r*epair *c*omplementing defective repair in *C*hinese hamster cells). Transfection of CHO cells from complementation group 2 with cosmids containing this gene results in enhanced resistance to killing by mitomycin C or u.v. radiation, as well as enhanced levels of unscheduled DNA synthesis and excision of thymine-containing pyrimidine dimers (Westerveld *et al.* 1984; Rubin *et al.* 1985).

Using a portion of the *ERCC-1* gene as a hybridization probe, van Duin and his colleagues (1986) isolated a series of overlapping cDNAs from which a complete cDNA was reconstructed. This cDNA complements the u.v. sensitivity of appropriate CHO mutants, but to date has not been shown to complement human XP cells (D. Bootsma, personal communication). DNA sequence analysis of the *ERCC-1* cDNA revealed an open reading frame consisting of 297 codons, which could encode a protein of calculated molecular weight 32562. As indicated previously, comparison of the predicted amino acid sequence of the Ercc1 polypeptide reveals considerable homology with the yeast Rad10 protein. It is also remarkable that a cDNA missing 302 bp from the 5' end of the gene (including 162 bp of 5' coding sequence) still complements the phenotype of mutant CHO cells (van Duin *et al.* 1986). At the time of writing, it has not been established whether the *ERCC-1* gene complements the phenotype of yeast *rad10* mutants. Attempts to complement CHO cells from complementation group 2 with the cloned yeast *RAD10* gene are in progress in my laboratory. The human *ERCC-1* gene has been mapped to chromosome 19, consistent with a recent report that this chromosome complements the phenotype of a CHO mutant from complementation group 2 (Thompson *et al.* 1985*b*).

The use of CHO (and possibly other rodent) cells, in which stable transformation by DNA-mediated transfection occurs at a reasonable frequency, would appear to be a useful procedure for screening the human genome for complementing sequences. One would expect that human genes identified in this way are involved in nucleotide excision repair in normal human cells, and the amino acid sequence homology between the human Ercc-1 and yeast Rad10 proteins is certainly consistent with this expectation. However, in view of the failure to demonstrate overlapping mutations in human XP and CHO cells, it would not be surprising if such human sequences do not complement XP cells and hence turn out to be uninformative with respect to the molecular basis of this human disease. Thus, there are compelling imperatives for the cloning of human genes by direct complementation of the phenotype of XP cells. In this regard, new strategies for phenotypic complementation by DNA transfer may be required, since to date XP cells have proven particularly resistant to conventional approaches to phenotypic complementation.

The author acknowledges the contributions of numerous post-doctoral fellows and students whose work on nucleotide excision repair in yeast and mammalian cells is described here. I also thank Aziz Sancar, Claude Backendorf and Lawrence Grossman for unpublished information, Jane Cooper, Linda Couto, Reinhard Fleer, Charles Nicolet, Gordon Robinson, Roger Shultz and William Weiss for critical review, Priscilla Cypiot for generating the hydropathicity profiles shown in Fig. 4, and Jean Oberlindacher and Margaret Beers for preparation of the manuscript. Work from the author's laboratory is supported by research grants from the National Cancer Institute, USPHS, the Council for Tobacco Research and the American Cancer Society, and by contract with the US Department of Energy.

REFERENCES

ARIKAN, E., KULKARNI, M. S., THOMAS, D. C. & SANCAR, A. (1986). Sequences of the *E. coli uvrB* gene and protein. *Nucl. Acids Res.* **14**, 2637–2650.

ARTHUR, H. M., BRAMHILL, D., EASTLAKE, P. B. & EMMERSON, P. T. (1982). Cloning of the *uvrD* gene of *E. coli* and identification of the product. *Gene* **19**, 285–295.

BACKENDORF, C., SPAINK, H., BARBEIRO, A. P. & VAN DE PUTTE, P. (1986). Structure of the *uvrB* gene of *Escherichia coli*. Homology with other DNA repair enzymes and characterization of the *uvrB5* mutation. *Nucl. Acids Res.* **14**, 2877–2890.

BARKER, D. G., WHITE, J. H. M. & JOHNSTON, L. H. (1985). The nucleotide sequence of the DNA ligase gene (*CDC9*) from *Saccharomyces cerevisiae*: a gene which is cell-cycle regulated and induced in response to DNA damage. *Nucl. Acids Res.* **13**, 8323–8337.

BEN-ISHAI, R. & SHARON, R. (1981). On the nature of the repair deficiency in *E. coli uvrE*. In *Chromosome Damage and Repair* (ed. E. Seeberg & K. Kleppe), pp. 147–151. New York: Plenum Press.

BRIDGES, B. A. (1975). An ultraviolet-resistant *tsDNA* mutant of *Escherichia coli* deficient in host cell reactivation ability for bacteriophage lambda and showing hypersensitivity towards induction of Weigle-reactivation. *Mutat. Res.* **29**, 489–492.

BRIDGES, B. A., MOTTERSHEAD, R. P. & LEHMANN, A. R. (1976). Error-prone DNA repair in *Escherichia coli*. IV. Excision repair and radiation-induced mutation in a *dnaB* strain. *Biol. Zbl.* **95**, 393–403.

CARON, P. R., KUSHNER, S. R. & GROSSMAN, L. (1985). Involvement of helicase II (*uvrD* gene product) and DNA polymerase I in excision mediated by the uvrABC protein complex. *Proc. natn. Acad. Sci. U.S.A.* **82**, 4925–4929.

CLEAVER, J. E. (1986). Xeroderma pigmentosum. In *Photomedicine* (ed. E. Ben-Hurand & I. Rosenthal), Boca Raton, Fla: CRC Press (in press).

EASTON, A. M. & KUSHNER, S. R. (1983). Transcription of the *uvrD* gene of *Escherichia coli* is controlled by the *lexA* repressor and by attenuation. *Nucl. Acids Res.* **11**, 8627–8641.

FINCH, P. W. & EMMERSON, P. T. (1984). The nucleotide sequence of the *uvrD* gene of *E. coli*. *Nucl. Acids Res.* **12**, 5789–5799.

FORSTER, J. W. & STRIKE, P. (1985). Organization and control of the *Escherichia coli uvrC* gene. *Gene* **35**, 71–82.

FRIEDBERG, E. C. (1985). *DNA Repair*. New York: W. H. Freeman and Co.

FRIEDBERG, E. C. (1986). Nucleotide excision repair of DNA in eukaryotes: comparisons between human cells and yeast. *Cancer Surveys* **4**, 529–555.

FRIEDBERG, E. C., FLEER, R., NAUMOVSKI, L., NICOLET, C., ROBINSON, G. W., WEISS, W. A. & YANG, E. (1986). Nucleotide excision repair genes from the yeast *Saccharomyces cerevisiae*. In *Mechanisms of Antimutagenesis and Anticarcinogenesis* (ed. D. M. Shankel, P. Hartman, T. Kada & A. Hollaender), pp. 231–242. New York: Plenum Press.

FUCHS, R. P. P. & SEEBERG, E. (1984). pBR322 plasmid DNA modified with 2-acetyl-aminofluorene derivatives: transforming activity and *in vitro* strand cleavage by the *Escherichia coli* uvrABC endonuclease. *EMBO J.* **3**, 757–760.

FULLER, R. S., FUNNELL, B. E. & KORNBERG, A. (1984). The dnaA protein complex with the *E. coli* chromosomal replication origin (*oriC*) and other DNA sites. *Cell* **38**, 889–900.

HAYNES, R. H. & KUNZ, B. A. (1981). DNA repair and mutagenesis in yeast. In *The Molecular Biology of the Yeast* Saccharomyces: *Life Cycle and Inheritance* (ed. J. N. Strathern, E. W. Jones & J. R. Broach), pp. 371–414. Cold Spring Harbor, NY: Cold Spring Harbor Laboratory Press.

HORIUCHI, T. & NAGATA, T. (1973). Mutations affecting growth of the *Escherichia coli* cell under a condition of DNA polymerase I deficiency. *Molec. gen. Genet.* **123**, 89–110.

HUSAIN, I., CHANEY, S. G. & SANCAR, A. (1985). Repair of *cis*–platinum–DNA adducts by ABC exinuclease *in vivo* and *in vitro*. *J. Bact.* **163**, 817–823.

HUSAIN, I., VAN HOUTEN, B., THOMAS, D. C., ABDEL-MONEM, M. & SANCAR, A. (1985). Effect of DNA polymerase I and DNA helicase II on the turnover rate of UvrABC excision nuclease. *Proc. natn. Acad. Sci. U.S.A.* **82**, 6774–6778.

HUSAIN, I., VAN HOUTEN, B., THOMAS, D. C. & SANCAR, A. (1986). Sequences of *E. coli uvrA* gene and protein reveal two potential ATP binding sites. *J. biol. Chem.* **261**, 4895–4901.

JOYCE, C. M., KELLEY, W. S. & GRINDLEY, N. D. F. (1982). Nucleotide sequence of the *Escherichia coli polA* gene and primary structure of DNA polymerase I. *J. biol. Chem.* **257**, 1958–1964.

KACINSKI, B. M. & RUPP, W. D. (1984). Interaction of the UVRABC endonuclease *in vivo* and *in vitro* with DNA damage produced by antineoplastic anthracyclines. *Cancer Res.* **44**, 3489–3492.

KENYON, C. J. & WALKER, G. C. (1980). DNA-damaging agents stimulate gene expression at specific loci in *Escherichia coli*. *Proc. natn. Acad. Sci. U.S.A.* **77**, 2819–2823.

KLINKERT, M.-Q., KLEIN, A. & ABDEL-MONEM, M. (1980). Studies on the functions of DNA helicase I and DNA helicase II of *Escherichia coli*. *J. biol. Chem.* **255**, 9746–9752.

KORNBERG, A. (1980). *DNA Replication*. New York: W. H. Freeman.

KUHN, B. & ABDEL-MONEM, M. (1982). DNA synthesis at a fork in the presence of DNA helices. *Eur. J. Biochem.* **125**, 63–68.

KUMURA, K. & SEKIGUCHI, M. (1984). Identification of the *uvrD* gene product of *Escherichia coli* as DNA helicase II and its induction by DNA-damaging agents. *J. biol. Chem.* **259**, 1560–1565.

KUMURA, K., SEKIGUCHI, M., STEINUM, A.-L. & SEEBERG, E. (1985). Stimulation of the UvrABC enzyme-catalyzed repair reactions by the UvrD protein (DNA helicase II). *Nucl. Acids Res.* **13**, 1483–1492.

KYTE, J. & DOOLITTLE, R. F. (1982). A simple method for displaying the hydropathic character of a protein. *J. molec. Biol.* **157**, 105–132.

LU, A.-L., CLARK, S. & MODRICH, P. (1983). Methyl-directed repair of DNA base-pair mismatches *in vitro*. *Proc. natn. Acad. Sci. U.S.A.* **80**, 4639–4643.

MADURA, K. & PRAKASH, S. (1986). Nucleotide sequence, transcript mapping, and regulation of the *RAD2* gene of *Saccharomyces cerevisiae*. *J. Bact.* **166**, 914–923.

MAPLES, V. F. & KUSHNER, S. R. (1982). DNA repair in *Escherichia coli*: Identification of the *uvrD* gene product. *Proc. natn. Acad. Sci. U.S.A.* **79**, 5616–5620.

MCCLANAHAN, T. & MCENTEE, K. (1984). Specific transcripts are elevated in *Saccharomyces cerevisiae* in response to DNA damage. *Molec. cell. Biol.* **4**, 2356–2363.

MCCLANAHAN, T. & MCENTEE, K. (1986). DNA damage and heat shock dually regulate genes in *Saccharomyces cerevisiae*. *Molec. cell. Biol.* **6**, 90–96.

MORIMYO, M. & SHIMAZU, Y. (1976). Evidence that the gene *uvrB* is indispensable for a polymerase I deficient strain of *Escherichia coli* K-12. *Mol. gen. Genet.* **147**, 243–250.

NAUMOVSKI, L., CHU, G., BERG, P. & FRIEDBERG, E. C. (1985). *RAD3* gene of *Saccharomyces cerevisiae*: nucleotide sequence of wild-type and mutant alleles, transcript mapping and aspects of gene regulation. *Molec. cell. Biol.* **5**, 17–26.

NAUMOVSKI, L. & FRIEDBERG, E. C. (1986). Analysis of the essential and excision repair functions of the *RAD3* gene of *S. cerevisiae* by mutagenesis. *Molec. cell. Biol.* **6**, 1218–1227.

NICOLET, C. M., CHENEVERT, J. M. & FRIEDBERG, E. C. (1985). The *RAD2* gene of *Saccharomyces cerevisiae*: nucleotide sequence and transcript mapping. *Gene* **36**, 225–234.

PETERSON, T. A., PRAKASH, L., PRAKASH., S., OSLEY, M. A. & REED, S. I. (1985). Regulation of *CDC9*, the *Saccharomyces cerevisiae* gene that encodes DNA ligase. *Molec. cell. Biol.* **5**, 226–235.

PLANQUE, K., BACKENDORF, C. F., LEKKERKERK, J. & VAN DE PUTTE, P. (1984). Expression of bacterial *uvrA* and *uvrB* in *Saccharomyces cerevisiae*. *Twelfth Int. Conf. Yeast Genet. Mol. Biol. Edinburgh*, p. 211 (Abstr.).

PRAKASH, L., HINKLE, D. & PRAKASH, S. (1979). Decreased UV mutagenesis in *cdc-8*, a DNA replication mutant of *Saccharomyces cerevisiae*. *Molec. gen. Genet.* **172**, 249–258.

REYNOLDS, P., HIGGINS, D. R., PRAKASH, L. & PRAKASH, S. (1985*a*). The nucleotide sequence of the *RAD3* gene of *Saccharomyces cerevisiae*: a potential adenine nucleotide binding amino acid sequence and a non-essential acidic carboxyl terminal region. *Nucl. Acids Res.* **13**, 2357–2372.

REYNOLDS, P., PRAKASH, L., DUMAIS, D., PEROZZI, G. & PRAKASH, S. (1985*b*). Nucleotide sequence of the *RAD10* gene of *Saccharomyces cerevisiae*. *EMBO J.* **4**, 3549–3552.

ROBINSON, G. W., NICOLET, C. M., KALAINOV, D. & FRIEDBERG, E. C. (1986). A yeast excision repair gene is inducible by DNA damaging agents. *Proc. natn. Acad. Sci. U.S.A.* **83**, 1842–1846.

ROEDER, G. S., BEARD, C., SMITH, M. & KERANEN, S. (1985). Isolation and characterization of the *SPT2* gene, a negative regulator of Ty-controlled yeast gene expression. *Molec. cell. Biol.* **5**, 1543–1553.

RUBIN, J. S., JOYNER, A. L., BERNSTEIN, A. & WHITMORE, G. F. (1983). Molecular identification of a human DNA repair gene following DNA-mediated gene transfer. *Nature, Lond.* **306**, 206–208.

RUBIN, J. S., PRIDEAUX, V. R., WILLARD, H. F., DULHANTY, A. M., WHITMORE, G. F. & BERNSTEIN, A. (1985). Molecular cloning and chromosomal localization of DNA sequences associated with a human DNA repair gene. *Molec. cell. Biol.* **5**, 398–405.

RUBY, S. & SZOSTAK, J. W. (1985). Specific *Saccharomyces cerevisiae* genes are expressed in response to DNA-damaging agents. *Molec. cell. Biol.* **5**, 75–84.

SANCAR, A., CLARKE, N. D., GRISWOLD, J., KENNEDY, W. J. & RUPP, W. D. (1981*b*). Identification of the *uvrB* gene product. *J. molec. Biol.* **148**, 63–76.

SANCAR, A., FRANKLIN, K. A., SANCAR, G. & TANG, M.-S. (1985). Repair of psoralen and acetylaminofluorene DNA adducts by ABC excinuclease. *J. molec. Biol.* **184**, 725–734.

SANCAR, A. & RUPP, W. D. (1983). A novel repair enzyme: UVRABC excision nuclease of *Escherichia coli* cuts a DNA strand on both sides of the damaged region. *Cell* **33**, 249–260.

SANCAR, A., SANCAR, G. B., LITTLE, J. W. & RUPP, W. D. (1982*a*). The *uvrB* gene of *Escherichia coli* has both *lexA*-repressed and *lexA*-independent promoters. *Cell* **28**, 523–530.

SANCAR, A., SANCAR, G. B., RUPP, W. D., LITTLE, J. W. & MOUNT, D. W. (1982*b*). LexA protein inhibits transcription of the *E. coli uvrA* gene *in vitro*. *Nature, Lond.* **298**, 96–98.

SANCAR, A., WHARTON, R. P., SELTZER, S., KACINSKI, B. M., CLARKE, N. D. & RUPP, W. D. (1981*a*). Identification of the *uvrA* gene product. *J. molec. Biol.* **148**, 45–62.

SANCAR, G. B., SANCAR, A. & RUPP, W. D. (1984). Sequences of the *E. coli uvrC* gene and protein. *Nucl. Acids Res.* **12**, 4593–4608.

SCHULTZ, R. A., BARBIS, D. & FRIEDBERG, E. C. (1985). Studies on gene transfer and on reversion to UV resistance in xeroderma pigmentosum cells. *Somat. cell. molec. Genet.* **11**, 617–624.

SEDGWICK, S. G. (1986). Stability and change through DNA repair. In *Accuracy in Molecular Processes* (ed. D. J. Galas, T. B. L. Kirkwood & R. F. Rosenberger). London: Chapman and Hall (in press).

SEEBERG, E. (1978). Reconstitution of an *Escherichia coli* repair endonuclease activity from the separated *uvrA$^+$* and *uvrB$^+$/uvrC$^+$* gene products. *Proc. natn. Acad. Sci. U.S.A.* **75**, 2569–2573.

SEEBERG, E. (1981). Multiprotein interactions in strand cleavage of DNA damaged by UV and chemicals. *Prog. nucl. Acid Res. molec. Biol.* **26**, 217–226.

SEEBERG, E., NISSEN-MEYER, J. & STRIKE, P. (1978). Incision of ultraviolet-irradiated DNA by extracts of *E. coli* requires three different gene products. *Nature, Lond.* **263**, 524–526.

SEEBERG, E. & STEINUM, A.-L. (1982). Purification and properties of the uvrA protein from *Escherichia coli*. *Proc. natn. Acad. Sci. U.S.A.* **79**, 988–992.

SHIZUYA, H. & DYKHUIZEN, D. (1972). Conditional lethality of deletions which include *uvrB* in strains of *Escherichia coli* lacking deoxyribonucleic acid polymerase I. *J. Bact.* **112**, 676–681.

SIEGEL, E. C. (1973). Ultraviolet-sensitive mutator *mutU4* of *Escherichia coli* inviable with *polA*. *J. Bact.* **113**, 161–166.

SIEGEL, E. C. (1983). The *Escherichia coli uvrD* gene is inducible by DNA damage. *Molec. gen. Genet.* **191**, 397–400.

SMIRNOV, G. B., FILKOVA, E. V., SKAVRONSKAYA, A. G., SAENKO, A. S. & SINZINIS, B. I. (1973). Loss and restoration of viability of *E. coli* due to combinations of mutations affecting DNA polymerase I and repair activities. *Molec. gen. Genet.* **121**, 139–150.

THOMAS, D. C., LEVY, M. & SANCAR, A. (1985). Amplification and purification of UvrA, UvrB, and UvrC proteins of *Escherichia coli*. *J. biol. Chem.* **260**, 9875–9883.

THOMPSON, L. H., MOONEY, C. L. & BROOKMAN, K. W. (1985*a*). Genetic complementation between UV sensitive CHO mutants and xeroderma pigmentosum fibroblasts. *Mutat. Res.* **150**, 423–429.

THOMPSON, L. H., MOONEY, C. L., BURKHART-SCHULTZ, K., CARRANO, A. V. & SICILIANO, M. J. (1985*b*). Correction of a nucleotide-excision-repair mutation by human chromosome 19 in hamster–human hybrid cells. *Somat. Cell molec. Genet.* **11**, 87–92.

VAN DEN BERG, E. A., GEERSE, R. H., MEMELINK, J., BOVENBERG, R. A. L., MAGNEE, F. A. & VAN DE PUTTE, P. (1985). Analysis of regulatory sequences upstream of the *E. coli uvrB* gene; involvement of the DnaA protein. *Nucl. Acids Res.* **13**, 1829–1840.

VAN DEN BERG, E. A., GEERSE, R. H., PANNEKOEK, H. & VAN DE PUTTE, P. (1983). *In vivo* transcription of the *E. coli uvrB* gene: both promoters are inducible by UV. *Nucl. Acids Res.* **11**, 4355–4363.

VAN DUIN, M., DE WIT, J., ODIJK, H., WESTERVELD, A., YASUI, A., KOKEN, M., HOEIJMAKERS, J. H. J. & BOOTSMA, D. (1986). Molecular characterization of the human excision repair gene *ERCC-1*: cDNA cloning and amino acid homology with the yeast DNA repair gene *RAD10*. *Cell* **44**, 913–923.

van Sluis, C. A., Moolenaar, G. F. & Backendorf, C. (1983). Regulation of the *uvrC* gene of *Escherichia coli* K12: localization and characterization of a damage-inducible promoter. *EMBO J.* **12**, 2313–2318.

Walker, G. C. (1985). Inducible DNA repair systems. *A. Rev. Biochem.* **54**, 425–454.

Walker, G. C., Marsh, L. & Dodson, L. A. (1985). Genetic analysis of DNA repair: inference and extrapolation. *A. Rev. Genet.* **19**, 103–126.

Walker, J. E., Saraste, M., Runswick, M. J. & Gay, N. J. (1982). Distantly related sequences in the α- and β-subunits of ATP synthase, myosin, kinase and other ATP-requiring enzymes and a common nucleotide binding fold. *EMBO J.* **1**, 945–951.

Weiss, B. & Grossman, L. (1986). Phosphodiesterases involved in DNA repair. *Adv. Enzymol.* (in press).

Weiss, W. A. & Friedberg, E. (1985). Molecular cloning and characterization of the yeast *RAD10* gene and expression of RAD10 protein in *E. coli. EMBO J.* **4**, 1575–1582.

Westerveld, A., Hoeijmakers, J. H. J., van Duin, M., de Wit, J., Odijk, H., Pastink, A. Wood, R. D. & Bootsma, D. (1984). Molecular cloning of a human DNA repair gene. *Nature, Lond.* **310**, 425–428.

Yang, E. & Friedberg, E. C. (1984). Molecular cloning and nucleotide sequence analysis of the *Saccharomyces cerevisiae RAD1* gene. *Molec. cell. Biol.* **4**, 2161–2169.

Yeung, A. T., Mattes, W. B. & Grossman, L. (1986). Protein complexes formed during the incision reaction catalyzed by the *Escherichia coli* UvrABC endonuclease. *Nucl. Acids Res.* **14**, 2567–2582.

Yeung, A. T., Mattes, W. B., Oh, E. Y. & Grossman, L. (1983). Enzymatic properties of purified *Escherichia coli* uvrABC proteins. *Proc. natn. Acad. Sci. U.S.A.* **80**, 6157–6161.

Yoakum, G. H. & Grossman, L. (1981). Identification of the *E. coli* UvrC protein. *Nature, Lond.* **292**, 171–173.

J. Cell Sci. Suppl. 6, 25–38 (1987)
Printed in Great Britain © The Company of Biologists Limited 1987

EXCISION REPAIR IN THE YEAST, *SACCHAROMYCES CEREVISIAE*

SHIRLEY J. McCREADY, JOY M. BOYCE AND BRIAN S. COX

Department of Plant Sciences, University of Oxford, South Parks Road, Oxford, OX1 3RA, UK

SUMMARY

cdc9 mutants of yeast lack detectable DNA ligase activity at restrictive temperatures. They also appear to be more sensitive than wild-type cells to ultraviolet (u.v.) radiation and it has been assumed that this is because the *CDC9* ligase is needed for the final ligation step in excision repair. The fact that single-strand breaks have been demonstrated in u.v.-irradiated *cdc9* mutants has been regarded as evidence for this interpretation. However, the kinetics of appearance of nicks in the DNA do not support this since maximal levels of strand breaks appear almost immediately after exposure to u.v. light and not progressively as repair events are initiated. We believe, therefore, that these strand breaks are connected with a u.v.-dependent preincision event, possibly connected with reorganization of chromatin.

INTRODUCTION

This work is concerned with excision of pyrimidine dimers after ultraviolet (u.v.) irradiation of yeast and involves nine yeast mutants: *rad1, -2, -3, -4, -7, -10, -14* and *-16* and *cdc9*. These eight *rad* mutants were originally classified as being defective in the same or related repair processes by epistasis studies and have all been shown to be defective to some degree in dimer excision (Unrau *et al.* 1971; Game & Cox, 1972; Prakash, 1977*a,b*; Reynolds, 1978; Prakash & Prakash, 1979). *CDC9* is the gene for either the sole or the major DNA ligase in yeast (Barker *et al.* 1985). Mutations, therefore, have to be conditional lethals and appear to be somewhat more sensitive than wild-type to u.v. irradiation (Johnston, 1979).

Table 1 gives a summary of the categories of DNA found in yeast cells. We shall not be concerned with mitochondrial DNA, since dimers are not removed from it by excision repair (Moustacchi & Heude, 1982), but we use repair assays in our laboratory for the other two sets of DNA. We analyse intact chromosomal DNA on alkaline sucrose gradients (Resnick *et al.* 1981). Plasmid molecules are analysed on agarose gels, assaying for dimers by nicking with u.v.-endonuclease to convert covalently closed circles to open circles (McCready & Cox, 1980).

MATERIALS AND METHODS

These are essentially as described by Resnick *et al.* (1981) and McCready & Cox (1980). Brief outlines of the methods are given in Figs 1 and 2.

Table 1. *DNA in* S. cerevisiae

Chromosomal DNA	
17 chromosomes	
260–1500 kb	total 12 000 kb
Plasmid DNA	
2 μm 'minichromosome'	
50–100 copies per cell in nucleus	
Mitochondrial DNA	
0–60 copies per cell	
75 kb each	not repaired by excision

RESULTS

Fig. 3 shows a typical profile of DNA from unirradiated cells and the same DNA treated with u.v.-endonuclease. This shows the chromosomal DNA as a broad peak unaffected by u.v.-endonuclease and a minor peak of mitochondrial DNA further up the gradient. Fig. 4 shows DNA from cells irradiated at 6 J m^{-2} with and without u.v.-endonuclease treatment. Repair is monitored by incubating cells in unlabelled growth medium before harvesting and Fig. 5 shows a set of gradient profiles super-imposed to show repair over a 1-h period after irradiation at 10 J m^{-2}. Repair is not quite complete at the end of this period.

Fig. 6 shows rates of repair of chromosomal DNA in the various *rad* mutants. These rates vary somewhat between different alleles of some genes (data not shown) suggesting, perhaps, that the reason *rad7*, *-10*, *-14* and *-16* are able to remove some dimers may simply be because we are using leaky alleles. This may be so in the case

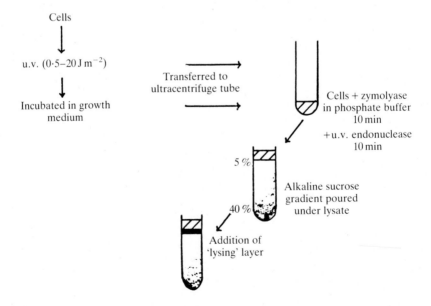

Fig. 1. Preparation of DNA for sucrose gradients.

of *rad10* since a strain with a deletion in the *rad10* gene is as sensitive to u.v. light as our *rad1* mutant (Friedberg, 1987). However, in the case of *rad7*, we find that a deletion mutant gives us an identical rate of dimer excision to that shown (unpublished observation). We do not have deletion mutants in *rad14* or *-16*.

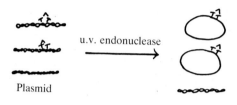

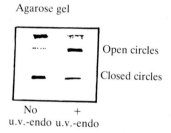

Fig. 2. Assay for pyrimidine dimers in the $2\,\mu$m plasmid. endo, endonuclease.

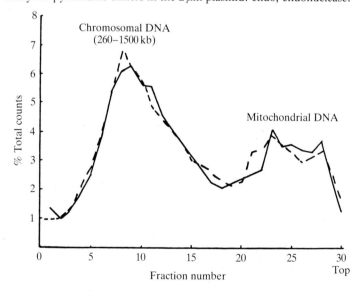

Fig. 3. Sedimentation of unirradiated yeast DNA treated (-----) and untreated (——) with u.v.-endonuclease. kb, 10^3 bases.

Dimers in the plasmid are assayed on gels. Total DNA is extracted carefully so as to avoid nicking. There is no selection for supercoiled DNA, or indeed for plasmid, as we want to be able to detect whether post-u.v. incubation results in nicking of circles. In this system the DNA is purified and all dimers can be cut by the micrococcal u.v.-endonuclease. Fig. 7 shows the results of such an assay. Repair of dimers after $20\,\mathrm{J\,m^{-2}}$ is complete after incubation for 3 h in the wild-type strain.

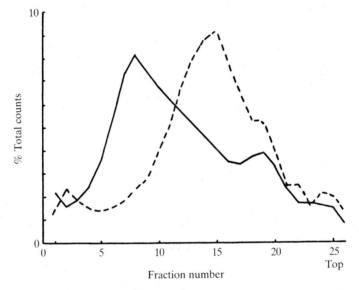

Fig. 4. Sedimentation of DNA from cells irradiated at $6\,\mathrm{J\,m^{-2}}$ and treated (-----) and untreated (——) with u.v.-endonuclease.

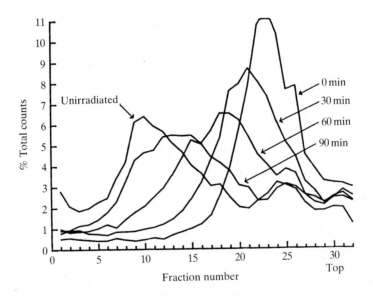

Fig. 5. Sedimentation of u.v.-endonuclease-treated DNA from cells irradiated at $10\,\mathrm{J\,m^{-2}}$ and incubated for up to 90 min.

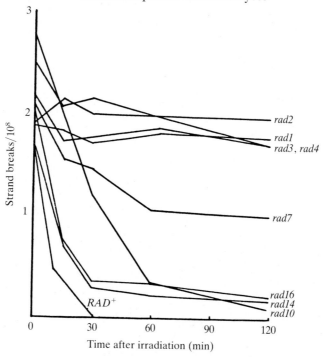

Fig. 6. Rates of repair of chromosomal DNA in *rad* mutants.

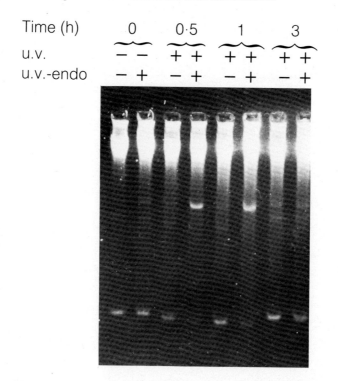

Fig. 7. Disappearance of dimers from $2\,\mu$m plasmid during 3-h incubation following u.v. irradiation at $20\,\mathrm{J\,m^{-2}}$. Pairs of tracks represent samples untreated and treated with u.v.-endonuclease. Conversion of closed circles to open circles indicates the presence of pyrimidine dimers.

Fig. 8 shows what happens in a *rad1* mutant incubated for 5 h, after a 20 J m^{-2} dose of u.v., and shows very clearly that:

(1) There is no removal of dimers.

(2) There is no accumulation of open circles in the cells during the post-u.v. incubation period, suggesting a pre-incision block.

(3) There is no increase in dimer-free circles, suggesting that not only is there no repair, but also there is no synthesis of new plasmid molecules, even using undamaged templates.

Such assays have shown that none of these *rad* mutants exhibits an increase in open circles during post-u.v. incubation, suggesting that all the blocks are either at or before incision. This is in agreement with work done by Reynolds & Friedberg (1981), who showed that no nicks accumulated in high molecular weight DNA in these mutants except after very high doses of u.v. light. The rates of repair of the 2 μm plasmid (Fig. 9) are similar to the rates shown for chromosomal DNA in wild type and in all mutants except *rad16*, which does not repair dimers in the plasmid at all, but repairs chromosomal DNA rather well.

CDC9 is the structural gene for the only ligase detected to date in yeast cells. In temperature-sensitive mutants there is accumulation of unligated Okazaki fragments at the restrictive temperature (Johnston & Nasmyth, 1978) and a temperature-sensitive ligase activity is found (Barker *et al.* 1985). Mutants are apparently more sensitive than normal cells to u.v. light, though this is quite difficult to assess, since cells have to be grown at the permissive temperature to measure survival. It may be

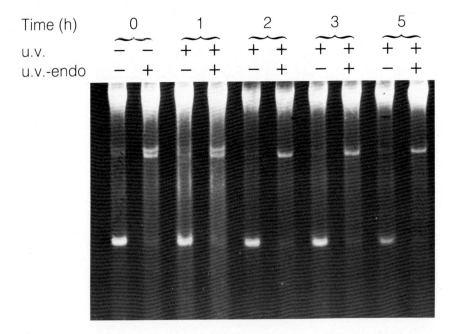

Fig. 8. Failure of a *rad1* mutant to remove dimers during 5-h post-u.v. incubation.

supposed that the increased sensitivity is due to a failure in the final ligation step of excision repair. So let us now see whether this is indeed the case.

Figs 10 and 11 show what happens in the $2\,\mu$m plasmid during the first 2 h of incubation at the restrictive temperature after irradiation at $20\,\text{J m}^{-2}$ in a *cdc9* strain. This is sufficient to introduce an average of 1.2 dimers per plasmid molecule. There are several features to notice. First, in unirradiated plasmid there is, as we would expect, an increase in open circles during the 2 h, due to aborted replication. Second, there is clearly repair of the plasmid at a rate comparable with wild-type repair. After 1 h only about a third of those plasmids originally containing dimers still do so. Third, there is an accumulation of open circles in the irradiated plasmid. This could either be a build-up of unligated repair intermediates or of replication intermediates. The latter seems more likely because repair is being completed at normal rates in at least the majority of the DNA. This interpretation has been confirmed by coupling the *cdc9* mutation with the *cdc7* mutation (Fig. 12). *cdc7* mutants fail to initiate DNA synthesis at the restrictive temperature, and these completely block the appearance of replication-dependent open circles. In the *cdc7 cdc9* double mutant u.v.-endonuclease-sensitive sites are lost at a rate similar to the wild type during post-u.v. incubation. In other words, the open circles that appear in *cdc9* mutants result from aborted replication rather than from a fault in repair.

We conclude that the *CDC9*-encoded ligase is not required for repair of the $2\,\mu$m plasmid. The plasmid appears to be repaired perfectly normally in *cdc9* mutants. This implies either that there is a second DNA ligase present (but so far undetected) in yeast cells, as there is in other eukaryotes, or that another enzyme is able to seal the nicks resulting from excision repair. There is no evidence of a second ligase activity even in the most sensitive assays used to date (Barker *et al.* 1985). However, it is

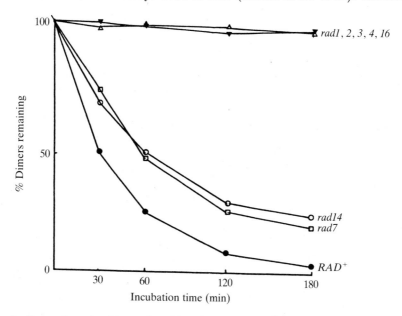

Fig. 9. Rates of repair of $2\,\mu$m plasmid molecules in *RAD*$^+$ and *rad*$^-$ mutant strains.

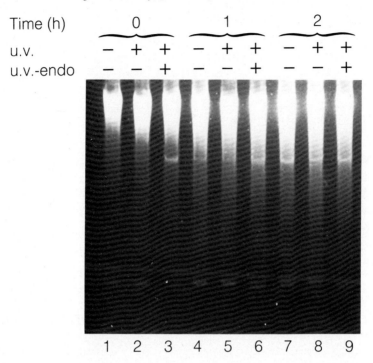

Fig. 10. Repair of 2 μm plasmid in a *cdc9.7* mutant at 36 °C. Tracks 1, 4 and 7 show the increase in open circle forms of the plasmid in the absence of u.v. irradiation. Tracks 2 and 3 show the effect of u.v.-endonuclease on the plasmid immediately after irradiation at 20 J m⁻². Tracks 5 and 6 show that after 1 h most of the covalently closed molecules are now unaffected by u.v.-endonuclease.

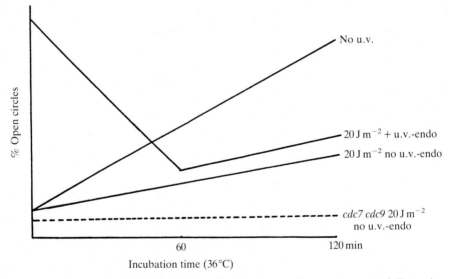

Fig. 11. Graph showing appearance of replication intermediates and repair of dimers in *cdc9.7* mutant. The amounts of DNA in the bands on gel (Fig. 9) were estimated using a densitometer.

possible that the second ligase represents a very minor component of ligase activity in yeast as in mammalian cells (Soderhall & Lindahl, 1976) or that the ligase is not extracted by the methods used for making cell-free extracts to test for ligase activity.

Moving now to repair of chromosomal DNA, the results are more difficult to analyse. Fig. 13 shows a gradient of DNA from a *cdc9* mutant incubated at 36 °C and irradiated with $10 \, \text{J m}^{-2}$ compared with that from unirradiated cells both without u.v. endonuclease. It is clear that u.v.-dependent nicks are appearing on incubation. The DNA is prelabelled, so we are looking entirely at non-replicating DNA. So the *CDC9* ligase may indeed be required for the final ligation step of excision repair in chromosomal DNA. However, partly because it is clear that the plasmid DNA is repaired successfully, we studied the *cdc9* mutant more closely to test the validity of this interpretation.

At all doses analysed $(0.5-10 \, \text{J m}^{-2})$ all nicks are present in the DNA 5 min after irradiation. There is no further increase after this time. In contrast to this nearly 2 h of incubation are needed to complete repair after the same dose of u.v. If we were really looking at nicks arising as a result of failure in the last step of repair, we would expect the rate of appearance of nicks at a given dose to follow closely the kinetics of repair at that dose (Fig. 14). In addition, there are many fewer nicks than dimers. After $2 \, \text{J m}^{-2}$ there is about 1 nick per 10 dimers and at $8 \, \text{J m}^{-2}$ about 1 nick per 5 dimers. One way of accounting for this would be to suppose that repair complexes reach saturation at a low number of dimers and that, after that, repair ceases. In that case we would expect a higher ratio of nicks per dimer at low doses than at high doses, which is the opposite of what we observe.

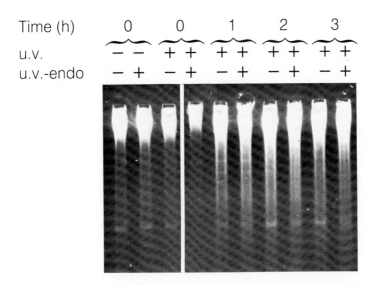

Time (h)	0	0	1	2	3
u.v.	− −	+ +	+ +	+ +	+ +
u.v.-endo	− +	− +	− +	− +	− +

Fig. 12. The effect of introducing a *cdc7* mutation (which causes failure to initiate DNA synthesis) into the *cdc9* strain. There is now no accumulation of replication intermediates and it is clear that dimers in plasmids are removed at the normal rate during post-u.v. incubation.

Neither of these sets of observations (the fast rate of appearance of nicks and ratios of nicks to dimers) fits at all well with the standard interpretation of the appearance of *cdc9*-dependent nicks after u.v. irradiation. For this reason, we have tried to find another interpretation of our results. Because of the very rapid appearance of the

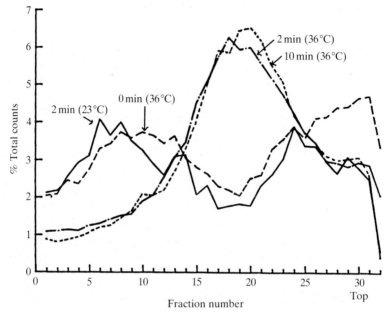

Fig. 13. Sedimentation of DNA from a *cdc9* mutant incubated at 36°C and irradiated with u.v. at 10 J m^{-2}.

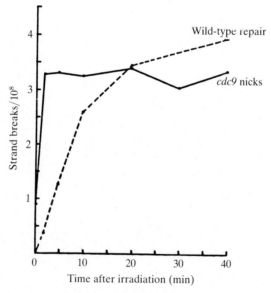

Fig. 14. Rapid appearance of *cdc9*-dependent nicks after irradiation at 8 J m^{-2} compared with the predicted rate of appearance of strand breaks derived from measurements of the rate of early repair after the same dose of u.v. light.

Table 2. *Strand breaks in* rad cdc9 *double mutants*

rad	Strand breaks/10^8
RAD^+	6·58
rad1	0·15
rad2	0·20
rad3	0·18
rad4	0·53
rad7	6·95
rad10	1·11
rad16	1·27

Strains were preincubated at 36 °C, irradiated with 15 J m^{-2} and given 30 min further incubation.

nicks after irradiation, we must consider the possibility that they are associated with some event occurring even before incision.

We know very little about preincision events, either in yeast or in higher eukaryotes, still less about what events are likely to involve nicking and immediate resealing of DNA strands. However, it is possible that these may include chromatin rearrangement, either at the nucleosome level (e.g. see Smerdon, 1985) or at the level of chromatin loops (Schor *et al.* 1975; McCready & Cook, 1984).

We have tried to understand more clearly what is going on in yeast, by looking at *cdc9 rad* double mutants. Do any of the *rad* blocks prevent appearance of the *cdc9* nicks? The answer is yes, almost all of them. Table 2 compares the number of nicks induced in a *cdc9 RAD$^+$* strain with nicks induced in the double mutants. *rad1* to *rad4* all block appearance of nicks. Nicks appear at very reduced levels in *rad10, -14* and *-16*. *rad7 cdc9* is the only double mutant showing the same levels of nicking as a *cdc9 RAD$^+$* strain.

We have two possible models, then, to explain the *cdc9* nicks and the effects of the *rad* mutations in the double mutants.

Model 1: cdc9-*dependent nicks are a result of unligated repair patches*

In this model the *cdc9*-dependent nicks do represent incision and incomplete repair, but only at the earliest repair sites, i.e. at the first 10–20 % of dimers normally to be repaired (because we only see 10–20 % as many nicks as there are dimers in the DNA). We have to infer that no further incision takes place if these remain unrepaired, perhaps because nucleosome or chromosomal domain rearrangement is required and only happens when repair is complete.

We have seen that *rad10, -14* and *-16* all show some accumulation of nicks in *cdc9 rad* double mutants. This is in agreement with the results of Wilcox & Prakash (1981), who concluded that *rad14* and *-16* must be blocked in post-incision events. We would interpret the result differently, however. Since we know that *rad10, -14* and *-16* are able to repair some dimers it would seem reasonable to expect to see some nicks as a result of attempted repair, and indeed nicks do appear at much reduced levels compared to those seen in the *cdc9 RAD$^+$* cells. These mutants are either leaky, therefore, or else they are able to recognize and repair only a subset of the dimers present. In either case they are not performing normal levels of incision and there is no indication of a post-incision rather than a preincision block.

Only the *rad7 cdc9* double mutant shows the same levels of nicking as the *cdc9* RAD^+. The simplest interpretation of this is that in a *rad7* strain, the same subset of dimers (i.e. 10–20 % of the sites) is recognized and incised as in the wild type. Perhaps in *rad7* it is nucleosome rearrangement or some other mechanism of making dimers accessible that is faulty. Why is there no further initiation of repair even at low doses, when the first set of incisions fail to result in complete repair? Since proportionally more nicks appear per dimer at higher than at lower doses we are clearly not looking at saturation of repair complexes. It must be concluded that if the dimers normally repaired first are incised but not completely repaired then other dimers never become accessible to the repair complexes. One explanation for this would be that the chromatin rearrangement needed to make more dimers accessible fails to occur if early repair is not completed.

Why do nicks in the chromosomal DNA appear at a rate far exceeding the rate of even very early repair (Fig. 14)? We have no ready explanation for this except that for some reason, if unligated repair patches persist in the DNA, new repair sites are incised more readily (until the critical 10–20 %, after which no further incisions occur). This seems very unlikely, especially since incision is generally thought to be the rate-limiting step in excision repair.

How is it that the *CDC9* ligase is required for ligation of repair patches in chromosomal DNA (in this model) but not in plasmid DNA? (We have never observed any rapidly appearing nicks in plasmid DNA comparable to that seen in chromosomal DNA even at u.v. doses up to $100 \, \mathrm{J \, m^{-2}}$.) We have to conclude either that a very small amount of active *CDC9* ligase is present and used preferentially for plasmid repair (rather than for replication or repair in chromosomes) or that another enzyme, perhaps a topoisomerase or a second, u.v.-dependent, ligase can seal nicks in the plasmid but not in chromosomal DNA.

Model 2: cdc9-dependent nicks are a result of preincision events

In this model the *cdc9*-dependent nicks result from a preincision event. This event would need the gene products of *RAD1*, *-2*, *-3* and *-4* (since in *rad1–4 cdc9* double mutants nicks do not appear). *RAD10*, *-14* and *-16* may also be required but our alleles are leaky. The *rad7* block is after this event (because *rad7 cdc9* double mutants show *cdc9* RAD^+ levels of nicks).

This model would explain the kinetics of appearance of the nicks and, if the preincision event involved a structural rearrangement of chromatin, for example, could explain why we do not see as many nicks as there are dimers. Nicks do not even have to be at dimers. The nature of the preincision event(s) can only be guessed at, but could be attachment of chromosome domains to repair complexes or re-arrangement of chromatin.

The 2 μm plasmid does not show evidence of *cdc9*-dependent nicks and, therefore, cannot require the preincision event unless the nicks are sealed by a different enzyme. However, plasmid molecules are deficient in dimer excision in the *rad* mutants (Fig. 9). Therefore, the *RAD* gene products may be involved in both very early and later repair events (as has also been suggested by White, 1985). This could be, for example, if the *RAD* gene products 'flag' the sites of damage immediately after u.v. and the flagging is essential both for the preinclusion event and for incision. Another possibility is that the first step in excision repair is attachment to a multi-enzyme repair complex. If a *RAD* gene product in this complex is defective then neither the preincision event nor later steps can be completed efficiently.

Neither model fully explains all the data. Nor are the two models mutually exclusive. It is possible that the *CDC9* ligase is involved during both preincision and postincision events. Certainly a proportion of repair can be completed in its absence (e.g. repair of 2 μm plasmid) whilst the repair of other categories may require it. This is perhaps more easily explained by the second model if, for example, some DNA but not all, needs to be reorganized to be repaired. This seems likely since plasmid and chromosomal DNA are quite differently arranged.

REFERENCES

BARKER, D. G., JOHNSON, A. L. & JOHNSTON, L. H. (1985). An improved assay for DNA ligase reveals temperature-sensitive activity in *cdc9* mutants of *Saccharomyces cerevisiae*. *Molec. gen. Genet.* **200**, 458–462.

FRIEDBERG, E. C. (1987). The molecular biology of nucleotide excision repair of DNA: recent progress. *J. Cell Sci. Suppl. 6*, 1–24.

GAME, J. C. & COX, B. S. (1972). Epistatic interactions between four rad loci in yeast. *Mutat. Res.* **16**, 353–362.

JOHNSTON, L. (1979). The DNA repair capacity of *cdc9*, the *Saccharomyces cerevisiae* mutant defective in DNA ligase. *Molec. gen. Genet.* **170**, 89–92.

JOHNSTON, L. H. & NASMYTH, K. A. (1978). *Saccharomyces cerevisiae* cell cycle mutant *cdc9* is defective in DNA ligase. *Nature, Lond.* **274**, 891–893.

MCCREADY, S. J. & COOK, P. R. (1984). Lesions induced in DNA by ultraviolet light are repaired at the nuclear cage. *J. Cell Sci.* **70**, 189–196.

MCCREADY, S. J. & COX, B. S. (1980). Repair of the 2 μm plasmid DNA in *Saccharomyces cerevisiae*. *Curr. Genet.* **2**, 207–210.

MOUSTACCHI, E. & HEUDE, M. (1982). Mutagenesis and repair in yeast mitochondrial DNA. In *Molecular and Cellular Mechanisms of Mutagenesis* (ed. J. F. Lemontt & W. M. Generoso), pp. 273–301.

PRAKASH, L. (1977*a*). Repair of pyrimidine dimers in radiation sensitive mutants, *rad3*, *rad4*, *rad6* and *rad9* of *Saccharomyces cerevisiae*. *Mutat. Res.* **45**, 13–20.

PRAKASH, L. (1977*b*). Defective thymine dimer excision in radiation sensitive mutants *rad10* and *rad16* of *Saccharomyces cerevisiae*. *Molec. gen. Genet.* **152**, 125–128.

PRAKASH, L. & PRAKASH, S. (1979). Three additional genes involved in pyrimidine dimer removal in *Saccharomyces cerevisiae*: RAD7, RAD14 and MMS19. *Molec. gen. Genet.* **176**, 351–359.

RESNICK, M. A., BOYCE, J. M. & COX, B. S. (1981). Postreplication repair in *Saccharomyces cerevisiae*. *J. Bact.* **146**, 285–290.

REYNOLDS, R. (1978). Removal of pyrimidine dimers from *Saccharomyces cerevisiae* nuclear DNA under nongrowth conditions as detected by a sensitive, enzymic assay. *Mutat. Res.* **50**, 43–46.

REYNOLDS, R. & FRIEDBERG, E. (1981). Molecular mechanisms of pyrimidine dimer excision in *Saccharomyces cerevisiae*: incision of ultraviolet irradiated deoxyribonucleic acid *in vivo*. *J. Bact.* **146**, 692–704.

SCHOR, S. L., JOHNSON, R. T. & WALDREN, C. A. (1975). Changes in the organisation of chromosomes during the cell cycle: response to ultraviolet light. *J. Cell Sci.* **17**, 539–565.

SODERHALL, S. & LINDAHL, T. (1976). DNA ligases of eukaryotes. *FEBS Lett.* **67**, 1–8.

SMERDON, M. J. (1985). Completion of excision repair in human cells. *J. biol. Chem.* **261**, 244–252.

UNRAU, P. R., WHEATCROFT, R. & COX, B. S. (1971). The excision of pyrimidine dimers from DNA of ultraviolet irradiated yeast. *Molec. gen. Genet.* **113**, 359–362.

WHITE, C. I. (1985). Ph.D. thesis, National Institute for Medical Research, Mill Hill, London.

WILCOX, D. R. & PRAKASH, L. (1981). Incision and postincision steps of pyrimidine dimer removal in excision-defective mutants of *Saccharomyces cerevisiae.J. Bact.* **148**, 618–623.

J. Cell Sci. Suppl. 6, 39–60 (1987)
Printed in Great Britain © The Company of Biologists Limited 1987

A GENETIC AND MOLECULAR ANALYSIS OF DNA REPAIR IN *DROSOPHILA*

JAMES B. BOYD[1,*], JAMES M. MASON[2], AKI H. YAMAMOTO[2], ROBERT K. BRODBERG[1], SATNAM S. BANGA[1] AND KENGO SAKAGUCHI[1]

[1]*Department of Genetics, University of California, Davis, California 95616, USA*

[2]*Cellular and Genetic Toxicology Branch, National Institutes of Environmental Health Sciences, PO Box 12233, Research Triangle Park, North Carolina 27709, USA*

SUMMARY

Overview
Mutant isolation and characterization
   Mutant sources
      Mutagen-sensitive mutants (*mus*)
      Meiotic mutants (*mei*)
      Mutations producing gene and chromosome instability
   Genetic and cytological analyses
      Mutant influences on meiosis
      Mutant influences on mutation
   Identification of defects in DNA repair
      Photorepair
      Excision repair
      Postreplication repair
      Additional repair processes
Molecular cloning of DNA repair genes
   Cloning strategy
   Mutation induction by transposon tagging
   Progress report
Enzymology related to DNA repair

OVERVIEW

In the analysis of eukaryotic DNA repair *Drosophila* provides a valuable link between studies being conducted in unicellular organisms and mammals. On the one hand, many of the refined genetic tools available in fungi for identifying and characterizing repair-related genes have been employed with *Drosophila* (see Generoso *et al.* 1980). Like mammals, however, *Drosophila* is a complex multi-cellular organism with separate somatic and germ cell lines. This combination of properties permits a detailed genetic analysis of repair functions and their influence on mutagenesis and recombination in both cell types. In addition to its genetic strengths, *Drosophila* provides a number of unique experimental advantages for the molecular analysis of DNA repair. Because embryonic cells are readily introduced into tissue culture, mutant repair deficiencies can be compared directly with related

* Author for correspondence.

mammalian deficiences (see Boyd *et al.* 1983). The capacity of embryos to replicate the entire *Drosophila* genome within 3·4 min (Rabinowitz, 1941), furthermore, makes this tissue an extraordinary source of DNA metabolic enzymes (see section on Enzymology Related to DNA Repair), many of which undoubtedly play a role in DNA repair as well as replication. The utility of *Drosophila* as a model for mammalian repair is also strengthened by observations that it uses similar mechanisms to activate procarcinogens to mutagens (Baars *et al.* 1980; Waters *et al.* 1982; Porsch-Hallström *et al.* 1983).

Current attempts to clone repair-related genes in *Drosophila* are greatly facilitated by its small genome size (Laird, 1973). The high resolution of *in situ* hybridization with giant polytene chromosomes has furthermore made this one of the best eukaryotes for performing chromosomal walking (Bender *et al.* 1983). Finally, *Drosophila* is one of the most accessible multicellular organisms for cloning by transposon tagging (Bingham *et al.* 1981) and for testing cloned functions by transformation (Rubin & Spradling, 1982). Application of these experimental systems to DNA repair in *Drosophila* is summarized in this article. Emphasis is placed on work that has appeared since this subject was last reviewed (Boyd *et al.* 1983). We start with a discussion of the available mutants and the contribution that their analysis has made to our understanding of the role of DNA repair in mutagenesis and recombination (in the following section). In the third section we describe strategies currently being employed in our laboratories to define the functions of key repair genes through their molecular cloning. Finally, an emerging body of enzymological analysis, which is relevant to DNA repair in *Drosophila*, is summarized in the last section. As an overview of the mutant analysis, the properties of the major known repair related genes in *Drosophila* are presented in Table 1. The individual entries in that table are discussed in the body of this review.

MUTANT ISOLATION AND CHARACTERIZATION

Mutant sources

Mutagen-sensitive mutants (mus). Genes in prokaryotes that are required for DNA repair have been identified through an analysis of mutants that increase the mutation frequency, decrease recombination, or are hypersensitive to mutagens (see Friedberg, 1985). In *Drosophila* the same three phenotypes have been used to identify genes potentially involved in repair. The most direct search for such functions has been performed by selecting mutants that are conditionally lethal upon exposure to moderate doses of mutagens (Smith *et al.* 1980). An example of a commonly employed selection scheme is presented in Fig. 1. In this approach DNA in spermatids and spermatozoa is modified by exposure of males to a chemical mutagen. Treated males are mated with virgin females carrying an attached X chromosome. This cross ensures that each son carries a unique mutagenized X chromosome. By next crossing individual F_1 males to attached X females, separate stocks are established in which the males of each stock carry the same mutagenized X chromosome. Those stocks in which the male larvae prove to be hypersensitive to a

Table 1. *Properties of the major* repair-related genes in* Drosophila

Repair function	Locus affected	Map position	Hypersensitivity	Meiotic effects	Mitotic chromosome stability
Photorepair	phr	2–57		NT	NT
Excision repair	mei-9	1–7	HN2, u.v., X-rays, MMS, AAF, 4-NQO, BP, MNNG, DEB, EMS	Recombination reduced by 90 %	Reduced
	mus201	2–23	u.v., MMS, HN2, EMS	None detected	NT
Postreplication repair	mei-41	1–53	Hydroxyurea, u.v., X-rays, MMS, AAF, 4-NQO, BP, MNNG, aflatoxin	Recombination reduced by 60 %	Strongly reduced
	mus205	2–64	u.v., MMS	None detected	NT
	mus302	3–45	MMS, HN2, X-rays, u.v.	None detected	Reduced
	mus310	3–47	MMS, X-rays, u.v.	None detected	Reduced

The information in this Table is soon to be summarized (Lindsley & Zimm, unpublished).
Abbreviations: HN2, nitrogen mustard; AAF, 2-acetylaminofluorene; BP, benzo(a)pyrene; MMS, methyl methane sulphonate; MNNG, *N*-methyl-*N'*-nitro-*N*-nitrosoguanidine; DEB, diepoxybutane; EMS, ethyl methane sulphonate; 4-NQO, 4-nitroquinolin oxide.
*Only those loci are included whose mutants exhibit the strongest repair defects.

mutagen potentially carry a lesion in an X-linked repair function. Analogous schemes have been employed to recover mutants on the major autosomes (Boyd *et al.* 1981; Snyder & Smith, 1982).

Mutants recovered by this procedure are termed mutagen-sensitive or *mus* mutants. The designation for a typical allele is *mus101*[D1]; in which the allele is distinguished by a superscript that includes a letter indicating the city of origin (Davis). Genetic loci identified by such mutants are given numbers starting with 101, if they are on the X chromosome; 201 for the second chromosome; etc.

Complementation analysis between mutagen-sensitive strains has led to the identification of 27 genes in *Drosophila* whose mutants exhibit this phenotype. Nine of these loci are on the X chromosome (*mus101*, *mus102*, *mus105*, *mus106*, *mus108*, *mus109*, *mus111*, *mei-9* and *mei-41*; see Generoso *et al.* 1980; Mason *et al.* 1981; Yamamoto, unpublished observations); seven are on the second chromosome (*mus201-mus207*; Boyd *et al.* 1982; Snyder & Smith, 1982); and 11 are on the third chromosome (*mus301*, *mus302*, *mus304-mus312*; Boyd *et al.* 1981). Mutagens used to select the *mus* mutants include γ-rays (Nguyen *et al.* 1978), methyl methane sulphonate (Smith, 1973; Boyd *et al.* 1976*a*), *N*-acetoxyacetylaminofluorene and nitrogen mustard (Boyd *et al.* 1981). The isolated mutants exhibit several patterns of mutagen sensitivity (Smith *et al.* 1980; Snyder & Smith, 1982; Boyd *et al.* 1983). All mutants, with the exception of those at the *mus308* locus, are hypersensitive to methyl methane sulphonate (MMS). The predominant sensitivity of mutants at the *mus308* locus is to nitrogen mustard. Since mutants at all tested loci are also sensitive

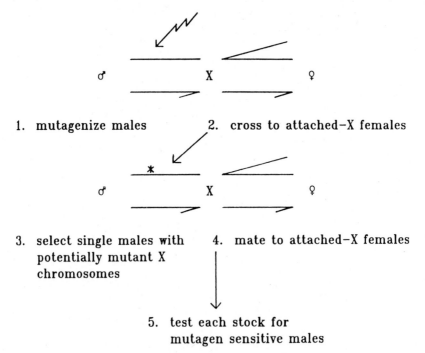

1. mutagenize males   2. cross to attached−X females

3. select single males with   4. mate to attached−X females
   potentially mutant X
   chromosomes

5. test each stock for
   mutagen sensitive males

Fig. 1. Isolation of X-linked mutants that are hypersensitive to mutagens.

to at least one form of radiation, it is unlikely that the observed sensitivity is due to defects in the metabolism or transport of chemical mutagens. The lack of radiation-resistant mutants, therefore, increases the probability that the recovered mutants influence DNA repair.

It is important to note that although the selection schemes are all designed to recover mutants that are conditional lethals, the genes identified by those mutants may be essential for survival. This possibility was demonstrated by the subsequent isolation of lethal alleles at the *mus101*, *mus105* and *mus109* loci (Baker & Smith, 1979). Studies of a temperature-sensitive *mus101* allele (Gatti *et al.* 1983; Smith *et al.* 1985) have raised the possibility that some of these genes primarily function in the maintenance of chromosome structure rather than in DNA metabolism.

Meiotic mutants (mei). Genetic investigations of the mutagen-sensitive mutants have revealed that nearly 50% of the tested *mus* genes are essential for normal meiosis (Snyder & Smith, 1982; see next section). That observation suggested that the large collection of meiotic (*mei*) mutants that have been isolated in *Drosophila* over the past 60 years (Baker *et al.* 1976*b*) could also be a valuable source of repair-defective mutants. Early genetic studies of the *mei-9* mutants (Carpenter & Sandler, 1974) had strongly implicated that locus in DNA metabolism. In confirmation of that suggestion, those mutants were subsequently found to be hypersensitive to methyl methane sulphonate (Boyd *et al.* 1976*b*) and new alleles of the *mei-9* gene were recovered in screens for mutagen-sensitive strains (Baker & Smith, 1979; Graf *et al.* 1979*b*; Mason *et al.* 1981). Allelism has also been demonstrated between a *mei-41* mutation and mutations recovered in a search for *mus* mutants (Smith, 1976). However, since mutants at only two of several tested meiotic loci exhibit mutagen sensitivity (Mason *et al.* 1981; Boyd, unpublished observations), a relatively small proportion of the *mei* mutants are likely to be involved in DNA repair.

Mutations producing gene and chromosome instability. Two additional mutant sources can potentially lead to the identification of repair-related genes. Smith *et al.* (1985) have recovered a number of temperature-sensitive lethal mutants, 15 of which exhibit mitotic chromosome instability. Since mutants at a majority of the *mus* loci exhibit similar chromosome instability (Baker *et al.* 1980; Gatti *et al.* 1984), complementation tests were performed between the two mutant classes. That analysis revealed that a new *mus101* allele had been recovered (Smith *et al.* 1985). It opened the possibility further for future identification of new *mus* mutants with this approach. Finally, the mutator strains of *Drosophila*, which exhibit a high spontaneous mutation frequency, are also a potential source of mutants in repair functions (Green, 1973). Although the correlation of this phenotype with defects in DNA repair is more tenuous, mutationally unstable giant (*gt*) strains were recently shown to exhibit altered DNA metabolism (Narachi & Boyd, 1985).

Genetic and cytological analyses

Mutant influences on meiosis. As mentioned in the previous section, many *mus* mutants disrupt meiosis. Mutations at four X-linked loci and in six autosomal *mus* genes increase the frequencies of meiotic non-disjunction from which it has been inferred that these mutations reduce meiotic exchange (Smith, 1976; Boyd *et al.* 1976*a*, 1981). Confirmation of this inference comes from reports that mutations at two loci on the first chromosome, *mei-9* and *mei-41*, two loci on the second chromosome, *mus203* and *mus204*, and at least two loci on the third chromosome, *mus312* and *mus304*, decrease meiotic recombination, as expected (Baker & Carpenter, 1972; Snyder & Smith, 1982; Green, 1981, 1982).

Three recombination-defective meiotic mutants have been examined in detail for their effects on the structure of the synaptonemal complex (SC) and recombination nodules (Carpenter, 1979). Recombination nodules have been inferred to be intimately associated with meiotic recombination because: (1) their numbers and distribution at pachytene correspond closely with the frequency and distribution of crossovers observed genetically; (2) they are closely associated with the central element of the SC (Carpenter, 1975); and (3) they occur at or are very close to the sites of DNA synthesis during meiosis (Carpenter, 1981). Two of the three mutants examined, *mei-9* and *mei-41*, have been shown to be defective in DNA repair (Boyd & Setlow, 1976; Boyd *et al.* 1976*b*), whereas the third, *mei-218*, exhibits normal sensitivity to mutagens and is probably not repair-defective (Boyd *et al.* 1976*a*). None of these mutants affects the structure, continuity or temporal behaviour of the SC. Mutants at the *mei-218* and *mei-41* loci, however, reduce the number of recombination nodules as well as change their morphology. In a *mei-218* mutant the nodule abnormality involves patchy, irregular condensation or formation of nodule material, whereas in a *mei-41* mutant the nodules are uniformly less dense than normal. In both *mei-41* and *mei-218* mutants the distribution of nodules along a chromosome arm is more uniform than in wild type (Carpenter, 1979). These observations are consistent with the hypothesis proposed by Baker & Carpenter (1972) that these two loci function in setting up the preconditions for exchange, that is, that they are involved in the choice or preparation of sites for exchange.

In contrast, the number, morphology and distribution of recombination nodules in a *mei-9* mutant are normal (Carpenter, 1979), consistent with the idea that the wild-type allele functions after the exchange preconditions have been established (Baker & Carpenter, 1972; Carpenter & Sandler, 1974) and after recombination nodules have been formed (Carpenter, 1979). Further evidence that *mei-9*$^+$ functions in the exchange process *per se* comes from observations that in homozygous *mei-9* females crossing over is reduced to less than 10% of normal levels although gene conversion is normal. Unlike the majority of meiotic mutants, which are postulated to mediate precondition events, the distribution of residual recombination events in *mei-9* mutants is normal. Finally, since postmeiotic segregation is elevated, mismatch repair is presumed to be reduced. These results have led Carpenter (1982) to conclude that the repair of heteroduplex mismatches and the isomerization step of recombination are closely related and are under the genetic control of the *mei-9* gene.

Mutant influences on mutation. Two approaches have been employed to measure the effect of mutagen-sensitive mutants on chromosome stability. In a genetic approach, flies are constructed that carry the mutant of interest and are simultaneously heterozygous for somatic cell markers affecting the colour or morphology

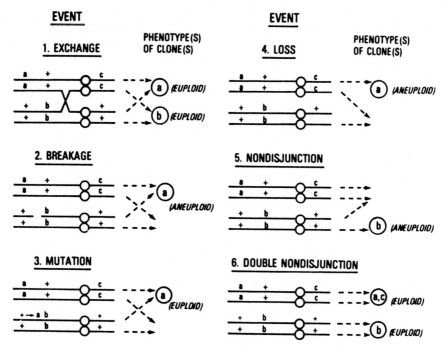

Fig. 2. Examples of mitotic events generating cells homozygous or hemizygous for one or more cell markers in heterozygous genotypes. (From Smith *et al.* (1985).)

of cuticular bristles. The effects of these mutants on the frequencies of mutation, chromosome breakage, somatic recombination, non-disjunction and chromosome loss can be detected by monitoring the frequency and size of cell clones that express the somatic cell marker (Fig. 2). Since clones resulting from each of these processes have distinguishable properties, the particular source of chromosome instability in any mutant may be identified. Using this approach, mutagen-sensitive alleles of six loci (*mei-9, mei-41, mus101, mus102, mus105, mus109*) were identified as increasing the frequency of somatic spots (Baker *et al.* 1978; Baker & Smith, 1979). Analysis of the size distribution of clones produced by mutants at these loci suggests that most of the chromosome instability in each of the mutants is the consequence of chromosome breakage.

In addition, the effects of mutagen-sensitive mutations on chromosome stability have been assessed by examining somatic chromosomes cytologically (Gatti, 1979; Gatti *et al.* 1984). Mutants at 12 loci (*mei-9, mei-41, mus101, mus102, mus105, mus109, mus301, mus304, mus305, mus308, mus309, mus312*) cause significant increases in the frequency of aberrations. In X-linked mutants the aberrations detected were predominantly chromatid and isochromatid breaks that had arisen during the previous cell cycle. In mutants at four X-linked loci, close to one half of the aberrations involve both chromatids, whereas in *mei-9* mutants the majority of aberrations are single chromatid breaks (Gatti, 1979).

After X-irradiation, neuroblasts from *mei-9* or *mei-41* mutants exhibit a large increase in the frequency of chromosome aberrations, compared with the *mei*[+]

control (Gatti *et al.* 1980). As was seen with unirradiated cells, chromatid and isochromatid breaks were recovered equally frequently in *mei-41*-bearing cells, but in *mei-9*-bearing cells most aberrations are chromatid breaks. Furthermore, chromatid interchanges were slightly reduced in *mei-41* cells and could not be induced in *mei-9* cells.

Since lethal alleles of *mus101*, *mus105* and *mus109* have been found, the functions defined by these loci are essential for survival (Baker *et al.* 1982; Gatti *et al.* 1983). Larvae carrying lethal alleles of *mus105* and *mus109* have degenerate imaginal discs and die at the time of pupation. Mitotically dividing cells in those larvae exhibit high frequencies of chromosome aberrations, which probably lead to high levels of cell death (Baker *et al.* 1982). An allele of *mus101* has been shown to abolish the amplification of chorion genes that normally occurs during oogenesis (Orr *et al.* 1984; Baker, personal communication). Data derived from a temperature-sensitive allele of *mus101* suggest that this locus is required for proper condensation of heterochromatin and that the mutagen sensitivity and inhibition of DNA repair found in viable alleles of *mus101* are secondary consequences of a primary defect in chromatin condensation (Gatti *et al.* 1983).

Chromatin structure may play an important role in mutagenesis by determining which DNA repair pathways are operative. This statement is supported by observations that in *mus105* and *mus109* mutants the distribution of chromosome breaks is altered. In *mus105* mutants about 80 % of the breaks are euchromatic and in *mus109* mutants about 80 % of the breaks occur at the heterochromatic–euchromatic junctions (Gatti, 1979). Mutants of *mus101*, a locus controlling chromatin condensation, decrease the frequency of nitrogen mustard-induced mutations (Graf *et al.* 1979a, 1982). Further support for this hypothesis is derived from studies of chromosome aberrations induced by X-rays in the presence of the *mu-2* mutation. Mutations at this locus potentiate the recovery of X-ray-induced terminal deficiencies from homozygous females (Mason *et al.* 1984), but do not cause hypersensitivity to killing by either MMS or X-rays. Homozygous *mu-2* males are indistinguishable from wild-type males in potentiating the recovery of partial Y losses (Mason, unpublished). In *mu-2* females, partial Y loss can be induced at a high frequency when the Y chromosome is irradiated in mature oocytes but not when the Y chromosome is irradiated in mature sperm, suggesting that *mu-2* can distinguish between maternally derived and paternally derived chromosomes. Furthermore, conformation of partial Y losses in progeny of *mu-2* females suggests that *mu-2* can distinguish between lesions in heterochromatin and those in euchromatin. X-ray-induced breaks in euchromatin give rise primarily to terminal deficiencies, whereas breaks in heterochromatin give rise to two break rearrangements (Mason, unpublished). Rather than controlling DNA repair directly, it is therefore more likely that the *mu-2* gene modulates the activity of DNA repair systems at the chromatin level.

The phenomenon of ribosomal DNA magnification in *Drosophila* reverses the loss of deleted ribosomal cistrons. Magnification has been shown by Polito *et al.* (1982) to be dependent upon the *mei-9* function under specified experimental conditions.

Hawley & Tartof (1983), using a somewhat different assay, were subsequently able to show that this process can also be altered by mutants at the *mei-41* locus. A similar dependence has also been reported for the *mus101* and *mus108* loci (Hawley *et al.* 1985). Each of these repair-related genes has therefore been implicated in yet another aspect of DNA metabolism.

The repair-defective mutants have been incorporated into experiments designed to examine their effect on mutagenesis during germ cell development. Early evidence for the timing of repair functions during spermatogenesis was based on the lack of a dose fractionation effect for radiation-induced mutations in mature sperm (Muller, 1940) and spermatids (Sobels, 1972). These observations suggested the absence of repair of X-ray-induced lesions in postmeiotic male germ cells. The repair-defective mutants provide a more direct test of this hypothesis. Using two different alkylating agents, Smith *et al.* (1983) were able to show that alkylation-induced mutation frequencies in meiotic and postmeiotic germ cells are similar for *mei-9* and wild-type males, but that in premeiotic cells the mutation frequency falls to a low level in wild-type, but not *mei-9* males. This result strongly suggests that the low induced mutation frequency normally seen in premeiotic cells is due to repair of the alkylation-induced lesions. Similar experiments using a *mus201* mutant in treated females indicate that excision repair is normally functional throughout oogenesis (Badaruddin *et al.* 1984). These results confirm earlier work on unscheduled DNA synthesis during oogenesis (Kelley & Lee, 1983; and section on Excision Repair, below).

Studies of the genetic control of mutagenesis in *Drosophila* have been conducted by crossing mutagenized males to repair-defective females to provide evidence of repair after fertilization (Graf *et al.* 1979a). Using this technique with eight different alkylating agents, Vogel *et al.* (1985) found that the hypermutability in the excision-deficient mutants *mei-9*[L1] and *mus201*[D1] correlates well with the Swain–Scott constant *s* (Swain & Scott, 1953). They interpreted this result to mean that excision repair has a significant effect on mutation induction at alkylated N atoms in DNA (induced by chemicals with high *s* values), but not at alkylated O atoms in DNA (more prominent lesions induced by chemicals with low *s* values). They further suggested that mutagenesis due to nitrogen alkylation in DNA occurs primarily through error-prone repair whereas mutagenesis due to base oxygen alkylation occurs predominantly by mispairing during replication (Smith & Dusenbery, 1985). These conclusions are consistent with the observation that base nitrogen alkylation in repair-proficient *Drosophila* is correlated with high frequencies of chromosome breakage while base oxygen alkylation produced primarily point mutations (Vogel & Natarajan, 1979a,b). That conclusion is not consistent, however, with the observation that two compounds with low Swain–Scott constants (DEN, ENU) induce high frequencies of partial Y loss when treated Y-bearing males are crossed with *mei-9*[a] females (Zimmering, 1983).

Very little is known about the role that cellular DNA-metabolizing enzymes play in controlling the frequency or precision of transposition in *Drosophila*. Rasmuson (1984) demonstrated that both *mei-9* and *mei-41* mutants increase the spontaneous mutation frequency of an unstable white mutation that contains an insertion sequence (IS) element. The MMS-induced somatic mutation rate was, however, reduced by a *mei-41* allele. That approach has been extended to additional *mus* mutants and alternate alkylating agents by Fujikawa & Kondo (1986). It has been suggested that the frequencies of germ line mutations induced by P element mutagenesis at the *sn* and *ras* loci are increased by the presence of mutations at *mei-9* and *mei-41* (Eeken & Sobels, 1981). Slatko *et al.* (1984), however, were unable to detect any effect of *mei-9*, *mei-41*, *mus101* or *mus102* mutations on the frequencies of P-element-induced sex-linked recessive lethals or recombination in the male germ line. Similarly, Voelker *et al.* (1984) found that mutations at *mei-9* and *mei-41* have no influence on the frequency of reversion of a lethal caused by the insertion of a P element but suggested that these mutations may increase the proportion of imprecise excision. If such imprecise excision results in large deletions, they could account for the observation that *mei-41* and *mus101* mutations decrease the recovery of P-bearing chromosomes from hybrid dysgenic males (Slatko *et al.* 1984).

Identification of defects in DNA repair

Mutants at 24 of the 31 loci associated with mutagen sensitivity have been tested for defects in at least one form of DNA repair. That analysis, which has recently been reviewed (Boyd *et al.* 1983), has revealed one locus that is required for photorepair, two that are necessary for excision repair and four whose mutants are strongly deficient in postreplication repair (Table 1). Although less extensive defects have been identified in mutants at 11 additional loci, those genes are presently accorded less emphasis because, with the exception of *mus101*, it is not known whether the moderate defects are due to leaky mutants in key functions or to mutants in genes whose functions are ancillary to the repair process under study. The following discussion accordingly emphasizes the seven loci identified in that table.

Photorepair. Early experiments demonstrating the existence of photorepair in *Drosophila* have been reviewed (Boyd *et al.* 1980). Because of the difficulty of selecting mutants in *Drosophila* with u.v. treatment (P. D. Smith & J. B. Boyd, unpublished observations), however, defects in this process have not been recovered in mutant screens. Recently, Boyd & Harris (1985) identified a photorepair-deficient mutant (*phr*) in a standard laboratory stock. Embryonic cells, which are homozygous for this second chromosomal mutation, are entirely devoid of photorepair. Analyses of this mutant have demonstrated that the *phr*$^+$ allele is essential for the enhanced survival of u.v.-treated larvae that is afforded by irradiation with visible light (unpublished observation). Because similar mutants in *Escherichia coli* (Sancar *et al.* 1983) have been shown to fall in the structural gene for a photolyase, it is likely that the *phr* gene in *Drosophila* codes for the photorepair enzyme recently characterized by Beck & Sutherland (1979) and Beck (1982). Both the photorepair defect and a partial defect in excision repair have been mapped genetically to position 57 on the 2nd chromosome. Since coincident defects in excision and photorepair have also been observed in *E. coli* (Yamamoto & Shinagawa, 1985), *Neurospora* (Inoue & Ishii, 1985) and man (Sutherland *et al.* 1975), it is becoming increasingly likely that those two repair systems do not function independently of one another *in vivo*. Further characterization of such mutants should serve to illuminate the molecular basis of that interaction. A partial defect in photorepair observed by Ferro (1985) has not been characterized thoroughly enough to know if it represents an allele of the *phr* gene.

Excision repair. Of the two identified loci in *Drosophila* that are absolutely required for excision repair, the *mus201* gene most closely resembles excision-defective mutants in other organisms (Boyd *et al.* 1982). Since that mutant is hypersensitive to u.v. and several carcinogens but is relatively insensitive to X-rays (Boyd *et al.* 1982; Dusenbery *et al.* 1983; Todo *et al.* 1985), it is likely to be defective in repair of lesions that distort the DNA helix as is true of excision-defective mutants in other organisms (see Cerutti, 1975). This expectation is born out by observations that cells homozygous for *mus201*^{D1} quantitatively retain pyrimidine dimers in their DNA after incubation times that permit wild-type cells to remove 80 % of those lesions (Boyd *et al.* 1982). In addition, the incision event associated with normal excision repair is not detected in *mus201*^{D1} cells following treatment with either u.v. or *N*-acetoxy-*N*-acetyl-2-aminofluorene, agents that generate bulky DNA lesions. Cytological studies of unscheduled DNA synthesis in *mus201*^{D1} have, however, revealed a deficiency in repair of at least a portion of the lesions generated by alkylating agents (Dusenbery *et al.* 1983) in addition to a defect in u.v.-induced unscheduled DNA synthesis (Boyd *et al.* 1982). Since *mus201*^{D1} cells lack most of the X-ray-induced unscheduled DNA synthesis but are relatively insensitive to X-rays, the lesions being repaired by the *mus201* pathway are probably not the primary lethal lesions induced by X-rays. The *mus201*^{D1} allele fails to exhibit any detectable effect on meiotic chromosome segregation or recombination. That mutant also exhibits a normal capacity for postreplication repair following u.v. treatment and the capability to seal single-strand breaks induced by X-rays. A *mus201*^{D1} mutant has recently been introduced into permanent cell culture by Todo *et al.* (1985).

Mutants at the *mei-9* locus also exhibit an absolute block in excision repair. Repair replication is abolished (Nguyen & Boyd, 1977) and pyrimidine dimers are retained (Boyd *et al.* 1976*b*) due to a block in the initial incision event (Harris & Boyd, 1980). The *mei-9* mutants are unique among excision-defective mutants in any organism in that they are hypersensitive to all classes of mutagens including X-rays (Baker *et al.* 1976*a*; Nguyen *et al.* 1979; Smith *et al.* 1980) and they exhibit a strong meiotic effect (section on Mutant Sources). In a molecular analysis of DNA repair in *Drosophila* oocytes, Kelley & Lee (1983) demonstrated that the *mei-9*^{a} mutation reduces repair replication induced by alkylation damage. Analysis of unscheduled DNA synthesis has also revealed a block in the repair of alkylation-induced lesions in somatic cells of mutant *mei-9* cells (Dusenbery *et al.* 1983). Although the molecular mechanisms of alkylation repair that are interrupted in either the *mei-9* or *mus201* mutants have not been investigated directly, repair of bases modified at nitrogen atoms is strongly implicated as the relevant repair target (section on Genetic and Cytological Analyses).

Utilization of the excision-deficient mutants has permitted the identification of a previously undetected step in excision repair that can occur in the absence of excision (Boyd *et al.* 1983; Harris & Boyd, unpublished observations). This step includes an apparent alteration in chromatin structure, which renders DNA lesions more accessible to repair. This function is more easily detected in excision-defective cells because of the lack of competing excision repair. The increase in accessibility is apparently not necessary for initial repair involving a subset of the chromatin; rather this process is postulated to permit repair of initially less-accessible regions through a topoisomerase-mediated alteration of chromatin structure.

Postreplication repair. The term postreplication repair refers to those mechanisms that permit DNA synthesis to proceed on a damaged template (Lehmann & Karran, 1981). Although the mechanism of this process in eukaryotes is not understood, the classical recombination mechanism in *E. coli* (Ganesan, 1974) is not a major component of postreplication repair in *Drosophila* (Boyd *et al.* 1983) or mammals (Lehmann & Kirk-Bell, 1978). Mutants defective in this process produce abnormally small polynucleotide chains during DNA synthesis following mutagen treatment (Lehmann *et al.* 1977). In *Drosophila* mutations in four different genes (Table 1) exhibit strong defects in this process (Boyd & Setlow, 1976; Boyd & Shaw, 1982). The deficiency in these mutants is similar to that exhibited by human xeroderma pigmentosum variant patients with the exception that caffeine does not have as strong a potentiating effect in *Drosophila* as it does in man (Lehmann *et al.* 1977; Boyd & Shaw, 1982).

The *mei-41* locus is unique among the four strong post-replication repair-deficient genes in that most of its mutants are hypersensitive to all tested mutagens (Smith *et al.* 1980; Nguyen *et al.* 1979) and they disturb meiosis (Baker *et al.* 1980; Mason *et al.* 1981). Recently, a strong hypersensitivity of *mei-41* mutants to hydroxyurea has been correlated with the generation of excessive chromosomal aberrations by that compound (Banga, Shenkar & Boyd, unpublished observations). Since the primary target of that inhibitor is thought to be ribonucleotide reductase (Tyrsted, 1982), it is possible that alterations in nucleotide pools play a role in the *mei-41* defect. Either the pools themselves may be altered or the replication complex may be particularly sensitive to variations in pool levels. Sensitivity to hydroxyurea is not a general feature of strong postreplication-deficient mutants, however, because mutants at the other three loci are not hypersensitive to that compound (Table 1).

Additional repair processes. Human cells from patients with ataxia telangiectasia fail to reduce DNA synthesis following exposure to X-rays (de Wit *et al.* 1981). A related phenomenon has been observed in the *giant* (*gt*) mutants of *Drosophila* (Narachi & Boyd, 1985), in which mutant larval cells fail to respond to u.v. treatment with the usual reduction in DNA synthesis. These mutants, which exhibit additional abnormalities in DNA metabolism, should ultimately contribute to an improved understanding of the response of DNA synthesis in eukaryotes to DNA damage. Although mutants at 24 loci have been tested for their capacity to repair single-strand breaks induced by X-rays (Boyd & Setlow, 1976; Oliveri, unpublished observations), all exhibit a normal repair capacity.

MOLECULAR CLONING OF DNA REPAIR GENES

Cloning strategy

As this symposium has documented, many of the recent advances in our knowledge of DNA repair in unicellular organisms are due to the application of DNA cloning. An in-depth analysis of repair mechanisms in multicellular eukaryotes is, therefore, likely to require cloning of the corresponding repair genes in these organisms as well. Gene cloning in *Drosophila* not only offers the potential for elucidating the structure and function of repair genes in this organism, but it may also facilitate parallel analyses in less genetically accessible organisms by providing heterologous probes. In our laboratories we have chosen the *mei-9* and *mei-41* genes as the initial targets for gene cloning because isolation of these two genes will provide an entry into the mechanisms of both excision (*mei-9*) and postreplication repair (*mei-41*).

The current strategy for cloning these genes is based upon a combination of transposon tagging and chromosome walking, which was initially developed by Bingham *et al.* (1981). An outline of this approach as it applies to the *mei-41* gene is depicted in Fig. 3. This method begins with the isolation of mutants that are generated by the insertion of a transposable element. In *Drosophila* the most convenient means of 'tagging' a gene in this way is using dysgenic crosses to mobilize transposable P elements as described below. The presence of a P insert at the locus of interest can then be verified by using a previously cloned P element as a probe for *in situ* hybridization to polytene chromosomes. In the appropriate mutant that probe will hybridize to the chromosomal region 14B13–14D1,2, which is the cytogenetic map position of the *mei-41* gene (Mason *et al.* 1981). In the second step of this procedure, fusion fragments of the *mei-41* gene and the P insert are recovered from a genomic library of the mutant stock by probing with labelled P sequences. Recovery of the correct genomic sequences is verified by *in situ* hybridization of the clones to wild-type salivary gland chromosomes lacking P elements. Finally, the fusion fragments are used as probes to recover the complete gene sequence from a wild type genomic library.

Mutation induction by transposon tagging

The phenomenon of hybrid dysgenesis in *Drosophila* has greatly expanded the applicability of transposon tagging because it is associated with a dramatic increase in the mobility of selected transposable elements (Engels, 1983). In the mating scheme depicted in Fig. 4 males carrying up to 50 P elements per genome are crossed to M females lacking such elements. Under these conditions the germ line of the progeny G_1 males experiences an elevated mutation frequency primarily due to increased P transposition. Stocks derived from individual G_2 males can then be tested for the presence of new mutations, which are usually due to the insertion of a P element into a gene of interest.

Progress report

We have used several variations of the basic strategy outlined in Fig. 4 to recover X-linked *mus* mutants with transposon insertions. These procedures differed primarily in the source of the G_0 parents and in the methods used to propagate the

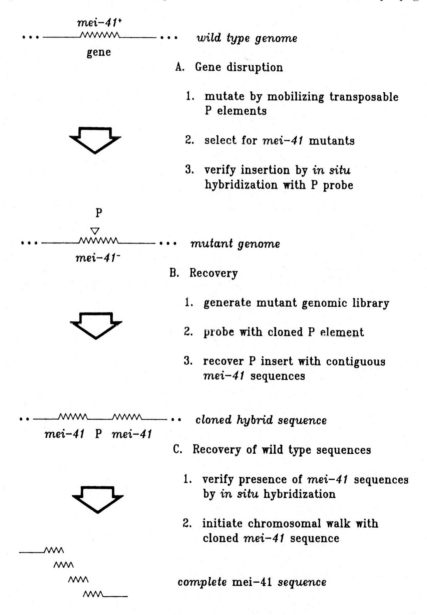

Fig. 3. Strategy for cloning the *mei-41* gene by transposon tagging.

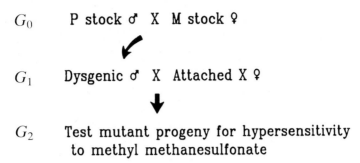

G_0 P stock ♂ X M stock ♀

G_1 Dysgenic ♂ X Attached X ♀

G_2 Test mutant progeny for hypersensitivity to methyl methanesulfonate

Fig. 4. Use of hybrid dysgenesis to generate *mus* mutants by transpositional insertion. Any mutant X chromosomes segregated by the dysgenic F_1 males are maintained in males, because the females carry attached X chromosomes.

recovered mutants. Essentially, the highest mutant yields were obtained when the resulting mutations were rapidly introduced into an *M* cytotype (a stock with a minimum number of P elements). A total of 10 mutants were recovered from 61 865 X chromosomes tested for hypersensitivity to methyl methane sulphonate and tested for complementation with the previously isolated mutants. Five mutations are *mei-41* alleles, four are allelic to *mei-9*, and one is a *mus102* allele. Consistent with their cytological map positions *in situ* hybridization has revealed the presence of a P insert at chromosomal position 4B in one of the *mei-9* mutants and P inserts at 14C in three of the *mei-41* mutants. We have, therefore, completed step A shown in Fig. 3 for both the *mei-41* and *mei-9* genes, and P-containing clones are currently being recovered from genomic libraries derived from those stocks. We are, therefore, confident that a thorough characterization of the structure and function of these two genes is now possible.

ENZYMOLOGY RELATED TO DNA REPAIR

The list of repair-related enzymes that have been identified in *Drosophila* has roughly doubled since this subject was reviewed three years ago. Although most of the newly recognized enzymes have not been extensively purified, they generally exhibit properties similar to those of more thoroughly purified mammalian enzymes. This correlation suggests that *Drosophila* will provide a valuable model for evaluating the relative importance of these enzymes in eukaryotic chromosome stability and mutagenesis once the corresponding genes have been identified. Within the same period *Drosophila* has also played a leading role in the analysis of eukaryotic polymerases and topoisomerases, primarily because of the extraordinary concentration of those enzymes in oocytes and embryos. At present, however, the genetic advantages of this organism have yet to be exploited in analysing the functions of any of these enzymes. In this section DNA metabolic enzymes that have been implicated either directly or indirectly in DNA repair are presented in alphabetical order.

Two classes of endonucleases have been identified that nick damaged DNA. In analogy with mammalian studies, the AP endonuclease activity of *Drosophila* embryos can be separated into two fractions by phosphocellulose chromatography

(Spiering & Deutsch, 1981). The variable levels and low purity of the flow-through fraction, however, indicate further work is needed before the identity and characterization of that activity are secure (Presley, unpublished observations). In parallel with analyses of xeroderma pigmentosum D cells, excision-deficient mutants at the *mei-9* and *mus201* loci in *Drosophila* exhibit reduced AP endonuclease activity (Osgood & Boyd, 1982).

An additional nuclease activity which degrades uracil-containing DNA has been detected in third instar larvae of *Drosophila* (Deutsch & Spiering, 1982). Although this activity may be due to a single enzyme similar to *E. coli* endonuclease V (Gates & Linn, 1977), the extensive nuclease activity present at this stage of development (Boyd, 1969) can complicate the interpretation of data obtained with impure preparations.

Previous failures to identify glycosylases in *Drosophila* have led to the suggestion that this organism might lack base-excision repair (Green & Deutsch, 1983). However, a glycosylase from *Drosophila* embryos that acts on oxidized thymine residues has recently been isolated (Breimer, 1986). This observation does not rule out the possibility that *Drosophila* repair enzymes may act on alkylated (Green & Deutsch, 1983) or uracil-containing (Deutsch & Spiering, 1982) DNA in a unique fashion.

Deutsch & Spiering (1985) have recently reported the presence of a purine-base insertase activity in *Drosophila* embryos that shares many properties with its mammalian counterpart (Deutsch & Linn, 1979). Since mutants affecting this activity are not available, its discovery in a genetically tractable eukaryote offers a possible clarification of the role of this activity.

A DNA ligase activity has recently been purified to virtual homogeneity from *Drosophila* embryos (Rabin & Chase, personal communication). This development should make it possible to identify the ligase structural gene.

The recent identification of a methyltransferase in *Drosophila* (Green & Deutsch, 1983) begins to fill the gap in our knowledge of alkylation repair in this organism. In view of the difficulty in identifying glycosylases that are specific for alkylated bases (Green & Deutsch, 1983), transferase activity may play a much greater role in the repair of alkylation damage in *Drosophila* than it does in other organisms.

Since the *phr*[+] gene described in the section on Photorepair is absolutely required for photorepair, there is a strong possibility that it encodes a photorepair enzyme. A probable candidate has been partially purified from *Drosophila* tissue culture cells by Beck & Sutherland (1979). That enzyme requires an RNA cofactor and exhibits assay requirements similar to those of the *E. coli* enzyme (Beck, 1982). Proof of the proposed gene–enzyme relationship would permit a refined definition of the biological role of that enzyme.

Although ribosylation of nuclear proteins by poly(ADP-ribose)synthetase has been strongly implicated in the regulation of eukaryotic DNA repair (Shall *et al.* 1982), no genetic proof of that relationship is available. Recently, however, Nolan & Kidwell (1982) have identified and partially characterized a poly(ADP-ribose)-synthetase in *Drosophila* tissue culture cells. Smulson *et al.* (1983) have furthermore demonstrated the specific accumulation of a protein at puffed regions of *Chironomous* polytene chromosomes as a result of its cross-reactivity to an antibody directed against poly(ADP-ribose)synthetase from man.

Three polymerases, which appear to be functionally homologous to the α, β and γ forms in mammals, have been purified to homogeneity from *Drosophila* embryos (Kaguni *et al.* 1983; Sakaguchi & Boyd, 1985; Sakaguchi, unpublished observations). On the basis of that homology each form is potentially involved in either nuclear (α, β) or mitochondrial (γ) DNA repair. The most complex and best-studied polymerase is the major synthetic enzyme polymerase α. That enzyme is composed of four different subunits with an aggregate molecular weight of 280 000 (Kaguni *et al.* 1983). Current efforts are being devoted to the development of an *in vitro* replication complex, which currently includes *Drosophila* DNA primase and ribonuclease H (DiFrancesco & Lehman, 1985). Analysis of that complex should ultimately contribute to an improved understanding of the synthetic aspects of repair and their impact on mutation and chromosome stability. Further characterization of the two smaller polymerases is expected to follow a similar pattern. The availability of these enzymes in pure form will greatly facilitate cloning of their structural genes, which will in turn permit a genetic analysis of enzyme function.

Topoisomerases, which are strongly implicated in DNA repair in other organisms, have also been extensively studied in *Drosophila* (Javaherian *et al.* 1982; Ackerman *et al.* 1985; Udvardy *et al.* 1985). *In situ* analysis of polytene chromosomes has revealed that topoisomerase II is a major chromosomal protein that is distributed evenly throughout the genome (Berrios *et al.* 1985). In contrast, topoisomerase I is associated primarily with the transcriptionally active regions of the chromosomes (Fleischmann *et al.* 1984). Identification of the corresponding genes through cloning is also expected to clarify the role of these enzymes in DNA repair.

The work reported from our laboratories is being supported by the Department of Energy (EV 70210) and the National Institutes of Health (GM 32040). We are grateful to Bruce Baker for permission to reproduce Fig. 2. The advice and participation of Paul Harris has been invaluable throughout this effort.

REFERENCES

ACKERMAN, P., GLOVER, C. V. C. & OSHEROFF, N. (1985). Phosphorylation of DNA topoisomerase II by casein kinase II: Modulation of eukaryotic topoisomerase II activity *in vitro*. *Proc. natn. Acad. Sci. U.S.A.* **82**, 3164–3168.

BAARS, A. J., BLIJLEVEN, W. G. H., MOHN, G. R., NATARAJAN, A. T. & BREIMER, D. D. (1980). Preliminary studies on the ability of *Drosophila* microsomal preparations to activate mutagens and carcinogens. *Mutat. Res.* **72**, 257–264.

BADARUDDIN, A. S., DUSENBERY, R. L. & SMITH, P. D. (1984). Mutagen sensitivity of *Drosophila melanogaster*. VII. Alkylation mutagenesis of mature and immature oocytes of the excision-deficient *mus(2)201^{D1}* mutant. *Environ. Mutagen.* **6**, 753–755.

BAKER, B. S., BOYD, J. B., CARPENTER, A. T. C., GREEN, M. M., NGUYEN, T. D., RIPOLL, P. & SMITH, P. D. (1976a). Genetic controls of meiotic recombination and somatic DNA metabolism in *Drosophila melanogaster*. *Proc. natn. Acad. Sci. U.S.A.* **73**, 4140–4144.

BAKER, B. S. & CARPENTER, A. T. C. (1972). Genetic analysis of sex chromosomal meiotic mutants in *Drosophila melanogaster*. *Genetics* **71**, 255–286.

BAKER, B. S., CARPENTER, A. T. C., ESPOSITO, M. S., ESPOSITO, R. E. & SANDLER, L. (1976*b*). The genetic control of meiosis. *A. Rev. Genet.* **10**, 53–134.

BAKER, B. S., CARPENTER, A. T. C. & RIPOLL, P. (1978). The utilization during mitotic cell division of loci controlling meiotic recombination and disjunction in *Drosophila melanogaster*. *Genetics* **90**, 531–578.

BAKER, B. S., GATTI, M., CARPENTER, A. T. C., PIMPINELLI, S. & SMITH, D. A. (1980). Effects of recombination-deficient and repair-deficient loci on meiotic and mitotic chromosome behavior in *Drosophila melanogaster*. In *DNA Repair and Mutagenesis in Eukaryotes* (ed. S. M. Generoso, M. D. Shelby & F. J. deSerres), pp. 189–208. New York, London: Plenum Press.

BAKER, B. S. & SMITH, D. A. (1979). The effects of mutagen-sensitive mutants of *Drosophila melanogaster* in nonmutagenized cells. *Genetics* **92**, 833–847.

BAKER, B. S., SMITH, D. A. & GATTI, M. (1982). Region specific effects on chromosome integrity of mutations at essential loci in *Drosophila melanogaster*. *Proc. natn. Acad. Sci. U.S.A.* **79**, 1205–1209.

BECK, L. A. (1982). Studies on a photoreactivating enzyme from *Drosophila melanogaster* cultured cells. Ph.D. dissertation, University of California, Irvine.

BECK, L. A. & SUTHERLAND, B. M. (1979). Purification of a photoreactivating enzyme from *D. melanogaster*. *Am. Soc. Photobiol.* **7**, 130 (abstract).

BENDER, W., SPIERER, P. & HOGNESS, D. S. (1983). Chromosomal walking and jumping to isolate DNA from *Ace* and *rosy* loci and the bithorax complex in *Drosophila melanogaster*. *J. molec. Biol.* **168**, 17–33.

BERRIOS, M., OSHEROFF, N. & FISHER, P. A. (1985). *In situ* localization of DNA topoisomerase II, a major polypeptide component of the *Drosophila* nuclear matrix fraction. *Proc. natn. Acad. Sci. U.S.A.* **82**, 4142–4146.

BINGHAM, P. M., LEVIS, R. & RUBIN, G. M. (1981). Cloning of DNA sequences from white locus of *D. melanogaster* by a novel and general method. *Cell* **25**, 693–704.

BOYD, J. B. (1969). *Drosophila* deoxyribonucleases. I. Variation of deoxyribonucleases in *Drosophila melanogaster*. *Biochim. biophys. Acta* **171**, 103–112.

BOYD, J. B., GOLINO, M. D., NGUYEN, T. D. & GREEN, M. M. (1976*a*). Isolation and characterization of X-linked mutants of *Drosophila melanogaster* which are sensitive to mutagens. *Genetics* **84**, 485–506.

BOYD, J. B., GOLINO, M. D. & SETLOW, R. B. (1976*b*). The *mei-9*ᵃ mutant of *Drosophila melanogaster* increases mutagen sensitivity and decreases excision repair. *Genetics* **84**, 527–544.

BOYD, J. B., GOLINO, M. D., SHAW, K. E. S., OSGOOD, C. J. & GREEN, M. M. (1981). Third-chromosome mutagen-sensitive mutants of *Drosophila melanogaster*. *Genetics* **97**, 607–623.

BOYD, J. B. & HARRIS, P. V. (1985). Isolation and characterization of a photorepair-deficient mutant in *Drosophila melanogaster*. *Genetics* **110**, s85.

BOYD, J. B., HARRIS, P. V., OSGOOD, C. J. & SMITH, K. E. (1980). Biochemical characterization of repair-deficient mutants of *Drosophila*. In *DNA Repair and Mutagenesis in Eukaryotes* (ed. W. M. Generoso, M. D. Shelby & F. J. deSerres), pp. 209–222. New York, London: Plenum Press.

BOYD, J. B., HARRIS, P. V., PRESLEY, J. M. & NARACHI, M. (1983). *Drosophila melanogaster*: A model eukaryote for the study of DNA repair. In *Cellular Responses to DNA Damage* (ed. E. C. Friedberg & C. A. Bridges), pp. 107–123. New York: Liss, Inc.

BOYD, J. B. & SETLOW, R. B. (1976). Characterization of postreplication repair in mutagen-sensitive strains of *Drosophila melanogaster*. *Genetics* **84**, 507–526.

BOYD, J. B. & SHAW, K. E. S. (1982). Postreplication repair defects in mutants of *Drosophila melanogaster*. *Molec. gen. Genet.* **186**, 289–294.

BOYD, J. B., SNYDER, R. D., HARRIS, P. V., PRESLEY, J. M., BOYD, S. F. & SMITH, P. D. (1982). Identification of a second locus in *Drosophila melanogaster* required for excision repair. *Genetics* **100**, 239–257.

BREIMER, L. H. (1986). A DNA glycosylase for oxidized thymine residues in *Drosophila melanogaster*. *Biochem. biophys. Res. Commun.* **134**, 201–204.

CARPENTER, A. T. C. (1975). Electron microscopy of meiosis in *Drosophila melanogaster* females. II. The recombination nodule – a recombination-associated structure at pachytene? *Proc. natn. Acad. Sci. U.S.A.* **72**, 3186–3189.

CARPENTER, A. T. C. (1979). Recombination nodules and synaptonemal complex in recombination-defective females of *Drosophila melanogaster*. *Chromosoma* **75**, 259–292.

CARPENTER, A. T. C. (1981). EM autoradiographic evidence that DNA synthesis occurs at recombination nodules during meiosis in *Drosophila melanogaster* females. *Chromosoma* **83**, 59–80.

CARPENTER, A. T. C. (1982). Mismatch repair, gene conversion, and crossing-over in two recombination-defective mutants of *Drosophila melanogaster*. *Proc. natn. Acad. Sci. U.S.A.* **79**, 5961–5965.

CARPENTER, A. T. C. & SANDLER, L. (1974). On recombination-defective meiotic mutants in *Drosophila melanogaster*. *Genetics* **76**, 453–574.

CERUTTI, P. A. (1975). Repairable damage in DNA: Overview. In *Molecular Mechanisms for Repair of DNA* (ed. P. C. Hanawalt & R. B. Setlow), pp. 3–11. New York: Plenum Press.

DE WIT, J., JASPERS, N. G. J. & BOOTSMA, O. (1981). The rate of DNA synthesis in normal human and ataxia telangiectasia cells after exposure to X-irradiation. *Mutat. Res.* **80**, 221–226.

DEUTSCH, W. A. & LINN, S. (1979). DNA-binding activity from cultured human fibroblasts that is specific for partially depurinated DNA and that inserts purines into apurinic sites. *Proc. natn. Acad. Sci. U.S.A.* **76**, 141–144.

DEUTSCH, W. A. & SPIERING, A. L. (1982). A new pathway expressed during a distinct stage of *Drosophila* development for removal of dUMP residues in DNA. *J. biol. Chem.* **257**, 3366–3368.

DEUTSCH, W. A. & SPIERING, A. L. (1985). Characterization of a depurinated-DNA purine-base-insertion activity from *Drosophila*. *Biochem. J.* **232**, 285–288.

DIFRANCESCO, R. A. & LEHMAN, I. R. (1985). Interaction of ribonuclease H from *Drosophila melanogaster* embryos with DNA polymerase-primase. *J. biol. Chem.* **260**, 14764–14770.

DUSENBERY, R. L., MCCORMICK, S. C. & SMITH, P. D. (1983). *Drosophila* mutations at the *mei-9* and *mus(2)201* loci which block excision of thymine dimers also block induction of unscheduled DNA synthesis by methyl methanesulfonate, ethyl methanesulfonate, *N*-methyl-*N*-nitrosource, UV light and X-rays. *Mutat. Res.* **112**, 215–230.

EEKEN, J. C. J. & SOBELS, F. H. (1981). Modification of MR mutator activity in repair-deficient strains of *Drosophila melanogaster*. *Mutat. Res.* **83**, 191–200.

ENGELS, W. R. (1983). The P family of transposable elements in *Drosophila*. *A. Rev. Genet.* **17**, 315–344.

FERRO, W. (1985). Studies on mutagen-sensitive strains of *Drosophila melanogaster*. V. Biochemical characterization of a strain (ebony) that is UV- and X-ray sensitive and deficient in photorepair. *Mutat. Res.* **149**, 339–408.

FLEISCHMANN, G., PFLUGFELDER, G., STEINER, E. K., JAVAHERIAN, K., HOWARD, G. C., WANG, J. C. & ELGIN, S. C. R. (1984). *Drosophila* DNA topoisomerase I is associated with transcriptionally active region of the genome. *Proc. natn. Acad. Sci. U.S.A.* **81**, 6958–6962.

FRIEDBERG, E. C. (1985). *DNA Repair*. New York: W. H. Freeman & Company.

FUJIKAWA, K. & KONDO, S. (1986). DNA repair dependence of somatic mutagenesis of transposon-caused *white* alleles in *Drosophila melanogaster* after treatment with alkylating agenets. *Genetics* **112**, 505–522.

GANESAN, A. K. (1974). Persistance of pyrimidine dimers during postreplication repair in ultraviolet light-irradiated *Escherichia coli* K12. *J. molec. Biol.* **87**, 103–119.

GATES, F. T. & LINN, S. (1977). Endonuclease V of *Escherichia coli*. *J. biol. Chem.* **252**, 1647–1653.

GATTI, M. (1979). Genetic control of chromosome breakage and rejoining in *Drosophila melanogaster*: Spontaneous chromosome aberrations in X-linked mutants defective in DNA metabolism. *Proc. natn. Acad. Sci. U.S.A.* **76**, 1377–1381.

GATTI, M., PIMPINELLI, S. & BAKER, B. S. (1980). Relationships among chromatid interchanges, sister chromatid exchanges, and meiotic recombination in *Drosophila melanogaster*. *Proc. natn. Acad. Sci. U.S.A.* **77**, 1575–1579.

GATTI, M., PIMPINELLI, S., BOVE, C., BAKER, B. S., SMITH, D. A., CARPENTER, A. T. C. & RIPOLL, P. (1984). Genetic control of mitotic cell division in *Drosophila melanogaster*. In *Genetics: New Frontiers*, vol. III (ed. V. L. Chopra, B. C. Joshi, R. P. Sharma & H. C. Bansal), pp. 193–204. New Delhi: Oxford & IBS Publishing Co.

GATTI, M., SMITH, D. A. & BAKER, B. S. (1983). A gene controlling condensation of heterochromatin in *Drosophila melanogaster*. *Science* **221**, 83–85.

GENEROSO, W. M., SHELBY, M. D. & DESERRES, F. J. (eds) (1980). *DNA Repair and Mutagenesis in Eukaryotes*, pp. 175–244. New York: Plenum Press.

GRAF, U., GREEN, M. M. & WÜRGLER, F. E. (1979*a*). Mutagen-sensitive mutants in *Drosophila melanogaster*: Effects on premutational damage. *Mutat. Res.* **63**, 101–112.

GRAF, U., KÄGI, A. & WÜRGLER, F. E. (1982). Mutagenesis in spermatozoa of *Drosophila melanogaster* by cross-linking agents depends on the *mus(1)101+* gene product in the oocyte. *Mutat. Res.* **95**, 237–249.

GRAF, U., VOGEL, E., BIBER, U. P. & WÜRGLER, F. E. (1979*b*). Genetic control of mutagen sensitivity in *Drosophila melanogaster*. A new allele at the *mei-9* locus on the X-chromosome. *Mutat. Res.* **59**, 129–138.

GREEN, M. M. (1973). Some observations and comments on mutable and mutator genes in *Drosophila*. *Genetics* **73**, s187–194.

GREEN, M. M. (1981). *mus(3)312*[D1], a mutagen sensitive mutant with profound effects on female meiosis in *Drosophila melanogaster*. *Chromosoma* **82**, 259–266.

GREEN, M. M. (1982). On the meiotic effects of mutants at the mutagen-sensitive locus, *mus(3)304*, in *Drosophila melanogaster*. *Biol. Zbl.* **101**, 223–226.

GREEN, D. A. & DEUTSCH, W. A. (1983). Repair of alkylated DNA: *Drosophila* have DNA methyltransferases but not DNA glycosylases. *Molec. gen. Genet.* **192**, 322–325.

HARRIS, P. V. & BOYD, J. B. (1980). Excision repair in *Drosophila*. Analysis of strand breaks appearing in DNA of *mei-9* mutants following mutagen treatment. *Biochim. biophys. Acta* **610**, 116–129.

HAWLEY, R. S., MARCUS, C. H., CAMERON, M. L., SCHWARTZ, R. L. & ZITRON, A. E. (1985). Repair-defect mutations inhibit rDNA magnification in *Drosophila* and discriminate between meiotic and premeiotic magnification. *Proc. natn. Acad. Sci. U.S.A.* **82**, 8095–8099.

HAWLEY, R. S. & TARTOF, K. D. (1983). The effect of *mei-41* on rDNA redundancy in *Drosophila melanogaster*. *Genetics* **104**, 63–80.

INOUE, H. & ISHII, C. (1985). A new ultraviolet-light sensitive mutant of *Neurospora crassa* with unusual photoreactivation property. *Mutat. Res.* **152**, 161–168.

JAVAHERIAN, K., TSE, Y.-C. & VEGA, J. (1982). *Drosophila* topoisomerase I: Isolation, purification and characterization. *Nucl. Acid Res.* **10**, 6945–6955.

KAGUNI, L. S., ROSSIGNOL, J. M., CONAWAY, R. C. & LEHMAN, I. R. (1983). The DNA polymerase–primase complex of *Drosophila melanogaster* embryos. In *Mechanisms of DNA Replication and Recombination* (ed. N. R. Cozarelli), pp. 495–510. New York: Liss.

KELLEY, M. R. & LEE, W. R. (1983). Mutagenesis in oocytes of *Drosophila melanogaster*. I. Scheduled synthesis of nuclear and mitochondrial DNA and unscheduled DNA synthesis. *Genetics* **104**, 279–299.

LAIRD, C. D. (1973). DNA of *Drosophila* chromosomes. *A. Rev. Genet.* **7**, 177–204.

LEHMANN, A. & KARRAN, P. (1981). DNA repair. *Int. Rev. Cytol.* **72**, 101–146.

LEHMANN, A. R. & KIRK-BELL, S. (1978). Pyrimidine dimer site associated with the daughter DNA strands in UV-irradiated human fibroblasts. *Photochem. Photobiol.* **27**, 297–307.

LEHMANN, A. R., KIRK-BELL, S., ARLETT, C. F., HARCOURT, S. A., DEWEIRD-KASTELEIN, E. A., KEIJZER, W. & HALL-SMITH, P. (1977). Repair of ultraviolet light damage in a variety of human fibroblast cell strains. *Cancer Res.* **37**, 904–910.

MASON, J. M., GREEN, M. M., SHAW, K. E. S. & BOYD, J. B. (1981). Genetic analysis of X-linked mutagen-sensitive mutants of *Drosophila melanogaster*. *Mutat. Res.* **81**, 329–343.

MASON, J. M., STROBEL, E. & GREEN, M. M. (1984). *mu-2*: Mutator gene in *Drosophila* that potentiates the induction of terminal deficiencies. *Proc. natn. Acad. Sci. U.S.A.* **81**, 6090–6094.

MULLER, H. J. (1940). An analysis of the process of structural change in chromosomes of *Drosophila*. *J. Genet.* **40**, 1–66.

NARACHI, M. A. & BOYD, J. B. (1985). The giant (*gt*) mutants of *Drosophila melanogaster* alter DNA metabolism. *Molec. gen. Genet.* **199**, 500–506.

NGUYEN, T. D. & BOYD, J. B. (1977). The meiotic-9 (*mei-9*) mutants of *Drosophila melanogaster* are deficient in repair replication of DNA. *Molec. gen. Genet.* **158**, 141–147.

NGUYEN, T. D., BOYD, J. B. & GREEN, M. M. (1979). Sensitivity of *Drosophila* mutants to chemical carcinogens. *Mutat. Res.* **63**, 67–77.

NGUYEN, T. D., GREEN, M. M. & BOYD, J. B. (1978). Isolation of two X-linked mutants in *Drosophila melanogaster* which are sensitive to γ-rays. *Mutat. Res.* **49**, 139–143.

NOLAN, N. L. & KIDWELL, W. R. (1982). Effect of heat shock on poly(ADP-ribose)synthetase and DNA repair in *Drosophila* cells. *Radiat. Res.* **90**, 187–203.

ORR, W., KOMITOPOULOU, K. & KAFATOS, F. C. (1984). Mutants suppressing in *tras* chorion gene amplification in *Drosophila. Proc. natn. Acad. Sci. U.S.A.* **81**, 3773–3777.

OSGOOD, C. J. & BOYD, J. B. (1982). Apurinic endonuclease from *Drosophila melanogaster*: reduced enzymatic activity in excision-deficient mutants of the *mei-9* and *mus(2)201* loci. *Molec. gen. Genet.* **186**, 235–239.

POLITO, L. C., CAVALIERE, D., ZAZO, A. & FURIA, M. (1982). A study of rDNA magnification phenomenon in a repair-recombination deficient mutant of *Drosophila melanogaster. Genetics* **102**, 39–48.

PORSCH-HALLSTRÖM, I., BLANCK, A. & ATUMA, S. (1983). Comparison of cytochrome P-450-dependent metabolism in different developmental stages of *Drosophila melanogaster. Chem.-Biol. Interact.* **46**, 39–54.

RABINOWITZ, M. (1941). Studies on the cytology and early embryology of the egg of *Drosophila melanogaster. J. Morph.* **69**, 1–49.

RASMUSON, A. (1984). Effects of DNA-repair-deficient mutants on somatic and germ line mutagenesis in the UZ system of *Drosophila melanogaster. Mutat. Res.* **141**, 29–33.

RUBIN, G. M. & SPRADLING, A. C. (1982). Genetic transformation of *Drosophila* with transposable element vectors. *Science* **218**, 348–352.

SAKAGUCHI, K. & BOYD, J. B. (1985). Purification and characterization of a DNA polymerase β from *Drosophila. J. biol. Chem.* **260**, 10 406–10 411.

SANCAR, G. B., SMITH, F. W. & SANCAR, A. (1983). Identification and amplification of the *E. coli phr* gene product. *Nucl. Acids Res.* **11**, 6667–6678.

SHALL, S., DURKACZ, B. W., GRAY, D. A., IRWIN, J., LEWIS, P. J., PERERA, M. & TAVARSOLI, M. (1982). (ADP-ribose)$_n$ participates in DNA excision repair. In *Mechanism of Chemical Carcinogenesis* (ed. C. C. Harris & P. A. Cerutti), pp. 389–407. New York: Liss, Inc.

SLATKO, B. E., MASON, J. M. & WOODRUFF, R. C. (1984). The DNA transposition system of hybrid dysgenesis in *Drosophila melanogaster* can function despite defects in host DNA repair. *Genet. Res.* **43**, 159–171.

SMITH, D. A., BAKER, B. S. & GATTI, M. (1985). Mutations in genes encoding essential mitotic functions in *Drosophila melanogaster. Genetics* **110**, 647–670.

SMITH, P. D. (1973). Mutagen sensitivity of *Drosophila melanogaster*. I. Isolation and preliminary characterization of a methyl methanesulfonate sensitive strain. *Mutat. Res.* **20**, 215–220.

SMITH, P. D. (1976). Mutagen sensitivity of *Drosophila melanogaster*. III. X-linked loci governing sensitivity to methyl methanesulphonate. *Molec. gen. Genet.* **149**, 73–85.

SMITH, P. D., BAUMEN, C. F. & DUSENBERY, R. L. (1983). Mutagen sensitivity of *Drosophila melanogaster*. VI. Evidence from the excision-defective *mei-9*^{AT1} mutant for the timing of DNA-repair activity during spermatogenesis. *Mutat. Res.* **108**, 175–184.

SMITH, P. D. & DUSENBERY, R. L. (1985). Mutagen sensitivity of *Drosophila melanogaster*. VIII. The influence of the *mei-41*^{D5}, *mus(1)101*^{D1}, *mus(1)102*^{D1}, *mus(1)103*^{D1}, *mus(2)205*^{A1} and *mus(3)310*^{D1} loci on alkylation-induced mutagenesis. *Mutat. Res.* **150**, 235–240.

SMITH, P. D., SNYDER, R. D. & DUSENBERY, R. L. (1980). Isolation and characterization of repair-deficient mutants of *Drosophila melanogaster*. In *DNA Repair and Mutagenesis in Eukaryotes* (ed. W. M. Generoso, M. D. Shelby & F. J. deSerres), pp. 175–188. New York, London: Plenum Press.

SMULSON, M., MALIK, N., WONG, M., POMATO, N. & THRACES, P. (1983). Fine resolution of the poly(ADP)-ribosylated domains of polynucleosomal chromatin: DNA gene and integrity analysis; mechanisms of histone H1 modification. In *ADP-Ribosylation, DNA Repair and Cancer* (ed. M. Miwa, O. Hayaishi, S. Shall, M. Smulson & T. Sugimura), pp. 49–70. Utrecht: Japan Sci. Soc. Press, Tokyo/VNU Science Press.

SNYDER, R. D. & SMITH, P. D. (1982). Mutagen sensitivity of *Drosophila melanogaster*. V. Identification of second chromosomal mutagen sensitive strains. *Molec. gen. Genet.* **188**, 249–255.

SOBELS, F. H. (1972). A dose-fractionation study to determine how long breaks induced in various stages of spermatogenesis stay open. *Revue suisse Zool.* **79**, 143–152.

SPIERING, A. L. & DEUTSCH, W. A. (1981). Apurinic DNA endonucleases from *Drosophila melanogaster* embryos. *Molec. gen. Genet.* **183**, 171–174.

SUTHERLAND, B. M., RICE, M. & WAGNER, E. K. (1975). Xeroderma pigmentosum cells contain low levels of photoreactivating enzyme. *Proc. natn. Acad. Sci. U.S.A.* **72**, 103–107.

SWAIN, C. G. & SCOTT, C. B. (1953). Quantitative correlation of relative rates: Comparison of hydroxide ion with other nucleophilic reagents toward alkyl halides, esters, epoxides and acyl halides. *J. Am. Chem. Soc.* **75**, 141–147.

TODO, T., HEDA, R., MIYAKE, T. & KONDO, S. (1985). Hypersensitivity to ultraviolet light and chemical mutagens of a cell line established from excisionless *Drosophila* strain *mus201*. *Mutat. Res.* **145**, 165–170.

TYRSTED, G. (1982). Effect of hydroxyurea and 5-fluorodeoxyuridine on deoxynucleoside triphosphate pools early in phytohemaglutinin-stimulated human lymphocytes. *Biochem. Pharmac.* **31**, 3107–3113.

UDVARDY, A., SCHEDL, P., SANDER, M. & HSIEH, T.-S. (1985). Novel partitioning of DNA cleavage sites for *Drosophila* topoisomerase II. *Cell,* **40**, 933–941.

VOELKER, R. A., GREENLEAF, A. L., GYURKOVICS, H., WISELY, G. B., HUANG, S.-M. & SEARLES, L. L. (1984). Frequent imprecise excision among reversions of a P element-caused lethal mutation in *Drosophila*. *Genetics* **107**, 279–294.

VOGEL, E. W., DUSENBERY, R. L. & SMITH, P. D. (1985). The relation between reaction kinetics and mutagenic action of monofunctional alkylating agents in higher eukaryotic systems. IV. The effects of the excision-defective *mei-9^{L1}* and *mus(2)201^{D1}* mutants on alkylation-induced genetic damage in *Drosophila*. *Mutat. Res.* **149**, 193–207.

VOGEL, E. W. & NATARAJAN, A. T. (1979*a*). The relationship between reaction kinetics and mutagenic action of mono-functional alkylating agents in higher eukaryotic systems. I. Recessive lethal mutations and translocations in *Drosophila*. *Mutat. Res.* **62**, 51–100.

VOGEL, E. W. & NATARAJAN, A. T. (1979*b*). The relation between reaction kinetics and mutagenic action of monofunctional alkylating agents in higher eukaryotic systems. II. Total and partial sex-chromosome loss in *Drosophila*. *Mutat. Res.* **62**, 101–123.

WATERS, L. C., NIX, C. E. & EPLER, J. L. (1982). Dimethylnitrosamine demethylase activity in *Drosophila melanogaster*. *Biochem. biophys. Res. Commun.* **106**, 779–785.

YAMAMOTO, K. & SHINAGAWA, H. (1985). Weigle reactivation of phage lambda in a *recA* mutant of *Escherichia coli*: Dependence on the excess amounts of photoreactivating enzyme in the dark. *Mutat. Res.* **145**, 137–144.

ZIMMERING, S. (1983). The *mei-9^a* test for chromosome loss in *Drosophila*: A review of assays of 21 chemicals for chromosome breakage. *Environ. Mutagen.* **5**, 907–921.

J. Cell Sci. Suppl. 6, 61–82 (1987)
Printed in Great Britain © The Company of Biologists Limited 1987

DNA REPAIR MUTANTS IN HIGHER EUKARYOTES

A. COLLINS

*Department of Biochemistry, University of Aberdeen, Marischal College, Aberdeen
AB9 1AS, UK*

AND R. T. JOHNSON

*Cancer Research Campaign Mammalian Cell DNA Repair Group, Department of
Zoology, Cambridge University, Cambridge CB2 3EJ, UK*

SUMMARY

Over the past ten years or so, we have seen a proliferation of reports of new cell lines of various vertebrate species, showing hypersensitivity to killing by DNA damaging agents. Regrettably, but predictably, there is no standard terminology to describe the mutants, and as a result the literature is liberally scattered with fragments of individualistic nomenclature. There is no way of imposing order at this stage, but it may be helpful to bring together in this chapter as much information as possible on the mutants now available. As well as being an aid for reference, this should serve as a pointer towards further investigation – either in characterizing the mutants we have, or in developing new ones to fill gaps in our knowledge.

INTRODUCTION

The purpose of this chapter is twofold. For those intending to enter the field of DNA repair mutants, we provide an introduction to the methodology of mutant production and characterization, with particular emphasis on rapid and simple techniques. We discuss potential uses and problems of such mutants. We also hope that the chapter will be of use to those already engaged in this work, since it provides a reasonably complete survey of permanent human cell lines showing DNA repair defects, together with tables cataloguing the artificially induced repair mutants so far available.

This survey will be limited to higher eukaryote cell lines. The genetics of repair in prokaryotes, in yeast and in *Drosophila*, have been dealt with in other chapters of this book. Mutants will be described in terms of their sensitivity (and their cross-sensitivities, i.e. sensitivities to agents other than that used for the original selection); and, where available, details will be given of the nature of the defect in the cells' response to DNA damage. In several cases, sets of mutant cell lines have been placed in different genetic complementation groups. Less commonly, complementation or the lack of it has been established between mutants originating in different laboratories.

As will be seen from the size of Table 2, the majority of known DNA repair mutants originate from two Chinese hamster cell lines, and it is more than likely that effort will be concentrated to an increasing extent on this material. No doubt this approach will quickly yield a unified view of DNA repair mechanisms – but it is already clear that different species display surprisingly distinct repair phenotypes, and we should beware of fishing exclusively in one small area of the eukaryote gene pool.

First, then, we shall give an outline of methods for obtaining DNA repair mutants, from the initial mutagenesis, through enrichment and selection, to a complete characterization.

INDUCTION AND SELECTION OF CELL LINES DEFECTIVE IN DNA REPAIR

Mutagenesis

Standard procedures are used for this step, treating exponentially growing cell populations with chemical mutagens such as ethyl methane sulphonate (EMS), or radiation, and allowing several days (subculturing if necessary so that cells do not enter a plateau phase of growth) for expression of the induced mutations. At this stage, stocks of mutagenized cells may be stored frozen for use in later screening experiments. (For general information on mutagenesis, see Thompson & Baker, 1973; Basilico & Meiss, 1974; Kao & Puck, 1974.)

Enrichment and selection

A common strategy is next to carry out an enrichment step, to exclude a large proportion of cells that are wild-type in terms of DNA repair. A 'suicide' procedure is adopted: for instance, after treatment with a DNA damaging agent, the cells are incubated with a DNA precursor analogue that will be incorporated into the DNA of normal cells in the course of repair synthesis, and will prove lethal; mutant cells defective in repair, unless they are in *S* phase, will tend to survive. Such protocols have been described by Isomura *et al.* (1973), Stefanini *et al.* (1982), and Fiorio *et al.* (1983), with bromodeoxyuridine (BrdUrd) as an analogue of thymidine; on subsequent irradiation with 'black light', photolysis of incorporated base causes lethal DNA damage. Schultz *et al.* (1981*b*) employed an analogous method but with high specific activity [^{3}H]thymidine ([^{3}H]dThd) substituted for BrdUrd–black light. In this case, death results from radiation damage caused by decaying incorporated tritium.

A complication with this strategy is its dependence on a DNA damaging treatment in order to produce the DNA resynthesis response; the DNA damage may be sufficient to remove from the population any highly sensitive mutants. Thus the enrichment is likely to produce a preponderance of moderate rather than extreme repair defects.

An alternative suicide approach involves infection of cells with virus previously treated with DNA damaging agent to inactivate it (Shiomi & Sato, 1979). Wild-type cells repair the virus, restoring its activity, and are killed by it; repair-defective cells survive. It is, of course, important to avoid the possibility of secondary infection of surviving cells with virus released from cells that have successfully repaired it.

The most productive technique so far for selecting those clones in a mutagenized population (with or without a preceding enrichment step) that represent repair defects is the simple criterion of reduced growth/cell division following a low level of DNA damage. Thompson *et al.* (1980) examined individual colonies microscopically and carefully recovered those most affected. Busch *et al.* (1980) used an automated photographic recording device to identify colonies that did not increase in size during a specified interval after irradiation. An alternative, labour-intensive approach (which has the advantage that mutants do not undergo any genotoxic treatment during selection) is that referred to as 'toothpicking', where cells from individual colonies are transferred manually (using toothpicks) to establish sets of replicate colonies in multiwell plates or on agar; one set is then treated with the selecting agent, hypersensitive colonies are identified, and a cell line established from the corresponding well on the replicate plate (Shiomi *et al.* 1982a; Jeggo & Kemp, 1983; Robson *et al.* 1985).

True replica plating, i.e. where a pattern of colonies is copied directly from one culture dish to another, one of which is tested, has been used in several versions. Stamato & Waldren (1977) established replicas of Chinese hamster ovary (CHO) colonies on nylon cloth and then irradiated the master plate with ultraviolet light (u.v.); a colony that readily detached was located on the replica and later characterized as the mutant UV-1. In a recent modification, Stamato *et al.* (1983) identified poorly growing colonies by matching photographic images taken at intervals after γ-irradiation. With the possibility of establishing multiple replicas on polyester mesh (Raetz *et al.* 1982; Collins, 1987), matching can be done between a reference, untreated stained replica and the master plate, treated with DNA damaging agent, incubated for preferential loss of hypersensitive colonies, and stained with a contrasting colour. There is the further possibility that assays specific for enzymic DNA repair activities can be carried out on one of the replicas. Stefanini *et al.* (1982) succeeded in identifying colonies showing low unscheduled DNA synthesis (UDS) in an autoradiographic assay on a replica.

A quite different, intriguingly elegant selection technique (Abbondandolo *et al.* 1982) makes use of a 'multiwire proportional chamber', which apparently discriminates between repairing and non-repairing colonies directly by comparison of levels of incorporation of $[^3H]$dThd.

Characterization

Following selection of clones that are possible DNA repair-defective mutants, the defect has to be confirmed and the phenotype characterized. The need is for quick and simple assays that can accommodate a large number of selected lines requiring testing at one time. We will describe here several such techniques that should make life easier for the collector of DNA repair mutants.

The parameter of fundamental importance in a mutant is its degree of sensitivity to genotoxic agents. The conventional plating assay, which measures single-cell colony-forming ability over a range of doses of the agent, is precise and reproducible but time-consuming; 1–2 weeks are required to allow development of colonies. As an alternative, cells can be plated at moderate density, treated with a range of doses of DNA damaging agent, and the combined effect of cell killing and growth inhibition assessed a few days later by visual inspection after fixing and staining, or by protein estimation or counting of attached cells. This procedure is similar to the 'differential cytotoxicity' assay developed by Hoy *et al.* (1984); an example is shown in Fig. 1. Arlett & Priestley (1983, 1984) introduced a useful method for quantifying the efficiency of repair of potentially lethal damage (PLD). In their procedure non-cycling, pre-*S*-phase cells were exposed to a DNA damaging agent and either replated immediately onto feeder layers to form colonies or replated after a 24 h period during which repair of PLD could occur. This method has proved to be extremely sensitive, maximizing discrimination between, for example, ataxia-telangiectasia (A-T), A-T heterozygote and wild-type fibroblasts. For permanent cell lines with less ability to arrest and therefore to repair PLD, this procedure may be more difficult to apply.

Repair DNA synthesis or UDS is a universally accepted parameter of excision repair capacity. Autoradiographic analysis of incorporated [³H]dThd is sound but slow (Pawsey *et al.* 1978). UDS can be measured by scintillation counting of acid-insoluble tritium, if replicative DNA synthesis is suppressed by hydroxyurea

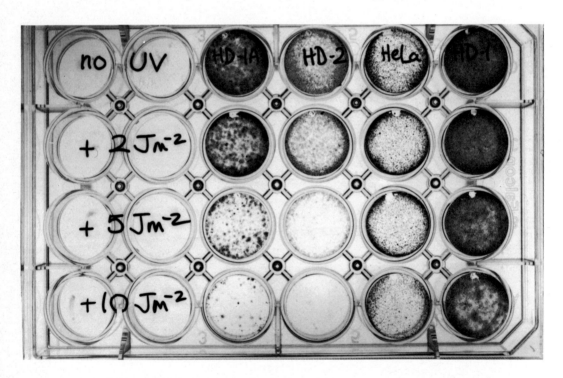

Fig. 1. Cytotoxicity assay using multiwell plates. Wells were inoculated with 10^5 cells each (suspended in PBS) in columns of four wells for each cell type: HD-1A, HD-2, HeLa and HD-1. They were irradiated with u.v. (0, 2, 5 or 10 J m^{-2} as shown), medium was added, and incubation continued for 4 days before fixing and staining. Different cell types give different staining intensities in the control, unirradiated wells, presumably as a result of differing rates of growth, cell size or morphology. But it can be seen, from the relative decrease in intensity with u.v. dose, that HD-1A suffers greater cytotoxicity than HD-1, and that HD-2 is particularly sensitive compared with HeLa. Qualitatively, this is in accord with known u.v. survival parameters (Johnson *et al.* 1985, 1986).

(Brandt *et al.* 1972); although there are theoretical objections to this procedure (Mullinger *et al.* 1983; Collins & Johnson, 1984), it is justified by the success of its results.

A near-universal feature of the cellular response to DNA damage is the temporary depression of replicative DNA synthesis (Painter, 1977). Generally the depression is more marked and the recovery slower in hypersensitive cell lines (Fig. 2). Although this assay is valuable for its generality, it cannot provide information on which aspect of repair is defective.

DNA breaks reflect the balance between production of damage and its removal, and measuring breaks at different times after DNA damage is inflicted may give clues as to the nature of a repair defect. Sucrose gradient sedimentation, nucleoid sedimentation, filter elution and alkaline unwinding are alternative methods for measuring breaks (Cook & Brazell, 1976; Friedberg & Hanawalt, 1981). The last – alkaline unwinding – is fairly sensitive and very quick. Many chemical agents, and ionizing radiation, produce frank DNA breaks that diminish with time of repair incubation. When u.v. damage is repaired, DNA breaks are only transiently present, but if the later stages of repair are blocked with DNA synthesis inhibitors incision events accumulate as readily measurable breaks, and so incision-defective lines can be easily identified. A particularly quick assay for breaks and repair is based on the use of Lab Tek 'chamber slides' (Collins *et al.* 1982); all steps are performed on these

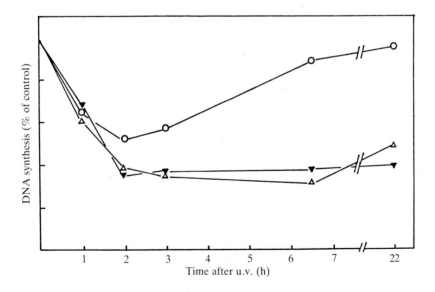

Fig. 2. Inhibition of thymidine incorporation after u.v. irradiation in HeLa-XPD hybrids. [^{14}C]dThd-labelled cultures were pulse-labelled for 1 h with [^{3}H]dThd at various times after u.v. (4 J m^{-2}). The points correspond to amounts of acid-insoluble radioactivity in irradiated *versus* mock-irradiated cells, expressed as a ratio of ^{3}H:^{14}C. Points represent the average of two experiments. HD-1 (○) shows normal u.v. sensitivity by comparison with the hypersensitive cells HD-1A (▼), and HD-2 (△) (Johnson *et al.* 1986, with permission of IRL Press Ltd).

slides, and the incision profile of several cell lines can be obtained within a day (Fig. 3).

Complementation analysis

Once a mutant cell line is characterized, it is important to know whether it is a novel variant or whether it fits into a known complementation group. For this, it is necessary in some way to combine the cells being tested with cells of a known complementation group and to assay for restoration of DNA repair activity (complementation), indicating whether or not the two cell lines are in the same complementation group. Complementation analysis is carried out on heterokaryons (the immediate product of fusion of cells of two distinct stocks, with two or more nuclei in a mixed cytoplasm; useful for short term studies); or, more rarely, on hybrids (i.e. the cell line derived from heterokaryons, carrying genetic components from each parent cell type). Complementation analysis by microinjection of cell extract of one type into cells of another type is a recent innovation, described by Hoeijmakers (1987). Complementation/non-complementation can be assessed on

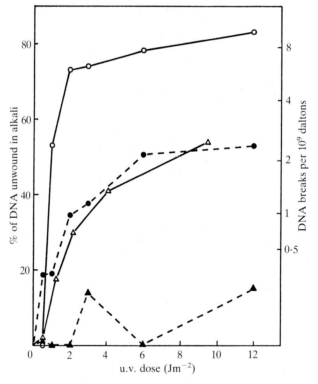

Fig. 3. Incision profiles of two hamster cell lines (K1, △———△; UV-5, ▲ – – – ▲) and two human cell lines (HeLa, ○———○; HD-2, ● – – – ●) following irradiation with a range of u.v. doses. Cells were prelabelled with [³H]dThd, incubated before and after u.v. irradiation with hydroxyurea and cytosine arabinoside, and accumulated DNA breaks (i.e. incomplete repair events) were measured by alkaline unwinding and S_1 nuclease digestion of unwound DNA, *in situ* on chamber slides (Collins *et al.* 1982).

the basis of whether the fused cells/hybrids/microinjected cells have restored the level of DNA repair or damage tolerance towards wild-type values.

In the case of heterokaryon analysis, it is crucial to be able to distinguish true heterokaryons from homokaryons where cells of the same type have fused. This can be done by growing the two cell lines with latex beads of different diameters; then only those binucleate cells with beads of both sizes need be scored (Murnane & Painter, 1982; Stefanini *et al.* 1985). Alternatively, one cell type may be heavily labelled with [³H]dThd for at least one generation before the fusion, so that heterokaryons are identified as binucleate cells with one densely labelled nucleus (e.g. see Johnson *et al.* 1985).

The assay for UDS in xeroderma pigmentosum (XP) heterokaryons by auto-radiography is described, for example, by Pawsey *et al.* (1979). Complementation between different ataxia-telangiectasia (A-T) strains is also assayed in heterokaryons by autoradiography but in this case recovery of the ability to inhibit replicative synthesis after X-irradiation is the index of complementation (Murnane & Painter, 1982; Jaspers & Bootsma, 1982). Conversely, restoration of the ability to replicate DNA after u.v. irradiation marks complementation between different Cockayne Syndrome (CS) strains (Tanaka *et al.* 1981). Lehmann (1982*a*) also demonstrated complementation between CS strains on the basis of the recovery of RNA synthetic ability after u.v. An approach that addresses a biological end-point of comp-lementation is that of Day *et al.* (1975). They infected XP heterokaryons with u.v.-irradiated adenovirus. If complementation of repair activity occurs between the two XP partners, the damaged virus is repaired and this is readily detected as a restoration of plaque-forming ability.

Hybrid cell lines are most easily produced when each parental variant involved in the fusion carries a different selectable genetic marker. Then, under appropriate selection, only successfully fused heterokaryons will survive to divide. Once estab-lished, hybrid cell cultures can be tested for a range of repair end-points such as UDS, incision capacity and host cell reactivation of virus; or for survival after treatment with DNA damaging agent, either by the standard plating assay for single cell colony-forming ability (Thompson *et al.* 1981, 1985*a*; Johnson *et al.* 1985, 1986; Duckworth-Rysiecki *et al.* 1985, 1986), or by a quick assay for cell survival and growth resembling the cytotoxicity assay described above (Cleaver, 1982; Thompson *et al.* 1985*a*).

In practice, provided sufficient clones are examined to remove the potential problems associated with chromosome segregation, hybrids should provide a wider view of complementation than can be achieved from heterokaryons. In one case hybrids have revealed discordance between UDS data and other repair assays. Johnson *et al.* (1985) backcrossed a permanent XP D-like hybrid with fibroblasts from different XP complementation groups. With XP C, E and F cells u.v. sensitivity and DNA repair ability were restored to normal; with XP D all hybrids remained u.v.-sensitive, and with the exception of somewhat elevated UDS levels, no other repair assay indicated complementation.

DNA REPAIR MUTANT CELL LINES

In this section, we list mutants that have been induced in established cell lines by techniques similar to those described above. Tables 1–4 cover cell lines representing four different species: human (Table 1), Chinese hamster (Table 2), mouse (Table 3), and frog (Table 4).

Table 1. *Human mutant cell lines*

Mutant cell line	Cell line of origin	Basis of selection	Cross-sensitivities	Process defective
S-1M[1]	HeLa S$_3$	Incompetence for u.v.		Dimer excision
S-2M[1]	HeLa S$_3$	repair (BrdUrd suicide)	4-NQO	Dimer excision
UVS-1[2]	FL	Incompetence for host cell reactivation of	(Not sensitive to X rays)	
UVS-2[2]	FL	u.v.-irradiated herpes simplex virus	(Not sensitive to X rays)	
8 clones[3]	EUE	Incompetence for u.v. repair (FdUrd suicide)		(UDS normal)
UVS20[4] UVS22[4] UVS24[4] UVS26[4] UVS38[4]	EUE	Incompetence for u.v. repair (BrdUrd suicide)		UDS reduced in all five lines

[1] Isomura *et al.* (1973); [2] Shiomi & Sato (1979); [3] Fiorio *et al.* (1981); [4] Fiorio *et al.* (1983).

As is well known, many human DNA repair mutants occur naturally, as clinical conditions. There are numerous reviews of the work done with primary cultures of cells from patients with autosomal recessive traits such as XP, A-T, etc. (see e.g., Lehmann, 1982*b*). In the following section, we will describe those cases in which permanent cell lines have been derived from such cultures, making them potentially useful in long-term molecular and cellular genetic analysis.

PERMANENT CELL LINES FROM PATIENTS WITH XP, AT ETC.

Permanent fibroblast cell lines have been derived from most of the complementation groups of XP. The line XP12ROSV is the simian virus 40 (SV40)-transformed counterpart of XP12RO, of group A, and was obtained by G. Veldhuisen and D. Bootsma. A well-characterized subclone, XP12RPO-MI, has been described (Royer-Pokora & Haseltine, 1984). Barbis *et al.* (1986) and Hashimoto *et al.* (1986) report other SV40-transformed XP A lines, derived from GM2009 and XP5NI, respectively. Immortal XP C lines have been produced by Daya-Grosjean *et al.* (1986), and by Canaani *et al.* (1986). In each case transformation was achieved by an origin-defective SV40 recombinant plasmid. One XP D line, derived from GM434 by means of the plasmid pSV7, has been described together with an XP E line from GM2415 (Moses *et al.* 1986). An immortal SV40-transformed XP F line was derived from XP2YO by Yagi & Takebe (1983), and an XP G line from GM3021 by Barbis *et al.* (1986). A permanent XP variant cell line (from GM2359) has also been reported (Barbis *et al.* 1986).

Another important source of immortal XP cell lines, this time lymphoblastoid in origin (following infection with Epstein Barr Virus (EBV)) was described many years ago by Andrews *et al.* (1974). Most XP complementation groups are now represented by lymphoblastoid derivatives (NIGMS Human Genetic Mutant Repository, 1985).

Permanent cell lines of Bloom's syndrome are available; one, SV889BL, was produced by SV40 transformation (K. Sperling, personal communication: see Squires *et al.* 1982), and two others, GM3498B-HV1 and -HV2, by transfection with DNA from a tumorigenic mouse cell line carrying a single copy of Harvey murine sarcoma virus (Doniger *et al.* 1983). The latter were found to exhibit the high spontaneous sister chromatid exchange (SCE) frequency characteristic of untransformed Bloom's syndrome cells (Doniger *et al.* 1983). Moses *et al.* (1986) reported an additional permanent Bloom's cell line derived from GM2548A by use of the recombinant plasmid pSV7, and Shiraishi *et al.* (1983) reported results with an EBV-transformed cell line.

Ataxia-telangiectasia is represented by the SV40-transformed fibroblast line AT5BIVA, by the pSVori⁻-transformed AT25F fibroblast line (Murnane *et al.* 1985) and the successful immortalization of A-T fibroblasts by transfection with a plasmid pSV3gpt containing the SV40 early region (Mayne *et al.* 1986*b*). Hashimoto *et al.* (1986) report the production of three A-T lines (from AT10S) using, for transformation, either the whole SV40 genome alone cloned into pBR322 or a combination of SV40 plus Moloney murine sarcoma virus. Henderson & Ribecky (1980) report the production of an AT lymphoblastoid cell line, and there are now many such lines listed in NIGMS Human Genetic Mutant Repository (1985).

The first permanent fibroblast cultures from Cockayne Syndrome (CS3BE, CSIAN) and the immunodeficient condition known as 46BR have been reported by Mayne *et al.* (1986*a*,*b*), while Henderson & Ribecky (1980) described the production and properties of an EBV-transformed CS lymphoblastoid line. Finally, permanent cell lines from Fanconi's anaemia have been described by Henderson & Ribecky (1980) and Duckworth-Rysiecki *et al.* (1985) (lymphoblastoid), and Duckworth-Rysiecki *et al.* (1986) (fibroblast-derived).

A fundamental problem with virally transformed cell lines such as these is the possibility that the process of transformation alters the phenotypic response to DNA damaging agents. This was illustrated some time ago for rat cells (Waters *et al.* 1977) and also for human cells (Heddle & Arlett, 1980). More recently, permanent AT lines were shown to be somewhat less sensitive to X-rays than their precursor fibroblasts (Murnane *et al.* 1985). It was known that the line XP12ROSV was hypersensitive to SCE formation after EMS treatment or u.v. irradiation (Wolff *et al.* 1977). Heddle & Arlett (1980) found that this line was also hypersensitive to killing by EMS; but the corresponding primary XP strain showed no hypersensitivity in either killing or SCE production by EMS. Furthermore, excision repair

Table 2. *Hamster mutant cell lines*

Mutant cell line	Cell line of origin	Basis of selection	Cross-sensitivities
UV-1[1]	CHO-K1 gly⁻*	u.v.-sensitive cell detachment	EMS[2], MNNG[3], MMC[3], AAAF[3] (methylation and cross-link sensitivities can be separated genetically[5])
UV-5 (representative of 4 clones)[6]	CHO-AA8*	u.v. sensitivity (poor colony growth)	4-NQO[6], MMC[7], most bulky adducts[8]
UV-20 (representative of 37 clones)[6]	CHO-AA8	u.v. sensitivity (poor colony growth)	cis-Pt[12], 4-NQO[6], EMS[6] MMC (extremely sensitive)[7]
UV-24 (representative of 2 clones)[14]	CHO-AA8	u.v. sensitivity (poor colony growth)	MMC[7]
UV-41 (sole representative)[14]	CHO-AA8	u.v. sensitivity (poor colony growth)	MMC (extremely sensitive)[7]
UV-135[14]	CHO-AA8	u.v. sensitivity (poor colony growth)	MMC[7]
UV-61[14]	CHO-AA8	u.v. sensitivity (poor colony growth)	
MC5[6]	CHO-AA8	MMC sensitivity	
EM7-2[6]	CHO-AA8	EMS sensitivity	γ-rays
EM9-1[6]	CHO-AA8	EMS sensitivity	γ-rays[6], MMS[17], ENU[17], MNNG[17], u.v.[17]
EU-1[14]	EM9-1	u.v. sensitivity	
EU-2[14]	EM9-1	u.v. sensitivity	
UVˢ-7[19]	V79	Incompetence for u.v. repair	
UVˢ-40[19]	V79	([³H]dThd suicide)	X-rays, MNNG, AAAF
UVˢ-44[19]	V79		X-rays, MNNG, AAAF
CHS-1[21]	V79	u.v. sensitivity	
CHO12RO[23]	CHO-K1	Low UDS, and growth inhibition after u.v.	MMC, CCNU, X-rays (hypoxic)[24]
CHO33RO[23]	CHO-K1		
CHO43RO[23]	CHO-K1		
43-3B[26]	CHO-9	u.v. sensitivity	4-NQO, MMC, alkylating agents (slight)[27]
27-1[26]	CHO-9	u.v. sensitivity	Alkylating agents[27]
XR-1[28]	CHO-K1 gly⁻	γ-ray sensitivity	Bleomycin
XR-2[28]	CHO-K1 gly⁻	γ-ray sensitivity	
*xrs*1,2,4,5,6,7[29]	CHO-K1	X-ray sensitivity	Bleomycin. Spectrum of different responses to various alkylating agents[29]
BLM1[33]	CHO-K1	Bleomycin sensitivity	Adriamycin
BLM2[33]	CHO-K1	Bleomycin sensitivity	X-rays, cis-Pt, u.v., chlorambucil, adriamycin

Table 2. *Continued*

Process(es) defective	Complementation	Other features
Post-replication recovery [2,4]	Cross-link sensitivity complements with hamster groups 2 and 4; methylation sensitivity does not[5]	Hypomutable after u.v./EMS[2]
Repair replication[6], incision[9], 7BrMeBA removal[10]	Hamster group 1[11]	Hypermutable after u.v.[9], 7BrMeBA[37]
Cross-link repair[12], incision[9], repair replication[6], 7BrMeBA removal[10]	Hamster group 2[11] (complements XP A,C,D,F,G)[15]	Defect corrected by gene on human chromosome 19[13]. Hypermutable after u.v.[9], 7BrMeBA[37]
Incision[9], 7BrMeBA removal[10]	Hamster group 3[11]	
Incision[9], 7BrMeBA removal[10]	Hamster group 4[11] (complements XP A,C,D,F)[15]	
Incision[9], 7BrMeBA removal[10]	Hamster group 5	
(UDS, and therefore probably incision, normal[16])	Hamster group 6[16]	
DNA break rejoining[17] (DNA ligase normal[18])		Hypermutable; high SCE (baseline and induced)[17]. Defect corrected by gene on human chromosome 19[36]
		Double mutant
	Hamster group 2	Double mutant
UDS		Hypermutable[20]
(UDS normal)		Hypermutable[20]
(UDS normal)		
Post-replication recovery[21,22]		
UDS[23]	CHO12RO complements XP groups A,B,C,D,F,G[25]	
	Hamster group 2[26]	Hypermutable after u.v.[26]
	Hamster group 3[16]	
		Sensitivity is cell cycle dependent
Rejoining of double-strand DNA breaks[30]	All six in same complementation group[31]	Reversion by azacytidine[32]
	In distinct complementation groups	

Continued overleaf

Table 2. *Continued*

Mutant cell line	Cell line of origin	Basis of selection	Cross-sensitivities
MMC1-10[34]	CHO-K1	MMC sensitivity	MMC-2 alone is u.v.-sensitive. Others: various sensitivities to range of agents[34]
A4, C11 and 2 others[35]	V79	X-ray sensitivity	Various
UVL-10[38]	CHO-AT3-2	u.v. sensitivity	Bulky adducts; cross-links (very sensitive)[40]
UVL-13[38]	CHO-AT3-2	u.v. sensitivity	Bulky adducts, cross-links[40]
UVL-1[39]	CHO-AT3-2	u.v. sensitivity	

* CHO-AA8, although ostensibly wild-type, is hypersensitive to alkylating agents when compared with CHO-K1 gly⁻; in this respect, CHO-AA8 resembles UV-1 (Hoy *et al.* 1985*b*). MNNG, *N*-methyl-*N'*-nitro-*N*-nitrosoguanidine; MMC, mitomycin C; AAAF, *N*-acetoxy-2-acetylaminofluorene; cis-Pt, *cis* platinum (II) diammine; MMS, methyl methane sulphonate; ENU, ethylnitrosourea; 7BrMeBA, 7-bromomethylbenz[a]-anthracene; CCNU, 1-(2-chloroethyl)-3-cyclohexyl-1-nitrosourea.

[1] Stamato & Waldren (1977); [2] Stamato *et al.* (1981); [3] Waldren *et al.* (1983); [4] Collins & Waldren (1982); [5] Hoy *et al.* (1985*b*); [6] Thompson *et al.* (1980); [7] Hoy *et al.* (1985*a*); [8] Thompson *et al.* (1983); [9] Thompson *et al.* (1982*c*); [10] Thompson *et al.* (1984); [11] Thompson *et al.* (1981); [12] Meyn *et al.* (1982); [13] Thompson *et al.*

Table 3. *Mouse mutant cell lines*

Mutant cell line	Cell line of origin	Basis of selection	Cross-sensitivities
Q31[1]	L5178Y	4-NQO sensitivity	u.v.[1]
US1–61[2]	L5178Y, subclone L51T/t	u.v. sensitivity	4-NQO, MMC[2]
M10[5]	L5178Y	MMS sensitivity	X-rays, EMS, MMC, 4-NQO[5,6]
LX830[7]	L5178Y	X-ray sensitivity	
MS1[6]	L5178Y	MMS sensitivity	EMS, MMC, caffeine[6]
FMS-1[8]	FM3A (derived from C3H mouse mammary ascites tumour)	u.v. sensitivity	
LSB1–5[8]	L5178Y	u.v. sensitivity	
LSC-1[8]	L5178Y	u.v. sensitivity	

See footnote to Table 2 for abbreviations in all Tables.

Table 2. *Continued*

Process(es) defective	Complementation	Other features
	MMC1–5 lie in 4 different complementation groups[34]. MMC-2 is in hamster group 3[16]	
A4 (but not C11) shows increased mis-repair of double-strand DNA breaks	At least 3 different groups. At least 2 of these differ from groups containing *xrs*1 and EM7-2	
Repair replication[38], dimer removal[38], Pyr(6-4)Pyo removal[39] (completely defective)	In hamster group 2[40]	
Repair replication[38], dimer removal[38] (partially defective) Pyr(6-4)Pyo removal[39] (partially defective)	In hamster group 1[40]	

(1985*b*); [14] Busch *et al.* (1980); [15] Thompson *et al.* (1985*a*); [16] Thompson *et al.* (1987); [17] Thompson *et al.* (1982*a*); [18] Chan *et al.* (1984); [19] Schultz *et al.* (1981*b*); [20] Schultz *et al.* (1981*a*); [21] Pinto *et al.* (1980); [22] Barenfeld (1984); [23] Stefanini *et al.* (1982); [24] Stefanini *et al.* (1986); [25] Stefanini *et al.* (1985); [26] Wood & Burki (1982); [27] Zdzienicka & Simons (1986); [28] Stamato *et al.* (1983); [29] Jeggo & Kemp (1983); [30] Kemp *et al.* (1984); [31] Jeggo & Kemp (1985); [32] Jeggo & Holliday (1986); [33] Robson *et al.* (1985); [34] Robson *et al.* (1986); [35] Jones *et al.* (1986); [36] Siciliano *et al.* (1985); [37] Thompson *et al.* (1982*b*); [38] Clarkson *et al.* (1983); [39] Mitchell *et al.* (1986); [40] G. M. Adair, personal communication.

Table 3. *Continued*

Process defective	Complementation	Other features
Dimer removal[3]	Group I	In hybrid, human chromosome 13 restores repair[4]
	Classified in groups I–IV[2]	
Abnormally fast recovery of DNA synthesis after X-rays[7]		
		Some lines lose sensitivity on continued growth in culture

[1] Sato & Hieda (1979*a*); [2] Shiomi *et al.* (1982*a*); [3] Sato & Setlow (1981); [4] Hori *et al.* (1983); [5] Sato & Hieda (1979*b*); [6] Shiomi *et al.* (1982*b*); [7] Hama-Inaba *et al.* (1983); [8] Kuroki & Miyashita (1977).

Table 4. Frog mutant cell lines

Mutant cell line	Cell line of origin	Basis of selection	Cross-sensitivities	Process defective
RRP601–605[1]	ICR 2A (haploid frog cells)	Incompetence for u.v. repair (BrdUrd suicide)		
DRP36[2]	ICR 2A	Poor colony growth after solar u.v. irradiation	γ-rays, EMS, cis-Pt, 4-NQO[2]	Reduced repair of non-pyrimidine-dimer lesions (dimers repaired normally)[3]

[1] Rosenstein & Ohlsson-Wilhelm (1979); [2] Rosenstein & Chao (1985a); [3] Rosenstein & Chao (1985b).

(indicated by u.v.-dependent incision of DNA) is drastically reduced in SV40-transformed normal human cells as well as in the SV40-transformed Bloom's syndrome line (Squires *et al.* 1982). Viral transformation is often associated with defective repair of O^6-alkylated purines (Day *et al.* 1987) and with enhanced rates of chromosome breakage and SCE (Wolff *et al.* 1977; Popescu *et al.* 1983), and Teo *et al.* (1983) suggest that the sensitivity of XP12ROSV to ethylating agents, and the defective removal of O^6-ethyl groups, results from transformation rather than from the XP phenotype. The report of poor O^6-alkyl removal from an XP C lymphoblastoid line by Altamirano-Dimas *et al.* (1979) may also be explained in this way. By contrast, there are several reports of transformed XP lines where DNA repair capabilities are much restored. The enhanced repair of cross-links in an SV40-transformed XP A line reported by Gantt *et al.* (1984) is one example. In other cases the complete wild-type, repair-competent phenotype is restored, as in the case of the spontaneously transformed XP line described by Thielmann *et al.* (1983), or the XP G line produced by Moses *et al.* (1986). Moreover, high rates of reversion of XP A cell lines to u.v.-resistant phenotypes have been reported (Takano *et al.* 1982; Royer-Pokora & Haseltine, 1984), while many AT lymphoblastoid cell lines display wild-type chromosome stability (Cohen *et al.* 1979). Clearly it is necessary to exercise great caution when regarding transformed cell lines as the accurate counterparts of the primary repair-defective or hypersensitive cell strains.

In the context of viral transformation u.v.- and 4-nitroquinoline-1-oxide (4-NQO)-sensitive permanent human fibroblast lines from a normal embryo have been reported in the absence of selection, by Suzuki & Kuwata (1979) and Suzuki & Fuse (1981), following complex double infection with Rous Sarcoma virus and SV40. From two of these clones revertants have been isolated after EMS mutagenesis and u.v. selection, though frequencies of reversion are not provided (Suzuki & Kuwata, 1979).

Finally, though from another species, the SV40-transformed Indian muntjac cell, SVM, should be mentioned in this section. SVM arose spontaneously from SV40 infection of a skin fibroblast culture and was not selected for the considerable sensitivity to u.v. and 4-NQO that it expresses (Pillidge, 1984). Its high spontaneous rate of chromosome aberrations suggested, however, that it might display repair defects and it was found to have aberrant post-replication recovery (daughter strand repair), as well as impaired ability to recover RNA synthesis after u.v. (Pillidge *et al.* 1986*a*). Moreover, u.v. induces numerous chromosome aberrations and abundant SCE in this cell (Pillidge *et al.* 1986*b*).

A quite different approach, not involving viral transformation, was adopted by Johnson *et al.* (1985) to establish a permanent line of XP D. HeLa (permanently growing heteroploid human) cells were fused in suspension with XP D fibroblasts, using inactivated Sendai virus. The HeLa cells had been X-irradiated prior to fusion, so that unfused HeLa cells would not be expected to proliferate. But some hybrid cells survived to form clones, having apparently gained the capacity for indefinite growth from a HeLa component, and of these one clone, HD2, closely resembles XP D in its u.v. sensitivity and DNA repair characteristics (Johnson *et al.* 1985).

DISCUSSION

The variety of DNA repair mutants that we have already might seem to indicate that there is no need to look for more. But DNA repair is likely to involve complex genetic systems, judging by what is now known for bacteria and by the plethora of complementation groups for XP representing just one step of repair, several of which clearly appear not to be allelic (Giannelli *et al.* 1982). It is unlikely, for instance, that the six complementation groups for CHO u.v. excision repair are all that exist (see Friedberg, 1987; Downes, 1986).

Mutants are invaluable for investigating the biochemistry of DNA repair. They are also, of course, exploited as recipients for transfected DNA in attempts to identify DNA repair genes. Before beginning a search for further mutants, it is wise to check that the cell line to be used will yield a suitable system; some otherwise valuable mutants are very poor at taking up foreign DNA (Schultz *et al.* 1985; Hoeijmakers *et al.* personal communication).

The frequency at which DNA repair mutants arise is remarkably high, around 1 in 10^4 or even higher (Thompson *et al.* 1980; Busch *et al.* 1980; Jeggo & Kemp, 1983; Robson *et al.* 1985). In common with other families of CHO mutants the abundance of DNA repair mutants lends support to the possibility that CHO cells might be physically or functionally hemizygous, so that mutation in only one allele is necessary to establish a mutant phenotype (Siminovitch, 1976). The hemizygous state may result from selective methylation; azacytidine, which blocks methylation, caused the reversion of *xrs* mutants to a normal phenotype (Jeggo & Holliday, 1986).

It is noteworthy that certain steps in the excision repair of u.v. damage (the most-studied pathway) seem to be over-represented among mutants. Almost all show defective incision; those that do not, tend to have ill-understood faults in post-replication recovery, i.e. tolerance mechanisms for replication in the presence of damage. The later stages of excision of damage, repair synthesis and ligation, seem genetically intractable (with the possible exception of a ligation anomaly in the human condition 46BR (Henderson *et al.* 1985) and several mouse cell lines (Pearson & Styles, 1984; Yin *et al.* 1973)). This may well be because the enzymes responsible for those steps are involved also in DNA replication or other essential processes, so mutations will tend to be lethal.

There is mounting evidence that defects in processes associated with DNA replication are often accompanied by elevated sensitivity to DNA damage. Thus, temperature-sensitive CHO cell lines ts13A and ts15C are hypersensitive to killing by alkylating agents (Srinivasan *et al.* 1980), as are deoxycytidine kinase-deficient CHO mutants (Meuth, 1983). Purine auxotroph CHO lines, in a purine-starved state, perform an abortive kind of DNA repair that appears to be mutagenic (Collins, 1985, and unpublished results). And an aphidicolin-resistant hamster (V79) mutant, aph^r 4-2, which has an altered DNA polymerase α with increased affinity for dCTP, is hypersensitive to both killing and mutation induction by u.v. light or MNNG (Liu *et al.* 1984).

It is important that DNA repair should be seen, not as an isolated phenomenon, but as one aspect of the integrated nucleic acid economy of the cell. The need now is for biochemical and genetic approaches that will allow us to investigate the relationship between normal DNA replication and the various mechanisms that the cell uses in order to cope with DNA damage and genetic misinformation.

We thank Dr Istvan Rasko for helpful comments on the manuscript.

REFERENCES

ABBONDANDOLO, A., BONATTI, S., BELLAZZINI, R., BETTI, G., DEL GUERRA, A., MASSAI, M. M., RAGADINI, M., SPANDRE, G. & TONELLI, G. (1982). Direct screening of living mammalian cell colonies for the identification of DNA repair deficient mutants by a multiwire proportional chamber. *Radiat. environ. Biophys.* **21**, 109–121.

ALTAMIRANO-DIMAS, M., SKLAR, R. & STRAUSS, B. (1979). Selectivity of the excision of alkylation products in a xeroderma pigmentosum-derived lymphoblastoid line. *Mutat. Res.* **60**, 197–206.

ANDREWS, A. D., ROBBINS, J. H., KRAEMER, K. H. & BUELL, D. N. (1974). Xeroderma pigmentosum long-term lymphoid lines with increased ultraviolet sensitivity. *J. natn. Cancer Inst.* **53**, 691–693.

ARLETT, C. F. & PRIESTLEY, A. (1983). Defective recovery from potentially lethal damage in some human fibroblast strains. *Int. J. Radiat. Biol.* **43**, 157–167.

ARLETT, C. F. & PRIESTLEY, A. (1984). Deficient recovery from potentially lethal damage in some gamma-irradiated human fibroblast cell strains. *Br. J. Cancer Suppl.* VI, 227–232.

BARBIS, D. P., SCHULTZ, R. A. & FRIEDBERG, E. C. (1986). Isolation and partial characterization of virus-transformed cell lines representing the A, G and variant complementation groups of xeroderma pigmentosum. *Mutat. Res.* **165**, 175–184.

BARENFELD, L. S. (1984). A study of DNA synthesis in the Chinese hamster cells of UV-sensitive and UV-resistant clones. *Tsitologia* **26**, 343–348.

BASILICO, C. & MEISS, H. K. (1974). Methods for selecting and studying temperature-sensitive mutants of BHK-21 cells. *Meth. Cell Biol.* **8**, 1–22.

BRANDT, W. N., FLAMM, W. G. & BERNHEIM, N. J. (1972). The value of hydroxyurea in assessing repair synthesis of DNA in HeLa cells. *Chem.-Biol. Interact.* **5**, 327–339.

BUSCH, D. B., CLEAVER, J. E. & GLASER, D. A. (1980). Large-scale isolation of UV-sensitive clones of CHO cells. *Somat. Cell Genet.* **6**, 407–418.

CANAANI, D., NAIMAN, T., TEITZ, T. & BERG, P. (1986). Immortalization of xeroderma pigmentosum cells by simian virus 40 DNA having a defective origin of DNA replication. *Somat. Cell molec. Genet.* **12**, 13–20.

CHAN, J. Y. H., THOMPSON, L. H. & BECKER, F. F. (1984). DNA-ligase activities appear normal in the CHO mutant EM9. *Mutat. Res.* **131**, 209–214.

CLARKSON, J. M., MITCHELL, D. L. & ADAIR, G. M. (1983). The use of an immunological probe to measure the kinetics of DNA repair in normal and UV-sensitive mammalian cell lines. *Mutat. Res.* **112**, 287–299.

CLEAVER, J. E. (1982). Rapid complementation method for classifying excision repair-defective xeroderma pigmentosum cell strains. *Somat. Cell Genet.* **8**, 801–810.

COHEN, M. M., SAGI, M., BEN-ZUR, Z., SCHAAP, T., VOSS, R., KOH, G. & BEN-BASSAT, H. (1979). Ataxia telangiectasia: chromosomal stability in continuous lymphoblastoid cell lines. *Cytogenet. Cell Genet.* **23**, 44–52.

COLLINS, A. (1985). Do mammalian cells control DNA repair according to the availability of DNA precursors. *Abst. Conf. Mechanisms of DNA Damage and Repair.* Gaithersburg, MD: National Bureau of Standards.

COLLINS, A. (1987). Replica plating of cultured human cells on polyester mesh. *J. Tiss. Culture Meth.* (in press).

COLLINS, A. R. S. & JOHNSON, R. T. (1984). The inhibition of DNA repair. *Adv. Radiat. Biol.* **11**, 71–129.

COLLINS, A., JONES, C. & WALDREN, C. (1982). A survey of DNA repair incision activities after ultraviolet irradiation of a range of human, hamster, and hamster-human hybrid cell lines. *J. Cell Sci.* **56**, 423–440.

COLLINS, A. & WALDREN, C. (1982). Cell cycle kinetics and ultraviolet light survival in UV-1, a Chinese hamster ovary cell mutant defective in post-replication recovery. *J. Cell Sci.* **57**, 261–275.

COOK, P. R. & BRAZELL, I. A. (1976). Detection and repair of single strand breaks in nuclear DNA. *Nature, Lond.* **263**, 679–682.

DAY, R. S. III, BABICH, M. A., YAROSH, D. B. & SCUDIERO, D. A. (1987). The role of O^6-methylguanine in human cell killing, sister chromatid exchange induction and mutagenesis: a review. *J. Cell Sci. Suppl.* 6, 333–353.

DAY, R. S., KRAEMER, K. H. & ROBBINS, J. H. (1975). Complementing xeroderma pigmentosum fibroblasts restore biological activity to UV damaged DNA. *Mutat. Res.* **28**, 251–255.

DAYA-GROSJEAN, L., JAMES, M., DROUGARD, C. & SARASIN, A. (1986). The establishment and characterisation of a xeroderma pigmentosum cell line transformed by an origin-defective SV40 recombinant plasmid. *Br. J. Cancer* **54**, 353 (abstr.).

DONIGER, J., DiPAULO, J. A. & POPESCU, N. C. (1983). Transformation of Bloom's syndrome fibroblasts by DNA transfection. *Science* **222**, 1144–1146.

DOWNES, C. S. (1986). Molecular biology of DNA repair. *Mutat. Res.* **166**, 221–226.

DUCKWORTH-RYSIECKI, G., CORNISH, K., CLARKE, C. & BUCKWALD, M. (1985). Identification of two complementation groups in Fanconi anemia. *Somat. Cell molec. Genet.* **11**, 35–41.

DUCKWORTH-RYSIECKI, G., TOJI, L., NG, I., CLARKE, C. & BUCHWALD, M. (1986). Characterization of a Simian virus 40-transformed Fanconi anemia fibroblast cell line. *Mutat. Res.* **166**, 207–214.

FIORIO, R., FROSINA, G. & ABBONDANDOLO, A. (1983). Isolation and preliminary characterization of UV-sensitive mutants from the human cell line EUE. *Carcinogenesis* **4**, 39–44.

FIORIO, R., QUINTAVALLE, A., ABBONDANDOLO, A., BONATTI, S. & MAZZACCARO, A. (1981). Characterization of UV-sensitive clones isolated in EUE human cells. *Mutat. Res.* **85**, 256 (abstr.).

FRIEDBERG, E. C. (1987). The molecular biology of nucleotide excision repair of DNA: recent progress. *J. Cell Sci. Suppl.* 6, 1–24.

FRIEDBERG, E. C. & HANAWALT, P. C. (1981). *DNA Repair: A Laboratory Manual of Research Procedures*, vol. 1B. New York, Basel: Marcel Dekker, Inc.

GANTT, R., TAYLOR, W. G., CAMALIER, R. F. & STEPHENS, E. V. (1984). Repair of DNA-protein cross-links in an excision repair-deficient human cell line and its Simian virus 40-transformed derivative. *Cancer Res.* **44**, 1809–1812.

GIANNELLI, F., PAWSEY, S. A. & AVERY, J. A. (1982). Differences in patterns of complementation of the more common groups of xeroderma pigmentosum: possible implications. *Cell* **29**, 451–458.

HAMA-INABA, H., HIEDA-SHIOMI, N. & SATO, K. (1983). Inhibition and recovery of DNA synthesis after X-irradiation in radiosensitive mouse-cell mutants. *Mutat. Res.* **120**, 161–165.

HASHIMOTO, T., NAKANO, Y., KOJI OWADA, M., KAKUNAGA, T. & FURNYAMA, J. (1986). Establishment of cell lines derived from ataxia telangiectasia and xeroderma pigmentosum patients with high radiation sensitivity. *Mutat. Res.* **166**, 215–220.

HEDDLE, J. A. & ARLETT, C. F. (1980). Untransformed xeroderma pigmentosum cells are not hypersensitive to sister-chromatid exchange production by ethyl methanesulphonate – implications for the use of transformed cell lines and for the mechanism by which SCE arise. *Mutat. Res.* **72**, 119–125.

HENDERSON, E. E. & RIBECKY, R. (1980). DNA repair in lymphoblastoid cell lines established from human genetic disorders. *Chem.-Biol. Interact.* **33**, 63–81.

HENDERSON, L. M., ARLETT, C. F., HARCOURT, S. A., LEHMANN, A. R. & BROUGHTON, B. C. (1985). Cells from an immunodeficient patient (46BR) with a defect in DNA ligation are hypomutable but hypersensitive to the induction of sister chromatid exchanges. *Proc. natn. Acad. Sci. U.S.A.* **82**, 2044–2048.

HOEIJMAKERS, J. H. J. (1987). Characterization of genes and proteins involved in excision repair of human cells. *J. Cell Sci. Suppl.* **6**, 111–125.

HORI, T.-A., SHIOMI, T. & SATO, K. (1983). Human chromosome 13 compensates a DNA repair defect in UV-sensitive mouse cells by mouse-human cell hybridization. *Proc. natn. Acad. Sci. U.S.A.* **80**, 5655–5659.

HOY, C. A., SALAZAR, E. P. & THOMPSON, L. H. (1984). Rapid detection of DNA-damaging agents using repair-deficient CHO cells. *Mutat. Res.* **130**, 321–332.

HOY, C. A., THOMPSON, L. H., MOONEY, C.-L. & SALAZAR, E. P. (1985a). Defective DNA cross-link removal in Chinese hamster cell mutants hypersensitive to bifunctional alkylating agents. *Cancer Res.* **45**, 1737–1743.

HOY, C. A., THOMPSON, L. H., SALAZAR, E. P. & STEWART, S. A. (1985b). Different genetic alterations underlie dual hypersensitivity of CHO mutant UV-1 to DNA methylating and cross-linking agents. *Somat. Cell molec. Genet.* **11**, 523–532.

ISOMURA, K., NIKAIDO, O., HORIKAWA, M. & SUGAHARA, T. (1973). Repair of DNA damage in ultraviolet-sensitive cells isolated from HeLa S3 cells. *Radiat. Res.* **53**, 143–152.

JASPERS, N. J. G. & BOOTSMA, D. (1982). Genetic heterogencity in ataxia-telangiectasia studied by cell fusion. *Proc. natn. Acad. Sci. U.S.A.* **79**, 2641–2644.

JEGGO, P. A. & HOLLIDAY, R. (1986). Reversion of a defect in DNA repair induced at high frequency by azacytidine. *Br. J. Cancer* **54**, 350 (abstr.).

JEGGO, P. A. & KEMP, L. M. (1983). X-ray sensitive mutants of Chinese hamster ovary cell line. Isolation and cross-sensitivity to other DNA damaging agents. *Mutat. Res.* **112**, 313–327.

JEGGO, P. A. & KEMP, L. M. (1985). Isolation and characterisation of X-ray sensitive mutants of the CHO cell line. *Br. J. Cancer* **51**, 609 (abstr.).

JOHNSON, R. T., SQUIRES, S., ELLIOTT, G. C., KOCH, G. L. E. & RAINBOW, A. J. (1985). Xeroderma pigmentosum D–Hela hybrids with low and high ultraviolet sensitivity associated with normal and diminished DNA repair ability, respectively. *J. Cell Sci.* **76**, 115–133.

JOHNSON, R. T., SQUIRES, S., ELLIOTT, G. C., RAINBOW, A. J., KOCH, G. L. E. & SMITH, M. (1986). Analysis of repair in XP–HeLa hybrids; lack of correlation between excision repair of UV damage and adenovirus reactivation in an XP(D)-like cell line. *Carcinogenesis* **7**, 1733–1738.

JONES, N. J., DEBENHAM, P. G. & THACKER, J. (1986). New X-ray-sensitive mutants of cultured hamster cells. *Br. J. Cancer* **54**, 349 (abstr.).

KAO, F.-T. & PUCK, T. T. (1974). Induction and isolation of auxotrophic mutants in mammalian cells. *Meth. Cell Biol.* **8**, 23–39.

KEMP, L. M., SEDGWICK, S. G. & JEGGO, P. A. (1984). X-ray sensitive mutants of Chinese hamster ovary cells defective in double-strand break rejoining. *Mutat. Res.* **132**, 189–196.

KUROKI, T. & MIYASHITA, S. Y. (1977). Isolation of UV-sensitive clones from mouse cell lines by Lederberg style replica plating. *J. cell. Physiol.* **90**, 79–90.

LEHMANN, A. R. (1982*a*). Three complementation groups in Cockayne's Syndrome. *Mutat. Res.* **106**, 345–356.

LEHMANN, A. R. (1982*b*). Xeroderma pigmentosum, Cockayne Syndrome and ataxia telangiectasia: Disorders relating DNA repair to carcinogenesis. *Cancer Surveys* **1**, 93–118.

LIU, P. K., CHANG, C.-C. & TROSKO, J. E. (1984). Evidence for mutagenic repair in V79 cell mutant with aphidicolin-resistant DNA polymerase-α. *Somat. Cell molec. Genet.* **10**, 235–245.

MAYNE, L. V., PRIESTLEY, A., JAMES, M. R. & BURKE, J. F. (1986*a*). Efficient immortalization and morphological transformation of human fibroblasts by transfection with SV$_{40}$ DNA linked to a dominant marker. *Expl Cell Res.* **162**, 530–538.

MAYNE, L. V., PRIESTLEY, A., JONES, T. & ARLETT, C. F. (1986*b*). Cloning of human DNA repair genes: 1. Immortalisation of primary strains. 2. Gene transfer and selection for resistance to DNA damaging agents. *Br. J. Cancer* **54**, 350 (abstr.).

MEUTH, M. (1983). Deoxycytidine kinase-deficient mutants of Chinese hamster ovary cells are hypersensitive to DNA alkylating agents. *Mutat. Res.* **110**, 383–391.

MEYN, R. E., JENKINS, S. F. & THOMPSON, L. H. (1982). Defective removal of DNA cross-links in a repair-deficient mutant of Chinese hamster cells. *Cancer Res.* **42**, 3106–3110.

MITCHELL, D. L., CLARKSON, J. M. & ADAIR, G. M. (1986). The DNA of UV-irradiated normal and excision-deficient mammalian cells undergoes relaxation in an initial stage of DNA repair. *Mutat. Res.* **165**, 123–128.

MOSES, R. E., TIMME, T. L. & WOOD, C. M. (1986). Immortalization of human DNA repair deficient fibroblasts. *Abst. 7th Int. Cong. Human Genetics*, West Berlin, vol. II, p. 690.

MULLINGER, A. M., COLLINS, A. R. S. & JOHNSON, R. T. (1983). Cell growth state determines susceptibility of repair DNA synthesis to inhibition by hydroxyurea and 1-β-D-arabinofuranosylcytosine. *Carcinogenesis* **4**, 1039–1043.

MURNANE, J. P., FULLER, L. F. & PAINTER, R. B. (1985). Establishment and characterization of a permanent pSVori⁻ transformed ataxia-telangiectasia cell line. *Expl Cell Res.* **158**, 119–126.

MURNANE, J. P. & PAINTER, R. B. (1982). Complementation of the defects in DNA synthesis in irradiated and unirradiated ataxia telangiectasia cells. *Proc. natn. Acad. Sci. U.S.A.* **79**, 1960–1963.

NIGMS HUMAN GENETIC MUTANT CELL REPOSITORY (1985). U.S. Department of Health and Human Services. Washington: N.I.H. Publication, no. 85-2011.

PAINTER, R. B. (1977). Rapid test to detect agents that damage human DNA. *Nature, Lond.* **265**, 650–651.

PAWSEY, S. A., MAGNUS, I. A., RAMSAY, C. A., BENSON, P. F. & GIANNELLI, F. (1978). Clinical, genetic and DNA repair studies on a consecutive series of patients with xeroderma pigmentosum. *Quart. J. Med.* **48**, 179–210.

PEARSON, C. & STYLES, J. A. (1984). Resistance of mouse lymphoma L5178YAII cells to alkylation with methylmethane sulphonate resides in a late step of excision repair. *J. Cell Sci.* **68**, 35–48.

PILLIDGE, L. (1984). Analysis of UV sensitivity and DNA repair in two Indian muntjac cell lines. PhD thesis, University of Cambridge.

PILLIDGE, L., DOWNES, C. S. & JOHNSON, R. T. (1986*a*). Defective postreplication recovery and UV sensitivity in a simian virus 40-transformed Indian muntjac cell line. *Int. J. Radiat. Biol.* **50**, 119–136.

PILLIDGE, L., MUSK, S. R. R., JOHNSON, R. T. & WALDREN, C. A. (1986*b*). Excessive chromosome fragility and abundance of sister chromatid exchanges induced by UV in an Indian muntjac cell line defective in postreplication (daughter strand) repair. *Mutat. Res.* **166**, 265–273.

PINTO, R. I., MANUKYAN, K. L., VIKHANSKAYA, F. L., MANUILOVA, E. S., SHAPIRO, N. I. & ZHESTYANIKOV, V. D. (1980). Post-replication repair of DNA in UV-sensitive clones of the Chinese hamster. *Tsitologia* **22**, 1085–1095.

POPESCU, N. C., AMSBAUGH, S. C. & DiPAULO, J. A. (1983). Human and rodent transformed cells are more sensitive to in vitro induction of SCE by N-methyl-N'-nitrosoguanidine (MNNG) than normal cells. *Hum. Genet.* **63**, 53–57.

RAETZ, C. R. H., WERMUTH, M. N., McINTYRE, T. M., ESKO, J. & WING, B. C. (1982). Somatic cell cloning in polyester stacks. *Proc. natn. Acad. Sci. U.S.A.* **79**, 3223–3227.

ROBSON, C. N., HARRIS, A. L. & HICKSON, I. D. (1985). Isolation and characterization of Chinese hamster ovary cell lines sensitive to mitomycin C and bleomycin. *Cancer Res.* **45**, 5305–5309.

ROBSON, C. N., HARRIS, A. L. & HICKSON, I. D. (1986). Characterisation of mitomycin C sensitive mutants of CHO-K1 cells and their use as hosts for the cloning of human DNA repair genes. *Br. J. Cancer* **54**, 350 (abstr.).

ROSENSTEIN, B. S. & CHAO, C. C.-K. (1985*a*). Isolation of a mutant cell line derived from ICR 2A frog cells hypersensitive to the induction of non-dimer DNA damages by solar ultraviolet radiation. *Somat. Cell molec. Genet.* **11**, 339–344.

ROSENSTEIN, B. S. & CHAO, C. C.-K. (1985*b*). Characterization of DNA repair in a mutant cell line derived from ICR 2A frog cells that is hypersensitive to non-dimer DNA damages induced by solar ultraviolet radiation. *Mutat. Res.* **146**, 191–196.

ROSENSTEIN, B. & OHLSSON-WILHELM, B. M. (1979). Isolation of UV-sensitive clones from a haploid frog cell line. *Somat. Cell Genet.* **5**, 117–128.

ROYER-POKORA, B. & HASELTINE, W. A. (1984). Isolation of UV-resistant revertants from a xeroderma pigmentosum complementation group A cell line. *Nature, Lond.* **311**, 390–392.

SATO, K. & HIEDA, N. (1979*a*). Isolation of a mammalian cell mutant sensitive to 4-nitroquinoline-1-oxide. *Int. J. Radiat. Biol.* **35**, 83–87.

SATO, K. & HIEDA, N. (1979*b*). Isolation and characterization of a mutant mouse lymphoma cell sensitive to methyl methanesulfonate and X rays. *Radiat. Res.* **78**, 167–171.

SATO, K. & SETLOW, R. B. (1981). DNA repair in a UV-sensitive mutant of a mouse cell line. *Mutat. Res.* **84**, 443–455.

SCHULTZ, R. A., BARBIS, D. P. & FRIEDBERG, E. C. (1985). Studies on gene transfer and reversion to UV resistance in xeroderma pigmentosum cells. *Somat. Cell molec. Genet.* **11**, 617–624.

SCHULTZ, R. A., CHANG, C.-C. & TROSKO, J. E. (1981*a*). The mutation studies of mutagen-sensitive and DNA repair mutants of Chinese hamster fibroblasts. *Environ. Mutagen.* **3**, 141–150.

SCHULTZ, R. A., TROSKO, J. E. & CHANG, C.-C. (1981*b*). Isolation and partial characterization of mutagen sensitive and DNA repair mutants of Chinese hamster fibroblasts. *Environ. Mutagen.* **3**, 53–64.

SHIOMI, T., HIEDA-SHIOMI, N. & SATO, K. (1982*a*). Isolation of UV-sensitive mutants of mouse L5178Y cells by a cell suspension spotting method. *Somat. Cell Genet.* **8**, 329–345.

SHIOMI, T., HIEDA-SHIOMI, N. & SATO, K. (1982*b*). A novel mutant of mouse lymphoma cells sensitive to alkylating agents and caffeine. *Mutat. Res.* **103**, 61–69.

SHIOMI, T. & SATO, K. (1979). Isolation of UV-sensitive variants of human FL cells by a viral suicide method. *Somat. Cell Genet.* **5**, 193–201.

SHIRAISHI, Y., YOSIDA, T. H. & SANDBERG, A. A. (1983). Analyses of bromodeoxyuridine-associated sister chromatid exchanges (SCEs) in Bloom syndrome based on cell fusion: single and twin SCEs in endoreduplication. *Proc. natn. Acad. Sci. U.S.A.* **80**, 4369–4373.

SICILIANO, M. J., CARRANO, A. V. & THOMPSON, L. H. (1985). Chromosome 19 corrects the complementing DNA repair mutations present in CHO cells. *Cytogenet. Cell Genet.* **40**, 744–745.

SIMINOVITCH, L. (1976). On the nature of hereditable variation in cultured somatic cells. *Cell* **7**, 1–11.

SQUIRES, S., JOHNSON, R. T. & COLLINS, A. R. S. (1982). Initial rates of DNA incision in UV-irradiated human cells. Differences between normal, xeroderma pigmentosum and tumour cells. *Mutat. Res.* **95**, 389–404.

SRINIVASAN, P. R., GUPTA, R. S. & SIMINOVITCH, L. (1980). Studies on temperature-sensitive mutants of Chinese hamster ovary cells affected in DNA synthesis. *Somat. Cell Genet.* **6**, 567–582.

STAMATO, T. D., HINKLE, L., COLLINS, A. R. S. & WALDREN, C. A. (1981). Chinese hamster ovary mutant UV-1 is hypomutable and defective in a postreplication recovery process. *Somat. Cell Genet.* **7**, 307–320.

STAMATO, T. D. & WALDREN, C. A. (1977). Isolation of UV-sensitive variants of CHO-K1 by nylon cloth replica plating. *Somat. Cell Genet.* **3**, 431–440.

STAMATO, T. D., WEINSTEIN, R., GIACCIA, A. & MACKENZIE, L. (1983). Isolation of cell-cycle-dependent gamma ray-sensitive Chinese hamster ovary cell. *Somat. Cell Genet.* **9**, 165–173.

STEFANINI, M., KEIJZER, W., WESTERVELD, A. & BOOTSMA, D. (1985). Interspecies complementation analysis of xeroderma pigmentosum and UV-sensitive Chinese hamster cells. *Expl Cell Res.* **161**, 373–380.

STEFANINI, M., MONDELLO, C., TESSERA, L., CAPUANO, V., GUERRA, B. R. & NUZZO, F. (1986). Sensitivity to DNA-damaging agents and mutation induction by UV light in UV sensitive CHO cells. *Mutat. Res.* **174**, 155–159.

STEFANINI, M., REUSER, A. & BOOTSMA, D. (1982). Isolation of Chinese hamster ovary cells with reduced unscheduled DNA synthesis after UV irradiation. *Somat. Cell Genet.* **8**, 635–642.

SUZUKI, N. & FUSE, A. (1981). A UV-sensitive human clonal cell line RSa, which has low repair activity. *Mutat. Res.* **84**, 133–145.

SUZUKI, N. & KUWATA, T. (1979). Establishment of ultraviolet-resistant cells from the highly sensitive human clonal cell line, RSb. *Mutat. Res.* **60**, 215–219.

TAKANO, T., NODA, M. & TAMURA, T. (1982). Transfection of cells from a xeroderma pigmentosum patient with normal human DNA confers UV resistance. *Nature, Lond.* **296**, 269–270.

TANAKA, K., KAWAI, K., KUMAHARA, Y., IKENAGA, M. & OKADA, Y. (1981). Genetic complementation groups in Cockayne Syndrome. *Somat. Cell Genet.* **7**, 445–455.

TEO, I. A., LEHMANN, A. R., MULLER, R. & RAJEWSKY, M. F. (1983). Similar rate of O^6-ethylguanine elimination from DNA in normal human fibroblast and xeroderma pigmentosum cell strains not transformed by SV40. *Carcinogenesis* **4**, 1075–1077.

THIELMANN, H. W., FISCHER, E., DZARLIEVA, R. T., KOMITOWSKI, D., POPANDA, O. & EDLER, L. (1983). Spontaneous *in vitro* malignant transformation in a xeroderma pigmentosum fibroblast line. *Int. J. Cancer* **31**, 687–700.

THOMPSON, L. H. & BAKER, R. M. (1973). Isolation of mutants of cultured mammalian cells. *Meth. Cell Biol.* **6**, 209–281.

THOMPSON, L. H., BROOKMAN, K. W., DILLEHAY, L. E., CARRANO, A. V., MAZRIMAS, J. A., MOONEY, C. L. & MINKLER, J. L. (1982*a*). A CHO-cell strain having hypersensitivity to mutagens, a defect in DNA strand-break repair, and an extraordinary baseline frequency of sister-chromatid exchange. *Mutat. Res.* **95**, 427–440.

THOMPSON, L. H., BROOKMAN, K. W., CARRANO, A. V. & DILLEHAY, L. E. (1982*b*). Role of DNA repair in mutagenesis of Chinese hamster ovary cells by 7-bromomethylbenz(a)anthracene. *Proc. natn. Acad. Sci. U.S.A.* **79**, 534–538.

THOMPSON, L. H., BROOKMAN, K. W., DILLEHAY, L. E., MOONEY, C. L. & CARRANO, A. V. (1982*c*). Hypersensitivity to mutation and sister-chromatid exchange induction in CHO cell mutants defective in incising DNA containing UV lesions. *Somat. Cell Genet.* **8**, 759–773.

THOMPSON, L. H., BUSCH, D. B., BROOKMAN, K., MOONEY, C. L. & GLASER, D. A. (1981). Genetic diversity of UV-sensitive DNA repair mutants of Chinese hamster ovary cells. *Proc. natn. Acad. Sci. U.S.A.* **78**, 3734–3737.

THOMPSON, L. H., MOONEY, C. L. & BROOKMAN, K. W. (1985*a*). Genetic complementation between UV-sensitive CHO mutants and xeroderma pigmentosum fibroblasts. *Mutat. Res.* **150**, 423–429.

THOMPSON, L. H., MOONEY, C. L., BURKHART-SCHULTZ, K., CARRANO, A. V. & SICILIANO, M. J. (1985*b*). Correction of a nucleotide-excision-repair mutation by human chromosome 19 in hamster-human hybrid cells. *Somat. Cell molec. Genet.* **11**, 87–92.

THOMPSON, L. H., RUBIN, J. S., CLEAVER, J. E., WHITMORE, G. F. & BROOKMAN, K. (1980). A screening method for isolating DNA repair-deficient mutants of CHO cells. *Somat. Cell Genet.* **6**, 391–405.

THOMPSON, L. H., SALAZAR, E. P., BROOKMAN, K. W., COLLINS, C. C., STEWART, S. A., BUSCH, D. B. & WEBER, C. A. (1987). Recent progress with the DNA repair mutants of Chinese hamster ovary cells. *J. Cell Sci. Suppl.* **6**, 000–000.

THOMPSON, L. H., SALAZAR, E. P., BROOKMAN, K. W. & HOY, C. A. (1983). Hypersensitivity to cell killing and mutation induction by chemical carcinogens in an excision repair-deficient mutant of CHO cells. *Mutat. Res.* **112**, 329–344.

WALDREN, C., SNEAD, D. & STAMATO, T. (1983). In *Cellular Responses to DNA Damage* (ed. E. C. Friedberg & B. R. Bridges), pp. 637–646. New York: Alan R. Liss.

WATERS, R., MISHRA, N., BOUCK, N., DIMAYORICA, G. & REGAN, J. (1977). Partial inhibition of postreplication repair and enhanced frequency of chemical transformation in rat cells infected with leukemia virus. *Proc. natn. Acad. Sci. U.S.A.* **74**, 238–242.

WOLFF, S., RODIN, B. & CLEAVER, J. E. (1977). Sister chromatid exchanges induced by mutagenic carcinogens in normal and xeroderma pigmentosum cells. *Nature, Lond.* **265**, 347–349.

WOOD, R. D. & BURKI, H. J. (1982). Repair capability and the cellular age response for killing and mutation induction after UV. *Mutat. Res.* **95**, 505–514.

YAGI, T. & TAKEBE, H. (1983). Establishment by SV40 transformation and characteristics of a cell line of xeroderma pigmentosum belonging to complementation group F. *Mutat. Res.* **112**, 59–66.

YIN, L., CHUN, E. H. L. & RUTMAN, R. J. (1973). A comparison of the effects of alkylation on the DNA of sensitive and resistant Lettre-Ehrlich cells following in vivo exposure to nitrogen mustard. *Biochim. biophys. Acta* **324**, 472–481.

ZDZIENICKA, M. Z. & SIMONS, J. W. I. M. (1986). Analysis of repair processes by the determination of the induction of cell killing and mutation in 2 repair deficient Chinese hamster ovary cell lines. *Mutat. Res.* **166**, 59–69.

J. Cell Sci. Suppl. 6, 83–96 (1987)
Printed in Great Britain © The Company of Biologists Limited 1987

FUNCTIONAL EXPRESSION OF THE *ESCHERICHIA COLI* ALKYLTRANSFERASE GENE IN MAMMALIAN CELLS

G. P. MARGISON[1] AND J. BRENNAND[2]

Departments of [1]Carcinogenesis and [2]Biochemical Genetics, Paterson Laboratories,
Christie Hospital, Manchester M20 9BX, UK

SUMMARY

Alkylating agents can produce a variety of biological effects in mammalian cells and organisms including toxicity, mutagenicity and malignant transformation. These agents react with oxygen and nitrogen atoms in DNA resulting in 12 products some of which are known to be eliminated from DNA by repair systems. One method of assessing the relative importance of a specific product in any of the biological effects of DNA alkylation would be to convert a cell line that is deficient in a particular repair function into a repair-proficient cell line and to determine whether this influences the magnitude of the effect. The cloning and expression in mammalian cells of the *Escherichia coli* DNA repair gene coding for the O^6-alkylguanine–alkylphosphotriester dual alkyltransferase will be described. The *E. coli* gene product acts on damage produced in host cell DNA by treatment with methylnitrosourea, and reduces the toxicity and mutagenicity of this agent. The effects on the toxicity of a variety of other mono and bifunctional alkylating agents have also been assessed.

INTRODUCTION

The mechanism by which alkylating agents induce tumours in experimental animals has been the subject of much research since the first demonstration of liver tumour induction in rats by dimethylnitrosamine (DMN; Magee & Barnes, 1956), which was later shown to alkylate cellular molecules such as protein (Magee & Hultin, 1962) and DNA (Magee & Farber, 1962). The alkylating agents are now known to be a large family of chemical compounds that includes *N*-nitrosamines such as DMN and also nitrosamides, sulphates, sulphonates, triazenes and others, and they can produce a wide range of biological effects including not only malignant transformation but also mutagenicity, cytotoxicity, chromosome aberrations and teratogenicity (reviewed by Magee *et al.* 1976; Preussmann & Stewart, 1984).

The N-nitroso compounds may have particular relevance to human cancer since these agents are present in the environment and can be generated from ingested inactive precursors (see Bartsch & Montesano, 1984). It has long been known that human liver is capable of the appropriate metabolic activation processes from DMN that give rise to DNA alkylation products (Montesano & Magee, 1970) and these products have been detected in liver DNA after known human exposure to DMN Herron & Shank, 1980).

Most of the nitrogen and oxygen atoms in DNA are potential sites for reaction of alkylating agents but the possible relevance of most of these has essentially been ignored since 1969 when it was first suggested that O^6-alkylation of guanine might be responsible for the mutagenic and possibly carcinogenic effects of alkylating agents (Loveless, 1969). The interest in this product was polarized by several factors: (1) the observation that the extent of formation of the major base alkylation product 7-methylguanine (7MeG) did not correlate with the carcinogenicity of a series of methylating agents (Swann & Magee, 1968). (2) The demonstration that O^6-methylguanine (O^6MeG) miscoded when present in oligonucleotides (Gerchman & Ludlum, 1973). (3) Another major alkylation product, 3-alkyladenine was unstable in DNA *in vivo* and *in vitro*, and its biological relevance was difficult to investigate (Margison & O'Connor, 1973). (4) Alkylphosphotriesters, though being the major product with some ethylating agents and a minor product with the methylating agents, were relatively difficult to quantify (Warren *et al.* 1979; O'Connor *et al.* 1975) and also more difficult to envisage as giving rise to mutagenic events. (5) At that time most of the other products, principally pyrimidine adducts in DNA, were present in such small amounts as to be unmeasurable for practical purposes (e.g. see Lawley, 1972).

The probable adverse biological effects of O^6-alkylguanine (O^6-AG) were also suggested by the early observation that *Escherichia coli* (Lawley & Orr, 1970) and rat liver (O'Connor *et al.* 1973) contained systems for the repair of such damage in DNA. The importance of this repair process in reducing the susceptibility of a tissue to tumour induction was demonstrated in numerous experiments in which the effectiveness of the process was compared in target and non-target tissues and organisms (reviewed by O'Connor *et al.* 1979).

Work with bacteria and cultured mammalian cells strongly implicated the mutagenic and in some cases toxic effects of O^6-AG in DNA (reviewed by Yarosh, 1985; Saffhill *et al.* 1985) and, more recently, evidence that O^6MeG is responsible for cell transformation by methylating agents has been produced (Doniger *et al.* 1985).

In order to examine further the role of O^6-AG in the various biological effects of alkylating agents, we have cloned the *E. coli* gene that codes for this repair function and produced vectors that permit its expression in cultured mammalian cells. Initially, a transient expression vector was used, but later a retrovirus-based drug-selectable plasmid was employed. Clones of repair-proficient cells have been generated and, by comparing their susceptibility to the toxic and mutagenic effects of alkylating agents with those of the parent line, the contribution of O^6-AG to these effects can be deduced.

The repair of O^6-AG in DNA in *E. coli* takes place by the transfer of the alkyl group to a cysteine residue within the 18K (K represents $10^3 M_r$) repair protein itself (Olsson & Lindahl, 1980; Demple *et al.* 1982). This is probably true in mammalian cells, although in this case the protein has not been purified to homogeneity (e.g. see Bogden *et al.* 1981). Exposure of *E. coli* to low doses of alkylating agents increases their resistance to the toxic and mutagenic effects of these agents and this, the 'adaptive' response (Samson & Cairns, 1977), was found to be under the control of a gene, *ada*, which was cloned by mutant rescue (Sedgwick, 1983). Since the relationship between the *ada* gene and *E. coli* O^6-AG AT (alkyltransferase) activity had not

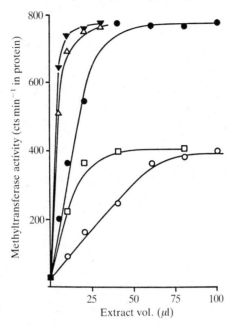

Fig. 1. Methyltransferase activity in extracts of *E. coli* harbouring various plasmids: (O——O) p061; (●——●) p062; (□——□) p062SX; (▼——▼) p062H; (△——△) p062C (see Fig. 3B). Extracts were prepared and assayed as described by Margison *et al.* (1985) except that the substrate was prepared using [³H]methylnitrosourea (23 Ci mmol l⁻¹) and an amount of this corresponding to 25 fmol of O^6MeG was used.

then been shown (Teo *et al.* 1984), we decided to attempt the cloning of the AT gene using a functional assay for the gene product that we had devised for the rapid assay of activity in mammalian cell extracts.

CLONING OF THE *E. COLI* ALKYLTRANSFERASE GENE

An *E. coli* genomic DNA library was made by partial digestion with *Sau*III AI, ligation into the *Bam*HI site of pUC8 and transformation into *E. coli* JM83. Colonies harbouring plasmids containing inserts were selected and pools of eight colonies were grown up. Extracts of these were screened for AT activity as described (Margison *et al.* 1985) using JM83 as a negative control. From two slightly positive pools three highly positive colonies were identified and plasmids from these were transformed into *E. coli* DH1 to avoid recombinational loss. The two resulting colonies were called 061 and 062. By comparing the stoichiometry of the transfer of methyl groups from O^6MeG in the substrate to the protein it was concluded that the former expressed only O^6-AG AT activity. Transfer of methyl groups to protein in 062 extracts was higher than could be attributed to O^6MeG alone and we concluded that these extracts contained an additional AT function (Fig. 1). This was shown to act on both methyl and ethyl phosphotriesters (Margison *et al.* 1985), and was probably the function identified earlier in extracts of adapted *E. coli* (McCarthy *et al.* 1983). It

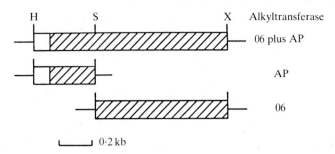

Fig. 2. Arrangement of AP and O^6-AG (06) AT activities in the p062HX subclone. Hatched area indicates approximate position of protein coding sequence. H, *Hin*dIII; S, *Sal*I; X, *Xho*I.

has recently been shown that this function acts only on the S stereoisomer of methylphosphotriesters (MeP) (McCarthy & Lindahl, 1985).

We carried out further characterization of extracts of 062 and its plasmids p062 and various subclones thereof (Fig. 1), and concluded that we had isolated a gene from *E. coli* that codes for a 37K protein containing both O^6-AG (3' region) and alkylphosphotriester (AP) (5' region) AT activities (Fig. 2). This was later shown to be identical to the earlier cloned *ada* gene the sequence of which has since been published (Demple *et al.* 1985; Nakabeppu *et al.* 1985).

Initially, we thought that p061 contained the O^6-AG AT section of this dual function gene (SX fragment, see Fig. 2). However, a limited restriction endonuclease map showed no common sites and Southern analysis has shown no sequence homology. Other evidence (P. M. Potter, J. Brennand & G. P. Margison, unpublished results) also suggests that this is a separate gene and sequence analysis is in progress to establish if this is the case.

EXPRESSION OF THE AT GENE IN COS7 MONKEY FIBROBLASTS

In order to show whether the bacterial gene could be expressed in mammalian cells we initially chose a simian virus 40 (SV40)-based transient expression vector, which had been used for the expression of the rabbit β-globin gene in COS7 monkey fibroblasts (Mulligan *et al.* 1979). The β-globin sequences were removed and a section of p062 containing the *E. coli* dual function AT gene was ligated into the gap to produce pSV206 as shown in Fig. 3A. Since this *E. coli* sequence contained an ATG upstream from the known dual AT protein initiation ATG, in a separate series of experiments (Fig. 3B) this was removed and the resulting fragment (062C) was used as above to generate pSV206C (Fig. 3A). COS7 monkey fibroblasts express an endogenous AT gene, which codes for a 24K protein acting on O^6MeG in substrate DNA. In pSV2βg-transfected cells the AT specific activity was 140 fmol mg^{-1} but in pSV206- and pSV206C-transfected cells it was increased to 460 and 810 fmol mg^{-1}, respectively. The increase varied between transfections and was time-dependent (Brennand & Margison, 1986a). It was essential to show that this increase was not due to upregulation of the endogenous gene, and this was achieved by preparing

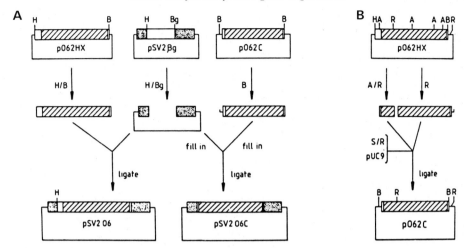

Fig. 3. Manipulations of p062HX to generate p062C, and the construction of pSV206 and pSV206C from p062HX or p062C and pSV2βg. A, *Alu*I; B, *Bam*HI; Bg, *Bgl*II; H, *Hin*dIII; R, *Eco*RI; S, *Sma*I.

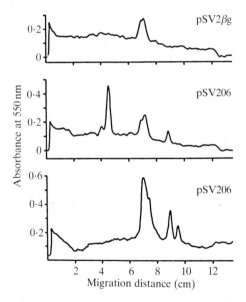

Fig. 4. Scanning densitometric traces of fluorographs of extracts of COS7 cells harbouring pSV2βg (top) or pSV206 (centre and bottom, representing two different experiments) following incubation with substrate DNA and SDS–PAGE (see Margison *et al.* 1985, for details). The peak around 4·5 cm corresponds to an M_r of around 37K. Those at 7 and 9 cm correspond to approx. 24K and 18K, respectively.

extracts of pSV2βg- and pSV206-transfected cells, and by sodium dodecyl sulphate–polyacrylamide gel electrophoresis (SDS–PAGE)–fluorography following incubation with substrate DNA. Scanning densitometry of the fluorographs shows that the pSV206-transfected population contained, in addition to the endogenous 24K protein, 37K and 18K proteins which correspond to the *E. coli* dual function and O^6-AG AT function proteins, respectively (Fig. 4).

In *E. coli* we found that the extent to which the 37K protein was broken down to subfragments was host-dependent (Margison *et al.* 1985). In further experiments with pSV206-transfected COS7 cells we found that a similar effect could take place giving rise in extreme cases to 18K and 16K bands exclusively (Fig. 4). Whether this degradation occurs before (giving rise to active subfragments) or after reaction with substrate DNA has not been elucidated.

Although we could have used these pSV206C-transfected cells to study the repair of AP, the presence of the endogenous O^6-AG AT activity and the relatively small increase in specific activity of the combined function in transfected cells obviated investigation of any changes in the biological effects of alkylating agents in this

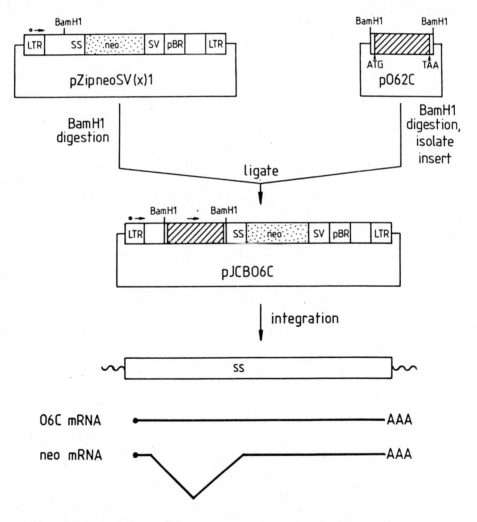

Fig. 5. Construction from p062C and pZipneoSV(X)1 and putative transcription in mammalian cells of pJCB06C.

system. However, the feasibility of the approach had been adequately demonstrated and we turned to vectors with a less restricted host range so that we could achieve *E. coli* AT gene expression in AT-deficient cell lines.

EXPRESSION OF THE AT GENE IN V79 CHINESE HAMSTER FIBROBLASTS

The plasmid pJCB06C was constructed as shown in Fig. 5 and transfected into O^6-AG AT-deficient V79 Chinese hamster fibroblasts (Warren *et al.* 1979; Brennand & Margison, 1986*a*). Cells incorporating this plasmid into their genome should be capable of producing two mRNA molecules (Fig. 5). One is a full-length mRNA starting transcription in the 5′LTR (long terminal repeat) and terminating in the 3′LTR, which, by initiation at the first AUG encountered, directs *E. coli* AT translation. The other is a spliced version of this, which does not contain the *E. coli* sequence and which directs translation from the initiation AUG of the *neo* gene, the product of which confers resistance to the antibiotic G418.

Of the extracts of the 12 clones of G418-resistant pJCB06C-transfected cells that were assayed, only four expressed high levels of AT activity (see Fig. 6A) and when corrected for protein concentration, extracts of clone 8 had the highest level (Fig. 6B, 1600 fmol mg^{-1} AT protein extracted). Transfection with control plasmid pZipneoSV(X)1 did not increase endogenous gene expression (Fig. 6B) and one clone (clone 2, AT sp. act. 4 fmol mg^{-1} protein) was used as the control in subsequent experiments. Southern analysis of DNA from clone 2 and clone 8 cells

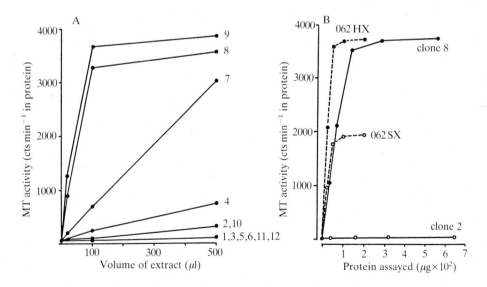

Fig. 6. A. Methyltransferase (MT) activity in clones of G418-resistant V79 Chinese hamster cells following transfection with pJCB06C (3–12) or pZipneo SV(X)1 (1 and 2). B. Substrate-limiting assay for methyltransferase activity in extracts of *E. coli* harbouring p062SX (O---O) or p062HX (●---●), or V79 cells harbouring pZipneoSV(X)1 (O——O) or pJCB06C (●——●).

using 06C as a probe showed that the *E. coli* AT gene had been incorporated into the genome of clone 8 cells (data not shown).

CHARACTERIZATION OF THE AT GENE PRODUCT IN V79 CELLS

Substrate-limiting experiments showed that extracts of pJCB06C-transfected cells contained the same AT activities as extracts of *E. coli* harbouring the dual-function gene plasmid p062HX (Fig. 6B). In most experiments this protein had a molecular weight of approx. 37K as shown by PAGE and fluorography (Fig. 7, lane A). In some cases, however, there was evidence for degradation to 18K and 20K proteins

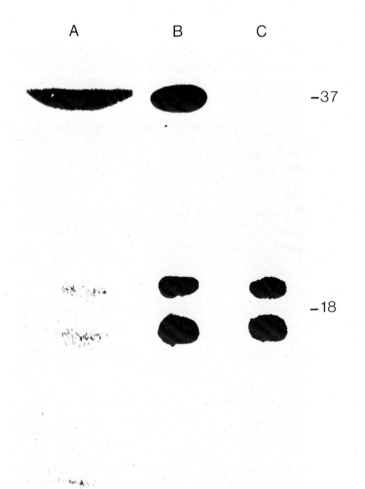

Fig. 7. Fluorographs of extracts of pJCB06C-transfected G418-resistant V79 cells following incubation with substrate DNA and SDS–PAGE. Lane A, a sample undergoing little degradation; lane B, bands around 18K prominent, but 37K material still present; lane C, no 37K material detectable.

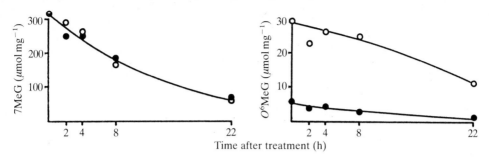

Fig. 8. Levels of 7-methylguanine (7MeG, left) and O^6-methylguanine (O^6MeG, right) in DNA of clone 8 (●——●) or clone 2 (○——○) cells various times after exposure to ^{3}H-labelled *N*-methyl-*N*-nitrosourea.

(Fig. 7, lanes B, C) as had been found in COS7 extracts (see above). Again, whether this breakdown occurs before or after incubation with substrate DNA is not known.

ACTION OF THE AT GENE PRODUCT ON HOST-CELL DNA DAMAGE

Although the *E. coli* AT gene was clearly present in clone 8 cells and was being expressed in an active form, it was necessary to show that the protein was capable of penetrating the nucleus and acting on alkylation damage in host cell DNA. Clone 2 and clone 8 cells were exposed to radiolabelled *N*-methyl-*N*-nitrosourea (MNU) for 1 h and harvested up to 22 h later. DNA was extracted and the amounts of the major product 7MeG and one of the substrates for the dual-function protein, O^6MeG, were determined by radiochromatography of acid hydrolysates of the DNA. Fig. 8 shows that the amounts detected immediately after treatment and the loss of 7MeG were identical in both clones, whereas the amounts of O^6MeG were much lower in clone 8 cells. This indicated that the *E. coli* gene product was capable of repairing host cell DNA damage very rapidly since even by the end of 1-h treatment with MNU (the 'zero' time) the O^6MeG level in clone 8 cells was only about 20 % of that in clone 2 cells.

EFFECT ON MNU-INDUCED MUTATION FREQUENCY

Exposure of clone 2 cells to increasing doses of MNU resulted in the generation of thioguanine(TG)-resistant cells with a frequency of about 1 in 10^3 at a survival rate of about 35 % (see Fig. 9). In contrast, in clone 8 cells there was no increase in TG-resistant clones above the spontaneous level of 0.5×10^5 to 1.0×10^5. *E. coli* AT gene expression therefore protects these cells against the mutagenic effect of MNU.

EFFECT ON THE TOXICITY OF MONOFUNCTIONAL ALKYLATING AGENTS

The survival curves of clone 2 and clone 8 cells after exposure to increasing doses of MNU or methylmethanesulphonate (MMS) are shown in Fig. 10. Clone 8 cells are more resistant than clone 2 cells to the toxic effects of MNU and this suggests that

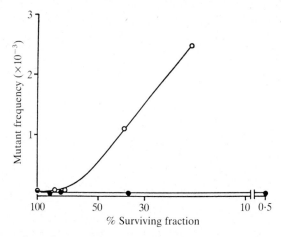

Fig. 9. Frequency of HPRT⁻ mutants (thioguanine-resistant cells) in relation to the % of cells surviving after exposure to increasing doses of *N*-methyl-*N*-nitrosourea; (O——O) clone 2; (●——●) clone 8.

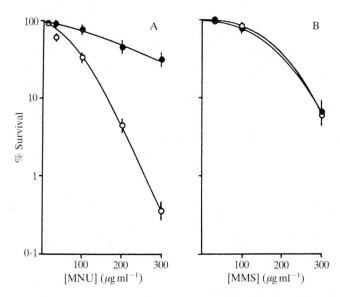

Fig. 10. Survival of clone 2 (O——O) or clone 8 (●——●) cells following exposure to increasing doses of MNU (A) or MMS (B).

E. coli AT-repairable DNA damage is responsible for part of this effect. Further work is needed to decide if the toxicity in clone 8 cells is a consequence of saturation of the repair function or the toxic effects of another lesion. This latter possibility appears to be more likely since both clones of cells are (equally) susceptible to killing by MMS, an agent that produces only a very small proportion of its total DNA damage in the form of AT-repairable lesions.

EFFECT ON THE TOXICITY OF BIFUNCTIONAL ALKYLATING AGENTS

Clone 8 cells were much less susceptible than clone 2 cells to the toxic effects of four chloroethylating agents, bis-chloroethylnitrosourea (BiCNU), taurine chloro-ethylnitrosourea (TCNU), chlorozotocin and nitrozolamide (Fig. 11). It has been suggested that these kinds of agents are toxic to cells because of their ability to form crosslinks that occur slowly *via* an initial mono addition to guanine to form O^6-chloroethylguanine (Tong *et al.* 1982). Circumstantial evidence of this is that the mono adduct can be dealkylated by the AT and this prevents crosslinking (Robins *et al.* 1983), and that cells that contain low levels of this AT protein either normally (Erickson *et al.* 1980), or after depletion by low doses of methylating agents (Zlotogorski & Erickson, 1983), are more susceptible to the toxic effects of these agents than cells containing high levels. Our results suggest that *E. coli* AT-repairable damage is almost exclusively responsible for cell killing by these agents, with the possible exception of BiCNU, which though much more toxic for clone 2 cells did show extensive killing of clone 8 cells (Fig. 11). The higher toxicity of BiCNU may be related to its carbamoylating activity.

Both clones were equally susceptible to the toxic effects of nitrogen mustard (Brennand & Margison, 1986*b*), which is thought to crosslink DNA *via* the N7

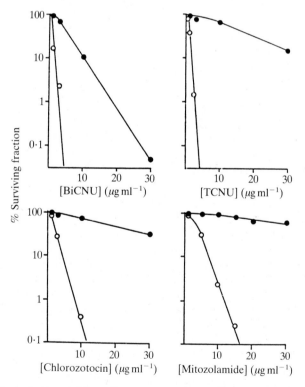

Fig. 11. Survival of clone 2 (O——O) or clone 8 (●——●) cells following exposure to increasing doses of bis-chloroethylnitrosourea (BiCNU, top left), taurine chloroethyl-nitrosourea (TCNU, top right), chlorozotocin (bottom left) or nitrozolamide (bottom right).

atoms of guanine residues (Kohn *et al.* 1966). This result further indicates that AT-repairable damage is not a cause of death in nigrogen-mustard-treated cells (see also Robins *et al.* 1983; Gibson *et al.* 1985).

DISCUSSION

From these experiments we can conclude that damage in DNA that can be repaired by the *E. coli* dual AT is responsible for the mutagenic effects of MNU and to a greater or lesser extent responsible for the toxic effects of MNU and chloro-ethylating agents but not nitrogen mustard or MMS. This conclusion is possible because the two clones we have generated differ only in their capacity to repair oxygen atom alkylation products in DNA: in all other respects they are identical.

The *E. coli* AT expressed in clone 8 cells has been shown to act on O^6-AG (see above) and this same repair function has also been shown to act on O^4-methyl-thymine in DNA (McCarthy *et al.* 1984). Another function in the protein acts on the S stereoisomers of MeP (McCarthy & Lindahl, 1985). By generating clones that express only the former or latter function we can now indicate precisely which effects can be attributed to these lesions. Initial results (Brennand & Margison, 1986c) show that clones expressing only the O^6-AG AT function have the same resistance to MNU as clone 8 cells, indicating that MeP S isomers are not toxic lesions. The same cells are, however, more susceptible to the toxic effects of chlorozotocin and nitrozolamide (but more resistant than clone 2 cells). There are several possible explanations for this observation, one of them being that chloroethylphosphotriesters may form lethal crosslinks if not repaired. Clones expressing only the AP AT function, which are now being generated, should help to resolve these questions.

Other biological effects of alkylating agents in these cells are being investigated. Initial results (White *et al.* 1986) indicate that expression of the *E. coli* O^6-AG AT protects V79 cells against MNU-induced sister chromatid exchanges, chromatid damage and micronucleus formation, indicating a role for O^6MeG in these effects. This approach is being extended to other classes of agents, and experiments intended to integrate *E. coli* DNA repair genes into cells and organisms that are susceptible to the transforming effects of alkylating agents are in hand.

We thank Sean Baker, Geoffrey Clarke, Martin Greaves, Brian C. Keenan, Yemisi Obisesan and Shrilene Oh for assistance in various aspects of this work, which was supported by grants from the Cancer Research Campaign. The saintly patience of Linda Evans deserves special mention! Mitozolamide was kindly provided by Dr E. Lunt of May and Baker Ltd.

REFERENCES

BARTSCH, H. & MONTESANO, R. (1984). Relevance of nitrosamines to human cancer. *Carcinogenesis* **5**, 1381–1393.

BOGDEN, J. M., EASTMAN, A. & BRESNICK, E. (1981). A system in mouse liver for the repair of O^6-methylguanine lesions in methylated DNA. *Nucl. Acids Res.* **9**, 3089–3103.

BRENNAND, J. & MARGISON, G. P. (1986a). Expression of the *E. coli* O^6-methylguanine-methylphosphotriester methyltransferase gene in mammalian cells. *Carcinogenesis* **7**, 185–188.

BRENNAND, J. & MARGISON, G. P. (1986b). Reduction in the toxicity and mutagenicity of alkylating agents in mammalian cells harbouring the *Escherichia coli* alkyltransferase gene. *Proc. natn. Acad. Sci. U.S.A.* (in press).

BRENNAND, J. & MARGISON, G. P. (1986c). Expression in mammalian cells of a truncated *E. coli* gene coding for O^6-alkylguanine alkyltransferase reduces the toxic effects of alkylating agents. *Carcinogenesis* (in press).

DEMPLE, B., JACOBSSON, A., OLSSON, M., ROBINS, P. & LINDAHL, T. (1982). The repair of alkylated DNA in *Escherichia coli*. Physical properties of O^6-methylguanine-DNA methyltransferase. *J. biol. Chem.* **257**, 13 776–13 780.

DEMPLE, B., SEDGWICK, B., ROBINS, P., TOTTY, N., WATERFIELD, M. D. & LINDAHL, T. (1985). Active site and complete sequence of the suicidal methyltransferase that counters alkylation mutagenesis. *Proc. natn. Acad. Sci. U.S.A.* **82**, 2688–2692.

DONIGER, J., DAY, R. S. & DiPAOLO, J. A. (1985). Quantitative assessment of the role of O^6-methylguanine in the initiation of carcinogenesis by methylating agents. *Proc. natn. Acad. Sci. U.S.A.* **82**, 421–425.

ERICKSON, L. C., BRADLEY, M. O., DUCORE, J. M., EWIG, R. A. G. & KOHN, K. W. (1980). DNA crosslinking and cytotoxicity in normal and transformed human cells treated with antitumour nitrosoureas. *Proc. natn. Acad. Sci. U.S.A.* **78**, 6766–6770.

GERCHMAN, L. L. & LUDLUM, D. B. (1973). The properties of O^6-methylguanine in templates for RNA polymerase. *Biochim. biophys. Acta* **308**, 310–316.

GIBSON, N. W., ZLOTOGORSKI, C. & ERICKSON, L. C. (1985). Specific DNA repair mechanisms may protect some human tumour cells from DNA interstrand crosslinking by chloroethylnitrosoureas but not from crosslinking by other antitumour alkylating agents. *Carcinogenesis* **6**, 445–450.

HERRON, D. C. & SHANK, R. (1980). Methylated purines in human liver DNA after probable dimethylnitrosamine poisioning. *Cancer Res.* **40**, 3116–3117.

KOHN, K. W., SPEARS, C. L. & DOTY, P. (1966). Interstrand crosslinking of DNA by nitrogen mustard. *J. molec. Biol.* **19**, 266–273.

LAWLEY, P. D. (1972). The action of alkylating agents on nucleic acids: N-methyl-N-nitroso compounds as methylating agents. In *Topics in Chemical Carcinogenesis* (ed. W. N. Kakahara *et al.*), pp. 237–256. Tokyo: University of Tokyo Press.

LAWLEY, P. D. & ORR, D. J. (1970). Specific excision of methylation products from DNA of *Escherichia coli* treated with N-methyl-N'-nitro-N-nitrosoguanidine. *Chem.-Biol. Interact.* **2**, 154.

LOVELESS, A. (1969). Possible relevance of O^6-alkylation of deoxyguanosine to the mutagenicity and carcinogenicity of nitrosamines and nitrosamides. *Nature, Lond.* **223**, 206–207.

MAGEE, P. N. & BARNES, J. M. (1956). The production of malignant primary hepatic tumours in the rat by feeding dimethylnitrosamine. *Br. J. Cancer* **10**, 114–122.

MAGEE, P. N. & FARBER, E. (1962). Toxic liver injury and carcinogenesis. Methylation of rat liver nucleic acids by dimethylnitrosamine. *Biochem. J.* **83**, 114–124.

MAGEE, P. N. & HULTIN, T. (1962). Toxic liver injury and carcinogenesis. Methylation of proteins of rat liver slices by dimethylnitrosamine *in vitro*. *Biochem. J.* **83**, 106–114.

MAGEE, P. M., MONTESANO, R. & PREUSSMANN, R. (1976). N-nitroso compounds and related carcinogens. *Chemical Carcinogens. ACS Monograph 173* (ed. C. E. Searle), pp. 491–625. Washington, DC: Am. Chem. Soc.

MARGISON, G. P., COOPER, D. P. & BRENNAND, J. (1985). Cloning of the *E. coli* O^6-methylguanine and methylphosphotriester methyltransferase gene using a functional DNA repair assay. *Nucl. Acids Res.* **13**, 1939–1952.

MARGISON, G. P. & O'CONNOR, P. J. (1973). Biological implications of the instability of the N-glycosidic bond of 3-methyldeoxyadenosine in DNA. *Biochim. biophys. Acta* **331**, 349–356.

McCARTHY, J. G., EDINGTON, B. V. & SCHENDEL, P. F. (1983). Inducible repair of phosphotriesters in *Escherichia coli*. *Proc. natn. Acad. Sci. U.S.A.* **80**, 7380–7384.

McCARTHY, T. V., KARRAN, P. & LINDAHL, T. (1984). Inducible repair of O-alkylated DNA pyrimidines in *Escherichia coli*. *EMBO J.* **3**, 545–550.

McCARTHY, T. V. & LINDAHL, T. (1985). Methylphosphotriesters in alkylated DNA one repaired by the ada regulatory protein of *E. coli*. *Nucl. Acids Res.* **13**, 2683–2698.

MONTESANO, R. & MAGEE, P. N. (1970). Metabolism of dimethylnitrosamine by human liver slices *in vitro*. *Nature, Lond.* **228**, 173–174.

MULLIGAN, R. C., HOWARD, B. H. & BERG, P. (1979). Synthesis of rabbit β-globin in cultured monkey kidney cells following infection with a SV40–β-globin recombinant genome. *Nature, Lond.* **277**, 108–114.

NAKABEPPU, Y., KONDO, H., KAWABATA, S., IWANAGA, S. & SEKIGUCHI, M. (1985). Purification and structure of the intact ada regulatory protein of *Escherichia coli* K12, O^6-methylguanine-DNA methyltransferase. *J. biol. Chem.* **260**, 7281–7288.

O'CONNOR, P. J., CAPPS, M. J. & CRAIG, A. W. (1973). Comparative studies of the hepatocarcinogen *N,N*-dimethylnitrosamine *in vivo*: reaction sites in rat liver DNA and the significance of their relative stabilities. *Br. J. Cancer* **27**, 153–166.

O'CONNOR, P. J., MARGISON, G. P. & CRAIG, A. W. (1975). Phosphotriesters in rat liver DNA after the administration of the carcinogen N,N-dimethylnitrosamine *in vivo*. *Biochem. J.* **145**, 475–482.

O'CONNOR, P. J., SAFFHILL, R. & MARGISON, G. P. (1979). N-nitroso compounds: biochemical mechanisms of action. In *Environmental Carcinogenesis* (ed. P. Emmelot & E. Kriek), pp. 73–96. Amsterdam: Elsevier/North Holland Biomedical Press.

OLSSON, M. & LINDAHL, T. (1980). Repair of alkylated DNA in *E. coli*: methyl group transfer from O^6-methylguanine to a protein cysteine residue. *J. biol. Chem.* **255**, 10569–10571.

PREUSSMANN, R. & STEWART, B. W. (1984). N-nitroso compounds and related carcinogens. In *Chemical Carcinogens* (ed. C. E. Searle), 2nd edn, pp. 643–828. Washington, DC: Am. Chem. Soc.

ROBINS, P., HARRIS, A. L., GOLDSMITH, I. & LINDAHL, T. (1983). Cross-linking of DNA induced by chloroethylnitrosourea is prevented by O^6-methylguanine-DNA methyltransferase. *Nucl. Acids Res.* **11**, 7743–7758.

SAFFHILL, R., MARGISON, G. P. & O'CONNOR, P. J. (1985). Mechanisms of carcinogenesis induced by alkylating agents. *Biochim. biophys. Acta* **823**, 111–145.

SAMSON, L. & CAIRNS, J. (1977). A new pathway for DNA repair in *Escherichia coli*. *Nature, Lond.* **267**, 281–283.

SEDGWICK, B. (1983). Molecular cloning of a gene which regulates the adaptive response to alkylating agents in *Escherichia coli*. *Molec. gen. Genet.* **191**, 466–472.

SWANN, P. F. & MAGEE, P. N. (1968). Nitrosamine induced carcinogenesis: The alkylation of nucleic acids of the rat by *N*-methyl-*N*-nitrosourea, dimethylnitrosamine, dimethylsulphate and methylmethanesulphonate. *Biochem. J.* **110**, 39–47.

TEO, I., SEDGWICK, B., DEMPLE, B., LI, B. & LINDAHL, T. (1984). Induction of resistance to alkylating agents in *E. coli*: the ada^+ gene product serves both as a regulatory protein and as an enzyme for repair for mutagenic damage. *EMBO J.* **3**, 2151–2157.

TONG, W. P., KOHN, K. W. & LUDLUM, D. B. (1982). Modifications of DNA by different haloethylnitrosoureas. *Cancer Res.* **42**, 4460–4464.

WARREN, W., CRATHORN, A. R. & SHOOTER, K. V. (1979). The stability of methylated purines and of methylphosphotriesters in the DNA of V79 cells after treatment with *N*-methyl-*N*-nitrosourea. *Biochim. biophys. Acta* **563**, 82–88.

WHITE, G. R. M., OCKEY, C. H., BRENNAND, J. & MARGISON, G. P. (1986). Chinese hamster cells harbouring the *E. coli* O^6-alkylguanine alkyltransferase gene are less susceptible to SCE induction and chromosome damage by methylating agents. *Carcinogenesis* (in press).

YAROSH, D. B. (1985). The role of O^6-methylguanine DNA methyltransferase in cell survival, mutagenesis and carcinogenesis. *Mutat. Res.* **145**, 1–16.

ZLOTOGORSKI, C. & ERICKSON, L. C. (1983). Pretreatment of normal human fibroblasts and human colon carcinoma cells with MNNG allows chloroethylnitrosourea to produce DNA interstrand crosslinks not observed in cells treated with chloroethylnitrosourea alone. *Carcinogenesis* **4**, 759–763.

J. Cell Sci. Suppl. 6, 97–110 (1987)
Printed in Great Britain © The Company of Biologists Limited 1987

RECENT PROGRESS WITH THE DNA REPAIR MUTANTS OF CHINESE HAMSTER OVARY CELLS

L. H. THOMPSON, E. P. SALAZAR, K. W. BROOKMAN,
C. C. COLLINS, S. A. STEWART, D. B. BUSCH* AND C. A. WEBER

*Biomedical Sciences Division, L452, Lawrence Livermore National Laboratory,
PO Box 5507, Livermore, CA 94550, USA*

SUMMARY

Repair-deficient mutants of Chinese hamster ovary (CHO) cells are being used to identify human genes that correct the repair defects and to study mechanisms of DNA repair and mutagenesis. Five independent tertiary DNA transformants were obtained from the EM9 mutant, which is noted for its very high sister-chromatid exchange frequencies. In these clones a human DNA sequence was identified that correlated with the resistance of the cells to chlorodeoxy-uridine (CldUrd). After *Eco*RI digestion, Southern transfer, and hybridization of transformant DNAs with the BLUR-8 *Alu* family sequence, a common fragment of 25–30 kilobases (kb) was present. Since the DNA molecules used to produce these transformants were sheared to <50 kb in size, the correcting gene should be small enough to clone in a cosmid vector.

Using drug-resistance markers to select for hybrids after fusion, we have done complementation experiments with ultraviolet light (u.v.)-sensitive mutants and have identified a sixth complementation group, line UV61. Additionally, CHO mutants UV27-1 and MMC-2, isolated in other laboratories, were found to belong to UV group 3, which is represented by line UV24.

To study the behaviour of transfected DNA molecules in repair-deficient cells, we treated plasmid pSV2*gpt* with either u.v. radiation or *cis*-diamminedichloroplatinum(II) (*cis*-DDP) and introduced the damaged DNA into normal CHO cells (AA8) and mutants UV4 and UV5. Unrepaired damage to the plasmid was indicated by loss of colony-forming ability of the transfected cells in selective medium containing mycophenolic acid. With u.v. damage, the differential survival of the cell lines was similar to that seen when whole cells are treated with u.v. However, with *cis*-DDP damage, mutant UV4 did not exhibit the extreme hypersensitivity (50-fold) that occurs when cells are treated. This result suggests that UV4 cells may be able to repair cross-links in transfected DNA.

INTRODUCTION

In our laboratory we have been characterizing DNA repair mutants of Chinese hamster ovary (CHO) cells as a tool for studying mechanisms of genetic change and mutagenesis (Thompson, 1985; Thompson & Hoy, 1986; Thompson *et al.* 1986). It is evident that repair mutants of rodent cells provide an important approach for isolating human (and rodent) genes involved in repair pathways. Westerveld *et al.* (1984) recently cloned a human gene that corrects ultraviolet light (u.v.)-sensitive mutants belonging to UV complementation group 2 described by Thompson *et al.* (1981). Efforts are under way in our laboratory and others to isolate genes that correct additional mutants that have sufficient hypersensitivity to provide an efficient selection system.

*Present address: Department of Environmental and Drug-Induced Pathology, Armed Forces Institute of Pathology, Washington, DC 20306-6000, USA.

Earlier in our laboratory we identified five complementation groups of u.v. mutants (Thompson *et al.* 1981; Thompson & Carrano, 1983), all of which involve a defect in the incision step of repair (Thompson *et al.* 1982*a*). These mutants, therefore, have properties quite similar to those of xeroderma pigmentosum (XP) cells (Friedberg *et al.* 1979; Cleaver, 1983). Mutants from each of the groups show a stable phenotype in response to 5-azacytidine treatment, suggesting that they did not arise by gene inactivation associated with methylation (Jeggo & Holiday, unpublished). We have obtained evidence from chromosome mapping studies that the five complementation groups represent at least four different human genes. In hybrid cells, the mutation of line UV20 (group 2) was corrected by a gene on human chromosome 19 (Thompson *et al.* 1985; Rubin *et al.* 1985). Mutant UV5 (group 1) also appears to be corrected by human chromosome 19, but the mutants of groups 3, 4 and 5 show correction by chromosomes 2, 16 and 13, respectively (L. Thompson, M. Siciliano & A. Carrano, unpublished data). Correction by different chromosomes indicates that different human genes are involved. It is conceivable that the two complementation groups corrected by chromosome 19 are due to interallelic complementation of a single gene. However, this possibility seems unlikely because the mutants in groups 1 and 2 consistently show very different phenotypes in terms of their sensitivity to DNA cross-linking agents (Hoy *et al.* 1985). The fact that two of the u.v. repair genes are linked on chromosome 19 could have functional significance, especially if they are close together. The isolation of the UV5-complementing gene is needed to give the appropriate DNA probes to determine the linkage. Gene transfer experiments in progress indicate that the human gene that corrects UV5 is functional in purified DNA and small enough to clone in a cosmid vector (unpublished data).

We are also proceeding to clone a human gene that corrects the EM9 mutant line, which is noted for its greatly elevated frequency of sister-chromatid exchange (SCE), defective repair of strand breaks, and reduced rate of DNA maturation when bromodeoxyuridine (BrdUrd) is in the template strand (Thompson *et al.* 1982*b*; Dillehay *et al.* 1983). The SCEs in EM9 cells result primarily from the BrdUrd incorporation that is used in the standard SCE protocol (Pinkel *et al.* 1985). All the enzymes involved in DNA metabolism that have been examined in EM9 cells were found to be normal (for references, see Thompson *et al.* 1985).

In hybrid cells, the EM9 defect is corrected by human chromosome 19 (Siciliano *et al.* 1986). DNA isolated from one of these resistant hybrids was also shown to correct EM9 in the DNA transfection procedure (Thompson *et al.* 1985). The data presented here on recent DNA transformants give our progress toward isolating the transferred human gene. We hope to use this gene to determine what gene product is defective in EM9 cells and to use this product to study the mechanism of SCE formation.

In addition, we present the results of recent efforts to identify new UV complementation groups of CHO cells. A sixth group has been found with line UV61. We also describe the behaviour of mutants UV5 (group 1) and UV4 (group 2) in response to transfected plasmid DNA that has been damaged with u.v. or *cis*-diamminedichloroplatinum(II) (*cis*-DDP).

MATERIALS AND METHODS

Culture conditions

Stock cell lines were grown in suspension as described earlier (Thompson *et al.* 1980, 1982*a,b*) in α-MEM medium supplemented with 10 % foetal bovine serum (K. C. Biological, Lenexa, KA). Medium contained 100 units ml^{-1} of penicillin and 100 μg ml^{-1} of streptomycin sulphate. Stocks were renewed every 3 months from material in liquid nitrogen and periodically tested for mycoplasma. The mutant lines were checked about once a month for sensitivity. Plasticware for monolayer culture and colony formation was from Corning.

Cell fusion complementation tests

For fusion, 2×10^6 cells (1:1 ratio of each type) were inoculated into a 6 cm dish and allowed several hours for attachment. Cells were exposed for 60 s to 2 ml of a solution containing 47 % polyethylene glycol 1000 (Baker Chemical Co.) and 10 % dimethyl sulphoxide (DMSO) in medium. The cells were rinsed twice with 10 % DMSO in medium and incubated in normal medium for ≈24 h for hybrid cell formation. Cells were then trypsinized, counted, and plated at 2×10^5 cells per 10 cm dish. After 4 h dishes were rinsed with phosphate-buffered saline and irradiated with far u.v. as described by Thompson *et al.* (1980). For colony formation, cells were then incubated 10 days in normal medium or medium containing 1 mM-ouabain (Sigma) plus hypoxanthine (74 μM), amethopterin (550 nM), and thymidine (41 μM), HAT medium. Colonies around the periphery of the dish, where shielding occurs during irradiation, were not counted.

Transfection of EM9 with sheared DNA

DNA from the secondary transformant 9TT3 (Thompson *et al.* 1986) was sheared so that almost all the molecules were below 50 kb. This was done by passing the DNA four times through a 30 gauge needle. Sheared genomic DNA was combined with pSV2*gpt* DNA in a 1:1 ratio (w/w). Calcium phosphate precipitates were prepared as described by Corsaro & Pearson (1981). To each dish of 2×10^6 EM9 cells containing 10 ml of medium, 40 μg of DNA in 1 ml was added. Sixty dishes were exposed to DNA for 20 h. Dishes were rinsed with 10 ml of medium and given 30 ml of fresh medium for a 48 h incubation for expression. Each dish was trypsinized and replated into three replicates with 30 ml of medium containing both MAXTA supplements and CldUrd (chlorodeoxyuridine) as described by Thompson *et al.* (1985) for selection of *gpt*-positive, repair-proficient cells. On days 4 and 8, 15 ml of fresh medium was added, and only the CldUrd selection was continued. Eleven to 15 days after plating, five colonies were isolated and grown to mass culture under CldUrd selection.

Transfer of pSV2gpt DNA treated with u.v. radiation or cis-DDP

For exposure to u.v. radiation, pSV2*gpt* DNA was diluted into a solution containing 0·25 M-CaCl$_2$, 1 mM-Tris·HCl (pH 8), and 10 mM-NaCl; 0·5 ml was irradiated in a 35 mm plastic dish. A 3 μg sample of precipitated DNA (see above) was added in a volume of 0·5 ml to each 10 cm dish containing 2×10^6 cells. A lower volume of precipitate was used here, compared to the case of genomic DNA, to reduce toxicity. The precipitate was left on the cells for 16–20 h. Then the dishes were rinsed, given fresh medium, and incubated for 24 h for expression of *gpt* function. Cells were trypsinized and replated at 1×10^6 to 2×10^6 cells per 10 cm dish in MAXTA-supplemented medium (Thompson *et al.* 1985) containing 2·5 times the standard concentration of glutamine. Three replicate dishes were plated for each dose point, and duplicate untreated controls were used in each experiment. Plating efficiency was determined at each dose by plating 300 cells into three replicate dishes, and these values (0·7–0·95) were used to calculate the frequency of MAXTA-resistant colonies per viable cell plated. MAXTA selection dishes were incubated 12–14 days, and plating efficiency dishes were incubated 7–9 days.

For exposure to *cis*-DDP, the DNA in 0·4 ml of 10 mM-Tris·HCl buffer (pH 8) was combined with *cis*-DDP (100 μg ml^{-1} in 10 mM-Tris·HCl) and incubated at 37°C for 1 h. The DNA in 0·3 M-sodium acetate (pH 5) was precipitated with ethanol at −70°C, then redissolved in 10 mM-Tris·HCl, 10 mM-EDTA (pH 7·4) for calcium phosphate precipitation. A 2 μg sample of DNA in 1 ml was added to each 10 cm dish containing 4×10^6 cells in 10 ml of medium, and the cells were incubated at 37°C for 4h. The medium was aspirated gently, and 2·5 ml of 20% glycerol in medium (v/v) at room temperature was added to the side of the dish. After 1 min, the glycerol was removed, and the dishes were rinsed three times with serum-free medium and given 20 ml of growth medium. After 24 h incubation the cells were plated for MAXTA selection as described above for u.v.-treated DNA.

Molecular hybridization

DNAs were digested with restriction enzymes, separated by electrophoresis, and transferred from agarose gels to nitrocellulose filters by the method of Southern (1975). Prehybridization of filters was done at 65°C with 25 ml of a solution containing 5×SSC (1×SSC is 150 mM-NaCl, 15 mM-sodium citrate), 50 μg ml^{-1} of denatured salmon sperm DNA, and 0·1% each of Ficoll, bovine serum albumin (BSA), polyvinylpyrrolidone (PVP), and sodium dodecyl sulphate (SDS). Hybridization was carried out for 18 h in 20 ml of a solution consisting of the prehybridization ingredients plus 10% dextran sulphate and the probe DNA, which contained 4·6×10^6 cts min^{-1} in ≈300 ng of the *Alu* family BLUR-8 sequence (Deininger *et al.* 1981) isolated as a *Bam*HI fragment. The probe was labelled with [α-^{32}P]dCTP by nick translation. Filter washes were done as follows: first, in 2×SSC + 0·1% each of Ficol, BSA, PVP and SDS (once for 5 min, three times for 15 min each); second, in 1×SSC + 0·1% each of SDS, Ficoll, BSA and PVP (four times for 30 min each); third, in 1×SSC at room temperature. The filter was exposed to Kodak X-OMAT AR5 film with an intensifying screen (Cronex Lightning-Plus, DuPont) for ≈3 days.

RESULTS AND DISCUSSION

Progress toward isolating a human DNA repair gene that corrects the EM9 mutation

Earlier, we introduced into EM9 cells human DNA sequences that normalized the SCE level and restored resistance to mutagens (Thompson *et al.* 1985). It is interesting to note that, unlike SCEs, chromosomal aberrations induced by BrdUrd remained slightly elevated in the primary transformants (Thompson *et al.* 1985). This result suggested that the transfected human gene was unable to correct fully all aspects of the biochemical defect in EM9.

Our strategy has been to identify the correcting human gene in the background of EM9 hamster DNA on the basis of the linkage of the gene to the human *Alu* family repetitive sequences. These repetitive sequences are associated with most genes (Schmid & Jelinek, 1982). The initial transfection was done with high molecular weight DNA (>160 kb) isolated from hybrid cells, which were derived by fusing EM9 cells with normal human lymphocytes. A 3·8 kilobase (kb) human *Eco*RI restriction fragment, which was present in 6/6 primary transformants (Thompson *et al.* 1985), looked promising as being part of the repair gene, and this sequence was isolated from a cosmid library of DNA from one of the primary transformants (see below). However, this fragment was later found to be absent in 3/6 secondary transformants (Thompson *et al.* 1986). To determine whether the repair gene was small enough to clone in a cosmid vector, a DNA transfer was performed using sheared DNA. DNA from the secondary transformant 9TT3 was sheared such that most of the molecules were 25–50 kb in size. This DNA was coprecipitated with pSV2*gpt* DNA and used to treat 1·2×10^8 EM9 cells. Five independent colonies were obtained that were able to grow in medium containing both MAXTA and CldUrd, implying that cotransfer of functional *gpt* and repair genes had occurred.

During the course of these experiments the resolution of the human restriction fragments on Southern blots was improved by using the 300 base-pair (bp) *Alu* family sequence (BLUR-8) as the probe and by optimizing the hybridization conditions. (The analysis of the primary clones was done using total human DNA, and the presence of large human restriction fragments could not be discerned in the high molecular weight region of the blots.)

The DNAs of the five tertiary clones were analysed for the presence of human sequences (Fig. 1). The prominent feature of these *Eco*RI-digested DNAs was the presence of a band corresponding to a human fragment of 25–30 kb in each of the transformants. The restriction fragment at 3·8 kb in the lane of 9TT3 donor DNA was not present in any of the tertiary clones. This result implies that the 3·8 kb fragment was a sequence flanking the complementing gene and was lost when the DNA was sheared. No bands were visible in the control lane of CHO DNA (from mutant UV135). The important large common fragment has similar intensity in each of the five independent transformants, suggesting that it is present as a single copy in each cell line. Lane 1 of Fig. 1, which illustrates the detection of human repetitive sequences, contains the recombinant cosmid pH9T12-1 present at a level equivalent to five copies per cell. This cosmid clone contains an insert of about 40 kb of human DNA, which includes the 3·8 kb fragment seen in the primary transformants.

As an additional control, two of the lanes in Fig. 1 contained UV135 DNA to which was added the equivalent of 1× or 10× copies per cell of the pSV2*gpt* DNA. Because of the cotransfer procedure used, all the transformants contain pSV2*gpt*. Since the 300 bp BLUR-8 sequence was isolated from pBR322, which has homology with pSV2*gpt*, we wanted to ensure that the BLUR-8 probe was not contaminated with vector sequences. No bands were evident in these two control lanes. Because these transformants were made from DNA <50 kb, the human fragment at ≈30 kb probably contains at least a part of the correcting gene. The gene may extend beyond this fragment since none of the transformants recovered show evidence of breakage of this fragment. The gene should be small enough to clone in a cosmid vector, which can accept inserts up to about 45 kb. Efforts toward reaching this objective are under way.

Line UV61 represents a sixth complementation group for u.v. sensitivity

Preliminary tests on the mutant line UV61 (previously designated 6-56-37 by Busch (1980)) were performed by the rapid complementation procedure described earlier (Thompson *et al.* 1981). These results suggested that this mutant might complement the five existing groups (Thompson *et al.* 1981; Thompson & Carrano, 1983) but were equivocal because the u.v. sensitivity of UV61 is less than that of the other mutants. As shown in Fig. 2, the u.v. fluence required to cause a given level of killing of UV5 cells is only about 60% as much as that required to give the same killing of UV61. The D_{37} values for UV5, UV61 and parental AA8 cells are 2·2, 3·8 and 10·6 J m^{-2}, respectively. It is of interest to note that these D_{37} values for UV5 and AA8 are somewhat higher than our previously published values (Thompson

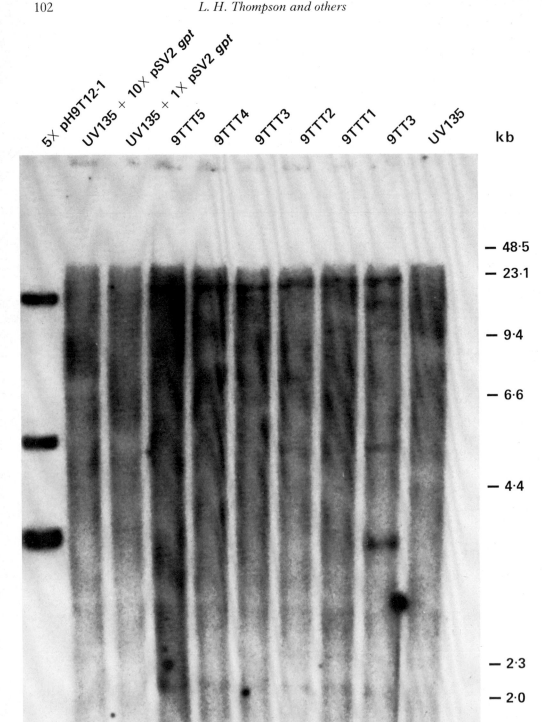

et al. 1980, 1981). We attribute these differences to changes in culture conditions, possibly the use of dialysed serum in earlier experiments.

Drug resistance markers were used to make the complementation tests more efficient. This approach is illustrated by the data in Table 1 for the mutants UV4 and UV41, which have been assigned to complementation groups 2 and 4, respectively (Thompson *et al.* 1981). The use of one line having both thioguanine and ouabain resistance (shown by the designation TOR) allows one to select for hybrids without having a selectable marker on each of the fusion partners (Baker *et al.* 1974). By selecting for hybrids after u.v. treatment, the background of colonies from surviving parental cells is eliminated. As shown in the last line of Table 1, when UV4 was fused with UV41-TOR, the frequency of hybrids was 0·0012 in the absence of u.v. irradiation. After exposure to $6 \, \mathrm{J \, m^{-2}}$, about 50% of these hybrids survived, indicating that they were relatively resistant although not as resistant as AA8 cells. (This incomplete complementation was shown previously by survival curves of individual hybrid clones (Thompson *et al.* 1981).) When UV41 was crossed with its derivative line UV41-TOR, no u.v.-resistant hybrids were formed, which was the expected result. Also, in the three self-cross controls, there were no detectable u.v.-resistant colonies, again as expected.

Similarly, UV61 was fused with mutants from each of the five complementation groups that had the 'TOR' phenotype, as shown in Table 2. The lines used were derivatives of UV5, UV20, UV24, UV41 and UV135, which belong to groups 1 through 5, respectively. These mutants were all isolated from the AA8 parental line. Mutant UV27-1, which belongs to group 3 (see below), has a different origin. In each cross of UV61 with a TOR line, a high frequency of u.v.-resistant hybrids was formed. These frequencies were in the same range as that seen with the complementing pair of mutants shown in Table 1. In each of the self-crosses in Table 2, no colonies were seen. These results indicate that UV61 complements each of the first five groups.

We showed above that the u.v. sensitivity of UV61 differs from that of the other mutants shown in Table 2. It is interesting to note that the biochemical defect in UV61 also appears to differ. Groups 1 through 5 have essentially no incision after u.v. treatment (Thompson *et al.* 1982*a*), but UV61 has an intermediate level of unscheduled DNA synthesis (D. Bootsma, personal communication), suggesting partial incision activity.

Fig. 1. Autoradiogram of a Southern transfer of DNA and hybridization to detect human sequences in tertiary transformants of mutant EM9. DNA from the secondary transformant 9TT3 was sheared to <50 kb and used to produce the five transformants designated 9TTT1, 9TTT2, 9TTT3, 9TTT4 and 9TTT5. DNAs were digested with *Eco*RI, subjected to electrophoresis in a 0·8% agarose gel, transferred to nitrocellulose, and probed with nick-translated BLUR-8 *Alu* family sequence. The common fragment at ≈25 kb in the five transformants probably contains repair gene sequences. The lanes containing UV135 DNA are negative controls (see the text), and the lane containing DNA from the cosmid pH9T12-1 is a positive control. The positioning of the molecular weight (in kb) markers (lambda phage DNA intact and digested with *Hind*III) takes into account the curvature of the gel. See Materials and Methods for hybridization conditions.

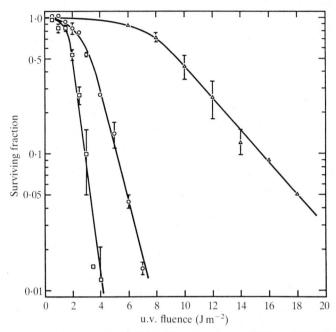

Fig. 2. u.v. survival curves of parental AA8 and mutants UV5 and UV61. Cells were irradiated at a density of 2×10^6 cells per 10 cm dish, trypsinized, and plated at varying densities for colony formation. Error bars are standard errors of the means for values from two or three experiments. Average plating efficiencies for UV5, UV61 and AA8 were 0·86, 0·88 and 0·90, respectively. Symbols: ($\triangle$) AA8; ($\bigcirc$) UV61; ($\square$) UV5.

Mutant UV27-1 belongs to complementation group 3

Clone '27-1' was isolated by Wood & Burki (1982). (We added the 'UV' prefix to indicate that it belongs to the collection of u.v.-sensitive lines.) On the basis of the data in Table 3, we have assigned UV27-1 to group 3, which contains UV24. In each cross with the TOR lines several hundred colonies were obtained, except with UV24-TOR. (We previously reported (International Conference on Mechanisms of Antimutagenesis and Anticarcinogenesis, Lawrence, KA, Oct. 6–10, 1985) that UV24 complemented UV27-1, but this result was in error due to mislabelling of a

Table 1. *Illustration of complementation tests using drug resistance markers with mutants from groups 2 and 4*

Cross	No. colonies $(0\,\mathrm{J\,m^{-2}})$	No. colonies $(6\,\mathrm{J\,m^{-2}})$
UV4 × UV4	4, 4, 3	0, 0, 0
UV41 × UV41	4, 2, —	0, 0, 0
UV41-TOR × UV41-TOR	0, 0, 0	0, 0, 0
UV41 × UV41-TOR	83, 79, 101	0, 0, 0
UV4 × UV41-TOR	244, 226, 242	111, 103, 121

Each number is the colony count on a replicate dish seeded with 2×10^5 cells and incubated with 1 mM-ouabain + HAT ingredients for 10 days (see Materials and Methods).

frozen stock.) Another mutant line MMC-2, which was isolated by Robson *et al.* (1985), was also found to belong to group 3 (results not shown).

*Survival of plasmid pSV2*gpt *in normal and u.v.-sensitive lines*

The plasmid pSV2*gpt* provides a convenient system for evaluating the repair of damaged DNA molecules introduced by the calcium phosphate precipitation procedure. In MAXTA selection medium, which includes mycophenolic acid, the bacterial *gpt* gene serves as a dominant selectable marker (Mulligan & Berg, 1981). Loss of *gpt* function can be determined by measuring the survival of transfected cells in MAXTA medium. One advantage of this approach to studying repair is that the damage is localized to the target DNA sequence.

In the present study we were interested in the question of whether the u.v. repair mutants would exhibit a repair-deficient phenotype when the plasmid was damaged with mutagens and transfected into the cells. Cells that can repair damage that would otherwise inactivate the plasmid should express a functional *gpt* gene and form colonies in selective medium. Thus, frequencies of transformation were determined as a function of the dose of DNA-damaging agent to which the plasmid was exposed.

As seen in Fig. 3, when the plasmid was treated with u.v. radiation, it was three to four times more resistant when transfected in the normal CHO cells (AA8) compared with the repair-deficient lines UV5 and UV4 (groups 1 and 2, respectively). These two mutants, which have similar survival responses to u.v. (Thompson *et al.* 1980; Busch *et al.* 1980), also showed the same response with irradiated plasmid. The differential survival between the normal and mutant cells was slightly less than that obtained with irradiated cells. Perhaps the repair of transfected plasmid DNA is

Table 2. *Line UV61 complements mutants from UV groups 1 through 5*

Cross	Average no. colonies $(6\,\mathrm{J\,m^{-2}})$	Average no. colonies $(8\,\mathrm{J\,m^{-2}})$
UV61 × UV5-TOR	287	167
UV61 × UV20-TOR	120	121
UV61 × UV24-TOR	175	161
UV61 × UV41-TOR	76	86
UV61 × UV135-TOR	274	175
UV61 × UV27-1-TOR	478	414*
UV61 self-cross	0	0
UV5-TOR self-cross	0	0
UV20-TOR self-cross	0	0
UV24-TOR self-cross	0	0
UV41-TOR self-cross	0	0
UV135-TOR self-cross	0	0
UV27-1-TOR self-cross	0	0

The data represent results of two experiments. Each value is the average number of colonies on three replicate dishes seeded with 2×10^5 cells. Dishes were incubated in medium containing 1 mM-ouabain + HAT.

*Dishes seeded with 1×10^5 cells.

Table 3. *UV27-1 belongs to complementation group 3*

Cross	Average no. colonies $(8\,\mathrm{J\,m^{-2}})$
UV27-1 × UV5-TOR	381
UV27-1 × UV20-TOR	178
UV27-1 × UV24-TOR	3, 1*
UV27-1 × UV41-TOR	200
UV27-1 × UV135-TOR	342
All self-crosses	0

Each value is the average of colonies on three replicate dishes. Dishes seeded with 2×10^5 cells were incubated in medium containing 1 mм-ouabain + HAT.
* Values from two different experiments.

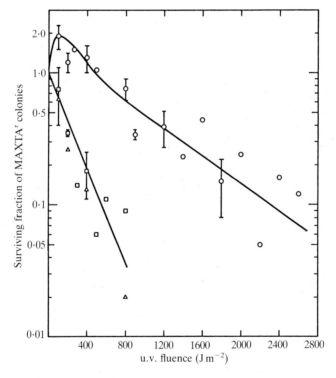

Fig. 3. Relative frequency of MAXTA-resistant colonies of AA8, UV4 and UV5 cells transfected with u.v.-irradiated pSV2*gpt* DNA. The absolute frequencies of MAXTA-resistant colonies in the absence of u.v. damage were 5×10^{-5} to 18×10^{-5}, 3×10^{-5}, and 8×10^{-5} to 18×10^{-5} for AA8, UV4 and UV5, respectively. Error bars show standard errors of the mean for repeat experiments of AA8 and UV5. For the AA8 data an exponential best fit was done for the points between 400 and 2600 J m^{-2} and the remainder of the curve was drawn by eye. For UV5, a linear best fit with a line going through a survival of 1·0 at zero dose was performed. Symbols: (○) AA8; (△) UV4; (□) UV5.

less efficient than genomic DNA. At low u.v. fluence we observed a twofold enhancement of the frequency of transformation to the gpt^+ phenotype in normal CHO cells, but the u.v.-sensitive lines showed no evidence of this effect. Overall, our results with irradiated plasmid differ in several respects from those seen with normal and XP human cell lines. The normal human cells showed higher levels of enhancement of transformation by u.v., and the same effect was seen with XP cells (Spivak *et al.* 1984; van Duin *et al.* 1985). In both studies the XP cells showed transformation frequencies that were as high as those obtained with normal cells, suggesting that in the plasmid transformation assay the XP (group A) cells could repair u.v. damage. However, with damaged viral DNA a repair defect has been seen in XP cells. Using a plaque assay for host cell reactivation of adenovirus 2, Day (1974) consistently found XP lines to have a more sensitive response to u.v.-irradiated virus than did normal human cells.

In a second set of transfection experiments we used the compound *cis*-diammine-dichloroplatinum(II) (*cis*-DDP), which, like u.v., produces bulky adducts but also produces DNA cross-links. This compound has been shown to produce DNA intrastrand cross-links as well as low, but potentially toxic, levels of interstrand cross-links (Plooy *et al.* 1985) in CHO cells. Under our conditions of treatment of the plasmid a very high percentage of the molecules should have interstrand cross-links (Poll *et al.* 1984). The pattern of responses with the three cell lines was similar to that seen with u.v. except that the mutants showed less difference compared with AA8 (Fig. 4). UV5 cells had a response that was about twice as sensitive as that of AA8 cells, and UV4 cells had a threefold more sensitive response. This result for UV5 is similar to the differential sensitivity seen with *cis*-DDP-treated cells in a cytotoxicity assay (Hoy *et al.* 1985). However, the behaviour of UV4 contrasts sharply with our finding that UV4 cells were 50 times more sensitive than AA8 in the cytotoxicity assay (Hoy *et al.* 1985). Since UV4 cells were also very sensitive to many other agents known to produce DNA interstrand cross-links, the results obtained with *cis*-DDP-treated plasmid were unexpected.

These results suggest that cross-links might not be nearly as toxic to UV4 when introduced in the plasmid as when present in the genomic DNA molecules. One interpretation is that in UV4 cells cross-links in naked DNA molecules can be repaired rapidly and efficiently compared with DNA in nucleosomes. For example, evidence has been presented that many of the mutations in the u.v. excision repair pathway in human cells act at the level of chromatin rather than unprotected DNA (Mortelmans *et al.* 1976; Kano & Fujiwara, 1983). In addition, the critical unhooking event for cross-links may have much faster kinetics than the removal of pyrimidine dimers (Reid & Walker, 1969) and occur before integration of the plasmid DNA into the genome can occur. Our results with UV4 are analogous to those seen with Fanconi's anaemia (FA) cells, which are characteristically very hypersensitive to killing by cross-linking agents (Ishida & Buchwald, 1982). Poll *et al.* (1984) found FA cells to be very sensitive to killing by *cis*-DDP, but in a host cell reactivation assay in which simian virus 40 (SV40) DNA was treated with *cis*-DDP, the FA cells showed a normal response. Alternatively, the unexpected results with

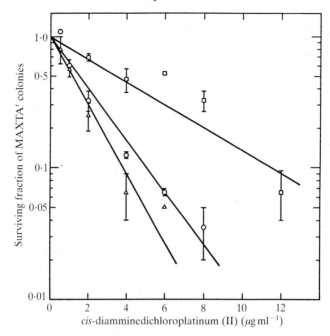

Fig. 4. Relative frequency of MAXTA-resistant colonies of AA8, UV4 and UV5 cells transfected with pSV2*gpt* DNA treated with *cis*-DDP. The absolute frequencies of MAXTA-resistant colonies in the absence of *cis*-DDP were 19×10^{-5} to 23×10^{-5}, 14×10^{-5}, and 13×10^{-5} to 20×10^{-5} for AA8, UV4 and UV5, respectively. Error bars show standard errors of the mean for repeat experiments. For each cell line an exponential best fit was obtained with a line going through a survival of $1 \cdot 0$ at zero dose. Plasmid DNA was exposed to *cis*-DDP for 1 h at 37 °C. Symbols: (□) AA8; (△) UV4; (○) UV5.

UV4 might be due to a different spectrum of lesions formed *in vitro versus in vivo*. Clearly much remains to be learned about the role of chromatin and other factors in the nucleotide excision repair process in both rodent and human cells.

This work was performed under the auspices of the US Department of Energy by the Lawrence Livermore National Laboratory under contract no. W-7405-ENG-48.

REFERENCES

BAKER, R. M., BRUNETTE, D. M., MANKOVITZ, R., THOMPSON, L. H., WHITMORE, G. F., SIMINOVITCH, L. & TILL, J. E. (1974). Ouabain-resistant mutants of mouse and hamster cells in culture. *Cell* **1**, 9–21.

BUSCH, D. B. (1980). Large scale isolation of DNA repair mutants of Chinese hamster ovary cells. Ph.D. dissertation, University of California, Berkeley.

BUSCH, D. B., CLEAVER, J. E. & GLASER, D. A. (1980). Large scale isolation of UV-sensitive clones of CHO cells. *Somat. Cell Genet.* **6**, 407–418.

CLEAVER, J. E. (1983). Xeroderma pigmentosum. In *The Metabolic Basis of Inherited Disease* (ed. J. B. Stanbury, J. B. Wyngaarden, D. S. Fredrickson, J. L. Goldstein & M. S. Brown), 5th edn, pp. 1227–1248. New York: McGraw-Hill.

CORSARO, C. M. & PEARSON, M. L. (1981). Enhancing the efficiency of DNA-mediated gene transfer in mammalian cells. *Somat. Cell Genet.* **7**, 603–616.

DAY, R. S. (1974). Cellular reactivation of ultraviolet-irradiated human adenovirus 2 in normal and xeroderma pigmentosum fibroblasts. *Photochem. Photobiol.* **19**, 9–13.

DEININGER, P. L., JOLLY, D. J., RUBIN, C. M., FRIEDMANN, T. & SCHMID, C. W. (1981). Base sequence studies of 300 nucleotide renatured repeated human DNA clones. *J. molec. Biol.* **151**, 17–33.

DILLEHAY, L. E., THOMPSON, L. H., MINKLER, J. L. & CARRANO, A. V. (1983). The relationship between sister-chromatid exchange and perturbations in DNA replication in mutant EM9 and normal CHO cells. *Mutat. Res.* **109**, 283–296.

FRIEDBERG, E. C., EHMANN, U. K. & WILLIAMS, J. J. (1979). Human diseases associated with defective DNA repair. *Adv. Radiat. Biol.* **8**, 85–174.

HOY, C. A., THOMPSON, L. H. & SALAZAR, E. P. (1985). Defective cross-link removal in Chinese hamster cell mutants hypersensitive to bifunctional alkylating agents. *Cancer Res.* **45**, 1737–1743.

ISHIDA, R. & BUCHWALD, M. (1982). Susceptibility of Fanconi's anemia lymphoblasts to DNA-cross-linking and alkylating agents. *Cancer Res.* **42**, 4000–4006.

KANO, Y. & FUJIWARA, Y. (1983). Defective thymine dimer excision from xeroderma pigmentosum chromatin and its characteristic catalysis by cell-free extracts. *Carcinogenesis* **4**, 1419–1424.

MORTELMANS, K., FRIEDBERG, E. C., SLOR, H., THOMAS, G. & CLEAVER, J. E. (1976). Defective thymine dimer excision by cell-free extracts of xeroderma pigmentosum cells. *Proc. natn. Acad. Sci. U.S.A.* **73**, 2757–2761.

MULLIGAN, R. C. & BERG, P. (1981). Selection for animal cells that express the *Escherichia coli* gene coding for xanthine-guanine phosphoribosyltransferase. *Proc. natn. Acad. Sci. U.S.A.* **78**, 2072–2076.

PINKEL, D., THOMPSON, L. H., GRAY, J. W. & VANDERLAAN, M. (1985). Measurement of sister chromatid exchanges at very low bromodeoxyuridine substitution levels using a monoclonal antibody in Chinese hamster ovary cells. *Cancer Res.* **45**, 5795–5798.

PLOOY, A. C. M., FICHTINGER-SCHEPMAN, A. M. J., SCHUTTE, H. H., VAN DIJK, M. & LOHMAN, P. H. M. (1985). The quantitative detection of various platinum–DNA-adducts in Chinese hamster ovary cells treated with cisplatin; application of immunochemical techniques. *Carcinogenesis* **6**, 561–566.

POLL, E. H. A., ABRAHAMS, P. J., ARWERT, F. & ERIKSSON, A. W. (1984). Host-cell reactivation of *cis*-diamminedichloroplatinum(II)-treated SV40 DNA in normal human, Fanconi anaemia and xeroderma pigmentosum fibroblasts. *Mutat. Res.* **132**, 181–187.

REID, B. D. & WALKER, I. G. (1969). The response of mammalian cells to alkylating agents. II. On the mechanism of the removal of sulfur-mustard-induced cross-links. *Biochim. biophys. Acta* **179**, 179–188.

ROBSON, C. N., HARRIS, A. L. & HICKSON, I. D. (1985). Isolation and characterization of Chinese hamster ovary cell lines sensitive to mitomycin C and bleomycin. *Cancer Res.* **45**, 5304–5309.

RUBIN, J. S., PRIDEAUX, V. R., WILLARD, H. F., DULHANTY, A. M., WHITMORE, G. F. & BERNSTEIN, A. (1985). Molecular cloning and chromosomal localization of DNA sequences associated with a human DNA repair gene. *Molec. cell. Biol.* **5**, 398–405.

SCHMID, C. W. & JELINEK, W. R. (1982). The *Alu* family of dispersed repetitive sequences. *Science* **216**, 1065–1070.

SICILIANO, M. J., CARRANO, A. V. & THOMPSON, L. H. (1986). Assignment of a human DNA repair gene associated with sister chromatid exchange to chromosome 19. *Mutat. Res.* **174**, 303–308.

SOUTHERN, E. M. (1975). Detection of specific sequences among DNA fragments separated by gel electrophoresis. *J. molec. Biol.* **98**, 503–517.

SPIVAK, G., GANESAN, A. K. & HANAWALT, P. C. (1984). Enhanced transformation of human cells by UV-irradiated pSV2 plasmids. *Molec. cell. Biol.* **4**, 1169–1171.

THOMPSON, L. H. (1985). DNA repair mutants. In *Molecular Cell Genetics* (ed. M. Gottesman), pp. 641–667. New York: John Wiley & Sons.

THOMPSON, L. H., BROOKMAN, K. W., DILLEHAY, L. E., CARRANO, A. V., MAZRIMAS, J. A., MOONEY, C. L. & MINKLER, J. L. (1982*b*). A CHO-cell strain having hypersensitivity to mutagens, a defect in DNA strand-break repair, and an extraordinary baseline frequency of sister chromatid exchange. *Mutat. Res.* **95**, 427–440.

THOMPSON, L. H., BROOKMAN, K. W., DILLEHAY, L. E., MOONEY, C. L. & CARRANO, A. V. (1982a). Hypersensitivity to mutation and sister-chromatid-exchange induction in CHO cell mutants defective in incising DNA containing UV lesions. *Somat. Cell Genet.* **8**, 759–773.

THOMPSON, L. H., BROOKMAN, K. W., SALAZAR, E. P., FUSCOE, J. C. & WEBER, C. A. (1986). DNA repair genes of mammalian cells. In *Antimutagenesis and Anticarcinogenesis: Mechanisms* (ed. D. M. Shankel, P. E. Hartman, T. Kada, & A. Hollaender), pp. 349–358. New York: Plenum Press.

THOMPSON, L. H., BUSCH, D. B., BROOKMAN, K., MOONEY, C. L. & GLASER, D. A. (1981). Genetic diversity of UV-sensitive DNA repair mutants of Chinese hamster ovary cells. *Proc. natn. Acad. Sci. U.S.A.* **78**, 3734–3737.

THOMPSON, L. H. & CARRANO, A. V. (1983). Analysis of mammalian cell mutagenesis and DNA repair using *in vitro* selected CHO cell mutants. In *Cellular Responses to DNA Damage, UCLA Symposia on Molecular and Cellular Biology*, New Series, vol. 11 (ed. E. C. Friedberg & B. A. Bridges), pp. 125–143. New York: Alan R. Liss.

THOMPSON, L. H. & HOY, C. A. (1986). Using repair-deficient Chinese hamster ovary cells to study mutagenesis. In *Chemical Mutagens* (ed. F. J. de Serres), pp. 285–325. New York: Plenum Press.

THOMPSON, L. H., MOONEY, C.L., BURKHART-SCHULTZ, K., CARRANO, A. V. & SICILIANO, M. J. (1985). Correction of a nucleotide-excision-repair mutation by human chromosome 19 in hamster–human hybrid cells. *Somat. Cell molec. Genet.* **11**, 87–92.

THOMPSON, L. H., RUBIN, J. S., CLEAVER, J. E., WHITMORE, G. F. & BROOKMAN, K. (1980). A screening method for isolating DNA repair-deficient mutants of CHO cells. *Somat. Cell Genet.* **6**, 391–405.

VAN DUIN, M., WESTERVELD, A. & HOEIJMAKERS, J. H. J. (1985). UV stimulation of DNA-mediated transformation of human cells. *Molec. cell. Biol.* **5**, 734–741.

WESTERVELD, A., HOEIJMAKERS, J. H. J., VAN DUIN, M., DE WIT, J., ODIJK, H., PASTINK, A., WOOD, R. D. & BOOTSMA, D. (1984). Molecular cloning of a human DNA repair gene. *Nature, Lond.* **310**, 425–429.

WOOD, R. D. & BURKI, H. J. (1982). Repair capability and the cellular age response for killing and mutation induction after UV. *Mutat. Res.* **95**, 505–514.

J. Cell Sci. Suppl. 6, 111–125 (1987)
Printed in Great Britain © *The Company of Biologists Limited 1987*

CHARACTERIZATION OF GENES AND PROTEINS
INVOLVED IN EXCISION REPAIR OF HUMAN CELLS

JAN H. J. HOEIJMAKERS

Department of Cell Biology and Genetics, Erasmus University, PO Box 1738, 3000 DR Rotterdam, The Netherlands

SUMMARY

To extend our knowledge of the excision repair system in mammalian cells we have focussed on the isolation of genes and proteins involved in this process. For the purification and characterization of human repair proteins the microneedle injection assay technique is utilized. This system is based on the transient correction of the excision repair defect of xeroderma pigmentosum (XP) fibroblasts (scored as increase of ultraviolet (u.v.)-induced unscheduled DNA synthesis (UDS)) upon microinjection of crude extracts from complementing XP or normal cells. Specific correction is observed in fibroblasts of all (9) excision-deficient XP complementation groups. The XP-A and G correcting factors were found to be proteins and several purification steps (including $(NH_4)_2SO_4$ fractionation, chromatography of phosphocellulose, heparin and u.v.-irradiated DNA-cellulose) have been worked out for the XP-A correcting protein.

The microinjection system was also used for the introduction of (partially) purified repair enzymes of lower organisms. *Micrococcus luteus* endonuclease and bacteriophage T4 endonuclease V were able to correct all XP complementation groups tested, in marked contrast to the more sophisticated *Escherichia coli uvrABC* complex injected with *uvrD*. Photoreversal of dimers could be registered after introduction of the yeast photoreactivating enzyme in repair-competent, XP-variant, XP-C and XP-I fibroblasts (monitored as decrease of (residual) UDS). Remarkably, no effect was noticed in XP-A, D, E and H, suggesting that something prevents dimers in these cells from being monomerized by the injected enzyme.

Using DNA-mediated gene transfer we have cloned a human gene (designated *ERCC-1*) that compensates for the excision defect of the u.v. and mitomycin C-sensitive Chinese hamster ovary cell (CHO) mutant 43-3B (complementation group 2). Characterization of this gene and its cDNA revealed the following features:

(1) *ERCC-1* corrects the full spectrum of repair deficiencies in mutants of complementation group 2. No correction is observed in mutants of the other CHO complementation groups.

(2) The *ERCC-1* gene has a size of 15×10^3 base-pairs (bp) and consists of 10 exons, one of which appears to be differentially spliced.

(3) It encodes two largely identical mRNAs, which differ in the presence or absence of a 72 bp coding exon, situated in the 3′ half of the mRNA. Only the cDNA of the large transcript is able to confer repair proficiency to 43-3B cells. No effect of u.v. treatment is found at the level of *ERCC-1* transcription in HeLa cells.

(4) Sequence analysis of full-length cDNA copies of the two *ERCC-1* mRNAs revealed open reading frames for proteins of 297 and 273 amino acids, respectively. Significant amino acid sequence homology was found between portions of the putative *ERCC-1* product and the protein encoded by the yeast excision-repair gene *RAD10*. Regional homology was also discovered between a part of *ERCC-1* and *uvrA*. On the basis of homology with functional protein domains a tentative nuclear location signal, DNA binding domain and ADP-ribosylation site could be identified in the *ERCC-1* aa sequence.

INTRODUCTION

The implication of DNA repair systems in vital processes such as mutagenesis, carcinogenesis and maintenance of primary DNA structure stresses the importance of investigating how these systems operate at the molecular level. Availability of genes and proteins involved in DNA repair is of basic interest to such studies. The isolation of genes, and subsequent purification of the products, functioning in repair systems of *Escherichia coli* (particularly in the excision repair pathway and the removal of alkylation lesions) has led to a considerable extension of our knowledge about mechanisms and genetic control of these processes in prokaryotes (Walker, 1985; Teo *et al.* 1986; for an extensive review on DNA repair in general, see Friedberg, 1985). For lower eukaryotes the phase of cloning repair genes has been reached with the recent isolation of a series of genes involved in three major repair pathways in the yeast *Saccharomyces cerevisiae* (e.g. see Yasui & Chevallier, 1983; Adzuma *et al.* 1984; Naumovski *et al.* 1985; Nicolet *et al.* 1985; Reynolds *et al.* 1985*a,b*; Perozzi & Prakash, 1986). As far as higher eukaryotes are concerned, valuable tools for the isolation of repair genes and proteins are available in the form of naturally occurring and laboratory-induced mutant cells. These are mainly of human and rodent origin. The most extensively characterized class of mutants is disturbed in the excision repair process, one of the major repair systems in the cell. Fibroblasts from many patients suffering from the autosomal recessive human syndrome xeroderma pigmentosum (XP) fall into this category (Cleaver, 1968). Genetic studies involving cell hybridization have disclosed the existence of nine complementation groups within the excision-deficient class of XP individuals (de Weerd-Kastelein *et al.* 1972; Fischer *et al.* 1985) and at least five within excision-deficient mutants generated from Chinese hamster ovary (CHO) cells (Thompson *et al.* 1981, 1982; Thompson & Carrano, 1983). It is not known whether some of these complementation groups are the same in both species; however, none of the mutants is able to perform efficiently the first step postulated in the excision pathway, i.e. the incision of the damaged DNA strand at or near the photolesion. This suggests the participation of at least nine, and possibly more than 13, genes and proteins in nucleotide excision. To date, progress with regard to the isolation of the components involved is limited, due to the complexity of the system and the experimental limitations of the organisms. Recently, we have cloned the first human gene (designated *ERCC-1*), implicated in the excision of lesions induced by ultraviolet (u.v.) light and cross-linking agents (Westerveld *et al.* 1984). Using microneedle injection we are in the process of purifying and characterizing proteins deficient in XP. Furthermore, we are investigating whether well-characterized repair proteins of heterologous organisms can interact with mammalian repair systems. In this chapter we will summarize results obtained on these topics. Part of the work reviewed here has been published in detail elsewhere (de Jonge *et al.* 1983, 1985; Zwetsloot *et al.* 1985; Hoeijmakers *et al.* 1987*a,b*; Van Duin *et al.* 1986; Vermeulen *et al.* 1986; Zwetsloot *et al.* 1986*a,b*).

MICROINJECTION EXPERIMENTS

The microinjection system

Notwithstanding many attempts the establishment of a reliable mammalian *in vitro* repair system has not been a very rewarding enterprise. As an alternative we have developed an *in vivo* test system suitable for at least some of the factors involved in excision repair. This system utilizes living human (XP) fibroblasts as test-tubes in which repair components are introduced by microneedle injection (de Jonge *et al.* 1983). u.v.-induced unscheduled DNA synthesis (UDS) is used as a single cell parameter to determine the effect on the excision repair of the injected cells. This test-system has a wide range of possibilities and applications to the study of nucleotide excision.

(1) Crude protein extracts from various cells can be screened for the presence of proteins that transiently compensate for the defect in one of the XP complementation groups (see e.g. Fig. 1A). On the basis of this property these polypeptides can then be isolated and characterized.

(2) As shown by Legerski *et al.* (1984), microinjection of mRNA can, after *in vivo* translation into protein, also temporarily alleviate some of the XP deficiencies. In principle this opens the possibility of isolating the responsible gene by cDNA cloning of the correcting RNA.

(3) Purified repair proteins from various prokaryotes and eukaryotes can be tested individually or in specific combinations for their effect on human excision repair or repair defects.

(4) The role of endogenous polypeptides that might be implicated in the excision pathway can be directly assessed *in vivo* by injection of (monoclonal) antibodies into human fibroblasts (e.g. monoclonal antibodies against DNA polymerase α).

(5) Finally, microinjection might be used to introduce certain repair substrates (in the form of DNA molecules carrying specific lesions) or inhibitors of specific steps in the excision process.

There are also obvious limitations inherent in the microinjection assay technique. Only a small number of samples can be tested in one experiment; it is a laborious, time-consuming procedure and yields only semi-quantitative results. We have concentrated mainly on the first and third application listed above and this section focusses on some of the results obtained thus far.

Injection of repair proteins of prokaryotes and eukaryotes into human fibroblasts

The effect of microinjection of defined prokaryotic proteins involved in excision repair on UDS of wild-type or XP fibroblasts of various complementation groups is summarized in Table 1 (for quantitative data see de Jonge *et al.* 1985). *Micrococcus luteus* endonuclease and bacteriophage T4 endonuclease V (which both catalyse the incision of damaged DNA at the site of cyclobutane dimers by a combined glycosylase and apyrimidinic endonuclease activity; Haseltine *et al.* 1980; Grafstrom *et al.* 1982) correct the defect of all XP complementation groups tested as judged by a significant increase in u.v.-induced UDS. This aspecific bypass of different excision

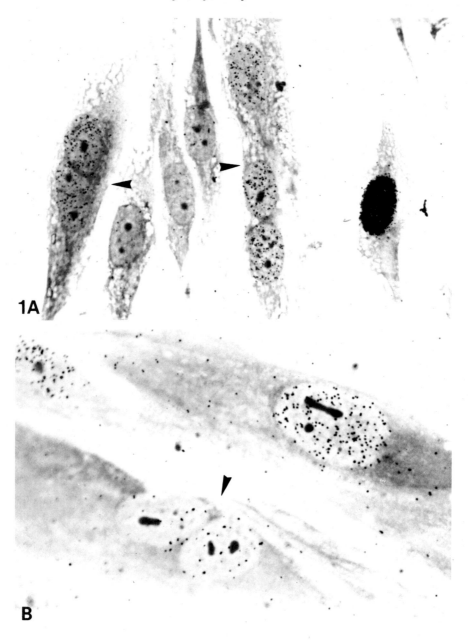

Fig. 1. A. Photomicrograph of XP25RO(XP-A) homopolykaryons (arrowheads) after microinjection of a crude HeLa cell extract, assay for u.v.-induced UDS and autoradiography. The monokaryons (one of which in *S*-phase) have not been injected. B. Photomicrograph of a C5RO (repair-proficient) homodikaryon (arrowhead) after injection of purified photoreactivating enzyme from *S. cerevisiae*. The monokaryons have not been injected. After microinjection the fibroblasts were u.v.-irridiated ($10\,\mathrm{J\,m^{-2}}$), illuminated with photoreactivating light, assayed for UDS, followed by autoradiography. Homopolykaryons are used for microinjection for reasons specified by de Jonge *et al.* (1983). The micrographs are of different magnification.

defects in XP, which was noted earlier for the T4 enzyme by Tanaka *et al.* (1975, 1977) and in the case of XPA-E and XP-F by Hayakawa *et al.* (1981), indicates that these prokaryotic enzymes are able to act on pyrimidine lesions in mammalian chromatin and that the cellular repair machinery can recognize the resulting incision products and use them as substrates for repair synthesis.

In contrast to the two u.v. endonucleases examined above, microinjection of the *E. coli* UvrABC and D proteins into XP-A, C and H fibroblasts did not result in restoration of u.v.-induced UDS (Table 1; Zwetsloot *et al.* 1986*a*). The *E. coli* excinuclease was assayed under conditions in which a T4 endonuclease preparation with the same *in vitro* incising activity was able to induce significant repair synthesis in the three XP complementation groups. To exclude the possibility that the negative results with the *E. coli* proteins could be due to potential problems in transport of this bulky enzyme complex (total mass $\sim 350 \times 10^3 M_r$, compared to $16 \times 10^3 M_r$ for T4 endonuclease) through the nuclear membrane both endonucleases were also tested by direct microinjection into the nucleus of XP-A and C fibroblasts. The same results were obtained (see Table 1). Although various explanations of a negative result are possible (as discussed elsewhere; Zwetsloot *et al.* 1986*a*) the most likely interpretation is that the *E. coli* excinuclease does not act on DNA photoproducts in a mammalian chromatin context.

A different manner of removing dimer lesions induced by u.v. is exemplified by enzymic photoreactivation accomplished by a single protein: the photoreactivating enzyme (PRE). This flavoprotein binds specifically to dimers and after absorption of a quantum of the visible to near-u.v. spectrum it simply reverses the dimerization regenerating two unlinked pyrimidine bases. This reaction does not involve repair synthesis and can compete with the excision repair of cyclobutane dimers. To examine whether PRE is active on pyrimidine dimers in chromatin of mammalian cells purified photolyase from yeast was injected into repair-proficient fibroblasts. Since photoreactivation of these lesions should be at the expense of repair synthesis a reduction of the UDS level is expected in the injected cells if photoreactivation occurs. Fig. 1B and Table 1 show that indeed a strong decrease in UDS of injected wild-type fibroblasts (to 20 % of non-injected control cells) was found. The fact that this reduction is photoreactivating light-dependent, proteinase κ-sensitive and not

Table 1. *Effect of various injected repair enzymes on XP UDS*

Enzyme	XP complementation group	u.v. ⚡ UDS	Conclusion
M. luteus endonuclease	A–I	↑	Correction
T4 endonuclease V	A*, C*–G	↑	Correction
E. coli uvrABCD	A*, C*, H	—	No correction
Yeast PRE + phr ⚡‡	WT†, XP-var, C, I, (F)	↓	Photoreactivation
Yeast PRE + phr ⚡‡	A, D, E, H	—	No photoreactivation

* Also tested by microinjection into nucleus.
† WT, wild-type.
‡ ⚡ phr, photoreactivating light.

observed with extracts prepared from phr^- yeast mutants (in contrast to extracts from phr^+ cells) argues in favour of the idea that it is due to photoreactivation of dimers by the injected enzyme (Zwetsloot *et al.* 1985). To determine whether lesions in XP cells also can be photoreactivated by the exogenous photolyase, the yeast protein was injected into fibroblasts from excision-deficient XP strains representing different complementation groups (all displaying more than 10% of the UDS of wild-type cells) and fibroblasts from two excision-proficient XP variant strains. In XP variant cells UDS was reduced to the same extent as in normal fibroblasts. Injected cells from XP complementation groups C, I and to a lesser extent XP-F also exhibited a reduced level of UDS (up to 50% of non-injected XP cells) indicating that pyrimidine dimers in these cells are accessible to and can be monomerized by the injected enzyme. In contrast, fibroblasts from groups A, D, E and H (with residual UDS activities up to 50% of wild-type cells) did not show any reduction in UDS upon PRE-injection and illumination with photoreactivating light (Zwetsloot *et al.* 1986b). These findings strongly suggest that the photoproducts are not equally well accessible in both sets of XP complementation groups. In the latter XP dimers might be 'protected' against injected PRE by a defective repair complex. At present, we are characterizing CHO transformants containing the yeast and *E. coli* PRE genes inserted in a mammalian expression vector with the eventual aim of studying the long-term effects of selective dimer removal on survival, mutability and induction of chromosomal aberrations.

Purification and characterization of XP correcting proteins

As mentioned above, crude extracts of human cells upon injection transiently compensate for the excision defect in XP fibroblasts. Table 2 shows that temporary correction is found for all excision-deficient XP complementation groups as indicated

Table 2. *Levels of u.v.-induced UDS in homopolykaryons of various XP complementation groups after microinjection of human cell extracts*

Injected cell*	Source extract*	UDS (grains/nucleus)† (% of wild-type ± S.E.M.)	
		Non-injected	Injected
XP25RO (A)	HeLa	2 ± 1	102 ± 7
XP11BE (B)	XP12ROSV40 (A)	5 ± 1	15 ± 2
XP21RO (C)	XP12ROSV40 (A)	13 ± 1	18 ± 1
XP1BR (D)	XP4ROSV40 (C)	17 ± 1	28 ± 2
XP2RO (E)	HeLa	47 ± 2	75 ± 3
XP126LO (F)	XP12ROSV40 (A)	16 ± 1	46 ± 3
XP2B1 (G)	HeLa	6 ± 1	33 ± 3
XPCS2 (H)	XP4ROSV40 (C)	39 ± 2	63 ± 2
XP3MA (I)	XP4ROSV40 (C)	14 ± 1	29 ± 2

*The XP complementation group is shown in parenthesis.

†In each experiment the average number of grains per nucleus was calculated and expressed as % of the mean number of grains per nucleus of repair-competent fibroblasts (C5RO), assayed in parellel under the same conditions. For further details see Vermeulen *et al.* (1986).

by an increase in UDS. In the complementation groups examined extracts prepared from complementing XP (as well as normal) cells induce correction, in contrast to extracts from non-complementing XP fibroblasts. We conclude, therefore, that in each instance specific factors are responsible for the observed phenotypic correction. The data in Table 2 display a wide variation in the level of correction between different complementation groups. Undoubtedly, this reflects at least in part differences in concentration of the various correcting factors in the injected extract, particularly in those XP groups in which the correcting component is rate-limiting. Another factor that influences the level of UDS is the kinetics of complementation, which is found to vary between different complementation groups. Cell fusion and microinjection experiments have demonstrated that, e.g. the XP-A defect is fully corrected within 30 min after introduction of the correcting factor (e.g. see Vermeulen *et al.* 1986). In contrast, complete compensation for the XP-C and D deficiencies is not achieved within 16–24 h after fusion with repair-competent fibroblasts (Giannelli *et al.* 1982; Keijzer *et al.* 1982). Characterization of the XP-A and XP-G factors established that both of them are sensitive to proteolytic degradation, suggesting that they are proteins (de Jonge *et al.* 1983; Vermeulen *et al.* 1986). Both proteins were found to precipitate at between 25% and 40% $(NH_4)_2SO_4$ saturation. Testing of subsequent purification steps revealed that the XP-A correcting factor is retained on phosphocellulose and heparin columns and that it has high affinity for single-stranded DNA as well as u.v.-irradiated double-stranded DNA attached to cellulose. A weaker affinity was found for non-irradiated double-stranded DNA (preliminary results). These findings support the idea that the XP-A correcting protein exerts its function in the nucleus presumably by involving binding to the u.v.-induced DNA lesions. At present, we are attempting large-scale purification of this polypeptide by a combination of the steps described above. Successful combinations of $(NH_4)_2SO_4$ fractionation and phosphocellulose chromatography using a total HeLa cell extract, and phosphocellulose followed by u.v.-irradiated DNA-cellulose chromatography using a placenta extract have been achieved. However, one of the problems (in addition to the laborious assay procedure) is that the protein seems to be more labile upon further purification.

ISOLATION AND CHARACTERIZATION OF THE HUMAN REPAIR GENE *ERCC-1*

Isolation of human repair genes

Although simian virus 40 (SV40)-transformed XP fibroblasts seem to be the ideal source for the cloning of complementing excision repair genes they have thus far failed to yield genuine repair-proficient transformants upon genomic DNA transfections (Lehmann, 1985). In a number of laboratories, u.v.-resistant repair-competent revertants have been obtained instead at a low frequency (e.g. see Royer-Pokora & Haseltine, 1984). The revertants probably arise in the course of long-lasting selection protocols using low doses of u.v. light. We think that the reason for the failure to obtain genuine transformants originates at least in part from the fact that XP cells (and also other human cells tested) are very restricted in the amount of DNA that becomes stably integrated in their genome after genomic DNA transfection. This problem may be overlooked because the relative ease and high efficiency by which transformants containing dominant marker genes are obtained in certain XP cell lines suggests that gene transfer is very efficient. However, dominant marker genes are present in the transfected DNA in vast molar excess and they are in general very small (less than 2 kilobases (kb)), increasing the chance that the gene remains intact during the transfection process. Relying on the transfection efficiency of dominant markers alone is deceptive. We have found that on average a 20- to 100-fold smaller amount of exogenous DNA is present per human transformant compared with e.g. CHO, Ltk⁻ and NIH3T3 transformants (Hoeijmakers *et al.* 1987*a*). It is, therefore, not surprising that to date most promising results have been obtained using CHO repair mutants induced in the laboratory. Transformants corrected by the uptake of human genes have been isolated for a number of excision-deficient CHO complementation groups (Rubin *et al.* 1983; MacInnes *et al.* 1984; Thompson *et al.* 1985; our unpublished results). The first human repair gene has been cloned using one such mutant (Westerveld *et al.* 1984) and more genes are on the way. The repair gene isolated was obtained by DNA-mediated gene transfer of the excision-deficient CHO mutant 43-3B (constructed by Wood & Burki, 1982) that falls in the u.v. and mitomycin C (MM-C)-sensitive CHO complementation group 2 described by Thompson. The fact that linked transfer of the correcting human gene and a covalently attached dominant marker gene could be achieved in secondary transformations greatly facilitated the eventual cloning of the gene (Westerveld *et al.* 1984). The gene (designated *ERCC-1*) induces concomitant u.v. and MM-C resistance after transfection to 43-3B cells and other mutants of the same complementation group. Mutants of the other four excision-deficient CHO complementation groups are not corrected by this gene (results obtained in collaboration with Dr L. Thompson).

Phenotypic characterization of ERCC-1 *correction*

ERCC-1 corrects the repair defect of the 43-3B mutant for all repair parameters tested: u.v. and MM-C survival, sensitivity to 4NQO, NAcAAF and alkylating agents, u.v.-induced UDS, dimer removal as measured by the T4 endonuclease assay, mutability and induced chromosomal aberrations (Zdzienicka *et al.* 1987; Daroudi, unpublished results). Although the human repair gene restores the full spectrum of impaired repair functions of 43-3B, the complementation is not for all end-points to the wild-type level. In particular, u.v. and MM-C survival is generally lagging behind that of the parental line, even when multiple *ERCC-1* gene copies are integrated in the 43-3B genome. This suggests that it is not due to a gene dose effect. A plausible explanation might be that the human gene product is unable to substitute fully for the CHO counterpart in the excision process.

Molecular characterization of ERCC-1

ERCC-1 was cloned on cosmid 43-34. Subsequent analysis of the insert by various methods revealed that *ERCC-1* resided in a 15–17 kb region of cosmid 43-34. Unique probes derived from this area were used to probe Northern filters and to screen cDNA libraries. On Northern blots hybridization was found mainly with an RNA species of 1·0–1·1 kb, present in HeLa and a number of other human cell lines. A similarly sized transcript is found in CHO cells (including the 43-3B mutant), mouse testis and brain (unpublished results). The fact that the CHO mutant shows a hybridization pattern indistinguishable from that of the parental wild-type cells, suggests that the gene is not inactivated by gross deletions or promotor and processing mutations. (This was confirmed by Southern blot analysis of the mutant and normal gene.) To investigate whether *ERCC-1* gene expression is induced by DNA-damaging treatments, HeLa cells were irradiated with u.v. (1 and 10 J m^{-2}). At various times after irradiation poly(A)$^+$ RNA was extracted and analysed by Northern hybridization. No significant quantitative differences were observed, suggesting that *ERCC-1* does not belong to a u.v.-inducible set of genes, like the SOS genes in *E. coli* and some of the yeast repair genes. Analysis of the *ERCC-1* promotor region is in progress to obtain more information on the regulation of *ERCC-1* transcription.

Screening of the Okayama/Berg (1983) cDNA library with genomic *ERCC-1* probes resulted in the isolation of three cDNA clones, all of which appeared to be incomplete. However, by recombining different parts of each clone we succeeded in producing complete cDNA versions of the *ERCC-1* transcript, which permitted analysis of the *ERCC-1* gene structure and its gene product (van Duin *et al.* 1986). Comparison of the cDNA sequence with the genomic DNA revealed that the gene is split over 10 exons. Sequence analysis of different cDNAs and nuclease S$_1$ digestion experiments indicated that one exon of 72 base-pairs (bp) (encoding an internal 24 amino acid portion of the predicted amino acid sequence of the *ERCC-1* gene product) is alternatively spliced. Hence, the 1·0–1·1 kb mRNA band, visible on Northern blots is in fact made up of two unresolved mRNA species, differing by 72 bp in size. To investigate the function of the two cDNAs, transfection experiments were carried out to 43-3B cells. The cDNA derived from the larger transcript (pcDE) inserted into an Okayama/Berg (1983) mammalian expression vector was able to confer both u.v. and MM-C resistance on the mutant, in contrast to the cDNA of the small transcript (pcDE-72). Apparently, the presence of the 72 bp exon is essential for the excision repair process. The function of the small RNA (if any) remains obscure. Using the Maxam & Gilbert (1980) sequencing technique the nucleotide sequences of both the 1098 and 1026 bp *ERCC-1* cDNAs were determined and are presented in Fig. 2 along with the deduced amino acid sequence of the only likely open reading frame. The alternatively spliced 72 bp exon, absent in pcDE-72 is underlined. The predicted *ERCC-1* gene products have sizes of 297 and 274 amino acids (M_r 32 562 and 29 993, respectively). At present, we are utilizing

E. coli expression systems and gene amplification in CHO cells to produce large quantities of the *ERCC-1* gene products for isolation and functional characterization.

Homology of ERCC-1 *gene products with other polypeptides*

To obtain information on the role of *ERCC-1* in excision repair the deduced *ERCC-1* amino acid sequence was compared with those of other proteins and functional protein domains to search for homology. Within the class of repair polypeptides extensive amino acid homology was detected with the yeast excision repair protein *RAD10*, which is predicted to have a size of 210 amino acid residues

```
                                                                                      5'  AAGTGCTGCGAGCCCTGGGCCAC
GCTGGCCGTGCTGGCAGTGGGCCGCCTCGATCCCTCTGCAGTCTTTCCCTTGAGGCTCCAAGACCAGCAGGTGAGGCCTCGCGGCGCTGAAACCGTGAGGCCCGGACCACAGGCTCCAG
                             50                                                     100
                                                                        NLS
  1
Met Asp Pro Gly Lys Asp Lys Glu Gly Val Pro Gln Pro Ser Gly Pro Pro Ala Arg Lys Lys Phe Val Ile Pro Leu Asp Glu Asp Glu
ATG GAC CCT GGG AAG GAC AAA GAG GGG GTG CCC CAG CCC TCA GGG CCG CCA GCA AGG AAG AAA TTT GTG ATA CCC CTC GAC GAG GAT GAG
        150                                                                 200
 31
Val Pro Pro Gly Val Ala Lys Pro Leu Phe Arg Ser Thr Gln Ser Leu Pro Thr Val Asp Thr Ser Ala Gln Ala Ala Pro Gln Thr Tyr
GTC CCT CCT GGA GTG GCC AAG CCC TTA TTC CGA TCT ACA CAG AGC CTT CCC ACT GTG GAC ACC TCG GCC CAG GCG GCC CCT CAG ACC TAC
                    250                                                     300
 61
Ala Glu Tyr Ala Ile Ser Gln Pro Leu Glu Gly Ala Gly Ala Thr Cys Pro Thr Gly Ser Glu Pro Leu Ala Gly Glu Thr Pro Asn Gln
GCC GAA TAT GCC ATC TCA CAG CCT CTG GAA GGG GCT GGG GCC ACG TGC CCC ACA GGG TCA GAG CCC CTG GCA GGA GAG ACG CCC AAC CAG
                                    350                                                     400
 91
Ala Leu Lys Pro Gly Ala Lys Ser Asn Ser Ile Ile Val Ser Pro Arg Gln Arg Gly Asn Pro Val Leu Lys Phe Val Arg Asn Val Pro
GCC CTG AAA CCC GGG GCA AAA TCC AAC AGC ATC ATT GTG AGC CCT CGG CAG AGG GGC AAT CCC GTA CTG AAG TTC GTG CGC AAC GTG CCC
                                                450          helix                  turn                  helix    500
121
Trp Glu Phe Gly Asp Val Ile Pro Asp Tyr Val Leu Gly Gln Ser Thr Cys Ala Leu Phe Leu Ser Leu Arg Tyr His Asn Leu His Pro
TGG GAA TTT GGC GAC GTA ATT CCC GAC TAT GTG CTG GGC CAG AGC ACC TGT GCC CTG TTC CTC AGC CTC CGC TAC CAC AAC CTG CAC CCA
                                                            550
151
Asp Tyr Ile His Gly Arg Leu Gln Ser Leu Gly Lys Asn Phe Ala Leu Arg Val Leu Leu Val Gln Val Asp Val Lys Asp Pro Gln Gln
GAC TAC ATC CAT GGC CGG CTG CAG AGC CTG GGG AAG AAC TTC GCC TTG CGG GTC CTG CTT GTC CAG GTG GAT GTG AAA GAT CCC CAG CAG
        600                                                             650
181
Ala Leu Lys Glu Leu Ala Lys Met Cys Ile Leu Ala Asp Cys Thr Leu Ile Leu Ala Trp Ser Pro Glu Glu Ala Gly Arg Tyr Leu Glu
GCC CTC AAG GAG CTG GCT AAG ATG TGT ATC CTG GCC GAC TGC ACA TTG ATC CTC GCC TGG AGC CCC GAG GAA GCT GGG CGG TAC CTG GAG
                    700                                                     750
                                                                  ADP-rs          ▼
211
Thr Tyr Lys Ala Tyr Glu Gln Lys Pro Ala Asp Leu Leu Met Glu Lys Leu Glu Gln Asp Phe Val Ser Arg Val Thr Glu Cys Leu Thr
ACC TAC AAG GCC TAT GAG CAG AAA CCA GCG GAC CTC CTG ATG GAG AAG CTA GAG CAG GAC TTC GTC TCC CGG GTG ACT GAA TGT CTG ACC
                                    800                                                         850
241
Thr Val Lys Ser Val Asn Lys Thr Asp Ser Gln Thr Leu Leu Thr Thr Phe Gly Ser Leu Glu Gln Leu Ile Ala Ala Ser Arg Glu Asp
ACC GTG AAG TCA GTC AAC AAA ACG GAC AGT CAG ACC CTC CTG ACC ACA TTT GGA TCT CTG GAA CAG CTC ATC GCC GCA TCA AGA GAA GAT
                                                900                                                                 950
271
Leu Ala Leu Cys Pro Gly Leu Gly Pro Gln Lys Ala Arg Arg Leu Phe Asp Val Leu His Glu Pro Phe Leu Lys Val Pro  *  *
CTG GCC TTA TGC CCA GGC CTG GGC CCT CAG AAA GCC CGG AGG CTG TTT GAT GTC CTG CAC GAG CCC TTC TTG AAA GTA CCC TGATGACCCCAG
                                                            1000

CTGCCAAGGAAACCCCCAGTGTAATAATAAATCGTCCTCCCAGGCCAGGCTCA  3'
  1050
```

Fig. 2. Nucleotide and deduced amino acid sequence of the *ERCC-1* cDNA clone pcDE. The alternatively spliced 72 bp exon, absent in pcDE-72, is underlined. Regions exhibiting homology with functional protein domains are boxed. NLS, nuclear location signal; helix-turn-helix, DNA binding domain; ADP-rs, ADP-ribosylation site. The arrowhead points to the arginine residu that by homology with other ADP-ribosylation sites is suggested to be the actual site for mono-ADP-ribosylation, e.g. by cholera toxin (see Hoeijmakers *et al.* 1987*b*, for details). Asterisk, stop codon. Interrupted underlining, polyadenylation signal.

(Reynolds *et al.* 1985*a*). The level of sequence identity is highest between the C-terminal half of *RAD10* and the middle 120 amino acids of *ERCC-1* (34% identity). However, detectable homology exists also in the N-terminal parts of both proteins (Fig. 3). This finding supports the idea that *ERCC-1* and *RAD10* are descendants of the same primordial gene and that they fulfil similar functions. The apparent C-terminal extension of the *ERCC-1* gene product compared to the deduced *RAD10* protein might suggest that *ERCC-1* has gained (or retained) additional functions not encoded by *RAD10*. In this respect it is worth noting that the 72 bp alternatively spliced exon, which is essential for excision repair in 43-3B, is located in the 'extra' part of *ERCC-1*. Transfection experiments of *ERCC-1*, *RAD10* and *ERCC-1/RAD10* hybrid genes to the yeast and CHO repair mutants will have to be done to reveal to what extent the two proteins are functionally related.

Amino-acid sequence homology between *ERCC-1*, *RAD10* and part of *uvrA*

```
        1                                    20
RAD10   M N N T D P T S F  E S I L    A  G V  A K L R K E K S G A      D T T G S Q S L
ERCC-1      M D P G K D K E G V P Q P S G P P A R  K K F V I P L D E D E V P P G V A
            1                                    20

                   40                               60
RAD10   E  I D A S K L Q Q Q E P Q T S R R I N S N Q V I  N A F N Q Q K P E E   W T D
ERCC-1  K P L F R S T Q S L P T V D T S A Q A A P Q T Y A E Y A I S Q P L E G A G A T C
             40                               60

                        80                            100
RAD10   S K A T D D Y N R K R P F R S T R P G  K   T V L V N T T Q K E N P L L N H L
ERCC-1  P T G S E P L A G E T P N Q A L K P G A K S N S I I V S P R Q R G N P V L K F V
              80                            100

                          120                        140
RAD10   K S T N W R Y V S S T G I N M I Y Y D Y L V R G R S   V L F L T L T Y H K L Y
ERCC-1  R N V P W E   F     G   D   V I P D Y V L  G Q S T C A L F L S L R Y H N L H
              120                        140

                              160                        180
RAD10   V D Y I S R R M Q P L S R N   E N N I L I F I V D D N N S E D T L N D I T K L C
ERCC-1  P D Y I H G R L Q S L G K N F A L R V L L V Q V D V K D P Q Q A L K E L A K N C
                      160                        180

                          200
RAD10   M F N G F T L L L A F N F E Q A A K Y I E Y L N L          220
ERCC-1  I L A D C T L I L A W S P E E A G R Y L E T Y K A Y E Q K P A D L L M E K L E Q
uvrA                        E G Q R R Y V E S L S A Y   A R Q F L S L M E K P D V
                            50                                            70

                          240                              260
ERCC-1  D F V S R V T E C L T T V  K S V N K T D S Q T L L L T T F G S L E Q L I A A S R
uvrA    D H I E G L S P A I S I E Q K S
                                    90
                          280

ERCC-1  E D L A L C P G L G P Q K A R R L F D V L H E P F L K V P
```

Fig. 3. Homology of the predicted protein sequence of *ERCC-1* to that of *RAD10* and *uvrA*. Sequence identities are indicated by thick boxes. Physicochemically closely related amino acids (K, R; D, E; I, L, V) by thin boxes and weakly related amino acids (see Schwartz & Dayhoff, 1978, for group classification) by thin underlining. The standard one-letter amino acid abbreviations are used. Numbering corresponds with the residue in the respective protein. The *RAD10*, and *uvrA* sequences are from Reynolds *et al.* (1985*a*), and Husain *et al.* (1986), respectively.

In addition to homology with *RAD10*, computer analysis indicated the existence of a 42 amino acid homologous region between *ERCC-1* and *uvrA* (31% identity) (Fig. 3). In *ERCC-1* this stretch includes the point where the alignment with *RAD10* stops. If this region represents a functional domain shared by *uvrA* and *ERCC-1* it is remarkable that it is only for the first part present in *RAD10*, since *uvrA* and *ERCC-1* are from such distant organisms and *RAD10* should be closer to both of them. Further analysis has to be done to clarify the significance of this observation.

A search for homology of *ERCC-1* amino acid sequences with identified functional protein domains revealed homology with nuclear location signals (NLS), DNA binding domains (helix-turn-helix motive) and adenosine phosphate (ADP) ribosylation sites found in other polypeptides. The position of these tentative functional domains in *ERCC-1* is indicated in Fig. 2. Details on the amino acid sequence comparisons have been published elsewhere (Hoeijmakers *et al.* 1987*b*). The NLS is situated in the N terminus of the *ERCC-1* protein and suggests that the *ERCC-1* gene product is actively transported into the nucleus. Transfection experiments with a *ERCC-1* cDNA clone lacking the first 53 amino acids have shown that this part of the *ERCC-1* protein, which includes the tentatively identified NLS, is not essential for correction of the 43-3B cells (Van Duin *et al.* 1986). It is possible that passive diffusion of the protein through the nuclear pore complex is sufficient to allow the transformants to survive our u.v. and MM-C selection conditions. Alternatively, the *ERCC-1* protein molecules might take the opportunity to reach (and possibly bind to) the DNA when the nuclear membrane is temporarily absent during mitosis. The proposed DNA binding property of *ERCC-1* could be relevant in this respect. The potential DNA binding domain is located in the middle part of *ERCC-1*. It coincides with the region that exhibits the highest level of sequence conservation with *RAD10* (Van Duin *et al.* 1986). Finally, the tentative ADP ribosylation site is located in the C-terminal portion. Intriguingly, it is positioned precisely at the border between exon 7 and the alternatively spliced exon 8. Transcripts lacking this exon would specify a gene product that lacks amino acid sequences thought to be essential for the ADP-ribosyl acceptor function. Although this and the other suggested properties of the *ERCC-1* gene product(s) are not unexpected for repair proteins, definite proof awaits experiments with the isolated protein. Production and purification of the *ERCC-1* protein(s) therefore have a high priority in our research programme, as well as the isolation of additional repair genes. It is hoped that this will lead to a detailed understanding of the mechanism of excision repair in higher organisms, as in *E. coli*.

The following persons were involved in the work presented here: Mr M. Van Duin, Dr A. Yasui, Mr W. Vermeulen, Mrs J. Zwetsloot, Mrs H. Odijk, Mr J. de Wit, Dr A. Westerveld and Dr D. Bootsma.

We are very grateful to Mr M. Koken and P. ten Dyke for help in some of the experiments, Dr R. van Gorcom (Medical Biological Laboratory, TNO, Rijswijk, The Netherlands) for valuable assistance in operating the computer and Dr H. Okayama for the generous gift of the cDNA library. Drs Eker (Delft), van Zeeland and Backendorf (Leiden) are thanked for the gift of enzymes. Furthermore, we thank Mrs R. Boucke for skilful typing of the manuscript and Mr T.

van Os for photography. This work was supported by FUNGO (Foundation of Medical Scientific Research in the Netherlands) and EURATOM contract no. B16-141-NL.

REFERENCES

ADZUMA, K., OGAWA, T. & OGAWA, H. (1984). Primary structure of the *RAD52* gene in *Saccharomyces cerevisiae*. *Molec. cell. Biol.* **4**, 2735–2744.

CLEAVER, J. E. (1968). Defective repair replication of DNA in xeroderma pigmentosum. *Nature, Lond.* **218**, 652–656.

DE JONGE, A. J. R., VERMEULEN, W., KEIJZER, W., HOEIJMAKERS, J. H. J. & BOOTSMA, D. (1985). Microinjection of *Micrococcus luteus* UV-endonuclease restores UV-induced unscheduled DNA synthesis in cells of 9 xeroderma pigmentosum complementation groups. *Mutat. Res.* **150**, 99–105.

DE JONGE, A. J. R., VERMEULEN, W., KLEIN, B. & HOEIJMAKERS, J. H. J. (1983). Microinjection of human cell extracts corrects xeroderma pigmentosum defect. *EMBO J.* **2**, 637–641.

DE WEERD-KASTELEIN, E. A., KEIJZER, W. & BOOTSMA, D. (1972). Genetic heterogeneity of xeroderma pigmentosum demonstrated by somatic cell hybridization. *Nature, new Biol.* **238**, 80–83.

FISCHER, E., KEIJZER, W., THIELMANN, H. W., POPANDA, O., BOHNERT, E., EDLER, L., JUNG, E. G. & BOOTSMA, D. (1985). A ninth complementation group in xeroderma pigmentosum, XP-I. *Mutat. Res.* **145**, 217–225.

FRIEDBERG, E. C. (1985). *DNA Repair*. San Francisco: Freeman & Company.

GIANNELLI, F., PAWSEY, S. A. & AVERY, J. A. (1982). Differences in patterns of complementation of the more common groups of xeroderma pigmentosum: possible implications. *Cell* **29**, 451–458.

GRAFSTROM, R. H., PARK, L. & GROSSMAN, L. (1982). Enzymatic repair of pyrimidine dimer-containing DNA: a 5'-dimer DNA glycosylase-3' apyrimidinic endonuclease mechanism from *Micrococcus luteus*. *J. biol. Chem.* **257**, 3465–3473.

HASELTINE, W. A., GORDON, L. K., LINDAN, C. P., GRAFSTROM, R. H., SHAPER, N. L. & GROSSMAN, L. (1980). Cleavage of pyrimidine dimers in specific DNA sequences by a pyrimidine dimer DNA-glycosylase of *M. luteus*. *Nature, Lond.* **285**, 634–641.

HAYAKAWA, H., ISHIZAKI, K., INOUE, M., YAGI, T., SEKIGUCHI, M. & TAKEBE, H. (1981). Repair of ultraviolet radiation damage in xeroderma pigmentosum cells belonging to complementation group F. *Mutat. Res.* **80**, 381–388.

HOEIJMAKERS, J. H. J., ODIJK, H. & WESTERVELD, A. (1987*a*). Differences between rodent and human cell lines in the amount of integrated DNA after transfection. *Expl Cell Res.* (in press).

HOEIJMAKERS, J. H. J., VAN DUIN, M., WESTERVELD, A., YASUI, A. & BOOTSMA, D. (1987*b*). Identification of DNA-repair genes in the human genome. *Cold Spring Harbor. Symp. quant. Biol.* (in press).

HUSAIN, I., VAN HOUTEN, B., THOMAS, D. C. & SANCAR, A. (1986). Sequence of *Escherichia coli* uvr A gene and protein reveal two potential ATP binding sites. *J. biol. Chem.* **261**, 4895–4901.

KEIJZER, W., VERKERK, A. & BOOTSMA, D. (1982). Phenotypic correction of the defect in xeroderma pigmentosum after fusion with isolated cytoplasts. *Expl Cell Res.* **140**, 119–125.

LEGERSKI, R. J., BROWN, D. B., PETERSON, C. A. & ROBBERSON, D. L. (1984). Transient complementation of xeroderma pigmentosum cells by microinjection of poly(A)⁺RNA. *Proc. natn. Acad. Sci. U.S.A.* **81**, 5676–5679.

LEHMANN, A. R. (1985). Use of recombinant DNA techniques in cloning DNA repair genes and in the study of mutagenesis in human cells. *Mutat. Res.* **150**, 61–67.

MACINNES, M. A., BINGHAM, J. D., THOMPSON, L. H. & STRNISTE, G. F. (1984). DNA-mediated cotransfer of excision repair capacity and drug resistance into Chinese hamster ovary cell line UV-135. *Molec. cell. Biol.* **4**, 1152–1158.

MAXAM, A. M. & GILBERT, W. (1980). Sequence end-labeled DNA with base-specific chemical cleavages. *Meth. Enzym.* **65**, 499–560.

NAUMOVSKI, L., CHU, G., BERG, P. & FRIEDBERG, E. C. (1985). *RAD3* gene of *Saccharomyces cerevisiae*: nucleotide sequence of wild type and mutant alleles, transcript mapping, and aspects of gene regulation. *Molec. cell. Biol.* **5**, 17–26.

NICOLET, C. M., CHENEVERT, J. M. & FRIEDBERG, E. C. (1985). The *RAD2* gene of *Saccharomyces cerevisiae*: nucleotide sequence and transcript mapping. *Gene* **36**, 225–234.

OKAYAMA, H. & BERG, P. (1983). A cDNA cloning vector that permits expression of cDNA inserts in mammalian cell. *Molec. cell. Biol.* **3**, 280–289.

PEROZZI, G. & PRAKASH, S. (1986). *RAD7* gene of *Saccharomyces cerevisae*: Transcripts, nucleotide sequence analysis, and functional relationship between the *RAD7* and *RAD23* gene products. *Molec. cell. Biol.* **6**, 1497–1507.

REYNOLDS, P., PRAKASH, L., DUMAIS, D., PEROZZI, G. & PRAKASH, S. (1985*a*). Nucleotide sequence of the *RAD10* gene of *Saccharomyces cerevisiae*. *EMBO J.* **4**, 3549–3552.

REYNOLDS, P., WEBER, S. & PRAKASH, L. (1985*b*). *RAD6* gene of *Saccharomyces cerevisiae* encodes a protein containing a tract of 13 consecutive aspartates. *Proc. natn. Acad. Sci. U.S.A.* **82**, 168–172.

ROYER-POKORA, B. & HASELTINE, W. A. (1984). Isolation of UV-resistant revertants from a xeroderma pigmentosum complementation group A cell line. *Nature, Lond.* **311**, 390–392.

RUBIN, J. S., JOYNER, A. I., BERNSTEIN, A. & WHITMORE, G. F. (1983). Molecular identification of a human repair gene following DNA-mediated gene transfer. *Nature, Lond.* **306**, 206–208.

SCHWARTZ, R. M. & DAYHOFF, M. D. (1978). Matrices for detecting distant relationships. In *Atlas of Protein Sequence and Structure* (ed. M. D. Dayhoff), vol. 5, suppl. 3, pp. 353–358. Washington, DC: National Biomedical Research Foundation.

TANAKA, K., HAYAKAWA, H., SEKIGUCHI, M. & OKADA, Y. (1977). Specific action of T4 endonuclease V on damaged DNA in xeroderma pigmentosum cells *in vivo*. *Proc. natn. Acad. Sci. U.S.A.* **74**, 2958–2962.

TANAKA, K., SEKIGUCHI, M. & OKADA, Y. (1975). Restoration of ultraviolet-induced unscheduled DNA synthesis of xeroderma pigmentosum cells by the concomittant treatment with bacteriophage T4 endonuclease V and HVJ (Sendai virus). *Proc. natn. Acad. Sci. U.S.A.* **72**, 4071–4075.

TEO, I., SEDGWICK, B., KILPATRICK, M. W., McCARTHY, T. V. & LINDAHL, T. (1986). The intracellular signal for induction of resistance to alkylating agents in *E. coli*. *Cell* **48**, 315–324.

THOMPSON, L. H., BROOKMAN, K. W., DILLEHAY, L. E., MOONEY, C. L. & CARRANO, A. V. (1982). Hypersensitivity to mutation and sister-chromatid exchange induction in CHO cell mutants defective in incising DNA containing UV-lesions. *Somat. Cell Genet.* **8**, 759–773.

THOMPSON, L. H., BROOKMAN, K. W., MINKLER, J. L., FUSCOE, J. C., HENNING, K. A. & CARRANO, A, V. (1985). DNA-mediated transfer of a human DNA repair gene that controls sister chromatid exchange. *Molec. cell. Biol.* **5**, 881–884.

THOMPSON, L. H., BUSCH, D. B., BROOKMAN, K. W., MOONEY, C. L. & GLASER, P. A. (1981). Genetic diversity of UV-sensitive DNA-repair mutants of Chinese hamster ovary cells. *Proc. natn. Acad. Sci. U.S.A.* **78**, 3734–3737.

THOMPSON, L. H. & CARRANO, A. V. (1983). Analysis of mammalian cell mutagenesis and DNA repair using in vitro selected CHO cell mutants. In *Cellular Responses to DNA Damage* (ed. E. C. Friedberg & B. R. Bridges), *U.C.L.A. Symp. Molec. Cell. Biol. New Series*, vol. 11, pp. 125–143. New York: Alan R. Liss.

VAN DUIN, M., DE WIT, J., ODIJK, H., WESTERVELD, A., YASUI, A., KOKEN, M. H. M., HOEIJMAKERS, J. H. J. & BOOTSMA, D. (1986). Molecular characterization of the human excision repair gene *ERCC-1*: cDNA cloning and amino acid homology with the yeast DNA repair gene *RAD10*. *Cell* **44**, 913–923.

VERMEULEN, W., OSSEWEIJER, P., DE JONGE, A. J. R. & HOEIJMAKERS, J. H. J. (1986). Transient correction of excision repair defects in fibroblasts of 9 xeroderma pigmentosum complementation groups by microinjection of crude human cell extracts. *Mutat. Res.* **165**, 199–206.

WALKER, G. C. (1985). Inducible DNA repair systems. *A. Rev. Biochem.* **54**, 425–457.

WESTERVELD, A., HOEIJMAKERS, J. H. J., VAN DUIN, M., DE WIT, J., ODIJK, H., PASTINK, A. & BOOTSMA, D. (1984). Molecular cloning of a human DNA repair gene. *Nature, Lond.* **310**, 425–429.

WOOD, R. D. & BURKI, H. J. (1982). Repair capability and the cellular age response for killing and mutation induction after UV. *Mutat. Res.* **95**, 505–514.

YASUI, A. & CHEVALLIER, M.-R. (1983). Cloning of photoreactivation repair gene and excision repair gene of the yeast *Saccharomyces cerevisiae*. *Curr. Genet.* **7**, 191–194.

ZDZIENICKA, M. Z., ROZA, L., WESTERVELD, A., BOOTSMA, D. & SIMONS, J. W. I. M. (1987). Biological and biochemical consequences of the human *ERCC-1* gene after transfection into a repair-deficient CHO cell line. *Mutat. Res.* (in press).

ZWETSLOOT, J. C. M., BARBEIRO, A. P., VERMEULEN, W., ARTHUR, H. M., HOEIJMAKERS, J. H. J. & BACKENDORF, C. (1986a). Microinjection of *Escherichia coli* uvrA,B,C and D proteins into fibroblasts of xeroderma pigmentosum groups A and C does not result in restoration of UV-induced unscheduled DNA synthesis. *Mutat. Res.* **166**, 89–98.

ZWETSLOOT, J. C. M., HOEIJMAKERS, J. H. J., VERMEULEN, W., EKER, A. P. M. & BOOTSMA, D. (1986b). Unscheduled DNA synthesis in xeroderma pigmentosum cells after microinjection of yeast photoreactivating enzyme. *Mutat. Res.* **165**, 109–115.

ZWETSLOOT, J. C. M., VERMEULEN, W., HOEIJMAKERS, J. H. J., YASUI, A., EKER, A. P. M. & BOOTSMA, D. (1985). Microinjected photoreactivating enzymes from *Anacystis and Saccharomyces* monomerize dimers in chromatin of human cells. *Mutat. Res.* **146**, 71–77.

J. Cell Sci. Suppl. 6, 127–137 (1987)
Printed in Great Britain © The Company of Biologists Limited 1987

A GAMMA-RAY-RESISTANT DERIVATIVE OF AN ATAXIA TELANGIECTASIA CELL LINE OBTAINED FOLLOWING DNA-MEDIATED GENE TRANSFER

MICHAEL H. L. GREEN*, JILL E. LOWE, COLIN F. ARLETT, SUSAN A. HARCOURT, JULIAN F. BURKE†, MICHAEL R. JAMES‡, ALAN R. LEHMANN

MRC Cell Mutation Unit, University of Sussex, Falmer, Brighton BN1 9RR, UK

AND SUSAN M. POVEY

MRC Human Biochemical Genetics Unit, The Galton Laboratory, University College, Wolfson House, 4 Stephenson Way, London NW1 2HE, UK

SUMMARY

Genomic DNA from normal human or mouse cells was transfected together with the selectable marker *gpt* into the simian virus 40-transformed ataxia telangiectasia fibroblast line, AT5BIVA. From a series of experiments involving over 400 000 clones selected for the *gpt* marker, one unambiguously radiation-resistant clone (clone 67) was recovered following selection with repeated cycles of gamma irradiation.

The normal level of radiation resistance of clone 67 has been maintained for at least 11 months in the absence of further selection by radiation. The resistant clone contains one copy of the *gpt* gene. Its DNA synthesis following gamma-irradiation is inhibited to an extent intermediate between that of ataxia telangiectasia and normal cells.

Three out of four thioguanine-resistant derivatives of clone 67 have either lost or do not express the *gpt* sequence and show almost the same sensitivity to gamma irradiation as the original AT5BIVA line. This suggests that the radiation resistance of clone 67 may be linked to the *gpt* sequence and may have arisen as a consequence of the transfection, rather than as the result of an independent mutation to radiation resistance.

INTRODUCTION

Ataxia telangiectasia (AT) is a recessive genetic disease, which in homozygous individuals leads to neurological disorders, immune deficiency and a high incidence of cancers, especially of the lymphatic system (Bridges & Harnden, 1982). Acute sensitivity to ionizing radiation has been observed in affected individuals (e.g. see Gotoff *et al.* 1967) and in cells cultured from them (Taylor *et al.* 1975). In order to obtain a better understanding of the nature of the genetic defect we are attempting to clone the normal gene that complements the defect in AT. As the first step we have transfected DNA sequences from normal human cells into simian virus 40 (SV40)-transformed AT fibroblasts.

---

* Author for correspondence.

† Present address: School of Biological Sciences, University of Sussex, Falmer, Brighton BN9 1QG, UK.

‡ Present address: Institut de Recherches Scientifiques sur le Cancer, B.P. No. 8, 94802 Villejuif Cedex, France.

One-step or two-step DNA transfection has proved a valuable tool in the identification of human oncogenes (Land *et al.* 1983) and it has been used to transfer a number of mammalian genes, such as those for hypoxanthine phosphoribosyltransferase (HPRT) (de Jonge *et al.* 1982) and adenine phosphoribosyltransferase (Lowy *et al.* 1980) to deficient cells. With these genes, a powerful positive selection system was available. In the case of human syndromes such as AT, which are characterized by enhanced radiation sensitivity, such one-step selection procedures are not possible since repair-deficient cells such as the AT cell line used in our study may only be about twofold more sensitive than the wild-type. In order to select for a possible resistant transfectant in such cases, it is necessary to use a procedure of repeated selective enrichment. This prolonged selection, followed by the subsequent study of resistant transfectants, requires the use of an immortalized human cell line as recipient. In this paper we report the isolation and characterization of a radiation-resistant cell line derived from an SV40-transformed (immortal) AT cell line following DNA-mediated gene transfer.

MATERIALS AND METHODS

Cell lines

The SV40-transformed AT cell line used as recipient in our experiments, AT5BIVA, was generously provided by Dr L. Toji, Institute for Medical Research, Camden, NJ, USA. Two SV40-transformed normal cell lines were used. GM0637 was obtained from the Camden Cell Repository (New Jersey) and MRC5-V1 (Huschtscha & Holliday, 1983) was obtained through Dr R. Cox, Harwell.

DNA preparations

High molecular weight genomic DNA was prepared from frozen human placenta, mouse embryos or MRC5-V1 cell cultures by lysis in sodium dodecyl sulphate, digestion with RNase and proteinase K followed by successive extraction with phenol, phenol/chloroform/isoamyl alcohol (50:48:2, by vol.) and chloroform/isoamyl alcohol (24:1, v/v). The plasmids pSV2*gpt* (containing the *gpt* gene under SV40 control cloned into pBR322 (Mulligan & Berg, 1981) and pL10 (containing the *gpt* gene cloned into pBR322) were generously provided by Dr P. Berg. They were extracted from bacteria by an alkaline lysis procedure (Ish-Horowicz & Burke, 1981).

Selection for radiation resistance

Since AT5BIVA is only about twofold more sensitive to gamma-irradiation than SV40-transformed normal cells (Fig. 1A), we have been obliged to use a procedure of repeated selective enrichment in order to select for potential resistant transfectants. In a typical DNA-mediated gene transfer experiment 2×10^5 to 5×10^5 AT5BIVA cells were seeded onto 100 9-cm plates. Two days later DNA transfection was carried out by the calcium phosphate precipitation method (Graham & van der Eb, 1973; Wigler *et al.* 1978) using 20 μg of genomic DNA and 10 μg of pSV2*gpt* DNA. After 16 h the DNA-containing medium was removed and replaced with fresh medium. Twenty-four hours later this medium was in turn replaced with selective "MAX" medium (after Mulligan & Berg, 1981) containing 25 μg ml^{-1} mycophenolic acid, 10 μg ml^{-1} xanthine, 15 μg ml^{-1} hypoxanthine, 0·2 μg ml^{-1} aminopterin, 5 μg ml^{-1} thymidine, 2·3 μg ml^{-1} deoxycytidine, 5 μg ml^{-1} glycine. The basis of this selection protocol is that mycophenolic acid inhibits the *de novo* synthesis of GMP. Cells are therefore dependent on an exogenous purine source. Xanthine, supplied exogenously, can be used by xanthine-guanine phosphoribosyltransferase (XPRT), the product of the *gpt* gene, but not by the endogenous *hprt* gene. Thus only cells harbouring the *gpt* gene can survive in MAX medium.

About 20 days after transfection, plates contained between 100 and 1000 gpt^+ colonies. These were trypsinized, pooled and half the cells frozen down. The other half were transferred to small flasks (approx. 10^6 cells per 25 cm^2 flask) and gamma-irradiated (3 Gy). At 7–10 days later, the flasks were again irradiated with the same dose and after a further 7–10 days the cycle of trypsinization, pooling and irradiation was repeated. This procedure, which permits approximately 1 % survival of AT cells and 10 % survival of cells with normal radiation-resistance following each cycle of radiation treatment, was continued until either the culture died out, or an apparently radiation-resistant culture emerged. Clone 67 arose from one such experiment using donor DNA from MRC5-V1.

Survival curves

Survival curves following gamma-irradiation from a ^{60}Co source were obtained using techniques described elsewhere (Arlett & Harcourt, 1980).

Assay for xanthine-guanine phosphoribosyltransferase (XPRT) in cell extracts

XPRT activity in sonicated cell extracts was assayed by the starch gel electrophoresis technique for HPRT as described by Harris & Hopkinson (1977). The substrate, [^{14}C]hypoxanthine ($2 \cdot 5 \, \mu$Ci ml^{-1}) can be used by both the endogenous HPRT and the exogenous XPRT enzymes (Miller *et al.* 1972), so that both enzymes can be detected in a single assay.

Southern analysis

A 25 μg sample of genomic DNA was digested with restriction enzymes for 4 h at 2 units μg^{-1} DNA. The DNA was electrophoresed in 0·7 % agarose gels and transferred onto nitrocellulose filters. The filters were hybridized at 42°C, in the presence of 50 % formamide, with pL10 DNA ^{32}P-labelled by nick translation to a specific activity of about 3×10^8 disints min^{-1} μg^{-1}. Standard procedures were used (Maniatis *et al.* 1982).

Selection of thioguanine-resistant derivatives

Clone 67 cells were plated in the presence of 2·5 ml^{-1} or 5 μg ml^{-1} 6-thioguanine (TG) at a density of 10^5 cells per dish. After 3 weeks, individual TG-resistant clones were picked and expanded into mass cultures in the presence of 5 μg ml^{-1} TG.

RESULTS

Selection of clone 67

All our experiments have involved cotransfection of AT5BIVA cells with human or mouse genomic DNA (see Table 1) and the plasmid pSV2gpt, which codes for the dominant selectable gpt gene. The cultures were selected first for the presence of the gpt gene, thus eliminating the vast majority of the cell population that had not incorporated any foreign DNA. The frequency of transfer of the gpt gene to these cells was generally greater than 10^{-3}. The gpt^+ transfectants were then allowed to grow to form clones before applying several cycles of radiation selection. Irradiation of clones should provide the same degree of enrichment for resistance as irradiation of individual cells, but the chance of eliminating an entire clone of resistant cells should be minimal with an appropriate choice of dose. Approximately 400 000 gpt^+ clones from mycophenolic acid selection have been grown up and screened for radiation resistance. Table 1 provides a summary of the selection experiments performed to date. Clone 67 was isolated from an experiment using MRC5-V1 DNA for transfection, followed by five cycles of approximately 3 Gy ^{60}Co irradiation.

Table 1. *Summary of experiments designed to correct the defect in AT5BIVA cells and select for radiation-resistant derivatives*

| | | Estimated number of | |
| | | | Gamma-ray-resistant clones |
Expt	Donor DNA	gpt^+ clones	
65	MRC5-V1	12 000	0
67	MRC5-V1	15 000	1
90	MM	12 000	0
92	MM	44 000	0
119	MM	2 500	0
121	MM	3 200	0
146	H or M	3 000	0
185	H	180 000	(1)*
186	M	51 000	0
188	M	85 000	0
	Total	408 700	1

Cells were treated with a calcium phosphate precipitate of 10 μg pSV2*gpt* DNA and 20 μg chromosomal DNA from various sources: H, high molecular weight human placenta DNA; M, high molecular weight mouse embryo DNA; MM, mouse embryo DNA partially digested with *Mbo*I to give fragments 15–20 ($\times 10^3$) bases in size.

* This clone showed increased radiation resistance in two experiments but lost mycophenolic acid and radiation resistance on subsequent culture.

Survival of clone 67

Some 20 flasks were found to contain apparently radiation-resistant clones in these experiments. Clone 67 was the only one to show good growth, stability and clearly enhanced radiation resistance. Clone 67 was found to have gamma-ray sensitivity within the normal range, approximately equal to that of GM0637 and slightly lower than that of MRC5-V1 (Fig. 1). This normal sensitivity was maintained during a 3-month test period in the absence of the gpt^+ selection, and for more than 11 months in the absence of further gamma-radiation selection (Fig. 1B). It should be noted that SV40 transformation in its own right increases the resistance of fibroblasts to gamma-irradiation. The distinction between AT and wild-type is nevertheless preserved (Green *et al.* 1985; Murnane *et al.* 1985).

Southern analysis

The DNA from clone 67 was subjected to digestion with restriction enzymes and Southern analysis. The probe used in these experiments was the plasmid pL10, which is very similar to pSV2*gpt* but lacks all the SV40 sequences. Digestion of DNA from clone 67 with *Sac*I, which has no cutting site in pSV2*gpt*, followed by hybridization with ^{32}P-labelled pL10 DNA showed a single band of 15–20 ($\times 10^3$) bases (Fig. 2A, lane 2). Digestion with *Eco*RI, which cuts at a single site in pSV2*gpt*, revealed a major hybridizing band of about 12×10^3 bases and a minor band of slightly higher molecular weight (Fig. 2B, lane 1). These results indicate that clone 67 contains a single integrated copy of the pSV2*gpt* plasmid. It is not possible to estimate the amount of exogenous human DNA that has been integrated into the recipient genome. However, analogous experiments using mouse genomic DNA as donor suggest that no more than 500×10^3 bases of exogenous mammalian DNA

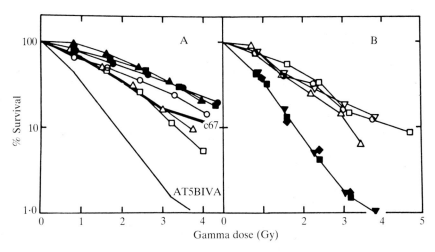

Fig. 1. Gamma-ray survival curves. A. Survival curves of normal cell lines, MRC5-V1 (filled symbols, 3 experiments), and GM0637 (open symbols, 3 experiments), and of AT5BIVA and clone 67 (c67)$^-$ mean line of data shown in Fig. 1B. B. Survival curves of clone 67 (open symbols) after 5 ($\square$), 8 ($\triangledown$), 10 ($\bigcirc$) or 11 ($\triangle$) months in the absence of gamma-ray selection. Equivalent filled symbols show data for AT5BIVA obtained in the same experiments.

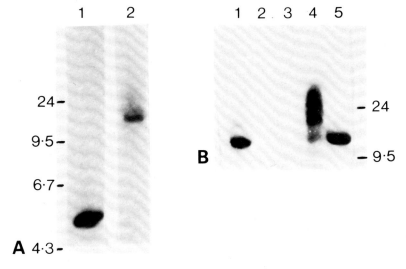

Fig. 2. *gpt* sequences in clone 67. DNA from clone 67 or AT5BIVA was digested with *Sac*I or *Eco*RI. The digests were run on 0·7% agarose gels and then transferred to nitrocellulose. A. Lane 1, pSV2*gpt* linearized with *Eco*RI (25 pg DNA); lane 2, clone 67 DNA digested with *Sac*I. B. *Eco*RI digestion of DNA from clone 67 and TG-resistant derivatives. Lane 1, clone 67; lane 2, 1332.1; lane 3, 1332.2; lane 4, 1338.3; lane 5, 1332.5. Numbers at the sides denote sizes ($\times 10^3$ bases) of *Hin*dIII-digested lambda DNA fragments, used as molecular weight markers.

Table 2. *Isoenzyme patterns in AT5BIVA, clone 67 and their TG-resistant derivatives*

Enzyme	AT5BIVA	Clone 67	1332.1	1332.2	1338.3	1332.5	Frequency*
Phosphoglucomutase 1	1	1	1	1	1	1	0·57
Phosphoglucomutase 3	2	2	2	2	2	2	0·07
Glutamate oxaloacetate transaminase 2	1	1	1	1	1	1	0·97
Esterase D	1	1	1	1	1	1	0·82
Adenosine deaminase	1	1	1	1	1	1	0·90
Acid phosphatase	B	B	B	B	B	B	0·35
Glyoxalase	2	2	2	2	2	2	0·36
α-Fucosidase	1	1	1	1	1	1	0·54
Phosphoglycollate phosphatase	2	2	2	2	2	2	0·016

Determinations were carried out as described by Harris & Hopkinson (1977).
*Frequency of this phenotype in Europeans. The combined probability of having this particular phenotype is 0·003 %.

(and maybe much less; this being the limit of detection in these experiments) is incorporated into the genome of AT5BIVA cells (unpublished observations).

DNA synthesis following gamma-irradiation

A characteristic of all primary AT fibroblasts studied to date is that there is less inhibition of DNA synthesis by gamma-irradiation in these cells than in normal cells (Houldsworth & Lavin, 1980; Painter & Young, 1980; Bridges & Harnden, 1982). We found that even though the resistance to gamma-irradiation of clone 67 was indistinguishable from that of normal cells (Fig. 1), the inhibition of DNA synthesis was only slightly greater than in AT5BIVA cells (Lehmann *et al.* 1986). It did not approach the level seen in normal cells. This finding in clone 67 of normal gamma-ray sensitivity associated with the reduced inhibition of DNA synthesis typical of AT clearly separates these two phenotypes.

Isoenzyme analysis

We have ruled out the possibility that clone 67 is a contaminant, by isoenzyme analysis of the parental line and of clone 67 (Table 2). The probability of finding this identical isoenzyme pattern with these nine enzymes in two independently derived cell lines is 0·003 %.

Effect of loss of gpt on radiation sensitivity of clone 67

Clone 67 could have arisen from a spontaneous reversion or second-site mutation to radiation resistance, in which case its radiation resistance would be completely independent of the transfected DNA. In order to investigate this possibility we attempted by selecting in thioguanine (TG) to obtain derivatives of clone 67 that had lost the *gpt* gene.

Clone 67 contains both the mammalian hypoxanthine phosphoribosyltransferase *hprt* and the bacterial guanine xanthine phosporibosyltransferase *gpt* genes and we were therefore surprised to find that TG-resistant derivatives could be isolated with relatively high frequency. In one experiment in which the selective concentration of TG was $2 \cdot 5 \, \mu g \, ml^{-1}$, TG-resistant clones arose at a frequency of $2 \cdot 5 \times 10^{-4}$; in a subsequent experiment using $5 \, \mu g \, ml^{-1}$ TG, the frequency was about 10^{-5}. Four TG-resistant lines designated 1332.1, 1332.2, 1338.3 and 1332.5 were examined for *gpt* sequences, for the activity of the *gpt* gene product XPRT, and for radio-sensitivity. Isoenzyme analysis confirmed that these four lines were indeed derived from clone 67 (Table 2).

The DNA from the TG-resistant derivatives was digested with *Eco*RI followed by Southern analysis and hybridization with ^{32}P-labelled pL10. Fig. 2B shows that in lines 1332.1 and 1332.2 the pSV2*gpt* sequences are completely deleted (lanes 2, 3) and line 1338.3 contains rearranged sequences (lane 4). In contrast in line 1332.5 (lane 5) the *gpt* sequences were indistinguishable from those of line 67 (lane 1).

The activities of the endogenous mammalian HPRT and the bacterial XPRT enzymes have been measured on starch gel electrophoresis. As anticipated, XPRT activity was not detected in the AT5BIVA parental line (Fig. 3A, lane 7), but it was present in line 67 (lane 8). In the TG-resistant derivatives 1332.1 and 1332.2 in which the *gpt* gene had been deleted there was no activity (lanes 5, 6). Some residual activity could be detected in 1338.3 (lane 3). Line 1332.5 had the unusual property of being able to grow in the presence of TG (selection against the *gpt* gene), in neutral medium, or in MAX (selection for the presence of the *gpt* gene). In all cases the *gpt* gene was expressed as demonstrated by the band of XPRT activity in Fig. 3A, lane 4, and Fig. 3B.

If the *gpt* gene were linked to the gene responsible for the increased radiation resistance of clone 67, some of these derivatives may also have deleted or altered the expression of linked sequences, and they may thus show loss of radiation resistance. From Fig. 4 it can be seen that this is indeed the case. All four independent derivatives were more sensitive than clone 67 to gamma-irradiation and were almost as sensitive as AT5BIVA.

DISCUSSION

We have isolated a radiation-resistant derivative of AT5BIVA (clone 67) following DNA-mediated gene transfer. Four derivatives of this line that have been selected for TG resistance have radiation sensitivity restored to a level close to that of AT5BIVA. In two of these lines the *gpt* gene has been deleted and in a third line it is rearranged. These findings suggest that the radiation resistance in clone 67 is linked to the *gpt* gene, which in turn suggests that the radiation resistance has arisen through trans-fection rather than by mutation during selection. The properties of the fourth derivative, however, weaken this argument. In this derivative radiation resistance is lost despite the fact that the *gpt* gene is maintained and continues to be expressed. The properties of this cell line are bizarre. It is able to grow in MAX or TG despite the fact that XPRT activity is expressed in both media. Moreover, its radiation

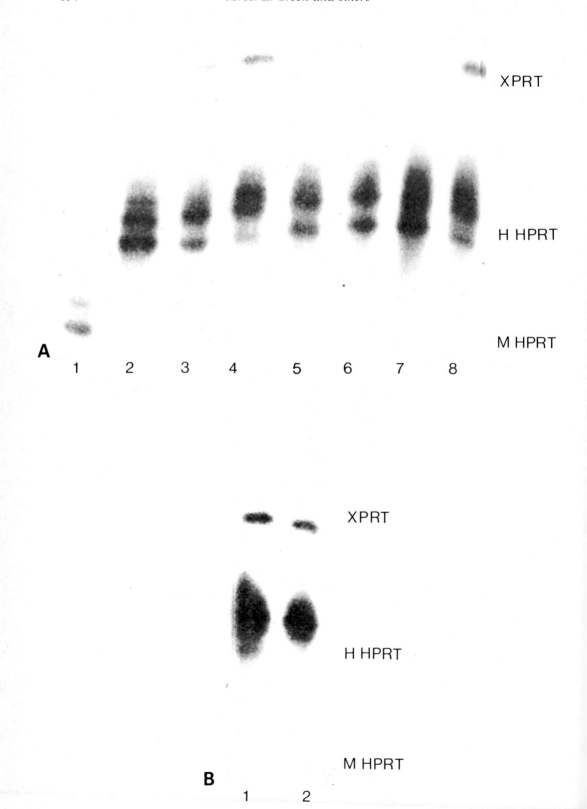

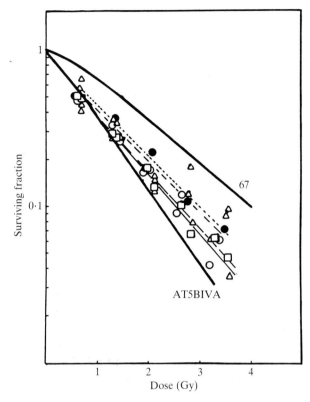

Fig. 4. Gamma-ray survival curves of TG-resistant derivatives of clone 67. Survival curves of AT5BIVA and clone 67 (heavy lines). TG-resistant derivatives of clone 67: 1332.1 (□——□); 1332.2 (△---△); 1338.3 (●·····●); 1332.5 (○——○). Best fit curves were determined by a NAG library subroutine.

sensitivity is also dependent on the growth medium (results not shown). We have no satisfactory explanation for these observations with line 1332.5.

For the rest of this Discussion we will assume that the *gpt* gene is linked to radiation resistance in line 67 and therefore that the radiation resistance has arisen by transfection, whilst keeping in mind that our evidence for this is not conclusive. The radiation resistance could then have arisen in a number of different ways. First, the wild-type allele of the gene responsible for the radiation sensitivity of AT5BIVA has itself been transferred and is now linked to the *gpt* gene. If this were the case, however, one would have expected restoration of post-irradiation DNA synthesis to wild-type levels since the two phenotypes are linked in all the AT complementation groups identified to date. Second, another gene complementing the radiation sensitivity but otherwise unrelated to AT may have been transferred. A third possibility is

Fig. 3. XPRT activity in various derivatives. XPRT and HPRT were assayed by starch gel electrophoresis using [^{14}C]hypoxanthine. A. Lane 1, mouse LMTK$^-$ cells; lane 2, human lymphoblastoid line BRI-8; lanes 3–6, TG-resistant derivatives of clone 67 (3, 1338.3; 4, 1332.5; 5, 1332.2; 6, 1332.1); lane 7, AT5BIVA; lane 8, clone 67. Extracts prepared from cells grown in non-selective medium. M, mouse; H, human. B. Extracts of line 1332.5 grown in MAX (lane 1) or TG (lane 2).

that no other gene has been transferred, but that the pSV2*gpt* has become integrated in such a manner as to alter expression of an adjacent gene affecting radiation resistance. In the very large number of *gpt* transfectants that we have examined, radiation resistance is unaffected, so that this is clearly not a general property of the integrated pSV2*gpt* plasmid.

Experiments attempting to transfer radiation resistance to repair-deficient human cells have been performed in several laboratories (Royer-Pokora & Haseltine, 1984; reviewed by Lehmann, 1985) with remarkably little success. An early promising result (Takano *et al.* 1982) has not been reproduced despite attempts in numerous laboratories. This contrasts with the successful correction of repair deficiencies in rodent cell lines using human DNA (Rubin *et al.* 1983; Westerveld *et al.* 1984; MacInnes *et al.* 1984; Thompson *et al.* 1985). In one case (Westerveld *et al.* 1984) this has led to the successful cloning of a human repair gene. One difficulty in the present gene-transfer experiments is the lack of an all-or-none selective system. The approach that we have adopted here should select clones with a moderate increase in radiation resistance, but if, as with xeroderma pigmentosum (Royer-Pokora & Haseltine, 1984), there is an appreciable frequency of mutation to radiation resistance the experiments are likely to become uninterpretable. Our failure to find more than one stable resistant clone among 400 000 transfectants suggests that this may not be a problem with the AT line used here. A second problem concerns the amount of genomic DNA incorporated by our recipient. In experiments with good rodent recipient cells (e.g. mouse L cells or 3T3 cells), on average only 10 000 clones need to be screened to detect a particular transferred gene of moderate size. If, as appears to be the case, our recipient takes up genomic DNA less efficiently, a correspondingly larger experiment is likely to be required.

Irrespective of the origin of the radiation resistance in clone 67, the separation of radiation sensitivity from the lack of inhibition of DNA synthesis is of considerable interest with respect to the molecular defect in AT, as discussed in detail earlier (Lehmann *et al.* 1986). Our isolation of a radiation-resistant derivative of AT in which the *gpt* gene may be linked to a gene influencing radiation sensitivity may provide an opportunity for cloning a gene that affects DNA repair in humans. We are currently cloning sequences linked to the *gpt* gene from the DNA of line 67.

This work was supported in part by Euratom contract BIO-E-414-81-UK.

REFERENCES

ARLETT, C. F. & HARCOURT, S. A. (1980). Survey of radiosensitivity in a variety of human cell strains. *Cancer Res.* **40**, 926–932.
BRIDGES, B. A. & HARNDEN, D. G. (eds) (1982). *Ataxia-Telangiectasia – a Cellular and Molecular Link between Cancer, Neuropathology and Immune Deficiency.* London: Wiley.
DE JONGE, A. J. R., ABRAHAMS, P. J., WESTERVELD, A. & BOOTSMA, D. (1982). Expression of human hprt gene on the inactive X chromosome after DNA-mediated gene transfer. *Nature, Lond.* **295**, 624–626.
GOTOFF, S. P., AMIRMOKRI, G. & LIEBNER, E. (1967). Ataxia-telangiectasia. Neoplasia, untoward response to X-irradiation and tuberous sclerosis. *Am. J. Dis. Child.* **114**, 617–625.

GRAHAM, F. L. & VAN DER EB, A. J. (1973). A new technique for the assay of human adenovirus 5 DNA. *Virology* **52**, 456–457.

GREEN, M. H. L., LOWE, J. E., JAMES, M. R. & ARLETT, C. F. (1985). An attempt to transfer radiation-resistance to an ataxia-telangiectasia cell line. In *Ataxia-Telangiectasia: Genetics, Neuropathology, and Immunology of a Degenerative Disease of Childhood* (ed. R. A. Gatti & M. Swift), pp. 173–179. New York: Alan R. Liss Inc.

HARRIS, H. A. & HOPKINSON, D. A. (1977). *Handbook of Enzyme Electrophoresis in Human Genetics*. Amsterdam: North-Holland.

HOULDSWORTH, J. & LAVIN, M. F. (1980). Effect of ionizing radiation on DNA synthesis in ataxia-telangiectasia cells. *Nucl. Acids Res.* **16**, 3709–3720.

HUSCHTSCHA, L. I. & HOLLIDAY, R. (1983). Limited and unlimited growth of SV40-transformed cells from human diploid MRC-5 fibroblasts. *J. Cell Sci.* **63**, 77–99.

ISH-HOROWICZ, D. & BURKE, J. F. (1981). Rapid and efficient cosmid cloning. *Nucl. Acids Res.* **9**, 2989–2998.

LAND, H., PARADA, L. F. & WEINBERG, R. A. (1983). Cellular oncogenes and multistep carcinogenesis. *Science* **222**, 771–777.

LEHMANN, A. R. (1985). Minireview: use of recombinant DNA techniques in cloning DNA repair genes and in the study of mutagenesis in mammalian cells. *Mutat. Res.* **150**, 61–67.

LEHMANN, A. R., ARLETT, C. F., BURKE, J. F., GREEN, M. H. L., JAMES, M. R. & LOWE, J. E. (1986). A derivative of an ataxia-telangiectasia (A-T) cell line with normal radiosensitivity but A-T-like inhibition of DNA synthesis. *Int. J. Radiat. Biol.* **49**, 639–643.

LOWY, I., PELLICER, A., JACKSON, J. F., SIM, G.-K., SILVERSTEIN, S. & AXEL, R. (1980). Isolation of transforming DNA: cloning the hamster aprt gene. *Cell* **22**, 817–823.

MACINNES, M. A., BINGHAM, J. M., THOMPSON, L. H. F. & STRNISTE, G. F. (1984). DNA-mediated co-transfer of excision repair capacity and drug resistance into Chinese hamster ovary mutant line UV-135. *Molec. cell. Biol.* **4**, 1152–1158.

MANIATIS, T., FRITSCH, E. F. & SAMBROOK, J. (1982). *Molecular Cloning*. Cold Spring Harbor Laboratory, New York: CSHL Press.

MILLER, R. L., RAMSEY, G. A., KRENITSKY, T. A. & ELION, G. B. (1972). Guanine phosphoribosyltransferase from *Escherichia coli*, specificity and properties. *Biochemistry* **11**, 4723–4731.

MULLIGAN, R. C. & BERG, P. (1981). Selection for animal cells that express the *Escherichia coli* gene coding for xanthine-guanine phosphoribosyl-transferase. *Proc. natn. Acad. Sci. U.S.A.* **78**, 2072–2076.

MURNANE, J. P., FULLER, L. F. & PAINTER, R. B. (1985). Establishment and characterization of a permanent pSVori⁻-transformed ataxia-telangiectasia cell line. *Expl Cell Res.* **158**, 119–126.

PAINTER, R. B. & YOUNG, B. R. (1980). Radiosensitivity in ataxia-telangiectasia: a new explanation. *Proc. natn. Acad. Sci. U.S.A.* **77**, 7315–7317.

ROYER-POKORA, B. & HASELTINE, W. (1984). Isolation of UV-resistant revertants from a xeroderma pigmentosum complementation group A cell line. *Nature, Lond.* **311**, 390–392.

RUBIN, J. S., JOYNER, A. L., BERNSTEIN, A. & WHITMORE, G. F. (1983). Molecular identification of a human DNA repair gene following DNA mediated gene transfer. *Nature, Lond.* **306**, 206–208.

TAKANO, R., NODA, M. & TAMURA, T. (1982). Transfection of cells from a xeroderma pigmentosum patient with normal human DNA confers UV resistance. *Nature, Lond.* **296**, 269–270.

TAYLOR, A. M. R., HARNDEN, D. G., ARLETT, C. F., HARCOURT, S. A., LEHMANN, A. R., STEVENS, S. & BRIDGES, B. A. (1975). Ataxia telangiectasia: a human mutation with abnormal radiation sensitivity. *Nature, Lond.* **258**, 427–429.

THOMPSON, L. H., BROOKMAN, K. W., MINKLER, J. L., FUSCOE, J. C., HENNING, K. A. & CARRANO, A. V. (1985). DNA-mediated transfer of a human DNA repair gene that controls sister chromatid exchange. *Molec. cell. Biol.* **5**, 881–884.

WESTERVELD, A., HOEIJMAKERS, J. H. J., VAN DUIN, M., DE WIT, J., ODIJK, H., PASTINK, A., WOOD, R. D. & BOOTSMA, D. (1984). Molecular cloning of a human DNA repair gene. *Nature, Lond.* **310**, 425–429.

WIGLER, M., PELLICER, A., SILVERSTEIN, S. & AXEL, R. (1978). Biochemical transfer of single-copy eucaryotic genes using total cellular DNA as donor. *Cell* **14**, 725–731.

J. Cell Sci. Suppl. 6, 139–146 (1987)
Printed in Great Britain © *The Company of Biologists Limited 1987*

PROPERTIES AND MECHANISM OF ACTION OF EUKARYOTIC 3-METHYLADENINE-DNA GLYCOSYLASES

D. E. HELLAND, R. MALE, B. I. HAUKANES, L. OLSEN,
I. HAUGAN AND K. KLEPPE

*Laboratory of Biotechnology and Department of Biochemistry, University of Bergen,
PO 3152, Årstad N-5001, Bergen, Norway*

SUMMARY

3-Methyladenine-DNA glycosylase activities have been identified in all eukaryotic cell systems studied. Some of the results from these studies are reviewed here. The enzymes possess molecular weights between 24×10^3 and 34×10^3, they have a broad pH optimum at approximately pH 8, require double-stranded DNA and act in the absence of any cofactors. The enzyme can excise several different methylated bases from DNA such as 3-methyladenine, 7-methylguanine and 3-methylguanine.

The specific activity of this DNA glycosylase in mouse L-cells was found to be a function of the proliferative state of the cell. *In vitro* quantification of this DNA repair activity in synchronized mouse L-cells suggests that it is regulated within a defined temporal sequence prior to the onset of DNA replication.

Using DNA fragments of defined sequences it was observed that the efficiency of removal of the methylated bases is sequence-dependent.

INTRODUCTION

Following exposure to alkylating agents DNA is modified at many sites, in particular at the ring nitrogen and the exocyclic oxygen atoms of the bases. The oxygen atoms of the phosphate internucleotide linkages are also attacked by alkylating agents (Singer & Kusmierek, 1982). In both bacteria and higher organisms, the alkylated bases or phosphate groups may either be repaired by a direct transfer of the modifying alkyl group from DNA to the repair protein or by direct cleavage of the glycosylic bond of the alkylated base by a specific DNA glycosylase (for a review, see Friedberg, 1985). In *Escherichia coli* several DNA glycosylases have evolved to deal with specific lesions (Lindahl, 1982). Two distinct 3-methyladenine-DNA glycosylases (types I and II) have been purified from this organism. The genetics and biochemistry of these two DNA glycosylases have been thoroughly studied (Friedberg, 1985). While 3-methyladenine-DNA glycosylase I releases only 3-methyladenine from DNA, 3-methyladenine-DNA glycosylase II has a much wider substrate specificity (Thomas *et al.* 1982; Karran *et al.* 1982). One major problem in the study of similar DNA repair activities in eukaryotic cells is that such cells are poorly characterized genetically with regard to DNA repair function. However, a number of observations made in different laboratories suggest that an activity similar to the type II DNA glycosylase from *E. coli* exists in eukaryotic cells.

In order to elucidate the role of DNA repair in the maintenance of a biological system one has to identify the different enzymic activities responsible for the removal of damaged regions of the DNA. Furthermore, it is important to examine how these different enzymes are regulated throughout the cell cycle and during differentiation of the eukaryotic cell.

This article reviews studies on 3-methyladenine-DNA glycosylases in higher organisms and compares the properties of these enzymes with the well-characterized bacterial counterpart. Some recent data from our laboratory are presented concerning the influence of DNA sequence on the removal of methylated purines by the 3-methyladenine-DNA glycosylase purified from calf thymus, and the cell cycle-dependent regulation of the same activity in cultured mouse cells.

PURIFICATION AND PHYSIOCHEMICAL CHARACTERIZATION

3-Methyladenine-DNA glycosylases have been purified from several different mammalian systems. Some of the properties and characteristics of the different enzymes isolated are listed in Table 1. For comparison, the properties of the two 3-methyladenine-DNA glycosylases present in *E. coli* are also provided.

Only the enzyme isolated from calf thymus has been obtained in an apparent homogeneous form, as judged by SDS–polyacrylamide gel electrophoresis and silver staining (Male *et al.* 1985*a*).

All the reported enzyme activities are associated with proteins of rather low molecular weights of around 30×10^3. In calf thymus and mouse cells we have found that multiple molecular weight species are present. Only the low molecular weight form has been purified to homogeneity. The presence of multiple species indicates that mammalian cells either have several gene products for these repair enzymes, that the enzymes are processed in the cell or that the enzymes are degraded by proteases during the purification procedure. Since the smaller molecular weight species is the only one present in the nucleus in calf thymus cells we conclude that the larger molecular weight form found only in the cytoplasm is a precursor of the chromatin-associated enzyme (Male *et al.* 1985*a*). Experiments verifying this hypothesis are in progress in our laboratory.

A striking difference is observed between the pI for the calf thymus enzyme and the two bacterial enzymes. The rather high pI for the calf thymus enzyme indicates a stronger affinity for DNA by the mammalian enzyme as compared to the *E. coli* enzyme.

The two 3-methyladenine-DNA glycosylases in *E. coli* differ in specificity. While the 3-methyladenine-DNA glycosylase I only releases 3-methyladenine, the type II enzyme catalyses the release of 3-methyladenine, 3-methylguanine, 7-methylguanine, O^2-methylcytosine and O^2-methylthymine from alkylated DNA (Thomas *et al.* 1982; McCarthy *et al.* 1984). The eukaryotic 3-methyladenine-DNA glycosylases are similar to the *E. coli* type II DNA glycosylase in this respect (Table 1). Gallagher & Brent (1984) have reported evidence that these different activities are associated with a single DNA glycosylase in human placenta. Our data on the

Table 1. *Properties of mammalian 3-methyladenine-DNA glucosylases*

Source	Human lymphoblasts	Human placenta	Rat liver	Calf thymus	Mouse L-cells	*E. coli* 3-methyladenine-DNA glycosylase I	*E. coli* 3-methyladenine-DNA glycosylase II
References	Brent (1979); Singer & Brent (1981)	Gallagher & Brent (1984)	Margison & Pegg (1981)	Male et al. (1985a,b, 1986)	Male et al. (1981)	Thomas et al. (1982); Reiazudin & Lindahl (1978)	Thomas et al. (1982); McCarthy et al. (1984)
Bases released	3mA, 3eA, 7mG, 7eG, 3mG, 3eG	3mA, 7mG, 3mG	3mA, 7mG	3mA, 7mG, 3mG, 7mA	3mA, 7mG	3mA	3mA, 7mA, 3mG, 7mG, O^2-mT, O^2-mC
Molecular weights ($\times 10^{-3}$)	34	25	24	42, 27	68, 47, 27	20	27
pI	N.D.	N.D.	N.D.	9·50	N.D.	6·0	7·0
Optimal assay conditions: NaCl (mM)		50		50	100		
pH	7·5–8·5	7·2–7·7		8·0–9·0	6·5	7·8	8·0
Divalent cation requirement	No	No, but slightly stimulated by Mg^{2+}	No	No	No	No	No

Abbreviations: 3mA, 3-methyladenine; 3eA, 3-ethyladenine; O^2-mT, O^2-methylthymidine; 7mG, 7-methylguanine; 7eG, 7-ethylguanine; O^2-mC, O^2-methylcytosine; 3mG, 3-methylguanine; 3eG, 3-ethylguanine; N.D., not determined.

purified calf thymus enzyme confirm that the wide specificity observed for the other mammalian 3-methyladenine-DNA glycosylases is associated with one protein.

A general property of all known DNA glycosylases is that no divalent cations are required for the enzyme-catalysed release of the modified bases. The mammalian 3-methyladenine-DNA glycosylases seem to be dependent on a cysteine residue in the reduced form since p-hydroxymercuribenzoate totally abolishes the activity (Gallagher & Brent, 1984; Male *et al.* 1985*a*).

KINETICS AND DNA SEQUENCE SPECIFICITY OF BASE RELEASE

We have shown that the rate of release of 3-methyladenine is much faster than that for the other methylated bases. In the case of the enzyme from calf thymus the ratio of release of 3-methyladenine *versus* 7-methyladenine residues was approximately 10:1 when methylated calf thymus DNA was used as a substrate. This ratio is, however, dependent on the structure of the DNA (Male *et al.* 1986). The interpretation of these observations is that following alkylation of DNA in the cell some sites are less efficiently repaired than others by the 3-methyladenine-DNA glycosylase. In order to elucidate further the influence of different DNA structures and base sequences on the rate of removal of methylated bases from DNA, we have used as substrates DNA fragments of defined sequences.

A 186 base-pair (bp) *Sal*I–*Hae*II fragment from the plasmid pUC18 was labelled at the 5′ end by bacteriophage T4 polynucleotide kinase, followed by methylation according to the Maxam–Gilbert procedure (Maxam & Gilbert, 1980), and then subsequently treated with the 3-methyladenine-DNA glycosylase. To induce nicks at the depurinated sites the DNA was then incubated with the Mg^{2+}-independent apurinic/apyrimidinic (AP)-endonuclease associated with the redoxy endonuclease from calf thymus (Doetsch *et al.* 1986). Determination of the sites of incision in the DNA fragment was carried out by analysis of the products on a 12% denaturing polyacrylamide sequencing gel alongside the Maxam–Gilbert sequencing reactions. To quantify the incision sites made by the enzyme, the autoradiograms of the sequencing gels were subjected to densitometer scanning. The results from one analysis are shown in Fig. 1. The efficiency of incision is indicated by the size of the histogram at a certain purine site. Some variations in the alkylation of DNA are known for the guanine-specific reaction. However, these variations are minor compared to the enzyme-induced nicking found in the DNA fragment. To minimize the effect of possible sequence preference by the redoxy endonuclease (Doetsch *et al.* 1986; Helland *et al.* 1986), a great excess of this enzyme was included in the assay mixtures to ensure that all AP sites generated by the action of the 3-methyladenine-DNA glycosylase were nicked.

Some of the alkylated purine sites are apparently seldom or never nicked by the combined action of these enzymes. These purine residues are frequently found in a sequence of several pyrimidines; in particular, adenine residues 5′ to another adenine were rarely removed. The most efficient substrates appear to be a base residue with a purine next to it on the 5′ side, or bases situated within a sequence of several purines.

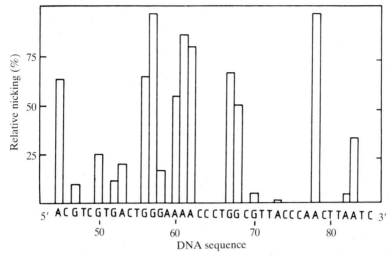

Fig. 1. DNA sequence preference of 3-methyladenine-DNA glycosylase. The graph represent the results of a densitometer scan of the autoradiogram of the 5′ end-labelled fragments generated from the 186 bp *Sal*I–*Hae*II fragment of the plasmid pUC18. The DNA had been methylated by dimethyl sulphate according to the A+G reaction in the Maxam–Gilbert sequencing protocol (Maxam & Gilbert, 1980) before being treated with the 3-methyladenine-DNA glycosylase (13 milli units) purified from calf thymus (Male *et al.* 1985*a*). Nicks in the DNA at the apurinic sites generated by the action of the glycosylase were introduced by adding an excess of the Mg^{2+}-independent AP-endo-nuclease associated with the calf thymus redoxyendonuclease (Doetsch *et al.* 1986) to the reaction mixture. The bases are numbered from the ^{32}P-labelled 5′ end of the restriction enzyme fragment.

Further experiments are required to determine the relationship between sequence specificity and the removal of methylated bases *in vivo*.

REGULATION OF 3-METHYLADENINE-DNA GLYCOSYLASE ACTIVITY

In addition to the differences in substrate specificity, the two 3-methyladenine-DNA glycosylase activities present in *E. coli* also differ in the way they are regulated. Thus the *E. coli* 3-methyladenine-DNA glycosylase I is constitutively expressed, while the glycosylase II is inducible (Karran *et al.* 1982). The biological conse-quence of this phenomenon is that bacteria may respond to exposure to alkylating agents by increasing the DNA repair capacity for the damage caused by these agents (Friedberg, 1985).

Several studies with mammalian cells have shown that both replicative DNA synthesis and the activities of both uracil-DNA glycosylase and 3-methyladenine-DNA glycosylase are increased following exposure to DNA damaging agents. The increase, however, is always found to be linked to an enhanced proliferation of the cells (Sirover & Gupta, 1985).

In a previous study we reported the effect of exposure to subtoxic doses of alkylating agents on C3H/10T1/2 cells and mouse L-cells (Male *et al.* 1985*b*). No significant differences between treated and control cells were observed when the

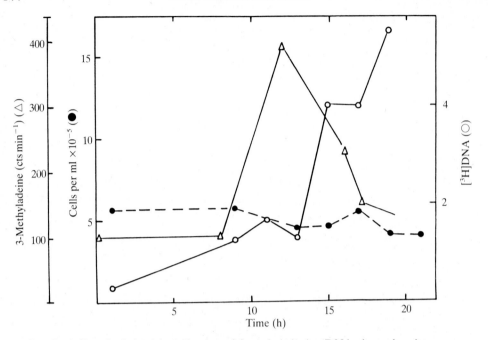

Fig. 2. Cell cycle-dependent induction of 3-methyladenine-DNA glycosylase in mouse L-cells. L-cells from suspension culture in logarithmic growth were separated on the basis of their size in a Beckman elutriation system. The DNA content and the cell cycle distribution of the different populations from the elutriation were established by means of flow cytometry. G_1 cells were incubated further and the cell number was corrected for the presence of dead cells by means of vital staining. The onset of DNA synthesis was followed by measuring the incorporation of [³H]thymidine. At different times after the start of the synchronous growth, samples of the cells were collected for enzyme extraction. Enzyme activity of the 3-methyladenine-DNA glycosylase was measured as cts min⁻¹ released from [³H]methyl methane sulphonate-treated calf thymus DNA per 10^5 cells. The procedure for measuring 3-methyladenine-DNA glycosylase activity has been described elsewhere (Male *et al.* 1985a).

survival of the cells was measured as a function of different concentrations of dimethylsulphate (from 2·5 μM to 25 μM). However, a twofold increase in the specific activity of 3-methyladenine-DNA glycosylase was found in L-cells following exposure to 130 μM-methyl methane sulphonate for 24 h. This increase could be due to a general stimulus to cell proliferation caused by the alkylating agent, similar to the response in bacteria.

Sirover & Gupta (1985) have documented a general increase in the activity of individual DNA repair enzymes as quiescent cells are stimulated to proliferate. Their primary approach has been to examine the regulation of DNA repair in human fibroblasts, growth-arrested by serum depletion, and then stimulated to proliferate by the readdition of serum. From these results the authors suggest that normal cells regulate excision repair genes in a defined sequence with respect to the induction of DNA replication, such that DNA repair is stimulated prior to DNA synthesis.

In order to study the regulation of the 3-methyladenine-DNA glycosylase activity as a function of the cell cycle phase L-cells in logarithmic suspension growth (Fig. 2) were sorted according to size by means of the Beckman elutriation system. The DNA content of the different populations obtained was analysed by flow cytometry and the distribution of cells in the cell cycle established. G_1 cells were allowed to progress through the cycle and their S-phase index (measured by incorporation of [^{3}H]thymidine) and viability were assessed.

At different times during synchronous growth cells were harvested and analysed for enzyme activity. It is evident from Fig. 2 that the activity of 3-methyladenine-DNA glycosylase in these cells increases substantially, reaching its maximum before the onset of DNA synthesis. During S-phase the 3-methyladenine-DNA activity drops to the basal level. It may be concluded from these observations that 3-methyladenine-DNA glycosylase activity in mammalian cells is regulated in a cell cycle-dependent manner. These results also indicate that no specific signal, such as alkylation of the DNA, is likely to increase the specific activity of this enzyme in the cells.

FUTURE ASPECTS OF MAMMALIAN DNA REPAIR ENZYMOLOGY

In order to understand better the function and biological role of mammalian DNA repair enzymes, these enzymes will have to be purified to homogeneity so that the amino acid sequence can be determined. On the basis of the amino acid sequence it should be possible to identify the genes coding for these activities and elucidate their structure and regulation. This approach, which is now pursued in several laboratories, will open up a new area in the knowledge of the role of DNA repair in eukaryotic systems. So far the main problem in this approach has been to obtain enough of the pure enzymes.

This study was supported by grants from the Norwegian Cancer Society (Landsforeningen mot Kreft). R.M. and D.E.H. are research fellows of this society. The authors thank Mrs Kirsten Selvik for excellent technical assistance.

REFERENCES

BRENT, T. P. (1979). Partial purification and characterization of a human 3-methyladenine-DNA glycosylase. *Biochemistry* **18**, 911–916.

DOETSCH, P. W., HELLAND, D. E. & HASELTINE, W. A. (1986). Mechanism of action of a mammalian DNA repair endonuclease. *Biochemistry* **25**, 2212–2220.

FRIEDBERG, E. C. (1985). *DNA Repair.* New York: W. H. Freeman and Company.

GALLAGHER, P. E. & BRENT, T. P. (1982). Partial purification and characterization of 3-methyladenine-DNA glycosylase from human placenta. *Biochemistry* **21**, 6404–6409.

GALLAGHER, P. E. & BRENT, T. P. (1984). Further purification and characterization of human 3-methyladenine-DNA glycosylase. *Biochim. biophys. Acta* **782**, 394–401.

HELLAND, D. E., DOETSCH, P. W. & HASELTINE, W. A. (1986). Substrate specificity of a mammalian DNA repair endonuclease that recognizes oxidative base damage. *Molec. cell. Biol.* **6**, 1983–1990.

KARRAN, P., HJELMGREN, T. & LINDAHL, T. (1982). Induction of a DNA glycosylase for N-methylated purines is part of the adaptive response to alkylating agents. *Nature, Lond.* **296**, 770–773.

LINDAHL, T. (1982). DNA repair enzymes. *A. Rev. Biochem.* **51**, 61–87.

MALE, R., HAUKANES, B. I., HELLAND, D. E. & KLEPPE, K. (1987). Substrate specificity of 3-methyladenine DNA glycosylase from calf thymus. *Eur. J. Biochem.* (in press).

MALE, R., HELLAND, D. & KLEPPE, K. (1985*a*). Purification and characterization of 3-methyladenine-DNA glycosylase from calf thymus. *J. biol. Chem.* **260**, 1623–1629.

MALE, R., HELLAND, D. E., LILLEHAUG, J. R. & KLEPPE, K. (1985*b*). Properties of mammalian 3-methyladenine-DNA glycosylases. In *Repair of DNA Lesions Introduced by* N-*nitroso Compounds* (ed. B. Myrnes & H. Krokan), pp. 230–241. Oslo: Norwegian University Press.

MALE, R., NES, I. F. & KLEPPE, K. (1981). Purification and properties of 3-methyladenine-DNA glycosylase from L-cells. *Eur. J. Biochem.* **121**, 243–248.

MARGISON, G. P. & PEGG, A. E. (1981). Enzymatic release of 7-methylguanine from methylated DNA by rodent liver extracts. *Proc. natn. Acad. Sci. U.S.A.* **78**, 861–865.

MAXAM, A. M. & GILBERT, W. (1980). Sequencing end-labelled DNA with base-specific chemical cleavages. In *Methods in Enzymology*, vol. 65, part I, (ed. L. Grossman & K. Moldave), pp. 499–560. New York: Academic Press.

MCCARTHY, T. V., KARRAN, P. & LINDAHL, T. (1984). Inducible repair of *O*-alkylated DNA pyrimidines in *Escherichia coli. EMBO J.* **3**, 545–550.

REIAZUDIN, S. & LINDAHL, T. (1978). Properties of 3-methyladenine-DNA glycosylase from *Escherichia coli. Biochemistry* **17**, 2110–2118.

SINGER, B. & BRENT, T. P. (1981). Human lymphoblasts contain DNA glycosylase activity exising N-3 and N-7 methyl and ethyl purines but not *O*⁶-alkylguanines or 1-alkyladenines. *Proc. natn. Acad. Sci. U.S.A.* **78**, 856–860.

SINGER, B. & KUSMIEREK, J. T. (1982). Chemical mutagenesis. *A. Rev. Biochem.* **52**, 655–693.

SIROVER, M. A. & GUPTA, P. K. (1985). Regulation of DNA repair in human cells. In *Human Carcinogenesis* (ed. H. Autrup & C. Harris), pp. 255–280. New York: Plenum Press.

THOMAS, L., YANG, C.-H. & GOLDWAIT, D. A. (1982). Two DNA glycosylases in *Escherichia coli* which release primarily 3-methyladenine. *Biochemistry* **21**, 1162–1169.

J. Cell Sci. Suppl. 6, 147–160 (1987)
Printed in Great Britain © The Company of Biologists Limited 1987

GENETIC EVIDENCE FOR NUCLEOTIDE EXCISION REPAIR OF O^6-ALKYLGUANINE IN MAMMALIAN CELLS

J. M. BOYLE, L. G. DURRANT, C. P. WILD, R. SAFFHILL
AND G. P. MARGISON

*Paterson Laboratories, Christie Hospital & Holt Radium Institute,
Manchester M20 9BX, UK*

SUMMARY

Human cells that lack O^6-alkylguanine DNA alkyltransferase (AT) activity can remove O^6-butylguanine (O^6-nBuG) produced in cellular DNA by exposure to N-n-butyl-N-nitrosourea as determined by radioimmunoassay of enzyme digests of DNA. Fibroblasts from xeroderma pigmentosum (XP) complementation groups A and G that show <5% unscheduled DNA synthesis following exposure to UVC failed to remove O^6-nBuG. Hence it appears that O^6-alkylguanine is repaired in cells that lack AT by a process that is defective in XP cells, presumably nucleotide excision repair. Neither V79 nor V79/79 Chinese hamster cell lines have AT activity and both are able to remove O^6-nBuG from DNA. However, only V79/79 is able to remove O^6MeG, suggesting some substrate specificity of the excision repair process. Comparison of relative levels of O^6-alkylation by N-methyl-, N-ethyl-, N-propyl- and N-n-butyl-nitrosourea indicate that approximately equal levels of O^6-alkylation are produced by equitoxic doses of these agents.

INTRODUCTION

Alkylation of DNA at the O^6 atom of guanine by monofunctional alkylating agents produces an adduct that introduces miscoding errors in transcription and replication of DNA (reviewed by Saffhill *et al.* 1985). The mutagenic and carcinogenic potential of this adduct is reduced in most cells by O^6-alkylguanine DNA alkyltransferase (AT), a protein that transfers the alkyl residue from the O^6-alkylguanine to a cysteine in its polypeptide chain, a process that inactivates the catalytic function (Harris *et al.* 1983). Cells that lack AT are sensitive to the cytotoxic and mutagenic action of mono- and some bi-functional alkylating agents whose primary attack is at O^6-guanine. Included in the latter class are the chloroethyl nitrosoureas, which form DNA crosslinks if the initial O^6-adduct is not repaired (Erickson *et al.* 1980; Scudiero *et al.* 1984a).

Human cells possess a nucleotide excision repair pathway that can excise bulky DNA adducts that are assumed to be similar to the archetypal lesion, the ultraviolet light (u.v.)-induced pyrimidine dimer, in causing topological distortions of the DNA double helix. In this paper we show that O^6-n-butylguanine (O^6-nBuG) can be repaired in cell lines deficient in AT, probably by nucleotide excision repair since xeroderma pigmentosum cells, defective in excision repair of pyrimidine dimers, are also defective in repair of the butyl adduct. We show also that a similar process appears to act on O^6-methylguanine (O^6MeG) in Chinese hamster V79 cells, and present some preliminary data concerning the expression of this activity in clones derived from cell fusion experiments.

MATERIALS AND METHODS

Cell lines

Human fibroblast cell lines, MRC-5 (Jacobs *et al.* 1970) and its simian virus 40 (SV40)-transformed derivative MRC-5 SV2 (Hoschtscha & Holliday, 1983) were kindly donated by Dr S. Fairweather. Xeroderma pigmentosum fibroblasts XP25RO (De Weerd-Kastelein *et al.* 1972) and the SV40-transformed line XP12RO(SV) (Teo *et al.* 1983), which carries the same XP group A mutation, were provided by Dr C. Arlett. These cells were maintained in Eagle's minimal essential medium (MEM) supplemented with 15 % foetal calf serum.

The origins of the cloned Chinese hamster lines V79A-2 and its u.v.-, X-ray- and alkylation-sensitive derivative V79/79-1 have been described previously (Durrant & Boyle, 1982). Both lines were maintained in MEM plus 10 % foetal calf serum. All cell lines were routinely screened for mycoplasma infection (Chen, 1977) and penicillin (100 IU ml^{-1}) and streptomycin (50 μg ml^{-1}) were added to experimental cultures but not to stock cultures.

Alkylation of calf thymus DNA in vitro

Calf thymus DNA was dissolved in 50 mM-potassium phosphate buffer, pH 7·4, at 1 mg ml^{-1} and alkylated by incubation at 37°C for 2 h with appropriate quantities of specific *N*-alkyl-*N*-nitrosoureas.

Radioimmunoassay of O^6-nBuG and O^6MeG

The formation and persistence of O^6-*n*BuG and O^6MeG in DNA were quantified in radio-immunoassay (RIA) systems developed with monoclonal antibodies specific for either of these adducts (Saffhill *et al.* 1982; Wild *et al.* 1983) and validated by comparison with standard radiochromatographic estimations (Wild *et al.* 1983; Saffhill, 1984).

O^6-alkylguanine DNA alkyltransferase activity

Pellets of up to 2×10^8 cells harvested by trypsinization were washed with PBS and resuspended in 1–4 ml buffer containing 50 mM-Tris · HCl, pH 7·8, 1 mM-EDTA and 3 mM-dithiothreitol. The suspensions were exposed to three 10-s pulses at 10 μm peak-to-peak in an MSE sonicator and 87 μg phenylmethylsulphonyl fluoride (PMSF) was added in 10 μl of ethanol. Sonicates were centrifuged at 4°C for 10 min at 20 000 revs min^{-1} in a Coolspin microcentrifuge. The supernatants were assayed for AT activity either by HPLC analysis (Cooper *et al.* 1982) in early experiments, or by a more rapid and sensitive assay that measures the transfer of radioactively labelled methyl groups from substrate DNA to the AT protein (Margison *et al.* 1985). Substrates were prepared (Margison *et al.* 1985) using *N*-[^{3}H]methyl-*N*-nitrosourea ([^{3}H]MNU) of 1·6 or 5·4 Ci mmol^{-1} (HPLC assays) or 5·4 or 30 Ci mmol^{-1} (protein assays).

Dot-blot and Southern analysis

High molecular weight DNA was extracted by a method similar to that of Blin & Stafford (1976). Optical density ratios of 260/280 nm were close to 2·0 and molecular weights in excess of 100 kilobases (kb) were demonstrated by electrophoresis in 0·3 % agarose.

The high molecular weight DNA was nick-translated by *Escherichia coli* DNA polymerase I using [α-^{32}P]dCTP (Rigby *et al.* 1977). Labelled DNA was separated from excess α-^{32}P by centrifugation through a column of Sephadex G50/80. By this method specific activities of $>1 \times 10^8$ cts min^{-1} μg^{-1} DNA were obtained.

Further fractions of high molecular weight DNA were digested with *Eco*RI and the fragments were separated by electrophoresis in 1 % agarose, then transferred from the gel to a nitrocellulose filter by capillary action (Southern, 1975). Filters were baked *in vacuo* for 2 h at 80°C and prehybridized in BLOTTO (Johnson *et al.* 1984). They were then probed with nick-translated MRC-5 total DNA at a stringency of 2×SSC (SSC is 0·15 M-NaCl, 0·015 M-sodium citrate, pH 7·0) at 65°C overnight and processed for autoradiography using AR X-ray film in a cassette with an intensifying screen.

For dot blots, cells were harvested and dilutions of 2×10^7, 7×10^6, 2×10^6, 7×10^5, 2×10^5 and 7×10^4 cells per ml were prepared and 50 μl of each dilution was applied to wells of a Bio-rad dot blot manifold. The cells were lysed by contact with 3MM papers soaked in 0·5 M-NaOH, 1·5 M-NaCl. The filter was neutralized and baked in a vacuum oven for 2 h at 80°C, prehybridized in BLOTTO, then probed with nick-translated DNA as above.

Alkylation schedule and cell survival assay

Exponentially growing monolayers of cells were treated in T30 flasks with *N-n*-butyl-*N*-nitrosourea (BNU) or MNU for 30 min at 37°C as previously described (Boyle *et al.* 1986*b*). Survival of colony-forming ability of human cells was measured in the presence of gamma-irradiated feeder cells (Boyle *et al.* 1986*a*).

RESULTS

With human cells

Alkyltransferase activity. Typical protein dependence curves for AT activity in cell sonicates are shown in Fig. 1, from which specific activities in terms of fmol methyl transferred per mg protein were calculated as 200 (MRC-5), 2 (MRC-5 SV2), 625 (XP25RO) and 0 (XP12RO (SV)). Values less than 10 fmol mg^{-1} protein are

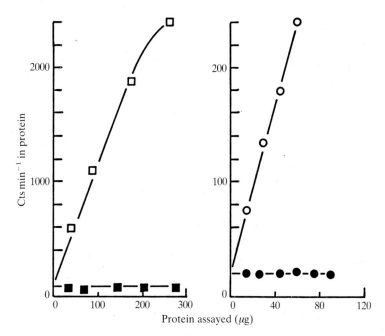

Fig. 1. AT activity in sonicates of human cells. The protein dependence of AT activity was measured by the protein assay (Materials and Methods) using sonicates of MRC-5 (O), MRC-5(SV2) (●), XP25RO (□) and XP12RO(SV) (■). The incubation time was 30 min.

within the range of background determinations. Thus the two SV40-transformed lines are devoid of AT activity, consistent with the findings of others (Day *et al.* 1980; Teo *et al.* 1983).

Formation and persistence of O^6*-nBuG.* The formation of O^6*-n*BuG (O^6*-n*-butylguanine) was measured by RIA immediately after treatment of cells with 4 mM-BNU for 30 min at 37 °C. A value of $13 \cdot 0 \pm 2 \cdot 0 \, \mu$mol adduct per mol guanine was obtained in six experiments, indicating that the rate of alkylation was similar in all cell lines.

Fig. 2 shows the persistence of the adduct during the 24 h following alkylation. The curves indicate that half the adduct was removed from MRC-5 and MRC-5 SV2 in 17 h and 22 h, respectively, whereas the XP lines removed only 5 % in 24 h. Thus normal human cell lines are able to remove O^6*-n*BuG efficiently whereas XP cells are deficient in this ability.

Evidence that AT can repair O^6*-nBuG in vivo.* To determine whether AT can remove O^6*-n*BuG *in vivo* we treated MRC-5 cells with doses of MNU or BNU that resulted in 10 % survival of colony-forming ability. Immediately and at intervals after treatment cells were harvested and residual AT activity in sonicates was

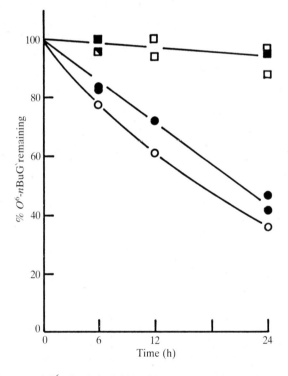

Fig. 2. Persistence of O^6*-n*BuG in DNA of human cells treated with BNU. Cells were exposed to 4 mM-BNU for 30 min, then harvested immediately or incubated in fresh medium for the indicated times. Cellular DNA was extracted and processed as described in Materials and Methods and the O^6*-n*BuG measured by RIA. Points represent individual determinations expressed as a percentage of the amount of adduct induced ($13 \cdot 0 \pm 2 \cdot 0 \, \mu$mol per mol guanine; $n = 6$). Symbols as for Fig. 1.

measured. On the basis of the assumption that transfer of butyl residues would inactivate AT stoichiometrically as in the case of methyl transfer, a decline in AT in cells treated with BNU would imply that AT can accept butyl residues, although this would give no information concerning the origin of the residues, whether from O^6-nBuG or from phosphotriesters.

Table 1 shows that butylation causes an immediate loss of 40 % AT activity from which the cells recover during subsequent incubation. The greater loss of activity seen with MNU may reflect the fact that at equitoxic doses the alkylation of the O^6 atom of guanine by MNU is 50 % greater than by BNU (see Discussion). Alternatively, AT might act more slowly on O^6-nBuG, the abundance of which is reduced by excision repair. Further experiments are in progress to establish the relative stoichiometry of inactivation of AT by these agents and the kinetics of resynthesis.

Relative sensitivity of human cells to killing by monofunctional alkylnitrosoureas. Dose–response curves for survival of colony-forming ability of each of the four human cell lines were determined with N-methyl-, N-ethyl-, N-propyl- and N-n-butyl-N-nitrosoureas. Fig. 3 shows the D_{10} (dose at which 10 % of cells survive to form colonies) values from those curves plotted as a function of alkyl chain length. The extreme sensitivity of SV40-transformed cells to methylation rapidly disappears when higher alkylating species are used. However, an approximately twofold increase in sensitivity due to the presence of the XP mutation is seen with all alkylating agents.

To determine the relative yields of O^6-alkylguanine from different nitrosoureas under standard conditions, calf thymus DNA was alkylated in 50 mM-phosphate and adduct yields were measured by radiochromatography or RIA (Table 2).

With Chinese hamster cells

Repair of O^6MeG and O^6-nBuG in V79, V79/79 and hybrid cells. Previously (Wild *et al.* 1983) we showed that V79/79 cells can repair O^6MeG whereas the parent line V79 cannot. However, both cell lines are capable of repairing O^6-nBuG at about equal rates (Fig. 4). These results are summarized in Table 3, which also shows

Table 1. *Changes in AT activity in MRC-5 cells exposed to equitoxic doses of MNU and BNU*

Agent	Time (h)	AT activity*
Control	—	616
MNU (1·0 mM)†	0	13
	2	7
BNU (3·5 mM)†	0	366
	2	401
	24	565

* fmol methyl transferred per mg protein in cell sonicate.
† D_{10} dose.

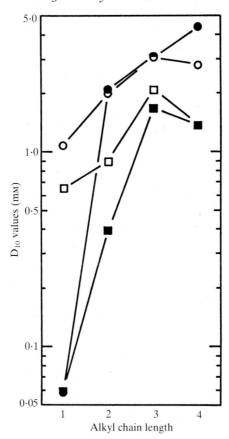

Fig. 3. Effect of alkyl chain length on sensitivity of human cells to cell killing by alkyl nitrosoureas. Survival of colony-forming ability was measured following exposure of each of the cell lines to MNU, ENU, PNU or BNU for 30 min. Survival curves were constructed from the results of duplicate experiments, some of which have been reported previously (Boyle *et al.* 1986*a*). D_{10} values derived from these curves are plotted as a function of the carbon chain length of the alkyl adducts. Symbols as for Fig. 1.

the half-times for removal of O^6MeG, 7-MeG and 3-MeA obtained by radio-chromatography of acid hydrolysed DNA extracted from MNU-treated cells. The differential removal of O^6MeG by the two cell lines is clearly not reflected in the removal of the other adducts, implying that removal of O^6MeG in V79/79 is mediated by a specific pathway and is not the result, for example, of enhanced non-specific nuclease attack.

The repair capacity was also determined by radiochromatography of three hybrid clones from fusion of V79A-2 HPRT$^-$ × V79/79-1 APRT$^-$ (Table 3). Two of the lines were able to repair O^6MeG whilst the other, which had a reduced chromosome complement, behaved like the V79 parent and lacked repair of this adduct.

AT activity in Chinese hamster cell lines. Table 3 also shows the AT activity of the cell lines. All the assays performed on sonicates of Chinese hamster cells gave values

Table 2. *Relative* in vitro *yields of O⁶-alkylguanine*

Alkylating agent	Concentration (mM)	Yield* O^6-alkylG	Total reaction
MNU†·‡	2	48	820§
	4	104	1760§
ENU‡	2	25	260§
	4	44	460§
PNU‡	2	23	
	4	38	
BNU‡·¶	1	7	77
	2	17	173
	4	25	324
	6	41	442

* μmol adduct per mol DNA phosphate.
† Measured by [³H]MNU and/or RIA.
‡ Measured by RIA.
§ Calculated from present results and those of Beranek *et al.* (1980).
¶ Measured by [¹⁴C]BNU and/or RIA.

that were indistinguishable from background even when relatively large amounts of protein were used.

The repair of O⁶MeG in hamster cells lacking AT activity is not unique to V79/79 cells. In order to investigate genetic factors controlling the repair of O^6-alkylguanine a series of fusions was performed between MRC-5 and an HPRT⁻ derivative of V79A-2 with selection in HAT medium plus 1×10^{-5} M-ouabain. The majority of colonies isolated were true hybrids containing human and hamster chromosomes. However, human DNA could not be detected in the colonies listed in Table 3 when tested by dot-blot and Southern analysis using nick-translated MRC-5 DNA as the probe (data not shown). Clones MV34 and MV4.4 contained 32 and 33 chromosomes, respectively, whereas clones MV33, MV7 and MV9 contained either 22 or 24 chromosomes, similar to that of the V79A-2 parent.

None of these clones had AT activity above background, but clones MV34, MV33 and MV4.4 removed 40% or more O^6MeG in 24 h following alkylation with 2 mM-MNU (Table 4).

DISCUSSION

Day *et al.* (1980) have demonstrated host cell reactivation of methylated viral DNA in human cells designated mer^+ (methyl *r*epair), but not in others designated mer^-, which lack AT activity. The finding that some mer^- cells showed more repair replication of cellular DNA than did wild-type cells following exposure to *N*-methyl-*N*′-nitro-*N*-nitrosoguanidine (MNNG), but not after dimethylsulphate (DMS) or u.v., provided the first indication that O^6-alkylguanine might be repaired by a specific excision repair process (Scudiero *et al.* 1984*b*). We have now shown that AT-deficient normal human cells, but not XP cells, are able to remove chemically stable O^6-*n*BuG from their DNA, an observation that strongly suggests that this

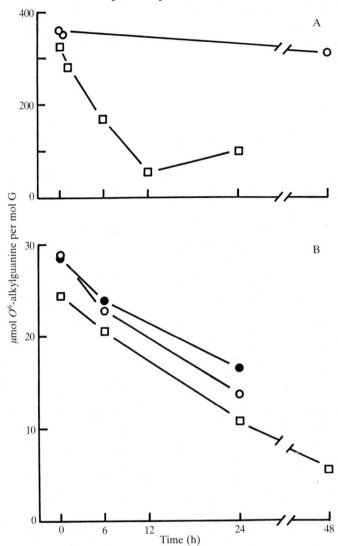

Fig. 4. Persistence of O^6-alkylguanine in Chinese hamster cells. Chinese hamster V79
(○, ●) and V79/79 (□) cells were exposed to MNU or BNU and the relevant O^6 adduct
in the DNA of cells harvested immediately or at intervals after alkylation was determined
by RIA. A is reproduced from Wild *et al.* (1983) by kind permission of IRL Press.
A. 2 mM-MNU for 30 min at 37 °C; B, 4 mM-BNU for 30 min at 37 °C.

adduct is repairable by nucleotide excision repair. This interpretation is supported
by preliminary evidence of O^6-nBudG in the culture medium supernatants of
excision-proficient cells (Saffhill & Boyle, unpublished data). Support for excision
repair of O^6-nBuG also comes from experiments in bacteria where *uvr* and *rec*
mutations have been shown to influence the frequency of site-specific transition
mutations induced in phage ϕX174 by this adduct (Chambers *et al.* 1985). The
possibility that cells of XP complementation group A have a special deficiency in this
respect is ruled out by the finding that group G cells, which are like group A cells in

Table 3. *Repair of alkyl purines and AT activity in Chinese hamster cell lines*

Cell line	Chromosome number	Half-time (h) for removal of alkyl purines					AT activity‡
		7MeG*	3MeA*	O^6MeG*	O^6MedG†	O^6-nBudG†	
V79A-2	21	27	3·6	>100	>100	23	0·0
				>100		28	0·5
V79/79-1	22	17	5·1	20	7	19	0·0
				27			
Hybrids [V79A-2 HPRT⁻ × V79/79-1 APRT⁻]							
AD2	36	20	5·0	>100			0·0
							5·5
AD4	42	16	n.d.§	16			0·0
AD10	40	23	n.d.	53			0·0
							3·8

* By radiochromatography.
† By RIA.
‡ fmol methyl transferred per mg protein.
§ n.d., not determined.

being strongly deficient in nucleotide excision of pyrimidine dimers, are also strongly defective in O^6-nBuG repair (Boyle *et al.* 1986a).

In Chinese hamster cells an alternative pathway to AT also exists, which we tentatively assume to be excision repair. Neither V79 nor V79/79 has detectable AT activity, but both lines are able to repair O^6-nBuG, a situation analogous to MRC-5 SV2 cells. The analogy can be strengthened semi-quantitatively. A dose of $1\,\mathrm{J\,m^{-2}}$ produces about 54000 dimers per cell and 4mM-BNU produces a roughly comparable yield of 26000 O^6-nBuG per cell. At this level of damage, which is non-saturating for excision of dimers, the ratio of excision (strictly, incision) of dimers in normal untransformed human *versus* hamster cells was 5·3 (Collins *et al.* 1982). Human cells transformed by SV40 showed a reduced rate of excision of dimers

Table 4. *Persistence of O^6MeG and AT activity in Chinese hamster cell lines after exposure to polyethylene glycol*

Cell line	Chromosome number	O^6MeG repair*	AT activity†
MRC-5	46	67	200
V79A2 TGʳ	22	1	0
V79/79-1	22	69	0
Fusion-derived clones:			
MV34	32	75	0
MV33	22	43	0
MV4.4	33	40	
MV7	24	0	0
MV9	22	0	

* % Adduct removed in 24 h.
† fmol methyl transferred per mg protein.

(Squires *et al.* 1982) so that it is likely that the ratio of excision of dimers in MRC-5 SV2 *versus* V79 is nearer 1 as is the ratio for excision of O^6-nBuG (Figs 1, 2). V79/79 cells appear somewhat exceptional compared to other Chinese hamster cell lines in that they can also remove O^6MeG by excision repair. As yet we have no data concerning excision of O^6MeG in human cells.

The ability of V79/79 cells to repair O^6MeG was inherited in two hybrid cell lines. We cannot identify the origins of individual chromosomes in these intraspecies hybrids, but because they contain nearly the sum of the chromosome numbers of the parent cells, whilst another hybrid has a reduced chromosome number and lacks O^6 repair, our tentative conclusion is that the repair activity is dominantly expressed in hybrids, suggesting that the lack of repair in V79 is not due to a *trans*-acting repressor.

Repair of O^6MeG was also observed in another group of clones derived from V79 and MRC-5 cells that had been subjected to a polyethylene glycol fusion protocol followed by selection in HAT plus ouabain. No human chromosomes could be distinguished in these cell lines and no human DNA was detected when dot-blot and Southern blot analysis were performed under conditions used to detect single copy genes. Following growth in HAT-free medium for several passages after isolation, all were found to be resistant to 6-thioguanine. Hence it would appear that these lines represent transient HAT-resistant phenocopies of V79 that survived the initial selection. An alternative explanation, that they represent hybrids that rapidly lost all human chromosomes, is possible but unlikely, since they were isolated at a frequency similar to that of true hybrids obtained from the same fusion experiment.

We favour the idea that the appearance of excision activity in these clones may be the result of hypomethylation of deoxycytidine. An analogous situation appears to cause the switching on of HPRT in fusions involving a partner thought to possess a deletion in HPRT because of its resistance to reverse mutagenesis (Watson *et al.* 1972; Bakay *et al.* 1973). In one series of experiments the fusogen was omitted but switching on of the repressed HPRT still occurred when the cells were incubated at high density under fusion conditions (Shin *et al.* 1973). In retrospect, it seems likely that these conditions were favourable for hypomethylation of HPRT, a known cause of activation of this gene (Migeon *et al.* 1985).

Some alkyl adducts, e.g. 3-methylpurines, are cytotoxic because they block DNA synthesis. Others, e.g. 7-MeG and methyl phosphotriesters, appear to have little effect on cell survival. The question whether O^6-alkylguanine is cytotoxic as well as promutagenic is contentious. The fact that *mer*[+] cells with AT activity are more resistant to MNU than are *mer*[−] cells, which lack AT activity, has been considered cogent evidence that O^6MeG is cytotoxic. Furthermore, transfection of the *E. coli* AT gene into V79 cells increased their resistance to alkylating agents (Margison & Brennand, 1987). On the other hand, selective inactivation of AT by incubation of cells with O^6MeG either had no effect (Karran & Williams, 1985) or only slightly increased sensitivity to monofunctional alkylating agents (Dolan *et al.* 1985), but increased sensitivity to bifunctional alkylating agents to a greater extent (Dolan *et al.* 1985). The argument centres upon the uncertainty that it is O^6MeG rather than

Table 5. *Calculation of O^6-alkylguanine molecules per cell per lethal hit*

Cell line	Agent	D_{37} (mM)*	In vitro† yield	In vivo‡ yield	Calculated yield per lethal hit*·†·‡
MRC-5	MNU	0·65	25·0	6500	15 100
	ENU	0·85	11·4		9 000
	PNU	1·4	10·2		13 300
	BNU	1·5	7·0		9 750
MRC-5(SV2)	MNU	0·02	25·0	6500	500
	ENU	1·0	11·4		10 600
	PNU	1·70	10·2		16 100
	BNU	2·10	7·0		13 650
XP25RO	MNU	0·35	25·0	6500	8 100
	ENU	0·40	11·4		4 200
	PNU	0·90	10·2		8 500
	BNU	0·65	7·0		4 200
XP12RO(SV)	MNU	0·02	25·0	6500	500
	ENU	0·15	11·4		1 600
	PNU	0·80	10·2		7 600
	BNU	0·65	7·0		4 200

* D_{37} = dose producing 37 % surviving fraction.

† The yield of μmol O^6-alkylG per mol DNA P per 1 mM-nitrosourea for alkylation of calf thymus DNA under standard conditions (Table 2). The ratio of the value for a particular nitrosourea divided by 7·0, the value for BNU, is given.

‡ The *in vivo* yield of O^6-nBuG ($\pm$s.E.M.) after 4 mM-BNU was $13·0 \pm 2·0\ \mu$mol adduct per mol G. Assuming 2×10^9 G per diploid genome this results in 6500 adduct residues per cell per 1 mM-BNU.

some other lesion produced with a similar dose response that causes lethality. The lack of AT activity in SV40-transformed fibroblasts means that MRC-5 cells are hypersensitive to the effects of MNU, but they show normal sensitivity to higher alkyl nitrosoureas. Against the background of excision deficiency of XP, SV40 transformation also adds an increment of sensitivity towards ENU. However, the excision defect in XP25RO gives an approximately twofold increase in sensitivity towards all the nitrosoureas tested.

According to target theory, the D_{37} dose, at which 37 % of cells survive to form colonies, will on average produce one lethal hit per cell. Knowing the extent of alkylation produced *in vivo* by 4 mM-BNU and the relative extents of O^6-alkylation produced *in vitro* under standard conditions by BNU, PNU, ENU and MNU (Table 2) we can gain an approximate estimate of the numbers of O^6-alkyl residues per lethal hit per cell (Table 5). This shows that the differential sensitivity to MNU associated with SV40 transformation is correlated with a difference of about 15 000 O^6MeG molecules per human cell (Harris *et al.* 1983). In a similar manner the excision defect of XP25RO is associated with a difference of 5000–7000 O^6-alkyl-guanine molecules, independent of alkyl chain length. It is of interest to note that in the AT-proficient, excision-proficient MRC-5 cells D_{37} values for all nitrosoureas are associated with $11\,800 \pm 3300$ O^6-alkylguanine molecules per cell, i.e. an almost constant value despite MNU being 3·6-fold more reactive than BNU at constant dosage and producing proportionately less O^6-alkylation (O^6/N^7 ratio, about $0\cdot1$) compared to other nitrosoureas (O^6/N^7 ratios $= 0\cdot6-0\cdot7$). Therefore, this observation tends to support the idea that O atom, rather than N atom, alkylation is predominant in the cytotoxicity of alkylnitrosoureas. A further inference is that the sparsity of O^6 lesions (on average 1 per 300 kilobase-pairs) makes it unlikely that cytotoxicity results from the overlapping of single strand breaks produced during excision of these lesions.

Bacterial and mammalian AT activities accept a range of alkyl groups including some chloroethyl derivatives. *In vitro*, transfer of methyl is more efficient than that of higher alkyl groups, including butyl (Morimoto *et al.* 1985). We do not know the relative rates of repair *in vivo* of methyl and butyl adducts; however, our present results show that in human cells O^6-nBuG is accepted by AT in a reaction that is rapid compared with that of excision repair. The present rough estimates (Table 5) show that D_{37} doses of MNU produce 15 100 O^6MeG and 9750 O^6-nBuG molecules per cell. Since human cells contain 10000–20000 AT molecules per cell, further work is necessary to determine to what extent the greater loss of AT in MNU-treated cells (Table 1) is due to stoichiometric inactivation of all AT molecules or due to a faster rate of reaction.

We thank Josie Hopkins, Ann Hallam, Gail McGown, Menna Davies, Janice Smith and Brian Keenan for skilled technical help in different phases of this work, and the Cancer Research Campaign for financial support.

REFERENCES

BAKAY, B., GRAF, M., CAREY, S., NISSINEN, E. & NYHAN, W. L. (1973). Re-expression of HPRT activity following cell fusion with polyethylene glycol. *Biochem. Genet.* **16**, 227–237.

BERANEK, D. T., WEISS, C. C. & SWENSON, D. H. (1980). A comprehensive quantitative analysis of methylated and ethylated DNA using high pressure liquid chromatography. *Carcinogenesis* **1**, 595–606.

BLIN, N. & STAFFORD, D. W. (1976). Isolation of high molecular weight DNA. *Nucl. Acids Res.* **3**, 2303–2308.

BOYLE, J. M., MARGISON, G. P. & SAFFHILL, R. (1986a). Evidence for the excision repair of O^6-nButyl deoxyguanosine in human cells. *Carcinogenesis* **7**, 1987–1990.

BOYLE, J. M., SAFFHILL, R., MARGISON, G. P. & FOX, M. (1986b). A comparison of cell survival, mutation and persistence of putative promutagenic lesions in chinese hamster cells exposed to BNU or MNU. *Carcinogenesis* **7**, 1981–1985.

CHAMBERS, R. W., SLEDZIEWSKA-GOJSKA, E., HIRANI-HOJATTI, S. & BOROWY-BOROWSKI, H. (1985). UvrA and recA mutations inhibit a site-specific transition produced by a single O^6-methylguanine in gene G of bacteriophage ϕX174. *Proc. natn. Acad. Sci. U.S.A.* **82**, 7137–7177.

CHEN, T. R. (1977). In situ dectection of mycoplasma contamination by fluorescent Hoechst 33258 stain. *Expl Cell Res.* **104**, 255–264.

COLLINS, A., JONES, C. & WALDREN, C. (1982). A survey of DNA repair incision activities after ultraviolet irradiation of a range of human, hamster and human–hamster hybrid cell lines. *J. Cell Sci.* **56**, 423–440.

COOPER, D. P., O'CONNOR, P. J. & MARGISON, G. P. (1982). Effect of acute doses of 2-acetylaminofluorine on the capacity of rat liver to repair methylated purines in DNA in vivo and in vitro. *Cancer Res.* **42**, 4203–4209.

DAY, R. S., ZIOLKOWSKI, C. H. J., SCUDIERO, D. A., MEYER, S. A., LUBINIECKI, A. S., GIRARDI, A. J., GALLOWAY, S. M. & BYNUM, G. D. (1980). Defective repair of alkylated DNA by human tumor and SV40 transformed human cell strains. *Nature, Lond.* **288**, 724–727.

DE WEERD-KASTELEIN, E. A., KEIJZER, W. & BOOTSMA, D. (1972). Genetic heterogeneity of xeroderma pigmentosum demonstrated by somatic cell hybridisation. *Nature, new Biol.* **238**, 80–83.

DOLAN, M. E., CORSICO, C. D. & PEGG, A. E. (1985). Exposure of HeLa cells to O(6)-alkyl-guanines increases sensitivity to the cytotoxic effects of alkylating agents. *Biochem. biophys. Res. Commun.* **132**, 178–185.

DURRANT, L. G. & BOYLE, J. M. (1982). Potentiation of cell killing by inhibitors of poly (ADP-ribose) polymerase in four rodent cell lines exposed to N-methyl-N-nitrosourea or UV light. *Chem.-Biol. Interact.* **38**, 325–338.

ERICKSON, L. C., BRADLEY, M. O., DUCORE, J. M., EWIG, R. A. G. & KOHN, K. W. (1980). DNA crosslinking and cytotoxicity in normal and transformed human cells treated with antitumor nitrosoureas. *Proc. natn. Acad. Sci. U.S.A.* **77**, 467–471.

HARRIS, A. L., KARRAN, P. & LINDAHL, T. (1983). O⁶-methylguanine-DNA methyltransferase of human lymphoid cells. Structural and kinetic properties and absence in repair deficient cells. *Cancer Res.* **43**, 3247–3252.

HOSCHTSCHA, L. I. & HOLLIDAY, R. (1983). Limited and unlimited growth of SV40 transformed cells from human diploid MRC-5 fibroblasts. *J. Cell Sci.* **63**, 77–99.

JACOBS, J. P., JONES, C. M. & BAILLE, J. P. (1970). Characterisation of a human diploid cell designated MRC-5. *Nature, Lond.* **227**, 168–170.

JOHNSON, D. A., GAUTSCH, J. W., SPORTSMAN, J. R. & ELDER, J. H. (1984). Improved technique utilizing nonfat dry milk for analysis of proteins and nucleic acids transferred to nitrocellulose. *Gene Analyt. Tech.* **1**, 3–8.

KARRAN, P. & WILLIAMS, S. A. (1985). The cytotoxic and mutagenic effects of alkylating agents on human lymphoid cells are caused by different DNA lesions. *Carcinogenesis* **6**, 789–792.

MARGISON, G. P. & BRENNAND, J. (1987). Functional expression of the *Escherichia coli* alkyltransferase gene in mammalian cells. *J. Cell Sci. Suppl. 6*, 83–96.

MARGISON, G. P., COOPER, D. P. & BRENNAND, J. (1985). Cloning of the *E. coli* O⁶-methylguanine and methyl-phosphotriester methyltransferase gene using a functional DNA repair assay. *Nucl. Acids Res.* **13**, 1939–1952.

MIGEON, B. R., JOHNSON, G. G., WOLF, S. F., AXELMAN, J. & SCHMIDT, M. (1985). Hyperexpression of HPRT induced by 5-azacytidine in mouse-human hybrid reactivants. *Am. J. hum. Genet.* **37**, 608–611.

MORIMOTO, K., DOLAN, M. E., SCICCHITANO, D. & PEGG, A. E. (1985). Repair of O⁶-propyl-guanine and O⁶-butylguanine in DNA by O⁶-alkylguanine-DNA-alkyltransferase from rat liver and *E. coli*. *Carcinogenesis* **6**, 1027–1031.

RIGBY, P. W. J., DIECKMANN, M., RHODES, C. & BERG, P. (1977). Labeling deoxyribonucleic acid to high specific activity *in vitro* by nick translation with DNA polymerase I. *J. molec. Biol.* **113**, 237–251.

SAFFHILL, R. (1984). *In vitro* reaction of N-n-butyl-N-nitrosourea and n-butylmethane sulphonate with guanine and thymine bases of DNA. *Carcinogenesis* **5**, 621–625.

SAFFHILL, R., MARGISON, G. P. & O'CONNOR, P. J. (1985). Mechanisms of carcinogenesis induced by alkylating agents. *Biochim. biophys. Acta* **823**, 111–145.

SAFFHILL, R., STRICKLAND, P. T. & BOYLE, J. M. (1982). Sensitive radioimmunoassays for O⁶-nbutyl deoxyguanosine, O²-nbutyl thymidine and O⁴-nbutyl thymidine. *Carcinogenesis* **3**, 547–552.

SCUDIERO, D. A., MEYER, S. A., CLATTERBUCK, B. E., MATTERN, M. R., ZIOLKOWSKI, C. H. J. & DAY, R. S. (1984*b*). Relationship of DNA repair phenotypes of human fibroblasts and tumor strains to killing by N-methyl-N'-nitro-N-nitrosoguanidine. *Cancer Res.* **44**, 961–969.

SCUDIERO, D. A., MEYER, S. A., CLATTERBUCK, B. E., MATTERN, M. R., ZIOLKOWSKI, C. H. J. & DAY, R. S. (1984*a*). Sensitivity of human cell strains having different abilities to repair O⁶-methylguanine in DNA to inactivation by alkylating agents including chloroethyl nitrosoureas. *Cancer Res.* **44**, 2467–2474.

SHIN, S., CANEVA, R., SCHILDKRAUT, C. L., KLINGER, H. P. & SINISCALO, M. (1973). Cells with phosphoribosyltransferase activity recovered from mouse cells resistant to 8-azaguanine. *Nature, Lond.* **241**, 194–196.

SOUTHERN, E. (1975). Detection of specific sequences among DNA fragments by gel electro-phoresis. *J. molec. Biol.* **98**, 503–517.

Squires, S., Johnson, R. T. & Collins, A. R. S. (1982). Initial rates of DNA incision in UV-irradiated human cells. Differences between normal, xeroderma pigmentosum and tumour cells. *Mutat. Res.* **95**, 389–404.

Teo, I. A., Lehmann, A. R., Muller, R. & Rajewsky, M. F. (1983). Similar rate of elimination of O^6-ethylguanine elimination from DNA in normal human fibroblast and xeroderma pigmentosum cell strains not transformed by SV40. *Carcinogenesis* **4**, 1075–1077.

Watson, B., Gormley, I. P., Gardiner, S. E., Evans, H. J. & Harris, H. (1972). Reappearance of murine hypoxanthine guanine phosphoribosyl transferase activity in mouse A9 cells after attempted hybridisation with human cell lines. *Expl Cell Res.* **75**, 401–409.

Wild, C. P., Smart, G. M., Saffhill, R. & Boyle, J. M. (1983). Radioimmunoassay of O^6-methyl deoxyguanosine in DNA of cells alkylated in vitro. *Carcinogenesis* **4**, 1605–1609.

J. Cell Sci. Suppl. 6, 161–176 (1987)
Printed in Great Britain © The Company of Biologists Limited 1987

MOLECULAR EVIDENCE FOR CLEAVAGE OF INTRADIMER PHOSPHODIESTER LINKAGE AS A NOVEL STEP IN EXCISION REPAIR OF CYCLOBUTYL PYRIMIDINE PHOTODIMERS IN CULTURED HUMAN CELLS

M. C. PATERSON[1,2], M. V. MIDDLESTADT[1,2], S. J. MacFARLANE[2], N. E. GENTNER[2], M. WEINFELD[1,2]

[1] *Molecular Genetics and Carcinogenesis Laboratory, Department of Medicine, Cross Cancer Institute, Edmonton, Alberta T6G 1Z2, Canada*

[2] *Health Sciences Division, Chalk River Nuclear Laboratories, Chalk River, Ontario K0J 1J0, Canada*

AND A. P. M. EKER

Biochemical and Biophysical Laboratory, Delft University of Technology, Delft 2628 BC, The Netherlands

SUMMARY

A re-analysis of the metabolic fate of ultraviolet light (u.v.)-induced cyclobutyl pyrimidine dimers in the DNA of dermal fibroblasts from patients with different genetic forms of xeroderma pigmentosum (XP), a rare cancer-prone skin disorder, has provided new insight into the mode of dimer repair in normal human cells. When DNA isolated from post-u.v. incubated cultures was subjected to enzymic photoreactivation (PR) to probe dimer authenticity, single-strand scissions were produced in the damaged DNA of incubated XP group A and D cells, but not in DNA from XP group C cells or normal controls. Since enzymic PR treatment ruptures only the cyclobutane ring, these results suggested that in dimer excision-defective XP group A and D strains, the intradimer phosphodiester bond may have been cleaved without site restoration. Such a cleavage event had not previously been detected; the possibility that this reaction may be an early step in the normal excision-repair process is supported by the observed release of free thymidine (dThd) and its monophosphate (TMP), but not of thymine, upon photochemical reversal of the dimer-containing excision fragments isolated from post-u.v. incubated normal cells. The combined number of dThd and TMP molecules released was equal to ≈80% of the number of dimers photoreversed; for such release to occur, the dimer must both be at one end of an excised fragment and contain an internal phosphodiester break. Taken together, these data lead us to propose a novel model for dimer repair in human cells in which hydrolysis of the intradimer phosphodiester linkage precedes the concerted action of a generalized 'bulky lesion-repair complex' involving conventional strand incision/lesion excision/repair resynthesis/strand ligation reactions.

INTRODUCTION

A milestone in the study of enzymic DNA repair processes in *Homo sapiens* occurred in 1968 with the disclosure by Cleaver that defective repair of ultraviolet light (u.v.)-induced cyclobutyl pyrimidine dimers is an intrinsic property of cultured cells from patients with xeroderma pigmentosum (XP), an autosomal recessive disorder predisposing to sunlight-associated skin cancer (Kraemer, 1983). Aside from demonstrating the crucial role of DNA repair systems in protecting mankind

Table 1. *Pertinent laboratory hallmarks of xeroderma pigmentosum complementation groups**

| Group | u.v. dose reduction factor[†] | Excision repair (% of normal) | |
		UV endonuclease site removal	Repair synthesis
A	18	~0	<5[‡]
B	?[§]	<10	3–7
C	5	15–35	10–25
D	10	~0	20–55
E	1·4	60	40–60
F	5	70	10–20
G	3	~0	<5
H	3	?	30

* Modified from Paterson *et al.* (1984).
† Ratio of 10 % survival fluences (normal strain/XP strain), as measured by post-u.v. colony-forming ability.
‡ One strain, XP8LO, exhibits 30 % of normal repair synthesis.
§ ? = unknown.

against an otherwise intolerable incidence of solar u.v.-induced malignancies, this seminal discovery unmasked a ready (indeed to date the sole) repository of mutant strains for detailed investigation into repair pathways that are operative on pyrimidine dimers in human cells. In the intervening two decades considerable effort has been expended in numerous laboratories in an attempt to define the full range of DNA repair anomalies associated with the syndrome (reviewed by Friedberg *et al.* 1979; Paterson *et al.* 1984; Kraemer, 1983). As indicated in Table 1, cultured dermal fibroblasts from no fewer than 119 genetically unrelated XP donors have now been subjected to one or more assays designed to monitor different parameters of the DNA repair machinery in general and the excision-repair process in particular. The cardinal biochemical anomaly in 98 of these unrelated XP strains (i.e. in ≈80 % of those examined) is a malfunction in the so-called nucleotide mode of excision repair; in this pathway a bulky lesion, such as a pyrimidine dimer, is excised as part of an oligonucleotide; this is followed by insertion of a normal nucleotide sequence using the intact complementary strand as template (Haseltine *et al.* 1980; Sancar & Rupp, 1983; Paterson *et al.* 1984). On the basis of a biochemical complementation test, somatic cell fusion studies have thus far assigned the excision repair-defective XP strains to eight mutually complementing and hence genetically distinct groups designated A–H (see Table 1). The remaining 21 XP strains display a pronounced deficiency in executing postreplication repair (also called replicative or daughter-strand repair), a poorly defined process that is believed to promote base-pairing fidelity when the *de novo* DNA synthesis machinery is called upon to replicate past dimers or other non-coding lesions in template DNA (Cleaver, 1980). Pending the development of a suitable complementation assay, all of these 21 XP strains have been lumped together to form the ninth complementation group, termed variant.

Despite the numerous inquiries into the DNA repair abnormalities in excision repair-defective strains belonging to XP complementation groups A–H (Kraemer, 1983; Paterson *et al.* 1984), little progress has been made in identifying the precise biochemical defect underlying any one of these eight genetic forms of the disease. This poor understanding of the root causes of the different XP genotypes has prompted us to undertake a new line of experimentation, one that promises not only to provide new insight into the basic deficiency in certain XP complementation groups but may also lead to a clearer definition of early reactions in the nucleotide repair mode that are operative on dimers in normal cells. A brief account of our findings to date forms the subject of this chapter.

BACKGROUND OVERVIEW

As a prelude to a description of our investigations into the molecular mechanism of dimer repair in cultured human cells, we shall first outline contemporary models, derived from the more comprehensive and sophisticated experimentation that is possible in simpler prokaryotic systems, of different mechanisms for the nucleotide excision-repair mode. This is followed by a concise account of the relevant hallmarks of excision repair-defective XP strains; this latter review will emphasize group D cells, for it was the bizarre and seemingly inconsistent excision-repair traits of these cells that moved us to initiate the studies reported here.

Models of dimer excision-repair mechanisms

Extensive research into the metabolic fate of pyrimidine dimers in bacteria and bacteriophages has led to the identification of two closely related but distinct mechanisms by which the nucleotide excision-repair mode can operate on these u.v. photoproducts (for particulars, see Haseltine, 1983; Sancar & Rupp, 1983; Friedberg, 1985). While details concerning the innermost workings of these complex multistep systems remain to be elucidated, the basic biochemical reactions in each pathway are reasonably well-defined and candidate enzymes capable of catalysing most of these reactions have been detected and characterized to varying degrees (Friedberg, 1985). The most widely accepted models of the two mechanisms for effecting dimer excision in prokaryotes are diagrammatically illustrated in Fig. 1. The first mechanism, which was discovered in *Escherichia coli* over two decades ago, is thought to consist of the following sequential reactions (see right-hand 'loop' of Fig. 1): (1) the phosphodiester backbone of the dimer-containing strand is incised upstream from (i.e. on the 5′ side of) the lesion by a damage-specific enzyme referred to as 'UV endonuclease'; (2) a second scission is introduced downstream from (i.e. on the 3′ side of) the u.v. photoproduct by an exonuclease, thereby facilitating the release of the lesion as part of a short oligonucleotide (N.B. in *E. coli*, these two cleavage steps may be performed concurrently by the concerted action of the so-called UVRABC excinuclease complex, leading to the liberation of the dimer near the middle of a single-strand fragment 12–13 nucleotides in length; the gap thus formed may be subsequently enlarged by exonucleolytic degradation of the chain in the $5' \rightarrow 3'$ direction); (3) nucleotides complementary to those in the opposite intact strand are then inserted into the resultant gap by the action of a DNA polymerase in an operation termed DNA repair synthesis; and finally (4) the repair patch and the juxtaposed pre-existing material are covalently linked by a DNA ligase, thus completing restoration of the site to normal structure and function (Sancar & Rupp, 1983; Friedberg, 1985).

The second mechanism by which nucleotide excision repair is known to operate on pyrimidine dimers was detected recently in *Micrococcus luteus* and bacteriophage T4-infected *E. coli*. As depicted in the left-hand 'loop' of Fig. 1, the UV endo-nucleases encoded by the *M. luteus* and phage T4 genomes accomplish the initial

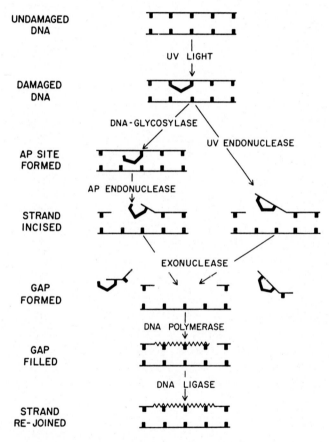

Fig. 1. Popular model for the two distinctive mechanisms by which the nucleotide mode of the excision-repair process is believed to operate on u.v.-induced pyrimidine dimers in different prokaryotic systems. In this model a dimer in either chain of the duplex DNA is excised as part of a short oligonucleotide, as described in the text. The term nucleotide excision distinguishes this mode from a second excision-repair mode called base excision. (In the latter, a carcinogen-damaged or non-conventional base is released in its free form (rather than in the nucleotide, or actually oligonucleotide, form) by the action of a highly specific DNA glycosylase, and the resultant AP site is then restored by sequential strand incision/AP site excision/repair patch insertion/strand ligation reactions (for details, consult Friedberg, 1985).) (From Paterson *et al.* (1985) by permission of Plenum Press.)

strand incision event by performing two concerted reactions: a dimer-recognizing DNA glycosylase activity hydrolyses the N-glycosyl bond between the 5′-pyrimidine member of the dimer and its corresponding deoxyribose, and the phosphodiester linkage 3′ to the newly formed 'denuded' sugar is then severed by an apyrimidinic/apurinic (AP) endonuclease activity (Haseltine *et al.* 1980; McMillan *et al.* 1981; Nakabeppu & Sekiguchi, 1981). In all likelihood, the repair pathway then proceeds to completion in a manner similar to the last three steps in the first mechanism; that is, exonucleolytic cleavage downstream from the dimer (thus releasing a single-strand fragment containing a dimerized pyrimidine-pyrimidylate moiety at its 5′ end), followed by insertion of a repair patch mediated by a DNA polymerase, and restitution of strand continuity at the site by the action of a DNA ligase (Friedberg, 1985).

Properties of excision repair-defective XP strains

In a number of laboratories representative strains of XP complementation groups A–H have been subjected to various assays monitoring different steps in excision repair in an attempt to pinpoint the stage at which blockage occurs in each complementation group. On the basis of these analyses, it appears that all eight XP groups are impaired at the same (strand incision) step (Friedberg *et al.* 1979; Kraemer, 1983; Paterson *et al.* 1984). The simplest interpretation of this unexpected finding is that no fewer than eight loci in the human genome may be involved in effecting the initial step in the nucleotide mode of excision repair. Other, less-direct, explanations cannot be excluded, however; these include the possibility that the action of otherwise normal strand-incising enzymic machinery may be precluded in some XP complementation groups, due to faulty execution of an unidentified pre-incision event(s) (e.g. the likely requirement that at particular structural and/or functional domains in the genetic material of higher organisms, the basic excision-repair process cannot be initiated at a dimer-containing site unless some form of localized processing of chromatin takes place first, such as ridding the DNA of associated histones and other nucleoproteins in order for repair enzymes to gain access to their substrates (Mortelmans *et al.* 1976; Mansbridge & Hanawalt, 1983; Mullenders *et al.* 1984; Karentz & Cleaver, 1986)).

These aforementioned assays also provide a quantitative estimate of the residual repair capacity in a given XP strain relative to that found in normal controls from healthy volunteers (see, e.g., Table 1). As a rule, XP strains assigned to a particular excision repair-defective complementation group carry out a similar amount of residual dimer repair, the particular value being characteristic of that specific group. This generally holds irrespective of which assay is utilized. XP group A cells, for example, appear to be extremely deficient in handling dimers *via* the nucleotide excision-repair mode, as judged by several criteria, including the following two: (1) a negligible ability to effect the removal of dimer-containing sites in DNA during incubation of u.v.-treated cells (detected in retrospect as u.v.-induced sites in extracted cellular DNA which are susceptible to the strand-incising activity of a UV endonuclease present in a crude protein extract of *M. luteus*; such sites are henceforth referred to as UV endonuclease-sensitive sites); and (2) a marked inadequacy in performing u.v.-induced DNA repair synthesis during postirradiation cell incubation (measured as unscheduled DNA synthesis or DNA repair replication) (see Table 1). (NB The first criterion of repair capability, UV endonuclease-sensitive site removal, is presumed to monitor the second (lesion excision) step in the excision-repair process whereas the second, u.v.-induced DNA repair synthesis, is customarily taken as a direct measure of the third (repair patch insertion) step in the pathway (Paterson, 1978).) In some other excision repair-defective XP groups, while a deficiency in dimer repair is evident, an appreciable residual level still remains, especially in groups E and F and, to a lesser extent, group C; this is the case for both repair hallmarks in Table 1.

A notable exception to this general inter-assay consistency when quantifying residual repair capacities of XP strains is readily apparent in group D. Strains belonging to this group are markedly, if not completely, deficient in acting upon UV endonuclease-sensitive sites but, paradoxically, still manage to accomplish a considerable amount of u.v.-induced DNA repair synthesis (see Table 1). (A second exception is evident in group F; in this case, however, the paradox is just the opposite of that seen in group D. That is to say, group F cells appear to be much more efficient at eliminating UV endonuclease-sensitive sites than would be predicted on the basis of their ability to carry out u.v.-stimulated DNA repair synthesis (Table 1).)

Several additional pieces of assorted evidence support the notion that the primary defect in XP group D is distinct from that arising in the other seven XP groups defective in excision repair. Aside from their uniqueness in lacking one of the two AP endonucleases normally present in human cells (Kuhnlein *et al.* 1978), XP group D cells exhibit the peculiar and unprecedented property of being *more* competent than normal cells in performing host-cell reactivation of partially depurinated SV40 DNA (Kudrna *et al.* 1979). Furthermore, in contradistinction to other XP strains harbouring a defect in excision repair, group D strains are much less deficient at excising angelicin adducts from DNA relative to their deficit in removing pyrimidine dimers (Cleaver & Gruenert, 1984).

ACCUMULATION OF MODIFIED DIMER-CONTAINING SITES IN u.v.-TREATED XP GROUP D CELLS

In attempting to resolve the apparent discrepancy in the excision-repair properties of XP group D strains, we first considered a possible trivial explanation, namely that the reported disparity in residual levels of UV endonuclease-sensitive site removal and of u.v.-induced DNA repair synthesis in these mutant strains may be simply due to some unidentified confounding variable in experimental protocol or cell culture methodology in different laboratories. Adopting a common experimental approach for both assays, we therefore monitored normal and XP group D cultures for their relative abilities: (1) to eliminate UV endonuclease-sensitive sites; and (2) to carry out u.v.-stimulated DNA repair replication. Our findings, like those of others (Zelle

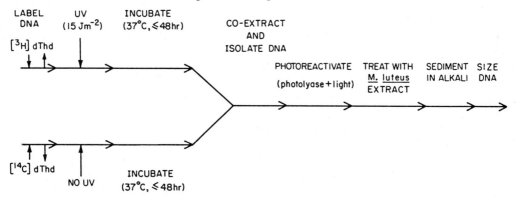

Fig. 2. Experimental protocol developed to assay for aberrant repair of u.v.-induced pyrimidine dimers in XP complementation group D fibroblasts. The treatment schedule was, in effect, identical to that followed in a conventional enzymic assay for dimer measurement (Paterson *et al.* 1981), except for the introduction of an enzymic PR step (to convert any intact dimers that remain back to constitutive monomeric bases *in situ*) before incubation with an *M. luteus* protein extract. The ^{14}C-labelled DNA from sham-irradiated cultures served as an internal control, which permitted correction for non-specific strand breakage arising from the various physical manipulations and enzymic treatments to which the isolated DNA is subjected in performing the assay. (From Paterson (1982) by permission of Elsevier Biomedical Press.)

& Lohman, 1979; Kraemer *et al.* 1975) indicated that XP group D cells do indeed perform a significant amount of u.v.-induced repair synthesis even though they are markedly impaired in recognizing dimer-containing sites in their DNA (for details, see Paterson, 1982).

Having ruled out inter-laboratory differences in experimental conditions as a viable explanation for the peculiar excision-repair hallmarks reported for XP group D strains, an alternative working hypothesis was constructed. This hypothesis was based on the supposition that, on exposure to u.v. radiation, XP group D cells may operate on only a portion of the dimer-containing sites in their DNA, and do so in a faulty manner, somehow replacing pre-existing nucleotides (presumably down-stream from the dimer) with new ones, thus accounting for the residual level of DNA repair synthesis, while at the same time failing to excise the photoproduct and thereby explaining the continued presence of all UV endonuclease-sensitive sites initially introduced. We further postulated that the insertion of such a putative 'pseudo-repair patch' could conceivably be accompanied by some structural modification in the immediate vicinity of the dimer. As a test of this postulate, we re-investigated the metabolic fate of dimer-containing sites in XP group D fibroblasts by measuring the photoreactivability (a well-documented diagnostic probe of dimer authenticity; Harm, 1976) of such sites in naked DNA isolated from normal and XP group D strains as a function of cell incubation time after exposure to germicidal light (far u.v. of chiefly 254 nm wavelength). A flow chart of our protocol is shown in Fig. 2. In short, after co-incubation for appropriate periods, parallel ^{3}H-labelled, u.v.-irradiated and ^{14}C-labelled, unirradiated cultures of each strain were lysed; the cellular DNAs were then co-extracted, subjected to enzymic photoreactivation (PR) treatment (using extensively purified *Streptomyces griseus* photolyase, an enzyme that binds to a dimer-containing site and, upon absorption of fluorescent light energy, ruptures the cyclobutane ring *in situ*, thereby regenerating the two constitutive pyrimidines (Sutherland, 1978)), and incubated with an *M. luteus* protein extract containing UV endonuclease activity. It was reasoned that this succession of treatments might uncover dimer-containing sites that may have been metabolically altered *in vivo* so as to render them refractory to restoration by enzymic PR but still susceptible to the strand-incising action of UV endonuclease. Finally, the incidence of single-strand nicks arising in the u.v.-damaged DNA as a result of this course of treatments, and hence the frequency of modified dimer-containing sites present in this DNA at the time of cell lysis, was quantified by the classical technique of velocity sedimentation in alkaline sucrose gradients (see Paterson *et al.* 1981).

In keeping with our reasoning, the protocol disclosed the appearance of strand breaks in the DNA of u.v.-irradiated and incubated group D (XP2NE and XP3NE) strains that was not observed in an identically treated normal (GM38) strain (for a fuller description of these initial results, see Paterson, 1982). As revealed in Fig. 3, the incidence of these peculiar strand breaks in the DNA of XP2NE cells reached a plateau value of ≈ 8 per 10^8 daltons by 48 h post-u.v. irradiation. This maximal yield was equivalent to approximately 15 % of the number of dimers acted upon by normal cells in the same 48-h period and was similar in relative magnitude to the residual

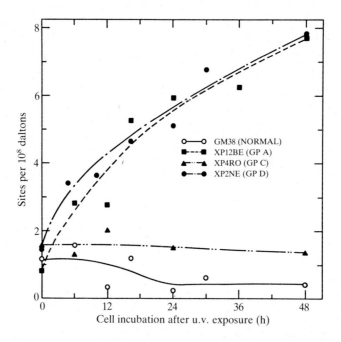

Fig. 3. Incidence of novel sites, as detected by subsequent enzymic PR and *M. luteus* extract treatments, accumulating in the DNA of normal and XP strains as a function of postirradiation time. The experimental protocol was as outlined in Fig. 2. Each datum point is the mean of multiple determinations (s.e. < 15 %). (From Paterson *et al.* (1985) by permission of Plenum Press.)

amount of u.v.-induced DNA repair replication ($\approx$15–20% of normal) occurring in this same XP group D strain. These comparable residual levels of modified dimers and of DNA repair synthesis in group D strains are consistent with the notion that the sites of presumed dimer modification and pseudo repair-patch insertion are one and the same.

Accumulation of such novel sites in cellular DNA in response to germicidal light was not restricted to XP strains belonging to complementation group D. These same sites also appeared at similar rates in XP group A (XP12BE) fibroblasts; on the other hand, group C (XP4RO), E or variant fibroblasts responded like normal controls (Fig. 3; Paterson, 1982; Paterson *et al.* 1985).

In a later, more extensive experimental series, we ran controls in which the *M. luteus* extract treatment was omitted from the protocol of Fig. 2, expecting to observe no strand breaks, even though the modified sites presumably still accumulated. Much to our surprise, however, essentially the same incidence of strand breaks was detected in XP group A and D cells (but not in normal or XP group C cells) when the purified DNA from postirradiation-incubated cultures were subjected to enzymic PR treatment alone. This unforeseen observation led us to modify our original postulate: we supposed that during incubation of u.v.-damaged XP group A or D fibroblasts, the intradimer phosphodiester linkage at certain dimer-containing sites may be severed and that at such modified sites the physical continuity of individual polynucleotide chains is then maintained solely by the cyclobutane bridge joining the two pyrimidine bases. In group A fibroblasts, the excision-repair process very probably aborts at this stage, given that these cells carry out little, if any, DNA repair synthesis in response to u.v. treatment (Table 1). In contrast, in group D cells, cleavage of the intradimer phosphodiester bond is possibly accompanied by insertion of an abnormal repair patch judging from, as pointed out above, the excellent correlation between residual levels of altered dimer-containing sites and of u.v.-stimulated repair synthesis in such cells.

The relationship between the accumulation of modified dimer-containing sites in u.v.-treated group D strains and the other abnormalities peculiar to these XP strains upon sustaining other forms of genotoxic damage (see Background Overview) must await further experimentation.

PHOTORELEASE OF THYMIDINE AND THYMIDINE MONOPHOSPHATE FROM DIMER-CONTAINING EXCISION FRAGMENTS ISOLATED FROM u.v.-DAMAGED NORMAL CELLS

In contemplating the significance of the modified dimer-containing sites discovered in XP group A and D strains, it struck us that the occurrence of such sites may not necessarily be solely confined to these mutant strains. Instead, their accumulation in XP group A and D fibroblasts may represent a piling up of an intermediate reaction product (because of a defect in a later reaction) that is usually seen only transiently in normal human fibroblasts. If so, then our inability to detect these modified dimer-containing sites in u.v.-damaged normal cells may have been simply because such 'internally incised dimer' structures, once formed, are immediately released from genomic DNA by subsequent reactions that rapidly follow in a fully functional excision-repair system. It was further reasoned that if: (1) hydrolysis of the intradimer phosphodiester linkage does indeed occur in normal cells before excision of an oligonucleotide containing a thymine (Thy)-thymine (T<>T) dimer, for example; and (2) the lesion is located at one end of the excision fragment, then exposure of isolated excision products to a photochemically reversing (i.e. cyclobutane ring-rupturing) fluence of germicidal light should lead to the release of either free thymidine (dThd) or thymidine monophosphate (TMP). (It was assumed that one member of the dimer pair was not present as Thy, since such a structure would have been detected by La Belle & Linn (1982) in an earlier study designed to determine whether the excision of dimers in human cells is initiated by rupture of an intradimer N-glycosyl bond.)

To test the validity of this reasoning, we adopted an experimental protocol that was very similar to that used by La Belle & Linn (1982). This approach takes advantage of the fact that the dimer-containing excision products, which are released from genomic DNA by the enzymic excision-repair machinery, are retained within human fibroblasts for prolonged periods ($\geqslant 24$ h); consequently, these excision fragments can be easily recovered in the trichloroacetic acid (TCA)-soluble fraction of cell cultures that have been incubated for appropriate times after u.v. irradiation. In brief, our experimental approach went as follows: normal (GM38) fibroblast cultures, whose DNA had been prelabelled with [^{3}H]dThd, were exposed to 40 J m^{-2} of germicidal light, incubated for 24 h, and then lysed in 5 % TCA; finally, the dimer-containing excision fragments were isolated from the acid-soluble fraction and subjected to a six-step procedure utilizing reverse-phase high performance liquid chromatography (HPLC) in order to determine the quantitative relationship between Thy, dThd and TMP released, on the one hand, and Thy-containing dimers monomerized by a photoreversing fluence (5·5 kJ m^{-2}) of germicidal light, on the other. The general protocol and rationale behind inclusion of each of the six steps are outlined in Fig. 4. It should be noted that in our chromatographic system, TMP migrates in the same region as the excision products and hence its presence has to be measured indirectly as the increase in dThd following bacterial alkaline phosphatase digestion.

The results obtained for each of the six steps in Fig. 4 are summarized in Table 2. It can be seen that exposure of isolated excision fragments to photoreversing irradiation did not result in an elevated level of free Thy, thus confirming the earlier observation of La Belle & Linn (1982). This inability to demonstrate the liberation of Thy upon photochemical monomerization of Thy-containing dimers in excision products strongly implies that hydrolysis of N-glycosyl bonds on dimerized pyrimidines is not an intermediate reaction in the excision-repair pathway operating on these photoproducts in human cells.

In contrast to the findings for Thy, 3·0 % (5·3 %−2·3 %) and 5·4 % (5·9 %−0·5 %) of the total TCA-soluble radioactivity was released as dThd and TMP, respectively, by the dimer-photoreversing treatment. The same u.v. fluence reduced

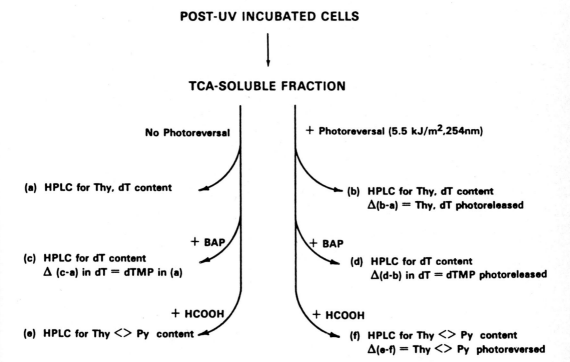

Fig. 4. Six-step protocol developed to assay for dimer photoreversal-induced liberation of Thy, dThd and TMP from TCA-soluble excision fragments isolated from u.v.-irradiated $(40\,J\,m^{-2})$ and incubated (24 h) normal human (GM38) fibroblasts. (From Weinfeld *et al.* (1986) by permission of the American Chemical Society.)

Table 2. *HPLC analysis of TCA-soluble material from post-u.v. $(40\,J\,m^{-2})$-incubated (24 h) normal human (GM38) fibroblasts for release of Thy, dThd and TMP upon photochemical reversal of pyrimidine dimers in isolated excision fragments**

				Free DNA constituents (% of total acid-soluble counts)			Excised dimers (% of total acid-soluble counts)	
Step†	Photoreversal	BAP	HCOOH	Thy	dT	TMP	T$\diamond$T	U$\diamond$T§
a	−	−		12·3	2·3			
b	+	−		9·1	5·3			
c	−	+			2·8	(0·5)		
d	+	+			11·2	(5·9)		
e	−		+	35·8			25·2	23·8
f	+		+	58·2			14·6	13·4

*From Weinfeld *et al.* (1986).
† Step in six-stage procedure for characterization of excision fragments, as depicted in Fig. 4.
‡ Minus, sham-treated; plus, treated; no entry, not done. BAP, bacterial alkaline phosphatase.
§ Derived from C$\diamond$T dimers by deamination as a result of formic acid hydrolysis.

the fraction of the total acid-soluble radioactivity in Thy-containing (i.e. T<>T and cytosine-thymine (C<>T)) dimers from 49 % (25·2 %+23·8 %) to 28 % (14·6 %+ 13·4 %), indicating that 21 % of the radioactivity was photochemically converted

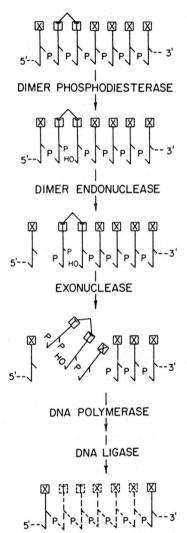

Fig. 5. Proposed model for the nucleotide mode of excision repair acting on cyclobutyl pyrimidine dimers induced in the DNA of cultured human fibroblasts by u.v. irradiation. For simplicity, only the dimer-containing strand of the duplex DNA macromolecule is shown. The notable difference between this model and that for prokaryotic systems in Fig. 1 is that here the first reaction in the multi-step repair pathway is mediated by a putative pyrimidine dimer-DNA phosphodiesterase instead of a dimer-DNA glycosylase, as in *M. luteus* and phage T4-infected *E. coli*, or an excinuclease complex, as in uninfected *E. coli*. In the scheme outlined here, the dimer is located at the 5′ end of the excised oligonucleotide and the scission of the intradimer phosphodiester bond yields 3′-P and 5′-OH end groups. Our current data are equally compatible with other schemes, and the precise location and nature of the breaks leading to dimer removal must await further experimentation. (From Paterson *et al.* (1985) by permission of Plenum Press.)

from dimers to monomers. Assuming that: (1) the genomic DNA was uniformly labelled with [^{3}H]dThd; (2) dimers were situated at one end of the isolated excision fragments; and (3) the intradimer phosphodiester bond was hydrolysed, then each photochemically monomerized T$\Longleftrightarrow$T or C$\Longleftrightarrow$T dimer should have released, on average, half of its radioactivity as dThd and/or TMP. Hence it follows that a maximum of 50 % of the tritium in photomonomerized Thy-containing dimers, that is, 10·5 % of the total acid-soluble counts, would be liberated as dThd and/or TMP. The actual amount of labelled dThd plus TMP recovered (8·4 %) was equal to ≈80 % of this theoretical maximum, and we therefore estimate that about 80 % of the Thy-containing dimers have their intradimer phosphodiester linkage ruptured and are also located at one extremity of the excised oligonucleotides. This shortfall in dThd/TMP molecules photoliberated compared to dimers photoreversed can be easily rationalized if, for example, the second aforementioned assumption (namely, that the dimer lies at one end of the excision fragment) does not hold for every fragment: photochemical monomerization of a dimer with at least one adjoining nucleotide on both sides would generate two shorter pieces, each at least dimeric in number. Whatever the reason, our assumptions nonetheless seem to fit the vast majority of the excision fragments.

CONCLUDING REMARKS

It is not feasible at present to ascertain whether the dimer-containing excision products from postirradiation-incubated normal fibroblasts have remained unaltered in length from the time of their enzymic excision from genomic DNA until their isolation from cultures at 24 h after u.v. treatment. It is, of course, entirely possible that the excision pieces examined by us first undergo postexcision degradation by non-specific endogenous nucleases. In fact, exonuclease activities operative on single-stranded DNA have been detected in various human sources (Doniger & Grossman, 1976; Friedberg *et al.* 1977). These and related nucleases may routinely catalyse the release of nucleotides from one or both termini of the excision fragments, until presumably becoming arrested upon encountering the distorted conformation of the oligonucleotides in the neighbourhood of the dimer. The average size of the repair patch inserted in the gap left by the release of a dimer is estimated to be approximately 20–25 nucleotides (derived from fig. 5 of Smith & Okumoto, 1984); consequently, the average size of the dimer-containing oligonucleotides at the time of their release from genomic DNA may well be considerably larger than their estimated size (≈3·7 nucleotides; Weinfeld *et al.* 1986) at the time of their isolation. (Alternatively, of course, this repair patch size may represent subsequent gap-widening.) Along a similar vein, our findings do not rule out the possibility that the apparent scission of the intradimer phosphodiester linkage in excision products may also be a consequence of postexcision exonucleolytic activity. We regard this latter possibility to be unlikely, however, in view of our evidence that the excision-repair apparatus appears to malfunction in XP group A and D fibroblasts after this intradimer incision reaction has occurred.

Instead, our preferred interpretation of the data presented here is that hydrolysis of the phosphodiester linkage between dimerized pyrimidines may constitute the initial reaction in the nucleotide excision-repair process that acts on these u.v. photoproducts in human dermal fibroblasts. In this model, which is illustrated in Fig. 5, the postulated role of the putative pyrimidine dimer–DNA phosphodiesterase activity is to induce a conformational change at the dimer-containing site such that the site becomes a substrate for a generalized 'bulky lesion-repair complex', possibly similar to the UVRABC excinuclease complex, which appears to recognize a vast array of chemically diverse lesions in the DNA of *E. coli* (Sancar & Rupp, 1983). Breakage of the intradimer phosphodiester bond may also serve to relieve conformational stress introduced by the rigid cyclobutane ring fusing the two pyrimidines, thus restoring hydrogen bonding of nearby base-pairs in the double-stranded helix and, by so doing, presumably increasing the fidelity of *de novo* DNA synthesis on a u.v.-damaged template. According to our model, cleavage of the intradimer phosphodiester linkage is then followed by classical strand incision/lesion excision/patch insertion/strand ligation steps. This scheme for dimer repair in human cells differs from that postulated for *M. luteus* and phage T4-infected *E. coli* in that the *N*-glycosyl bond on the 5′-pyrimidine of the dimer remains intact. It should be noted, however, that in both models the *same* phosphodiester bond is cut; in human cells this is proposed as the initial step, whereas in the two bacterial systems depyrimidination of the sugar moiety on the 5′ side of this bond is believed to precede the intradimer backbone-incision reaction.

This work was supported primarily by Atomic Energy of Canada Limited and the US National Cancer Institute through contract NO1-CP-21029 (Basic) with the Clinical and Environmental Epidemiology Branches, NCI, Bethesda, MD, and in the final stages of the study by a Heritage Medical Scientist award to M.C.P. and a Postdoctoral Fellowship to M.W. from the Alberta Heritage Foundation for Medical Research. We are grateful to V. Bjerkelund for secretarial assistance.

REFERENCES

CLEAVER, J. E. (1980). DNA damage, repair systems and human hypersensitive diseases. *J. environ. Path. Toxicol.* **3**, 53–68.

CLEAVER, J. E. & GRUENERT, D. C. (1984). Repair of psoralen adducts in human DNA: Differences among xeroderma pigmentosum complementation groups. *J. invest. Derm.* **82**, 311–315.

DONIGER, J. & GROSSMAN, L. (1976). Human correxonuclease. Purification and properties of a DNA repair exonuclease from placenta. *J. biol. Chem.* **251**, 4579–4587.

FRIEDBERG, E. C. (1985). *DNA Repair*, pp. 141–322. New York: W. H. Freeman & Co.

FRIEDBERG, E. C., COOK, K. H., DUNCAN, J. & MORTELMANS, K. (1977). DNA repair enzymes in mammalian cells. *Photochem. Photobiol. Rev.* **2**, 263–322.

FRIEDBERG, E. C., EHMANN, U. K. & WILLIAMS, J. I. (1979). Human diseases associated with defective DNA repair. *Adv. Radiat. Biol.* **8**, 85–174.

HARM, H. (1976). Repair of UV-irradiated biological systems: Photoreactivation. In *Photochemistry and Photobiology of Nucleic Acids*, vol. 2 (ed. S. Y. Wang), pp. 219–263. New York: Academic Press.

HASELTINE, W. A. (1983). Ultraviolet light repair and mutagenesis revisted. *Cell* **33**, 13–17.

HASELTINE, W. A., GORDON, L. K., LINDAN, C. P., GRAFSTROM, R. H., SHAPER, N. L. & GROSSMAN, L. (1980). Cleavage of pyrimidine dimers in specific DNA sequences by a pyrimidine dimer DNA-glycosylase of *M. luteus*. *Nature, Lond.* **285**, 634–641.

KARENTZ, D. & CLEAVER, J. E. (1986). Excision repair in xeroderma pigmentosum group C but not group D is clustered in a small fraction of the total genome. *Mutat. Res.* **165**, 165–174.

KRAEMER, K. H. (1983). Heritable diseases with increased sensitivity to cellular injury. In *Update: Dermatology in General Medicine* (ed. T. B. Fitzpatrick, A. Z. Eisen, K. Wolff, I. M. Freedberg & K. F. Austen), pp. 113–142. New York: McGraw-Hill Book Co.

KRAEMER, K. H., COON, H. G., PETINGA, R. A., BARRETT, S. F., RAHE, A. E. & ROBBINS, J. H. (1975). Genetic heterogeneity in xeroderma pigmentosum: Complementation groups and their relationship to DNA repair rates. *Proc. natn. Acad. Sci. U.S.A.* **72**, 59–63.

KUDRNA, R. D., SMITH, J., LINN, S. & PENHOET, E. E. (1979). Survival of apurinic SV40 DNA in the D complementation group of xeroderma pigmentosum. *Mutat. Res.* **62**, 173–181.

KUHNLEIN, U., LEE, E., PENHOET, E. E. & LINN, S. (1978). Xeroderma pigmentosum fibroblasts of the D group lack an apurinic DNA endonuclease species with a low apparent K_m. *Nucl. Acids Res.* **5**, 951–960.

LA BELLE, M. & LINN, S. (1982). *In vivo* excision of pyrimidine dimers is mediated by a DNA *N*-glycosylase in *Micrococcus luteus* but not in human fibroblasts. *Photochem. Photobiol.* **36**, 319–324.

MANSBRIDGE, J. N. & HANAWALT, P. C. (1983). Domain-limited repair of DNA in ultraviolet irradiated fibroblasts from xeroderma pigmentosum complementation group C. In *Cellular Responses to DNA Damage* (ed. E. C. Friedberg & B. N. Bridges), pp. 195–207. New York: Alan R. Liss.

McMILLAN, S., EDENBERG, H. J., RADANY, E. H., FRIEDBERG, R. C. & FRIEDBERG, E. C. (1981). *denV* gene of bacteriophage T4 codes for both pyrimidine dimer-DNA glycosylase and apyrimidinic endonuclease activities. *J. Virol.* **40**, 211–223.

MORTELMANS, K., FRIEDBERG, E. C., SLOR, H., THOMAS, G. & CLEAVER, J. E. (1976). Defective thymine dimer excision by extracts of xeroderma pigmentosum cells. *Proc. natn. Acad. Sci. U.S.A.* **73**, 2757–2761.

MULLENDERS, L. H. F., VAN KESTEREN, A. C., BUSSMAN, C. J. M., VAN ZEELAND, A. A. & NATARAJAN, A. T. (1984). Preferential repair of nuclear matrix associated DNA in xeroderma pigmentosum complementation group C. *Mutat. Res.* **141**, 75–82.

NAKABEPPU, Y. & SEKIGUCHI, M. (1981). Physical association of pyrimidine dimer DNA glycosylase and apurinic/apyrimidinic DNA endonuclease essential for repair of UV-damaged DNA. *Proc. natn. Acad. Sci. U.S.A.* **78**, 2742–2746.

PATERSON, M. C. (1978). Use of purified lesion-recognized enzymes to monitor DNA repair *in vivo*. *Adv. Radiat. Biol.* **7**, 1–53.

PATERSON, M. C. (1982). Accumulation of non-photoreactivable sites in DNA during incubation of UV-damaged xeroderma pigmentosum group A and D cells. *Prog. Mutat. Res.* **4**, 183–192.

PATERSON, M. C., GENTNER, N. E., MIDDLESTADT, M. V., MIRZAYANS, R. & WEINFELD, M. (1985). Hereditary and familial disorders linking cancer proneness with abnormal carcinogen response and faulty DNA metabolism. In *Epidemiology and Quantitation of Environmental Risk in Humans from Radiation and Other Agents* (ed. A. Castellani), pp. 235–267. New York: Plenum Press.

PATERSON, M. C., GENTNER, N. E., MIDDLESTADT, M. V. & WEINFELD, M. (1984). Cancer predisposition, carcinogen hypersensitivity, and aberrant DNA metabolism. *J. cell. Physiol. Suppl.* **3**, 45–62.

PATERSON, M. C., SMITH, B. P. & SMITH, P. J. (1981). Measurement of enzyme-sensitive sites in UV- or γ-irradiated human cells using *Micrococcus luteus* extracts. In *DNA Repair: A Laboratory Manual of Research Procedures*, vol. 1, part A (ed. E. C. Friedberg & P. C. Hanawalt), pp. 99–111. New York: Marcel Dekker, Inc.

SANCAR, A. & RUPP, W. D. (1983). A novel repair enzyme: UVRABC excision nuclease of *Escherichia coli* cuts a DNA strand on both sides of the damaged region. *Cell* **33**, 249–260.

SMITH, C. A. & OKUMOTO, D. S. (1984). Nature of DNA repair synthesis resistant to inhibitors of polymerase α in human cells. *Biochemistry* **23**, 1383–1391.

SUTHERLAND, B. M. (1978). Enzymatic photoreactivation of DNA. In *DNA Repair Mechanisms* (ed. P. C. Hanawalt, E. C. Friedberg & C. F. Fox), pp. 113–122. New York: Academic Press.

WEINFELD, M., GENTNER, N. E., JOHNSON, L. D. & PATERSON, M. C. (1986). Photoreversal-dependent release of thymidine and thymidine monophosphate from pyrimidine dimer-containing DNA excision fragments isolated from ultraviolet-damaged human fibroblasts. *Biochemistry* **25**, 2656–2664.

ZELLE, B. & LOHMAN, P. H. M. (1979). Repair of UV-endonuclease-susceptible sites in the 7 complementation groups of xeroderma pigmentosum A through G. *Mutat. Res.* **62**, 363–368.

J. Cell Sci. Suppl. 6, 177–189 (1987)
Printed in Great Britain © The Company of Biologists Limited 1987

MOLECULAR STUDIES ON THE NATURE OF THE REPAIR DEFECT IN ATAXIA-TELANGIECTASIA AND THEIR IMPLICATIONS FOR CELLULAR RADIOBIOLOGY

P. G. DEBENHAM, M. B. T. WEBB, N. J. JONES AND R. COX

Division of Cell and Molecular Biology, MRC Radiobiology Unit, Chilton, Oxon, UK

SUMMARY

We have utilized DNA transfer and recombinant DNA techniques to probe DNA double-strand break repair in the human ionizing radiation-sensitive genetic syndrome ataxia-telangiectasia (A-T). Using restriction enzyme-generated double-strand breaks in the coding sequence of a selectable gene we have detected a significantly greater frequency of mis-repair of such breaks in a permanent A-T cell line compared with cell lines of normal radiosensitivity. This mis-repair in A-T can plausibly explain many of the clinical features of the disease but was insufficiently detailed to address the broad problem of DNA repair mechanisms relevant to ionizing radiation-induced damage. To extend these observations of DNA double-strand break mis-repair we have now applied this type of repair assay to novel, *de novo* induced mammalian X-ray-sensitive cell lines and to appropriate *Escherichia coli* mutants. In both cellular systems we have now found some equivalence to the A-T repair defect. In particular, studies on one *E. coli* mutant have provided evidence suggesting an involvement of a topoisomerase activity in DNA double-strand break mis-repair, which may be relevant to the biochemical defect in A-T.

INTRODUCTION

Mechanisms of DNA repair may be resolved through detailed *in vitro* studies on cellular mutant phenotypes that, through specific DNA-repair deficiencies, exhibit increased sensitivity to DNA damaging agents. However, it is a paradox that while radiobiological studies were instrumental in the discovery of cellular repair phenomena we now have a much better understanding of the mechanisms of repair of ultraviolet light-induced and chemically induced DNA damage than for the repair of damage induced by ionizing radiation. However, the advent of recombinant DNA techniques and their application to radiobiological problems is now beginning to change this rather dismal picture and in this chapter we summarize recent studies in this laboratory on radiosensitive cellular mutant phenotypes that may provide new insights into mechanisms of DNA repair following exposure to ionizing radiation.

While the main focus of these studies has been the resolution of the putative DNA-repair defect in ionizing radiation-sensitive cells cultured from patients with the human genetic disorder, ataxia-telangiectasia, we also discuss recent unpublished data from studies on other mammalian and bacterial radiosensitive mutants that contribute to our understanding of the problem.

ATAXIA-TELANGIECTASIA, CLINICAL AND CELLULAR DESCRIPTION

Ataxia-telangiectasia (A-T) is an autosomal recessive genetic disease presenting during childhood and associated with a number of progressive and variable clinical features. These include neuromotor dysfunction associated with neuronal loss (Sedgewick, 1982), variable immunodeficiency (Waldman, 1982), susceptibility to sinopulmonary infection, a high frequency of lymphoreticular neoplasia and other cancers (Spector *et al.* 1982), high levels of serum alpha fetoprotein (Waldman & McIntire, 1972), cytogenetic abnormalities of peripheral lymphocytes (Taylor, 1982) and the development of occulocutaneous telangiectases. Following adverse reaction of A-T patients to conventional radiotherapy (see Cox, 1983), cells cultured from a large number of patients have been shown to be hypersensitive to ionizing radiation both in terms of induction of chromosome aberration (Taylor, 1982) and loss of reproductive capacity (Taylor *et al.* 1975; Cox *et al.* 1978).

The observation that A-T cells are specifically sensitive to ionizing radiation has been the motivation for many cellular and biochemical studies, which have attempted to relate A-T radiosensitivity to specific defects in DNA metabolism. Many of these studies have been collated (Bridges & Harnden, 1982), forming an important resource for those interested in the broad aspects of the disorder. However, the published studies on A-T present a wide array of observed cellular phenomena with little consensus as to the underlying deficiency present. Thus whilst there is general agreement as to its clinical description, research into A-T has not provided a coherent biochemical or enzymic definition to explain the cellular radiosensitivity, let alone the clinical features of the disease. Of the various radiobiological characteristics described there is, though, broad agreement on a few cellular manifestations of the genetic defect in A-T. These include the lack of post-irradiation DNA synthesis delay that is observed in cells of normal radiosensitivity, a normal sensitivity to ultraviolet light (u.v.), relatively less hypersensitivity to ionizing radiations of increasing linear energy transfer (LET), and a hypersensitivity to strand breaking agents such as bleomycin (Lehmann, 1982; Cox, 1982). Most importantly, and central to an understanding of A-T, following exposure to ionizing radiation A-T cells rejoin the radiation-induced DNA double-strand breaks as efficiently as normal cells (Lehmann, 1982). This characteristic distinguishes A-T cells from other reported mutants hypersensitive to ionizing radiation, which are defective in the rejoining of ionizing radiation-induced DNA double-strand breaks, i.e. *xrs* mutants of hamster cells (Kemp *et al.* 1984), *rad*52 series mutants in yeast (Resnick & Martin, 1976) and *ror*A and *rec*N mutants in *Escherichia coli* (Glickman *et al.* 1971; Picksley *et al.* 1984). DNA double-strand breaks constitute a major genetic lesion with great potential to cause recombination, rearrangements and deletions. An inability to repair such lesions, which are directly induced in the cellular DNA by ionizing radiation, would logically explain a cellular sensitivity to ionizing radiation. Such a repair defect would not necessarily also impart increased sensitivity to u.v. as DNA double-strand breaks are not efficiently induced directly by u.v. With one possible exception (Coquerelle & Weibezahn, 1981) A-T cells are quantitatively proficient in DNA double-strand break repair and, overall, it would seem that a gross deficiency in such repair cannot account for A-T radiosensitivity.

DNA DOUBLE-STRAND BREAK REPAIR FIDELITY IN A-T CELLS

Accepting that DNA double-strand breaks are one of the most potent DNA lesions induced by ionizing radiation it is important to recognize that the conventional assay techniques (see Lehmann, 1982) used to measure repair of such lesions are only quantitative and cannot comment on the fidelity of the whole process. We have developed an experimental approach that enables the fidelity of DNA double-strand break repair to be examined using DNA-mediated gene transfer techniques (Cox *et al.* 1984). This approach involves the introduction of a unique double-strand break in the coding sequence of a dominant, selectable gene (*gpt*) in a normally circular DNA vector by restriction enzyme cleavage. For more detailed studies an improved vector (Fig. 1) was subsequently developed and utilized (unpublished observations). This DNA vector contains a linked second dominant and selectable gene (G418^R), which acts as a control for DNA transfer and gene expression. If the double-strand break introduced into the non-selected gene is not rejoined or is rejoined incorrectly within the recipient cell, then the gene will be inactive and this can be detected by subsequent lack of expression of its function. Because this technique involves gene transfer it is unfortunately not easily applied to primary diploid cell cultures and is most suitable for transformed cell lines (Debenham *et al.* 1984). However, using this approach we have shown that the one transformed A-T cell line available at present (AT5BIVA) rejoins DNA double-strand breaks with at least a 7- to 10-fold higher frequency of mis-repair than cell lines of normal ionizing radiation sensitivity (Cox *et al.* 1984, 1986).

The simplest explanation for such a mis-repair phenotype is that either exonuclease activities, which degrade DNA at double-strand breaks, are over-produced, or factors that normally protect DNA termini from such degradation are altered or lacking. Since no gross elevation of exonuclease activity was detected in crude extracts of A-T cells (data not shown) some form of deficiency of protection of DNA termini seems a more plausible explanation. In order to explain the observed misrepair in A-T it was postulated that an equilibrium exists, at DNA termini, between their correct rejoining and exonuclease degradation (Cox *et al.* 1986). In normal cells a protein factor/complex is present that concomitantly protects the termini from exonuclease activity and promotes their correct repair. In A-T cells the equilibrium is perturbed by the alteration or deficiency of this factor so that sequence information is more frequently lost at the termini of a DNA double-strand break than in the wild-type cell. Consequently, a variable, and unpredictable, degree of mis-repair may occur at any DNA double-strand break.

Are the data on which this hypothesis is based sufficient to warrant further extrapolation and experimentation? Given the controversy surrounding the basis of the A-T disorder it is important to establish whether the results obtained are due to

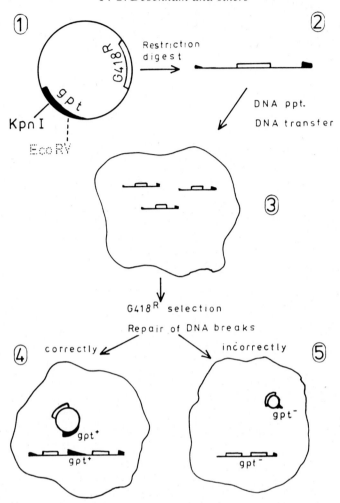

Fig. 1. A schematic representation of the experimental protocol to detect mis-repair of a restriction enzyme generated break in the *gpt* gene. (1) pPM17 or pPMHSV16 DNA is linearized by cleavage with either *Kpn*I or *Eco*RV. Both enzymes cut in the coding sequence of the *gpt* gene. (2) The linearized DNA is precipitated onto a monolayer of cells *via* a standard calcium phosphate procedure. (3) Cells that take up the DNA (often more than one copy) and express the undamaged G418^R gene will grow in medium containing G418. The transferred DNA is eventually integrated into the cellular DNA, so that on division each daughter cell will contain the same configuration of this DNA. (4) If during the growth in G418 medium the cell has correctly joined one or more *Kpn*I (or *Eco*RV) sites the cell will have an active *gpt* gene and survive in XHATM medium (Mulligan & Berg, 1981). (5) If no correct joining of *Kpn*I (or *Eco*RV) sites occurs the recipient cell will not have an active *gpt* gene and this cell (colony) will die in XHATM medium.

experimental artefacts or are essentially unique to the single transformed A-T cell line investigated to date. Since DNA transfer remains a poorly understood cellular process it may be that this component of the experimental approach is the most vulnerable to misinterpretation.

The most relevant aspect of the DNA transfer process that might artefactually produce an apparent mis-repair phenotype in AT5BIVA is the copy number of linearized vector taken up/maintained by the normal and A-T cell lines. A single functional copy of the *gpt* gene (the gene cleaved in the mis-repair assay) is sufficient to provide resistance to the selective medium (XHATM; Thacker *et al.* 1983). Other things being equal, a cell receiving or maintaining many copies of the linearized vector has a higher probability of producing at least one correctly repaired gene than does a cell receiving a small number of copies. Southern blot analysis in the initial study showed that for both the normal cell line used (MRC5CV) and AT5BIVA only a small number of copies of the vector (pPM17) were found per cell (Cox *et al.* 1986). We have subsequently found that the effective copy number can be further reduced to approximately one by using a vector (pPMHSV16) with a more efficiently expressed $G418^R$ gene such that one copy of this gene is now sufficient to establish cell growth in the initial selection following DNA transfer (Fig. 1; and unpublished observations). The $G418^R$ gene in pPM17 is not sufficiently active to achieve this in single copy. Consequently, using pPMHSV16 more transformant colonies are obtained for a given amount of transferred DNA reflecting successful growth of cells with only one or a few copies of the vector. With pPM17 such colonies were only poorly viable in the selective medium. Therefore, the use of the pPMHSV16 vector should more precisely monitor the nature of repair of each restriction enzyme generated break.

It was found that monitoring the rejoin fidelity of the *Kpn*I site using pPMHSV16 as the vector, rather than pPM17, reduces the observed wild-type (MRC5CV) fidelity from ≈88% to 56% as scored by *gpt* expression in transformed colonies (Table 1). It has long been known that transferred DNA molecules are subject to DNase activity during DNA transfer and, for MRC5CV, the effect on DNA transfer of reducing the copy number of transferred DNA molecules it consistent with the activity of degradative cellular processes (Goebel & Schiess, 1975; Wigler *et al.* 1978). Although the same non-specific degradative events appear to be occurring in AT5BIVA, reducing the observed fidelity from ≈12% to ≈6%, the differential rejoin fidelity, thought to be a consequence of the genetic defect in A-T, is still clearly apparent. As far as is known MRC5CV and AT5BIVA were not derived from related donors, and numerous other genetic differences may also exist that influence the observed repair fidelity. Additional genetic differences may also derive from the establishment of these cell lines by simian virus 40 (SV40) infection. However, other unrelated SV40 established cell lines of normal sensitivity to ionizing radiation were examined in earlier studies and found to give results comparable to MRC5CV (Cox *et al.* 1984, 1986). Given the increased sensitivity of using the pPMHSV16 vector the repair of the *Kpn*I site in XP12ROSV cells has been re-examined. These cells are extremely sensitive to u.v. (from a patient with xeroderma pigmentosum, group A; see Lehmann & Stevens, 1980) but have a normal response to ionizing radiation. In these studies it was found that although the fidelity of rejoining of double-strand breaks in XP12ROSV cells was not quite as high as in MRC5CV cells, it was more than five times higher than in AT5BIVA cells (Table 1). The difference between

MRC5CV and XP12ROSV responses may merely reflect a natural range in repair fidelity that, on the basis of the data presented here and elsewhere, remains clearly distinct from the A-T cell response.

DNA DOUBLE-STRAND BREAK MIS-REPAIR IN OTHER IONIZING RADIATION-SENSITIVE CELL LINES

Unfortunately, no other suitable A-T cell lines are available at present to extend and confirm the results obtained with AT5B1VA. However, it is still possible to ask whether the mis-repair defect observed in AT5BIVA is unique or whether parallels exist in other equivalent mutant cell lines. A-T cells clearly differ from other published examples of ionizing radiation-hypersensitive cell lines in being competent at rejoining ionizing radiation induced DNA double-strand breaks. Recently, however, four new X-ray-sensitive mammalian sub-lines derived from V79 hamster cells have been isolated in this laboratory (Jones, unpublished), which have been placed in different genetic complementation groups from previously characterized mutants such as the *xrs* series (Jeggo & Kemp, 1983) or EM 9.1/EM 7.2 (Thompson *et al.* 1980). The vector-mediated assay has recently been applied to two of these mutant lines that show the greatest sensitivity to ionizing radiation, at present termed A4 (D_{37} for X-rays of 134 rad) and C11 (D_{37} for X-rays of 141 rad), as well as their parental cell line V79 (D_{37} for X-rays of 420 rad (Jones, unpublished). Obviously these cell lines all have the same genetic background and allow for more direct comparison than is possible in the available human cell lines. It appears that in hamster cell lines (V79 and CHO; Table 2, and unpublished observations) there is a

Table 1. *Rejoin fidelity of linearized pPM17 and pPMHSV16 vectors* $(XHATM^R/G418^R)$

Recipient cell line	Transforming DNA species	Total G418^R transformants tested	gpt^+	gpt^-	Fidelity of rejoining (%)
	pPM17				
MRC5CV	KpnI	138*	122	16	88·4
AT5BIVA	KpnI	161*	20	141	12·4
	pPMHSV16				
MRC5CV	KpnI	59	33	26	56·0
AT5BIVA	KpnI	32	2	30	6·2
XP12ROSV	KpnI	289	99	190	34·2

KpnI-linearized pPM17 or pPMHSV16 DNA was transferred into MRC5CV, AT5BIVA and XP12ROSV cells by a standard calcium phosphate precipitation procedure (see Cox *et al.* 1984). The cells used are SV40 transformed lines derived from human diploid cultures of MRC5 (normal), AT5BI (classical A-T) and XP12RO (classical XP). After 2 days expression the cells were plated into medium containing 1 mg ml^{-1} G418. Colonies arising after 2 weeks incubation were noted and then refed with XHATM medium, which selects for *gpt* gene expression (Mulligan & Berg, 1981). Colony degeneration over the next 7 days was indicative of an absence of a functional *gpt* gene.
* Data pooled from Cox *et al.* (1986).

Table 2. *Rejoin fidelity of linearized pPMHSV16 vector (XHATM^R/G418^R)*

No. of experiments	Cut site	V79	A4	C11
4	*Kpn*I	0·10 (±0·03)	0·021 (±0·006)	0·10 (±0·01)*
2	*Eco*RV	0·17 (±0·04)	0·05 (±0·02)	0·20†

*Kpn*I or *Eco*RV linearized pPMHSV16 DNA was transferred into V79 hamster cells and two mutant derivative cell lines A4 and C11 that are hypersensitive to ionizing radiation. In each of a number of independent experiments the fidelity of rejoining of the restriction site was assessed by detecting *gpt* function in G418-resistant transformants (see Table 1 for protocol). Numbers represent the fraction of *gpt*$^+$ colonies observed. Numbers in parenthesis indicate the s.D. between experiments.

* Data from 2 experiments.

† Data from one experiment only.

high degree of degradative action at the *Kpn*I site in the *gpt* gene such that only approximately 10 % of transformed colonies have functional *gpt* gene activity. The *Kpn*I site is clearly subject to mis-repair in rodent cells, which may mask mis-repair in the ionizing radiation-sensitive cell lines. However, even with this possible masking effect A4 mutant cells have been reproducibly observed to show a fivefold reduction in the fidelity of rejoining at the *Kpn*I site compared with V79 (Table 2). This mis-repair phenomenon in A4 cells is also apparent if the *gpt* gene is linearized by *Eco*RV, which cleaves DNA to leave flush termini as opposed to the 3′ single-strand ends generated by *Kpn*I. Thus A4 shows a mis-repair that appears independent of the nature of the DNA double-strand break and is therefore qualitatively equivalent to the defect in human A-T cells. Conversely, C11 and *xrs*1 (data not shown), although hypersensitive to ionizing radiation, are both as proficient as their parental cell lines at correctly rejoining restriction-enzyme-generated DNA double-strand breaks at the *Kpn*I and *Eco*RV sites. This is particularly intriguing as *xrs*1 has been shown to be quantitatively defective in the repair of ionizing radiation-induced DNA double-strand breaks (Kemp *et al.* 1984).

Comparable studies have also been undertaken in three *E. coli* mutants specifically sensitive to ionizing radiation (*ror*A, *ror*B and *rec*N). Mutants *ror*A and *rec*N have been shown to be defective in the rejoining of ionizing radiation-induced double-strand breaks (Glickman *et al.* 1971; Picksley *et al.* 1984). Mutant *ror*B is a newly isolated mutant that appears to be competent with respect to ionizing radiation-induced DNA double-strand break repair (unpublished observations). Unlike *ror*A and *rec*N, *ror*B appears to rejoin erroneously restriction enzyme-generated double-strand breaks in plasmid DNA molecules (unpublished observations). Thus *ror*B, like AT5BIVA appears to be an example of a cellular phenotype showing competent rejoining of ionizing radiation-induced DNA double-strand breaks, but which may involve low fidelity in the rejoining process. Conversely, *ror*A and *rec*N competently rejoin the simple, restriction enzyme-generated double-strand breaks in plasmid DNA molecules (unpublished observations). Thus *ror*B, like AT5BIVA appears to be an example of a cellular phenotype showing competent rejoining of ionizing radiation-induced DNA double-strand breaks, but which may involve low fidelity in the rejoining process. Conversely, *ror*A and *rec*N competently rejoin the simple, restriction enzyme-generated double-strand breaks with high fidelity but are deficient in processes rejoining a proportion of perhaps more complex ionizing radiation-induced strand breaks. It is possible that the hamster mutant *xrs*1 falls into a repair class similar to that of *ror*A and *rec*N.

THE CAUSE OF DNA DOUBLE-STRAND BREAK MIS-REPAIR

Is there any clue as to the nature of the two distinct repair pathways (described above) acting on DNA double-strand breaks? The pathway deficient in *E. coli* mutants *ror*A and *rec*N, and also yeast mutants *rad*52 etc., has for some time been argued to involve DNA recombination, which in turn had been thought to be the major process by which cells repair ionizing radiation-induced DNA double-strand breaks (Resnick, 1976).

It has been shown here that a second aspect of DNA double-strand break repair that influences the fidelity of the process is also of major importance. A possible clue to the enzymic basis of this mis-repair was the surprising finding (unpublished observations) that two independently isolated *ror*B mutants appear hypersensitive to coumermycin A1, a specific antagonist of the ATP binding subunit (*gyr*B) of *E. coli* gyrase (Sugino *et al.* 1978). Mutants *ror*A and *rec*N have a normal sensitivity to coumermycin A1. *ror*B has a normal sensitivity to nalidixic acid, which inhibits the other subunit of *E. coli* gyrase (*gyr*A; Gellert *et al.* 1977), suggesting *ror*B has a very specific change in its gyrase activity. However, the gene complementing *ror*B is not *gyr*B and the cloned *gyr*B gene when introduced into *ror*B cells does not complement the radiation sensitivity of this mutation. Thus, it seems that the *ror*B gene codes for a factor that alters gyrase activity.

The similarities to *ror*B, with respect to a DNA mis-repair phenotype associated with a hypersensitivity to ionizing radiation, prompted the question whether A-T cells and A4 cells also showed alteration in a topoisomerase type II activity that is the equivalent of gyrase in *E. coli*. Novobiocin is the mammalian equivalent of coumermycin A1, inactivating topoisomerase type II in mammalian cells (Gellert, 1981), although it is thought to affect other cellular processes without acting *via* topoisomerase (e.g. see Gottesfield, 1986). Fig. 2 shows the novobiocin sensitivities of MRC5CV, XP12ROSV and AT5BIVA cells and it is clear that AT5BIVA is considerably more novobiocin-sensitive than MRC5CV and XP12ROSV. These analyses of pooled data were made difficult by the form of the cellular response to novobiocin and there was some variation in individual sensitivity with different drug preparations, nevertheless there were consistent differences in each experiment between AT5BIVA and MRC5CV/XP12ROSV.

In a similar study the novobiocin sensitivities of V79, A4 and C11 cells were also studied . V79 hamster cells were also found to show rapidly decreasing survival with increasing novobiocin concentration. V79 and mutant C11 did not differ markedly in their response to the drug but mutant A4 was clearly more novobiocin-sensitive (unpublished observations). Thus a consistent picture may be arising in which the repair of at least some DNA double-strand breaks involves or is associated with a topoisomerase type II activity and, overall, the studies summarized here imply that alteration in this process may cause the relevant breaks to be repaired with relatively low fidelity.

THE MIS-REPAIR OF DNA DOUBLE-STRAND BREAKS AND THE A-T CELLULAR PHENOTYPE

The hypothesis that DNA double-strand breaks are subjected to a high frequency of mis-repair in A-T cells appears from the data discussed here to receive plausible support from studies with other radiosensitive cellular phenotypes. How well does this model of repair specifically address the many aspects of the A-T phenotype? The hypothesis can explain, in broad terms, cellular radiosensitivity in A-T and some aspects of the more readily understood clinical features of this genetic disorder (Cox *et al.* 1986). Since the misrepair is focussed on DNA double-strand breaks it is also consistent with the lack of A-T hypersensitivity to u.v. exposure and the majority of base-damaging chemical agents. A-T cells are sensitive to bleomycin (see Lehmann, 1982), which directly induces single-strand breaks and thus could also produce double-strand DNA breaks from two closely adjacent scissions. While it is therefore possible to consider the repair of DNA double-strand breaks as the principal

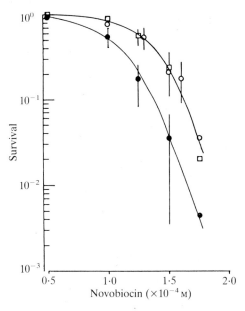

Fig. 2. MRC5CV (○), XP12ROSV (□) and AT5BIVA (●) cells were plated into 10 ml medium in 9-cm diam. dishes containing freshly prepared novobiocin at the indicated concentrations. The cells were incubated, without change, for 14 days at 37 °C. Viable colonies were scored relative to the viability of the cells in medium without novobiocin (approx. 36 %, 45 % and 40 %, respectively). Data presented are the means (±S.D., shown by bars, where appropriate) from three experiments for MRC5CV and AT5BIVA, and two experiments for XP12ROSV.

biochemical problem for A-T, some degree of deficiency in single-strand break repair fidelity is quite feasible and, indeed, cytogenetic observation of excessive chromatid type damage in irradiated G_0 A-T cells lends some support to this possibility (Taylor, 1982).

A-T cells are relatively less hypersensitive to radiations of increasing linear energy transfer (high LET; Cox, 1982). High LET radiation tracks (e.g. those of α particles) will tend to cause greater deposition of energy in a greater number of bases on traversal of a DNA duplex. This increase in energy depositions must result in many more chemical interactions such that sites of high LET radiation-induced double-strand breaks will probably be associated with aberrant chemical structures such as intra- and inter-strand cross-linking, and cross-linking with neighbouring proteins. In a genetic context, many of these lesions in both normal and A-T cells may be irreparable through simple rejoining, and only recombination processes would be expected to reconstitute the sequence information lost from both DNA strands. Consequently, as the inherent 'rejoinability' of lesions decreases so the difference in sensitivity of A-T cells to such radiation, relative to normal cells would decrease. Thus the mis-repair hypothesis can accommodate the reduced relative sensitivity of A-T cells to radiations of increasing LET (Cox, 1982).

However, it is not so obvious why a perturbation of the fidelity of DNA double-strand break repair should influence the progression of the cell through the DNA replicative cycle. Following exposure to ionizing radiation, normal cells do not continue their progression through S-phase but are delayed for several hours (Houldsworth & Lavin, 1980; Edwards & Taylor, 1980). In A-T cells S-phase progression is not greatly influenced by such exposure. It is thought that one DNA strand break is enough to stop initiation of DNA synthesis within a group of replicons (Povirk, 1977). However, as the majority of A-T cell strains are both kinetically and quantitatively competent at rejoining double-strand breaks the explanation does not seem to be related to the repair or mis-repair of DNA double-strand breaks. An explanation may be found by examining possible subsidiary rôles of the cellular factor that is deficient in A-T. Is it possible, for example, that following irradiation normal DNA replication is retarded by the consumption of a factor normally required at sites of DNA double-strand break repair? To address this possibility we need to know what factors are associated with the process of correctly rejoining DNA double-strand breaks. The previous section of this chapter has indicated the possibility that a topoisomerase type II activity could have an important rôle in this process.

TOPOISOMERASE TYPE II ACTIVITY AND CELLULAR RADIOSENSITIVITY

Topoisomerase type II function in cells is thought to regulate the conformation of the DNA by generating transient DNA double-strand breaks and passing the double helix through them, thus altering the degree of supercoiling of the DNA. During this process the DNA termini are protected (Morrison & Cozzarelli, 1981). It is thus tempting to speculate that a topoisomerase type II activity, particularly its termini protection activity, is in some way utilized to promote the correct rejoining of DNA double-strand breaks including those produced by ionizing radiation. In A-T cells it is this function that would be altered. However, the mutation in A-T may not reside in a gene structurally constituting topoisomerase type II activity and may act indirectly. On this point it may be relevant that the gene complementing the *E. coli* *ror*B mutation is neither *gyr*A or *gyr*B (the only genes required to determine structurally DNA gyrase activity in *E. coli*).

The increased sensitivity to novobiocin/coumermycin of the ionizing radiation-sensitive mammalian and bacterial cells characterized by a mis-repair of DNA double-strand breaks may reflect a defective and potentially lethal process in the cell normally counteracted or controlled by topoisomerase type II activity. Recently, and independently, it has been shown that AT5BI cells are hypersensitive to the drug VP16, which mediates its cellular toxicity *via* the topoisomerase type II enzyme (P. J. Smith, personal communication). These studies reveal that the intrinsic sensitivity of topoisomerase type II activity to VP16 in A-T cells is normal but that accumulation of VP16-induced DNA damage is greater than normal. Thus a process controlling topoisomerase type II enzyme level or its sites of activity is proposed to be altered.

The A-T defect, as discussed earlier, causes a lack of control of DNA replication following exposure to ionizing radiation. In the normal cell, replication is curtailed for several hours following exposure but the mechanism involved is unknown. The unwinding of condensed (supercoiled) chromosome structures by topoisomerase II (and possibly also topoisomerase I) probably plays an essential role in replicative DNA synthesis. It may therefore be argued that in normal cells, following exposure to ionizing radiation, topoisomerase type II activity is temporarily consumed in protecting DNA double-strand breaks from degradation, thus hindering initiation of new replicons. In A-T cells the factor interacting with topoisomerase type II activity for DNA double-strand break repair is defective, allowing continued availability of topoisomerase type II activity for the de-condensation of replicons. On this basis it may be expected that, in A-T, DNA replication will continue without major perturbation in the presence of radiation-induced DNA strand breaks.

CONCLUSION

We present initial evidence and arguments to link three phenomena: a cellular hypersensitivity to ionizing radiation, an ability to rejoin DNA double-strand breaks but with a higher frequency of misrepair than comparable wild-type cells, and a sensitivity to novobiocin that may reflect altered topoisomerase type II function. The evidence is derived from cell lines hypersensitive to ionizing radiation from *E. coli*, hamsters and humans. Taken together, these data highlight DNA double-strand breaks as crucial lesions induced by ionizing radiation and link their correct repair with post-irradiation DNA synthesis through regulation of topoisomerase II enzyme activity. Further to this, we suggest that the primary genetic defect in radiosensitive cells from human ataxia-telangiectasia patients may reside in the regulation of topoisomerase II activity.

This study is supported in part by C.E.C. Contract 816-144-UK.

REFERENCES

BRIDGES, B. A. & HARNDEN, G. D. (1982). *Ataxia-telangiectasia*. New York: Wiley.

COQUERELLE, T. M. & WEIBEZAHN, K. F. (1981). Rejoining of DNA double strand breaks in human fibroblasts and its impairment in one ataxia-telangiectasia and two Fanconi strains. *J. supramolec. Struct. cell. Biochem.* **17**, 369–376.

COX, R. (1982). A cellular description of the repair defect in ataxia-telangiectasia. In *Ataxia-telangiectasia* (ed. B. A. Bridges & D. G. Harnden), pp. 141–153. New York: Wiley.

COX, R. (1983). *In vivo* and *in vitro* radiosensitivity in ataxia-telangiectasia. In *The Biological Basis of Radiotherapy* (ed. G. G. Steel, G. E. Adams & M. J. Peckham), pp. 105–112. Oxford: Elsevier.

COX, R., DEBENHAM, P. G., MASSON, W. K. & WEBB, M. B. T. (1986). Ataxia-telangiectasia: A human mutation giving high frequency misrepair of DNA double strand scissions. *Molec. Biol. Med.* **3**, 229–244.

COX, R., HOSKING, G. P. & WILSON, J. (1978). Ataxia-telangiectasia: Evaluation of radio-sensitivity in cultured skin fibroblasts as a diagnostic test. *Archs Dis. Childh.* **53**, 386–390.

COX, R., MASSON, W. K., DEBENHAM, P. G. & WEBB, M. B. T. (1984). The use of recombinant DNA plasmids for the determination of DNA repair and recombination in cultured mammalian cells. *Br. J. Cancer* **49**, Suppl. VI, 67–72.

DEBENHAM, P. G., WEBB, M. B. T., MASSON, W. K. & COX, R. (1984). DNA-mediated gene transfer into human diploid fibroblasts derived from normal and ataxia-telangiectasia donors: parameters for DNA transfer and properties of DNA transformants. *Int. J. Radiat. Biol.* **45**, 525–536.

EDWARDS, M. J. & TAYLOR, A. M. R. (1980). Unusual levels of (ADP-ribose)$_n$ and DNA synthesis in ataxia-telangiectasia cells following γ-irradiation. *Nature, Lond.* **287**, 745–747.

GELLERT, M. (1981). DNA topoisomerases. *A. Rev. Biochem.* **50**, 879–910.

GELLERT, M., MIZUUCHI, K., O'DEA, M. H., ITOH, T. & TOMIZAWA, J.-I. (1977). Nalidixic acid resistance: A second genetic character involved in DNA gyrase activity. *Proc. natn. Acad. Sci. U.S.A.* **74**, 4772–4776.

GLICKMAN, B. W., ZWENK, H., VAN SLUIS, C. A. & RORSCH, A. (1971). The isolation and characterisation of an X-ray sensitive ultraviolet-resistant mutant of Escherichia coli. *Biochim. biophys. Acta* **254**, 144–154.

GOEBEL, W. & SCHIESS, W. (1975). The fate of bacterial plasmid DNA in mammalian cells. *Molec. gen. Genet.* **138**, 213–223.

GOTTESFIELD, J. M. (1986). Novobiocin inhibits RNA polymerase III transcription *in vitro* by a mechanism distinct from DNA topoisomerase II. *Nucl. Acids Res.* **14**, 2075–2087.

HOULDSWORTH, J. & LAVIN, M. F. (1980). Effect of ionising radiation on DNA synthesis in ataxia-telangiectasia. *Nucl. Acids Res.* **8**, 3709–3720.

JEGGO, P. A. & KEMP, L. M. (1983). X-ray sensitive mutants of Chinese hamster ovary cell line. Isolation and cross-sensitivity to other DNA-damaging agents. *Mutat. Res.* **112**, 313–327.

KEMP, L. M., SEDGWICK, S. G. & JEGGO, P. A. (1984). X-ray sensitive mutants of Chinese hamster ovary cells defective in double-strand break rejoining. *Mutat. Res.* **132**, 189–196.

LEHMANN, A. R. (1982). The cellular and molecular responses of ataxia-telangiectasia cells to DNA damage. In *Ataxia-telangiectasia* (ed. B. A. Bridges & D. G. Harnden), pp. 83–101. New York: Wiley.

LEHMANN, A. R. & STEVENS, S. (1980). A rapid procedure for measurement of DNA repair in human fibroblasts and for complementation analysis of xeroderma pigmentosum cells. *Mutat. Res.* **69**, 177–190.

MORRISON, A. & COZZARELLI, N. R. (1981). Contacts between DNA gyrase and its binding site on DNA: Features of symmetry and asymmetry revealed by protection from nucleases. *Proc. natn. Acad. Sci. U.S.A.* **78**, 1416–1420.

MULLIGAN, R. C. & BERG, P. (1981). Selection for animal cells that express the *Escherichia coli* gene coding for xanthine-guanine phosphoribosyltransferase. *Proc. natn. Acad. Sci. U.S.A.* **78**, 2072–2076.

PICKSLEY, S. M., ATTFIELD, P. V. & LLOYD, R. G. (1984). Repair of DNA double strand breaks in *Escherichia coli* K12 requires a functional *recN* product. *Molec. gen. Genet.* **195**, 267–274.

POVIRK, L. F. (1977). Localisation of inhibition of replicon initiation to damaged regions of DNA. *J. molec. Biol.* **114**, 141–151.

RESNICK, M. A. (1976). The repair of double strand breaks in DNA: A model involving recombination. *J. theor. Biol.* **59**, 97–106.

RESNICK, M. A. & MARTIN, P. (1976). The repair of double strand breaks in the nuclear DNA of *Saccharomyces cerevisiae* and its genetic control. *Molec. gen. Genet.* **143**, 119–129.

SEDGEWICK, R. P. (1982). Neurological abnormalities in ataxia-telangiectasia. In *Ataxia-telangiectasia* (ed. B. A. Bridges & D. G. Harnden), pp. 23–35. New York: Wiley.

SPECTOR, B. D., FILIPOVITCH, A. H., PERRY, G. S. & KERSER, J. H. (1982). Epidemiology of cancer in ataxia-telangiectasia. In *Ataxia-telangiectasia* (ed. B. A. Bridges & D. G. Harnden), pp. 103–138. New York: Wiley.

SUGINO, A., HIGGINS, N. P., BROWN, P. O., PEEBLES, C. L. & COZZARELLI, N. R. (1978). Energy coupling in DNA gyrase and the mechanism of action of novobiocin. *Proc. natn. Acad. Sci. U.S.A.* **75**, 4838–4842.

TAYLOR, A. M. R. (1982). Cytogenetics of ataxia-telangiectasia. In *Ataxia-telangiectasia* (ed. B. A. Bridges & D. G. Harnden), pp. 53–81. New York: Wiley.

TAYLOR, A. M. R., HARNDEN, D. G., ARLETT, C. F., HARCOURT, S. A., LEHMANN, A. R., STEVENS, S. & BRIDGES, B. A. (1975). Ataxia-telangiectasia: a human mutation with abnormal radiation sensitivity. *Nature, Lond.* **258**, 427–429.

THACKER, J., DEBENHAM, P. G., STRETCH, A. & WEBB, M. B. T. (1983). The use of a cloned bacterial gene to study mutation in mammalian cells. *Mutat. Res.* **111**, 9–23.

THOMPSON, L. H., RUBIN, J. S., CLEAVER, J. E., WHITMORE, G. F. & BROOKMAN, K. (1980). A screening method for isolating DNA repair-deficient mutants of CHO cells. *Somat. Cell Genet.* **6**, 391–405.

WALDMAN, T. A. (1982). Immunological abnormalities in ataxia-telangiectasia. In *Ataxia-telangiectasia* (ed. B. A. Bridges & D. G. Harnden), pp. 37–51. New York: Wiley.

WALDMAN, T. A. & MCINTIRE, K. R. (1972). Serum alpha-fetoprotein levels in patients with ataxia-telangiectasia. *Lancet* **ii**, 1112–1115.

WIGLER, M., PELLICER, A., SILVERSTEIN, S. & AXEL, R. (1978). Biochemical transfer of single-copy eucaryotic genes using total cellular DNA as donor. *Cell* **14**, 725–731.

J. Cell Sci. Suppl. 6, 191–206 (1987)
Printed in Great Britain © The Company of Biologists Limited 1987

RECOVERY OF DNA SYNTHESIS FROM INHIBITION BY ULTRAVIOLET LIGHT IN MAMMALIAN CELLS

ARMANDO M. VENTURA, J. MIGUEL ORTEGA, R. IVAN SCHUMACHER AND ROGERIO MENEGHINI*

Department of Biochemistry, Institute of Chemistry, University of São Paulo, CP 20780, 01498 São Paulo, SP, Brazil

SUMMARY

In general mammalian cells recover from DNA synthesis inhibition by ultraviolet light (u.v.) before most of the pyrimidine dimers have been removed from the genome. This is a complex phenomenon whose biological significance has not been fully assessed. In Chinese hamster V79 cells this recovery seems to be directly coupled to an enhanced rate of double-stranded DNA elongation. The presence of the DNA polymerase α inhibitor, aphidicolin, after u.v. irradiation produces two different responses. At low concentration, sufficient to inhibit 95 % of DNA replication but having no effect on excision repair, the drug has no effect on the recovery. This shows that ongoing replicative DNA synthesis is not required for recovery. At higher concentrations of aphidicolin, sufficient to block excision repair, the recovery phenomenon was prevented. The recovery was also prevented by actinomycin D at a concentration that inhibits 60 % of RNA synthesis. In quantitative autoradiography experiments in which previously irradiated cells were fused with unirradiated cells the nuclei of the latter exhibited a higher resistance to inhibition by u.v. than nuclei from non-fused cells. These results indicate that: (1) even the low repair rate exhibited by V79 cells (relative to human cells) is important for recovery; although most of the dimers remain in the V79 genome after recovery of DNA synthesis, either the removal of lesions from some important region of chromatin or the activity of the repair process itself is important for the recovery; (2) the recovery mechanism is induced and depends on RNA synthesis and the production of specific factors.

Finally, we have observed that cells previously treated with fluorodeoxyuridine become more resistant to inhibition by u.v. After irradiation these cells replicate DNA faster than untreated cells. Since it has been shown that this drug activates unused origins of replication in Chinese hamster cells, reducing the average replicon size, we assume that the acquired resistance has to do with the operation of a larger number of smaller replicons. This may also be the mechanism whereby recovery from inhibition occurs after u.v. irradiation.

INTRODUCTION

Damage to DNA elicits several biological responses. Besides the immediate mobilization to eliminate the burden of lesions the cells exhibit a slower response, whose kinetics are compatible with an inducible process, and which consists ultimately of acquiring tolerance to the remaining lesions (Meneghini *et al.* 1981). This tolerance is reflected by a recovery from DNA synthesis inhibition (Meneghini *et al.* 1981), an enhanced capability to reactivate infecting virus whose genome has been damaged (Bockstahler & Lytle, 1970; Sarasin & Hanawalt, 1978), and an increasing resistance to lethal injuries produced by ultraviolet light (u.v.) (Domon & Rauth, 1973; Todd, 1973; Menck & Meneghini, 1982). At present we do not know

* Author for correspondence.

whether these phenomena are causally related. From the molecular point of view the recovery from DNA synthesis inhibition is interesting because it may reveal the occurrence of inducible tolerance mechanisms in the eukaryotic cell perhaps resembling the SOS mechanism in bacteria. It is well established that pyrimidine dimers arrest the replication fork movement (Meneghini *et al.* 1981), and the recovery might be related to an inducible mechanism that somehow overcomes the block. Such recovery could also be related to induced mutagenesis and transformation. To study recovery of DNA synthesis, many investigators have used the method of DNA sedimentation in alkaline sucrose gradients (Meyn & Humphrey, 1971; Lehmann & Kirk-Bell, 1972; D'Ambrosio & Setlow, 1976). However, this technique has its drawbacks; it does not permit a direct analysis of the rate of DNA elongation because of the formation of daughter-strand gaps (Lehmann, 1972; Cordeiro-Stone *et al.* 1979). Moreover, possible artefacts may arise from an expanded pool of longer DNA strands after u.v. irradiation, which remain as a source of further chain elongation at later pulse-labelling times (Painter, 1978). The method of DNA-fibre autoradiography has been used to measure directly the elongation rate of double-stranded DNA (Edenberg, 1976; Doniger, 1978; Dahle *et al.* 1980). In Chinese hamster cells, this technique has revealed that, along with a recovery from inhibition by u.v. of [^{3}H]thymidine incorporation, there occurs a recovery in the rate of elongation of double-stranded DNA (Dahle *et al.* 1980). To speed up analysis of recovery, we have used a technique based on CsCl gradient centrifugation of DNA pulse-labelled with BrdUrd (bromodeoxyuridine), which also measures the rate of elongation of double-stranded DNA (Cordeiro & Meneghini, 1973). We found that recovery of [^{3}H]thymidine incorporation in V79 cells is accompanied by a recovery of DNA elongation rate (Ventura & Meneghini, 1984). Rodent cells have been used in many of these experiments because, in spite of a limited excision repair capacity, they recover from DNA synthesis inhibition, suggesting that other mechanisms are involved. However, even in human cells excision repair, though it appears to be necessary (Moustacchi *et al.* 1979), is not sufficient for recovery (Lehmann *et al.* 1979). More recently, studies with Chinese hamster ovary (CHO) cells defective in excision repair have confirmed that the low, wild-type repair ability is required for recovery (Griffiths & Ling, 1985). However, another u.v.-sensitive CHO mutant, normal in excision repair but defective in postreplication repair, has been shown to be defective in DNA synthesis recovery (Collins & Waldren, 1982). Thus again excision repair does not seem to be sufficient for recovery.

Several points remain obscure. There are doubts about whether the recovery is an inducible process, dependent on previous transcription and protein synthesis. In addition, the mechanism of recovery itself is unknown. In principle, it can be ascribed to a larger number of active replicons or to an acquired capacity of the replication machinery to bypass a lesion (Park & Cleaver, 1979; Meneghini & Mello-Filho, 1983). In both cases the net result would be a faster overall DNA elongation rate.

We set about testing some of these points, using several metabolic inhibitors. The use of inhibitors involves some risks because of their lack of absolute specificity, but it can reveal aspects that otherwise would be difficult to assess. We took care to ascertain that, upon removal of the inhibitors, the level of DNA synthesis in unirradiated cells returned to the level of untreated cells, and also that the drug had no secondary effects on chromatin structure. The three main areas of investigation were: (1) the importance of the limited excision repair in V79 cells for recovery; (2) the inducibility of recovery; (3) the activation of unused replication origins during recovery.

MATERIALS AND METHODS

Cells

V79 Chinese hamster fibroblasts were kindly provided by Dr M. Taylor from Indiana University. A clone (C-1) was used throughout the experiments. Cells were routinely grown in Dulbecco's modified Eagle's medium, pH 7·0, supplemented with 10% foetal calf serum, 472 units ml^{-1} penicillin and 94 μg ml^{-1} streptomycin. The cells were kept in a 5% CO_2-humidified atmosphere at 37°C. For irradiation, cultures were rinsed with phosphate-buffered saline (PBS), and exposed in this same solution to 254 nm u.v. from a low-pressure mercury lamp at a dose rate of 0·5 J m^{-2} s^{-1}. The rates of semiconservative replication and RNA synthesis were determined by labelling cultures for 20–30 min with 5 μCi ml^{-1} of [^{3}H]thymidine (dThd) (72 Ci mmol^{-1}) or 5 μCi ml^{-1} [^{3}H]uridine (27·1 Ci mmol). The cultures were rinsed twice with PBS and once with 5% trichloroacetic acid for 10 min at 5°C. After two more washings with trichloroacetic acid the cells were rinsed with 95% ethanol and treated with 1·5 ml of 0·3 M-NaOH for 2 h at 37°C for lysis. Measurements of A_{260} and radioactivity in this solution gave the final values of DNA synthesis in cts min^{-1} unit^{-1} A_{260}.

CsCl density gradient and neutral sucrose density gradient centrifugation

The methods described previously were followed (Ventura & Meneghini, 1984). These two techniques were used to measure the values of D and M_n, respectively, which were in turn used to determine the relative rate of elongation of double-stranded DNA. D represents the fraction of the BrdUrd-pulse-labelled DNA that remained within the density range of the unsubstituted DNA after CsCl centrifugation, and M_n is the number average molecular weight (Ventura & Meneghini, 1984).

Autoradiography and cell fusion

The cells were first synchronized in medium containing 2 mM-hydroxyurea for 14 h before releasing and pulse-labelling for 30 min with 10 μCi ml^{-1} of [^{3}H]dThd (cells D). They were then irradiated with 5 J m^{-2} of 254 nm u.v. or sham-irradiated, trypsinized and transferred to vials containing cells growing on slides (cells R). After 9 h the mixed cells were fused with polyethylene glycol (Pontecorvo et al. 1977) incubated for a further 3 h and irradiated with 5 J m^{-2} or sham-irradiated. One hour later the cells were pulse-labelled with 0·5 μCi ml^{-1} of [^{3}H]dThd for 30 min after which they were washed, fixed and exposed to AR-10 Kodak stripping-film. After developing, the cells were stained with Toluidine Blue and grains in R cell nuclei were scored. Under these conditions D nuclei appeared heavily labelled and R nuclei contained from 40–90 grains. Separate experiments (not shown) indicated that the number of grains is proportional to the pulse-labelling time.

Nucleoid sedimentation

Cells were pre-labelled for 17 h with 0·3 μCi ml^{-1} of [^{3}H]dThd and 10^{-6} M-dThd. After experimental treatment the cells were trypsinized and resuspended in 3 ml of PBS, centrifuged for 15 min at 600 g at 4°C and resuspended in 50 μl of PBS containing 10 mM-EDTA; 250 μl of lysis solution containing 2·28 M-NaCl, 24 mM-EDTA, 0·6% Triton X-100 and 10 mM-Tris·HCl, pH 8·0, was added to the cell suspension, the mixture was layered over 4·5 ml of a 15% to 30%

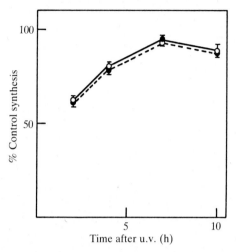

Fig. 1. Recovery of DNA synthesis from inhibition by u.v. and effect of aphidicolin. Cells were irradiated with 5 J m^{-2} and incubated for the indicated periods of time with medium with (●) or without (○) 1 μg ml^{-1} of aphidicolin. The cells were further incubated for 1 h in normal medium and pulse-labelled with [^{3}H]dThd for 20 min. Bars indicate deviation for duplicate. 'Control synthesis' relates to incorporation of [^{3}H]dThd in unirradiated cultures with or without aphidicolin as appropriate.

sucrose gradient containing 1·9 M-NaCl, 10 mM-EDTA, 10 mM-Tris·HCl, pH 8·0, and left for 15 min before centrifugation at 20 °C for 30 min at 10 000 rev. min^{-1} in a SW-50.1 Beckman rotor. Fractions (0·2 ml) were collected on strips of Whatman paper 17. After drying the paper strips were cut, placed in vials with 5·0 ml of PPO–POPOP–toluene and their radioactivity was counted in a scintillation spectrometer.

RESULTS

In u.v.-irradiated mammalian cells DNA synthesis is inhibited mainly because of the arrest of the replication fork by the pyrimidine dimer. u.v. irradiation also prevents initiation of DNA synthesis but this is mainly observed at very low doses (Kaufmann & Cleaver, 1981). Fig. 1 shows that in V79 cells the inhibition of [^{3}H]dThd incorporation produced by a dose of 5 J m^{-2} is overcome by 7–10 h. This recovery cannot be attributed to the accumulation of cells in S phase by u.v. irradiation. Though there is a slight increase in the proportion of cells in S phase from 4–6 h after u.v. (rising from 60–70 %), by 9–10 h, when recovery has been fully attained, the percentage of u.v.-irradiated cells in S phase is the same as in the control population (results not shown). We have shown that recovery of [^{3}H]dThd incorporation is linked to a recovery in the rate of elongation of double-stranded DNA, as measured by centrifugation of DNA in CsCl density gradients (Ventura & Meneghini, 1984). Thus, it seems appropriate to designate this phenomenon as recovery of DNA synthesis from inhibition by u.v. irradiation.

Recovery and excision repair

By 9 h after 5 J m^{-2} only 23 % of the dimers have been excised, as measured by sites sensitive to the *Microccus luteus* u.v. endonuclease (results not shown). This

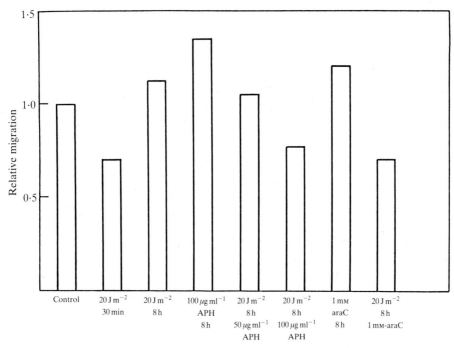

Fig. 2. Relative sedimentation distance of nucleoids after u.v. irradiation and the effects of araC and aphidicolin (APH). The cells were irradiated with $20\,\mathrm{J\,m^{-2}}$ of u.v. and left for 30 min or 8 h before nucleoid preparation. In some samples aphidicolin or araC at the indicated concentrations was present during the 8-h period.

result seems to make less likely any role for excision repair in the recovery of DNA synthesis in V79 cells. However, Griffiths & Ling (1985) showed that CHO cells that are completely defective in excision repair do not recover from inhibition by u.v. We decided therefore to determine whether the low level of repair exhibited by repair-competent V79 cells was important for the recovery. Aphidicolin, an inhibitor of DNA polymerase α is an inhibitor of excision repair (Ciarrocchi *et al.* 1979). At a concentration of $1\,\mu\mathrm{g\,ml^{-1}}$, aphidicolin reduced [^{3}H]thymidine incorporation to less than 5 % of control levels in V79 cells, but had no effect on excision repair of dimers as determined by the nucleotide sedimentation technique. DNA strand breaks accumulate in u.v.-irradiated cells incubated with inhibitors of repair, and in preparations of nucleoids this is reflected in a lasting reduction in sedimentation rate under neutral conditions (Mattern *et al.* 1982). Fig. 2 shows that in exponentially growing V79 cells only high concentrations of aphidicolin (50 and $100\,\mu\mathrm{g\,ml^{-1}}$) effectively block DNA repair. We have found that upon removal of this drug, even at such high concentration, there occurs a reversal of replicative DNA synthesis inhibition to 80 % of the control in 1 h (results not shown). Incubation with aphidicolin at a concentration of $1\,\mu\mathrm{g\,ml^{-1}}$ for up to 10 h has no effect on the recovery of DNA synthesis (Fig. 1). However, at a concentration of $100\,\mu\mathrm{g\,ml^{-1}}$ the drug prevented recovery (Fig. 3). These results argue in favour of the idea that recovery does not depend on continuous DNA synthesis, but does require normal excision

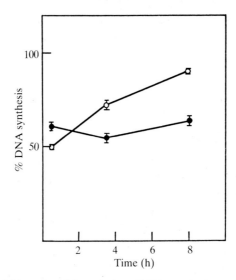

Fig. 3. Effect of inhibition of excision repair on DNA synthesis recovery. The cells were irradiated with 5 J m^{-2} and incubated for the indicated times with (●) or without (○) 100 μg ml^{-1} of aphidicolin. The cells were further incubated for 1 h in normal medium and pulse-labelled with [^{3}H]dThd for 30 min. Bars indicate deviation for duplicate.

repair. It is interesting to note that the inhibition of RNA synthesis by u.v. irradiation, a phenomenon that is only detected at relatively high u.v. doses, is also followed by recovery, but with faster kinetics than DNA synthesis recovery (Fig. 4). It is also clear that 100 μg ml^{-1} of aphidicolin prevents recovery of RNA synthesis. At 1 μg ml^{-1} aphidicolin has no effect on this recovery (results not shown). A similar prevention of RNA synthesis recovery was observed with 1 mM-arabinocytidine (araC), which is also (Fig. 2) an efficient inhibitor of excision repair. However, neither 1 mM-araC nor a mixture of 20 μM-araC plus 2 mM-hydroxyurea, an effective combination of excision repair inhibitors (Cleaver, 1982), could be used to test for prevention of DNA synthesis recovery, since removal of these compounds did not bring a prompt reversal of DNA synthesis inhibition, as was the case for aphidicolin.

Inducibility of recovery

Using a split-dose protocol, D'Ambrosio & Setlow (1976) observed that two doses of u.v. separated by an interval had significantly less effect on the rate of DNA elongation than a single u.v. dose equivalent to the total of the split doses. We followed similar protocols to see whether the first dose has some effect on the kinetics of recovery after a second dose. Fig. 5 shows that this is not the case, the degree of inhibition and the kinetics of recovery being the same whether or not the cells had been previously irradiated. Similar responses were obtained when the first dose was diminished or the time between the two doses was reduced. These results of [^{3}H]dThd incorporation are corroborated by measurements of the elongation of double-stranded DNA by means of CsCl density gradient centrifugation (Fig. 6). As previously reported (Ventura & Meneghini, 1984) a dose-dependent decrease in

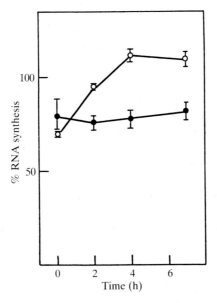

Fig. 4. Effect of inhibition of excision repair on RNA synthesis recovery. Cells were incubated for 30 min with 100 μg ml^{-1} of aphidicolin or normal medium, irradiated with 15 J m^{-2} and incubated for the indicated periods of time with (●) or without (○) 100 μg ml^{-1} of aphidicolin. At the end of these periods they were pulse-labelled for 40 min with [^{3}H]uridine. Bars represent deviation for duplicate.

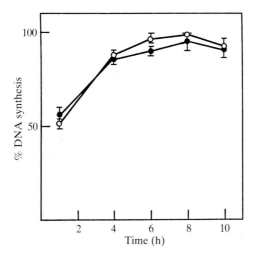

Fig. 5. Effect of a previous u.v. dose on the recovery of DNA synthesis after a second dose. Cells were previously irradiated with 0 (○) or 5 J m^{-2} (●) and 20 h later irradiated again with 5 J m^{-2}. After the indicated times they were pulse-labelled for 30 min with [^{3}H]dThd. Bars indicate deviation for duplicate.

elongation is observed initially, followed by a recovery 8 h later. A second dose then brings the elongation rate down to a level similar to that observed after a single dose. These results suggest that the phenomenon of recovery is not inducible. However, we have now carried out experiments that suggest quite the contrary. In the experiment shown in Fig. 7 we irradiated the cells with $5\,\mathrm{J\,m^{-2}}$ and followed the recovery in the presence of actinomycin D at a concentration of $0{\cdot}05\,\mu\mathrm{g\,ml^{-1}}$. At this concentration the antibiotic has only a negligible effect on DNA synthesis while it reduces RNA synthesis to 40% of the control level. It is clear that the recovery phenomenon is strongly inhibited under these conditions. We found a similar effect by using $10^{-5}\,\mathrm{M}$-cycloheximide. However, this compound has a strong inhibitory effect on DNA synthesis, which is not reversed upon its removal. We used a different approach to test the inducibility of recovery. Cells, previously u.v. irradiated (D), were fused with unirradiated cells (R) and, after u.v. irradiation of the fused cells, the extent of DNA synthesis in the R nuclei was measured by quantitative auto-radiography. In this experiment D cells were heavily prelabelled with $[^3\mathrm{H}]\mathrm{dThd}$ so as to distinguish their nuclei from those of the R cells, which were much more lightly labelled. The results in Fig. 8 show that, of the various experimental protocols, the only one resulting in a significant difference between the amounts of DNA synthesis in the R nuclei in R+D fused cells compared with unfused R cells was when both R and D were irradiated. In this case DNA synthesis was elevated in the fused cells. This is consistent with the hypothesis that factors produced in previously irradiated D cells are transferred to R nuclei, which, upon irradiation, recover faster from DNA synthesis inhibition.

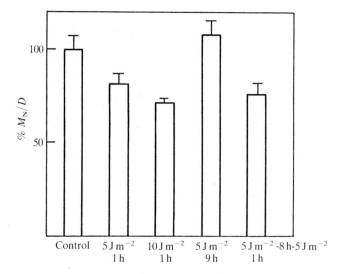

Fig. 6. Effect of a previous u.v. dose on the degree of inhibition of DNA elongation after a second dose. Cells were irradiated with the indicated doses and after the indicated times pulse-labelled for 1 h in medium containing $10^{-5}\,\mathrm{M}$-BrdUrd, $39\,\mu\mathrm{Ci\,ml^{-1}}$ of $[^3\mathrm{H}]\mathrm{dThd}$ ($5\times10^{-7}\,\mathrm{M}$), $10^{-5}\,\mathrm{M}$-uridine and $10^{-6}\,\mathrm{M}$-FdUrd. In the sample represented by the right-most bar, the cells were irradiated twice with $5\,\mathrm{J\,m^{-2}}$, separated by 8 h, and 1 h after the second dose they were incubated in the medium above. The DNAs were extracted and submitted to CsCl density gradient centrifugation or sucrose gradient centrifugation for determinations of D and M_n, respectively (Ventura & Meneghini, 1984). M_n/D for control cells is regarded as 100%. The deviation for duplicate samples is indicated.

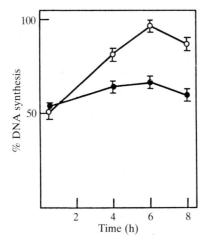

Fig. 7. Action of actinomycin D on DNA synthesis recovery. Cells were incubated for 30 min prior to irradiation with $5 \, J \, m^{-2}$ and for the indicated periods of time after irradiation in medium with (●) or without (○) $0 \cdot 05 \, \mu g \, ml^{-1}$ of actinomycin D. At the end they were pulse-labelled for 30 min with [^{3}H]dThd. Bars indicate deviation for duplicate.

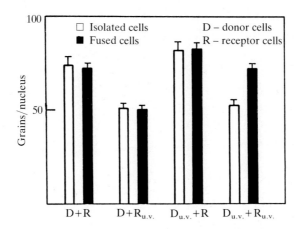

Fig. 8. Cell fusion to test for inducibility of the recovery phenomenon. Donor cells were irradiated with 0 (D) or $5 \, J \, m^{-2}$ ($D_{u.v.}$) and 9 h later fused to receptor cells (R). Three hours later the fused cells were irradiated with 0 (R) or $5 \, J \, m^{-2}$ ($R_{u.v.}$) and 1 h later they were pulse-labelled with [^{3}H]dThd for 30 min. After developing, the autoradiography grains on the R cell nuclei were counted in both fused and isolated cells. The standard deviation of the mean of 50 nuclei is indicated.

The possible role of utilization of new replication origins in the recovery phenomenon

Park & Cleaver (1979) proposed that when replication forks are blocked by pyrimidine dimers the arrest of DNA replication could be relieved by chain growth from adjacent unblocked forks. According to this idea, initiation of replication at origins that are not normally utilized would permit a recovery from DNA synthesis

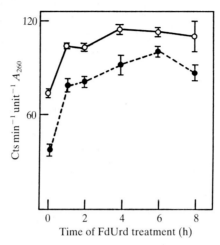

Fig. 9. Effect of FdUrd on inhibition of DNA synthesis by u.v. The cells were incubated for the indicated times with 10^{-6} M-FdUrd, irradiated with 0 (○) or $5 \, J \, m^{-2}$ (●) of u.v. incubated for 1 h in 10^{-5} M-dThd and pulse-labelled for 30 min with [^{3}H]dThd.

inhibition. Taylor (1977) has shown that when Chinese hamster cells are held at the beginning of S phase by the thymydilate synthase inhibitor, fluorodeoxyuridine (FdUrd), new origins are activated and the inter-origin distance is diminished. We decided to submit cells to FdUrd treatment to see whether they became more resistant to u.v. irradiation, as might be expected. The experiment depicted in Fig. 9 shows that exposure to FdUrd for increasing time before irradiation does in fact bring about a resistance of DNA synthesis to inhibition by u.v. In this experiment the resistance was maximum after 6 h of exposure of cells to FdUrd; at this time [^{3}H]dThd incorporation in irradiated cells was 89 % of that in unirradiated cells, whereas with no FdUrd the relative incorporation was only 51 %. After removal of FdUrd and before the [^{3}H]dThd pulse-labelling the cells were exposed for 1 h to 10^{-5} M-dThd in an attempt to restore the TTP pool, depleted by the FdUrd treatment. An alteration in [^{3}H]dThd incorporation does not necessarily indicate altered DNA synthesis, especially when the TTP pool has been disturbed. However, it was confirmed that a real increase in DNA synthesis takes place on incubation with FdUrd in experiments in which the cells were pre-labelled for 26 h with [^{3}H]dThd, treated with FdUrd and labelled with cold BrdUrd (Fig. 10). The area of the hybrid peak represents the real amount of template DNA that was replicated, whereas the shift represents the concentration of BrdUrd in the TTP pool. This latter parameter is the same in the four profiles, whereas DNA synthesis was more than doubled in FdUrd-treated cells. This is not due only to an accumulation of cells in S phase, which changed from 68 % in untreated cells to 91 % in treated cells. From the areas of the hybrid DNA peaks it can be calculated that the inhibition of DNA synthesis by u.v. was 28 % in untreated cells and 10 % in FdUrd-treated cells.

The resistance to inhibition by u.v. detected in the experiments of Figs 9, 10 was observed over a range of u.v. doses up to $12 \, J \, m^{-2}$. Moreover, the resistance disappeared after a prolonged period (18 h) in which the cells were kept in the presence of

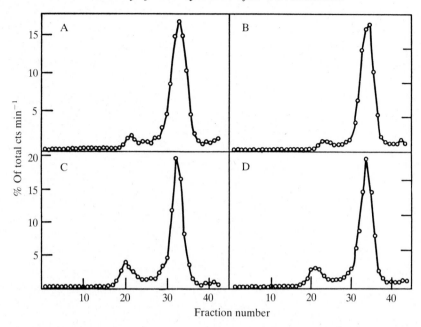

Fig. 10. Stimulation of DNA synthesis by previous FdUrd treatment. The cells were labelled for 13 h with $0.2\,\mu\text{Ci ml}^{-1}$ [^{3}H]dThd plus 10^{-6} M-dThd. Culture was rinsed in PBS, and incubated for 6 h in 10^{-6} M-FdUrd. This medium was removed, the cells were irradiated with $5\,\text{J m}^{-2}$ and incubated for 1 h in 10^{-5} M-dThd. At the end the medium was replaced by new medium containing 10^{-5} M-BrdUrd and after 2 h the DNA was extracted for DNA centrifugation in a CsCl density gradient. The fractions of radioactivity shifted to the hybrid position in relation to total counts were: A (control), 0.085; B (u.v.-irradiated, untreated), 0.062; C (treated with FdUrd, unirradiated), 0.190; D (treated with FdUrd, u.v.-irradiated), 0.171.

10^{-5} M-dThd. We carried out the experiment shown in Fig. 11 to see whether the phenomenon of resistance can be ascribed to an increased rate of double-stranded DNA elongation. What the results in Fig. 11 seem to indicate is that in spite of a higher level of DNA synthesis in FdUrd-treated *versus* control cells, revealed in the experiments of Figs 9, 10, the overall rate of double-stranded DNA elongation in FdUrd-treated cells is no greater than in control cells. However, in u.v.-irradiated cells the situation is different; with FdUrd present there is a significantly higher rate of DNA elongation than in untreated cells, indicating a coupling of resistance to inhibition to faster DNA elongation in u.v.-irradiated cells.

DISCUSSION

Chinese hamster V79 cells are inefficient in excision of pyrimidine dimers compared with normal human fibroblasts. However, it has been shown that in transcriptionally active regions of the Chinese hamster genome the excision of dimers is very efficient (Bohr *et al.* 1985; Smith, 1987). In human cells excision of dimers plays an important role in recovery from DNA synthesis inhibition by u.v. (Moustacchi *et al.* 1979). More recently, Griffiths & Ling (1985) have shown that mutants of CHO cells, in which the excision of dimers is virtually non-existent, are defective in the recovery phenomenon. In this chapter we have described experiments designed to determine the effect of excision repair inhibition on recovery. Our results clearly show that at concentrations that inhibit repair aphidicolin is a strong inhibitor of recovery as well, while at a concentration that inhibits only DNA synthesis the drug has no effect on recovery. These data sustain the hypothesis that at least some type of excision repair is required for the recovery of DNA synthesis. In this connection it is noteworthy that the recovery of RNA synthesis from u.v. inhibition is also prevented by inhibition of excision repair (Fig. 4), in agreement with the data of Mayne (1984). Because excision repair seems to be particularly efficient in transcriptionally active regions (Bohr *et al.* 1985) we are tempted to suggest that excision of dimers from these regions enables DNA synthesis to occur, which in turn is required for the recovery of DNA synthesis. An alternative hypothesis suggests that excision repair is important because of the alterations of chromatin organization that are required for the recovery phenomenon.

Our finding that the recovery of DNA synthesis is not dependent on ongoing DNA synthesis requires further comment. We have used aphidicolin to inhibit DNA synthesis, and our results are in agreement with those of Lehmann *et al.* (1979), who have used FdUrd for the same purpose in human cells. Griffiths *et al.* (1981) concluded that continuous DNA synthesis is required for the recovery phenomenon to occur in Chinese hamster cells, using hydroxyurea as an inhibitor of semiconservative replication. We have obtained similar results using hydroxyurea but we have also noticed that this drug relaxed DNA supercoiling in nucleoids. This is not the case for aphidicolin and FdUrd, which in contrast bring about additional

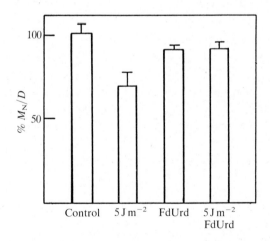

Fig. 11. Rate of elongation of double-stranded DNA after FdUrd treatment. The cells were exposed to 10^{-6} M-FdUrd for 6 h and then u.v.-irradiated with 0 or 5 J m^{-2} of u.v. There followed a 1-h incubation in 10^{-5} M-dThd after which the cells were pulse-labelled for 1 h with 10^{-5} M-BrdUrd, 10^{-6} M-FdUrd, 10^{-5} M-uridine and 39 μCi ml^{-1} of [^{3}H]dThd (5×10^{-7} M). The DNAs were extracted and submitted to CsCl density gradients centrifugation and sucrose density gradient centrifugation for determination of D and M_n, respectively. The deviation for duplicates is indicated.

condensation of the nucleoids (Fig. 2; and unpublished results). We therefore ascribe the inhibition of recovery of hydroxyurea to a secondary effect on chromatin structure and conclude that recovery is not dependent on ongoing DNA synthesis. In fact, the prevention of recovery by $100\,\mu\mathrm{g}\,\mathrm{ml}^{-1}$ of aphidicolin may be due to a persistence of unsealed breaks in u.v.-irradiated cells.

Our results with actinomycin D and with fused cells indicate that transcription of DNA is required for a recovery of DNA synthesis. That u.v. irradiation elicits synthesis of new proteins and RNA has been shown by others (Miskin & Ben-Ishai, 1981; Schorpp *et al.* 1984). We have noticed that in V79 cells the gene c-*fos* is activated after u.v. irradiation with kinetics similar to those of the recovery phenomenon (unpublished results). These results are consistent with the observation that inhibition of excision repair prevents recovery of RNA synthesis, which in turn inhibits recovery of DNA synthesis. The question then arises of why this faster recovery does not occur in the split-dose experiment described above when it is apparent in the fusion experiment. As yet, we have no answer to this question, but must suppose that a difference exists between the nuclei analysed in the fused cells, which carry a burden of dimers resulting from $5\,\mathrm{J\,m}^{-2}$, and the nuclei from cells submitted to a split-dose irradiation, which carry a burden of dimers resulting from two irradiations with $5\,\mathrm{J\,m}^{-2}$. Under split-dose conditions a larger amount of putative inducible factors may be required for recovery to occur. In fact, the kinetics of recovery from a single dose are much slower when the dose is increased (Dahle *et al.* 1980; and our unpublished results). In contrast, in human cells splitting the dose does enhance the recovery from inhibition produced by the second dose (Moustacchi *et al.* 1979).

The resistance of FdUrd pre-treated cells to DNA synthesis inhibition by u.v. is interesting and may shed some light on the recovery phenomenon. Brozmanova (1984) has observed a similar phenomenon in HeLa cells and has attributed it to a mechanism similar to that SOS mechanism described for bacteria. We prefer to think that it has to do with the induction of new origins of replication reported to occur in CHO cells exposed to FdUrd (Taylor, 1977). This would lead to a decrease in the average size of the replicon (Taylor, 1977) and, in fact, Cleaver *et al.* (1983) have reported that the initial inhibition of DNA synthesis after u.v. irradiation was dependent on replicon size in different cells, those with smaller replicons being more resistant to inhibition. This is the result expected if the arrest of a replication fork at a dimer is alleviated by another fork approaching from an adjacent origin.

According to the above model, a given fibre of DNA would replicate faster in FdUrd-treated cells, because the origins of replication are closer to each other. This has not been observed in unirradiated cells (Fig. 11). However, Taylor (1977) has reported that the activation of unused replicons by FdUrd in CHO cells was accompanied by a drop in the rate of fork movement, as if there were a compensation for the larger number of replicons. In the case of irradiated cells the effect of FdUrd pre-treatment is clearer (Fig. 11), probably because the activation of an unused replicon means the relief of a replication fork that otherwise would remain blocked at a dimer. The recovery phenomenon observed after u.v. irradiation may have a similar nature, reinitiation between blocked replication forks leading to recovery (Painter, 1985). Interestingly, nucleoids of cells that have been exposed either to u.v. or FdUrd a few hours earlier sediment faster than control nucleoids (our unpublished results). It is possible that a larger number of activated replicons causes more points of attachment of chromatin to the nuclear cage, rendering the nucleoids more condensed. It is attractive to think of reinitiation *via* usually silent origins as an SOS type of response in mammalian cells, requiring the synthesis of specific factors that are necessary as catalysts of DNA synthesis or as inducers of modification in the chromatin structure, for instance creating more points of attachment of chromatin and nuclear matrix. Excision-deficient Chinese hamster cells may be incapable of recovery either because even the low level of excision in wild-type cells is important for synthesis of the required RNA, or because it facilitates the attachment of the chromatin to the nuclear matrix.

We thank the Natural Product Branch of the N.C.I. for making aphidicolin available to us. This work was supported by grants from FAPESP, FINEP and CNPq, Brazilian foundations of scientific support. A.M.V. and J.M.O. hold fellowships from FAPESP.

REFERENCES

BOCKSTAHLER, L. E. & LYTLE, D. D. (1970). UV light enhanced reactivation of a mammalian virus. *Biochem. biophys. Res. Commun.* **41**, 184–189.

BOHR, V. A., SMITH, C. A., OKUMOTO, D. S. & HANAWALT, P. C. (1985). DNA repair in an active gene: removal of pyrimidine dimers from the DHFR gene of CHO cells is much more efficient than in the genome overall. *Cell* **40**, 359–369.

BROZMANOVA, J. (1984). Stimulation of postirradiation DNA synthesis in ultraviolet irradiated HeLa cells by fluorodeoxyuridine. *Neoplasma* **31**, 169–173.

CIARROCHI, G., JOSE, J. G. & LINN, S. (1979). Further characterization of a cell-free system for measuring replicative and repair synthesis with cultured fibroblasts and evidence for the involvement of polymerase α in DNA repair. *Nucl. Acids Res.* **7**, 1205–1219.

CLEAVER, J. E. (1982). Normal reconstruction of DNA supercoiling and chromatin structure in Cockayne syndrome during repair of damage from ultraviolet light. *Am. J. hum. Gen.* **34**, 566–575.

CLEAVER, J. E., KAUFMANN, W. K., KAPP, L. N. & PARK, S. D. (1983). Replication size and excision repair as factors in the inhibition and recovery of DNA synthesis from UV damage. *Biochim. biophys. Acta* **739**, 207–215.

COLLINS, A. & WALDREN, C. (1982). Cell cycle kinetics and UV light survival in UV-1, a CHO mutant defective in post replication recovery. *J. Cell Sci.* **57**, 265–275.

CORDEIRO, M. & MENEGHINI, R. (1973). The rate of DNA replication in the polytene chromosome of *Rhynchosciara angelae*. *J. molec. Biol.* **78**, 261–274.

CORDEIRO-STONE, M., SCHUMACHER, R. I. & MENEGHINI, R. (1979). Structure of replication fork in UV light irradiated human cells. *Biophys. J.* **27**, 287–300.

DAHLE, D., GRIFFITHS, T. D. & CARPENTER, J. G. (1980). Inhibition and recovery of DNA synthesis in UV-irradiated Chinese hamster V-79 cells. *Photochem. Photobiol.* **32**, 157–165.

D'AMBROSIO, S. M. & SETLOW, R. B. (1976). Enhancement of post-replication repair in Chinese hamster cells. *Proc. natn. Acad. Sci. U.S.A.* **73**, 2396–2400.

DOMON, M. & RAUTH, A. M. (1973). Cell cycle specific recovery from fractionated exposures to UV light. *Radiat. Res.* **55**, 81–92.

DONIGER, J. (1978). DNA replication in UV light irradiated Chinese hamster cells: the nature of replicon inhibition and post-replication repair. *J. molec. Biol.* **120**, 433–446.

EDENBERG, H. J. (1976). Inhibition of DNA replication by UV light. *Biophys. J.* **16**, 849–859.

GRIFFITHS, T. D., DAHLE, D. B., MEECHAN, P. J. & CARPENTER, J. G. (1981). Effects of inhibitors of DNA synthesis on the rate of DNA synthesis after exposure of mammalian cells to UV light. *Biochim. biophys. Acta* **656**, 55–61.

GRIFFITHS, T. D. & LING, S. Y. (1985). Effect of ultraviolet light on thymidine incorporation, DNA chain elongation and replicon initiation in wild-type and excision deficient Chinese hamster ovary cells. *Biochim. biophys. Acta* **826**, 121–128.

KAUFMANN, W. K. & CLEAVER, J. E. (1981). Mechanisms of inhibition of DNA replication by ultraviolet light in normal human and xeroderma pigmentosum fibroblasts. *J. molec. Biol.* **149**, 175–187.

LEHMANN, A. R. (1972). Postreplication repair of DNA in UV-irradiated mammalian cells. *J. molec. Biol.* **66**, 319–337.

LEHMANN, A. R. & KIRK-BELL, S. (1972). Postreplication repair of DNA in UV-irradiated mammalian cells. No gaps in DNA synthesized late after UV-irradiation. *Eur. J. Biochem.* **31**, 438–445.

LEHMANN, A. R., KIRK-BELL, S. & MAYNE, L. (1979). Abnormal kinetics of DNA synthesis in UV-irradiated cells from patients with Cockayne's syndrome. *Cancer Res.* **39**, 4237–4241.

MATTERN, M. R., PAONE, R. F. & DAY, R. S. III (1982). Eukaryotic DNA repair is blocked at different steps by inhibitors of DNA topoisomerases and of DNA polymerases α and β. *Biochim. biophys. Acta* **697**, 6–13.

MAYNE, L. V. (1984). Inhibitors of DNA synthesis (aphidicolin and cytosine arabinoside/hydroxyurea) prevent the recovery of RNA synthesis after UV-irradiation. *Mutat. Res.* **131**, 187–191.

MENCK, C. F. M. & MENEGHINI, R. (1982). Recovery in survival capacity of UV-irradiated 3T3 mouse cells at Go cannot be solely dependent on the excision of pyridine dimers. *Mutat. Res.* **96**, 273–280.

MENEGHINI, R., MENCK, C. F. M. & SCHUMACHER, R. I. (1981). Mechanisms of tolerance to DNA lesions in mammalian cells. *Q. Rev. Biophys.* **14**, 381–432.

MENEGHINI, R. & MELLO-FILHO, A. C. (1983). Rate of DNA synthesis in mammalian cells irradiated with ultraviolet light: a model based on the variations in the rate of movement of the replication fork and in the number of active replicons. *J. theor. Biol.* **100**, 359–372.

MEYN, R. E. & HUMPHREY, R. M. (1971). DNA synthesis in UV-light irradiated Chinese hamster cells. *Biophys. J.* **11**, 295–301.

MISKIN, R. & BEN-ISHAI, R. (1981). Induction of plasminogen activator by UV light in normal and xeroderma pigmentosum fibroblasts. *Proc. natn. Acad. Sci. U.S.A.* **78**, 6236–6240.

MOUSTACCHI, E., EHMANN, U. K. & FRIEDBERG, E. C. (1979). Defective recovery of semi-conservative DNA synthesis in XP cells following split dose UV-irradiation. *Mutat. Res.* **62**, 159–171.

PAINTER, R. B. (1978). Does UV light enhance postreplication repair in mammalian cells? *Nature, Lond.* **275**, 243–245.

PAINTER, R. B. (1985). Inhibition and recovery of DNA synthesis in human cells after exposure to ultraviolet light. *Mutat. Res.* **145**, 63–69.

PARK, S. D. & CLEAVER, J. E. (1979). Post-replication repair: questions of its definition and possible alteration in XP cells strains. *Proc. natn. Acad. Sci. U.S.A.* **76**, 3927–3931.

PONTECORVO, G., RIDDLE, P. N. & HALES, A. (1977). Time and mode of fusion of human fibroblasts treated with polyethylene glycol. *Nature, Lond.* **265**, 257–258.

SARASIN, A. R. & HANAWALT, P. C. (1978). Carcinogens enhance survival of UV-irradiated simian virus 40 in treated monkey kidney cells: induction of a recovery pathway. *Proc. natn. Acad. Sci. U.S.A.* **75**, 346–350.

SCHORPP, M., MALLICK, U., RAHMSDORF, H. J. & HERRLICH, P. (1984). UV-induced extracellular factor from human fibroblasts communicates the UV response to nonirradiated cells. *Cell* **37**, 861–868.

SMITH, C. A. (1987). DNA repair in specific sequences in mammalian cells. *J. Cell Sci. Suppl. 6*, 225–241.

TAYLOR, J. H. (1977). Increase in DNA replication sites in cells at the beginning of *S* phase. *Chromosoma* **62**, 291–300.

TODD, P. (1973). Fractionated UV light irradiation of cultured Chinese hamster cells. *Radiat. Res.* **55**, 93–100.

VENTURA, A. M. & MENEGHINI, R. (1984). Inhibition and recovery of the rate of DNA synthesis in V79 Chinese hamster cells following ultraviolet light irradiation. *Mutat. Res.* **131**, 81–88.

J. Cell Sci. Suppl. 6, 207–214 (1987)
Printed in Great Britain © The Company of Biologists Limited 1987

DNA SYNTHESIS IN IRRADIATED MAMMALIAN CELLS

ROBERT B. PAINTER[1,2] AND BARBARA R. YOUNG[1]

[1] *Laboratory of Radiobiology and Environmental Health* and
[2] *Department of Microbiology, University of California, San Francisco, CA 94143, USA*

SUMMARY

One of the first responses observed in S phase mammalian cells that have suffered DNA damage is the inhibition of initiation of DNA replicons. In cells exposed to ionizing radiation, a single-strand break appears to be the stimulus for this effect, whereby the initiation of many adjacent replicons (a replicon cluster) is blocked by a single-strand break in any one of them. In cells exposed to ultraviolet light (u.v.), replicon initiation is blocked at fluences that induce about one pyrimidine dimer per replicon. The inhibition of replicon initiation by u.v. in Chinese hamster cells that are incapable of excising pyrimidine dimers from their DNA is virtually the same as in cells that are proficient in dimer excision. Therefore, a single-strand break formed during excision repair of pyrimidine dimers is not the stimulus for inhibition of replicon initiation in u.v.-irradiated cells. Considering this fact, as well as the comparative insensitivity of human ataxia telangiectasia cells to u.v.-induced inhibition of replicon initiation, we propose that a relatively rare lesion is the stimulus for u.v.-induced inhibition of replicon initiation.

INTRODUCTION

In the past 20 years or so, DNA repair has developed from a vague, almost unacceptable, concept into a series of well-studied phenomena about which a tremendous amount of information has accumulated. It is probably only natural, then, that many investigators have attributed the whole of the cell's ability to withstand DNA damage to DNA repair alone. And yet, if the study of science has taught us anything, it is that simple concepts are often flawed just because they are too simple.

Attempts to correlate extent of DNA repair in mammalian cells with survival parameters have, in general, failed. The principal exception has been demonstrated by cells from patients with xeroderma pigmentosum (XP): cells from those patients with the most severe deficiencies in excision repair are in general the most sensitive to ultraviolet light (u.v.) (Andrews *et al.* 1978). But similar correlations do not exist for other comparisons between mammalian cells. Cultured mouse cells, which exhibit almost no excision repair of u.v.-induced DNA damage (Klímek, 1965), survive u.v. irradiation almost exactly as do excision-competent human cells (Rauth & Whitmore, 1966). The repair of single-strand breaks (ssbs) and double-strand breaks seems to be almost complete in cells irradiated with ionizing radiation at doses causing up to 99% killing (Hariharan *et al.* 1981; Lehmann & Stevens, 1977), and ionizing radiation-induced base damage seems to be rapidly and completely repaired in all normal mammalian cells (Remsen & Cerutti, 1977). Cell lines from many, but not all, patients with ataxia telangiectasia (AT) are defective in the excision of such base damage; yet survival curves of cells from all AT patients tested, whether or not defective in base damage repair, are virtually identical (Paterson & Smith, 1979).

One of the cellular responses that have been cited as candidates for cellular protection is the inhibition of DNA synthesis that is induced by DNA-damaging agents. It has been proposed that this slowing down of DNA synthesis increases the time for repair before replication can fix the damage (Tolmach *et al.* 1980). One of the components of DNA synthesis inhibition is DNA damage-induced delay of replicon initiation. This 'low-dose' effect is exhibited by many, perhaps all, DNA-damaging agents. The inhibition of replicon initiation by ionizing radiation, which induces large numbers of ssbs in cellular DNA, can be mimicked by exposing cells to 313 nm light after their DNA thymine has been partially replaced with bromouracil. Because of this, Povirk & Painter (1976) proposed that the lesion that causes the block to replicon initiation is the ssb.

Kaufmann *et al.* (1980) proposed that the u.v.-induced inhibition of replicon initiation in HeLa cells and normal human fibroblasts was mediated by ssbs formed during excision repair of pyrimidine dimers. However, when this hypothesis was tested, Kaufmann & Cleaver (1981) found that replicon initiation in XP cells of complementation group A, which exhibit virtually no excision repair of pyrimidine dimers (Kleijer *et al.* 1973), was inhibited by u.v. just as well as in excision-proficient normal cells. To determine if this phenomenon holds true for other mammalian cells, we examined the effects of u.v. on DNA synthesis in excision-deficient and excision-proficient Chinese hamster cells.

MATERIALS AND METHODS

Chinese hamster ovary (CHO) cell line AA8 was a gift from Lloyd Fuller, and CHO 43–3B, which is u.v.-sensitive and excision-deficient (Wood & Burki, 1982), was donated by Regine Goth-Goldstein. Both cell lines were grown in modified Eagle's medium with 10% bovine serum. Inhibition of DNA synthesis after u.v. or ionizing radiation was measured by preincubation of cells with [^{14}C]thymidine for 24 h and incubation of cells with [^{3}H]thymidine for 15 min after irradiation (Painter, 1977). Alkaline sucrose gradient analysis was performed as described previously (Painter & Young, 1976). Cells were exposed to u.v. under saline at a fluence rate of $1 \cdot 3 \, \text{J m}^{-2} \text{s}^{-1}$; cells were X-irradiated (250 kVp) at a dose rate of 1 gray (100 rad) per min.

RESULTS

After exposure to either $0 \cdot 3 \, \text{J m}^{-2}$ or $1 \cdot 0 \, \text{J m}^{-2}$, the initial decrease in rate of DNA synthesis was about the same for both the radiosensitive 43-3B cell line and the AA8 line; the AA8 cells then began to recover and reached virtually normal rates of DNA synthesis by 4 h after exposure, whereas the 43-3B cells continued at depressed rates of synthesis until at least 7 h after exposure (Fig. 1). Similar results were obtained with UV-5 cells, which are excision-defective cells derived from AA8 (data not

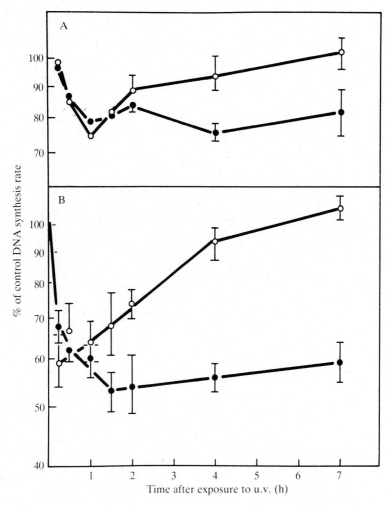

Fig. 1. Inhibition of DNA synthesis in CHO AA8 (○) and CHO 43-3B (●) cells as a function of time after exposure to $0.3\,\mathrm{J\,m^{-2}}$ (A) or $1.0\,\mathrm{J\,m^{-2}}$ (B) of u.v.

shown). Rudé & Friedberg (1977) observed a similar lack of recovery in repair-deficient human cells compared with normal human cells.

To determine the basis for the deficiency in recovery of DNA synthesis, we used alkaline sucrose gradient analysis to determine the status of nascent strands of DNA in the two cell lines at various times after exposure to u.v. At 30 min after irradiation, the inhibition of replicon initiation was about the same in both cell lines (Fig. 2), as indicated by a fluence-dependent decrease in radioactive DNA in the low molecular weight regions (fractions 5–13) of the gradients. In no case did the low fluences we used have a significant effect on chain elongation, as evidenced by virtually the same radioactivity in DNA of high molecular weight (fractions 14–24) from all cells. Thus, the early drop in DNA synthesis rate in both cell lines is due exclusively to inhibition of replicon initiation.

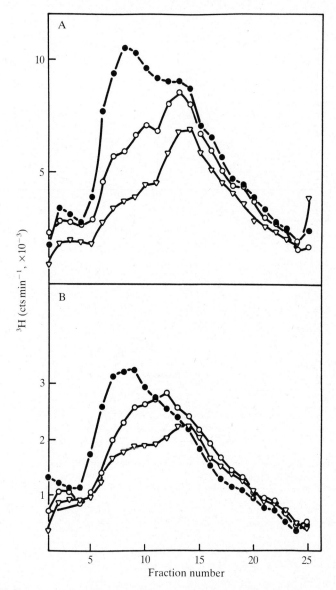

Fig. 2. Alkaline sucrose gradient profiles of nascent DNA labelled by incubating CHO AA8 cells (A) or CHO 43-3B cells (B) for 10 min with [³H]thymidine at 30 min after exposure to $0.3\,\mathrm{J\,m^{-2}}$ (○), $1.0\,\mathrm{J\,m^{-2}}$ (▽), or 0 (●) u.v. Sedimentation is from left to right.

At 60 min after u.v. irradiation, a difference between the two lines could be distinguished (Fig. 3). Although the status of nascent strands in cells of both lines exposed to $0.3\,\mathrm{J\,m^{-2}}$ was about the same, a continuing depression of replicon initiation was apparent in 43-3B cells, but not in AA8 cells. And at 90 min after irradiation, there was a marked difference between the two cell lines (Fig. 4). After both fluences, the AA8 cells had completely recovered from the inhibition of replicon

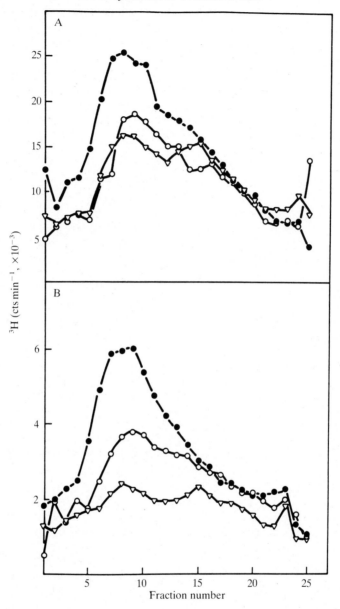

Fig. 3. Same as Fig. 2, but incubation with [³H]thymidine began 60 min after exposure to u.v.

initiation by this time, whereas in 43-3B cells, the inhibition of replicon initiation was greater than at earlier times. (The rate of recovery in experiments using alkaline sucrose gradient analysis was faster than in the experiments of Fig. 1, but the trend was the same.) Inhibition of DNA chain elongation in 43-3B cells was also evident at 90 min after exposure to u.v. When AA8 cells and 43-3B cells were exposed to X-rays, there was no difference between the two lines in the dose response for inhibition of DNA synthesis (data not shown).

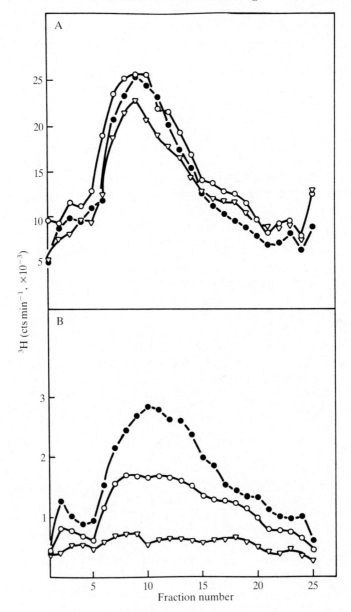

Fig. 4. Same as Fig. 2, but incubation with [³H]thymidine began 90 min after exposure to u.v.

DISCUSSION

The initial u.v.-induced inhibition of replicon initiation was the same in both excision-proficient and excision-deficient CHO cells. Kaufmann & Cleaver (1981) observed the same results for excision-proficient and excision-deficient human cells. It therefore seems certain that neither the ssb nor any other event associated with nucleotide excision repair is responsible for the inhibition of replicon initiation observed in u.v.-irradiated cells. However, the recovery of overall DNA synthesis was greatly delayed in excision-defective cells. The simplest interpretation of these results is that pyrimidine dimers are responsible for the original inhibition of replicon initiation in both cell types and for the delayed recovery of overall DNA synthesis in excision-defective cells. Again, however, the simplest explanation may not be the correct one.

Consider the case of the effects of u.v. on inhibition of DNA synthesis in human AT cells. Although it is generally true that AT cells are normal in their response to u.v., the inhibition of replicon initiation after exposure to u.v. is slightly but significantly less in AT cells than in normal human cells (Painter, 1985). If u.v.-induced lesions themselves were responsible for inhibition of replicon initiation, there would be no such difference between AT and normal cells. Therefore, some response of AT cells to u.v.-induced lesions must be abnormal. It is generally believed that the reduced inhibition of replicon initiation observed in X-irradiated AT cells is due to a defective effector, which in its normal state is activated by an ssb and causes the inhibition of replicon initiation. This is probably also the basis for the reduced inhibition of replicon initiation in u.v.-irradiated AT cells. Because there is no difference in inhibition of replicon initiation by u.v. between excision-proficient and excision-deficient cells, the effector must not be stimulated by ssbs formed during repair of pyrimidine dimers or the 6-4 photoproduct, neither of which is reparable by u.v.-sensitive cells (Mitchell *et al.* 1985). The lesion that causes the inhibition of replicon initiation in u.v.-irradiated cells may be a relatively rare photoproduct. Perhaps, like thymine glycol, it is repaired by the base-excision repair pathway in both normal and u.v.-sensitive cells. During this kind of repair, the endonucleolytic attack that follows glycosylase action causes an ssb. This ssb would be the stimulus for inhibition of replicon initiation in u.v.-irradiated normal cells but not in u.v.-irradiated AT cells, because of the abnormal effectors in AT. Such an interpretation is supported by results with both chick cells (Lehmann & Stevens, 1975) and cells of the fat-tailed marsupial mouse, *Sminthopsis crassicaudata* (Wilkins, 1983), in which photoreactivation of pyrimidine dimers failed to reverse the u.v.-induced inhibition of DNA synthesis.

In u.v.-irradiated cells, it is possible that the delay in initiation of replicons gives the cell extra time to repair DNA lesions before they are fixed by replication. The result of this would be complementary to the effect reported by Bohr *et al.* (1985) that CHO cells repair u.v.-induced pyrimidine dimers preferentially in transcribed genes such as that for dihydrofolate reductase. Removing damage from crucial DNA before it replicates seems to be a cellular priority.

This work was supported by the Office of Health and Environmental Research, U.S. Department of Energy (contract no. DE-AC03-76-SF01012).

REFERENCES

ANDREWS, A. D., BARRETT, S. F. & ROBBINS, J. H. (1978). Xeroderma pigmentosum neurological abnormalities correlate with colony-forming ability after ultraviolet radiation. *Proc. natn. Acad. Sci. U.S.A.* **75**, 1984–1988.

BOHR, V. A., SMITH, C. A., OKUMOTO, D. S. & HANAWALT, P. C. (1985). DNA repair in an active gene: Removal of pyrimidine dimers from the DHFR gene of CHO cells is much more efficient than in the genome overall. *Cell* **40**, 359–369.

HARIHARAN, P. V., ELECZKO, S., SMITH, B. P. & PATERSON, M. C. (1981). Normal rejoining of DNA strand breaks in ataxia telangiectasia fibroblast lines after low X-ray exposure. *Radiat. Res.* **86**, 589–597.

KAUFMANN, W. K. & CLEAVER, J. E. (1981). Mechanisms of inhibition of DNA replication by ultraviolet light in normal human and xeroderma pigmentosum fibroblasts. *J. molec. Biol.* **149**, 171–187.

KAUFMANN, W. K., CLEAVER, J. E. & PAINTER, R. B. (1980). Ultraviolet radiation inhibits replicon initiation in *S* phase human cells. *Biochim. biophys. Acta* **608**, 191–195.

KLEIJER, W. J., DE WEERD-KASTELEIN, E. A., SLUYTER, M. L., KEIJZER, W., DE WIT, J. & BOOTSMA, D. (1973). UV-induced DNA repair synthesis in cells of patients with different forms of xeroderma pigmentosum and of heterozygotes. *Mutat. Res.* **20**, 417–428.

KLÍMEK, M. (1965). Formation but no excision of thymine dimers in mammalian cells after UV-irradiation. *Neoplasma* **12**, 459–460.

LEHMANN, A. R. & STEVENS, S. (1975). Postreplication repair of DNA in chick cells: Studies using photoreactivation. *Biochim. biophys. Acta* **402**, 179–187.

LEHMANN, A. R. & STEVENS, S. (1977). The production and repair of double strand breaks in cells from normal humans and from patients with ataxia telangiectasia. *Biochim. biophys. Acta* **474**, 49–60.

MITCHELL, D. L., HAIPEK, C. A. & CLARKSON, J. M. (1985). (6-4) Photoproducts are removed from the DNA of UV-irradiated mammalian cells more efficiently than cyclobutane dimers. *Mutat. Res.* **143**, 112–115.

PAINTER, R. B. (1977). Rapid test to detect agents that damage human DNA. *Nature, Lond.* **265**, 650–651.

PAINTER, R. B. (1985). Inhibition and recovery of DNA synthesis in human cells after exposure to ultraviolet light. *Mutat. Res.* **145**, 63–69.

PAINTER, R. B. & YOUNG, B. R. (1976). Formation of nascent DNA molecules during inhibition of replicon initiation in mammalian cells. *Biochim. biophys. Acta* **418**, 146–153.

PATERSON, M. C. & SMITH, P. J. (1979). Ataxia-telangiectasia: An inherited human disorder involving hypersensitivity to ionizing radiation and related DNA-damaging chemicals. *A. Rev. Genet.* **13**, 291–318.

POVIRK, L. F. & PAINTER, R. B. (1976). The effect of 313 nanometer light on initiation of replicons in mammalian cell DNA containing bromodeoxyuridine. *Biochim. biophys. Acta* **432**, 267–272.

RAUTH, A. M. & WHITMORE, G. F. (1966). The survival of synchronized L cells after ultraviolet irradiation. *Radiat. Res.* **28**, 84–95.

REMSEN, J. F. & CERUTTI, P. A. (1977). Excision of gamma-ray induced thymine lesions by preparations from ataxia telangiectasia fibroblasts. *Mutat. Res.* **43**, 139–146.

RUDÉ, J. M. & FRIEDBERG, E. C. (1977). Semi-conservative deoxyribonucleic acid synthesis in unirradiated and ultraviolet-irradiated xeroderma pigmentosum and normal human skin fibroblasts. *Mutat. Res.* **42**, 433–442.

TOLMACH, L. J., HAWKINS, R. B. & BUSSE, P. M. (1980). The relation between depressed synthesis of DNA and killing in X-irradiated HeLa cells. In *Radiation Biology in Cancer Research* (ed. R. E. Meyn & H. R. Withers), pp. 125–142. New York: Raven Press.

WILKINS, R. J. (1983). Photoreactivation of UV damage in *Sminthopsis crassicaudata*. *Mutat. Res.* **111**, 263–276.

WOOD, R. D. & BURKI, H. J. (1982). Repair capability and the cellular age response for killing and mutation induction after UV. *Mutat. Res.* **95**, 505–514.

J. Cell Sci. Suppl. 6, 215–223 (1987)
Printed in Great Britain © The Company of Biologists Limited 1987

MOLECULAR SIGNAL FOR INDUCTION OF THE ADAPTIVE RESPONSE TO ALKYLATION DAMAGE IN *ESHERICHIA COLI*

B. SEDGWICK

Imperial Cancer Research Fund, Clare Hall Laboratories, South Mimms, Herts EN6 3LD, UK

SUMMARY

Exposure of *Escherichia coli* to simple alkylating agents, such as methylnitrosourea, causes the induction of at least three DNA repair functions that are under the control of the *ada* gene. The *ada* gene product itself repairs several O-methylated lesions in DNA, including methylphospho-triesters and the mutagenic adduct O^6-methylguanine. The methyl groups are transferred from these lesions on to two different cysteine residues within the Ada protein resulting in self-methylation. We have found that the Ada protein is converted to an activator of expression of genes involved in the adaptive response after accepting a methyl group from a methylphosphotriester, but not from O^6-methylguanine. This was shown using the *in vitro* techniques of DNA-dependent protein synthesis and run-off transcription. Delayed electrophoretic migration and footprinting experiments have shown that the methylated activator of transcription binds to specific DNA sequences immediately upstream from the RNA polymerase binding sites in the promoter regions of the inducible genes. The Ada protein-binding sites contain the common sequence d(A-A-A-N-N-A-A-A-G-C-G-C-A).

INTRODUCTION

The adaptive response to alkylation damage is induced in *Escherichia coli* on exposure to simple alkylating agents, such as N-methylnitrosourea (MNU) and N-methyl-N'-nitro-N-nitrosoguanidine (MNNG) (Samson & Cairns, 1977). This DNA repair pathway is not induced by ultraviolet irradiation and occurs in RecA mutants, and is therefore independent of the inducible SOS response (Jeggo *et al.* 1977). The increased resistance of the induced cells to both the mutagenic and toxic effects of alkylating agents is known to correlate with the induction of at least two enzymes that repair a wide range of methylation lesions in DNA (Karran *et al.* 1982).

AlkA mutants of *E. coli* are sensitive to the toxicity of alkylating agents and are deficient in one of the inducible enzymes, 3-methyladenine-DNA glycosylase II (Evensen & Seeberg, 1982). The *alkA* gene has been cloned and sequenced and shown to be the structural gene of the protein (Clarke *et al.* 1984; Nakabeppu *et al.* 1984). The enzyme excises 3-methyladenine and 3-methylguanine, which are toxic to the cell, and also the minor alkylated pyrimidines, O^2-methylcytosine and O^2-methylthymine (Karran *et al.* 1982; McCarthy *et al.* 1984). The second inducible enzyme, O^6-methylguanine-DNA methyltransferase, repairs the mutagenic lesions

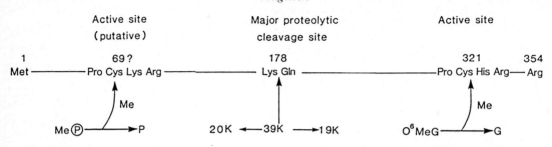

Fig. 1. Diagrammatic representation of the $39 \times 10^3 M_r$ (39 K) Ada protein, that is, the O^6-methylguanine (O^6MeG)-DNA methyltransferase. The putative position of the N-terminal active cysteine is within a similar amino sequence to the C-terminal active cysteine.

O^6-methylguanine and O^4-methylthymine by direct demethylation. The methyl groups are transferred from these lesions on to one of the enzyme's cysteine residues identified as cysteine 321 in the C-terminal half of the protein (Fig. 1) (Olsson & Lindahl, 1980; Demple *et al.* 1985). The same enzyme also repairs methylphosphotriester lesions in the DNA backbone. The 'S', but not the 'R', stereoisomer of methylphosphotriesters is repaired by methyl transfer to a different cysteine residue in the N-terminal region of the protein (McCarthy & Lindahl, 1985; Margison *et al.* 1985; Hamblin & Potter, 1985; Weinfeld *et al.* 1985). The location of this acceptor cysteine has yet to be determined. Cysteine 69 may be the second acceptor cysteine (Fig. 1) because it is within a protein sequence similar to the C-terminal active site. In accepting a methyl group from one O^6-methylguanine or O^4-methylthymine lesion and one methylphosphotriester lesion the methyltransferase is inactivated as a DNA repair enzyme.

The $39 \times 10^3 M_r$ methyltransferase is very sensitive to proteolysis on cell lysis (Teo *et al.* 1984). As a result of this, the enzyme was originally purified as a $19 \times 10^3 M_r$ C-terminal fragment, which can repair O^6-methylguanine and O^4-methylthymine but not methylphos photriesters (see Fig. 1) (Demple *et al.* 1982). The protease responsible has not been identified, but resembles an activity that cleaves the UvrB protein in over-producing cells (Teo, 1986; Arikan *et al.* 1986).

The $39 \times 10^3 M_r$ protein was shown, by immunological cross-reactivity, and DNA and protein sequencing, to be the product of the *ada* gene (Teo *et al.* 1984). Ada mutants were first characterized as regulatory mutants of the adaptive response as they lack both methyltransferase and glycosylase activities (Lindahl *et al.* 1983). The cloned *ada* gene product was found to stimulate *in vivo* expression of both its own gene and that of *alkA*, that is, it acts as a positive regulator of the adaptive response (Sedgwick, 1983; Demple *et al.* 1985; LeMotte & Walker, 1985). The Ada protein has, therefore, both regulatory and DNA repair activities, and in this respect is comparable with the RecA protein.

Two additional genes, *alkB* and *aidB*, have also been associated with the adaptive response. Expression of *aidB* is regulated by the Ada protein whereas *alkB* forms a small operon with *ada*. AlkB mutants are sensitive to alkylating agents whereas AidB mutants are resistant (Kataoka & Sekiguchi, 1985; Volkert & Ngyuen, 1984). The functions of the gene products are unknown.

MECHANISM OF ACTIVATION OF Ada PROTEIN AS A POSITIVE REGULATOR

We have recently been engaged in efforts to identify the inducing signal of the adaptive response produced in cells exposed to methylating agents, and to determine the role of the *ada* gene product in this regulatory mechanism.

Self-methylation of the Ada protein or its proteolytic cleavage have been proposed as possible mechanisms of its activation as a positive regulator of the adaptive response. The effects of addition of these various forms of the Ada protein on the expression of the *ada* and *alkA* genes were therefore examined *in vitro* using the techniques of DNA-directed protein synthesis and run-off transcription (Teo *et al.* 1986).

The plasmid pCS68 encodes three polypeptides, the products of the *amp*, *tet* and *ada* genes (Teo *et al.* 1984). The major ^{35}S-labelled polypeptide synthesized in the Zubay system (Zubay, 1973) directed by pCS68 was the $31 \times 10^3 M_r$ β-lactamase, the product of the *amp* gene. Little or no synthesis of the $36 \times 10^3 M_r$ Tet protein or the $39 \times 10^3 M_r$ Ada protein was observed. Various forms of the Ada protein were added to this Zubay system in attempts to stimulate expression of the *ada* gene. Addition of the $39 \times 10^3 M_r$ Ada protein or its $19 \times 10^3 M_r$ C-terminal fragment did not induce synthesis of new Ada protein. However, the $39 \times 10^3 M_r$ Ada protein, self-methylated by preincubation with MNU-treated DNA, was an efficient activator of *ada* gene expression (Teo *et al.* 1986). The methylated $19 \times 10^3 M_r$ fragment did not induce expression.

During repair of methylated DNA, the Ada protein can be self-methylated at two active cysteines by accepting methyl groups from O^6-methylguanine and methyl-phosphotriesters (see Fig. 1). To determine whether Ada protein methylated at only one of these sites could activate *ada* gene expression, the Ada protein was incubated with substrates containing only one of these sources of methyl groups. The substrate containing only O^6-methylguanine was a double-stranded symmetrical oligonu-cleotide containing two O^6-methylguanine·thymine base pairs. The substrate con-taining methylphosphotriesters but no O^6-methylguanine was poly(dA)·poly(dT) methylated in only one of the strands. Methylated poly(dT) contains some O^4-methylthymine but this was removed by mild acidic hydrolysis. The Ada protein singly methylated by repair of O^6-methylguanine did not stimulate new synthesis of Ada protein in the pCS68-directed Zubay system. However, Ada protein singly methylated by repair of methylphosphotriesters was an efficient activator of *ada* gene expression. Transfer of a methyl group from a methylphosphotriester lesion in DNA on to a cysteine residue in the N-terminal region of the Ada protein is there-fore the mechanism of activation of Ada protein as a positive regulator of its own expression.

In vivo observations made by LeMotte & Walker (1985) and Nakabeppu *et al.* (1986) have suggested that expression of the *ada* and *alkA* genes is regulated at the

B. Sedgwick

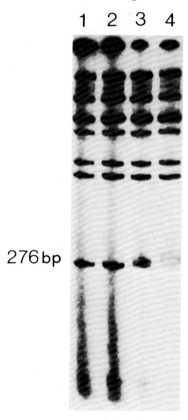

Fig. 2. Electrophoretic migration of an *ada* promoter DNA fragment was specifically delayed after incubation with methylated Ada protein. Ada protein was self-methylated by repair of MNU-treated DNA. An *Ava*I/*Eco*RI digest of the *ada*-carrying plasmid pCS42 (Sedgwick, 1983) was ^{32}P-end-labelled, incubated with methylated Ada protein at various molar excesses for 30 min at 20 °C, and then analysed on a 5 % polyacrylamide gel. The smallest fragment of 276 base-pairs (bp) contains the *ada* promoter region and 76 bp of the structural gene. The molar excesses of methylated Ada protein were: lane 1, no added protein; lane 2, 90-fold; lane 3, 370-fold; lane 4, 1750-fold.

transcriptional level. In our experiments, run-off transcription of fragments of the *ada* and *alkA* genes, carrying the promoter regions and part of the structural genes, was not observed in the absence of added Ada protein. Addition of unmethylated protein resulted in a small increase in transcription, but this was increased approximately 100-fold by addition of methylated protein. The sizes of the transcripts agreed with those expected from *in vivo* determinations of the transcriptional start sites (Nakabeppu & Sekiguchi, 1986). The ability of unmethylated Ada protein to act as a weak activator accounts for the low levels of methyltransferase and glycosylase in uninduced cells, and for the higher levels of glycosylase observed in cells containing the *ada* gene on a multicopy plasmid (Sedgwick, 1983). Self-methylation of the Ada protein therefore converts it to an efficient transcriptional activator of the *ada* and *alkA* genes (Teo *et al.* 1986).

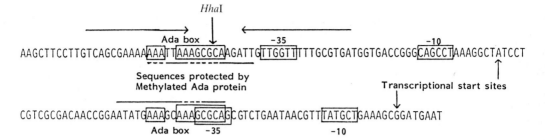

Fig. 3. DNA sequences of the promoters of the *ada* and *alkA* genes (upper and lower sequences, respectively) (Demple *et al.* 1985; Nakabeppu *et al.* 1984). The horizontal arrows indicate a region of dyad symmetry. The sequences protected by methylated protein from DNase I digestion are indicated. The broken lines indicate less well protected regions. The sequences common to the protected regions of both genes and the putative ribosome binding sites are boxed. The possible ribosomal binding sites of the *alkA* gene and the transcriptional start sites are from Nakabeppu & Sekiguchi (1986).

DNA BINDING SITES OF THE METHYLATED Ada PROTEIN

Digestion of the Ada fragment with *Hha*I in the promoter region upstream from the putative RNA polymerase binding site (see Fig. 3) resulted in a loss of the stimulatory effect of methylated Ada protein on run-off transcription. The methylated Ada protein may therefore be binding to the *ada* promoter in this region. Delayed migration on a polyacrylamide gel of an *ada* promoter fragment after incubation with methylated Ada protein also indicated that the protein was binding specifically to the *ada* promotor region. The *ada* plasmid pCS42 (Sedgwick, 1983) was cut with *Ava*I and *Eco*RI into eight fragments, which were ^{32}P-end-labelled and incubated with methylated Ada protein at a molar excess of zero to 1000-fold. Incubation with high concentrations of protein resulted in a slight but significant delayed migration on a polyacrylamide gel of the 276 base-pair fragment that contained the *ada* promoter region (Fig. 2). A shift to form a distinct new band of apparently higher molecular weight, as observed in similar experiments on other DNA binding proteins (Garner & Revzin, 1981; Hendrickson & Schleif, 1984) did not occur, possibly because of instability of the complex during migration through the polyacrylamide gel. The delayed migration of only the 276 base-pair fragment indicated that Ada protein was binding specifically to the *ada* promoter region.

The binding site was defined more precisely by DNase I footprinting experiments (Galas & Schmitz, 1978). End-labelled DNA fragments of the *ada* and *alkA* genes carrying the promoter regions and part of the structural genes were incubated with a 50-fold molar excess of methylated Ada protein and digested to a limited extent with DNase I. When the digests were examined on a denaturing polyacrylamide gel, the methylated Ada protein was observed to protect certain regions of the *ada* and *alkA* promoters (Teo *et al.* 1986; see Figs 3 and 4). The unmethylated protein did not protect these regions from DNase I digestion. The poor ability of the unmethylated protein to bind is in agreement with it being a weak activator of transcription. Self-methylation of the Ada protein therefore enables it to bind specifically and efficiently to the *ada* and *alkA* promoters.

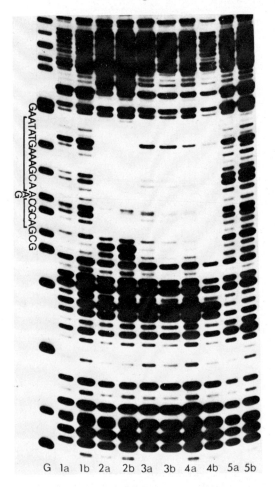

Fig. 4. Protection of the *alkA* promoter against DNase I by methylated forms of the Ada protein. Ada protein (5pmol) was incubated with various substrates and then added to 0·1pmol of a 267 bp *Acc*I–*Mlu*I fragment of the *alkA* gene labelled with ^{32}P at the 3′ end of the *Acc*I site. The complexes were partially digested with DNase I and analysed on a denaturing 8 % polyacrylamide gel. The DNA substrates were: lane 1, *Micrococcus luteus* DNA; lane 2, MNU-treated *Micrococcus luteus* DNA; lane 3, a mixture of the substrates in lanes 4 and 5; lane 4, poly(dA)·poly(dT) containing a MNU-treated poly(dA) strand; lane 5, a double-stranded oligonucleotide containing O^6-methyl-guanine. The mixtures were digested with various concentrations of DNase I to obtain similar levels of digestion of non-protected DNA. Lane 1, 1ng μl^{-1} for 15 s (a) and 30 s (b). Lanes 2, 3 and 4, 5ng μl^{-1} for 10 s (a) and 30 s (b). Lane 5, 5ng $\mu g l^{-1}$ for 30 s (a) and 60 s (b). Lane G is the Maxam–Gilbert G sequencing reaction of the same fragment. The DNA sequence is taken from Nakabeppu *et al.* (1984). The brackets indicate the promoter region protected by methylated Ada protein from DNase I digestion.

The Ada protein singly methylated by repair of methylphosphotriesters, but not O^6-methylguanine, was also found to bind specifically to the same region of the *ada* promoter, which agrees with its ability to stimulate *ada* gene expression in the DNA-directed protein synthesis experiments described above (Teo *et al.* 1986). This singly methylated protein also protected the *alkA* promoter against DNase I digestion, however, the effect was only partial (Fig. 4), suggesting that it binds more readily to the *ada* than to the *alkA* promoter. This would agree with data indicating that the methyltransferase is induced to a greater extent than the glycosylase (Lindahl *et al.* 1983).

The sequence protected in the *ada* promoter is in the region of the *Hha*I site, in the centre of a region of dyad symmetry and immediately upstream from the putative RNA polymerase binding site (Fig. 3). The sequence protected in the *alkA* gene actually overlaps the proposed RNA polymerase binding site (Nakabeppu & Sekiguchi, 1986). Ada protein bound in these regions may therefore facilitate binding of RNA polymerase and in this way stimulate initiation of transcription.

The regions of the *ada* and *alkA* promoters protected by the methylated Ada protein have a long sequence in common, A-A-A-N-N-A-A-A-G-C-G-C-A, now referred to as the Ada box. This sequence is not present in any other *E. coli* promoters that are in the data banks (M. Ginsburg, personal communication). The only other gene known to be positively regulated by *ada* is the *aidB* gene, but the DNA sequence of this gene is not yet available.

Methylation of a specific cysteine in the N-terminal region of the Ada protein may produce a conformational change that enables the protein to bind specifically to the Ada box. This mechanism of activation is comparable with that of the cyclic AMP-receptor protein, which undergoes a conformational change on binding cyclic AMP, enabling it to bind to the promoters of catabolite-sensitive operons immediately upstream or overlapping their RNA polymerase binding sites (reviewed by de Crombrugghe *et al.* 1984; Raibaud & Schwartz, 1984). This regulatory mechanism is, however, quite different from that of the SOS response and the heat-shock response, which are also induced by stressful environments. The RecA protein is activated as a protease that destroys the *lexA* and other repressors of the SOS genes (Little & Mount, 1982; Walker, 1985). The regulatory gene of the heat-shock response encodes an alternative sigma factor of RNA polymerase, and in this way stimulates transcription of the heat-shock genes (Grossman *et al.* 1984; Landick *et al.* 1984).

Methylation of the Ada protein is the first example of covalent modification leading to activation of a regulatory protein (Teo *et al.* 1986). The protein is therefore also apparently irreversibly activated. Proteolytic cleavage of the Ada protein, which occurs rapidly on cell lysis, has not been reproducibly demonstrated *in vivo*, but it could possibly be of importance in destroying the activated Ada protein, and therefore in switching off the adaptive response. Preliminary evidence suggests that the 20×10^3 and $19 \times 10^3 M_r$ proteolytic fragments can still repair methyl-phosphotriesters and O^6-methylguanine, respectively. Although the self-methylated N-terminal fragment was able to bind to the *ada* promoter, as determined by DNase I footprinting experiments, it was unable to stimulate run-off transcription of the *ada* gene. This fragment must, therefore, contain the DNA binding domain that recognizes the Ada box, but the Ada protein needs to be intact in order to enhance initiation of transcription.

Methylphosphotriesters in DNA are not known to have a toxic or mutagenic effect on the cells. DNA polymerase I is able to synthesize past these lesions although the rate of replication is reduced (Miller *et al.* 1982). The only known importance of actively repairing methylphosphotriesters in *E. coli* therefore appears to be the induction of the adaptive response.

The recent work reported in this review was performed at the Imperial Cancer Research Fund in collaboration with Drs I. Teo, M. Kilpatrick, T. McCarthy and T. Lindahl, and is described in greater detail by Teo *et al.* (1986).

REFERENCES

ARIKAN, E., KULKANI, M. S., THOMAS, D. C. & SANCAR, A. (1986). Sequences of the *E. coli uvrB* gene and protein. *Nucl. Acids Res.* **14**, 2639–2650.

CLARKE, N. D., KVAAL, M. & SEEBERG, E. (1984). Cloning of *E. coli* genes encoding 3-methyladenine DNA glycosylases I and II. *Molec. gen. Genet.* **197**, 368–372.

DE CROMBRUGGHE, B., BUSBY, S. & BUC, H. (1984). Cyclic AMP receptor protein: role in transcription activation. *Science* **224**, 831–837.

DEMPLE, B., JACOBSSON, A., OLSSON, M., ROBINS, P. & LINDAHL, T. (1982). Repair of alkylated DNA in *E. coli*. Physical properties of O^6-methylguanine-DNA methyltransferase. *J. biol. Chem.* **257**, 13776–13780.

DEMPLE, B., SEDGWICK, B., ROBINS, P., TOTTY, N., WATERFIELD, M. D. & LINDAHL, T. (1985). Active site and complete sequence of the suicidal methyltransferase that counters alkylation mutagenesis. *Proc. natn. Acad. Sci. U.S.A.* **82**, 2688–2692.

EVENSEN, G. & SEEBERG, E. (1982). Adaption to alkylation resistance involves the induction of a DNA glycosylate. *Nature, Lond.* **296**, 773–775.

GALAS, D. L. & SCHMITZ, A. (1978). DNase footprinting: a simple method for the detection of protein-DNA binding specificity. *Nucl. Acids. Res.* **5**, 3157–3170.

GARNER, M. M. & REVZIN, A. (1981). A gel electrophoresis method for quantifying the binding of proteins to specific DNA regions: application to components of the *Escherichia coli* lactose operon regulatory system. *Nucl. Acids Res.* **9**, 3047–3060.

GROSSMAN, A. D., ERICKSON, J. W. & GROSS, C. A. (1984). The htpR gene product of *E. coli* is a sigma factor for heat shock promoters. *Cell* **38**, 383–390.

HAMBLIN, M. R. & POTTER, B. V. L. (1985). *E. coli* Ada regulatory protein repairs the Sp diastereoisomer of alkylated DNA. *FEBS Lett.* **189**, 315–317.

HENDRICKSON, W. & SCHLEIF, R. F. (1984). Regulation of the *Escherichia coli* L-arabinose operon studied by gel electrophoresis DNA binding assay. *J. molec. Biol.* **174**, 611–628.

JEGGO, P., DEFAIS, M., SAMSON, L. & SCHENDEL, P. (1977). An adaptive response of *E. coli* to low levels of alkylating agent: comparison with previously characterized DNA repair pathways. *Molec. gen. Genet.* **157**, 1–9.

KARRAN, P., HJELMGREN, T. & LINDAHL, T. (1982). Induction of a DNA glycosylase for N-methylated purines is part of the adaptive response to alkylating agents. *Nature, Lond.* **296**, 770–773.

KATAOKA, H. & SEKIGUCHI, M. (1985). Molecular cloning and characterization of the *alkB* gene of *E. coli*. *Molec. gen. Genet.* **198**, 263–269.

LANDICK, R., VAUGHN, V., LAU, E. T., VANBOGELEN, R. A., ERICKSON, J. W. & NEIDHARDT, F. C. (1984). Nucleotide sequence of the heat shock regulatory gene of *E. coli* suggests its protein product may be a transcription factor. *Cell* **38**, 175–182.

LEMOTTE, P. K. & WALKER, G. C. (1985). Induction and autoregulation of *ada*, a positively acting element regulating the response of *E. coli* K-12 to methylating agents. *J. Bact.* **161**, 888–895.

LINDAHL, T., SEDGWICK, B., DEMPLE, B. & KARRAN, P. (1983). Enzymology and regulation of the adaptive response to alkylating agents. In *Cellular Responses to DNA Damage* (ed. E. C. Friedberg & B. A. Bridges), pp. 241–253. New York: Alan R. Liss.

LITTLE, J. W. & MOUNT, D. W. (1982). The SOS regulatory system of *Escherichia coli. Cell* **29**, 11–22.

MARGISON, G. P., COOPER, D. P. & BRENNAND, J. (1985). Cloning of the *E. coli* O^6-methylguanine and methylphosphotriester methyltransferase gene using a functional DNA repair assay. *Nucl. Acids Res.* **13**, 1939–1952.

MCCARTHY, T. V., KARRAN, P. & LINDAHL, T. (1984). Inducible repair of *O*-alkylated DNA pyrimidines in *E. coli. EMBO J.* **3**, 545–550.

MCCARTHY, T. V. & LINDAHL, T. (1985). Methyl phosphotriesters in alkylated DNA are repaired by the Ada regulatory protein of *E. coli. Nucl. Acids Res.* **13**, 2683–2698.

MILLER, P. S., CHANDRASEGARAN, S., DOW, D. L., PULFORD, S. M. & LOU SING KAN (1982). Synthesis and template properties of an ethyl phosphotriester modified decadeoxyribo-nucleotide. *Biochemistry* **21**, 5468–5474.

NAKABEPPU, Y., MIYATA, T., KONDO, H., IWANAGA, S. & SEKIGUCHI, M. (1984). Structure and expression of the *alkA* gene of *E. coli* involved in adaptive response to alkylating agents. *J. biol. Chem.* **259**, 13 730–13 736.

NAKABEPPU, Y. & SEKIGUCHI, M. (1986). Regulatory mechanism for induction of synthesis of repair enzymes in response to alkylating agents; Ada protein acts as a transcriptional regulator. *Proc. natn. Acad. Sci. U.S.A.* (in press).

OLSSON, M. & LINDAHL, T. (1980). Repair of alkylated DNA in *E. coli*. Methyl group transfer from O^6-methylguanine-DNA to a protein cysteine residue. *J. biol. Chem.* **255**, 10 569–10 571.

RAIBAUD, O. & SCHWARTZ, M. (1984). Positive control of transcription initiation in bacteria. *A. Rev. Genet.* **18**, 173–206.

SAMSON, L. & CAIRNS, J. (1977). A new pathway for DNA repair in *E. coli. Nature, Lond.* **267**, 281–282.

SEDGWICK, B. (1983). Molecular cloning of a gene which regulates the adaptive response to alkylating agents in *E. coli. Molec. gen. Genet.* **191**, 466–472.

TEO, I. A. (1986). Proteolytic processing of the Ada protein that repairs DNA O^6-methylguanine residues in *E. coli. Mutat. Res.* (in press).

TEO, I. A., SEDGWICK, B., DEMPLE, B., LI, B. & LINDAHL, T. (1984). Induction of resistance to alkylating agents in *E. coli*: the *ada* gene product serves both as a regulatory protein and as an enzyme for repair of mutagenic damage. *EMBO J.* **3**, 2151–2157.

TEO, I. A., SEDGWICK, B., KILPATRICK, M. W., MCCARTHY, T. V. & LINDAHL, T. (1986). The intracellular signal for induction of resistance to alkylating agents in *E. coli. Cell* **45**, 315–324.

VOLKERT, M. R. & NGUYEN, D. C. (1984). Induction of specific *E. coli* genes by sublethal treatments with alkylating agents. *Proc. natn. Acad. Sci. U.S.A.* **81**, 4110–4114.

WALKER, G. C. (1985). Inducible DNA repair systems. *A. Rev. Biochem.* **54**, 425–457.

WEINFELD, M., DRAKE, A. F., SAUNDERS, J. K. & PATERSON, M. C. (1985). Stereospecific removal of methylphosphotriesters from DNA by an *E. coli ada* extract. *Nucl. Acids Res.* **13**, 7067–7077.

ZUBAY, G. (1973). *In vitro* synthesis of protein in microbial systems. *A. Rev. Genet.* **7**, 267–287.

J. Cell Sci. Suppl. 6, 225–241 (1987)
Printed in Great Britain © The Company of Biologists Limited 1987

DNA REPAIR IN SPECIFIC SEQUENCES IN MAMMALIAN CELLS

CHARLES A. SMITH

Department of Biological Sciences, Stanford University, Stanford CA 94305-5020, USA

SUMMARY

To investigate the influence of function or activity of a DNA sequence on its repair, we have studied excision repair of a number of adducts in the non-transcribed, heterochromatic alpha DNA of monkey cells (by physically isolating the DNA) and also the removal of pyrimidine dimers in a number of genes in rodent and human cells (by an indirect assay using a dimer-specific endonuclease). In confluent cells, psoralen and aflatoxin B_1 (AFB_1) adducts are produced in similar frequencies in alpha and in the rest of the DNA, but removal from alpha is severely deficient. Adducts of N-acetoxyacetylaminofluorene (NA-AAF) are formed in slightly higher frequencies in alpha, and removal is slightly deficient. The removal of thymine glycols from alpha DNA in gamma-irradiated cells is proficient, as is repair synthesis elicited by exposure to methyl methane sulphonate, dimethyl sulphate, or 254 nm ultraviolet light (u.v.). Removal of AFB_1 and NA-AAF adducts from alpha is enhanced by small doses of u.v. but not by X-rays or DMS. The quantum efficiency of conversion of psoralen monoadducts to crosslinks is much lower in alpha DNA. Taken together, these results suggest that the highly condensed chromatin structure of alpha hinders access of the repair system that acts on bulky adducts but not of systems for repair of specific base damage. u.v. damage may alter this chromatin structure directly or facilitate the action of some system that changes accessibility of chromatin to repair. The repair deficiencies are not observed in actively growing cells, in which chromatin structure may be less condensed due to DNA replication.

We have also demonstrated preferential excision repair of pyrimidine dimers in active genes. Dimers are efficiently removed from the essential dihydrofolate reductase (DHFR) and hydroxy-methylglutaryl CoA reductase genes in Chinese hamster ovary (CHO) cells and from the transcribed c-*abl* proto-oncogene in the mouse cells. Both cell types remove few dimers from their overall genomes or from sequences distal to the DHFR gene; dimers are also removed poorly from the non-transcribed mouse c-*mos* gene. In human cells, dimers are removed more rapidly from the DHFR gene than from the genome as a whole. However, repair is as deficient in this gene in XP-C cells as it is in the entire genome.

These results suggest that resistance to DNA damage correlates better with repair of vital or active sequences than with overall repair levels and that mutagenic efficiency may vary according to the activity of the gene under study.

INTRODUCTION

In the past several years many of us* working in the laboratory of Philip Hanawalt have focused on the study of excision repair in specific DNA sequences in cultured mammalian cells. Unrepaired damage in DNA of different functional states would be expected to have differing consequences for the cell. Mutations in active sequences or blockage of their transcription could have direct effects on cell survival and function.

---

*This contribution summarizes and discusses research carried out primarily by M. Zolan and S. Leadon (alpha DNA), V. Bohr and I. Mellon (specific genes), and H. Madhani and D. Okumoto (both areas).

Most of the DNA in a cell in a complex organism contains information unnecessary or inappropriate to its own specialized function, and is not expressed. The interference with appropriate control of expression of such information by persisting damage is also likely to play a role in carcinogenesis. Different states of chromatin into which the DNA is packaged may modulate the actions of particular damaging agents and the various repair systems to different degrees. To determine how the function or state of activity of DNA relates to its repair one must study particular sequences in known states of expression and/or chromatin configuration. We have studied in some detail a repetitive DNA species in monkey cells called alpha DNA, a non-transcribed sequence that can be isolated in sufficient quantity for examination by a variety of well-established techniques. For non-repetitive DNA, we have begun to develop methods that utilize hybridization with specific probes. Here, I will summarize our results with alpha DNA and present information about removal of pyrimidine dimers from some specific genes.

ALPHA DNA OF MONKEY CELLS

Alpha DNA is a highly repetitive DNA (Singer, 1982), found primarily near chromosome centromeres (Segal et al. 1976) in constitutive heterochromatin, comprising 15–20% of the genome of African green monkey cells (Maio, 1971). It is generally considered to be a non-transcribed sequence (Kuff et al. 1978) and no function for it has been identified. Sequences highly homologous to alpha have been found in several other primates, but in much lower quantities than in green monkey, e.g. in human cells, an alpha-like species comprises about 1% of the DNA (Wu & Manuelidis, 1980). Musich et al. (1977) reported that alpha chromatin was depleted in histone H1 and enriched for other chromosomal proteins. Strauss & Varshavsky (1984) described a high mobility group protein that binds to alpha DNA and suggested it aids specific nucleosomal positioning with alpha arrays. More recently this protein has been shown to bind specifically to short runs of $A \cdot T$ base-pairs (Solomon et al. 1986), and it may play a role outside alpha chromatin. The repeating unit of alpha DNA in green monkey cells is a 172 base-pair (bp) monomer, which has been cloned and sequenced (Rosenberg et al. 1978). Most of the monomers contain a single recognition site for the restriction endonuclease HindIII, and a clustered subset (about 10%) also contain a site for EcoRI (Wu et al. 1983). The sequence does not differ significantly from total cellular DNA in base composition and nearest neighbour frequencies.

We recently investigated the lengths of alpha arrays by digesting genomic DNA with restriction endonucleases and determining the sizes of fragments that hybridized to alpha-specific probe (Madhani et al. 1986b). We determined an average array length of about 450 monomer units (about 80 kb), probably an underestimate due to unavoidable shearing of DNA during manipulation.

Alpha DNA can be isolated from cellular genomic DNA by separation of HindIII fragments on preparative 2% agarose gels. Alpha DNA and the remaining cellular DNA (which we refer to as bulk DNA) are excised and purified for further study. We have compared DNA repair in alpha to that in the bulk DNA, both by measuring repair synthesis and by quantifying the persisting lesions, using radioactively labelled adducts or specific antibodies. The results described in the following sections (summarized in Tables 1, 2) were obtained with confluent cultures.

Ultraviolet light

We found no significant differences in the extent, time course, or dose response of repair synthesis in alpha and bulk DNAs in cells irradiated with 254 nm ultraviolet light (u.v.) (Zolan *et al.* 1982*a*). Repair was determined after doses ranging from $5\,\mathrm{J\,m^{-2}}$ (about 2 pyrimidine dimers per 10^5 bases of DNA) to $50\,\mathrm{J\,m^{-2}}$ at 4 and 24 h after irradiation, and over the entire time course up to 48 h following $20\,\mathrm{J\,m^{-2}}$. Chromatographic analysis of hydrolysed DNA showed that $50\,\mathrm{J\,m^{-2}}$ induced pyrimidine dimers with the same quantum yield in both alpha and bulk DNAs.

Furocoumarins

These tricyclic compounds intercalate into DNA and can covalently bind to pyrimidines upon absorption of 360 nm light. Linear furocoumarins (psoralens) can form both monoadducts and interstrand crosslinks, because each of the two ends of the ring structure (called the pyrone and furan ends) is positioned to allow formation of a cyclobutyl linkage to the 5–6 carbons of a pyrimidine, one above the plane of the intercalated psoralen molecule and one below it, on opposite DNA strands. Crosslink formation is a two-photon, sequential process: in the majority of monoadducts a thymine is linked to the furan end of the psoralen (furan-T monoadducts) and the

Table 1. *Repair in alpha DNA measured as repair synthesis*

Damaging agent	Incubation times (h)	Dose	Adducts per 100 kb	Repair (% of bulk)	Patch size Alpha	Bulk
Furocoumarins						
Angelicin	4–48	$25\,\mu g\,ml^{-1}+15\,kJ*$	(30)	30	20	20
AMT	4–48	$100\,\mu g\,ml^{-1}+2{\cdot}5\,kJ$	(30)	30	20	20
	24	$6\,\mu g\,ml^{-1}+2{\cdot}5\,kJ$	8	30		
HMT	4–48	$30\,\mu g\,ml^{-1}+7{\cdot}5\,kJ$	—	20		
Aflatoxin B1	4–48	$0{\cdot}3\,\mathrm{mM}$	450	25	10	20
NA-AAF†	4–48	$6\,\mu g\,ml^{-1}$	—	60	20	20
u.v. (254 nm)	4–48	$5\text{--}50\,\mathrm{J\,m^{-2}}$	4–40	90–100	20	20
Methylating agents						
MMS	8	$1\,\mathrm{mM}$	—	80		
	8	$4\,\mathrm{mM}$	—	80	8	8
DMS	8	$1\,\mathrm{mM}$	—	72		

Values in parenthesis are estimated from indirect measurements.
*kJ refers to $kJ\,m^{-2}$ irradiation with black light-bulbs.
† NA-AAF, *N*-acetoxyacetylaminofluorene.

Table 2. *Repair in alpha DNA measured by lesion removal*

Damaging agent	Incubation times (h)	Adducts per 100 kb		Removal (% of bulk)	Fraction removed from bulk
Furocoumarins					
AMT	24	8		30	0·3
HMT	24, 48	0·6		20	0·3–0·4
Aflatoxin B1	8–48	0·3		[0]	0·4*
NA-AAF	24				
		Alpha	Bulk		
N²-AAF		0·06	0·05	—	0
C8-AAF		0·16	0·07	55	0·6
C8-AF		0·28	0·20	75	0·5
Gamma rays	2	Thymine glycol	0·3	90	0·8

* Removal above that seen in XP-A cells.

unreacted pyrone end can then react to form a crosslink if another pyrimidine is in the appropriate position on the opposite strand. Monoadducts of angelicin, an angular furocoumarin, do not have properly positioned unreacted ends and do not normally form crosslinks. Furocoumarins provide a kind of hybrid species between u.v. irradiation-induced pyrimidine dimers and direct-acting chemical agents. Their adducts form through the same cyclobutane bridge to pyrimidines as in pyrimidine dimers. The requirement for photochemical activation provides more precise control of the amount and type of damage introduced than that for direct-acting chemicals. However, like other chemicals, their interaction with DNA is strongly modulated by chromatin structure. In addition, the monoadducts and crosslinks present fundamentally different challenges to cellular repair systems as well as qualitatively different obstacles for DNA transactions such as replication or recombination.

In contrast to results with u.v., repair synthesis in response to either angelicin or the psoralen derivative aminomethyl-trimethylpsoralen (AMT) was markedly deficient in alpha, being only about 30% of that in the bulk DNA from 4–8 h after treatment. On the basis of previous measurements of angelicin adducts in DNA (Zolan *et al.* 1982*b*) and AMT crosslinkable sites (unpublished results) in human cells we estimate that about 30 adducts per 10^5 bases were formed in the bulk DNA under conditions used in these experiments. With radioactive AMT at 4- to 16-fold lower concentrations, we found adduct frequencies to be the same in alpha and bulk DNA, and repair synthesis in alpha was still only about 30% of that in bulk. At 0·8 AMT adducts per 10^5 bases, about 28% were removed in 24 h from bulk DNA, but only 9% were removed from alpha. These results (Zolan *et al.* 1982*a*) were the first demonstration of heterogeneous repair among different genomic sequences DNA in a single cell.

A possible explanation for these results was that some specific furocoumarin adduct that is inherently refractory to repair is formed to a much greater degree in alpha DNA. To test this, we investigated removal of another psoralen derivative, hydroxymethyl-trimethylpsoralen (HMT), because methods for analysing HMT adducts by high-pressure liquid chromatography (HPLC) and the proportions of the various adducts formed in purified DNA had been reported (Kanne *et al.* 1982). The major monoadduct species, the furan-T monoadduct, exists in either of two diastereomers, depending upon whether the psoralen is 5′ or 3′ to the thymine in the DNA. These are the only forms present in large enough quantity to be candidates for the hypothesis under test; the deficient repair observed with angelicin ruled out differential crosslink formation and repair as a primary cause of the deficiency.

Repair of HMT adducts in alpha DNA was only 20% of that in bulk, both at high adduct frequencies (repair synthesis) and much lower ones (removal of labelled adducts). Analysis by HPLC showed that the relative amounts of the two diastereomers of the furan-T adduct were the same in alpha and bulk DNA, whether irradiated in cells or as purified DNA. Using treatment conditions that gave only about 3% of the adducts as crosslinks, we found that in 48 h all the monoadduct species were removed from bulk DNA to about the same extent, roughly 40%. These studies (Zolan *et al.* 1984) ruled out differential formation and repairability of different individual adducts as a cause for repair deficiency in alpha. However, they did provide evidence for an altered chromatin structure of alpha. Although we always observed similar total adduct frequencies for bulk and alpha DNAs, the ratio of crosslinks to monoadducts formed *in vivo* was considerably lower in alpha than in the bulk DNA. This was observed at two different overall levels of modification, but not when purified alpha and bulk DNA were reacted with HMT. This lower apparent quantum yield for conversion of monoadducts to crosslinks in alpha could be due to a more condensed chromatin structure, restricting the flexibility of the nucleosomal linker DNA, in which most of the psoralen adducts are found. Model building studies (Peckler *et al.* 1982) show that a large kink must occur in the DNA at the site of a crosslink; a reduction of the flexibility might therefore lower the quantum yield for crosslink formation.

Aflatoxin adducts

We also examined repair in cells treated with activated aflatoxin B_1 (Leadon *et al.* 1983). At high levels (about 440 adducts per 10^5 bases for both alpha and bulk DNA, measured using radiolabelled compound) repair synthesis in alpha was only about 25% of that in the bulk DNA. At much lower levels (about 0·3 adduct per 10^5 bases), analysis by HPLC showed that 95% of the initial adducts were to the N-7 position of guanine, and that loss of these adducts was much slower in alpha DNA than in the bulk DNA, but was still appreciable. In fact the rate of loss of adducts from alpha resembled that reported for the total DNA in xeroderma pigmentosum (XP) group A cells by Leadon *et al.* (1981). The loss in XP cells is ascribed to spontaneous release of the AFB_1 moiety from some guanines and the release of some of the modified guanines to leave apurinic sites (AP) sites, rather than to enzymic repair. The residual repair synthesis in alpha might result from excision repair initiated at these AP sites, indicating that such repair is at least partly proficient in alpha. Evidence for this was provided by measurements of the sizes of the repair patches in alpha and bulk DNA (see below).

Adducts of NA-AAF

This compound makes adducts to guanine (primarily at the C-8 and N^2 positions) that are not subject to spontaneous release. In cells treated with 25 μM NA-AAF, repair synthesis in alpha was about 60 % of that in the bulk DNA, considerably more than observed for furocoumarin or aflatoxin adducts (Zolan *et al.* 1982*a*). Studies with radiolabelled compound at 0·3 μM (Leadon & Hanawalt, 1984) showed that more adducts formed in alpha DNA (about 0·5 per 10^5 bases) than in the bulk DNA (0·32 per 10^5 bases). This reflected primarily an increase in G-C8-acetylamino-fluorene, with only a slight increase in the major adduct, G-C8-aminofluorene. The minor G-N^2-AAF adduct was formed in about equal frequencies, and was not removed in 24 h from either DNA species. For NA-AAF, differences between adduct removal from alpha and bulk DNA were complex. When expressed as the fraction of initial G-C8 adducts removed, repair in alpha after 24 h was about 70 % as great as that in bulk, but if considered as number of adducts removed, it was 90 %. Both G-C8 adducts contributed to these minor repair deficiencies. However the kinetics of removal differed; removal from alpha appeared to taper off rapidly after about 8 h whereas adducts were progressively removed from bulk DNA up to 48 h, the longest period studied.

Alkylation damage

Repair synthesis in response to methylating agents is thought to be initiated by sequential action of glycosylases specific for methylated bases and AP endonucleases. We exposed cells to the alkylating agents methyl methane sulphonate (MMS) (at 1 and 4 mM) and dimethyl sulphate (DMS) (1 mM) and incubated them in medium for 8 h. Repair synthesis in alpha was 80 % of that in the bulk for either concentration of MMS and was 72 % for DMS.

Thymine glycols

Saturation of the 5–6 double bond of thymine to give various products occurs when cells are treated with oxidizing agents, ionizing radiation or u.v. One of these products, the thymine glycol, can be produced specifically in purified DNA by treatment with osmium tetroxide. This facilitated the isolation of a monoclonal antibody to this lesion in DNA by Leadon & Hanawalt (1983), who used it to demonstrate rapid removal of most of these adducts by BS-C-1 cells. Glycosylases that act on thymine glycols have been identified in bacteria and mammalian cells, and it is assumed that removal of this lesion is mediated by glycosylase/AP endonuclease. Exposure of cells to 25 krad of gamma radiation produced 0·3 reactive site per 10^5 bases for both bulk and alpha DNAs, 90 % of which were removed from each species within 2 h.

Repair patch sizes in alpha and bulk DNA

We measured the average tract length of DNA synthesis associated with removal of adducts in both bulk and alpha DNA for most of the damaging agents used in these studies. Patch sizes were measured from density shifts of alpha DNA (172 bp) or bulk DNA reduced in length to about 200 bp by sonication (Smith *et al.* 1981).

The density shifts observed both in bulk and alpha DNA from cells treated with u.v., AMT and NA-AAF (Zolan *et al.* 1982*a*), were all similar, and the patch size was calculated to be about 20 nucleotides. A similar shift was observed with the bulk DNA of cells treated with AFB_1. However, the alpha DNA from these cells had a markedly smaller density shift indicating a patch size of about 10 nucleotides. Measurements on total DNA of XP (group A) cells and normal human fibroblasts treated with AFB_1 showed that patches in XP were about half the size of those in normal cells. A patch size of about eight nucleotides was calculated for both bulk and alpha DNAs from monkey cells treated with MMS. The absolute values for patch sizes cited here are less important than the clearly observable differences noted, which suggest that the average patch resulting from the glycosylase/AP endonuclease pathway is smaller than that made by the 'bulky adduct' pathway, deficient in XP cells. This patch size difference was originally documented with the bromo-uracil–photolysis technique (Regan & Setlow, 1974), although absolute sizes measured by that technique for bulky adducts have generally been greater than those we have measured. The smaller patch size observed for repair in alpha DNA containing AFB_1 adducts lends support to the hypothesis that a considerable portion of this repair synthesis results from repair of AP sites and that bona fide enzymic repair of the original AFB_1 adducts in alpha is severely deficient. For furocoumarin and NA-AAF adducts, the lower repair synthesis observed in alpha appears to reflect normal repair at some lower efficiency.

Enhancement of repair in alpha

With the exception of u.v., deficient repair in alpha appeared to be confined to bulky adducts. To explain the proficient repair of u.v. photoproducts, we suggested that u.v. irradiation might itself alter the chromatin structure of alpha, or that u.v. photoproducts might be more efficient at stimulating factors that generally render chromatin accessible to repair. We therefore assessed the effect of u.v. irradiation on removal of chemical damage (Leadon *et al.* 1983; Leadon & Hanawalt, 1984). Cells were u.v.-irradiated and treated with small amounts of labelled AFB_1, and the amount of total adducts removed from bulk and alpha DNA was determined after 8 h. u.v. had no effect on removal from bulk DNA, but it increased removal from alpha up to a dose of 5 J m^{-2}. At this point it was the same in alpha as in bulk, and was not increased by higher u.v. doses. Increasing the time between u.v. irradiation and AFB_1 treatment decreased the effect in a manner that suggested the increased removal is a function of the absolute number of photoproducts remaining in the DNA at the time of AFB_1 treatment. The enhancement was not dependent upon new protein synthesis and was not observed when DMS or gamma rays were used in place of u.v. When 5 J m^{-2} u.v. and NA-AAF were combined, removal of NA-AAF adducts was also enhanced. However, in two experiments we did not observe enhancement of removal of AMT adducts by u.v.

Repair in actively growing cells

All the studies heretofore described used confluent cultures, in which the cells enter a G_0-like state and very little DNA synthesis or cell division occurs. In actively growing cells one might expect changes in chromatin structure preparatory to DNA replication or cell division to affect repair in alpha. Leadon & Hanawalt (1986) showed that for actively growing cells containing low frequencies of AFB_1 adducts, removal of adducts from alpha was nearly as fast as from bulk DNA. This was due both to an increased rate of removal from alpha and a decreased rate of removal from the bulk DNA, compared to confluent cells. This same result was obtained for repair in the 12-h period beginning 3 h after subculturing cells from the confluent state, a regimen that synchronizes the cells for about one cell cycle. Interestingly, very little removal was observed for either alpha or bulk DNA during the following 12-h period that corresponds to the S phase in this system, and removal was maximal for both species in a final 12-h period, corresponding to late S/G_2. Similar results were obtained with NA-AAF treatment. We also examined repair replication in alpha DNA in growing cells in the 8 h following exposure to $20 \, \text{J m}^{-2}$ u.v. or to high levels of HMT or AFB_1. For u.v., repair was the same in alpha and bulk DNA, and repair in alpha for the two chemical agents was indeed higher than we had found for confluent cells, being about 50 % of that in bulk DNA for AFB_1 and 75 % for HMT.

Conclusions from study of alpha DNA

The most striking feature of the interactions of alpha DNA with damaging agents and repair systems is its complexity. In non-dividing cells, something about the organization of alpha severely restricts the cell's ability to remove furocoumarin and AFB_1 adducts, both at frequencies that elicit maximal repair response in the bulk DNA and at frequencies 500–1000 times lower. Yet, overall frequencies of these adducts were the same in alpha and bulk DNA. It appears that repair systems for these adducts are somehow excluded from interacting with the DNA although the damaging agents are not. This exclusion does not extend to repair systems for AP sites, thymine glycols and alkylation damage under the same conditions. Repair deficiency for NA-AAF adducts is variable and appears to depend on adduct frequencies. u.v. damage presents a special case. In actively dividing cells all the repair deficiencies are eliminated or greatly reduced.

Our interpretation of these results involves ideas about the degree to which the DNA in chromatin must be made accessible to the incising activity of repair systems. Glycosylases and AP endonucleases are relatively small and recognize specific short-range aspects of DNA structure. They may be able to penetrate even compact chromatin, and recognize their substrates even when the DNA is tightly associated with chromatin proteins.

Repair pathways for the bulky adducts we studied are known to share common steps because they are all poorly repaired in XP cells. The complexity of the recognition step for such adducts is revealed by the large number of complementation groups of XP cells. Part of this complexity is probably due to a multiple subunit structure of the actual incising activity, which is assumed to recognize many different bulky adducts. Studies of the UVR-ABC nuclease of *Escherichia coli* suggest that such an incising activity recognizes a damage-induced change in DNA conformation rather than specific features of adducts themselves (see Sancar *et al.* 1985). Part of this complexity of recognition probably also reflects the need for alteration of chromatin structure prior to incision, both for physical access of the repair enzymes to the damage in compact chromatin, and at the actual lesion site to allow the incising activity to interact with DNA unconstrained by nucleosome structure.

Extracts of some XP cells are able to promote excision of pyrimidine dimers in pure DNA or heterologous chromatin (Mortelmans *et al.* 1976; Fujiwara & Kano, 1983), and XP-C cells appear to confine repair to certain regions of the chromatin (Mansbridge & Hanawalt, 1983; Mullenders *et al.* 1987). These and results described below suggest the existence of systems to make lesions accessible to repair enzymes, but little information is available on how they might function. The complexity of such systems is probably related directly to that of chromatin itself. Domains containing active or potentially active genes may require less 'opening up' than those containing genes not competent for transcription and domains containing DNA such as alpha. A 'scanning' system may operate on some domains constitutively, but extend its activity to the entire genome only after triggering by DNA damage or its repair. Pyrimidine dimers may be especially efficient at triggering such a system, or their presence in domains of compact chromatin may directly facilitate its function in them. Cycling cells may simply maintain alpha chromatin in a more accessible state, perhaps due to its location at centromeres.

REPAIR IN NON-REPETITIVE SEQUENCES

We are developing indirect methods to study repair in sequences in the cell that cannot be isolated in quantity. One such method uses bacteriophage T4 endonuclease V to provide specificity for u.v.-induced pyrimidine dimers and hybridization to specific probes to quantify repair in sequences present in as few as two copies per cell. The essential features of the method are as follows: after irradiation with u.v., cells are lysed either immediately or after incubation in bromodeoxyuridine for various periods. After proteinase digestion, high molecular weight DNA is extracted, freed of RNA, and digested with an appropriate restriction endonuclease. Unreplicated DNA isolated by centrifugation in CsCl is dialysed and concentrated. For each sample, two equal portions ($2-10\,\mu g$), one of which is treated with T4 endonuclease V), are electrophoresed in parallel lanes in 0.4% alkaline agarose gels, transferred to a support membrane and hybridized to ^{32}P-labelled probes specific for the sequences of interest. In DNA not treated with T4 endonuclease, bands with the expected electrophoretic mobility of the full-length restriction fragments under study are revealed by autoradiography of the membrane. In samples treated with the nuclease the amount of hybridization at the full-length position is diminished due to nicking of those fragments containing one or more pyrimidine dimers. Assuming a random production of pyrimidine dimers, their actual frequency can be calculated from the fraction of fragments with no endonuclease-sites (ESS), using the Poisson expression. The amount of hybridization at the position of intact fragments for each sample is quantified by densitometry of the autoradiograms or, in the case of sufficiently amplified sequences, by scintillation counting of excised regions of the membrane.

This method places constraints on usable fragment sizes and u.v. doses. The gel must adequately resolve the full-length restriction fragments from the products of T4 endonuclease digestion. The initial frequency of pyrimidine dimers must be great enough to result in measurable reduction of the amount of full-length fragments, but still low enough that repair results in significant re-appearance of full-length fragments, at least in positive controls. These conditions are met with 15–25 kilobase (kb) fragments and u.v. doses of $10–20 \, \text{J m}^{-2}$. To date, our studies have concentrated on a few well-characterized genes, using detailed genomic restriction maps to guide the choice of restriction nucleases and probes. Probes from genomic clones are advantageous because they may be used to examine sequences outside transcription units, they often hybridize to a single restriction fragment, and they usually have extensive homology to the genomic fragments under study. They do often contain repeated sequences, however, which necessitates pre-hybridization of the membranes with a preparation of non-radioactive highly repeated DNA.

The method was initially developed using Chinese hamster cells (CHO) that contain an intrachromosomal amplification of the dihydrofolate reductase (DHFR) gene, to about 100 copies (Bohr *et al.* 1985). This provided sufficient hybridization to permit quantification by scintillation counting. The formation of ESS as a function of u.v. dose $(5–40 \, \text{J m}^{-2})$ was 0·6 per 100 kb per J m^{-2} both for a 14 kb *Kpn*I fragment that comprises the 5′ half of the DHFR transcription unit and for a 22 kb *Hin*dIII fragment, most of which extends 3′ to the gene. This value is in reasonable agreement with that obtained by chromatographic assay (0·8), by van Zeeland *et al.* (1981).

To measure repair we determine the disappearance of sites sensitive to T4 endonuclease V. We assume that this reflects removal of pyrimidine dimers, although any alteration of dimers that rendered them insensitive to the nuclease would appear as removal, unless the altered site was alkali-labile. The following summarizes results obtained with this method to date (May 1986).

Chinese hamster cells

Much of our work has focused on the well-characterized DHFR gene in CHO cells. A number of investigators have generously provided us with extensive and detailed maps, cell lines, and cloned genomic fragments. In cells containing an amplification of a large region that includes the DHFR gene, we determined that repair in the DHFR gene itself was much more efficient than in the genome overall (Bohr *et al.* 1985). After $10 \, \text{J m}^{-2}$, almost 60 % of the ESS were removed from a 14 kb fragment in the gene in 8 h, and about 40 % were removed after $20 \, \text{J m}^{-2}$. We confirmed the expectation from the work of others that overall removal of dimers was poor in these CHO cells using a sensitive technique in which permeabilized cells are treated with T4 endonuclease, and their DNA is analysed on alkaline sucrose gradients (van Zeeland *et al.* 1981). Only about 15 % of the ESS had been removed in 24 h in cells irradiated with 5 J m^{-2}, a dose much lower than those used to measure repair in the DHFR gene. Repair in a 22 kb fragment also in the amplified unit, but located at least 40 kb from the DHFR gene, resembled repair in the genome as a whole: less than 10 % of the ESS formed by 20 J m^{-2} were removed after 24 h. This indicated that preferential repair was not a property of the entire amplified unit.

CHO and other rodent lines survive u.v. about as well as human cells, even though human cells remove pyrimidine dimers very efficiently. However, mutants of CHO cells that have lost their residual capacity to remove dimers are u.v.-sensitive, like human XP cells, demonstrating that the excision repair observed in CHO cells is necessary for their considerable u.v. resistance (see Thompson *et al.* 1987). Our results with the DHFR gene suggest that the u.v. resistance of CHO cells is achieved by selective repair of actively transcribed sequences, like the DHFR gene, that are vital to cell growth.

The use of cells in which a sequence of interest is amplified greatly facilitates the analysis, but a general method requires assay of sequences present in only one or two copies per genome. A number of technical refinements were made in the hybridization procedure to accomplish this, and we used scanning densitometry to quantify the hybridization. Repair in the parental CHO line was found to be similar to that in the amplified line (Bohr *et al.* 1986a). After 20 J m^{-2}, removal of ESS was substantial in the 14 kb intragenic fragment, but not detected in the fragment distal to the gene. Removal in the genome overall following 5 J m^{-2} was again about 15 %, confirming that the heterogeneity in repair is a property of the CHO cells and not related to sequence amplification.

More recently the region around the DHFR gene has been studied in more detail, again using the cells in which these sequences are amplified (Bohr *et al.* 1986b). Repair was assayed at 8 and 24 h following 20 J m^{-2} u.v. Removal of ESS from a 14 kb *Kpn*I fragment whose 5' end lies only about 8 kb from the 3' end of the transcription unit was nearly undetectable after 8 h and only 21 % after 24 h. Thus a sequence downstream from the transcription unit but very close to it exhibited the deficient repair characteristic of the overall genome. Within the gene itself, repair in a 7 kb fragment that lies at the 3' end of the gene was only about half of that observed for the 14 kb fragment that encompasses the 5' end of the gene. About 7 kb of unassayed DNA separates these two fragments. On the 5' side of the gene, repair was also very efficient. A fragment that includes the 5' end of the gene but also extends out about 19 kb in the 5' direction was repaired as well as the 14 kb fragment in the 5' end of the gene.

It has recently been reported that a transcription unit with polarity opposite to the DHFR gene is located just upstream from the DHFR 5' control region (Mitchell *et al.* 1986). The regions of most efficient repair thus correspond to the control region and the 5' ends of two transcription units. The region of efficient DNA repair in the DHFR locus is roughly 60 kb, a length similar to that calculated for some kind of structural 'domain' in chromatin by a number of different techniques (for review, see Pienta & Coffey, 1984). The low level of repair observed in fragments just 3′ to the transcription unit may reflect abrupt transition to chromatin structure characteristic of non-transcribed DNA, or it may result from transition to some other level of chromatin organization. The apparently lower repair in the 3′ region of the transcription unit itself may in part reflect the high u.v. doses necessary to study repair in the relatively small fragments available in that region, which place several dimers in the possibly more accessible 5′ region. Changes in chromatin structure along the gene or some processivity in repair may also account for this result. Detailed analysis of other genes and the surrounding sequences will be necessary to determine which if any of these features are general ones.

An experimental difficulty encountered with CHO cells is their extensive amount of replication: even after $20\,\mathrm{J\,m^{-2}}$ u.v., about half the DNA is replicated in 24 h. After longer times most of the DNA is therefore unavailable for analysis. To examine repair in non-cycling cells we used serum starvation, and followed repair for 48 h in the 14 kb fragment in the 5′ half of the gene and in the 14 kb fragment just downstream from the transcription unit. Replication under these conditions was only 4 %, and the difference in repair exhibited by the two fragments was about the same as observed in growing cells. After 48 h about 80 % of the ESS were removed from the fragment in the gene and less than 20 % were removed from the downstream fragment. Repair at early times also resembled that in the growing cells. These results indicate that the unreplicated DNA we assay in growing cells does not represent a selected population with abnormal repair characteristics, and that the heterogeneity in repair we observe is maintained for at least 48 h.

We have also begun to study the gene for hydroxymethyl glutaryl coenzyme A reductase, the pivotal gene in cholesterol biosynthesis, which has served as model for study of end-product regulation in mammalian cells (Osborne *et al.* 1985). Its rate of transcription in cultured cells can be varied over a large range by altering the lipid content of the medium. The low density lipoproteins (LDLs) present in serum result in a reduction of enzyme activity to about 5 % of that obtained in the absence of LDLs, mainly due to repression of the gene. Initial experiments with CHO cells growing in normal medium showed that repair of a large fragment wholly within the transcription unit is as efficient as that in the DHFR gene. Thus even moderately low activity may be sufficient to facilitate repair.

Mouse cells

Like CHO cells, cultured mouse cells exhibit only limited removal of pyrimidine dimers from their genomes overall (Yagi *et al.* 1984). We measured removal of ESS 24 h after a dose of $20\,\mathrm{J\,m^{-2}}$ in three different sequences in mouse 3T3 cells: a region upstream from the DHFR gene using a genomic probe, and the proto-oncogenes c-*abl* and c-*mos* using retroviral probes (Madhani *et al.* 1986a). Repair was efficient in a 20 kb intragenic fragment of the c-*abl* transcription unit, both in actively growing cells (60 % removed) and in contact-inhibited cells (85 % removed). This gene is known to be actively transcribed in these cells. In constrast, repair was relatively deficient in a 27 kb fragment upstream from the DHFR locus, a result similar to that observed for CHO cells. It was also deficient in fragments containing the silent c-*mos* locus. This locus contains a 14 kb open reading sequence identified by hybridization to retroviral probes. This sequence is hypermethylated and not represented in RNA in cultured cells, but is represented in RNA in mouse gonadal tissue and early embryos. A 15 kb fragment containing c-*mos* exhibited 22 % removal in confluent cells, and 9 % in growing cells. A 6·2 kb fragment containing the sequence exhibited little or no removal. These results extend the observation of preferential repair of active genes to another rodent system, and suggest that genes repressed for developmental reasons are not preferentially repaired. Implications for the role of repair in carcinogen-promoted activation of proto-oncogenes are discussed by Madhani *et al.* (1986*a*).

Human cells

Most pyrimidine dimers are removed by human cells in about 24 h; thus one would expect that preferential repair of active sequences might relate to the rate of their removal. Indirect evidence for rapid repair of active sequences was reported by Mayne & Lehmann (1982), who found that the rate of RNA synthesis in irradiated cells recovers after irradiation before overall repair is complete. To examine human cells for preferential repair we have used a line containing an intrachromosomal amplification for the region containing the human DHFR gene (Mellon *et al.* 1986). We analysed two different fragments, a 20 kb fragment located in the centre of the 30 kb gene, and a 25 kb fragment that contains only a few hundred bp of the 5' end of the gene and extends out in the 5' direction. For both of these fragments, more than 60 % of the dimers had been removed by 4 h after 10 J m^{-2}, a rate considerably greater than we expected for the genome as a whole, judging from our own previous work and published reports. We measured the removal of pyrimidine dimers in the overall genome of these same cells by treating permeabilized cells with T4 endonuclease V and analysing the molecular weight of the DNA on alkaline sucrose gradients. Only about 25 % had been removed in 4 h.

To ensure that the repair differences were not the results of using two different techniques, we devised a method to measure removal of ESS from DNA containing the DHFR gene region by the same technique used to assay total DNA. Besides determining the molecular weight average of the (T4 endonuclease-treated and untreated) mass-labelled cellular DNA in the sucrose gradients, we transferred the DNA in the gradient fractions of duplicate gradients to nitrocellulose, and hybridized to a 1·8 kb genomic probe, located at the 5' end of the gene. The molecular weight distribution for DNA that hybridized to the probe was identical to that for the total DNA for cells analysed immediately after irradiation. However, 4 or 8 h after irradiation, the molecular weight of DHFR-containing DNA was considerably greater than that of the total DNA. This was not due to replication of the DHFR-containing sequences, which was less than 6 %. In addition, using a probe for human alpha DNA, we found no such differences in molecular weights, indicating, as expected, that repair in alpha resembled that in the genome as a whole.

Calculations of the amount of removal (Table 3) were consistent with the values obtained by Southern analysis. The fragments containing the sequence that hybridizes to the probe could contain variable amounts of sequences outside the region in which rapid repair occurs. This would limit the increase in molecular weight used as an indicator of repair to the size of this region, resulting in an underestimate of repair within it.

These results indicate that at least the DHFR region is repaired in a preferential manner in these cells: the rate of its repair is considerably greater than that of the average sequence in the cell. The rapid repair of the fragment 5′ to the gene could indicate a divergent transcription unit, as has been shown in CHO and mouse cells, or might reflect some minimum size for preferentially repaired regions. We consider it unlikely that the preferential repair is related to amplification; preliminary experiments with unamplified cells also suggest rapid repair of the DHFR gene. We are currently examining DHFR and other genes in various human fibroblasts. The technique using slot blotting is sensitive enough for analysis of single-copy genes and promises to be useful for analysing repair of several different sequences in a single experiment without the requirement for extensive DNA preparation and digestion with different restriction nucleases.

We also compared the extent of repair in the DHFR gene in normal human cells to that in repair-deficient XP-C cells (Bohr *et al.* 1986a). Like CHO cells, XP-C cells remove only a small fraction of u.v.-induced pyrimidine dimers from their genomes, but unlike CHO cells, they are much more sensitive to u.v. than normal human cells. Recently it was demonstrated that the repair that does take place in XP-C cells seems to be clustered in certain regions of the genome (Mansbridge & Hanawalt, 1983), and also that this repair is associated with the nuclear matrix (see Mullenders *et al.* 1987). Measured 24 h after u.v., the repair in a 23 kb *Hin*dIII fragment that included the 5′ two-thirds of the DHFR gene was found to be nearly complete (70–90 %) in cultured normal skin fibroblasts or keratinocytes, but very low (0–20 %) in the XP-C cells. This indicates that the repaired regions in XP-C do not include all active genes. Taking the results for CHO and human XP-C cells together, it appears that u.v. resistance correlates better with efficient repair of active genes than with overall repair levels.

Table 3. *Removal of pyrimidine dimers (ESS) by human (6A3) cells*

Time (h)	% Removed				
	Southern analysis		Alkaline sucrose gradients		
	DHFR gene	5′ Flanking	DHFR region	Total DNA	Alpha DNA
1	6	14			
2	24	21		<10	
4	79	67	48	25	29
8		77	73	39	35
24		89		69	
48				91	

DISCUSSION

Our study of repair in coding sequences is only in its initial stage, but has already provided important insights. The demonstration of efficient repair in several genes in rodent cells suggests that these cells achieve high u.v. resistance despite low overall repair levels by repairing those sequences necessary for cell function. Whether this selective repair is a consequence of culture *in vitro* and whether it occurs for lesions other than pyrimidine dimers remains to be determined. For human cells, selective repair has been detected as a more rapid rate of repair for active sequences, although additional selectivity in the extent of repair could occur, but would be difficult to detect. If responsible for the rapid recovery of RNA synthesis reported by Mayne & Lehmann (1982), this selective repair would be an important factor in the resistance to u.v. of human cells, since rapid recovery of RNA synthesis appears deficient in u.v.-sensitive Cockayne's syndrome cells. At present we cannot adequately compare the rates of repair of active genes in human and rodent cells, because of the different u.v. doses and incubation times used.

Our results also indicate that damage in silent regions of the genome may have greater potential for engendering mutations and DNA re-arrangements than damage in or near transcriptive units.

The preferential repair of a given sequence could reflect greater accessibility, perhaps due to different chromatin condensation or to location in more accessible areas of the nucleus. The rodent cells may lack (or have lost during culture) a system present in human cells that renders the remaining DNA accessible.

Whatever its cause, the preferential DNA repair we observe mandates caution interpreting correlations, whether positive or not, between overall repair capacity and other biological parameters. Defects in preferential repair could have profound effects on such parameters without noticeably altering overall repair levels.

Research in our laboratory has been supported by grants to P. C. Hanawalt from the National Insitutes of Health of the U.S. Public Health Service, the American Cancer Society, and the U.S. Department of Energy. We are grateful to R. Schimke, R. Simoni, L. Chasin, G. Attardi and J. Hamlin for supplying us with cell lines and probes, P. Seawell and E. Wauthier in our laboratory for preparation of T4 endonuclease V, and many colleagues who have supplied expertise and materials.

REFERENCES

BOHR, V. A., OKUMOTO, D. S. & HANAWALT, P. C. (1986a). Survival of UV-irradiated mammalian cells correlates with efficient DNA repair in an essential gene. *Proc. natn. Acad. Sci. U.S.A.* **83**, 3830–3833.

BOHR, V. B., OKUMOTO, D. S., HO, L. & HANAWALT, P. C. (1986b). Characterization of a DNA repair domain containing the dihydrofolate reductase gene in Chinese hamster ovary cells. *J. biol. Chem.* (in press).

BOHR, V. B., SMITH, C. A., OKUMOTO, D. S. & HANAWALT, P. C. (1985). DNA repair in an active gene: removal of pyrimidine dimers from the DHFR gene of CHO cells is much more efficient than in the genome overall. *Cell* **40**, 359–369.

FUJIWARA, Y. & KANO, Y. (1983). Characteristics of thymine dimer excision from xeroderma pigmentosum chromatin. In *Cellular Responses to DNA damage* (ed. E. C. Friedberg & B. A. Bridges), pp. 215–221. New York: Alan R. Liss.

KANNE, D., STRAUB, K., HEARST, J. E. & RAPOPORT, M. (1982). Isolation and characterization of pyrimidine-psoralen-pyrimidine photoadducts from DNA. *J. Am. Chem. Soc.* **104**, 6754–6764.

KUFF, E. L., FERDINAND, F.-J. & KHOURY, G. (1978). Transcription of host-substituted simian virus 40 DNA in whole cells and extracts. *J. Virol.* **25**, 28–36.

LEADON, S. A. & HANAWALT, P. C. (1983). Monoclonal antibody to DNA containing thymine glycol. *Mutat. Res.* **112**, 191–200.

LEADON, S. A. & HANAWALT, P. C. (1984). Ultraviolet irradiation of monkey cells enhances the repair of DNA adducts in alpha DNA. *Carcinogenesis* **5**, 1505–1510.

LEADON, S. A. & HANAWALT, P. C. (1986). Cell cycle dependent repair of damage in alpha and bulk DNA of monkey cells. *Mutat. Res.* **166**, 71–77.

LEADON, S. A., TYRRELL, R. M. & CERUTTI, P. A. (1981). Excision repair of aflatoxin B1-DNA adducts in human fibroblasts. *Cancer Res.* **41**, 5125–5129.

LEADON, S. A., ZOLAN, M. E. & HANAWALT, P. C. (1983). Restricted repair of aflatoxin B1 induced damage in alpha DNA of monkey cells. *Nucl. Acids Res.* **11**, 5675–5689.

MADHANI, H. D., BOHR, V. A. & HANAWALT, P. C. (1986*a*). Differential DNA repair in transcriptionally active and inactive proto-oncogenes: c-*abl* and c-*mos*. *Cell* **45**, 417–422.

MADHANI, H. D., LEADON, S. A., SMITH, C. A. & HANAWALT, P. C. (1986*b*). Alpha DNA in African Green Monkey cells is organized into extremely long tandem arrays. *J. biol. Chem.* **261**, 2314–2318.

MAIO, J. J. (1971). DNA strand reassociation and polyribonucleotide binding in the African green monkey, *Cercopithecus acthiops*. *J. molec Biol.* **56**, 579–595.

MANSBRIDGE, J. N. & HANAWALT, P. C. (1983). Domain limited repair of DNA in ultraviolet irradiated fibroblasts from xeroderma pigmentosum complementation group C. In *Cellular Responses to DNA Damage*, UCLA Symp. on Mol. and Cell. Biol. New Series, vol. 2 (ed. E. C. Friedberg & P. C. Hanawalt), pp. 195–207. New York: Alan R. Liss.

MAYNE, L. V. & LEHMANN, A. R. (1982). Failure of RNA synthesis to recover after UV-irradiation: An early defect in cells from individuals with Cockayne's syndrome and xeroderma pigmentosum. *Cancer Res.* **42**, 1473–1478.

MELLON, I., BOHR, V. B., SMITH, C. A. & HANAWALT, P. C. (1986). Preferential DNA repair of an active gene in human cells. *Proc. natn. Acad. Sci. U.S.A.* (in press).

MITCHELL, P. J., CAROTHERS, A. M., HAN, J. H., HARDING, J. D., KAS, E., VENOLIA, L. & CHASIN, L. A. (1986). Multiple transcription start sites, DNase I hypersensitive sites, and an opposite-strand axon in the 5' region of the CHO DHFR gene. *Molec. cell. Biol.* **6**, 425–440.

MORTELMANS, K., FRIEDBERG, E. C., SLOR, H., THOMAS, G. & CLEAVER, J. E. (1976). Defective thymine dimer excision by cell-free extracts of xeroderma pigmentosum cells. *Proc. natn. Acad. Sci. U.S.A.* **73**, 2757–2761.

MULLENDERS, L. H. F., VAN ZEELAND, A. A. & NATARAJAN, A. T. (1987). The localization of ultraviolet light-induced excision repair in the nucleus and the distribution of repair events in higher-order chromatin loops in mammalian cells. *J. Cell. Sci. Suppl.* **6**, 243–262.

MUSICH, P. R., MAIO, J. J. & BROWN, F. L. (1977). Subunit structure of chromatin and the organization of eukaryotic highly repetitive DNA. *J. molec. Biol.* **117**, 657–677.

OSBORNE, T. F., GOLDSTEIN, J. L. & BROWN, M. S. (1985). 5' end of HMG CoA reductase gene contains sequences responsible for cholesterol-mediated inhibition of transcription. *Cell* **42**, 201–212.

PECKLER, S., GRAVES, B., KANNE, D., RAPOPORT, H., HEARST, J. E. & KIM, S.-H. (1982). Isolation and characterization of pyrimidine-psoralen photoadducts from DNA. *J. molec. Biol.* **162**, 157–172.

PIENTA, K. J. & COFFEY, D. S. (1984). A structural analysis of the role of the nuclear matrix and DNA loops in the organization of the nucleus and chromosome. *J. Cell Sci. Suppl.* **1**, 123–135.

REGAN, J. D. & SETLOW, R. B. (1974). Two forms of repair in the DNA of human cells damaged by chemical carcinogens and mutagens. *Cancer Res.* **34**, 3318–3325.

ROSENBERG, H., SINGER, M. & ROSENBERG, M. (1978). Highly reiterated sequences of simiansimiansimiansimiansimian. *Science* **200**, 394–402.

SANCAR, A., FRANKLIN, K. A., SANCAR, G. & TANG, M. S. (1985). Repair of psoralen and acetylaminofluorene DNA adducts by ABC exinuclease. *J. molec. Biol.* **184**, 725–734.

SEGAL, S., GARNER, M., SINGER, M. F. & ROSENBERG, M. (1976). In situ hybridization of repetitive monkey genomic sequences isolated from defective simian virus 40 DNA. *Cell* **9**, 247–257.

SINGER, M. F. (1982). Highly repeated sequences in mammalian genomes. *Int. Rev. Cytol.* **76**, 67–112.

SMITH, C. A., COOPER, P. K. & HANAWALT, P. C. (1981). Measurement of repair replication by equilibrium sedimentation. In *DNA Repair: A Laboratory Manual of Research Procedures,* vol. 1 (ed. E. C. Friedberg & P. C. Hanawalt), pp. 289–305. New York: Marcel Dekker.

SOLOMON, M. J., STRAUSS, F. & VARSHAVSKY, A. (1986). A mammalian high mobility group protein recognizes any stretch of six A·T base pairs in duplex DNA. *Proc. natn. Acad. Sci. U.S.A.* **83**, 1276–1280.

STRAUSS, F. & VARSHAVSKY, A. (1984). A protein binds to a satellite DNA repeat at 3 specific sites that would be brought into mutual proximity by DNA folding in the nucleosome. *Cell* **37**, 889–901.

THOMPSON, L. H., SALAZAR, E. P., BROOKMAN, K. W., COLLINS, C. C., STEWART, S. A., BUSCH, D. B. & WEBER, C. A. (1987). Recent progress with the DNA repair mutants of Chinese hamster ovary cells. *J. Cell Sci. Suppl. 6,* 97–110.

VAN ZEELAND, A. A., SMITH, C. A. & HANAWALT, P. C. (1981). Introduction of T4 endonuclease V into frozen and thawed cells. *Mutat. Res.* **82**, 173–189.

WU, J. C. & MANUELIDIS, L. (1980). Sequence definition and organization of a human repeated DNA. *J. molec. Biol.* **142**, 363.

WU, K. C., STRAUSS, F. & VARSHAVSKY, A. (1983). Nucleosome arrangement in green monkey alpha-satellite chromatin: superimposition of non-random and apparently random patterns. *J. Molec. Biol.* **170**, 93–117.

YAGI, T., NIKAIDO, O. & TAKEBE, H. (1984). Excision repair of mouse and human fibroblast cells, and a factor affecting the amount of UV-induced unscheduled DNA synthesis. *Mutat. Res.* **132**, 101–112.

ZOLAN, M. E., CORTOPASSI, G. A., SMITH, C. A. & HANAWALT, P. C. (1982a). Deficient repair of chemical adducts in alpha DNA of monkey cells. *Cell* **28**, 613–619.

ZOLAN, M. E., SMITH, C. A., CALVIN, N. M. & HANAWALT, P. C. (1982b) Rearrangement of mammalian chromatin structure following excision repair. *Nature, Lond.* **299**, 462–464.

ZOLAN, M. E., SMITH, C. A. & HANAWALT, P. C. (1984). Formation and repair of furocoumarin adducts in alpha deoxyribonucleic acid and bulk deoxyribonucleic acid of monkey cells. *Biochemistry* **23**, 63–69.

J. Cell Sci. Suppl. 6, 243–262 (1987)
Printed in Great Britain © The Company of Biologists Limited 1987

THE LOCALIZATION OF ULTRAVIOLET-INDUCED EXCISION REPAIR IN THE NUCLEUS AND THE DISTRIBUTION OF REPAIR EVENTS IN HIGHER ORDER CHROMATIN LOOPS IN MAMMALIAN CELLS

L. H. F. MULLENDERS, A. A. VAN ZEELAND AND A. T. NATARAJAN

Department of Radiation Genetics and Chemical Mutagenesis, University of Leiden, Wassenaarseweg 72, 2333 AL Leiden, The Netherlands and
J. A. Cohen Institute, Interuniversity Institute of Radiopathology and Radiation Protection, The Netherlands

SUMMARY

Several lines of evidence indicate that eukaryotic DNA is arranged in highly supercoiled domains or loops, and that the repeating loops are constrained by attachment to a nuclear skeletal structure termed the nuclear matrix. Active genes are transcribed at the nuclear matrix and during replication the loops are reeled through fixed matrix-associated replication complexes. We have investigated whether the repair of DNA damage also occurs in the nuclear matrix compartment. Biochemical analysis of confluent normal human fibroblasts, ultraviolet (u.v.)-irradiated with $30 \, \mathrm{J \, m^{-2}}$ and post-u.v. incubated in the presence of hydroxyurea, did not show any evidence for the occurrence of repair synthesis at the nuclear matrix either 30 min or 13 h after irradiation. Autoradiographic visualization of repair events in single DNA halo–matrix structures confirmed the biochemical observations. At a biologically more relevant dose of $5 \, \mathrm{J \, m^{-2}}$ repair synthesis seems to initiate at the nuclear matrix, although only part of the total repair could be localized there. In u.v.-irradiated $(30 \, \mathrm{J \, m^{-2}})$ normal human fibroblasts post-u.v. incubated in the presence of hydroxyurea and arabinosylcytosine for 2 h, multiple single-stranded regions are generated in a DNA loop as a result of the inhibition of the excision repair process. Different biochemical approaches revealed that most of the single-stranded regions are clustered, indicating that the repair process itself is non-random or that domains in the chromatin are repaired at different rates. Preferential repair of certain domains in the chromatin was shown to occur in xeroderma pigmentosum cells of complementation group C (XP-C). In XP-C cells these domains are localized near the attachment sites of DNA loops at the nuclear matrix. In contrast, xeroderma pigmentosum cells of complementation group D as well as Syrian hamster embryonic cells with limited excision-repair capacities, revealed a random distribution of repair events in DNA loops. The preferential repair of matrix-associated DNA in XP-C cells may be related partly to repair of transcriptionally active DNA and this may account for the ability of XP-C cells, in contrast to XP-D cells, to recover u.v.-inhibited synthesis of DNA and RNA.

INTRODUCTION

Models for the spatial and temporal organization of DNA replication and segregation of the duplicated DNA during mitosis imply the existence of a scaffold-like structure to which the DNA is attached (Comings, 1968; Dingman, 1974). Such a structure would provide binding sites for the origins of the tandemly arranged replicons.

Evidence for the binding of chromosomal DNA to a scaffold-like nuclear structure has been obtained from nuclei extracted with high concentrations of salt (Berezney & Coffey, 1977). This structure, termed nuclear matrix, appears to be a ubiquitous structure since it has been isolated from a wide variety of eukaryotic organisms. Different approaches indicate that the DNA is attached to the nuclear matrix *via* multiple supercoiled loops (Cook & Brazell, 1975; Mullenders *et al.* 1983*a*; Vogelstein *et al.* 1980) and that the anchorage points of the loops are organized non-randomly, transcriptionally active genes being in close proximity to the nuclear matrix (Mirkovitch & Laemmli, 1984; Small *et al.* 1985). Direct sequencing of matrix-associated DNA provides evidence for the involvement of specific sequences in the binding to the nuclear matrix (Goldberg *et al.* 1983).

The loop organization appears to be of relevance to DNA replication and transcription. A close relationship between average loop size and replicon size has been shown to exist (Buongiorno-Nardelli *et al.* 1982) and recent results suggest that the attachment sites of the loops at the nuclear matrix contain replication origins (Aelen *et al.* 1983). After initiation the DNA is reeled through fixed matrix-associated replication complexes (Dijkwel *et al.* 1979; Pardoll *et al.* 1980). Besides replication the nuclear matrix may also have a key function in transcription and RNA processing (van Eekelen *et al.* 1981). It is tempting to speculate that the association of regulatory elements with the matrix brings about functional compartmentalization of the nucleus.

Whether the matrix compartment also contains major binding sites for enzymes involved in repair synthesis is not known. We have investigated this question using similar methodology to that reported previously for the study of DNA replication (Dijkwel *et al.* 1979). Moreover, considering the non-random organization of DNA sequences in DNA loops, we have investigated whether different regions within DNA loops are repaired at different rates.

THE ROLE OF THE NUCLEAR MATRIX IN THE REPAIR OF ULTRAVIOLET-INDUCED DAMAGE

To study the extent of involvement of the nuclear matrix in DNA repair we have introduced damage into DNA by ultraviolet (u.v.) irradiation of the cells. For such a study u.v. irradiation as the source of DNA damage has a number of advantages. Since the distribution of u.v.-induced lesions within the genome is random (Rahn & Stafford, 1974), difficulties in interpretation of the data resulting from initial non-random distribution of damage are avoided. Moreover, the detection of excision repair sites by radioactive labelling is relatively simple and the effects of inhibitors on u.v.-induced repair synthesis have been investigated intensively. We have studied the localization of repair events in DNA loops by two approaches: a biochemical approach that involves progressively detaching DNA from the nuclear matrix with DNase I, and an autoradiographic approach that directly visualizes the distribution of repair events in DNA loops at the single cell level using the DNA halo–matrix technique (Vogelstein *et al.* 1980).

DNase digestion studies

In order to detect repair synthesis by radioactive labelling of u.v.-irradiated cells, it is necessary to reduce the incorporation of label by replicative synthesis to a sufficiently low level. In our studies this was achieved by using confluent human fibroblasts post-u.v. incubated in the presence of hydroxyurea (HU) or HU and arabinosylcytosine (araC). Under these conditions the label incorporated in un-irradiated cells amounted to about 8 % of the label incorporated in irradiated cells. However, since the rate of DNA synthesis after u.v. irradiation is reduced, the relative incorporation of label by replicative synthesis is expected to be even less in irradiated cells.

DNA attached to the nuclear matrix can be isolated as a rapidly sedimenting complex from nuclei, treated with 2 M-NaCl (nuclear lysate) and subsequently centrifuged in neutral sucrose gradients (Wanka *et al.* 1977; Fig. 1A). These complexes contain almost all the nuclear DNA arranged in supercoiled loops (Mullenders *et al.* 1983*a*). The relative positions of repair events (and replication forks) in DNA loops can be examined by cleaving the DNA with increasing concentrations of DNase I, since the probability of a DNA fragment being released from a loop by breaks will decrease the closer it is situated to a region bound on the nuclear matrix. DNase digestion of nuclear lysates prepared from unirradiated exponentially growing or confluent cells pulse-labelled for 10 min (Fig. 1B) indicates that nascent DNA is attached to the nuclear matrix by binding sites close to the replication forks (Dijkwel *et al.* 1979). The fact that the matrix is still enriched for nascent DNA after 30 or 60 min in the presence of inhibitors (Fig. 1C) is consistent with a reduction in DNA chain growth (Radford *et al.* 1982); under non-inhibitory conditions, the ^{3}H/^{14}C ratio decreases as the pulse length increases (Dijkwel *et al.* 1979). Since the attachment of replicating DNA to the nuclear matrix was also observed after u.v. irradiation, it is clear that the conditions used to reduce the replicative synthesis in favour of detection of repair synthesis do not alter the spatial organization of DNA replication at the nuclear matrix.

Measurement of repair synthesis was performed by short pulse-labelling of the cells at different times following u.v. irradiation at 30 J m^{-2}. In the presence of HU (or HU and araC) no preferential association of repair-labelled DNA with the nuclear matrix during either early repair (directly after irradiation) or late repair (13 h after irradiation) was observed (Fig. 2). Although these data suggest that repair synthesis after 30 J m^{-2} does not proceed *via* repair enzymes associated with the nuclear matrix, two aspects of the methodology employed have to be considered: the length of the pulse and the presence of HU. It is important, for this conclusion, to point out that pulses of 4–10 min are suitable for detecting matrix-associated repair. The time required to repair u.v.-induced dimers is about 3 min without inhibitor and about 15 min in the presence of HU (Erixon & Ahnström, 1979). Using the enzyme *Bal*31 nuclease we could show (see Fig. 6 and text below) that under our experimental conditions about 75 % of the repair patches made during a 10 min pulse, in the presence of HU, were not completed.

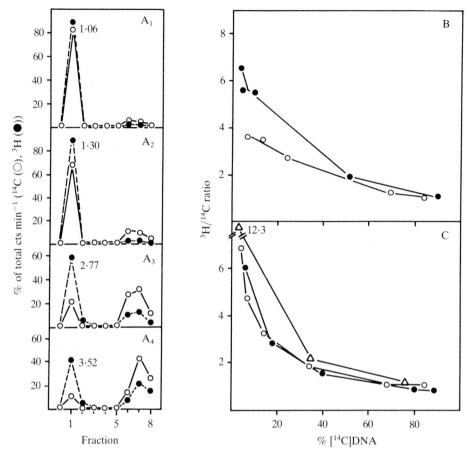

Fig. 1. Association of replicating DNA with the nuclear matrix (from Mullenders *et al.* 1983*b*). A. Exponentially growing ^{14}C-prelabelled cells were pulse-labelled for 10 min with [^{3}H]thymidine (25 μCi ml^{-1}) and nuclei were lysed in 2 M-NaCl (nuclear lysate). Samples of the nuclear lysate were incubated with 0 (A$_1$), 2 (A$_2$), 4 (A$_3$) and 6 (A$_4$) μg ml^{-1} DNase I and analysed in neutral sucrose gradients. Direction of centrifugation in this and other figures was from right to left. The numbers in the panels represent the ratios of the % of ^{3}H and ^{14}C cts min^{-1} in the DNA–nuclear matrix complex. B,C. Exponentially growing cells ($\bigcirc$, $\triangle$) or confluent cells ($\bullet$) pulse-labelled with [^{3}H]thymidine for 10 min without inhibitors (B) or 30 min in the presence of 10 mM-HU (C) or 60 min in the presence of 10 mM-HU and 0·1 mM-araC ($\triangle$; C). B and C, as well as Figs 3, 6, 8, show the ^{3}H/^{14}C ratio of the DNA–nuclear matrix complex *versus* the relative amount of prelabelled DNA remaining associated with the nuclear matrix.

It is unlikely that HU, which delays repair, may cause incomplete repair patches to detach from the matrix. The ligation of repair patches that is going on in the presence of HU is incompatible with a model in which the total repair process, i.e. from incision to final sealing by ligase, is localized at the nuclear matrix. Also the results of the autoradiographic analysis (see below) performed without HU show no evidence for a repair process occurring at the nuclear matrix.

A number of studies (Miller & Chinault, 1982; Dresler & Lieberman, 1983) suggest that the types of DNA polymerase involved in the repair of damage, not only depend on the kind of damage but also on the dose of damaging agent. On the basis of incorporation of [³H]thymidine in the presence of inhibitors, Dresler & Lieberman (1983) proposed that after low levels of u.v. damage, repair is largely carried out by polymerase β, while at high doses of polymerase α is the enzyme involved. However, at both low and high u.v. doses, under conditions of polymerase α inhibition, polymerase β may be responsible for the remaining repair (Smith & Okumoto, 1984). Since the location of repair processes in the nucleus may depend on the particular enzymes involved, we have investigated the repair process after a dose of $5 \, \mathrm{J \, m^{-2}}$. Fig. 3 shows that when a short pulse was given directly after u.v. irradiation, repair-labelled DNA was enriched at the nuclear matrix. The preferential labelling of matrix-associated DNA was dependent on the length of the time between

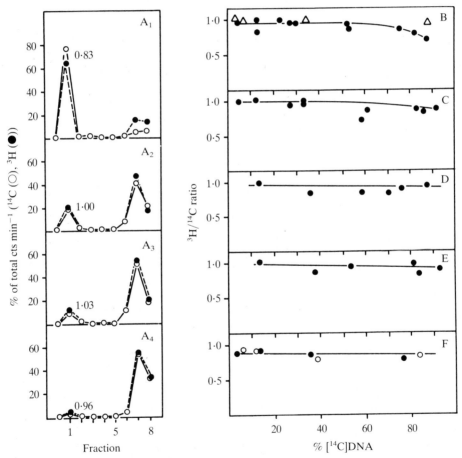

Fig. 2. Distribution of repair-labelled DNA in DNA–nuclear matrix complexes after $30 \, \mathrm{J \, m^{-2}}$ u.v. irradiation (from Mullenders *et al.* 1983*b*). Prelabelled confluent cells were u.v.-irradiated and pulse-labelled with [³H]thymidine ($50 \, \mu\mathrm{Ci \, ml^{-1}}$) in the presence of HU. Nuclear lysates were incubated with increasing concentrations of DNase I: A, 10 min pulse, directly after irradiation; B, 10 min pulse, directly after irradiation in the presence of HU (●) or HU and araC (△); C, irradiation, 10 min incubation, 10 min pulse; D, irradiation, 20 min incubation, 10 min pulse; E, irradiation, 20 min pulse; F, irradiation, 13 h incubation, 10 (●) or 20 (○) min pulse.

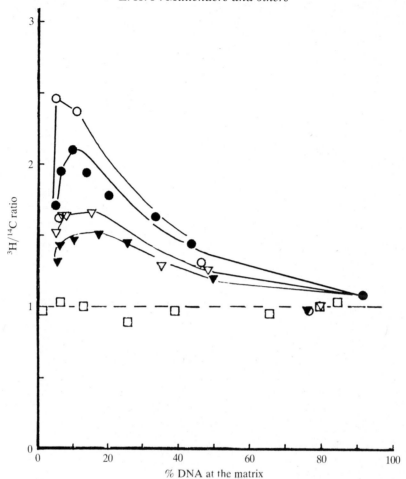

Fig. 3. Distribution of repair-labelled DNA in DNA–nuclear matrix complexes after 5 J m^{-2} u.v. irradiation. Confluent ^{14}C-prelabelled human fibroblasts were u.v.-irradiated and directly pulse-labelled with [^{3}H]thymidine (50 μCi ml^{-1}) for 5 min (○) or for 10 min (●) or for 2 h (□) in the presence of HU. In another set of experiments cells were u.v.-irradiated and incubated for 30 min (▽) or 2 h (▼) before starting 10 min pulse-labelling. Nuclear lysates were incubated with increasing concentrations of DNase I.

irradiation and pulse-labelling. Compared to a 10 min pulse given directly after irradiation a 10 min pulse given 2 h after irradiation results in a less preferential labelling of matrix-associated DNA. An obvious explanation of the data could be that at 5 J m^{-2} a dynamic repair process is operating that is localized at the nuclear matrix. However, considering the average repair time for a dimer in the presence of HU to be 10 min, an only two- to threefold enrichment is inconsistent with repair of lesions at the matrix. This may imply that matrix-associated repair is not inhibited by HU, or is inhibited to a lesser extent, resulting in a much shorter repair time (i.e. 3 min; Erixon & Ahnström, 1979) and that it may represent a fraction of repair, insensitive to inhibitors (Smith & Okumoto, 1984; Mullenders *et al.* 1985). If one assumes that the time required to repair a dimer by matrix-associated repair enzymes does not vary during the post-u.v. period, the distribution of repair patches after a short pulse is also not expected to vary at different times after u.v. However, we observed a variation in the distribution of repair label, which may be due to several factors. First, the time required to repair a dimer may be dependent on the period of post-u.v. incubation. Second, there may be two processes operating simultaneously: a matrix-localized repair process, and another that is not restricted to this substructure and is inducible. The relative contribution of the presumed inducible process to the total repair will increase during recovery and may increase also with increasing u.v. dose. The occurrence of such a process would account for the variation in the distribution of repair events at $5 \, \text{J m}^{-2}$, and for the absence of any sign of a matrix-associated process at $30 \, \text{J m}^{-2}$. There are some experimental data that are in favour of the hypothesis. The generation of DNA breaks in the presence of HU and araC is maximal 30–60 min after u.v. irradiation and this maximal number of breaks is dose-dependent (Erixon & Ahnström, 1979). An alternative explanation is that the two- to threefold enrichment is not a reflection of a dynamic repair process operating at the matrix, but merely a reflection of preferential repair of matrix-associated DNA sequences.

Autoradiographic analysis of repair events in DNA loops

To investigate the distribution of repair events at the single cell level we employed the DNA halo–matrix method (Vogelstein *et al.* 1980). Cells growing on coverslips are extracted with non-ionic detergent and high salt concentrations, including ethidium bromide in the final step. After relaxation of the DNA, the nuclear matrix surrounded by a halo of DNA can be seen in the fluorescence microscope (Fig. 4A). It is important to note that, in contrast to the biochemical experiments, the autoradiographic analyses are performed with exponentially growing cells in the absence of inhibitors. In our preparations about 18 % of the grains in prelabelled cells were associated with the nuclear matrix. In S-phase cells about 75 % of the label was overlying the nuclear matrix region after 6 min labelling. Following 6 min pulse-labelling directly after u.v. irradiation ($30 \, \text{J m}^{-2}$), grains were predominantly found in the halo region in non-S-phase cells (Fig. 4B). On average, about 33·9 % and 23·8 % of the grains were recovered from the nuclear matrix after 6 min and 10 min pulse-labelling, respectively. Although an enrichment of grains at the matrix was observed after a very short pulse (4–6 min), we did not see a very distinct preferential labelling of the nuclear matrix region compatible with the initiation of repair at the nuclear matrix as observed in the initiation of DNA replication. Thus the auto-radiographic analysis confirms the biochemical observations and suggests that at a dose of $30 \, \text{J m}^{-2}$ initiation of repair occurs in the DNA loops without requiring attachment of damaged sites to the nuclear matrix.

A similar approach has been used by McCready & Cook (1984) to investigate the initiation of u.v.-induced repair synthesis in HeLa cells. They reported a preferential labelling (2·5 or 5 min pulse) of matrix-associated DNA after high doses of u.v. light. However, as stated by the authors, the preferential labelling could be due to abortive

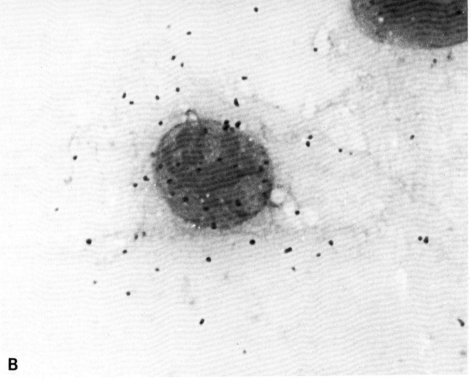

Fig. 4. Localization of u.v.-induced repair patches in DNA halo–nuclear matrix structures. A. Fluorescence micrograph of a DNA halo–matrix structure, prepared from normal human cells. B. Autoradiogram of a DNA halo–matrix structure prepared from cells pulse-labelled for 6 min directly after u.v. irradiation ($30\,\mathrm{J\,m^{-2}}$).

replication or to repair of transcriptionally active DNA. At least in the experiments in which we pulse-labelled the u.v.-irradiated cells for 10 min, we could distinguish the S-phase cells by prelabelling cells with [^{3}H]thymidine 2 h prior to irradiation. In experiments with shorter pulses prelabelling was omitted because it increased the background of grains too much.

DISTRIBUTION OF REPAIR EVENTS IN DNA LOOPS

As the data suggest that at least at 30 J m^{-2} u.v.-induced repair synthesis does not occur at the nuclear matrix, we have investigated whether the repair occurs in a coordinated non-random way within single DNA loops, and whether domains in DNA loops are repaired at different rates. Evidence for non-random repair in normal human cells has been recently reported by Cohn & Lieberman (1984) and in hamster cells by Bohr *et al.* (1985).

Biochemical experiments were performed with confluent human cells post-u.v. incubated for 2 h in the presence of HU or HU and araC. Nuclear lysates were incubated with nuclease S_1 and DNase I to elucidate the distribution of repair events in DNA loops. To visualize the repair events in DNA loops, DNA halo–matrix structures were prepared and processed for autoradiography.

Distribution of repair events in normal human cells

When DNA–nuclear matrix complexes were prepared from confluent human fibroblasts post-u.v. incubated for 2 h in the presence of HU or HU and araC, and digested with DNase I, the ^{3}H/^{14}C ratio remained at about 1, suggesting a random distribution of repair events in the total population of DNA loops (Fig. 8A). Identical results were found in exponentially growing HeLa cells (Mullenders *et al.* 1986). An alternative way of investigating the distribution of repair events is to use nuclease S_1. Using this enzyme, single-strand breaks accumulating in u.v.-irradiated cells in the presence of inhibitors can be converted to double-strand breaks and, consequently, when two or more breaks are present per DNA loop, DNA will be released from the matrix. Fig. 5 shows that in the presence of HU or HU and araC about 70 % and 80 %, respectively, of the DNA was released from the matrix by nuclease S_1, representing 3·5 or 5 single-strand breaks per DNA loop, assuming a random distribution. Thus it is obvious that the frequency of breaks is not limited to one at a time in each DNA loop as proposed by Collins *et al.* (1984). As shown in Fig. 5, nuclease S_1 released repair-labelled [^{3}H]DNA made in the presence of HU and araC to a greater extent than prelabelled DNA. This was also the case in the presence of HU, but only during the first 20 min of post-u.v. incubation. The preferential release of repair-labelled DNA is related to the extent of ligation of repair patches, which was determined by digestion with *Bal*31 nuclease. Owing to its mode of action, labelled repair patches near single-stranded regions, i.e. unligated patches, are rendered acid-soluble much more rapidly than ^{14}C-prelabelled DNA (Smith &

Okumoto, 1984; Mullenders *et al.* 1985). To compare digestion of repair-labelled [³H]DNA to prelabelled [¹⁴C]DNA we have plotted the relative ratio as ³H and ¹⁴C radioactivity *versus* the time of incubation (Fig. 6). As shown in Fig. 6, 90 % of the

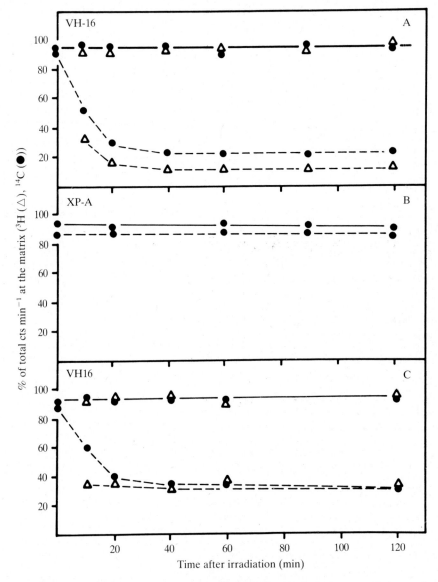

Fig. 5. Preferential release of repair-labelled DNA from the nuclear matrix by nuclease S₁ (from Mullenders *et al.* 1985). Confluent ¹⁴C-prelabelled cells were u.v.-irradiated (30 J m⁻²) and incubated in the presence of [³H]thymidine and HU and araC (A,B) or HU (C) for various periods of time. Nuclear lysates were treated with and without nuclease S₁ and analysed in sucrose gradients. A,C. Normal human fibroblasts. B. Xeroderma pigmentosum cells of complementation group A. ¹⁴C with (●‒‒‒●) and without (●——●) nuclease S₁; ³H with (△‒‒‒△) and without (△——△) nuclease S₁. The relative amount of DNA at the matrix is plotted *versus* the time of post-u.v. incubation.

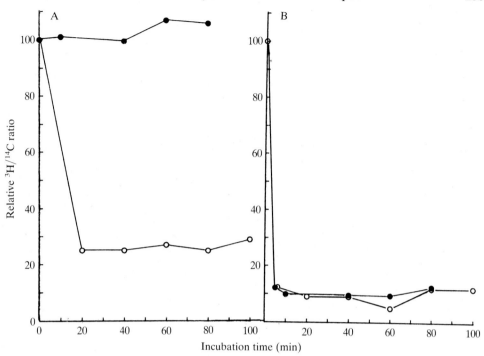

Fig. 6. Analysis of the structure of repair-labelled DNA. DNA–nuclear matrix complexes were isolated from u.v.-irradiated ($30 \, \text{J m}^{-2}$) cells post-u.v. incubated in the presence of [^{3}H]thymidine and HU (A) or HU and araC (B) for 10 min or 2 h. Samples of DNA–nuclear matrix preparations were digested with *Bal*31 nuclease and acid-precipitable radioactivity was determined; 10 min incubation (○), 2 h incubation (●).

repair patches made in the presence of HU and araC were unligated regardless of the duration of post-u.v. incubation, whereas in the presence of HU only during a 10 min pulse was the major part of the repair unligated.

Theoretically, a random distribution of repair patches within DNA loops is inconsistent with a preferential release of repair-labelled DNA from the matrix by nuclease S_1. To obtain more insight into the localization of repair events, the size distribution of matrix-associated DNA, as well as loop-DNA obtained after nuclease S_1 digestion of nuclear lysates, was analysed in neutral sucrose gradients. As shown in Fig. 7, the ^{14}C profile was displaced relative to the ^{3}H profile in matrix-associated as well as loop-DNA. This is due to the different distribution of label: ^{14}C label was uniformly distributed, while the ^{3}H label was located at the end of molecules, owing to incomplete repair patches and cleavage by nuclease S_1 (Cleaver, 1983). It is obvious that the ^{14}C profiles of matrix-associated and loop-DNA were very similar, which suggests that the incision events were distributed randomly along the DNA loops. Comparison of the ^{3}H profiles reveals that although there was a considerable similarity, loop-DNA was composed of smaller repair-labelled DNA fragments than matrix-associated DNA. These data suggest that although the majority of incision events are distributed randomly in DNA loops, there must also exist clusters of incision events. The probability of detecting these clusters in the ^{14}C profile in sucrose gradients will depend on the relative amount of DNA constituting the clusters. From the similarity in ^{14}C profiles of matrix-associated and loop-DNA (Fig. 7), it is obvious that this amount must be small. However, owing to ^{3}H-labelled repair patches at the end of the DNA fragments after nuclease S$_1$ digestion, small amounts of DNA will be visible in the ^{3}H profiles. The appearance of clustered repair events may indicate that at 30 J m^{-2} two different repair systems are operating simultaneously: a processive system resulting in clustered repair events, and a system operating by random collisions. Alternatively, non-random distribution of repair events could occur when domains of DNA are repaired at different rates, as a result of variation in chromatin organization rendering some regions more accessible to repair enzymes than others.

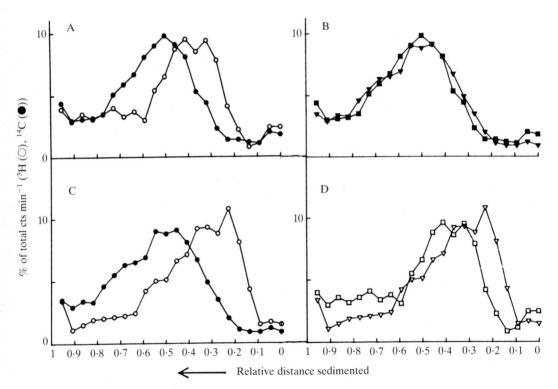

Fig. 7. Analysis of the size distribution of matrix-associated and loop-DNA after nuclease S$_1$ digestion. Nuclear lysates prepared from ^{14}C-prelabelled u.v.-irradiated (30 J m^{-2}) cells post-u.v. incubated for 2 h in the presence of HU and araC and [^{3}H]thymidine were digested with nuclease S$_1$. Matrix-associated DNA was separated from nuclease S$_1$ detached DNA by neutral sucrose gradient centrifugation. Both fractions were dialysed, incubated with proteinase K and again analysed in a neutral sucrose gradient. A. Matrix-associated DNA. C. Loop-associated DNA. B. ^{14}C-labelled DNA: loop-DNA (▼), matrix-associated DNA (■). D. ^{3}H-labelled DNA: loop-DNA (▽), matrix-associated DNA (□). The ^{3}H/^{14}C ratio of loop-DNA and matrix-associated DNA was 2·13 and 1·09, respectively. The matrix-associated DNA represented about 20 % of the total DNA.

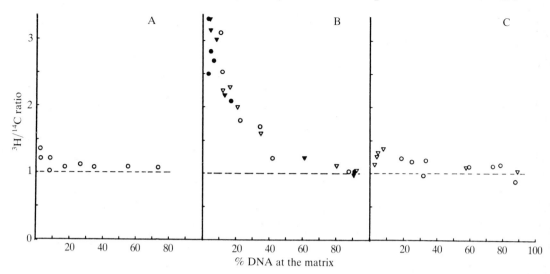

Fig. 8. Distribution of repair-labelled DNA in normal and in xeroderma pigmentosum cells (from Mullenders *et al.* 1986). ^{14}C-prelabelled confluent cells were u.v. irradiated (30 J m^{-2}) and incubated for 2 h in the presence of [^{3}H]thymidine and araC and/or HU. Samples of the nuclear lysates were treated with DNase I and analysed in sucrose gradients. A. Normal human cells. B. XP-C cells. XP21RO (○), XP6RO (●), XP1TE (▽), XP8CA (▼). C. XP-D cells: XP3NE (▽), XP7BE (○).

Distribution of repair events in xeroderma pigmentosum cells

A recent study by Mansbridge & Hanawalt (1983) has indicated that the residual level of excision repair in xeroderma pigmentosum cells of complementation group C (XP-C) occurs in localized domains of the chromatin. Since nothing was known about the localization of these domains in the chromatin, we have investigated the distribution of repair events in DNA loops using biochemical and autoradiographic approaches.

DNase I digestion of DNA–nuclear matrix complexes prepared from four different XP-C cell lines post-u.v. incubated for 2 h revealed that repair patches were preferentially situated near the attachment sites of DNA loops (Fig. 8B). In two xeroderma pigmentosum cell lines belonging to complementation group D (XP-D), which have a repair capacity comparable to XP-C (relative level of Unscheduled DNA Synthesis (UDS): 25 % in XP-D and 18 % in XP-C), no preferential localization of repair label at the nuclear matrix was observed (Fig. 8C). The enrichment of repair patches at the nuclear matrix in XP-C cells was independent of the duration of post-u.v. incubation (Mullenders *et al.* 1984), which suggests that the non-uniform distribution must be due to repair of particular DNA segments situated near the nuclear matrix.

Autoradiographic analysis of DNA halo–matrix structures was performed to check the biochemical observations by direct visualization of repair events in DNA loops. In XP-C cells post-u.v. incubated for 2 h in the presence of [^{3}H]thymidine, grains were preferentially overlying the nuclear matrix: 62·5 % of the grains were found in the matrix region compared to 18·9 % in normal cells (Fig. 9). In XP-D cells the

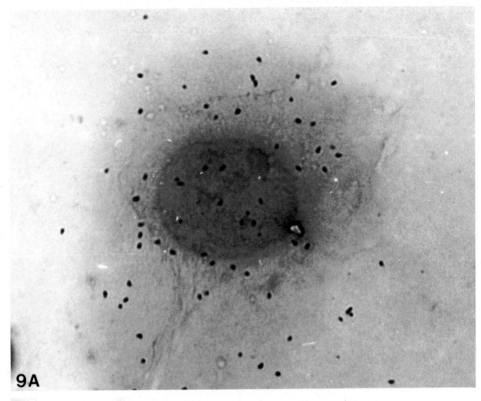

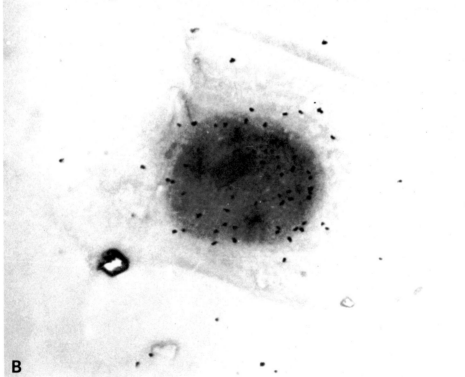

Fig. 9. Autoradiograms of DNA halo–matrix structures prepared from normal human and XP-C cells. Cells were u.v. irradiated ($30\,\mathrm{J\,m^{-2}}$) and incubated with [^{3}H]thymidine. A. Normal human cells incubated for 10 min. B. XP-C cells incubated for 2 h.

distribution of grains resembled the normal cells: $22 \cdot 4\%$ of the grains were found in the nuclear matrix region. Since DNA halo–matrix structures are prepared from exponentially growing cells not treated with inhibitors, it is clear that the non-uniform repair in XP-C cells is not dependent on the presence of inhibitors or on physiological conditions, i.e. confluent or proliferating state. Nuclease S_1 digestion of nuclear lysates prepared after 2 h post-u.v. incubation in the presence of HU and araC, resulted in a detachment of 30% of the ^{14}C-labelled DNA from the nuclear matrix compared to 80% in normal human cells.

Sedimentation analysis of the size distribution of DNA fragments released from the nuclear matrix by nuclease S_1 revealed striking differences between XP-C and normal cells (Fig. 10). Owing to endlabelling of DNA fragments, the ^{14}C profile is displaced relative to the ^{3}H profile. In normal human cells the molecular weight (M_r) of nuclease-S_1-released ^{14}C-labelled DNA fragments was about 2×10^7. In XP-C cells the enzyme detached DNA fragments of about $10^8\ M_r$, which is the average loop size in human fibroblasts (Mullenders *et al.* 1984, 1985). In contrast to lysates from normal human cells, the ^{3}H profile of XP-C lysates showed a non-homogeneous distribution. The high molecular weight part is slightly shifted relative to the ^{14}C profile, due to endlabelling. In addition the ^{3}H profile shows a second peak consisting of low molecular weight DNA fragments. We have interpreted this non-homogeneous distribution of ^{3}H-labelled DNA in XP-C cells as a consequence of preferential repair of DNA segments near the attachment sites of the DNA loops. The assumption is that in DNA regions near the nuclear matrix DNA repair events are very close to each other. Nuclease S_1 will then release loop-sized ^{14}C-labelled DNA as well as small ^{3}H-labelled fragments. Comparison of the M_r of the small DNA fragments (about 5×10^6) and the interdimer distance of $30\ J\ m^{-2}$ (2×10^6) suggests that repair events in the domains subject to repair do indeed occur very close to each other. Considering the accuracy of the M_r determinations at the very top of the gradient, the repair events may in fact be localized at the interdimer distance.

Since in XP-C cells about 70% of the DNA was still attached to the nuclear matrix upon nuclease S_1 digestion (Fig. 10A), we were interested in the distribution of repair events in this DNA. One way to examine this is to analyse the size of this matrix-associated DNA. The matrix-associated DNA can be converted to free DNA molecules by proteolytic digestion of the nuclear matrix (Wanka *et al.* 1977). Thus, we made a comparison of ^{3}H and ^{14}C profiles of nuclease-S_1-treated nuclear lysates with and without a final proteolytic digestion (Fig. 10). No differences were seen in normal cells post-u.v. incubated for 10 min in the presence of HU and araC (Fig. 10B,D). In XP-C cells two main differences were observed. First, even after proteolytic digestion about 25% of the DNA was collected on the sucrose shelf and consisted of very long molecules. Second, ^{3}H and ^{14}C profiles shifted towards positions of higher molecular weight, concomitant with a reduction in the relative amount of small molecules. This sedimentation analysis suggests a rather complex distribution of repair events in XP-C cells. The DNA fragments initially released by nuclease S_1 from the DNA–nuclear matrix complex, originate from loops with repair events at both attachment sites. This distribution occurs in about 30% of the

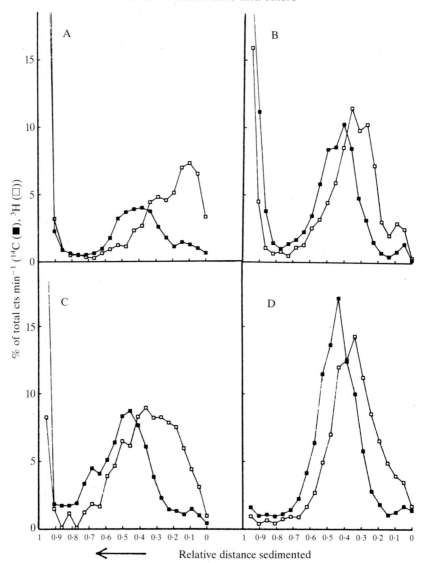

Fig. 10. Size distribution of nuclease-S_1-released DNA with and without proteolytic digestion (from Mullenders *et al.* 1986). ^{14}C-prelabelled normal human cells as well as XP-C cells were u.v. irradiated (30 J m^{-2}) and incubated for 10 min (normal cells) or 2 h (XP-C cells) in the presence of HU and araC, and [^{3}H]thymidine. Samples of nuclear lysates were incubated with nuclease S_1, and finally with and without proteinase K. A. XP-C, nuclease S_1. B. Normal cells, nuclease S_1. C. XP-C cells, nuclease S_1 and proteinase K. D. Normal cells, nuclease S_1 and proteinase K. % cts min^{-1} of ^{3}H and ^{14}C at the sucrose cushion: A, 40·6 % ^{3}H, 52 % ^{14}C; B, 15·9 % ^{3}H, 19·2 % ^{14}C; C, 8·1 % ^{3}H, 26·3 % ^{14}C, D, 1·0 % ^{3}H, 1·6 % ^{14}C.

loops. The DNA recovered from the sucrose shelf after the combined nuclease S_1/proteolytic digestion obviously consisted of regions comprising multiple loops, which are excluded from the repair process during the first 2 h after u.v. irradiation. The presence of DNA fragments of somewhat larger size than an average loop suggests that small clusters of loops with repair events at only one attachment site are also present. This DNA will not be detached from the matrix by nuclease S_1, since single-stranded gaps at *both* attachment sites are required to release DNA. An alternative explanation could be that a subset of cells is not carrying out repair at all. However, autoradiographic analyses of DNA halo–matrix structures as well as data published by Mansbridge & Hanawalt (1983) revealed no such inhomogeneity of repair between cells.

The non-uniform distribution of repair events in XP-C raises the question of what the characteristics are of DNA that is subject to repair. Actively transcribed genes remain close to the nuclear matrix by attachment at the 5' end of the genes (Small *et al.* 1985; Mirkovitch & Laemmli, 1984; Cook *et al.* 1982). From these anchorage points active genes are thought to extend into DNA loops. A three- to fourfold enrichment of repair events at the nuclear matrix in XP-C cells indicates that the domains subject to repair must extend beyond the attachment sites and may therefore cover the transcribed regions, at least partly (Mullenders *et al.* 1984). This hypothesis is supported by a study of Mayne & Lehmann (1982), who reported a partial recovery of u.v.-inhibited RNA synthesis in XP-C cells, but not in XP-D cells. They also showed that u.v.-inhibited DNA synthesis could recover appreciably in XP-C cells, but not in XP-D cells. Since inhibition of DNA replication after u.v. irradiation is due to inhibition of chain elongation, the matrix-associated replication forks may reside in the domains in XP-C cells subject to repair. Although the domains in XP-C cells are repaired to the same extent or even to a greater extent than the genome in normal cells (Mansbridge & Hanawalt, 1983; Mullenders *et al.* 1984) it is obvious that XP-C cells are much more sensitive to u.v. irradiation than normal cells. A number of reasons may account for this. Not all active regions may be covered by the domains subject to repair or be repaired to the same extent. Clusters of DNA loops that are not repaired at all may also include active regions. Furthermore, a large gene may extend beyond the domains, resulting in efficient repair of only parts of a gene. The factors that regulate the restricted repair in XP-C cells and factors that are necessary to repair damage outside the domains are not known. However, it seems unlikely that the repair of restricted areas in the genome is simply mediated by the accessibility of the chromatin. Exposure of confluent XP-C cells to sodium butyrate, which converts the chromatin into an 'active' configuration (Simpson, 1978), and stimulates the u.v.-induced repair synthesis twofold, does not influence the non-random distribution of repair events in XP-C cells (Mullenders *et al.* 1986).

Distribution of repair events in rodent cells

One of the striking properties of rodent cells is the high rate of survival after u.v. irradiation in spite of the very limited capacity to perform excision repair. Since recovery after u.v. irradiation seems to be directly related to repair capacity (Chan & Little, 1979; Simons, 1979), possible explanation for the apparent discrepancy may be the occurrence of preferential repair in domains covering active genes. Indeed, in established Chinese hamster ovary cells (CHO), Bohr *et al.* (1985) have shown that active DNA was repaired to a much greater extent than the total genome. On the other hand, Nairn *et al.* (1985) did not find evidence for preferential repair of active DNA in CHO cells. We have investigated the distribution of repair events in Syrian hamster primary cells. For biochemical experiments these cells have the advantage of growing to confluency. DNase I digestions of nuclear lysates prepared from cells post-u.v. incubated for 2 h did not result in any evidence for non-random repair in Syrian hamster cells. This was confirmed by an alternative approach, in which the distribution of bacteriophage T4 endonuclease-sensitive sites was analysed. In contrast to XP-C cells, there was no indication of a non-random distribution of repaired sites (Mullenders *et al.* 1986).

CONCLUDING REMARKS

Owing to increasing knowledge of the structure and organization of chromatin, it is possible to investigate the role of chromatin structure in cellular processes. The involvement of scaffold-like structures such as the nuclear matrix in DNA replication provides the possibility of functional compartmentalization of this process with respect to regulating factors as well as unwinding of parental DNA molecules. Excision repair induced by high doses of u.v. ($30 \, \mathrm{J \, m^{-2}}$) appears to proceed without participation of the nuclear matrix and this may provide an efficient and rapid way of restoring damaged DNA at any position in DNA loops. However, at low and biologically more relevant doses ($5 \, \mathrm{J \, m^{-2}}$) at least part of the total excision repair may initiate at the nuclear matrix. It is tempting to speculate that matrix-associated repair may be the important repair pathway at low u.v. doses and be related to that part of excision repair that is resistant to inhibitors of polymerase α. In fact we cannot rule out the possibility that the distribution of repair events at high doses may be due partly to abnormal repair activity.

Comparison of recovery of RNA synthesis and removal of lesions after u.v. irradiation suggests the existence of a process of preferential repair of damage in transcriptionally active chromatin. From the spatial distribution of repair events in DNA loops there is evidence for preferential repair of damage in transcriptionally active DNA in xeroderma pigmentosum cells of complementation group C, consistent with the appreciable recovery of RNA synthesis in these cells. However, using this methodology, there is no evidence for preferential repair of transcriptionally active chromatin in normal human and hamster primary cells.

We thank A. C. van Kesteren and C. J. M. Bussmann for excellent technical assistance.

This work was supported by the Association of the University of Leiden with Euratom, contract no. BIO-E-407-81-NL.

REFERENCES

AELEN, J. M. A., OPSTELTEN, R. J. G. & WANKA, F. (1983). Organization of DNA replication in *Physarum polycephalum*. Attachment of the origins of replicons and replication forks to the unclear matrix. *Nucl. Acids Res.* **11**, 1181–1195.

BEREZNEY, R. & COFFEY, D. S. (1977). Nuclear matrix. Isolation and characterization of a framework structure from rat liver nuclei. *J. Cell Biol.* **73**, 616–637.

BOHR, V. A., SMITH, C. A., OKUMOTO, D. S. & HANAWALT, P. C. (1985). DNA repair in an active gene: removal of pyrimidine dimers from the DHFR gene is much more efficient than in the genome overall. *Cell* **40**, 359–369.

BUONGIORNO-NARDELLI, M., MICHELI, G., CARRI, M. T. & MARILLY, M. (1982). A relation between replicon size and supercoiled loop domains in the eukaryotic genome. *Nature, Lond.* **298**, 100–102.

CHAN, G. L. & LITTLE, J. B. (1979). Resistance of plateau phase cell, human normal, and xeroderma pigmentosum fibroblasts to the cytotoxic effects of ultraviolet light. *Mutat. Res.* **63**, 401–412.

CLEAVER, J. E. (1983). Structure of repaired sites in human DNA synthesized in the presence of inhibitors of DNA polymerases alpha and beta in human fibroblasts. *Biochim. biophys. Acta* **739**, 301–311.

COHN, S. M. & LIEBERMAN, M. W. (1984). The distribution of DNA excision repair sites in human diploid fibroblasts following ultraviolet irradiation. *J. biol. Chem.* **259**, 12 463–12 469.

COLLINS, A. R. S., DOWNES, C. S. & JOHNSON, R. T. (1984). An integrated view of inhibited repair. In *DNA Repair and its Inhibition* (ed. A. R. S. Collins, C. S. Downes & R. T. Johnson). *Nucl. Acids Symp. Series*, no. 13, pp. 1–11. Oxford, Washington, DC: IRL Press.

COMINGS, D. E. (1968). The rationale for an ordered arrangement of chromatin in the interphase nucleus. *Am. J. hum. Genet.* **20**, 550–560.

COOK, P. R. & BRAZELL, I. A. (1975). Supercoils in human DNA. *J. Cell Sci.* **19**, 261–279.

COOK, P. R., LANG, J., HAYDAY, A., LANIA, L., FRIED, M., CHISWELL, D. & WYKE, J. A. (1982). Active viral genes in transformed cells lie close to the nuclear cage. *EMBO J.* **1**, 447–452.

DIJKWEL, P. A., MULLENDERS, L. H. F. & WANKA, F. (1979). Analysis of the attachment of replicating DNA to a nuclear matrix in mammalian interphase nuclei. *Nucl. Acids Res.* **6**, 219–230.

DINGMAN, C. W. (1974). Bidirectional chromosome replication: some topological considerations. *J. theor. Biol.* **43**, 187–195.

DRESLER, S. L. & LIEBERMAN, M. W. (1983). Identification of DNA polymerases involved in DNA excision repair in diploid human fibroblasts. *J. biol. Chem.* **258**, 9990–9994.

ERIXON, K. & AHNSTRÖM, G. (1979). Single-strand breaks in DNA during repair of UV-induced damage in normal human and xeroderma pigmentosum cells as determined by alkaline unwinding and hydroxylapatite chromatography. *Mutat. Res.* **59**, 257–271.

GOLDBERG, G. I., COLLIER, I. & CASSEL, A. (1983). Specific DNA sequences associated with the nuclear matrix in synchronized mouse 3T3 cells. *Proc. natn. Acad. Sci. U.S.A.* **80**, 6887–6891.

MANSBRIDGE, J. N. & HANAWALT, P. C. (1983). Domain-limited repair of DNA in ultraviolet irradiated fibroblasts from xeroderma pigmentosum complementation group C. In *Cellular Responses to DNA Damage* (ed. E. C. Friedberg & B. R. Bridges), pp. 195–207. New York: Alan Liss.

MAYNE, L. V. & LEHMANN, A. R. (1982). Failure of RNA synthesis to recover after UV irradiation: An early defect in cells from individuals with Cockayne's syndrome and xeroderma pigmentosum. *Cancer Res.* **42**, 1473–1478.

McCREADY, S. J. & COOK, P. R. (1984). Lesions induced in DNA by ultraviolet light are repaired at the nuclear cage. *J. Cell Sci.* **39**, 53–62.

MILLER, M. R. & CHINAULT, D. N. (1982). The roles of DNA polymerases α and β in DNA repair synthesis induced in hamster and human cells by different DNA damaging agents. *J. biol. Chem.* **257**, 10 204–10 209.

MIRKOVITCH, J. & LAEMMLI, U. K. (1984). Organization of the higher-order chromatin loop: Specific attachment sites on nuclear scaffold. *Cell* **39**, 233–232.

MULLENDERS, L. H. F., VAN KESTEREN, A. C., BUSSMANN, C. J. M., VAN ZEELAND, A. A. & NATARAJAN, A. T. (1984). Preferential repair of nuclear matrix associated DNA in xeroderma pigmentosum complementation group C. *Mutat. Res.* **141**, 75–82.

MULLENDERS, L. H. F., VAN KESTEREN, A. C., BUSSMANN, C. J. M., VAN ZEELAND, A. A. & NATARAJAN, A. T. (1986). Distribution of UV-induced repair events in higher-order chromatin loops in human and hamster fibroblasts. *Carcinogenesis* **7**, 995–1002.

MULLENDERS, L. H. F., VAN KESTEREN, A. C., VAN ZEELAND, A. A. & NATARAJAN, A. T. (1985). Analysis of the structure and spatial distribution of ultraviolet-induced DNA repair patches in human cells made in the presence of inhibitors of replicative synthesis. *Biochim. biophys. Acta* **826**, 38–48.

MULLENDERS, L. H. F., VAN ZEELAND, A. A. & NATARAJAN, A. T. (1983a). Comparison of DNA loop size and supercoiled domain size in human cells. *Mutat. Res.* **112**, 245–252.

MULLENDERS, L. H. F., VAN ZEELAND, A. A. & NATARAJAN, A. T. (1983b). Analysis of the distribution of DNA repair patches in the DNA–nuclear matrix complex from human cells. *Biochim. biophys. Acta* **740**, 428–435.

NAIRN, S. R., MITCHELL, D. L. & CLARKSON, J. M. (1985). Role of chromatin structure in the repair of DNA photoadducts in mammalian cells. *Int. J. Radiat. Biol.* **47**, 181–189.

PARDOLL, D. M., VOGELSTEIN, B. & COFFEY, D. S. (1980). A fixed site of DNA replication in eukaryotic cells. *Cell* **19**, 527–536.

RADFORD, I. A., MARTIN, R. F. & FINCH, L. R. (1982). Effects of hydroxyurea on DNA synthesis in mouse L-cells. *Biochim. biophys. Acta* **696**, 145–153.

RAHN, R. O. & STAFFORD, R. S. (1974). Measurements of defects in ultraviolet-irradiated DNA by the kinetic formaldehyde method. *Nature, Lond.* **248**, 52–54.

SMALL, D., NELKIN, B. & VOGELSTEIN, B. (1985). The association of transcribed genes with the nuclear matrix of *Drosophila* cells during heat shock. *Nucl. Acids Res.* **13**, 2413–2431.

SIMONS, J. W. I. M. (1979). Development of a liquid-holding technique for the study of DNA-repair in human diploid fibroblasts. *Mutat. Res.* **59**, 273–283.

SIMPSON, R. T. (1978). Structure of chromatin containing extensively acetylated H_3 and H_4. *Cell* **13**, 691–699.

SMITH, C. A. & OKUMOTO, D. S. (1984). Nature of DNA repair synthesis resistant to inhibitors of polymerase alpha in human cells. *Biochemistry* **23**, 1383–1391.

VAN EEKELEN, E. A. G. & VAN VENROOY, W. J. (1981). HnRNA and its attachment to a nuclear protein matrix. *J. Cell Biol.* **88**, 554–562.

VOGELSTEIN, B., PARDOLL, D. M. & COFFEY, D. S. (1980). Supercoiled loops and eukaryotic DNA replication. *Cell* **22**, 79–85.

WANKA, F., MULLENDERS, L. H. F., BEKERS, A. G. M., PENNINGS, L. J., AELEN, J. M. A. & EYGENSTEYN, J. (1977). Association of nuclear DNA with a rapidly sedimenting structure. *Biochem. biophys. Res. Commun.* **74**, 739–747.

J. Cell Sci. Suppl. 6, 263–288 (1987)
Printed in Great Britain © *The Company of Biologists Limited 1987*

DNA REPAIR UNDER STRESS

R. T. JOHNSON, A. R. S. COLLINS*, SHOSHANA SQUIRES,
ANN M. MULLINGER, G. C. ELLIOTT†, C. S. DOWNES
AND I. RASKO‡

Cancer Research Campaign Mammalian Cell DNA Repair Group, Department of Zoology, Cambridge University, Downing Street, Cambridge CB2 3EJ, UK

SUMMARY

When the excision repair process of eukaryote cells is arrested by inhibitors of repair synthesis including hydroxyurea (HU), 1-β-D-arabinofuranosylcytosine (araC) or aphidicolin, major cellular changes follow the accumulation of repair-associated DNA breaks. These changes, each of which reflects more or less severe cellular stress, include cycle delay, chromosome behaviour, fall in NAD level, the development of double-stranded DNA breaks, rapid chromosome fragmentation and cell killing. Disruption of the repair process by agents such as araC after therapeutic DNA damage may, therefore, have some potential value in cancer treatment. The extreme cellular problems associated with the artificial arrest of repair may have their subtler counterparts elsewhere, and we discuss several systems where delays in the completion of excision repair in the absence of repair synthesis inhibitors have marked repercussions on cell viability. We also show that the average completion time of an excision repair patch varies according to the state of cell culture, and that completion time is extended after treatment with insulin or following trypsin detachment. Under certain growth conditions ultraviolet irradiation followed by mitogenic stimulation results in double-stranded DNA breakage and additional cell killing, and we discuss these data in the light of protocols that have been used successfully to transform human or rodent cells *in vitro*. Finally, we consider whether the rejoining of DNA breaks accumulated by repair synthesis inhibitors is a valid model system for studying ligation, and show that this protocol provides an extremely sensitive assay for most incision events and, thereby, a means for discriminating between normal human cells on the one hand, and Cockayne's Syndrome cells and their heterozygotes on the other.

INTRODUCTION

The response of cells to DNA damaging agents is complex. In addition to long-term genetic changes (ranging from point mutations to chromosome aberrations) there are many profound shifts in metabolism that occur much earlier. These include dramatic changes in the size and composition of deoxyribonucleotide triphosphate pools (Newman & Miller, 1984), inhibition of transcription (Hackett *et al.* 1978), nucleolar disruption and inhibition of protein synthesis (Collins *et al.* 1981), induction of proteolytic activity (Miskin & Reich, 1980), and arrest of DNA replication (Painter, 1977). In addition, DNA repair pathways are activated. Clearly, these must function most actively in eukaryote cells under conditions of

* Present address: Department of Biochemistry, University of Aberdeen, Marischal College, Aberdeen AB9 1AS, UK.

† Present address: Department of Biochemistry, University of California, Berkeley, CA 94720, USA.

‡ Present address: Genetics Institute, Biological Research Center, Hungarian Academy of Sciences, P.O.B. 501, Szeged, Hungary.

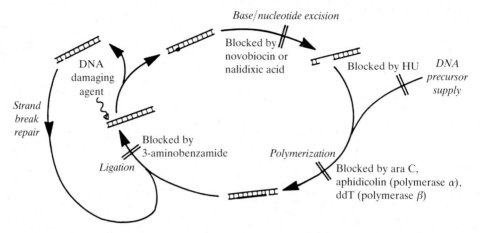

Fig. 1. A simplified scheme illustrating repair of DNA lesions and showing postulated sites of action of typical inhibitory agents. (From Collins & Johnson, 1984, with permission from Academic Press.)

serious cellular stress. Stress is a rather general term, though fairly widely used in a repair context (e.g. see Friedberg, 1985). In prokaryotes stress associated with DNA damage invokes the coordinated SOS response (Radman, 1974), one consequence being error-prone repair (Witkin, 1976). Though there is some evidence for an SOS response in eukaryote cells (e.g. see Sarasin & Benoit, 1986), the biochemical mechanism has not been identified. In this chapter the term stress is used in two ways. We examine the various cellular consequences that follow arrest of the excision repair process by inhibitors of repair synthesis. In general such inhibitors exacerbate and compound the cellular stress due to DNA damage. We also examine operation of the excision repair process itself when stress is applied to it by way of limiting the DNA precursor supply. One of the aims of this chapter is to chronicle some consequences of repair inhibition after ultraviolet (u.v.) damage and to consider how the stress induced by artificially blocking repair with inhibitors is a model for situations occurring normally in certain cells and conditions.

ARTIFICIAL INHIBITION OF u.v.-INDUCED EXCISION REPAIR

Complex enzymic mechanisms involving several steps should in theory be susceptible to a number of specific inhibitors whose application results in the accumulation of intermediate products. This is, as yet, only partly true in the case of the pathway for u.v.-induced excision repair. Fig. 1 shows a cartoon from 1984 (Collins & Johnson, 1984) depicting the points in the excision repair process at which different inhibitors were thought to act. For the best-characterized repair synthesis inhibitors, agents such as hydroxyurea, which reduces the supply of DNA precursors, and more or less specific inhibitors of DNA polymerase α such as aphidicolin or araC, the main application described in this chapter is that, in concert, such inhibitors can be used over short periods after u.v. irradiation to accumulate large numbers of DNA breaks created by the incision step of the repair process. The inhibition of repair synthesis by HU and polymerase inhibitors is thoroughly substantiated and has been reviewed recently (Collins & Johnson, 1984; Collins *et al.* 1984); it need concern us no further here except to note that it provides the most effective way of setting up abundant unligated excision repair sites with which to study subsequently the process of break sealing. This topic will be discussed later in the chapter.

Turning to novobiocin, a less-traditional inhibitor of replicative and repair DNA synthesis, the evidence in favour of its supposed mode of action *via* the inhibition of a topoisomerse-II-mediated preincision step must now be regarded as questionable. Novobiocin blocks the accumulation of u.v.-induced incision events by araC plus HU, monitored either by alkaline unwinding or nucleoid sedimentation (Collins & Johnson, 1979a; Mattern *et al.* 1982; Downes *et al.* 1985), and it also inhibits unscheduled DNA synthesis (Mattern & Scudiero, 1981). It is less effective when aphidicolin is used (Clarkson & Mitchell, 1983; Downes *et al.* 1985), probably because, unlike araC, aphidicolin does not require phosphorylation before it can act as an inhibitor. Despite an old observation (Frei *et al.* 1958) that novobiocin inhibits oxidative phosphorylation, it was only recently that its effect on mitochondria was revealed, when Downes *et al.* (1985) reported the massive (yet reversible) and rapid change in mitochondrial structure induced by the drug (Fig. 2). The shift in

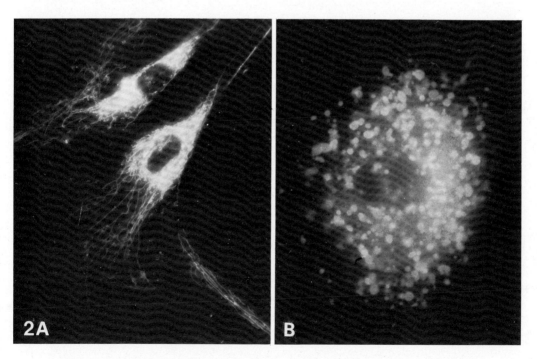

Fig. 2. Micrographs showing the effects of novobioicin on rhodamine 123 fluorescence in normal human fibroblasts. Cells were incubated for 10 min in medium with rhodamine, washed in normal medium and then incubated for another 30 min in: A, normal medium; or B, medium with 1 mM-novobiocin. A, ×450; B, ×1100. (From Downes *et al.* 1985, with permission from IRL Press.)

Table 1. *Consequences of repair inhibition*

Additional cell killing
Cell cycle arrest
Inhibition of transcription
Additional chromosome aberrations
Chromosome decondensation and fragmentation
DNA DS breaks
NAD depletion

structure was associated with a fivefold reduction over 30 min in the ratio of ATP to ADP, an effect that presumably helps to explain the reduction in the amount of phosphorylated araC in the soluble pool during this period. Given the considerable energy dependence of excision repair, the inhibitory effect of novobiocin can at present be as easily attributed to constraint of energy supply as to inhibition of a putative topoisomerase-mediated pre-incision step.

SOME CONSEQUENCES OF INHIBITED EXCISION REPAIR

Inhibition of repair synthesis by agents such as HU, araC and aphidicolin, acting after the incision step, results in an exaggeration of many cellular responses to u.v. Some of these are listed in Table 1. Not included in this table is the feedback inhibition of the repair process itself, due to immobilization of the repair polymerase, and presumably the associated endonuclease, at the inhibited site. Studies of feedback inhibition may thus yield information about the assembly and stability of excision repair components (Snyder *et al.* 1981; Squires *et al.* 1982). A detailed analysis of the process reveals considerable complexity in these interactions: the efficiency of feedback inhibition increases with time after irradiation, and the process culminates in a paradoxical state in which no further excision occurs, though many lesions remain unrepaired and the capacity to perform further incision in response to fresh lesions is only partly diminished (Downes, 1984). But we will not deal with this topic further in this chapter. An important general point to stress is that a brief treatment with inhibitors is usually sufficient to elicit the effects listed in Table 1.

Cell killing and the importance of DNA precursor pools

The most consistent feature of repair inhibition in u.v.-irradiated cells is additional cell killing, the extent of which depends on the stage in the cell cycle when u.v. was given and the type of inhibitor used. For many years it has been recognized that inhibitors of DNA synthesis (in the absence of DNA damage) selectively kill cells in S phase (Chu & Fischer, 1962; Sinclair, 1965, 1967; Pfeiffer & Tolmach, 1967; Burg *et al.* 1977), a not unexpected finding, though exactly *how* killing is achieved remains speculative; one possibility is that disruption of DNA replication results in the production of lethal chromosome aberrations (Yu & Sinclair, 1968). The effect of inhibitors after u.v. is best studied, therefore, in other stages of the cycle. For example, a 3 h incubation of HeLa cells in 10^{-2} M-HU, after u.v. irradiation in mitosis or early G_1, resulted in greater killing than u.v. alone (Schor *et al.* 1975). The cycle-related pattern of killing of synchronized Chinese hamster ovary cells, u.v.-irradiated and incubated for 90 min with HU, first suggested that the size of the DNA precursor pool is an important parameter in the overall DNA repair capability (Burg *et al.* 1977). Mitotic and G_2 CHO cells have large pools (Skoog *et al.* 1973; Walters *et al.* 1973) and show no, or only slight, additional u.v.-associated killing when a 90 min pulse of HU is given. In mid G_1, at a time when precursor pools are much smaller, HU promotes u.v. killing: an effect that is nullified by the simultaneous provision of DNA precursors. Burg *et al.* (1977) concluded from these results that, by inhibiting the synthesis of DNA precursors, HU can disrupt repair DNA synthesis to such an extent that cell death occurs. Since the main effect of HU is to inhibit ribonucleotide reductase, a key enzyme in DNA precursor provision (Thelander & Reichard, 1979) and since the lethal effect of HU after u.v. damage apparently varies in relation to precursor pool size, this suggests that variations in cell sensitivity to u.v. radiation are, in turn, reflections of the size or availability of the pool: a point to which we will return shortly.

araC on its own also causes additional killing of u.v.-irradiated mitotic and G_1 CHO cells; a 30 min exposure is not enough but 2 h is (Collins *et al.* 1980). As would be expected, in combination araC or aphidicolin plus hydroxyurea potentiate u.v. killing. Fig. 3 shows u.v. survival curves of a log phase repair-competent human cell, HD1, given 90 min exposures to HU plus aphidicolin at two different times after u.v. In this case, treatment immediately after u.v. markedly reduces survival whereas treatment at about 4 h after u.v., when there is much less repair activity, does not have much effect on survival. Given that inhibitors such as those used in the studies mentioned above result in the arrest of incision soon after u.v. (Snyder *et al.* 1981; Squires *et al.* 1982; Downes, 1984), with the consequence that continued dimer removal is blocked (Snyder *et al.* 1981), the prolonged presence of dimers in the DNA might be considered likely to account for the enhanced u.v. killing in the presence of inhibitor. However, calculations of the sort described by Collins *et al.* (1980), which take into account dimers that are not removed when inhibitors are used, strongly suggest that this is unlikely to be the case. For example, after $10 \, \text{J m}^{-2}$ HD1 cells incubated over a 30 min period with HU plus araC (a suitable substitute for aphidicolin) accumulate nine breaks per 10^9 daltons (Johnson *et al.* 1985), and so a 90 min incubation would temporarily prevent the removal of, at most, 27, dimers per 10^9 daltons, corresponding to a u.v. dose of about $2 \, \text{J m}^{-2}$. It is, however, clear from data in Fig. 3 that the effect on survival of 90 min post-u.v. exposure to aphidicolin/HU is greater than would be produced by delivering an extra $2 \, \text{J m}^{-2}$ of u.v. The 'extra' lethality associated with repair inhibition strongly suggests that breaks accumulated during this period are intrinsically more lethal then the dimers that would otherwise have been replaced.

Turning to the relationship between DNA precursor availability and survival after u.v., it is clear that supplementing medium with DNA precursors enhances survival after u.v., most spectacularly for unstimulated B and T lymphocytes (Yew & Johnson, 1979), but also very strongly for fibroblasts (Collins & Johnson, 1979*b*). The greatest improvements in survival promoted by precursor supplement are in those cells (such as quiescent lymphocytes) or cycle stages (G_0, early G_1) where DNA precursor pools are known or expected to be very small (Munch-Petersen *et al.* 1973; Skoog *et al.* 1973; Snyder, 1984). In these cases, therefore, we might conclude that precursor availability is likely to be a major rate-limiting factor in the repair of u.v. damage.

Cell killing and secondary consequences of inhibited repair

Survival curves of repair-inhibited cells, such as those in Fig. 3, should not be taken at face value. That is to say the cellular response to primary DNA damage may be modified by, among other things, changes in cycle progression. For example, as Mayne (1984) has shown, inhibitors greatly increase the u.v. arrest of transcription, a perturbation serious enough to result in cycle delay. Fig. 4 shows that u.v. irradiation of synchronized G_1 cells, followed by a short pulse of aphidicolin/HU or especially of araC/HU results in considerable delay in the onset of DNA synthesis (I. Rasko & R. T. Johnson, unpublished data), providing, in effect, an extended pre-S phase period when potentially lethal lesions might be removed (Simons, 1979). This is one possibility, but inspection of the survival curves suggests that it must be

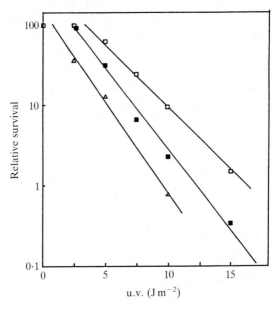

Fig. 3. Survival of human repair-competent cell, HD1 (Johnson *et al.* 1985), after u.v. irradiation, in the presence or absence of 1·5-h pulses of aphidicolin ($10 \mu g \, ml^{-1}$) plus hydroxyurea ($10^{-2} M$). One population was u.v.-irradiated with a graded series of fluences and incubated for the next 1·5 h with inhibitors ($\triangle$); another was incubated with inhibitors between 3·5 and 5 h after u.v. irradiation ($\blacksquare$); and a final population served as the u.v. control ($\square$). All populations were washed three times after exposure to inhibitors and the dishes (in triplicate) were incubated for 8 days to allow colonies to grow. The curves were fitted by least squares analysis. Standard errors for the D_0 and D_q values with their standard errors are as follows: control u.v., $D_0 \, 2·81 \pm 0·2$, $D_q \, 3·44 \pm 0·41$; first 1·5-h exposure, $D_0 \, 1·8 \pm 0·3$, $D_q \, 0·7 \pm 0·15$; $3\frac{1}{2}$–5 h exposure, $D_0 \, 2·17 \pm 0·1$, $D_q \, 2·31 \pm 0·34$. (I. Rasko & R. T. Johnson, unpublished results.)

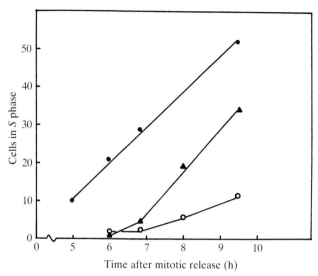

Fig. 4. Arrest in cell cycle progression after u.v. irradiation associated with repair synthesis inhibitors. HD1A, an excision repair defective, XPD-like hybrid cell line (Johnson *et al.* 1986), was reversibly blocked in mitosis by nitrous oxide arrest (Johnson *et al.* 1978), and released into G_1 phase 2·5 h later; when more than 90 % of cells had entered G_1 medium was removed and the cells u.v. irradiated *in situ* with $2 \mathrm{J\,m^{-2}}$ in warm phosphate-buffered saline. One dish was incubated with araC ($10^{-4}\mathrm{M}$) and HU ($10^{-2}\mathrm{M}$) for 1·5 h ($\bigcirc$); one dish with aphidicolin ($10\,\mu\mathrm{g\,ml^{-1}}$) plus $10^{-2}\mathrm{M}$-HU for 1·5 h ($\blacktriangle$), and another dish served as the u.v. control ($\bullet$). After washing each plate three times with warm medium the cultures were incubated with medium containing $0·5\,\mu\mathrm{Ci\,ml^{-1}}$ [^{3}H]thymidine ($50\,\mathrm{Ci\,mmol^{-1}}$), and at the times indicated cells were removed and cytocentrifuge preparations made. These were processed for autoradiography and the frequency of labelled nuclei was scored in 100–200 cells. (I. Rasko & R. T. Johnson, unpublished results.)

outweighed by more damaging consequences of the inhibited repair process itself. As we discussed earlier, diminished rates of dimer removal in the presence of inhibitors cannot entirely account for the substantial potentiation of killing observed and one must, therefore, suspect the development of secondary and more hazardous consequences, presumably at the DNA level.

Cell killing, DNA and chromosome fragmentation

We can obtain more precise and primary information about the potentiation of cell killing by repair synthesis inhibitors from a study of chromosome aberrations. In general, incubation with inhibitors is associated with increased frequencies of chromosome gaps and breaks, a phenomenon that, as Taylor *et al.* (1962) correctly inferred, results from the deprivation of precursor supply necessary to sustain adequate DNA repair. Several recent reviews have dealt with this area (e.g. see Collins & Johnson, 1984; Kihlman & Natarajan, 1984; Bryant & Iliakis, 1984) and these should be consulted for further details. However, it is clear that many uncertainties remain in the aetiology of chromosome aberrations, mostly related to the long time scale over which it is necessary to allow them to develop before cells reach mitotis. We (and others) have therefore been interested in developing more immediate chromosome techniques for exploring the relationship between DNA damage, repair and its inhibition, and the production of chromosome aberrations. Two procedures have been used: one, the cell fusion technique of premature chromosome condensation, which allows one to look directly at interphase chromosomes without waiting for them to enter mitosis (Johnson *et al.* 1982; Hittelman, 1984); and the second, metaphase repair, makes use exclusively of the mitotic cell (with fully packed chromosomes) to generate aberrations during this phase of the cycle (Mullinger & Johnson, 1985).

u.v. irradiation of metaphase or interphase cells followed by repair inhibition results in massive chromosome decondensation dependent on both time and dose. Metaphase and prematurely condensed chromosomes (PCC) finally lose all apparent structure (Schor *et al.* 1975; Mullinger & Johnson, 1985) (Fig. 5). Decondensation continues long after DNA strand breaks, as measured by alkaline unwinding, have saturated (Fig. 6). This figure also shows that accumulated breaks mostly disappear when the inhibitors, in this case araC and HU, are removed. Inspection of chromosomes from such cells, after reversal of inhibition (Mullinger & Johnson, 1985) reveals that though the bulk of strand breaks are rejoined there is an abundance of chromosome aberrations, mostly in the form of chromatid breaks (Fig. 7). The degree of chromosome fragmentation depends on the duration of repair inhibition and the u.v. dose (Mullinger & Johnson, 1985). For G_1 PCC the picture is similar (Hittelman, 1984; Hittelman & Pollard, 1984), with fragmentation revealed after a period of inhibition. Fig. 8 contrasts the appearance of normal G_1 PCC from a human fibroblast with those from a G_1 cell irradiated with $10 \mathrm{J m^{-2}}$ and incubated for 90 min with aphidicolin and HU before inhibitors were removed and cells fused to produce PCC. Fragmentation is evident. Table 2 supplies quantitative information and a comparison of the effects of araC/HU and aphidicolin/HU inhibition on PCC fragmentation in normal and Cockayne's Syndrome (CS) fibroblasts. Both cell types respond similarly at this u.v. dose, and it appears that araC has a stronger effect on fragmentation than aphidicolin, a point we will return to later.

Since virtually all single strand DNA breaks are removed after inhibitor reversal, this being particularly true for aphidicolin (see below), chromosome breakage probably reflects the small proportion of residual, barely detectable double strand (DS) DNA breaks. Using neutral elution or viscoelastometry, several groups have shown that DS DNA breaks develop in a time- and dose-related manner as a consequence of repair inhibition (Bradley & Taylor, 1983; Filatov & Noskin, 1983), while Hittelman (1984) and Mullinger & Johnson (1985) have related the appearance of DS breaks to the development of chromosome fragmentation. DS breaks can develop rapidly in these cells as the data in Fig. 9 show. Here a normal human fibroblast and a permanent human cell line, HD1, irradiated with $10 \mathrm{J m^{-2}}$, were incubated with araC/HU for up to 90 min and at various points the presence of DS breaks was assessed. Clearly, after 20 min of inhibition, elution behaviour has changed, implying the early development of DS lesions. The figure also shows that aphidicolin is as effective as araC in promoting DS breaks. Removal of the inhibitors

(Mullinger & Johnson, 1985, and Fig. 9), or removal plus addition of DNA precursors, results in some loss of DS breaks, a finding in agreement with the results of Bryant & Iliakis (1984) using araA in combination with X-irradiation. We assume that in our system remaining DS breaks are reflected in chromosome fragmentation, though we do not have a quantitative correlation between the two. A small proportion of the DS breaks may be accounted for by overlap of inhibited repair sites in opposite strands, an idea proposed by Filatov & Noskin (1983), and one that is marginally strengthened by data suggesting that the size of repair patch in the presence of inhibitors is greater than usual (Clarkson, 1978; Francis *et al.* 1979; Th'ng & Walker, 1986). It is worth pointing out, however, that the increased size of repair patch in the presence of inhibitors is likely to be trivial (from 20 to 50 bases)

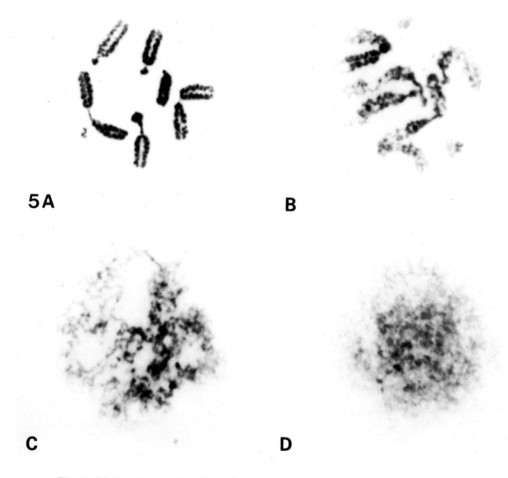

5A   **B**

C   **D**

Fig. 5. Light micrographs of Indian muntjac chromosome spreads illustrating progressive stages of condensation after u.v. irradiation of metaphase cells pre-incubated for 30 min and post-incubated for 90 min with araC (10^{-4} M) and HU (10^{-2} M). A, $0.4\,\mathrm{J\,m^{-2}}$; B, $2\,\mathrm{J\,m^{-2}}$; C, $2\,\mathrm{J\,m^{-2}}$; D, $5\,\mathrm{J\,m^{-2}}$. ×900. (From Mullinger & Johnson, 1985.)

compared to the distance between patches (about 100 000 base-pairs after $10\,\mathrm{J\,m^{-2}}$). Moreover, DS breaks and chromosome fragmentation develop even after rather low levels of u.v. (e.g. $5\,\mathrm{J\,m^{-2}}$), when rates of dimer coincidence in opposite strands

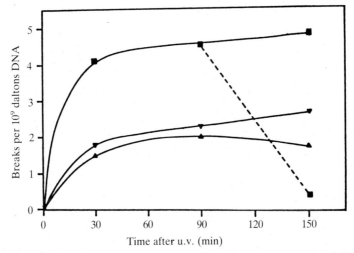

Fig. 6. DNA break accumulation in u.v.-irradiated, metaphase-arrested HeLa cells during incubation with araC ($10^{-4}\,\mathrm{M}$) plus HU ($10^{-2}\,\mathrm{M}$). Data are shown for 0·5 (▲), 1 (▼) and 5 (■) $\mathrm{J\,m^{-2}}$ u.v. At 90 min after u.v. inhibitors were removed from a parallel $5\,\mathrm{J\,m^{-2}}$ sample, which was incubated for a further 60 min in the presence of the four deoxyribonucleosides, each at $10^{-4}\,\mathrm{M}$. DNA breaks were assayed after alkaline unwinding and hydroxyapatite chromatography. (From Mullinger & Johnson, 1985.)

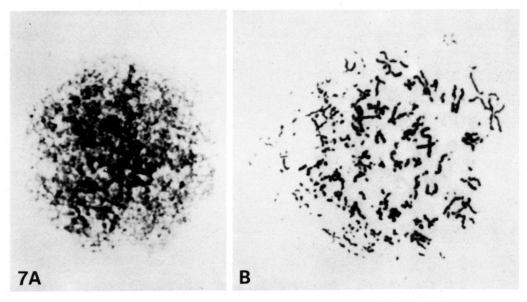

Fig. 7. Light micrographs of HeLa chromosomes showing reversal of decondensation leading to fragmented chromosomes. Metaphase cells were u.v.-irradiated ($20\,\mathrm{J\,m^{-2}}$), incubated with araC ($10^{-4}\,\mathrm{M}$) plus HU ($10^{-2}\,\mathrm{M}$) for 90 min, followed by a further 60 min either in the continued presence of inhibitors (A), or in their absence but presence of $10^{-4}\,\mathrm{M}$-deoxyribonucleosides (B). ×750. (From Mullinger & Johnson, 1985.)

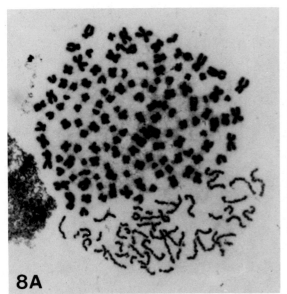
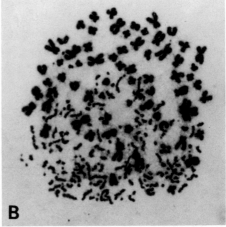

Fig. 8. u.v. irradiation and repair synthesis inhibition results in fragmentation of prematurely condensed chromosomes. Normal human fibroblasts in quiescent culture were either: A, fused with mitotic HeLa cells to induce premature chromosome condensation; or B, u.v. irradiated $(10 \, \mathrm{J \, m^{-2}})$ and incubated with araC $(10^{-4} \, \mathrm{M})$ plus HU $(10^{-2} \, \mathrm{M})$ for 60 min, at which point inhibitors were removed and the cells incubated for a further 30 min with $10^{-4} \, \mathrm{M}$-deoxyribonucleosides; this population was fused with mitotic HeLa cells to induce PCC. (A. M. Mullinger, S. Squires & R. T. Johnson, unpublished results.)

would be extremely low. It seems likely, therefore, that a proportion of DS breaks arise from (secondary) nuclease action opposite the gaps at inhibited repair sites: though, as Hittelman (1984) has shown by means of S_1 nuclease modification of neutral elution behaviour of DNA from repair arrested cells, not all single strand gaps are converted to DS breaks in the cells.

CONCLUSIONS DRAWN ABOUT STRESS ASSOCIATED WITH REPAIR SYNTHESIS INHIBITORS

Despite our rather general ignorance of detailed metabolic changes that follow u.v. irradiation and subsequent incubation with inhibitors of DNA repair synthesis, we are now in a stronger position to conclude that the substantial extra killing that is commonly found with HU, araC and aphidicolin is predominantly due to degradative changes occurring at many of the inhibited sites of repair. The most important change in terms of potential lethality is the DS DNA break. Some of these can be repaired; others will form the basis of chromosome fragmentation, probably the immediate cause of lethality. Metaphase repair and PCC techniques allow us to narrow the time-scale between DNA damage, repair events and their perturbation, and the development of chromosome aberrations. It remains possible, however, that brief distortions of the repair process by inhibitors have additional deleterious and, as

Table 2. *Inhibition of excision repair and the production of chromosome fragments in G_1 PCC from u.v.-irradiated human fibroblasts*

u.v. ($J\,m^{-2}$)	Preincubation 30 min	1st postincubation 60 min	2nd postincubation 30 min	Total G_1 chromosomes including fragments (mean ± S.D.) in:	
				Normal human fibroblasts	Cockayne's Syndrome fibroblasts
10	HU + araC	HU + araC	+DNA precursors	91·2 ± 23·9	103·6 ± 26·9
10	HU + aphidicolin	HU + aphidicolin	+DNA precursors	67·1 ± 11·7	73·6 ± 17·4
10	No inhibitors	No inhibitors	No DNA precursors	48·2 ± 2·5	45·8 ± 2·5

Quiescent normal human fibroblasts or Cockayne's Syndrome fibroblasts (GM1856) were plated into dishes, allowed to attach and 2 h later, where appropriate, inhibitors were added as follows: HU (10^{-2} M), araC (10^{-4} M), aphidicolin ($10\,\mu g\,ml^{-1}$) for 30 min pre u.v. incubation. u.v. was delivered *in situ* in PBS, and post-incubation with the appropriate inhibitors was given for 1 h. At this point inhibitors were removed; the cultures washed and each of the four deoxyribonucleosides (10^{-4} M) added, where indicated, for 30 min. At this time each culture was removed from its dish and fused with twice the number of mitotic HeLa cells to induce premature chromosome condensation (Johnson & Rao, 1970). Standard chromosome preparations were made and spreads containing PCC were photographed for scoring. 20 PCC were scored for each of the inhibited samples, and 10 for the u.v. control. (A. M. Mullinger, S. Squires & R. T. Johnson, unpublished material.)

yet, unknown consequences for excision repair and such disturbance may contribute to cell killing. The most likely interpretation of the effect of novobiocin on repair probably arises from the cellular stress it induces *via* its disturbance of ATP metabolism. This mechanism can account for its potency until other data are produced.

POTENTIAL THERAPEUTIC VALUE OF TREATMENT WITH DNA REPAIR INHIBITORS

The conversion of repair sites to lethal strand-breaks by DNA repair inhibitors offers possibilities in the chemotherapy of cancer. Potentially the most useful agent in this respect is araC, since its effect is not easily reversible. araC, acting as an inhibitor of replicative synthesis, is already widely used in chemotherapy, being the most effective agent for the treatment of myeloid leukaemia (Frei *et al.* 1969). Other tumours are more refractory to treatment with araC, in some cases because their replicative polymerase is less sensitive to inhibition (Tanaka & Yoshida, 1982). But even without replicative incorporation, the combination of araC and a DNA

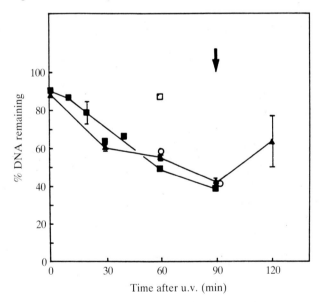

Fig. 9. Effect of repair inhibitors on the elution behaviour of u.v.-irradiated metaphase DNA under neutral (pH 9·6) conditions. Normal human fibroblasts (■), or human cell line HD1 (▲), uniformly prelabelled with [³H]thymidine, were u.v. irradiated (10 J m⁻²) and incubated with araC (10⁻⁴M) plus HU (10⁻²M) (filled symbols) or aphidicolin (10 μg ml⁻¹) plus HU (10⁻²M) (fibroblasts, (○)), for up to 90 min. At the indicated times samples were prepared for neutral elution as described by Mullinger & Johnson (1985). In this figure the resulting elution profiles are expressed in terms of the proportion of DNA radioactivity remaining on the filter after a 15 h elution period. Without inhibitors elution of the DNA from u.v.-irradiated HD1 cells is negligible (□). The arrow indicates the time of inhibitor removal from a fibroblast sample, which was then incubated for a further 30 min before cell lysis. Where bars are present they represent the range in duplicate samples. (R. T. Johnson, unpublished results.)

damaging agent is, as we have seen, more lethal than the damage alone. Kufe *et al.* (1984) have shown that the increased lethality correlates well with the incorporation of araCTP into repair patches. araC, or possibly other repair inhibitors, might therefore effectively increase the effectiveness of DNA damaging agents used therapeutically. In this context it is worth noting that the efficiency of discrimination against araCTP, as a substrate for incorporation, may be less with repair polymerases than with replicative polymerases, and be less in transformed than in diploid cells (Elliott & Downes, 1986).

PERTURBATION OF LATE STAGES IN THE EXCISION REPAIR PROCESS WITHOUT THE USE OF INHIBITORS

The gross effects associated with inhibited repair that have been chronicled may have their subtler counterparts elsewhere. For example, there are several cases where, without our interference, cells behave very much as though their post-incision repair processes were inhibited or delayed. Here, though the effects are less extreme, they may be far more biologicaly significant. The best examples of delayed repair are seen in the Chinese hamster mutant EM9 (see Thompson *et al.* 1987, this volume) and in the human fibroblast designated 46 BR (Webster *et al.* 1982). In both these cases, in the absence of inhibitors, the disappearance of repair-induced breaks is poor compared with wild-type counterparts (Thompson *et al.* 1982; Squires & Johnson, 1983; Teo *et al.* 1983). A survey of human cells has revealed that CS fibroblasts also accumulate breaks in the absence of inhibitors, but only if they have recently undergone trypsinization (Squires & Johnson, 1983). CS cells irradiated up to 6 h after trypsin treatment accumulated significant numbers of breaks by comparison with normal cells, though always to a lesser degree than 46 BR. Unlike 46 BR this disturbed CS state can be alleviated by providing DNA precursors, implicating a possible abnormality in CS cells of precursor production or of the polymerization process itself in CS cells.

Normally, human fibroblasts do not generate long-lived breaks (unless treated with repair inhibitors) but in special circumstances they can. Squires *et al.* (unpublished) have investigated conditions under which delayed repair occurs. In particular, we have examined the dependence of break accumulation on trypsin detachment of cells in different growth states, seeking to establish whether the protocols used to transform human or rodent cells also impede the repair process. One mitogen, insulin, has been employed with success in transformation studies (Milo *et al.* 1981; Umeda *et al.* 1963) and its effect on excision repair has been examined. Fig. 10 illustrates the excision repair behaviour of cells in three growth states given $4 \mathrm{J\,m^{-2}}$ of u.v. over a 60 min period. The three cell states are log cultures reseeded 3 h earlier (A), quiescent cultures (B); and cultures seeded 3 h earlier from quiescence (C). Each data set includes time courses of DNA break frequencies in the presence and absence of repair synthesis inhibitors, and both of these conditions have an additional variable, the presence or absence of insulin. Several points are clear. First, in the presence of inhibitors each culture shows a similar profile of break accumulation, and insulin has little or no effect. Second, in the absence of inhibitors there are few long-lived breaks in log reseeded or quiescent cultures; but there are many more in cultures recently reseeded from quiescence, amounting to about 10^3 per cell. Third, insulin increases the frequency of long-lived breaks in each culture, with the greatest net value in quiescent reseeded cells of about 5×10^3/cell.

Data such as these in Fig. 10 allow us to estimate the average time taken to complete a repair site in human fibroblasts (Squires *et al.* unpublished). We assume that for a given culture state all repair sites give rise to breaks in the presence of inhibitors, and that all sites take the same time to be completed in the absence of inhibitors. Clearly, not all repair sites *are* converted into breaks in the presence of inhibitors (Downes, 1984; Smith, 1984), but we note from the data in Fig. 10 that the frequency of inhibited repair sites in the three cultures is similar, and we assume for this argument that the required correction factor would not reduce completion

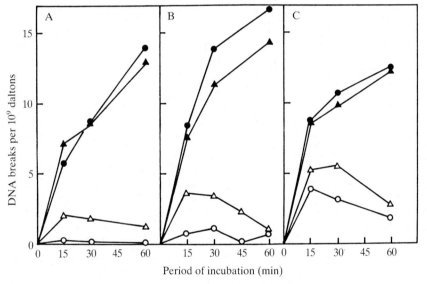

Fig. 10. The accumulation of u.v.-induced incomplete repair sites in human fibroblasts as a function of growth state and insulin treatment.

A. Logarithmic cultures of normal human fibroblasts, labelled with [³]thymidine were irradiated with 4 J m⁻² of u.v. light 3 h after seeding. The cells were incubated in growth medium either with insulin (1 unit ml⁻¹) (▲, △), or without (●, ○) for various periods in the presence of 10^{-2} M-HU and 5×10^{-5} M-araC (▲, ●), or without DNA synthesis inhibitors (△, ○). When inhibitors were used the cells were preincubated for 30 min before irradiation. The frequency of breaks in DNA was determined by alkaline lysis and hydroxyapatite chromatography.

B. Quiescent cell cultures were obtained 2–3 weeks after seeding, with at least two medium changes during the interim period. The contact-inhibited cells were irradiated with 4 J m⁻², 3 h after serum stimulation.

C. Cultures obtained by reseeding, in fresh medium, trypsinized quiescent cells. These were irradiated 3 h later. The results shown represent the mean of several experiments (A, at least 3; B, 6; C, over 10). At 15 min incubation standard errors of the mean break frequency per 10^9 daltons were: A. (●), ±1·4; (▲), ±2; (△), ±0·9. B. (●), ±3·4; (▲), ±3; (○), ±0·6; (△), ±2·8. C. (●), ±2; (▲), ±2·1; (○), ±1·8; (△), ±2·4. (From Squires, Elliott & Johnson, unpublished results.)

Table 3. *Estimated time for repair at a single site*

Cell type and growth state	m/n (relative DNA break frequency, without/with inhibitors)		Time for repair at a single site, t (min)	
	Without insulin	With insulin	Without insulin	With insulin
Normal fibroblasts (logarithmic)	0·025	0·31	0·37	4·6
Normal fibroblasts (quiescent)	0·1	0·45	1·4	6·8
Normal fibroblasts (quiescent, reseeded)	0·45	0·61	6·7	9·1
46BR fibroblasts (logarithmic)	0·8	—	12	—

n and m are, respectively, the DNA break frequencies observed after 15-min incubation with or without DNA synthesis inhibitors (see Fig. 1). We assume that represents the total number of incision events performed by the cell in that time (4). The parameter m, measured without inhibitors, represents those sites at which repair began in the last t min of the 15-min incubation period but has not yet finished. t, the time it takes to complete repair at a single site can be estimated from the relationship $t/15 = m/n$. (From Squires *et al.* unpublished data.)

time by more than 30%. Finally, we assume that the rate of incision is constant over a 15 min period of break accumulation in the presence of inhibitors. Breaks detected in the absence of inhibitors must therefore arise during a period after u.v. when there was too little incubation time left for completion at the site. Thus the fraction of repair sites that are incomplete at the end of 15 min equals the fraction of the 15 min needed to complete an incised site. These maximum estimates, shown in Table 3, indicate that the time required to complete a site varies with the growth state and also that insulin delays completion in all. For example, quiescent cells require four times longer to complete a repair site than proliferating cells and quiescent cells stimulated to cycle by trypsin treatment, and replating require about 18 times longer than their proliferating counterparts. The most extreme delays do not, however, exceed the 12 min duration of patch completion in 46BR fibroblasts, 40 times longer than a normal fibroblast (data taken from Squires & Johnson, 1983).

The intriguing question of how the mitogens insulin and trypsin act to exacerbate delays in rejoining of repair patches can be partly answered. We know, from the fact that added DNA precursors can alleviate their effect, that DNA precursor pools are likely to be a target (Squires *et al.* unpublished). Now we have preliminary, direct evidence that deoxyribonucleotide pools are reduced by both trypsin and insulin treatment (Collins, Squires & Johnson, unpublished data). While insulin specifically reduces purine pools by up to 50%, trypsin reduces purine and pyrimidine pools by 30–50%. How commonly mitogens act in this way remains to be seen; and how reduction in DNA precursor pools fits into the overall pattern of growth stimulation is, as yet, obscure. Trypsin effects are likely to be complex, especially since the enzyme can readily gain access into cells (Hodges *et al.* 1973); and also, by cleaving surface receptors such as those of insulin (Czech, 1985), it may radically change the cellular response to other mitogens.

Pre-*S*-phase fibroblasts irradiated with u.v. after detachment by trypsin rapidly develop double strand DNA damage, especially when insulin is present, though the effect is less marked than with repair inhibitors. Cells reseeded from quiescence show the greatest DS breakage, and with these cultures, also, insulin increases u.v. toxicity, reducing the D_0 by a factor of almost 3 (Squires *et al.* unpublished).

The stressed fibroblasts considered above were not the first example to be discovered, of cell hypersensitivity to u.v. related to limitations of DNA precursor supply. The extreme u.v. sensitivity of unstimulated lymphocytes can be attributed in part at least to the limited size of the DNA precursor pool (Munch-Petersen *et al.* 1973), since supplies of deoxyribonucleosides greatly improve both B and T cell survival, *and* also speed up the completion of the excision repair process (Yew & Johnson, 1979). We may now be in a position to resolve the paradox of why non-cycling lymphocytes should be so u.v.-sensitive even though they are in an extended holding state, which should allow repair to occur, however slowly, before the cells have to replicate their DNA. They may represent a repair-stressed situation where small pools are associated with delayed completion of the repair sites resulting in secondary DS DNA breaks and subsequent cell death. Additionally, however, a small proportion of lymphocytes may have advanced towards transformation because of this damage. This is an intriguing possibility. DS DNA breaks or gaps undergoing repair in mammalian cells may, as in yeast (Resnick, 1976; Orr-Weaver & Szostak, 1983), represent an excellent substrate for mitotic recombination. Resulting rearrangements, perhaps in the form of translocations and deletions, could form the basis of subsequent transformation. The work of Zajac-Kaye & Ts'o (1984) has shown a clear relationship between the production of DNA breaks with subsequent chromosome rearrangements and increased rates of transformation. In human fibroblasts the relationship between the induction after u.v. irradiation of long-lived repair sites by trypsin and insulin, and the promotion of genetic instability is speculative. However, several studies have demonstrated the usefulness of trypsin detachment and insulin treatment in promoting human and rodent cell mutagenesis and transformation from quiescent cultures (Milo *et al.* 1981; Zimmerman & Little, 1983; Grosovsky & Little, 1984; Terasima *et al.* 1985). Stressing the excision repair capacity after damage by reducing precursor availability and thereby delaying the completion of repair may be important general consequences of cell exposure to trypsin or other proteolytic enzymes, and to mitogens such as insulin. After tissues have experienced DNA damage they are subject to significant protease activity (Miskin & Reich, 1980, 1981), and also undertake rapid cell renewal presumably under control of growth factors.

Conclusions drawn about delays in the excision repair process not associated with repair synthesis inhibitors

There is now evidence that the completion time of the excision repair process is (1) related to the state of cell growth, and (2) greatly delayed by certain mitogenic stimuli. These statements relate to cells *in vitro* and are not necessarily associated with any mutant phenotype. Underlying each delay in completion is evidence of immediate DNA precursor limitation, either related to natural oscillations of pool size associated with growth state, or to induced pool depletion by agents other than those recognized as inhibitors of precursor production or DNA polymerization (Nicander & Reichard, 1985). In cell cultures the consequences of such delayed repair are clearly seen, though they are usually less extreme than when repair synthesis inhibitors have been used. In the organism there is no direct evidence for delayed repair associated with pool constraint and we must, therefore, be careful in making any extrapolation. However, given the evidence we have from cell cultures about the production of DS DNA breaks, chromosome aberrations, and transformation and mutagenesis associated with mitogenic stimulation of specific growth stages following DNA damage, we feel that some speculation is reasonable. We conclude that delay in the completion of repair *in vivo* may be an important consequence of the cellular response to DNA damage, especially since such repair behaviour is likely to occur in tissues where cell removal and renewal are commonplace. DNA templates suffering from such delay could act as substrates for recombination or deletion and both of these long-term genetic consequences could play a prominent role in cell transformation.

STUDIES WITH LIGATION

Earlier in this chapter, we noted that many of the DNA breaks accumulated with inhibitors after u.v. can be chased away when inhibitors are removed. This allows us to examine the kinetics of the ligation step in excision repair, and in particular its sensitivity to the ADP-ribosyl transferase inhibitor, 3-aminobenzamide (3AB); we will deal with this latter aspect first. Many laboratories have shown that DNA breakage, such as is caused by alkylation damage, results in the activation of ADP-ribosyl transferase, which utilizes NAD to produce polymers of ADP-ribose associated with nuclear proteins (Shall, 1984). Arrest of its activity by 3AB results in the retention of the NAD pool and the lack of sealing of alkylation-related breaks. One possible model for the action of 3AB is the dependence of DNA ligase II on ADP-ribosylation for its activation (Creissen & Shall, 1982).

Unlike alkylation damage, u.v. irradiation does not usually lead to the accumulation of many DNA strand breaks, and it produces only a slow, moderate fall in NAD levels. However, if repair synthesis inhibitors are used to accumulate DNA breaks in u.v.-irradiated cells, NAD levels fall further and faster as much additional poly(ADP-ribose) synthesis is induced (Jacobson *et al.* 1983; Collins, 1985; Squires *et al.* unpublished). NAD levels also fall by 20% in cultures of human fibroblasts reseeded from quiescence, which accumulate incomplete repair sites after u.v., especially in the presence of insulin (Fig. 10C) (Squires *et al.* 1986). Though the fall in NAD can be prevented entirely by 3AB, break sealing after removal of inhibitors (though still in the presence of 3AB) is normal (Collins, 1985; Squires *et al.* unpublished). A typical experiment is shown in Fig. 11. Panel A follows the NAD pool in u.v.-irradiated cells incubated with aphidicolin plus HU, with and without 3AB. In the absence of 3AB the pool falls to 40% of its starting level by 60 min; *with*

3AB, NAD levels remain constant. Panel B registers the accumulated DNA breaks in this material. With aphidicolin/HU about 10 breaks accumulate in 60 min whether or not 3AB is present. Restoring repair synthesis by removing inhibitors and providing DNA precursors at the time indicated results in rapid break sealing (and no further loss of NAD). Under these circumstances we conclude that whichever DNA ligase is involved in repair of u.v. damage in fibroblasts, ADP ribosylation is not crucial for this activity.

The reversal of DNA breaks accumulated after u.v. in the presence of inhibitors such as araC or aphidicolin provides a simple and quantitative measure of post-incision events including ligation, an activity that is otehwise difficult to study. Breaks accumulated by aphidicolin are rejoined much more rapidly than those associated with araC-arrested repair, a phenomenon attributed to the different modes of action of these agents (Cleaver, 1983; Collins, 1987). For aphidicolin reversal (Fig. 11) the rate of break rejoining can be extremely rapid (Squires *et al.* unpublished) and for human and Chinese hamster cells, Collins (1987) has computed rates of rejoining in excess of one or two breaks per min per 10^9 dalton over the first 10 min, surpassing by 15-fold the maximum rates of incision in these cells. Such data indicate that ligation can validly be studied in this artificial situation, especially when the period of break accumulation is short. Extending the length of inhibition results in slower rates of rejoining and less-complete reversal (Collins, 1987), symptoms typical of increasing cellular stress associated with inhibited repair; and it seems likely that the development of DS DNA breaks and chromosome fragmentation

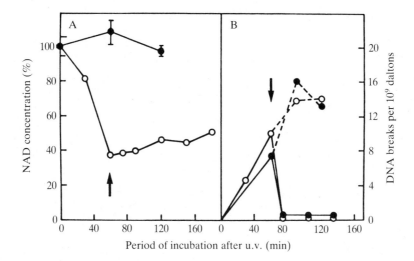

Fig. 11. Effect of 3AB on NAD levels and on the rate of gap sealing of DNA breaks accumulated after u.v. in the presence of repair synthesis inhibitors. Proliferating cultures were irradiated with $4\,\mathrm{J\,m^{-2}}$ of u.v. and incubated at $37\,^{\circ}\mathrm{C}$, with $10^{-2}\,\mathrm{M}$-HU and $10\,\mu\mathrm{g\,ml^{-1}}$ aphidicolin in the presence (●) or absence (○) of 5 mM-3AB. An hour after irradiation the medium containing inhibitors was replaced with medium plus $10^{-4}\,\mathrm{M}$-dX $\pm$ 5 mM-3AB (——) or not replaced (----) and the cells were incubated further. At various times samples were removed and NAD (A) or DNA breaks (B) were assayed as described (Squires *et al.* 1986). (From Squires *et al.* unpublished results.)

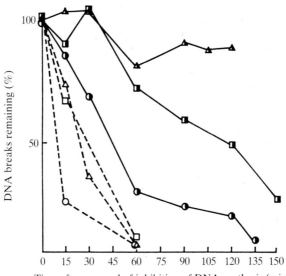

Fig. 12. Delays in break rejoining in fibroblasts from an individual with Cockayne's Syndrome (CS) and a Cockayne's Syndrome heterozygote (CSH). Confluent cultures of: (○ or ◑) normal human fibroblasts (embryonic lung); (△ or ▲) CS3BE (CS); and (□ or ▣) CSHIBI (CSH), were u.v.-irradiated (4 J m^{-2}) and incubated with aphidicolin (10 μg ml^{-1}) plus HU (10^{-2} M) for 30 min to accumulate repair-related DNA breaks. At this point inhibitors were removed and incubation continued for about 2 h either in the presence of 10^{-4} M-deoxyribonucleosides (broken lines, open symbols) or in standard growth medium (continuous lines, half-filled symbols). At different times samples were lysed in alkali, and the frequency of DNA breaks assessed by means of hydroxyapatite chromatography. (S. Squires & R. T. Johnson, unpublished results.)

during more prolonged inhibition could slow down or disrupt repair. Other explanations for less-efficient rejoining, involving DNA precursor availability, are also possible given the complex disturbance to the deoxyribonucleotide pools caused by u.v. light on the one hand (Das *et al.* 1983; Newman & Miller, 1984) and by inhibitors such as HU and aphidicolin on the other (Nicander & Reichard, 1985).

We have already seen that break rejoining is retarded in u.v.-irradiated normal fibroblasts by trypsin and insulin treatment (Fig. 10) (Squires *et al.* unpublished), and in CS fibroblasts by trypsin (Squires & Johnson, 1983). In both situations addition of DNA precursors restores normal break-rejoining behaviour, implying that the effect of trypsin/insulin was to disturb either precursor supply or precursor presentation to the repair polymerase. Given the exaggerated difficulties experienced by CS cells, we examined their capacity to rejoin accumulated breaks in a standard 'recoil' situation (Squires & Johnson, unpublished). Fig. 12 shows the time courses of break sealing for normal and CS fibroblasts and also for a CS heterozygous strain. Each culture had been reseeded recently from quiescence, before u.v. irradiation and incubation for 30 min with aphidicolin plus HU. One striking feature is the very marked difficulty experienced by CS cells in rejoining breaks compared with a normal cell strain. But the figure also reveals that the CS heterozygous strain is delayed, to an intermediate degree. Even when the reversal is carried out with DNA precursors present to speed up rejoining the behaviour of both CS and CS hetero-zygous cells still differs from wild type, suggesting that disruption of the repair mechanism in CS cells may not simply be explained in terms of precursor supply. Studies are in progress to establish the generality of this finding with several CS strains and their heterozygotes.

SLOW COMPLETION OF REPAIR SITES IN SEVERAL HUMAN HERITABLE CONDITIONS: RELATIONSHIP WITH DEFECTS IN DNA REPLICATION

Finally, it is worth pointing out that the susceptibility of post-incision steps of DNA repair processes to disruption by agents such as trypsin may be rather widespread among heritable human diseases. For example, in recently detached progeria cells, X-irradiated in suspension, there is clear evidence of slow break-rejoining compared with a normal control (Epstein *et al.* 1973). But when attached monolayers are irradiated, progeria cells reseal DNA breaks as rapidly as their normal counterparts (Setlow & Regan, 1974; Bradley *et al.* 1976). XP variant cells, without apparent defects in excision repair, have also been reported to accumulate long-lived breaks in parental DNA in the absence of inhibitors (Fornace *et al.* 1976) and, using the accumulated break-rejoining assay, Squires & Johnson (unpublished) have now confirmed that the only XP variant strain examined to date (XP30R0) *is* slow to remove breaks. Whether the ease with which excision repair steps can be dissociated in CS, progeria and XP variant cells is attributable in each case to abnormal DNA precursor provision or to defects in DNA polymerization/ligation steps remains uncertain. What does seem clear is that under most circumstances demands made on the precursor supply by repair synthesis will be met by the cell. Certainly this is the case for CS and XP variant in log growth, and in these conditions excision repair is apparently normal. For these cells the much more serious possi-bility lies in abnormal DNA replication behaviour when they are stressed either by damaging agents or by exposure to mitogenic signals. DNA damage in CS cells caused by u.v. is associated with prolonged inhibition of both DNA and RNA synthesis, and with failure of these cells to recover normally from potentially lethal u.v. damage when held in a non-dividing state (Lehmann *et al.* 1979; Mayne & Lehmann, 1982). We should like to know, by direct measurement, whether u.v. causes hyperinstability of nucleotide metabolism in CS. The stress induced in nucleotide metabolism by mitogenic stimulation is poorly understood, though the direct measurement of deoxyribonucleotide pool reduction associated with insulin or trypsin treatment mentioned above is perhaps the first evidence (Collins *et al.* unpublished data). But trypsin is also known to cause severe arrest of entry into *S* phase in normal cells (Campisi & Medrano, 1983), and can disturb precursor supply during *S* phase (S. Squires, unpublished). Extrapolating from the sensitivity of excision-related DNA synthesis in CS, these cells may also display an exaggerated sensitivity of replication to disturbance. This is currently being investigated. If, as seems likely, replication in CS is hypersensitive to the stresses involved in handling cells in culture, this would not be the first hereditary defect to display such behaviour. Bloom's Syndrome fibroblasts, for example, show exactly this pattern, with extremely slow rates of DNA chain growth by comparison with normal fibroblasts in sparse or recently reseeded cultures (Ockey, 1979). Each of these hereditary conditions might be regarded perhaps as a family of conditional replication mutants, defective in some aspect of DNA synthesis or synthesis-coupled step that is displayed most readily when an appropriate stress is applied. Given the complexity of the replication process and its roots in the synthesis and interconversion of precursors, the analysis may be prolonged.

We are grateful to the Cancer Research Campaign, of which R.T.J. is a Research Fellow, for their continued support, and to Ann Hill, Roger Northfield, David Oates, Peggy Pawley and Jacquie Whybrow for their excellent help.

REFERENCES

BRADLEY, M. O., ERICKSON, L. C. & KOHN, K. W. (1976). Normal DNA strand rejoining and absence of DNA crosslinking in progeroid and aging human cells. *Mutat. Res.* **37**, 279–292.

BRADLEY, M. O. & TAYLOR, V. I. (1983). Repair-induced DNA double strand breaks after ultraviolet light and either aphidicolin or 1-β-D-arabinofuranosylcytosine/hydroxyurea. *Carcinogenesis* **4**, 1513–1517.

BRYANT, P. E. & ILIAKIS, G. (1984). Possible correlations between cell killing, chromosome damage and DNA repair after X-irradiation. In *DNA Repair and its Inhibition, Nucl. Acids Symp., Series*, no. 13 (ed. A. R. S. Collins, C. S. Downes & R. T. Johnson), pp. 291–308. Oxford, Washington, D.C.: IRL Press.

BURG, K., COLLINS, A. R. S. & JOHNSON, R. T. (1977). Effects of ultraviolet light on synchronized Chinese hamster ovary cells; potentiation by hydroxyurea. *J. Cell Sci.* **28**, 29–48.

CAMPISI, J. & MEDRANO, E. E. (1983). Cell cycle perturbations in normal and transformed fibroblasts caused by detachment from the substratum. *J. cell. Physiol.* **114**, 53–60.

CHU, M. Y. & FISCHER, G. A. (1962). A proposed mechanism of action of 1-β-D-arabinofuranosylcytosine as an inhibitor of the growth of leukemic cells. *Biochem. Pharmac.* **11**, 423–430.

CLARKSON, J. M. (1978). Enhancement of repair replication in mammalian cells by hydroxyurea. *Mutat. Res.* **52**, 273–284.

CLARKSON, J. M. & MITCHELL, D. L. (1983). The effects of various inhibitors of DNA synthesis on the repair of DNA photoproducts. *Biochim. biophys. Acta* **740**, 417–427.

CLEAVER, J. E. (1983). Structure of repaired sites in human DNA synthesised in the presence of inhibitors of DNA polymerases α and β in human fibroblasts. *Biochim. biophys. Acta* **739**, 301–311.

COLLINS, A. R. S. (1985). Poly(ADP-ribose) is not involved in the rejoining of DNA breaks accumulated to high levels in UV-irradiated HeLa cells. *Carcinogenesis* **6**, 1033–1036.

COLLINS, A. R. S. (1987). Estimates of the rate of ligation during excision repair of ultraviolet damaged DNA in mammalian cells. *Biochim. biophys. Acta* (in press).

COLLINS, A. R. S., DOWNES, C. S. & JOHNSON, R. T. (1980). Cell cycle-related variations in UV damage and repair capacity in Chinese hamster (CHO-K1) cells. *J. cell. Physiol.* **103**, 179–191.

COLLINS, A. R. S., DOWNES, C. S. & JOHNSON, R. T. (1984). *DNA Repair and its Inhibition, Nucl. Acids Symp. Series*, no. 13. Oxford, Washington, D.C.: IRL Press.

COLLINS, A. R. S., ORD, M. J. & JOHNSON, R. T. (1981). Correlations of DNA damage and repair with nuclear and chromosomal damage in HeLa cells caused by methylnitrosamides. *Cancer Res.* **41**, 5176–5187.

COLLINS, A. & JOHNSON, R. (1979a). Novobiocin: an inhibitor of the repair of UV-ionduced but not X-ray-induced damage in mammalian cells. *Nucl. Acids Res.* **7**, 1311–1320.

COLLINS, A. R. S. & JOHNSON, R. T. (1979b). Repair and survival after UV in quiescent and proliferating *Microtus agrestis* cells: Different rates of incision and different dependence on DNA precursor supply. *J. cell. Physiol.* **99**, 125–138.

COLLINS, A. R. S. & JOHNSON, R. T. (1984). The inhibition of DNA repair. In *Advances in Radiation Biology*, vol. 11 (ed. J. T. Lett), pp. 71–129. London, New York: Academic Press.

CREISSEN, D. & SHALL, S. (1982). Regulation of DNA ligase activity by poly(ADP-ribose). *Nature, Lond.* **296**, 271–272.

CZECH, M. P. (1985). The nature and regulation of the insulin receptor: structure and function. *A. Rev. Physiol.* **47**, 357–381.

DAS, S. K., BENDITT, E. P. & LOEB, L. I. (1983). Rapid changes in deoxynucleoside triphosphate pools in mammalian cells treated with mutagens. *Biochem. biophys. Res. Commun.* **114**, 458–464.

DOWNES, C. S. (1984). Approaches to the quantitative analysis of repair through the use of inhibitors. In *DNA Repair and its Inhibition, Nucl. Acids Symp. series*, no. 13 (ed. A. Collins, C. S. Downes & R. T. Johnson), pp. 231–254. Oxford, Washington, D.C.: IRL Press.

DOWNES, C. S., ORD, M. J., MULLINGER, A. M., COLLINS, A. R. S. & JOHNSON, R. T. (1985). Novobiocin inhibition of DNA excision repair may occur through effects on mitochondrial structure and ATP metabolism, not on repair topoisomerases. *Carcinogenesis* **6**, 1343–1352.

ELLIOTT, G. C. & DOWNES, C. S. (1986). Qualitative differences between replicative and repair synthesis in normal and transformed mouse cells as measured by precursor discrimination. *Mutat. Res.* (in press).

EPSTEIN, J., WILLIAMS, J. R. & LITTLE, J. B. (1973). Deficient DNA repair in human progeroid cells. *Proc. natn. Acad. Sci. U.S.A.* **70**, 977–981.

FILATOV, M. V. & NOSKIN, L. A. (1983). Sensitization of human cells by inhibitors of DNA synthesis following the action of DNA damaging agents. *Mutat. Res.* **110**, 393–399.

FORNACE, A. J., KOHN, K. W. & KANN, H. E. (1976). DNA single strand breaks during repair of UV damage in human fibroblasts and abnormalities of repair in xeroderma pigmentosum. *Proc. natn. Acad. Sci. U.S.A.* **73**, 39–43.

FRANCIS, A. A., BLEVINS, R. D., CARRIER, W. L., SMITH, D. P. & REGAN, J. D. (1979). Inhibition of DNA repair in ultraviolet-irradiated cells by hydroxyurea. *Biochim. biophys. Acta* **563**, 385–392.

FREI, E., BICKERS, J., HEWLETT, J., LANE, M., LEARY, W. & TALLY, R. (1969). Dose schedule and antitumor studies of arabinosyl cytosine. *Cancer Res.* **29**, 1325–1332.

FREI, J., CANAL, N. & GORI, E. (1958). Novobiocin as an uncoupling agent. *Experimentia* **14**, 377–378.

FRIEDBERG, E. C. (1985). *DNA Repair*. New York: W. H. Freeman and Co.

GROSOVSKY, A. J. & LITTLE, J. B. (1983). Influence of confluent holding time on UV light mutagenesis in human diploid fibroblasts. *Mutat. Res.* **110**, 401–412.

HACKETT, P. B., TRAUB, P. & GALLWITZ, D. (1978). The histone genes in HeLa cells are on individual transcriptional units. *J. molec. Biol.* **126**, 619–635.

HITTELMAN, W. N. (1984). Prematurely condensed chromosomes: a model system for visualizing effects of DNA damage, repair and inhibition at the level of chromosome structure. In *DNA Repair and its Inhibition, Nucl. Acids Symp. Series*, no. 13 (ed. A. R. S. Collins, C. S. Downes & R. T. Johnson), pp. 341–371. Oxford, Washington, D.C.: IRL Press.

HITTELMAN, W. N. & POLLARD, M. (1984). Visualization of chromatin events associated with the repair of ultraviolet light-induced damage by premature chromosome condensation. *Carcinogenesis* **5**, 1277–1285.

HODGES, G., LIVINGSTONE, D. & FRANKS, C. (1973). The localisation of trypsin in cultured mammalian cells. *J. Cell Sci.* **12**, 887–902.

JACOBSON, E. L., ANTOL, K. M., JUAREZ-SALINAS, H. & JACOBSON, M. K. (1983). Poly(ADP-ribose) metabolism in ultraviolet-irradiated human fibroblasts. *J. biol. Chem.* **258**, 103–107.

JOHNSON, R. T., COLLINS, A. R. S. & WALDREN, C. A. (1982). Prematurely condensed chromosomes and the analysis of DNA and chromosome lesions. In *Premature Chromosome Condensation* (ed. P. N. Rao, R. T. Johnson & K. Sperling), pp. 253–308. London, New York: Academic Press.

JOHNSON, R. T., MULLINGER, A. M. & DOWNES, C. S. (1978). Human minisegregant cells. In *Methods in Cell Biology*, vol. 20 (ed. D. M. Prescott), pp. 255–314. London, New York: Academic Press.

JOHNSON, R. T. & RAO, P. N. (1970). Mammalian cell fusion: Induction of premature chromosome condensation in interphase nuclei. *Nature, Lond.* **226**, 717–722.

286   *R. T. Johnson and others*

JOHNSON, R. T., SQUIRES, S., ELLIOTT, G. C., KOCH, G. L. E. & RAINBOW, A. J. (1985). Xeroderma pigmentosum D–HeLa hybrids with low and high ultraviolet sensitivity associated with normal and diminished DNA repair ability respectively. *J. Cell Sci.* **76**, 115–133.

JOHNSON, R. T., SQUIRES, S., ELLIOTT, G. C., RAINBOW, A. J., KOCH, G. L. E. & SMITH, M. (1986). Analysis of DNA repair in XP–HeLa hybrids; lack of correlation between excision repair of UV damage and adenovirus reactivation in an XP(D)-like cell line. *Carcinogenesis* (in press).

KIHLMAN, B. A. & NATARAJAN, A. T. (1984). Potentiation of chromosomal alterations by inhibitors of DNA repair. In *DNA Repair and its Inhibition, Nucl. Acids Symp. Series*, no. 13 (ed. A. R. S. Collins, C. S. Downes & R. T. Johnson), pp. 319–339. Oxford, Washington, D.C.: IRL Press.

KUFE, D. W., WEICHSELBAUM, R., EGAN, M., DAHLBERG, W. & FRAN, R. J. (1984). Lethal effects of 1-β-D-arabinofuranosyl cytosine incorporation into deoxyribonucleic acid during ultraviolet repair. *Molec. Pharmac.* **25**, 322–326.

LEHMANN, A. R., KIRK-BELL, S. & MAYNE, L. V. (1979). Abnormal kinetics of DNA synthesis in ultraviolet-irradiated cells from patients with Cockayne's Syndrome. *Cancer Res.* **39**, 4238–4241.

MATTERN, M. R., PAONE, R. F. & DAY, R. S. (1982). Eukaryotic DNA repair is blocked at different steps by inhibitors of DNA topoisomerases and of DNA polymerases α and β. *Biochim. biophys. Acta* **697**, 6–13.

MATTERN, M. R. & SCUDIERO, D. A. (1981). Dependence of mammalian DNA synthesis on DNA supercoiling. III. Characterization of the inhibition of replicative and repair-type DNA synthesis by novobiocin and nalidixic acid. *Biochim. biophys. Acta* **653**, 248–258.

MAYNE, L. V. (1984). Inhibitors of DNA synthesis (Aphidicolin and araC/HU) prevent the recovery of RNA synthesis after UV-irradiation. *Mutat. Res.* **131**, 187–191.

MAYNE, L. V. & LEHMANN, A. R. (1982). Failure of RNA synthesis to recover after UV irradiation: an early defect in cells from individuals with Cockayne's Syndrome and xeroderma pigmentosum. *Cancer Res.* **42**, 1473–1478.

MILO, G. E., WEISBRODE, S. A., ZIMMERMAN, R. & MCCLOSKEY, J. A. (1981). Ultraviolet radiation-induced neoplastic transformation of normal human cells, *in vitro*. *Chem–Biol. Interact.* **36**, 45–59.

MISKIN, R. & REICH, E. (1980). Plasminogen activator: Induction of synthesis by DNA damage. *Cell* **19**, 217–224.

MISKIN, R. & REICH, E. (1981). Induction of plasminogen activator by UV light in normal and xeroderma pigmentosum fibroblasts. *Proc. natn. Acad. Sci. U.S.A.* **78**, 6236–6240.

MULLINGER, A. M. & JOHNSON, R. T. (1985). Manipulating chromosome structure and metaphase status with ultraviolet light and repair synthesis inhibitors. *J. Cell Sci.* **73**, 159–186.

MUNCH-PETERSEN, B., TYRSTED, G. & DUPONT, B. (1973). The deoxyribonucleoside 5'-triphosphate (dATP and dTTP) pool in phytohaemagglutinin-stimulated and non-stimulated human lymphocytes. *Expl Cell Res.* **79**, 249–256.

NEWMAN, C. N. & MILLER, J. H. (1983). Mutagen-induced changes in cellular deoxycytodine triphosphate and thymidine triphosphate in Chinese hamster ovary cells. *Biochem. biophys. Res. Commun.* **114**, 34–40.

NICANDER, B. & REICHARD, P. (1985). Evidence for the involvement of substrate cycles in the regulation of deoxyribonucleoside triphosphate pools in 3T6 cells. *J. biol. Chem.* **260**, 9216–9222.

OCKEY, C. H. (1979). Quantitative replicon analysis of DNA synthesis in cancer-prone conditions and the defects in Bloom's Syndrome. *J. Cell Sci.* **40**, 125–144.

ORR-WEAVER, T. L. & SZOSTAK, J. W. (1983). Yeast recombination: The association between double-strand gap repair and crossing-over. *Proc. natn. Acad. Sci. U.S.A.* **80**, 4417–4421.

PAINTER, R. B. (1977). Rapid test to detect agents that damage human DNA. *Nature, Lond.* **265**, 650–651.

PFEIFFER, S. E. & TOLMACH, L. J. (1967). Inhibition of DNA synthesis in HeLa cells by hydroxyurea. *Cancer Res.* **27**, 124–129.

RADMAN, M. (1974). Phenomenology of an inducible mutagenic DNA repair pathway in *Escherichia coli*: SOS repair hypothesis. In *Molecular and Environmental Aspects of Mutagenesis* (ed. L. Prakesh, F. Sherman, M. Miller, C. Lawrence & H. W. Tabor), p. 128. Springfield: Thomas.

RESNICK, M. (1976). The repair of double strand breaks in DNA: A model involving recombinations. *J. theor. Biol.* **59**, 97–106.

SARASIN, A. & BENOIT, A. (1986). Error-prone replication of ultraviolet-irradiated simian virus 40 occurs in mitomycin c-treated host cells only at low multiplicity of infection. *Molec. cell. Biol.* **6**, 1102–1107.

SCHOR, S. L., JOHNSON, R. T. & WALDREN, C. A. (1975). Changes in the organization of chromosomes during the cell cycle: Response to ultraviolet light. *J. Cell Sci.* **17**, 539–565.

SETLOW, R. B. & REGAN, J. D. (1974). DNA repair in human progeroid cells. *Fedn Proc. Fedn Am. Socs exp. Biol.* **33**, 1539.

SHALL, S. (1984). Inhibition of DNA repair by inhibitors of nuclear ADP-ribosyl transferase. In *DNA Repair and its Inhibition, Nucl. Acids Symp. Series*, no. 13 (ed. A. R. S. Collins, C. S. Downes & R. T. Johnson), pp. 143–191. Oxford, Washington, D.C.: IRL Press.

SIMONS, J. W. I. M. (1979). Development of a liquid-holding technique for the study of DNA repair in human diploid fibroblasts. *Mutat. Res.* **59**, 273–279.

SINCLAIR, W. K. (1965). Hydroxyurea: Differential lethal effects on cultured mammalian cells during the cell cycle. *Science* **150**, 1729–1731.

SINCLAIR, W. K. (1967). Hydroxyurea: Effects on Chinese hamster cells grown in culture. *Cancer Res.* **27**, 297–308.

SKOOG, K. L., NORDENSKJOLD, B. A. & BJURSELL, K. G. (1973). Deoxyribonucleoside-triphosphate pools and DNA synthesis in synchronized hamster cells. *Eur. J. Biochem.* **33**, 428–432.

SMITH, C. A. (1984). Analysis of repair synthesis in the presence of inhibitors. In *DNA Repair and its Inhibition, Nucl. Acids Symp. Series*, no. 13 (ed. A. R. S. Collins, C. S. Downes & R. T. Johnson), pp. 51–71. Oxford, Washington, D.C.: IRL Press.

SNYDER, R. D. (1984). The role of deoxyribonucleoside triphosphate pools in the inhibition of DNA excision repair and replication in human cells by hydroxyurea. *Mutat. Res.* **131**, 163–172.

SNYDER, R. D., CARRIER, W. L. & REGAN, J. D. (1981). Application of arabinofuranosyl cytosine in the kinetic analysis and quantitation of DNA repair in human cells after ultraviolet irradiation. *Biophys. J.* **35**, 339–350.

SQUIRES, S. & JOHNSON, R. T. (1983). UV induces long lived DNA breaks in Cockayne's Syndrome and cells from an immunodeficient individual (46BR): defects and disturbance in post incision steps of excision repair. *Carcinogenesis* **4**, 565–572.

SQUIRES, S., JOHNSON, R. T. & COLLINS, A. R. S. (1982). Initial rates of DNA incision in UV-irradiated human cells. Differences between normal, xeroderma pigmentosum and tumour cells. *Mutat. Res.* **95**, 389–404.

TANAKA, M. & YOSHIDA, S. (1982). Altered sensitivity to 1-α-D-arabinofuranosylcytidine-5'-triphosphate of DNA polymerase alpha from leukaemic blasts of acute lymphoblastic leukaemia. *Cancer Res.* **42**, 649–665.

TAYLOR, J. H., HAUT, W. F. & TUNG, J. (1962). Effects of fluorodeoxyuridine on DNA replication, chromosome breakage, and reunion. *Proc. natn. Acad. Sci. U.S.A.* **48**, 190–198.

TEO, I. A., BROUGHTON, B. C., DAY, R. S., JAMES, M. R., KARRAN, P., MAYNE, L. V. & LEHMANN, A. R. (1983). A biochemical defect in the repair of alkylated DNA in cells from an immunodeficient patient (46BR). *Carcinogenesis* **4**, 559–564.

TERASIMA, T., YASUKAWA, M. & KIMURA, M. (1985). Neoplastic transformation of plateau phase mouse 10T½ cells following single and fractionated doses of X rays. *Radiat. Res.* **102**, 367–377.

THELANDER, L. & REICHARD, P. (1979). Reduction of ribonucleotides. *A. Rev. Biochem.* **48**, 133–158.

TH'NG, J. P. H. & WALKER, I. G. (1986). Excision repair in the presence of aphidicolin. *Mutat. Res.* **165**, 139–150.

THOMPSON, L. H., BROOKMAN, D. W., DILLEHAY, L. E., CARRANO, A. V., MAZRIMAS, J. A., MOONEY, C. L. & MINKLER, J. L. (1982). A CHO-cell strain having hypersensitivity to mutagens, a defect in DNA strand-break repair, and an extraordinary baseline frequency of sister chromatid exchange. *Mutat. Res.* **95**, 427–440.

THOMPSON, L. H., SALAZAR, E. P., BROOKMAN, K. W., COLLINS, C. C., STEWART, S. A., BUSCH, D. B. & WEBER, C. A. (1987). Recent progress with DNA repair mutants of Chinese hamster ovary cells. *J. Cell Sci. Suppl.* **6**, 97–110.

UMEDA, M., TANAKA, K. & ONO, T. (1983). Effect of insulin on the transformation of BALB/3T3 cells by X-ray irradiation. *Gann* **74**, 864–869.

WALTERS, R. A., TOBEY, R. A. & RATLIFF, R. L. (1973). Cell cycle-dependent variations of deoxyribonucleoside triphosphate pools in Chinese hamster cells. *Biochim. biophys. Acta* **319**, 336–347.

WEBSTER, D., ARLETT, C. F., HARCOURT, S. A., TEO, I. A. & HENDERSON, L. (1982). A new syndrome of immunodeficiency and increased cellular sensitivity to DNA damaging agents. In *Ataxia-Telangiectasia – A Cellular and Molecular Link Between Cancer, Neuropathology and Immune Deficiency* (ed. B. A. Bridges & D. G. Harnden), pp. 379–386. London: John Wiley and Sons.

WITKIN, E. M. (1976). Ultraviolet mutagenesis and inducible DNA repair in *Escherichia coli*. *Bact. Rev.* **40**, 869–907.

YEW, F. H. & JOHNSON, R. T. (1979). Ultraviolet-induced DNA excision repair in human B and T lymphocytes II. Effect of inhibitors and DNA precursors. *Biochim. biophys. Acta* **562**, 240–251.

YU, C. K. & SINCLAIR, W. K. (1968). Cytological effects on Chinese hamster cells of synchronizing concentrations of hydroxyurea. *J. cell. Physiol.* **72**, 39–42.

ZAJAC-KAYE, M. & TS'O, P. O. P. (1984). DNAse I encapsulated in liposomes can induce neoplastic transformation of Syrian hamster embryo cells in culture. *Cell* **39**, 427–437.

ZIMMERMAN, R. J. & LITTLE, J. B. (1983). Characteristics of human diploid fibroblasts transformed in vitro by chemical carcinogens. *Cancer Res.* **43**, 2183–2189.

J. Cell Sci. Suppl. 6, 289–301 (1987)
Printed in Great Britain © The Company of Biologists Limited 1987

TOXICITY, MUTAGENESIS AND STRESS RESPONSES INDUCED IN *ESCHERICHIA COLI* BY HYDROGEN PEROXIDE

STUART LINN AND JAMES A. IMLAY

Department of Biochemistry, University of California, Berkeley, California 94720, USA

SUMMARY

Two modes of killing of *Escherichia coli* by hydrogen peroxide can be distinguished. Mode-one killing is maximal at 1–2 mM; at higher concentrations the killing rate is approximately half-maximal and is independent of H_2O_2 concentration but first order with respect to exposure time. Mutagenesis and induction of a phage lambda lysogen are similarly affected by H_2O_2 concentration, with reduced levels of response above 1–2 mM-H_2O_2. Mutagenesis is not affected by inactivation of *umuC*. Mode-one killing requires active metabolism during the H_2O_2 challenge and it results in *sfiA*-independent filamentation of both cells that survive and those that are killed by the challenge. This mode of killing is enhanced in *xth*, *polA*, *recA* and *recB* strains; however, it is unaffected by mutations in the *nth*, *uvrA*, *uvrB*, *uvrC*, *uvrD*, *rep*, *gyrA*, *htpR* and *rel* loci. Mode-one killing is normal in strains totally lacking catalase activity (*katE*, *katG*), glutathione reductase (*gor*) or glutathione synthetase (*gshB*), but enhanced in a strain lacking NADH dehydrogenase (*ndh*). Mode-one killing is accelerated by the presence of CN^- or by an unidentified function that is induced by anoxic growth and is under the control of the *fnr* locus. A strain carrying both *xth* and *recA* mutations and certain *polA* mutants appear to undergo spontaneous mode-one killing only under aerobic conditions. Taken together, these observations imply that mode-one killing results from DNA damage that normally occurs at a low, non-lethal level during aerobic growth. Models for the resistance to mode-one killing at doses above 1–2 mM-H_2O_2 will be discussed.

Mode-two killing occurs at high concentrations of H_2O_2 and longer times. It does not require active metabolism, and cells that are killed do not filament, although survivors demonstrate a dose-dependent growth lag followed by a period of filamentation. Mode-two killing is accompanied by enhanced mutagenesis, but strains with DNA repair defects were not observed to be especially sensitive to this mode of killing.

INTRODUCTION

Our laboratory has utilized H_2O_2 toxicity in *Escherichia coli* as a simple model system for studying DNA damage induced by free radical agents such as near-ultraviolet light, gamma-irradiation, and chemical carcinogens (Demple & Linn, 1982; Demple *et al.* 1983; Demple & Halbrook, 1983; Imlay & Linn, 1986). In essence, we hope to learn by what mechanism and to what species H_2O_2 is activated to cause DNA damage, what the nature of the damage is, and how it is repaired. *E. coli* was selected because of the wealth of biochemical and genetic knowledge of its DNA repair functions, and it is expected that the knowledge gained will be applicable to eukaryotic microorganisms and finally to mammalian systems.

One important discovery in this program has been the ability of *E. coli* to 'adapt' to H_2O_2, i.e. after exposure to low levels of the agent the bacteria become resistant to normally toxic doses of H_2O_2 and gamma radiation (Demple & Halbrook, 1983). Christman *et al.* (1985) have recently shown that this response is at least partially under the regulation of a locus, *oxyR*, which is apparently responsible for a positive regulator that induces increased levels of scavenger enzymes, notably peroxidases, catalase and superoxide dismutase. In addition, the response was shown to overlap with the heat-shock response.

This paper summarizes some of our most recent findings concerning killing and mutagenesis of *E. coli* by hydrogen peroxide, and the possible involvement of at least some aspects of the SOS response in surviving exposure to the agent.

MATERIALS AND METHODS

Challenges with H_2O_2 were for 15 min in K medium plus 1 % glucose, as described by Imlay & Linn (1986). *E. coli* strains utilized are either described therein or are as follows: C600(λ) was obtained from Dr H. Echols, University of California, Berkeley; GW2100 (as AB1157 plus *umuC122*::Tn5) was from Dr G. Walker, MIT; CSH7 (*lac7 rpsL thi-1*) and UM1 (as CSH7 plus *katE1 katG14*) were from Dr P. Lowen, University of Manitoba; RK4353 (Δ*lacY169 araD139 non thi rpsL gyrA*) and RK5279 (as RK4353 plus *fnr250*) were from Dr Valley Stewart, Stanford University; IY13 (F⁻*thi his ilv trp rspL*) and IY12 (as IY13 plus *ndh*) were from Dr Ian Young, Australian National University; JF511 (as JC7623 plus *gshB*::Kan) was from Dr James Fuchs, University of Minnesota.

RESULTS

Some DNA repair mutants are sensitive to relatively low concentrations of H_2O_2

When DNA repair-proficient strains of *E. coli* are exposed to various concentrations of H_2O_2, a small amount of killing is generally observed near 2·5 mM, but drastic toxicity is only observed above roughly 25 mM during a 15-min exposure (Fig. 1; and Imlay & Linn, 1986). The killing at low doses is enhanced in several mutants lacking DNA repair enzymes (Fig. 1), most notably *xth* mutants, which lack exonuclease III, *recB* mutants, which lack *recBC* enzyme (exonuclease V), and particularly *polA* mutants, which lack DNA polymerase I. The sensitivity of *recB* mutants appears to be due to a defect in recombinational repair, because suppression of this defect with a second, *recF*-activating *sbcB* mutation gives rise to cells that still lack the recBC enzyme, also lack exonuclease I, are recombinational repair-proficient, and regain resistance to low concentrations of H_2O_2 (Fig. 1).

A property that distinguishes the killing curves of the DNA repair-defective mutants is their unique shape: killing is maximal at roughly 2·5 mM, then somewhat reduced and independent of H_2O_2 concentration up to 20 mM-H_2O_2, where the rate of killing begins to increase with concentration. This relative independence of killing from H_2O_2 concentration at low and moderate doses, the enhancement of killing at these doses in certain mutants, and other properties described below define a mode of killing at the low and moderate exposures, which we denote as mode-one, that is different from that at high doses, which we denote as mode-two.

We have also noted that extremely repair-defective mutants such as an *xth recA* strain (Imlay & Linn, 1986) or a *polA* deletion mutant (Morimyo, 1982) appear to

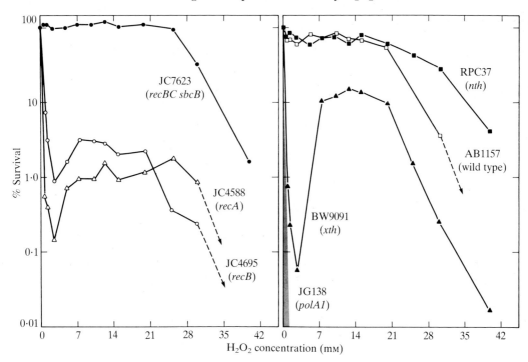

Fig. 1. Survival of DNA repair-defective strains after challenge with H_2O_2.

undergo mode-one killing during aerobic growth, probably due to the generation of endogenous H_2O_2. Under anoxic conditions these strains grow well and without any indication of such killing.

A notably resistant strain (Fig. 1) is one carrying a mutation in *nth*, the structural gene for endonuclease III, a DNA glycosylase recognizing oxidized thymine residues such as thymine glycol (Demple & Linn, 1980; Cunningham & Weiss, 1985). Also showing normal levels of killing by H_2O_2 are strains carrying *uvrA*, *uvrB*, *uvrC*, *uvrD*, *rep*, *gyrA* and *rel* mutations (not shown).

Mutagenesis and stress responses induced by exposure to H_2O_2

The sensitivity of *recA* mutants to mode-one killing by H_2O_2 (Fig. 1) implies that the SOS responses might be normally induced by H_2O_2 to protect cells against this agent. Indeed, a *lexA3* mutant also exhibits enhanced sensitivity to H_2O_2 and the peculiar dose-response seen for other DNA-repair mutants (Fig. 2). Moreover, when one scores for induction of phase λ in C600(λ), phage induction is seen at very low concentrations of H_2O_2, reaches a maximum below 0·5 mM, is constant until roughly 3 mM, then drops off with increasing concentration (Fig. 3). (In this experiment significant killing (<85 % survival) occurred only above 15 mM-H_2O_2.) Evidently the SOS response is induced by challenges of H_2O_2 that produce mode-one, but perhaps not mode-two, killing.

An important aspect of the SOS response in *E. coli* is the enhancement of mutagenesis due to the induction of the *umuC* and *umuD* genes (Walker, 1985).

When mutagenesis was measured after exposure to H_2O_2 by induction of trimetho-prim resistance (i.e. loss-of-function mutation of *thyA*, the structural gene for thymidylate synthetase), a dose-response similar to the killing dose-response was observed: a maximal level of mutagenesis near 2·5 mM, reduced mutagenesis at intermediate ranges, then enhanced mutagenesis at the high doses that give mode-two killing (Fig. 4). Most intriguing, induced mutagenesis was not altered in a strain carrying a *umuC*::Tn5 allele, i.e. mutagenesis by H_2O_2 does not appear to be affected by the product of the *umuC* gene.

Though Christman *et al.* (1985) reported an overlap in the proteins induced by H_2O_2 exposure and by heat-shock, we have observed normal dose-responses for killing by H_2O_2 of an *htpR* mutant (Imlay & Linn, 1986), i.e. the *htpR* stress responses do not obviously protect against killing by H_2O_2.

As noted by Christman *et al.* (1985), the *oxyR* locus is reponsible for regulating, probably in a positive manner, a stress response to H_2O_2. Mutants defective in the *oxyR*-regulated response are not abnormally sensitive to mode-one or mode-two killing if the cells are not pretreated (Imlay & Linn, 1986). However, pretreatment of

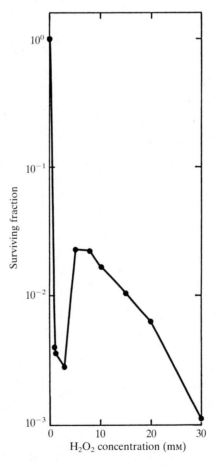

Fig. 2. Survival of DM49 (*lexA3*) after challenge with H_2O_2.

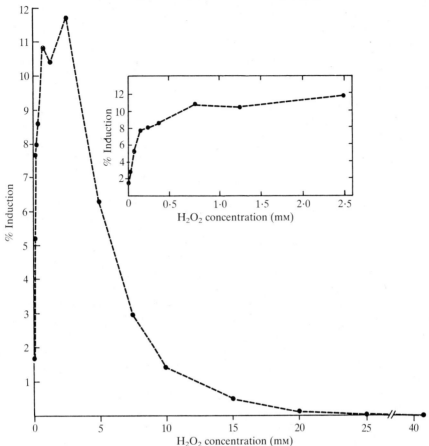

Fig. 3. Induction of C600(λ) after challenge with H_2O_2. After 15 min of exposure to H_2O_2, catalase was added and cells were diluted and plated with *E. coli* AB1157 as an indicator.

DNA repair-proficient cells with adapting doses of H_2O_2 results in protection against mode-two killing at high concentrations of H_2O_2 (Fig. 5), and this protection is not observed in the presence of chloramphenicol or in a mutant with a deletion of the *oxyR* locus (Imlay & Linn, 1986). Protection is also not seen in mutants that totally lack catalase (Fig. 5), so that the induction of catalase appears to be largely responsible for the induced protection of repair-proficient cells to mode-two killing. Remarkably, however, catalase mutants are not especially sensitive to H_2O_2 in the non-adapted state (Fig. 5).

When repair-deficient strains are adapted to H_2O_2, protection against mode-two killing at high H_2O_2 concentrations and against mode-one killing at intermediate concentrations is observed; however, the extent of mode-one killing at concentrations of H_2O_2 below 5 mM is not affected (Imlay & Linn, 1986). Therefore the *oxyR*-mediated adaptation appears not to be efficient against very low doses, i.e. those that themselves induce the adaptation.

In sum, it appears that the stress response by *E. coli* to H_2O_2 is quite complex and involves at least some functions of the *lexA*-regulated SOS response as well as the *oxyR*-regulated response. The former seems most effective at low H_2O_2

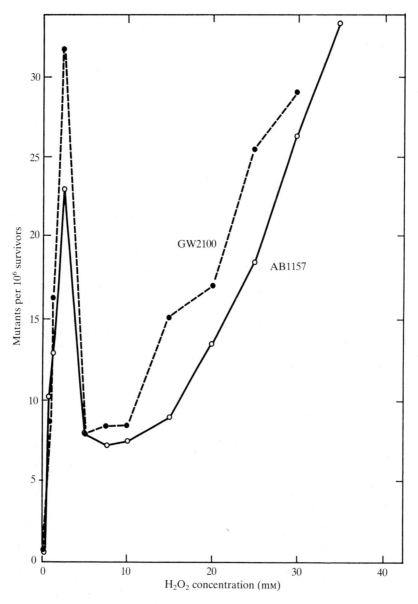

Fig. 4. Mutagenesis of AB1157 (*umuC*$^+$) and *GW2100* (*umuC*::Tn5) to trimethoprim resistance after challenge with H_2O_2. After 15 min of exposure to H_2O_2, catalase was added and cells were plated with 2 ml of top agar containing 2 mg of thymine to score survival, or 2 mg thymine plus 0·2 mg trimethoprim to score mutagenesis. Survival up to 20 mm-H_2O_2 for both strains was not significantly different than that of AB1157 shown in Fig. 1. Survival at 25, 30 and 35 mm-H_2O_2 was 86%, 20% and 4%, respectively, for AB1157, and 82%, 21% and 1%, respectively, for GW2100.

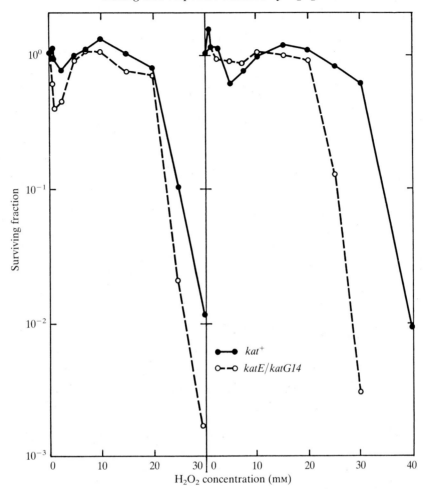

Fig. 5. Survival of CSH7 (*kat⁺*) and UM1 (*katE katG*) after challenge with H₂O₂. Cells in the left frame were not pretreated with adapting doses of H₂O₂; cells in the right frame were pretreated with 60 μM-H₂O₂ for 70 min before challenge.

concentrations, whereas the latter appears most effective at high concentrations. The involvement of the *htpR*-regulated, heat-shock response, if any, is at present unclear.

Anoxic growth sensitizes cells to mode-one killing through function(s) regulated by the fnr *locus*

When DNA repair-proficient *E. coli* strains are grown anoxically, they become sensitive to mode-one killing by H₂O₂ with a dose-response similar to that seen for DNA repair-deficient strains (Imlay & Linn, 1986; and Fig. 6). This sensitivity is synergistic with that induced by DNA-repair deficiency. It is also dependent upon a functional *fnr* gene (Fig. 6), a gene that positively regulates the adaptation to low-oxygen or anoxic growth conditions (*fnr = f*umarate, *n*itrate *r*eductase) (Shaw & Guest, 1982). Identification of the induced function that sensitizes the cells to

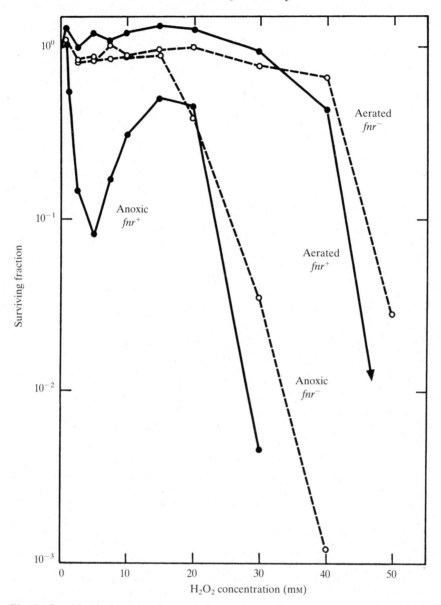

Fig. 6. Sensitization by anoxia to mode-one killing by H_2O_2 requires fnr function. RK4353 (*fnr+*) and RK5279 (*fnr-250*) were challenged after aerobic growth or after 60 min of anoxic growth. Similar resistance to mode-one killing was seen in a strain carrying the *fnr* allele, *nirR22*. The absence of a requirement for fnr function to enhance mode-two killing is a reproducible effect.

mode-one killing is a major goal; we have already ruled out the involvement of menaquinone, cytochrome D and fumarate reductase.

Distinguishing features of the two modes of killing

Table 1 summarizes properties that distinguish mode-one from mode-two killing by H_2O_2. The requirement for active metabolism for mode-one killing is immediately observed upon addition of glucose to starved cells, even if chloramphenicol is present (Imlay & Linn, 1986). The linearity of mode-one killing with time occurs for as long as 15 min at moderate doses; at very low doses killing eventually becomes slower because of medium detoxification, whereas at higher doses killing eventually increases as a result of the manifestation of mode-two killing. The phenotypic responses of mode-one killing challenges clearly differ from those of mode-two killing challenges. It appears that the former inhibit cell division, but not growth, whereas the latter inhibit growth as well. The ordered response noted for survival from mode-two killing challenges suggests, moreover, that mode-two killing lesions are repaired prior to mode-one killing lesions that might also be present.

Models to explain the peculiar dose-responses observed for mode-one killing and mutagenesis

Two important unknowns concerning H_2O_2 toxicity are: (1) the mechanism(s) by which H_2O_2 is activated to induce DNA damage and other killing lesions; and (2) the origin of the peculiar dose-response noted for mode-one killing. It appears to us that the solution to (2) will help to provide answer(s) to (1).

The unique resistance to mode-one killing observed at moderate *versus* low concentrations of H_2O_2 presumably can be due either to a blockage of lesion production or an enhanced ability to tolerate lesions at the higher H_2O_2 concentrations. All normal induction phenomena are ruled out by various chloramphenicol experiments and by the fact that similar dose-responses are seen over 90-s exposures

Table 1. *Properties of the two modes of killing by H_2O_2*

Mode-one killing
Observed at low or moderate H_2O_2 concentrations
Enhanced by DNA repair deficiencies
Enhanced by anoxic growth
Requires active metabolism
Rate of killing is:
essentially independent of H_2O_2 concentration
first order with respect to time
When exposed to mode-one killing challenges, all cells exhibit *sfiA*-independent filamentation; only the survivors divide
Mode-two killing
Observed at high H_2O_2 concentrations
Not enhanced by DNA repair deficiencies
Not enhanced by anoxic growth
Does not require active metabolism
Rate of killing is:
multiple order with respect to H_2O_2 concentration
multiple order with respect to time
When exposed to mode-two killing challenges, killed cells do not filament; survivors exhibit a growth delay that is proportional to exposure, then filament, then divide

Compilations are from Imlay & Linn (1986) and this paper.

(Imlay & Linn, 1986). Activation effects (e.g. delayed DNA replication, DNA repair enzyme activation, etc.) or inactivation effects (e.g. destruction of agents that activate H_2O_2) are ruled out by the linearity of mode-one killing with time, the observation that once cells are exposed to low doses of H_2O_2 they cannot be rescued at higher doses, and, most notably, the observation that when cells are diluted out of $10\,mM$-H_2O_2 into $0.5\,M$ or $1\,mM$-H_2O_2, they immediately start being killed at the enhanced rate typical of the lower concentration (Imlay & Linn, 1986). These observations, coupled with the fact that import and export of H_2O_2 are diffusion-limited, suggest that the resistance to higher doses results from suppression of activated intermediates by the higher H_2O_2 concentrations.

We should like to propose two very general types of models for this suppression. Both models assume that during electron flow from glucose to the ultimate electron acceptor, there is/are donor(s), D, which pass electrons (one or two at a time) to acceptors, A:

$$D^+ + e^- \rightarrow D$$
$$D + A \rightarrow D^+ + A^-.$$

H_2O_2 would be activated in this process when it accepts one electron from D in place of A so as to form the very toxic hydroxyl radical:

$$D + H^+ + H_2O_2 \rightarrow D^+ + H_2O + OH^{\cdot}.$$

This process is presumed to be saturated at some concentration of H_2O_2, however, due either to limiting D or to saturation by substrate of a reaction that follows standard enzyme kinetics.

To explain reduced toxicity as the H_2O_2 concentration is raised, the first model proposes a *chemical quenching* of the toxic $OH^{\cdot}$ species (or a related product) by the reaction:

$$OH^{\cdot} + H_2O_2 \rightarrow H_2O + HO_2^{\cdot}.$$

This reaction can be calculated from half-reaction potentials to have a favourable ΔG of $-9\,kcal$ ($1\,cal = 4.184\,J$). The superoxide formed by this quenching reaction is presumably less toxic; however, it too can react with peroxide by the Haber–Weiss reaction:

$$HO_2^{\cdot} + H_2O_2 \rightarrow O_2 + H_2O + OH^{\cdot}.$$

This situation can explain the dose-response as follows: at very low H_2O_2 concentrations killing increases as $OH^{\cdot}$ generation increases with increasing H_2O_2; however, killing begins to be suppressed at higher doses as the rate of $OH^{\cdot}$ generation is saturated, while $OH^{\cdot}$ is converted to $HO_2^{\cdot}$ by the quenching reaction. Finally, a kinetic steady-state is reached (Fig. 7) in which the quench and Haber–Weiss reactions serve to carry out the catalase reaction in a redox cycle that generates levels of $OH^{\cdot}$ and $HO_2^{\cdot}$ (and hence killing) that are independent of H_2O_2 concentration.

Activation $\quad$ $D + H^+ + H_2O_2 \rightarrow D^+ + H_2O + OH^{\cdot}$

Quench $\quad\quad$ $OH^{\cdot} + H_2O_2 \rightarrow H_2O + HO_2^{\cdot}$

Haber–Weiss $\quad$ $HO_2^{\cdot} + H_2O_2 \rightarrow O_2 + H_2O + OH^{\cdot}$

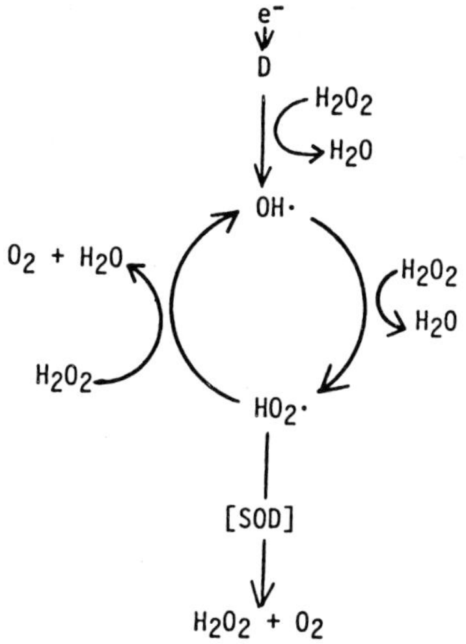

Cycle (sum of Quench and Haber–Weiss) is the catalase reaction:
$$2H_2O_2 \rightarrow H_2O_2 + O_2$$

Fig. 7. A hypothetical scheme for the production and redox cycling of free radicals.

In favour of this model is the effect of starvation, which stops the cycle, and of adaptation to H_2O_2, which reduces the killing at moderate doses but not very low ones. The latter effect could be explained by the induction of superoxide dismutase, an enzyme that would perturb the steady-state levels of $OH^{\cdot}$ and $HO_2^{\cdot}$ (hence killing) as shown in Fig. 7.

A second type of model to generate the dose-response would propose an *electron diversion* at higher H_2O_2 concentrations from one-electron H_2O_2 activation to a peroxidase function(s) that catalyses the two-electron reduction of H_2O_2 to H_2O (Fig. 8). By this scheme, higher H_2O_2 concentrations draw electrons away from activation of H_2O_2 to $OH^{\cdot}$ towards one or more peroxidase sites that have lower affinities for H_2O_2 than the one-electron activation reaction. If the peroxidase also can be saturated with H_2O_2, a constant level of killing would be observed above some H_2O_2 concentrations (Fig. 8).

Consistent with the feasibility of electron diversion is the sensitization of cells to mode-one killing by CN^- (Fig. 9). In this instance, one might envisage that blockage of haem-dependent electron flow with CN^- diverts electrons to activation, and, at higher H_2O_2 concentrations, to peroxidase(s) so as to generate the dose-response noted in Fig. 9.

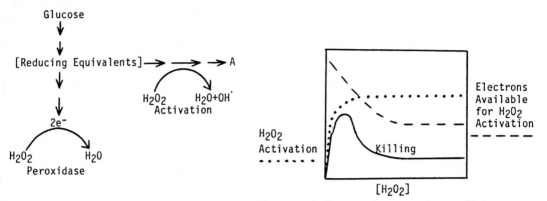

Fig. 8. A hypothetical scheme for the diversion of electrons from one-electron H_2O_2 activation to two-electron peroxidation. On the graph on the right: (———) the observed rate of killing; (·····) the saturable H_2O_2 activation reaction; (———) the electrons available for activation in the presence of electron diversion to peroxidase(s). The combination of the dotted and broken line dependences could generate the observed killing response by adjustment of the H_2O_2 activation rates.

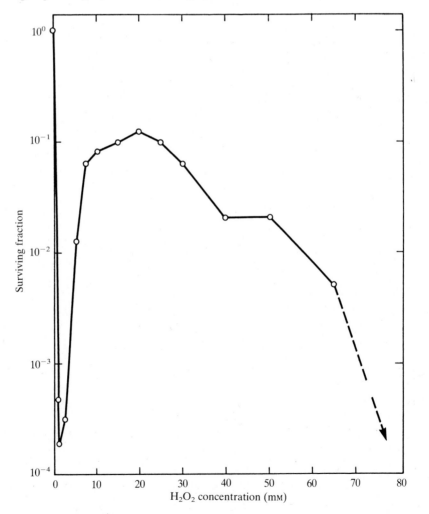

Fig. 9. Enhancement by KCN of mode-one killing by H_2O_2. Strain AB1157 was grown aerobically and challenged in the presence of 3 mM-KCN.

A recent further observation in this regard is that, while cells lacking glutathione reductase (*gor*) or glutathione synthetase (*gshB*) are not abnormally sensitive to H_2O_2, a strain lacking NADH dehydrogenase (*ndh*) gives a dose-response for mode-one killing that looks very much like that of Fig. 9 regardless of whether CN^- is present or not. Such an effect would be expected if the activation of H_2O_2 competes with respiration functions for NADH. Blockage of NADH oxidation might then divert electrons to the activation reaction as well as to peroxidase functions.

CONCLUSIONS

We are hopeful that a genetic and biochemical analysis will serve ultimately to validate and/or modify the above general models for H_2O_2 activation and the mode-one killing dose-response. In the process, it is also hoped that we will begin to understand how other DNA-damaging agents that act through the generation of H_2O_2, OH˙ or other free radicals serve to damage DNA and induce protective responses. Such knowledge gained in bacteria such as *E. coli* cannot help but be applicable to higher organisms.

Another objective is to begin to dissect mode-two killing and the lesions involved. The inhibition of growth by mode-two killing doses suggests that perhaps lipid oxidation is involved; however, enhanced mutagenesis suggests the presence of DNA damage. Whatever the site(s) of damage, the observation of mode-two killing in the absence of a carbon source predicts the occurrence of a novel and potentially interesting activation reaction that does not require electron flow.

This research was supported by grant GM19020 from the National Institutes of Health, US Department of Health and Human Services.

REFERENCES

CHRISTMAN, M. F., MORGAN, R. W., JACOBSON, F. S. & AMES, B. N. (1985). Positive control of a regulon for defenses against oxidative stress and some heat-shock proteins in *Salmonella typhimurium*. *Cell* **41**, 753–762.
CUNNINGHAM, R. P. & WEISS, B. (1985). Endonuclease III (*nth*) mutants of *Escherichia coli*. *Proc. natn. Acad. Sci. U.S.A.* **82**, 474–478.
DEMPLE, B. & HALBROOK, J. (1983). Inducible repair of oxidative DNA damage in *Escherichia coli*. *Nature, Lond.* **304**, 466–468.
DEMPLE, B., HALBROOK, J. & LINN, S. (1983). *E. coli xth* mutants are hypersensitive to hydrogen peroxide. *J. Bact.* **153**, 1079–1082.
DEMPLE, B. & LINN, S. (1980). DNA N-glycosylases and UV repair. *Nature, Lond.* **287**, 203–208.
DEMPLE, B. & LINN, S. (1982). 5,6-Saturated thymine lesions in DNA: Production by ultraviolet light or hydrogen peroxide. *Nucl. Acids Res.* **10**, 3781–3789.
IMLAY, J. A. & LINN, S. (1986). A bimodal pattern of killing of DNA repair-defective or anoxic *Escherichia coli* by hydrogen peroxide. *J. Bact.* **166**, 519–527.
MORIMYO, M. (1982). Anaerobic incubation enhances the colony formation of a *polArecB* strain of *Escherichia coli* K-12. *J. Bact.* **152**, 208–214.
SHAW, D. J. & GUEST, J. R. (1982). Amplification and product identification of the *fnr* gene of *Escherichia coli* K-12. *J. gen. Microbiol.* **128**, 2221–2228.
WALKER, G. (1985). Inducible DNA repair systems. *A. Rev. Biochem.* **54**, 425–457.

J. Cell Sci. Suppl. 6, 303–321 (1987)
Printed in Great Britain © *The Company of Biologists Limited 1987*

PLASMID GENES AFFECTING DNA REPAIR AND MUTATION

PETER STRIKE* AND DAVID LODWICK

Department of Genetics, University of Liverpool, PO Box 147, Liverpool L69 3BX, UK

SUMMARY

Many bacterial plasmids have the effect of increasing the ultraviolet (u.v.) resistance of host cells that harbour them, apparently by an error-prone repair mechanism that leads to a high level of mutation amongst the survivors. These plasmid systems are apparently analogues of the *Escherichia coli umuD/C* operon, which is absolutely required in this organism for mutation induced by u.v. light and by many chemical mutagens. This article reviews the extensive and sometimes conflicting literature relating to this phenomenon, and describes the further characterization of one such plasmid system, the *imp* (*I* group *m*utation and *p*rotection) operon of the I1 group plasmid TP110. It is demonstrated that each of the protection mutation systems well characterized to date shows a similar genetic arrangement, and that significant homology can be detected at the amino acid level between the proteins encoded by these different systems.

INTRODUCTION

The ability of certain bacterial plasmids to affect the survival and mutagenic responses of bacterial cells to ultraviolet irradiation was first recognized by Howarth (1965) in a study with the I1 group plasmid ColIb-P9 in *Salmonella typhimurium* LT2. She demonstrated a twofold effect of the presence of the plasmid in ultraviolet (u.v.)-irradiated cells, namely an increase in survival and an increase in the fraction of mutants found amongst the survivors (Howarth, 1965, 1966). Since these initial observations, a great deal has been learnt about the plasmid-encoded genes responsible for these effects, and it is the intention of this review to set recent developments in the context of the earlier work.

EXTENT OF THE PHENOMENON

Following these early demonstrations, it became apparent that many bacterial plasmids encoded similar functions. Drabble & Stocker (1965) reported one fi^+ and four fi^- plasmids, which protected *S. typhimurium* LT2 against the killing effects of u.v., while Marsh & Smith (1969) showed that the plasmids RE13 and RE1-290 improved the u.v. resistance of *Escherichia coli* K12 strains by up to 60 % in a process that appeared to depend upon the host strain's ability to undergo recombination. Further examples of u.v. protecting plasmids were reported by Siccardi (1969), who screened 31 different plasmids for their u.v. protection effects. It was observed that 15 protected, 11 had little or no effect and five caused a substantial decrease in u.v. resistance. The protecting plasmids included members of

* Author for correspondence.

the F, N and I incompatibility (Inc) groups. A number of other u.v. protecting plasmids have been listed by Novick (1974) and by Jacob *et al.* (1977), showing that this phenotype is common amongst IncI and IncN plasmids. This is probably a reflection of the limited number of plasmids that had been tested for this particular character, since more recently Molina *et al.* (1979) and Pinney (1980) have found examples of u.v. protecting plasmids in 10 different incompatibility groups.

Plasmid-mediated u.v. protection/mutation effects are not limited to the Enterobacteria. The u.v. protecting effect has been widely observed amongst conjugative and drug resistance plasmids of *Pseudomonas aeruginosa* (Jacoby, 1974; Krishnapillae, 1975; Lehrbach *et al.* 1977*a,b*; Stokes & Krishnapillai, 1978), in IncP plasmids introduced into *Myxococcus xanthus* (McCann & Clark, 1981), and may also be encoded by the SCP1 plasmid of *Streptomyces coelicolor* (Puglia *et al.* 1982; Misuraca, 1984). Naturally occurring plasmids of *Streptococcus faecalis* are also reported to encode a similar function (Miehl *et al.* 1980). In almost every case, the two plasmid-encoded effects are inseparable, i.e. the plasmids both increase u.v. survival of the host cells and also increase u.v.-induced mutation. With certain plasmids, for example R205 and pKM101, a third related phenotype is also observed, namely a significant increase in the spontaneous reversion of certain genetic markers (McCann *et al.* 1975; Mortelmans & Stocker, 1976; MacPhee, 1977). Although it is likely that this phenotype is encoded by the genes that encode u.v. survival and mutation, there is one report in the literature that the genes for these effects can be separated (Mortelmans & Stocker, 1979). The same genes have been shown to be responsible for both protection and mutation effects by the isolation of point and transposon insertion mutations that abolish both effects simultaneously. Plasmids in which such mutations have been isolated include pKM101 (Walker, 1978; Shanabruch & Walker, 1980), R205 (D. G. MacPhee, quoted by Kronish & Walker, 1979), pMG2 (Lehrbach *et al.* 1977*a*) and TP110 (Glazebrook *et al.* 1986).

THE PLASMID pKM101

Of this large number of plasmids, the most widely studied is pKM101, a deletion derivative of the naturally occurring N group plasmid R46 (also known as R-Brighton, R1818 and TP120). pKM101 was created from R46 by P22 transduction, and is about two-thirds of the size of the parent plasmid, due to the loss of DNA encoding many of the drug and metal resistances (Mortelmans & Stocker, 1979). The extent of the deletion has been characterized in a number of laboratories (Brown & Willetts, 1981; Langer & Walker, 1981; Dowden & Strike, 1982) and it appears to result in a slight increase in the efficiency of the mutagenic processes encoded by the plasmid (McCann *et al.* 1975), perhaps due to deletion of a function that, in R46, acts *in trans* to reduce plasmid-encoded error-prone repair (Dowden & Strike, 1982). The choice of pKM101 as the main target for study is largely a consequence of the use of this plasmid in the Ames *Salmonella* test system where it greatly increases the sensitivity of the test strains to the mutagenic effects of many carcinogens

(McCann *et al.* 1975). Again this is a common property of all of the plasmids tested to date; not only do they increase the number of mutations induced by u.v. light, but they also increase mutations caused by many chemical mutagens. The use of plasmids to enhance the sensitivity of bacterial test systems in this way was first suggested and shown to be a useful approach by MacPhee (1972, 1973*a,b*). Recent studies indicate that many of the u.v. protection/mutation systems carried by bacterial plasmids, and also in some instances by bacterial chromosomes, are functionally and structurally related to the pKM101 system, which is therefore proving to be an excellent model.

REQUIREMENTS FOR HOST GENES

One of the earliest observations of the protection/mutation systems of bacterial plasmids was that they appeared to require a functional recombination system in the host (Marsh & Smith, 1969). A thorough investigation of host genes required for expression of the plasmid-encoded phenotype has revealed that all plasmids tested to date require a functional *recA* gene product in the host (Upton & Pinney, 1983). This is true for R46 and R205 in *S. typhimurium* (Mortelmans & Stocker, 1976; MacPhee, 1973*c*), for pKM101 in *S. typhimurium* (McCann *et al.* 1975) and for pMG2 in *P. aeruginosa* (Lehrbach *et al.* 1977*a*). In *E. coli* K12 the same dependence on *recA*$^+$ is seen with R46 and pKM101 (Tweats *et al.* 1976; Monti-Bragadin *et al.* 1976; Walker, 1977; Goze & Devoret, 1979) and with the I1 group plasmid TP110 (Fig. 1A). Also in *E. coli* K12, the protection/mutation effects of R46 and pKM101 are not expressed in *lexA*(Ind$^-$) mutants such as *lexA*3 and *lexA*1 (Walker, 1977). Waleh & Stocker (1979) have shown, however, that care is needed to interpret the interaction of plasmid systems with the *lexA* gene product, since the effects depend to a large extent on the *lexA* allele involved and the genetic background of the strain used. In the *E. coli* WP2 strains there are indications that the protection/mutation genes of some plasmids can be well expressed in *lexA*(Ind$^-$) mutants, particularly in a *uvr*$^-$ background (Monti-Bragadin *et al.* 1976; Babudri & Monti-Bragadin, 1977; Nunoshiba & Nishioka, 1984). However, these observations seem to apply only to certain plasmid/mutagen combinations, for example pKM101 with u.v. irradiation (Venturini & Monti-Bragadin, 1978), and it is clear that in most cases the *lexA*(Ind$^-$) mutations, like *recA*$^-$ mutations, effectively block expression of the plasmid systems.

With the exception of the *recA* and *lexA* genes, no other host genes appear to be absolutely required for the plasmid effects, although some rather complex effects are seen in *uvrE* mutant hosts. The most comprehensive surveys have been performed in *E. coli* K12, but in the limited studies performed with other organisms the results are in good agreement. In *E. coli* K12, plasmids effectively protect and increase the mutation rate following u.v. irradiation of *uvrA*, *uvrB*, *uvrC*, *polA*, *lig*, *recB*, *recC*, *recL*, *uvrD*, *recF*, *dam*3 and *umuC/D* mutants (Tweats *et al.* 1976; Goze & Devoret, 1979; Monti-Bragadin *et al.* 1976; Venturini & Monti-Bragadin, 1978; Walker, 1977; Upton & Pinney, 1983; Nunoshiba & Nishioka, 1984). These observations appear to be true for all plasmids tested to date (Upton & Pinney,

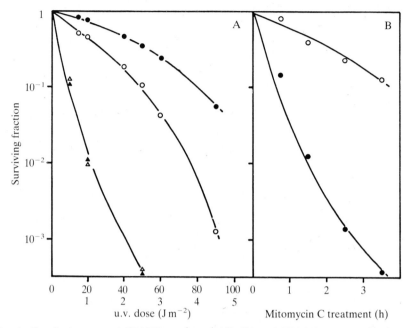

Fig. 1. Survival curves of AB1157 *uvr*⁺ *rec*⁺ (○, ●) and AB2463 *recA13* (△, ▲) with (filled symbols) and without (open symbols) the I1 groups plasmid TP110; A shows survival following u.v. irradiation; B shows survival following treatment with 1 μg ml⁻¹ mitomycin C for the times indicated. Note in A the two scales for u.v. dose: the range 0–100 J m⁻² applies to AB1157; the range 0–5 J m⁻² applies to AB2463.

1983), with the sole exception of the J group plasmid R391 and its relatives, as discussed below. Some variation is seen in the ability of plasmids to confer u.v. protection/mutation effects upon *uvrE* mutants. The reasons for this variation are not known, nor is there an obvious explanation for these observations since the plasmids unable to express their effects in a *uvrE* host are able to protect *uvrD* and *recL* mutants (Upton & Pinney, 1983), and these three mutant classes are actually all mutations within the same gene (now designated *uvrD*) affecting the *E. coli* DNA helicase II (Kushner *et al.* 1978; Siegal, 1981; Oeda *et al.* 1982).

The reports in the literature concerning the effects of *uvrD* alleles are also somewhat contradictory: for example, Upton & Pinney (1983) demonstrated that R46 can effectively protect *recL* mutants of *E. coli*, while Todd & Glickman (1979) showed that the R46 derivative pKM101 cannot protect these strains. Moreover, it is likely that the *uvrD*⁺ gene is needed only for the protection part of the phenotype and not for mutation, since plasmid-mediated enhancement of u.v.-mutagenesis has been shown to occur in *uvrD*, *recL* and *uvrE* mutants (Upton & Pinney, 1983; Todd & Glickman, 1979), with the proviso that Goze & Devoret (1979) demonstrated that plasmid-mediated Weigle mutagenesis of bacteriophage lambda was abolished by a *uvrE*502 mutation. Taken together, these observations suggest that the UvrD and plasmid-coded proteins may interact together in error-prone repair as suggested by Shanabruch & Walker (1983).

Plasmid R391 and other related plasmids of the J incompatibility group sensitize the bacterial host to u.v. irradiation, rather than protecting, but also increase the mutagenic response to u.v. (Pinney, 1980). This phenotype is not uncommon, several other sensitizing plasmids being described by Siccardi (1969). As with the protecting plasmids, the sensitization is not observed in $recA^-$ hosts, and is slightly reduced in $lexA(\text{Ind}^-)$ hosts (Upton & Pinney, 1983; Pembroke & Stevens, 1984). Enhancement of the mutagenic response is also abolished in these mutant host strains, indicating an involvement of the host SOS system in this plasmid-encoded phenomenon. Recent work indicates that the sensitization is due to inhibition of the host recombination system (Pembroke & Stevens, 1984), which leaves the possibility that the J group plasmids may encode a u.v. mutation-enhancing function that is under *rec/lex* control and is quite separate from the function that sensitizes.

INVOLVEMENT OF THE HOST 'SOS' SYSTEM

The observation that plasmid-coded u.v. protection and mutation effects are usually abolished in both $recA^-$ and $lexA(\text{Ind}^-)$ mutants of *E. coli* carries the clear implication that the plasmid genes interact with the 'SOS' (*rec/lex*) system of the host, and several options therefore seem possible. The plasmid-coded genes could be expressed constitutively, but need to interact with an inducible component of the SOS system in order to carry out error-prone repair, or the plasmid-coded genes could themselves be under the control of the *rec/lex* system. In fact the evidence indicates the true situation to be a combination of these two.

A variety of experiments have been reported that attempt to assess the inducibility of the plasmid genes. Walker (1978) reported that a large inducible Weigle-reactivation effect could be observed when u.v.-irradiated bacteriophage P22 was infected into u.v.-irradiated *S. typhimurium* containing pKM101, but not when it was infected into plasmid-free cells. Similar results were obtained when u.v.-irradiated bacteriophage lambda was infected into *E. coli* K12, although in this case a considerable effect was also seen in plasmid-free cells (Walker, 1977). Taken in conjunction with the observation that the presence of pKM101 in a *tif sfi*A mutant grown at 42 °C causes a substantial increase in the amount of reversion occurring, either spontaneously or following treatment with u.v. or chemical mutagens, this indicates that pKM101 does not simply cause the constitutive expression of the inducible host SOS system, but rather that it increases the amount of error-prone repair once the system is induced (Doubleday *et al.* 1977; Monti-Bragadin *et al.* 1976; Walker, 1977). In support of this conclusion, the introduction of pKM101 or TP110 into bacterial cells has no effect on the basal level of RecA protein, a change in which is usually taken as a measure of SOS induction (Little & Hanawalt, 1977; Dowden & Strike, unpublished observations), or on the induction of lambda prophage (Goze & Devoret, 1979). A rather different interpretation is placed by Goze & Devoret (1979) on Weigle reactivation data rather similar to those described above. They demonstrate that the presence of pKM101 in *E. coli* K12 cells is sufficient to give a 20-fold increase in phage survival compared to plasmid-free cells, even when the host cells are unirradiated. They take this to imply that the pKM101 system acts constitutively over and above the inducible host system, and conclude that repair mediated by pKM101 is different from SOS repair. In the light of recent data (discussed later) it seems likely that this conclusion is incorrect.

Conflicting reports have been given concerning the effects of chloramphenicol on the inducibility of the plasmid functions. Tweats *et al*. (1976) reported that R46 would protect cells treated with chloramphenicol before irradiation, but not cells treated after irradiation. Dobson & Walker (1980), however, observed that while post-irradiation chloramphenicol treatment abolished Weigle reactivation in non-plasmid-containing cells, cells containing pKM101 could still perform this process. Moreover, they showed that the u.v. protective effect of pKM101 and R46 was not affected by chloramphenicol. The reasons for the disparity in these results are not apparent, but may reflect the slightly different regimes adopted for chloramphenicol treatment.

The genetic data on the question of inducibility are also somewhat in conflict. The ability of some plasmids to express protection/mutation functions in *lexA*(Ind⁻) mutants of *E. coli* B has already been referred to, and indeed Babudri & Monti-Bragadin (1977) have used the ability to restore methyl methane sulphonate (MMS)-induced mutability to WP2 *lexA*(Ind⁻) strains as a means of classifying plasmids into different groups. Similar tests in *E. coli* K12, however, apparently show an absolute requirement for *lexA*⁺ in the expression of plasmid functions (Walker, 1977). An investigation of pKM101 protection/mutation effects in *lexB* and *zab*53 host strains, which are defective in SOS induction due to mutations within the *recA* structural gene, showed that these strains could be effectively protected and mutated by the plasmid system, which would not be expected of genes under *rec/lex* control. However, the efficiency of the processes was somewhat reduced, and the *lexB* mutation completely abolished the ability to promote Weigle reactivation and mutagenesis of u.v.-irradiated bacteriophage lambda (Blanco & Rebollo, 1981).

It seems likely that these apparently conflicting reports can be reconciled by a consideration of the relative ease with which plasmid protection/mutation systems and their chromosomal equivalents can be induced. That the plasmid-coded genes are under *rec/lex* control there can be no doubt. Gene fusion analysis using Mu d(*amp lac*) and promoter probe vectors has demonstrated unequivocally that the pKM101 protection/mutation genes (designated *muc*, *m*utation, *u*ltraviolet and *c*hemical) and the TP110 protection/mutation genes (designated *imp*, *I*-group *m*utation and *p*rotection) are under the direct control of the LexA repressor protein (Elledge & Walker, 1983*b*; Dowden *et al*. 1984). If the plasmid-coded functions were more easily induced than their chromosomal equivalents, perhaps requiring lower levels of activated RecA protein to achieve derepression, this would go a long way towards explaining many of the observations. The data of Goze & Devoret (1979), for example, could be taken to show that plasmid-coded protection/mutation genes could be rapidly induced by infection of the cells with u.v.-irradiated bacteriophage lambda, while induction of the chromosomal equivalent genes, *umuC/D*, required irradiation of the host cell prior to infection. Similarly, the reduced level of RecA protease in *lexB* mutants may be sufficient to induce the plasmid system, but not the chromosomal. Recent sequence data confirm that 5′ to both the pKM101 *muc* genes and the TP110 *imp* genes there lies a LexA binding site with an excellent match to the consensus sequence for such sites (Fig. 2; Perry *et al.* 1985). In this respect the plasmid genes are similar to their chromosomal equivalents *umuD* and *C* (Perry *et al.* 1985; Kitagawa *et al.* 1985).

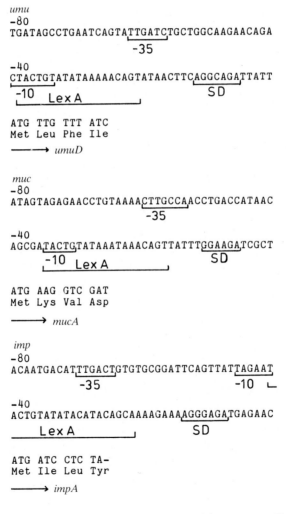

Fig. 2. Control sequences preceding the *umu*, *muc* and *imp* operons. For each operon, the positions of the −35 and −10 components of the promoter are shown, as is the ribosome binding site (Shine-Dalgarno sequence, SD), and the start of the structural gene. Notice that in each case a potential LexA binding site overlaps the promoter sequences. The data for *umu* and *muc* are taken from Perry *et al.* (1985).

INTERACTIONS WITH OTHER PLASMID GENES

In addition to interactions with chromosomal genes, the plasmid protection/ mutation systems also interact with other genes carried on the same plasmid. The increased mutagenic ability of pKM101 over its parent R46 has been referred to previously, and has been explained by the presence of a *trans*-acting gene on R46, which acts in some way to reduce the effectiveness of the *muc* genes. This effect is specific to the *muc* system; when cloned in high copy number vectors, the gene(s) responsible severely curtail the properties of *muc*, but have no effect on the *imp* genes of TP110 (Dowden & Strike, 1982).

A similar complex effect in pKM101 has been reported by Langer *et al.* (1985), who describe a mutation within pKM101 that abolishes the u.v. protection effect of the plasmid, and indeed leads to sensitization, but increases susceptibility to mutagenesis to a greater extent than the parent plasmid. Unexpectedly, the mutation lies within a 2·0 kilobase region just upstream from *mucAB*, and not within the structural genes. The reasons for these effects are not yet understood, but it seems possible that they may affect the level of expression of the *muc* genes. Similar effects have been observed when cloning the TP110 *imp* genes into high expression vectors in different orientations with respect to external promoters (Glazebrook & Strike, unpublished observations).

An interesting interaction between plasmid genes is seen in Fig. 1B. TP110 protects against the killing effects of u.v. light, due to the presence of the protection/mutation genes whose expression is under *rec/lex* control. Like many I group plasmids, however, TP110 carries a second SOS function directly controlled by the LexA protein, namely the colicin Ib production and immunity operon (Glazebrook *et al.* 1983). Induction of this operon leads to colicin production, a process that is lethal to the host cell. Thus TP110 contains two SOS-controlled operons; induction of one (*imp*) protects against the killing effects of u.v., induction of the other (*cib*) by u.v. causes cell death. Clearly, following u.v. irradiation, the effects of *imp* expression outweigh the effects of *cib* expression (Fig. 1A) and cell survival is improved. However, treatment with the radiomimetic drug mitomycin C (a particularly effective SOS-inducing agent against which the R46 protection/ mutation system shows little protection but a significant mutagenic response (Attfield & Pinney, 1984)), has the opposite effect. Colicin production is effectively induced and cell survival decreases.

RELATIONSHIP TO THE HOST *umuD/C* GENES

The most significant advance in the understanding of plasmid-coded protection/ mutation systems came with the demonstration that protecting/mutating plasmids could restore mutability to the non-mutable *umuC* and *umuD* mutants (Kato & Shinoura, 1977; Steinborn, 1979), first demonstrated for R46 and pKM101 (Walker, 1979; Walker & Dobson, 1979), and more recently for TP110 and a range of other plasmids (Dowden & Strike, 1982; Upton & Pinney, 1983). This behaviour appears to be a property of all protecting/mutating plasmids tested to date, including the sensitizing plasmid R391. The simplest explanation for these observations, namely that the plasmids all produce analogues of the *umuD/C* genes of *E. coli*, has now been shown to be correct for both pKM101 and TP110.

The *umu* operon of *E. coli* has now been well characterized and is known to contain two genes, *umuD* and *umuC*, which encode proteins of M_r 15 064 and 47 681, respectively (Elledge & Walker, 1983*a*; Perry *et al.* 1985; Kitagawa *et al.* 1985). Mutations in either of these genes have the same effect: the cell loses its ability to produce mutations in response to treatment with u.v. light or indirect chemical mutagens, and in an otherwise wild-type background the cells become slightly u.v.-sensitive. In an excision-repair defective background (*uvr⁻*), mutations in *umuD/C* cause a more dramatic increase in u.v. sensitivity (Kato & Shinoura, 1977; Walker & Dobson, 1979). The expression of the *umu* genes is under *rec/lex* control, with the LexA protein acting as a direct repressor (Bagg *et al.* 1981). The products appear to be involved only in the processes of error-prone repair, do not affect any other aspect of the SOS system, and are not essential for cell viability (Bagg *et al.* 1981; Elledge & Walker, 1983*a*). The induced *umu* gene products are not, by themselves, sufficient for error-prone repair to occur, and it has been demonstrated that activated RecA protein plays a mechanistic role in mutagenesis as well as its role in the control of SOS systems (Bagg *et al.* 1981; Blanco *et al.* 1982; Little & Mount, 1982). A two-stage model has been proposed by Bridges & Woodgate (1985) involving activated RecA protein in the misincorporation step of error-prone repair, followed by the *umuD/C* products acting to permit chain extension. This model is based on the observation that if *umuD/C⁻* mutants are allowed to synthesize DNA for a period following irradiation, and then subjected to photoreactivation, mutants are produced. The Bridges & Woodgate model proposes for the first time a consistent model of error-prone repair, although the recent observation that the *dnaQ49* (*mutD*) *umuC*::Tn*5* double mutant is still hypermutable may call for some reappraisal (Piechocki *et al.* 1986).

Whatever the role of the *umuD/C* gene products in indirect mutagenesis, it is quite clear that the plasmids well characterized to date, such as pKM101 and TP110, can provide analogues of these gene products that work as well as, if not better than, the chromosomally encoded functions. Moreover, in the case of these two plasmids, the gene products are structurally as well as functionally related to the UmuD/C proteins. As with *umu*, the pKM101 and TP110 protection/mutation functions are encoded by an operon of two genes, *mucA* and *mucB* in pKM101, *impA* and *impB* in TP110 (Perry & Walker, 1982; Glazebrook *et al.* 1986), which encode proteins of M_r 16 371 and 46 362 in pKM101 (Perry *et al.* 1985), and approximately 11 000 and 51 000 in TP110 (Glazebrook *et al.* 1986). It is surely significant that the sum of the sizes of these proteins coded for by the *umu*, *muc* and *imp* operons is constant, indicating perhaps that each of these operons has evolved from a common ancestor. In addition to the constant coding capacity of the protection/mutation operons, the proteins they encode show a remarkable degree of homology, particularly in conserved blocks. The degree of homology at the DNA level is significant, but is not sufficiently high to allow hybridization between *umu*, *muc* and *imp* operons (Perry *et* al. 1985; Table 1). Perry et al. (1985) have demonstrated that the UmuD and MucA proteins are 41% homologous, while UmuC and MucB are 55% homologous. Fig. 3 shows some of the results of our preliminary sequence analysis of the TP110 imp

Table 1. *Presence of sequences homologous to* imp *amongst plasmids that do or do not encode protection/mutation functions*

Plasmid	Incompatibility group	u.v. protection/ mutation	Homology with imp sequences
TP110	I1	+	+
R144	I1	+*	+
ColIBP9	I1	+†	+
R46	N	+	−
R64	I1	NT	+
R1-19	F2	−	−
N3	N	NT	−
TΔ	I1	NT	+
R16	B	+*	+
JR66a	I1	NT	−
R621a	I	+*	+
R648	I1	NT	−
pHH721	I2	NT	−
R805a	B/I1	+*	+
R821a	I2	NT	−

The probe contained sequences encoding both ImpA and ImpB proteins, with a small amount of non-coding sequence flanking both 5′ and 3′ sides. Hybridization was performed under conditions of moderate stringency (at 62°C, in the presence of 0·3 M-NaCl. Positive hybridization indicates a homology of greater than 78%.)
* Upton & Pinney (1983).
† Jacob et al. (1977).

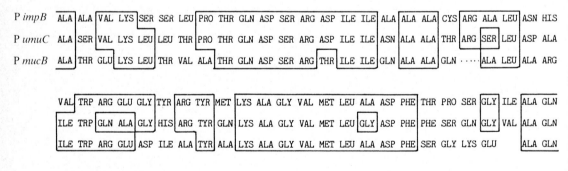

Fig. 3. Homology between the proteins encoded by *impB*, *umuC* and *mucB*. Amino acid residues conserved between the three proteins are boxed. The region shown lies towards the C-terminal end of the proteins. The data for *umuC* and *mucB* are taken from Perry et al. (1985).

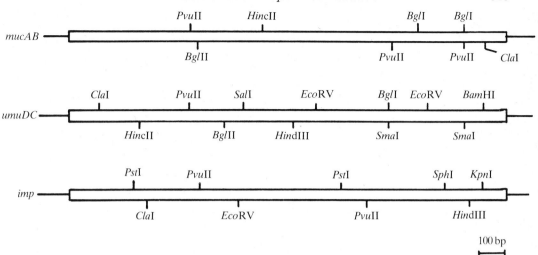

Fig. 4. Comparative restriction maps of the coding regions, *umu*, *muc* and *imp*. The data for *umu* and *muc* are taken from Perry *et al.* (1985).

operon: the region of the proteins shown, towards the carboxy terminus of UmuC, MucB and ImpB, shows a striking degree of conserved sequence between all three operons. Restriction maps of the operons are shown in Fig. 4, demonstrating the diversity of these systems at the DNA level.

One intriguing observation from the sequence data of Perry *et al.* (1985) is that the MucA protein contains a region homologous to the site at which the LexA protein is cleaved by activated RecA protein. It seems quite likely that in addition to controlling the expression of the *muc* operon, activated RecA protein may also be needed to process the MucA protein to an active form. An alternative role for this processing might be to allow efficient translation of the *mucB* gene product, the coding sequence for which overlaps the coding sequence of *mucA* by 13 base-pairs. Thus, a shift in reading frame is required for expression of *mucB* and initiation of *mucB* translation must be allowed within the coding sequence for *mucA*. Conceivably, this shift might be achieved by processing of the *mucA* gene product.

Functional tests also show that the plasmid-coded systems operate in a similar but perhaps not identical way to the chromosomal systems. Although there is no cross-complementation between plasmid-coded proteins and their chromosomal equivalents (Walker, 1984), an analysis of the types of agents against which the systems are effective, and investigations of the types of nucleotide changes induced as a consequence of DNA damage, all reveal strong similarities between the two systems with respect to both targeted and non-targeted mutagenesis. Thus Glickman (1983) has shown that while pKM101 increases the number of mutations obtained in both uvr^+ and $uvrB$ mutants of *E. coli* following u.v. irradiation, the spectrum of changes detected in the *lacI* system (i.e. the preferred sites for mutation) is exactly the same, irrespective of the presence of the plasmid. Eisenstadt *et al.* (1982) demonstrated similar effects with the chemical mutagens benzo (a) pyrene and cyclopenta (cd) pyrene, although Fowler *et al.* (1981) have reported that pKM101 does alter the mutational specificity of u.v. with respect to the reversion of certain *trpA* alleles of *E. coli*, and Todd *et al.* (1979) have reported that R46 alters the spectrum of arg^+

revertants obtained by MMS mutagenesis of AB1157. An analysis by Mattern *et al.* (1985) also shows that pKM101 alters the mutation specificity of the *trpA223* allele in *E. coli*, both after treatment with indirect mutagens (i.e. those that require SOS processing in order to give rise to a mutation) such as MMS and ethyl nitrosourea (ENU), and with direct-acting mutagens (those that are SOS-independent) such as 2,6-diaminopurine and ethyl methane sulphate (EMS). They suggest that the *muc* genes are involved in the induction of mutations not only during SOS error-prone repair, but also during misreplication. The effect is seen as a reduction in the number of A·T to G·C transitions, and an increase in the number of A·T transversions. It seems likely that while plasmid genes act in a similar way to the chromosomal genes, their activities are not identical and differences can be detected, depending upon the allele used to measure mutation and the type of mutagen used. The specificity of base changes is likely to be determined to some extent by the surrounding sequence, and by the mutagen used. It has been shown that, in *Salmonella*, the pKM101 system is capable of promoting every possible base-pair change, except perhaps for G·C to C·G (Youderian *et al.* 1982).

SPECTRUM OF ACTIVITY

In addition to restoring the mutagenic response of *umu* mutants to u.v. light and the polycyclic aromatic mutagens mentioned above (Eisenstadt *et al.* 1982), pKM101 also restores mutability by a variety of other agents including 4-nitro-quinoline oxide, methyl methane sulphonate, 2-(2-furyl)-3-(5-nitro-2-furyl)-acryl-amide (AF2), gamma rays, *cis*-platinum (II) diamminodichloride, mitomycin C and neocarzinostatin (Nuroshiba & Nishioka, 1984; Attfield & Pinney, 1983, 1984; Eisenstadt *et al.* 1980). An extensive list of mutagens for which pKM101 is effective in increasing the mutagenic sensitivity of the Ames *Salmonella* tester strains is given by McCann *et al.* (1975).

While the plasmid systems are effective in increasing the mutagenic response of bacterial cells to the agents listed, they do not confer resistance to the killing effects of all of them. Thus while R46 increases the u.v. resistance of a *uvrA umuC* mutant by over 1000-fold (Upton & Pinney, 1983), it has no effect on the resistance of the strain to mitomycin C (Attfield & Pinney, 1984). It has been demonstrated that both the plasmid-coded systems and the chromosomal *umu* system are able to increase the mutagenic effects of single- and double-stranded DNA damaging agents, but are only able to protect against those that cause single-stranded damage (Upton & Pinney, 1983; Attfield & Pinney, 1984). This similarity in function again emphasizes the relatedness of the plasmid and chromosomal systems.

FUNCTIONS OF THE ENCODED PROTEINS

A variety of suggestions have been made concerning the functions encoded by the *umu* and *muc* genes. MacPhee (1974) reported that a polymerase activity encoded by R205 could be detected in *polA* mutants of *S. typhimurium*, and Lehrbach *et al.*

(1977*a*,*b*) detected a similar activity apparently expressed by pMG2 in cell extracts of a *polA* strain of *P. aeruginosa*. However, Stokes & Krishnapillai (1978) were unable to repeat the observations in *P. aeruginosa* and neither Kronish & Walker (1979) nor Upton & Pinney (1979, 1981) could detect polymerase activity associated with R46, pKM101 or R205, even when the plasmid-containing cells had been induced with u.v. light. An endonuclease activity encoded by pKM101 has been reported (Lackey *et al.* 1977) but this enzyme is also produced by mutants of pKM101 that no longer protect and mutate, and is now thought to be associated with the conjugation system of the plasmid. Whatever the role of the plasmid-coded products, it has been shown that their chromosomal analogues, UmuD and UmuC, apparently interact in a specific way with the DNA replication processes in *E. coli*. Strains in which the *umu* gene products are over produced become cold-sensitive, due to an inhibition of DNA synthesis (Marsh & Walker, 1985). Indirect suppressors of the cold sensitivity appear to affect protein turnover in the cells, in a rather complex way. Whether this interaction of the Umu proteins with DNA replication holds a valuable clue to their mode of action is not yet clear. The reaction is specific to *umu* and does not occur with overproduced *muc* gene products, so this is apparently not an obligatory phenotype for protecting/mutating proteins. Overproduction of the *imp* gene products cannot be tolerated in *E. coli*, although whether this involves an inhibition of DNA replication is not known.

Most models of error-prone repair envisage an alteration in polymerase fidelity within the cell, allowing replication to proceed across DNA lesions (reviewed by Walker, 1984). It has been suggested that the *umu* gene products may play a role in this reduced fidelity, as mentioned above, although the model of Bridges & Woodgate (1985) ascribes this property to activated RecA protein and suggests a later role for UmuD/C. A *dnaQ* mutant has been described that has properties remarkably similar to those predicted for a strain possessing a DNA polymerase of altered fidelity; the mutation affects the 3′ to 5′ proof reading activity of DNA polymerase III (Piechocki *et al.* 1986). It is possible that this mutation creates the change in fidelity normally produced by interaction with *umu* or *muc* gene products. An alternative candidate is the altered form of DNA polymerase I isolated from SOS-induced cells by Lackey *et al.* (1982), although this can also be isolated from *umuC* mutant cells. The way in which protection/mutation genes interact with polymerases can at this stage only be speculative, until a detailed biochemical study becomes possible. It is perhaps worth emphasizing that much of the effect of the plasmid-encoded systems results in error-free repair of DNA damage; thus the *uvrA umuC* double mutant becomes over 1000 times more resistant to u.v. light upon intro-duction of R46, and the vast majority of the surviving cells are not mutants. Although the plasmid-coded process is error-prone, it does not always produce errors. Whatever model is devised to explain the activity of the protection/mutation genes must take into account the fact that the majority of repair is still accurate.

Several pieces of evidence also suggest that the plasmid-coded genes may encode products that do not interact in a specific way with host polymerases. N group plasmids such as R46 have a very wide host range, and confer u.v. protection and mutation upon most of their hosts. It is difficult to see how a specific interaction with DNA polymerases could take place in such different hosts. Moreover, it has been shown that pKM101 can be introduced into yeast cells, where the *muc* genes are expressed to a limited extent and a degree of protection is conferred (Potter *et al.* 1984); similar results have also been reported on introduction of TP120 into cultured mouse cells (Elli *et al.* 1983). The implication of these observations is clearly that the plasmid-coded proteins carry out some self-contained DNA modification, which can subsequently be acted upon by the host polymerase and converted into a repaired or mutated site.

ORIGIN OF THE PROTECTION/MUTATION SYSTEM

The widespread occurrence of protection/mutation genes across plasmids of many different incompatibility groups raises the question as to whether all of these different genes are related, and perhaps derived from a common ancestor. One can also consider the origin of the *umuD/C* genes in *E. coli* as they are clearly related to plasmid-borne genes. The spread of chromosomal protection/mutation genes is by no means universal, however. These genes are present in the laboratory K12 and B strains of *E. coli*, but are not found for example in *S. typhimurium*, *Proteus mirabilis* or *Deinococcus radiodurans* (Walker, 1983; Hofmeister *et al.* 1979; Tempest & Moseley, 1982). Moreover, even amongst *E. coli* strains there is no consistent picture. Sedgewick & Goodwin (1985) report that the *umuD/C* genes are not present in three of six species of *E. coli* tested, and that outside this genus inducible mutagenesis was rarely found, as judged by the presence of DNA homologous to the *umu* genes. It is clear that this variation applies only to the inducible mutagenesis component of SOS repair; all of the strains tested were inducible for other aspects of the SOS response. Even amongst those *E. coli* strains that carry DNA homologous to *umuD/C*, considerable variations are observed in the flanking DNA, and it is conceivable that the genes may occupy different map positions in different strains (S. G. Sedgewick, personal communication). In *S. typhimurium* the site corresponding to the map position of *umu* in *E. coli* is in fact occupied by one end of a major DNA rearrangement, which is a characteristic difference between these two strains (Sanderson & Roth, 1983). *Haemophilus influenzae* presents perhaps the most interesting indication of the relationship between chromosomal and plasmid-borne protection/mutation systems. This strain is non-mutable by u.v. light, and might be expected not to contain *umu*-like genes. However, Balganesh & Setlow (1985) have shown that mutability can be restored to this strain by the introduction of a recombinant plasmid carrying *only* the pKM101 *mucA* gene. Hybridization between the *muc* genes and *Haemophilus* chromosomal DNA shows that this strain actually contains, in a chromosomal location, a functional gene homologous to *mucB*, and that the combination of the chromosomal *mucB*-analogue with the cloned *mucA* gene not only restores mutability, but also restores post-replication repair to a Rec⁻

host. It is clear from these data that inducible mutation is not an inherent part of the SOS response, that *E. coli* B and K12 are the exception rather than the rule in having such genes on the chromosome, and that when the genes are integrated into the chromosome, perhaps from a plasmid donor, DNA rearrangements and instabilities occur.

In an attempt to determine whether such rearrangements and instabilities were also associated with plasmid-coded genes, we have used the cloned *imp* genes of TP110 as a probe in Southern blotting against a variety of protecting/mutating plasmids, the results being summarized in Table 1. Perry *et al.* (1982) have reported that sequences homologous to *muc* can be detected amongst several other N group plasmids. The data in Table 1 demonstrate that the homology between *imp* and *muc* is not sufficient to permit stable hybridization. However, *imp*-like sequences can be detected in many, but not all, I and B group plasmids. Even in plasmids that are homologous, however, we have detected considerable restriction site polymorphism, indicating divergent evolution of these closely related protection/mutation systems. Details of this work will be published elsewhere.

The widespread occurrence of protection/mutation genes in plasmids and chromosomes has led several workers to suggest that these genes may be carried on a transposon (Sedgewick & Goodwin, 1985; Balganesh & Setlow, 1985). However, a characteristic of transposons is that the same genetic element can be found associated with unrelated replicons. With the protection/mutation genes this does not appear to be the case. Homology to *muc* is found only amongst N group plasmids, homology to *imp* is found only amongst I and B group plasmids (which may be closely related, since some plasmids encode both I and B incompatibility), and the *umu* system seems unique to the *E. coli* chromosome. The model most consistent with these observations is that these functions may at one time have been carried on a transposable element, but that recent evolution has been strictly within groups and the functions can no longer transpose. In support of this theory, we have attempted to mobilize *mob*⁻ plasmids by cointegration with an otherwise transposon-free plasmid carrying the *imp* genes (ColIb-P9), and have found no evidence that such transposition can occur. It is possible that protection/mutation genes were never carried on a transposon, but were spread by replicon fusion promoted by insertion sequence (IS) elements and transposons not related to these genes. R46, for example, carries the active IS46 element that is capable of promoting just such integrations and DNA rearrangements (Brown *et al.* 1984). Future work, extending through an even wider range of plasmids, is in progress and may allow us to identify those features of the protection/mutation genes that must have been present on the archetypal gene from which many if not all of these systems appear to have evolved.

The work in our laboratory on TP110 has been supported by both the Science and Engineering Research Council, and the Medical Research Council. Thanks and credit are due to Martin Ramsden, Simon Dowden, Janice Glazebrook and Kanwal Grewal, who have all worked on this project over the years.

REFERENCES

ATTFIELD, P. V. & PINNEY, R. J. (1983). Plasmid R46 fails to protect *Escherichia coli* against double-strand DNA-binding agents but increases their mutagenic activities. *Mutat. Res.* **107**, 1–12.

ATTFIELD, P. V. & PINNEY, R. J. (1984). Comparison of the *Escherichia coli umu*+-encoded function with plasmid R46-mediated error-prone repair in DNA-damaged cells. *Mutat. Res.* **139**, 101–105.

BABUDRI, N. & MONTI-BRAGADIN, C. (1977). Restoration of mutability in non-mutable *Escherichia coli* carrying different plasmids. *Molec. gen. Genet.* **155**, 287–290.

BAGG, A., KENYON, C. J. & WALKER, G. C. (1981). Inducibility of a gene product required for UV and chemical mutagenesis in *Escherichia coli*. *Proc. natn. Acad. Sci. U.S.A.* **78**, 5749–5753.

BALGANESH, M. & SETLOW, J. K. (1985). Genes from plasmid pKM101 in *Haemophilus influenzae*: Separation of functions of *mucA* and *mucB*. *Proc. natn. Acad. Sci. U.S.A.* **82**, 7753–7756.

BLANCO, M., HERRERA, G., COLLADO, P., REBOLLO, J. & BOTELLA, L. M. (1982). Influence of RecA protein on induced mutagenesis. *Biochimie* **64**, 633–636.

BLANCO, M. & REBOLLO, J. (1981). Plasmid pKM101-dependent repair and mutagenesis in *Escherichia coli* cells with mutations *lexB30 tif* and *zab-53* in the *recA* gene. *Mutat. Res.* **81**, 265–275.

BRIDGES, B. A. & WOODGATE, R. (1985). Mutagenic DNA repair in *Escherichia coli*: Products of the *recA* gene and of the *umuD* and *umuC* genes act at different steps in UV-induced mutagenesis. *Proc. natn. Acad. Sci. U.S.A.* **82**, 4193–4197.

BROWN, A. M. C., COUPLAND, G. M. & WILLETTS, N. S. (1984). Characterization of IS46, an insertion sequence found on two IncN plasmids. *J. Bact.* **159**, 172–481.

BROWN, A. M. C. & WILLETTS, N. S. (1981). A physical and genetic map of the IncN plasmid R46. *Plasmid* **5**, 188–201.

DOBSON, P. P. & WALKER, G. C. (1980). Plasmid (pKM101)-mediated Weigle reactivation in *Escherichia coli* K12 and *Salmonella typhimurium* LT2: genetic dependence, kinetics of induction, and effect of chloramphenicol. *Mutat. Res.* **71**, 25–41.

DOUBLEDAY, O. P., GREEN, M. H. L. & BURIDGES, B. A. (1977). Spontaneous and ultraviolet-induced mutation in *Escherichia coli*: interaction between plasmid and *tif-1* mutator effects. *J. gen. Microbiol.* **101**, 163–166.

DOWDEN, S. B., GLAZEBROOK, J. A. & STRIKE, P. (1984). UV inducible UV protection and mutation functions on the I group plasmid TP110. *Molec. gen. Genet.* **193**, 316–321.

DOWDEN, S. B. & STRIKE, P. (1982). R46-derived recombinant plasmids affecting DNA repair and mutation in *E. coli*. *Molec. gen. Genet.* **186**, 140–144.

DRABBLE, W. T. & STOCKER, B. A. D. (1968). R. (transmissible drug-resistance) factors in *Salmonella typhimurium*: pattern of transduction of phage P22 and ultraviolet-protection effect. *J. gen. Microbiol.* **53**, 109–123.

EISENSTADT, E., WARREN, A. J., PORTER, J., ATKINS, D. & MILLER, J. H. (1982). Carcinogenic epoxides of benzo (a) pyrene and cyclopenta (cd) pyrene induce base substitutions via specific transversions. *Proc. natn. Acad. Sci. U.S.A.* **79**, 1945–1949.

EISENSTADT, E., WOLF, M. & GOLDBERG, I. H. (1980). Mutagenesis by neocarzinostatin in *Escherichia coli* and *Salmonella typhimurium*: requirement for *umuC*+ on plasmid pKM101. *J. Bact.* **144**, 656–660.

ELLEDGE, S. J. & WALKER, G. C. (1983a). Proteins required for ultraviolet light and chemical mutagenesis: identification of the products of the *umuC* locus of *Escherichia coli*. *J. molec. Biol.* **164**, 175–192.

ELLEDGE, S. J. & WALKER, G. C. (1983b). The *muc* genes of pKM101 are induced by DNA damage. *J. Bact.* **155**, 1306–1315.

ELLI, R., MARCUCCI, L., BOSI, R., OPPI-BATTAGLIA, P. A. & GIGILIANI, F. (1983). The pR UV+ plasmid transfected into mammalian cells enhances their UV survival. *Nucl. Acids Res.* **11**, 3679–3686.

FOWLER, R. G., MCGINTY, L. & MORTELMANS, K. E. (1981). Mutational specificity of ultraviolet light in *Escherichia coli* with and without the R plasmid pKM101. *Genetics* **99**, 25–40.

GLAZEBROOK, J. A., FORSTER, J. W. & STRIKE, P. (1983). Regulation of expression of the colicin gene of the I1 group plasmid TP110. *J. Bact.* **155**, 122–128.

GLAZEBROOK, J. A. (1986). Molecular analysis of the UV protection and mutation genes carried by the I incompatibility group plasmid TP110. *J. Bact.* **168**, 251–256.

GLICKMAN, B. (1983). Mutational specificity of UV light in *E. coli*: influence of excision repair and mutator plasmid pKM101. In *Induced Mutagenesis* (ed. C. W. Lawrence), pp. 135–170. New York: Plenum Publishing Corp.

GOZE, A. & DEVORET, R. (1979). Repair promoted by plasmid pKM101 is different from SOS repair. *Mutat. Res.* **61**, 163–179.

HOFMEISTER, J. M., KOHLER, H. & FILIPPOV, V. D. (1979). DNA repair in *Proteus mirabilis*. VI. Plasmid (R46-) mediated recovery and UV mutagenesis. *Molec. gen. Genet.* **176**, 265–273.

HOWARTH, S. (1965). Resistance to the bactericidal effects of ultraviolet radiation conferred on enterobacteria by the colicin factor ColI. *J. gen. Microbiol.* **40**, 43–55.

HOWARTH, S. (1966). Increase in frequency of ultraviolet induced mutation brought about by the colicin factor ColI in *Salmonella typhimurium*. *Mutat. Res.* **3**, 129–134.

JACOB, E. A., SHAPIRO, J. A., YAMAMOTO, L., SMITH, D. I., COHEN, S. W. & BERG, D. (1977). Plasmids studied in *Escherichia coli* and other enteric bacteria. In *DNA Insertion Elements, Plasmids and Episomes* (ed. A. L. Bukhari, J. A. Shapiro & S. L. Adhya), pp. 601–704. New York: Cold Spring Harbor Laboratory Press.

JACOBY, G. A (1974). Properties of R plasmids determining resistance by acetylation in *Pseudomonas aeruginosa*. *Antimicrob. Agents Chemother.* **6**, 239–252.

KATO, T. & SHINOURA, Y. (1977). Isolation and characterization of mutants of *Escherichia coli* deficient in induction of mutations by ultraviolet light. *Molec. gen. Genet.* **156**, 121–131.

KITAGAWA, Y., AKABOSHI, E., SHINAGAWA, H., HORII, T., OGAWA, H. & KATO, T. (1985). Structural analysis of the *umu* operon required for inducible mutagenesis in *Escherichia coli*. *Proc. natn. Acad. Sci. U.S.A.* **82**, 4336–4340.

KRISHNAPILLAI, V. (1975). Resistance to ultraviolet light and enhanced mutagenesis conferred by *Pseudomonas aeruginosa* plasmids. *Mutat. Res.* **29**, 363–372.

KRONISH, J. W. & WALKER, G. C. (1979). The effects of the ultraviolet-protecting plasmids pKM101 and R205 on DNA polymerase I activity in *Escherichia coli* K12. *Mutat. Res.* **60**, 135–142.

KUSHNER, S. R., SHEPHERD, J., EDWARD, G. & MAPLES, V. F. (1978). *uvrD*, *uvrE* and *recL* represent a single gene. In *DNA Repair Mechanisms* (ed. P. Hanawalt, E. C. Friedberg & C. F. Fox), pp. 251–254. New York: Academic Press.

LACKEY, D., KRAUSS, S. W. & LINN, S. (1982). Isolation of an altered form of DNA polymerase I from *Escherichia coli* cells induced for *recA*/*lexA* functions. *Proc. natn. Acad. Sci. U.S.A.* **79**, 330–334.

LACKEY, D., WALKER, G. C., KING, T. & LINN, S. (1977). Characterization of an endonuclease associated with the drug resistance plasmid pKM101. *J. Bact.* **131**, 583–588.

LANGER, P. J., PERRY, K. L. & WALKER, G. C. (1985). Complementation of a pKM101 derivative that decreases resistance to UV killing but increases susceptibility to mutagenesis. *Mutat. Res.* **150**, 147–158.

LANGER, P. J. & WALKER, G. C. (1981). Restriction endonuclease cleavage map of pKM101: relationship to parental plasmid R46. *Molec. gen. Genet.* **182**, 268–272.

LEHRBACH, P., KING, A. H. C. & LEE, B. T. O. (1977a). Loss of ultraviolet light protection and enhanced ultraviolet light-induced mutability in *Pseudomonas aeruginosa* carrying mutant R plasmids. *J. gen. Microbiol.* **101**, 135–141.

LEHRBACH, P., KING, A. H. C., LEE, B. T. O. & JACOBY, G. A. (1977b). Plasmid modification of radiation and chemical-mutagen sensitivity in *Pseudomonas aeruginosa*. *J. gen. Microbiol.* **98**, 167–176.

LITTLE, J. W. & HANAWALT, P. C. (1977). Induction of protein X in *Escherichia coli*. *Molec. gen. Genet.* **150**, 237–248.

LITTLE, J. W. & MOUNT, D. W. (1982). The SOS regulatory system of *Escherichia coli*. *Cell* **29**, 11–22.

MACPHEE, D. G. (1972). Effect of an R factor on resistance of *Salmonella typhimurium* to radiation of chemical treatment. *Mutat. Res.* **14**, 450–453.

MacPhee, D. G. (1973*a*). *Salmonella* hisG46 (R-Utrecht): possible use in screening mutagens and carcinogens. *Appl. Microbiol.* **26**, 1004–1005.

MacPhee, D. G. (1973*b*). Effects of an R factor and caffeine on ultraviolet mutability in *Salmonella typhimurium. Mutat. Res.* **18**, 367–370.

MacPhee, D. G. (1973*c*). Effect of *rec* mutations on the ultraviolet protecting and mutation-enhancing properties of the plasmid R-Utrecht in *Salmonella typhimurium. Mutat. Res.* **19**, 356–359.

MacPhee, D. G. (1974). DNA polymerase activity determined by the ultraviolet-protecting plasmid R-Utrecht. *Nature, Lond.* **251**, 432–434.

MacPhee, D. G. (1977). Spontaneous, ultraviolet and ionizing radiation mutagenesis in two auxotrophic strains of *Salmonella typhimurium* carrying an R plasmid. *Mutat. Res.* **45**, 1–6.

McCann, K. & Clarke, C. H. (1981). Plasmid-mediated UV-protection in *Myxococcus xanthus. Molec. gen. Genet.* **182**, 137–142.

McCann, J., Spingarn, N. E., Kabori, J. & Ames, B. N. (1975). Detection of carcinogens as mutagens: bacterial tester strains with R factor plasmids. *Proc. natn. Acad. Sci. U.S.A.* **72**, 979–983.

Marsh, E. G. & Smith, D. H. (1969). R factors improving survival of *Escherichia coli* K12 after ultraviolet irradiation. *J. Bact.* **100**, 128–139.

Marsh, L. & Walker, G. C. (1985). Cold sensitivity induced by overproduction of UmuDC in *Escherichia coli. J. Bact.* **162**, 155–161.

Mattern, I. E., Olthoff-Smith, F. P., Jacobs-Meijsing, B. L. M., Enger-Valk, B. E., Pouwels, P. H. & Lohman, P. H. M. (1985). A system to determine base pair substitutions at the molecular level, based on restriction enzyme analysis: influence of the *muc* genes of pKM101 on the specificity of mutation induction in *E. coli. Mutat. Res.* **148**, 35–45.

Miehl, R., Miller, M. & Yasbin, R. E. (1980). Plasmid mediated enhancement of UV resistance in *Streptococcus faecalis. Plasmid* **3**, 128–134.

Misuraca, F. (1984). Plasmid-mediated inducible reactivation of an actinophage. *Microbiologica* **7**, 323–329.

Molina, A. M., Babudri, N., Tamaro, M., Venturini, S. & Monti-Bragadin, C. (1979). Enterobacteriacae plasmids enhancing chemical mutagenesis and their distribution among incompatibility groups. *FEMS Lett.* **5**, 33–37.

Monti-Bragadin, C., Babudri, N. & Samer, L. (1976). Expression of the pKM101-determined repair system in *recA*⁻ and *lex*⁻ strains of *Escherichia coli. Molec. gen. Genet.* **145**, 303–306.

Mortelmans, K. E. & Stocker, B. A. D. (1976). Ultraviolet light protection, enhancement of ultraviolet light mutagenesis and mutator effect of plasmid R46 in *Salmonella typhimurium. J. Bact.* **128**, 271–282.

Mortelmans, K. E. & Stocker, B. A. D. (1979). Segregation of the mutator property of plasmid R46 from its ultraviolet-protecting property. *Mol. gen. Genet.* **167**, 317–327.

Novick, R. P. (1974). Bacterial plasmids. In *Handbook of Microbiology*, vol. 4 (ed. A. I. Laskin & H. A. Lechevalier), pp. 537–586. Cleveland, Ohio: C.R.C. Press.

Nunoshiba, T. & Nishioka, H. (1984). Protective effect of R-factor plasmid pKM101 on lethal damage by UV and chemical mutagens in *E. coli* strains with different DNA-repairing capacities. *Mutat. Res.* **141**, 135–139.

Oeda, K., Horiuchi, T. & Sekiguchi, M. (1982). The *uvrD* gene of *E. coli* encodes a DNA dependent ATPase. *Nature, Lond.* **298**, 98–100.

Pembroke, J. J. & Stevens, E. (1984). The effect of plasmid R391 and other IncJ plasmids on the survival of *Escherichia coli* after UV irradiation. *J. gen. Microbiol.* **130**, 1839–1844.

Perry, K. L., Elledge, S. J., Lichtman, M. R. & Walker, G. C. (1982). In *Proc. Third Int. Conf. Environ. Mutagens* (ed. T. Sugimura, S. Kondo & H. Takebe), pp. 113–120. Liss, New York: University of Tokyo Press.

Perry, K. L., Elledge, S. J., Mitchell, B. B., Marsh, L. & Walker, G. C. (1985). *UmuC* and *mucAB* operons whose products are required for UV light- and chemical-induced mutagenesis: UmuD, MucA and LexA proteins share homology. *Proc. natn. Acad. Sci. U.S.A.* **82**, 4331–4335.

Perry, K. L. & Walker, G. C. (1982). Identification of plasmid (pKM101)-coded proteins involved in mutagenesis and UV resistance. *Nature, Lond.* **300**, 278–281.

PIECHOCKI, R., KUPPER, D., QUINONES, A. & LANGHAMMER, R. (1986). Mutational specificity of a proof-reading defective *Escherichia coli dnaQ49* mutator. *Molec. gen. Genet.* **202**, 162–168.

PINNEY, R. J. (1980). Distribution among incompatibility groups of plasmids that confer UV mutability and UV resistance. *Mutat. Res.* **72**, 155–159.

POTTER, A. A., NESTMANN, E. R. & IYER, V. N. (1984). Introduction of the plasmid pKM101-associated *muc* gene into *Saccharomyces cerevisiae*. *Mutat. Res.* **131**, 197–204.

PUGLIA, A. M., MISURACA, F., RANDAZZO, R., SCIANDRELLO, G. & SERMONTI, G. (1982). Plasmid-dependent Co-mutation in *Streptomyces coelicolor* A3(2). *Curr. Genet.* **5**, 89–92.

SANDERSON, K. E. & ROTH, J. R. (1983). Linkage map of *Salmonella typhimurium*, edn VI. *Microbiol. Rev.* **47**, 410–553.

SEDGEWICK, S. G. & GOODWIN, P. (1985). Differences in mutagenic and recombinational DNA repair in Enterobacteria. *Proc. natn. Acad. Sci. U.S.A.* **82**, 4172–4176.

SICCARDI, A. G. (1969). Effect of R factors and other plasmids on ultraviolet susceptibility and host cell reactivation property of *Escherichia coli*. *J. Bact.* **100**, 337–346.

SIEGAL, E. C. (1981). Complementation studies with repair-deficient *uvrD3*, *uvrE156* and *recL152* mutations in *Escherichia coli*. *Molec. gen. Genet.* **184**, 526–530.

SHANABRUCH, W. G. & WALKER, G. C. (1980). Localization of the plasmid (pKM101) gene(s) involved in *recA⁺ lexA⁺*-dependent mutagenesis. *Molec. gen. Genet.* **179**, 289–297.

STEINBORN, G. (1979). Uvm mutants of *Escherichia coli* K12 deficient in UV mutagenesis: II. Further evidence for a novel function in error-prone repair. *Molec. gen. Genet.* **175**, 203–208.

STOKES, H. W. & KRISHNAPILLAE, V. (1978). Prevalence of *Pseudomonas aeruginosa* FP plasmids which enhance spontaneous and UV-induced mutagenesis. *Mutat. Res.* **50**, 19–28.

TEMPEST, P. R. & MOSELEY, B. E. B. (1982). Lack of ultraviolet mutagenesis in radiation-resistant bacteria. *Mutat. Res.* **104**, 275–280.

TODD, P. A. & GLICKMAN, B. W. (1979). UV protection and mutagenesis in *uvrD*, *uvrE* and *recL* strains of *Escherichia coli* carrying the pKM101 plasmid. *Mutat. Res.* **62**, 451–457.

TODD, P. A., MONTI-BRAGADIN, C. & GLICKMAN, B. W. (1979). MMS mutagenesis in strains of *Escherichia coli* carrying the R46 mutagenic enhancing plasmid: phenotypic analysis of Arg⁺ revertants. *Mutat. Res.* **62**, 227–237.

TWEATS, D. J., THOMPSON, M. J., PINNEY, R. J. & SMITH, J. T. (1976). R factor-mediated resistance to ultraviolet light in strains of *Escherichia coli* deficient in known repair functions. *J. gen. Microbiol.* **93**, 103–170.

UPTON, C. & PINNEY, R. J. (1979). Absence of plasmid-mediated DNA polymerase activity from UV induced strains of *Escherichia coli*. *J. Pharm. Pharmac.* **31**, 35P.

UPTON, C. & PINNEY, R. J. (1981). Absence of ultraviolet-inducible DNA polymerase I-like activity in *Escherichia coli* strains harbouring R plasmids. *J. gen. Microbiol.* **125**, 131–137.

UPTON, C. & PINNEY, R. J. (1983). Expression of eight unrelated Muc⁺ plasmids in eleven DNA repair-deficient *E. coli* strains. *Mutat. Res.* **112**, 261–273.

VENTURINI, S. & MONTI-BRAGADIN, C. (1978). R plasmid-mediated enhancement of mutagenesis in strains of *Escherichia coli* deficient in known repair functions. *Mutat. Res.* **50**, 1–8.

WALEH, N. S. & STOCKER, B. A. D. (1979). Effect of host *lex*, *recA*, *recF* and *uvrD* genotypes of plasmid R46 in *Escherichia coli*. *J. Bact.* **137**, 830–838.

WALKER, G. C. (1977). Plasmid (pKM101)-mediated enhancement of repair and mutagenesis: dependence on chromosomal genes in *Escherichia coli* K12. *Molec. gen. Genet.* **152**, 93–103.

WALKER, G. C. (1978). Inducible reactivation and mutagenesis of UV-irradiated bacteriophage P22 in *Salmonella typhimurium* LT2 containing the plasmid pKM101. *J. Bact.* **135**, 415–421.

WALKER, G. C. (1979). Mutagenesis and repair-enhancing activities associated with the plasmid pKM101. *Cold Spring Harbor Symp. quant. Biol.* **43**, 893–896.

WALKER, G. C. (1983). Molecular principles underlying the Ames *Salmonella*-microsome test: elements and design of short-term tests. In In Vitro *Toxicology Testing of Environmental Agents: Current and Future Possibilities* (ed. A. R. Kolber, T. K. Wang, L. D. Grant, R. S. De Woskink & T. J. Hughes), pp. 15–39. New York: Plenum.

WALKER, G. C. (1984). Mutagenesis and inducible responses. *Microbiol. Rev.* **48**, 60–93.

WALKER, G. C. & DOBSON, P. P. (1979). Mutagenesis and repair deficiencies on *Escherichia coli umuC* mutants are suppressed by the plasmid pKM101. *Molec. gen. Genet.* **172**, 17–24.

YOUDERIAN, P., BOUVIER, S. & SUSSKIND, M. M. (1982). Sequence determinants of promoter activity. *Cell* **30**, 843–853.

J. Cell Sci. Suppl. 6, 323–331 (1987)
Printed in Great Britain © The Company of Biologists Limited 1987

STRATEGIES TO ANALYSE MUTAGENESIS IN MAMMALIAN CELLS USING SIMIAN VIRUS 40 OR SHUTTLE VECTORS

CARLOS F. M. MENCK, MICHAEL R. JAMES, ALAIN GENTIL AND ALAIN SARASIN

Laboratory of Molecular Mutagenesis, Institut de Recherches Scientifiques sur le Cancer, B.P. no. 8, 94802, Villejuif Cedex, France

SUMMARY

The use of exogeneous DNA probes, which replicate extrachromosomally, is proposed in order to study spontaneous and induced mutagenesis in mammalian cells. Simian virus 40 has already proved to be very useful, since it has provided much important information in this field. Recently, several shuttle vectors have been designed for this purpose; however, it seems that these molecules have high spontaneous mutation frequencies when replicating in mammalian cells. We have developed new alternative systems, such as Epstein-Barr virus-based shuttle vectors that can be episomally maintained in human cells. Furthermore, we have constructed packageable shuttle vectors, which appear to be stable in the host cell and thus suitable for analysis of mutagenesis.

INTRODUCTION

Genetic instability in higher organisms seems to be correlated with several deleterious physiological phenomena such as carcinogenesis and aging. The processes involved in this instability, either gene rearrangements or point mutations, are not known. Although they may occur 'spontaneously', the presence of induced DNA lesions, as a result of either a metabolic product or an external agent, may play an important role in the origin of genome alterations (Smith & Sargentini, 1985). Mutations can activate some cellular oncogenes (Cooper, 1984) leading to dramatic effects on the regulation of cellular growth. Recent experimental data provide demonstrations that such mutations in oncogenes can be induced by DNA-damaging agents (Sukumar *et al.* 1983; Guerrero *et al.* 1984). The relationship between unrepaired genomic lesions, mutations and carcinogenesis is also evident in the classical human genetic disease xeroderma pigmentosum. The absence of excision repair of some classes of DNA lesions in cells from these patients is correlated with increased mutagenesis and with a cancer-prone phenotype (Cleaver & Bootsma, 1975).

The analysis of induced genomic mutations in mammalian cells has been possible due to the existence of a few cell lines in which the mutated phenotype can be selected with appropriate media (Thacker, 1985). However, these analyses present technical difficulties, are time-consuming and yield very limited information. Hence, the use of small and easily manipulatable DNA probes, which would depend on cellular enzymic machinery for replication and repair, is desirable. These requirements can be fulfilled by certain animal viruses, such as simian virus 40 (SV40), and shuttle vectors. Lesions can be induced in the DNA molecules *in vitro* by treatment with DNA-damaging agents. Subsequently, the damaged probes are introduced into the recipient cells, by infection (virus) or transfection (naked DNA), where they will be repaired and/or mutagenized. A suitable mutation screening permits isolation of selected mutants, which may then be genetically mapped and characterized at the molecular level. The mutation sites can be correlated with the presence of putative lesions and thus the mechanisms by which a DNA lesion is processed into a mutational event can be approached. An additional advantage of this system is that the DNA probe and the host cell genome can be independently damaged, which permits a search for inducible SOS responses in mammalian cells (Sarasin, 1985).

THE USE OF SIMIAN VIRUS 40 AS A PROBE

SV40 is in many ways ideally suited as a probe for studying mutagenesis in mammalian cells. SV40 is a papovavirus with a supercoiled double-stranded DNA genome (5243 base-pairs) entirely dependent on the host cell machinery for replication as well as for DNA repair. Few proteins are encoded by the virus. The early transcription genes give rise to two mRNAs, which are translated into two proteins, the small t-antigen and the large T-antigen. This latter binds near the origin of replication and is the only virus-encoded protein needed to initiate DNA replication. Late transcription gives rise to the messenger RNA of the three capsid proteins, VP_1, VP_2 and VP_3, and a fourth, agnoprotein, also involved in encapsidation. No enzyme is encoded for DNA replication or DNA repair. Moreover, SV40 DNA exists *in vivo* as a minichromosome resembling the chromatin organization of mammalian cells. One of the advantages in using such a viral probe is the facility to treat *in vitro* SV40 either as a virion or as DNA (when the compounds to be tested may react with the capsid proteins), and to treat the host cell separately.

Our mutation assay is based upon the reversion of a temperature-sensitive growth phenotype at the restrictive temperature of 41 °C to a wild-type growth phenotype. Two temperature-sensitive mutants are used, either the tsA58 SV40 mutant, unable to initiate DNA replication at 41 °C, or the tsB 201 late mutant, unable to produce virions at the restrictive temperature (Bourre *et al.* 1983).

Using the SV40 as probe, Sarasin & Hanawalt (1978) showed that a recovery pathway was acting in monkey cells, able to enhance the survival of the viral progeny from ultraviolet (u.v.)-irradiated virus, when cells were either u.v.-irradiated or treated with a chemical carcinogen prior to infection. This new recovery pathway has been shown to be error-prone since the mutation assay revealed an increased mutagenesis in the viral progeny of u.v.-irradiated virus grown in u.v.-irradiated cells (Sarasin & Benoit, 1986). Similar results have been obtained for human cells (Gentil *et al.* 1985). u.v.-induced revertants of the tsA58 mutant were isolated and their DNAs were analysed. The mutation responsible for the phenotype reversion, which leads to an active T-antigen at the restrictive temperature, was mapped by the marker rescue technique. DNAs of the revertants were digested by restriction enzymes, and the fragments obtained were hybridized with single-stranded tsA58 DNA. The restriction fragments that complement the tsA58 sequence carry the mutation. The nucleotide sequencing of these fragments was then carried out (Bourre & Sarasin, 1983). Our results showed that in all cases the tsA58 sequence was still present and that the reversion was always the result of a base substitution, changing one amino acid to another. All of these mutations were 'targeted', that is to say opposite a putative u.v. lesion, pyrimidine dimer or pyrimidine-(6-4)-pyrimidone.

As described above, one of the advantages of the system is the possibility of treating the DNA *in vitro* and therefore of quantifying precisely the number and type of lesions induced before transfection into permissive cells. This method has been used successfully to study the mutagenicity of u.v. lesions, abasic sites, and of acetoxy-acetylaminofluorene treatment (Bourre *et al.* 1983; Gentil *et al.* 1982). For u.v. treatment, identical viral data were obtained using DNA and using SV40 virion, except for a slight protective effect of the capsid proteins. When DNA is heated at 70°C under acidic conditions, abasic sites, chiefly apurinic sites (AP sites), are produced in SV40. One AP site is formed per 15 min of heating per SV40 genome (Gentil *et al.* 1984). This number is determined easily since these AP sites are alkali-labile and since AP endonucleases are available. We have shown that AP sites are very mutagenic for monkey cells and that they strongly decrease survival of the viral progeny with a lethal hit of three AP sites per SV40 genome. The use of SV40 DNA enabled us to compare the lethality and mutation efficiency of different kinds of lesion. Indeed, we showed that a great difference exists in cell killing potency between u.v. lesions, AP sites and acetylaminofluorene adducts. Four AP sites are as efficient in cell killing as 50 pyrimidine dimers or 200 acetylaminofluorene adducts. At these lethality levels similar mutation frequencies were obtained (Bourre *et al.* 1983).

These values, however, are the final result of many poorly understood phenomena that occur in the cell, including processes other than DNA metabolism. On this point we note that one restriction in the method we have used is that transfection of mammalian cells, itself, may well induce unusual phenomena. This is of relevance in the context of inducible repair. Indeed, one interpretation of our data is that AP sites are mutagenic *per se*, but an alternative interpretation is that mutator functions acting on AP sites may be induced by the transfection protocol. We have no data that bear directly on this possibility but we make the comparison with Shaaper & Loeb (1981) who, using ϕX174 bacteriophage, found that AP sites were mutagenic in bacteria only after SOS-induction of the host cells by u.v. irradiation. The molecular analysis of the mutations induced by AP sites and the carcinogen acetoxy-acetyl-aminofluorene is under investigation using the same experimental protocol as described above.

In conclusion, while it is valid to comment that this protocol is concerned with how viral DNA rather than chromosomal DNA is processed, the use of SV40 as a probe gives information that would not be accessible using other methods, given the complexity of a mammalian cell.

SHUTTLE VECTORS

As part of other projects in our laboratory we have been investigating the potential of shuttle vectors for improving the efficiency of introduction, expression and rescue of genetic loci that are of interest in mammalian cells, particularly those from DNA repair-deficient and cancer-prone genetic syndromes. In addition such a vector system may facilitate the analysis of mutagenesis similar to the viral system described above but with less effort, more rapidly and with greatly improved logistics (Calos *et al.* 1983; Razzaque *et al.* 1983). This convenience arises from the ability to manipulate the vectors in mammalian cells but subsequently rescue and analyse them in bacteria.

In the first instance, we have inserted the replication origins or entire early-gene regions of monkey and human papovaviruses into a small cosmid (see Fig. 1A). The mutation locus we have chosen to insert in the vectors is *lacZ'*, which may be scored easily in appropriate bacterial hosts. These vectors replicate transiently in monkey COS-7 cells (Gluzman, 1981) and in human cell lines, including a xeroderma pigmentosum strain XP4PA-SVwt (group C), transformed with an origin-defective SV40 recombinant, because these cells provide T-antigen *in trans* (Daya-Grosjean *et al.* 1987). Two to three days following transfection with the vectors, plasmid that has replicated may be rescued in bacteria. In agreement with the data from other laboratories, the spontaneous mutation frequency of shuttled vectors is high, greater than 10^{-2}, in all cell types with the exception of human 293 cells (Lebkowski *et al.* 1984). Agarose gel electrophoresis of rescued plasmids shows many insertions and deletions. The inclusion in these vectors of the hybrid neomycin resistance gene permits selection in mammalian cells using the drug G418. Selection of XP4PA-SVwt cells transfected with these vectors results in rapid establishment of cell clones that show episomally maintained plasmid, a phenomenon that appears much less toxic to the human cells than to monkey COS cells. A high copy-number of the vector was found in the low molecular weight DNA fraction of these XP cells, persisting for more than 2 months. When this persisting vector was rescued into bacteria, however, an even higher spontaneous mutation frequency was observed, and electrophoresis revealed a concomitant increase in gross alterations in the plasmid.

More recently we have inserted *lacZ'* into Epstein-Barr virus (EBV)-based shuttle vectors to investigate the claim by Yates *et al.* (1985) that these vectors may be maintained, without gross alteration, in an exclusively episomal manner in human cells. Indeed, preliminary results of several cell lines containing between 30 and 100 copies of the vector p205-Z (Fig. 1B) have indicated a far lower spontaneous mutation frequency of *lacZ'* (10^{-4} to 10^{-5}). These results suggest that this system may be suitable for examining induced mutagenesis and repair phenomena in a more systematic and efficient manner than has been possible previously.

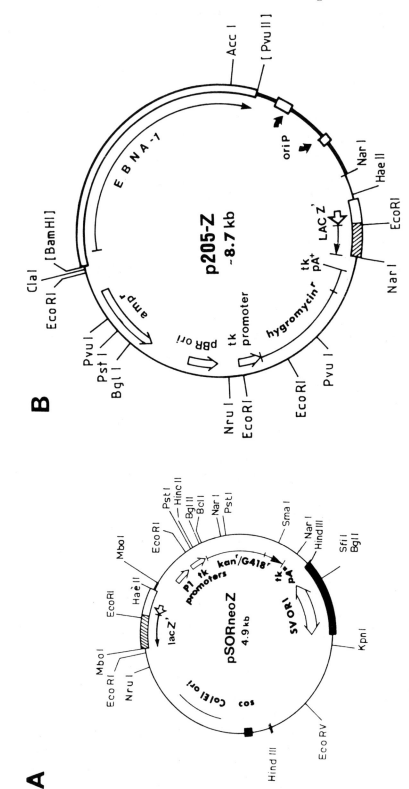

Fig. 1. General structure of SV40-based (A) and EBV-based (B) shuttle vectors. Divisions within the circles indicate functional components including bacterial-plasmid (ColE1, pBR) and SV40 replication origins, EBV sequences necessary for plasmid replication and maintenance in mammalian cells (EBNA-1 and *oriP*), selectable genes (kan^r/G418^r, amp^r and hygromycin^r), mutation locus (*lacZ'*). Inner arrows show major transcripts. Restriction enzyme sites indicated in brackets are deleted. Constructions will be described in detail elsewhere.

SV40-BASED SHUTTLE-VIRUS

Another possibility for studying mutagenesis is to combine the advantages of both virus and shuttle vectors by means of a packageable shuttle vector. Such a shuttle-virus would enable DNA to be introduced into mammalian cells without the need for transfection, which has certain disadvantages including variable and low efficiency and variable toxicity to many human cell lines. This method may also be one cause of the high spontaneous frequency of mutagenesis observed with shuttle vectors. It seemed feasible to construct a shuttle vector, similar to those described above, which was packageable as a mammalian virus by use of a helper system. We have accomplished this goal by the construction of a series of SV40-based shuttle vectors containing the entire SV40 late region, which codes for capsid proteins, and its intact replicon origin. These vectors, one of which is presented in Fig. 2, have part of the SV40 early genes, which normally transcribe for the small t- and large T-antigen, substituted by the miniplasmid $\pi\Delta$lac (Little *et al.* 1983). This plasmid has the minimal essential DNA sequences for replication in *Escherichia coli*, the *supF* suppressor tRNA gene, which provides selection in the appropriate host, and the *lacO* sequence. Although unable to produce the large T-antigen these plasmids can replicate efficiently in monkey COS-7 cells, which produce this protein constitutively, thus avoiding the use of a helper virus. Since all the other genetic information necessary for virus production is present in these vectors, they also produce infectious viral particles (Menck, James & Sarasin, unpublished data).

Plasmid DNA from cells infected with these viruses can be transferred back into *E. coli* for analysis of its stability during replication in mammalian cells. Many DNA alterations, mostly deletions, are observed in these plasmids and appear to be due to limits in the genome size that could be packaged as virus. Plasmids with sizes smaller than SV40 are more stable. Moreover, the *lac* operator sequence present in these vectors permits the analysis of mutations induced in this DNA target, which can be monitored by a sensitive colour assay. The presence of multiple copies of a non-mutated plasmid in a *lacZ*-proficient bacterial host leads to binding of the Lac repressor to the plasmid and thus to the derepression of the *lac* operon. In this situation, the bacteria metabolize the synthetic substrate X-gal to produce a chromogenic (blue) metabolite. Mutations in the *lacO* sequence that inhibit Lac repressor binding lead to formation of white colonies. Preliminary studies indicate that at least one of the vectors is very stable (*lacO* spontaneous mutation frequency after passage as shuttle-virus is lower than 0·03 %). Analysis of mutations induced by u.v. irradiation of the shuttle-virus is in progress.

CONCLUSION

We have outlined a variety of strategies that we are using to analyse, at the molecular level, mutagenesis in mammalian cells.

The EBV-based shuttle vectors show considerable promise as this system appears to function in all immortalized human cells tested to date. Such a stable episomal system offers unique advantages in experimental versatility; for example, time

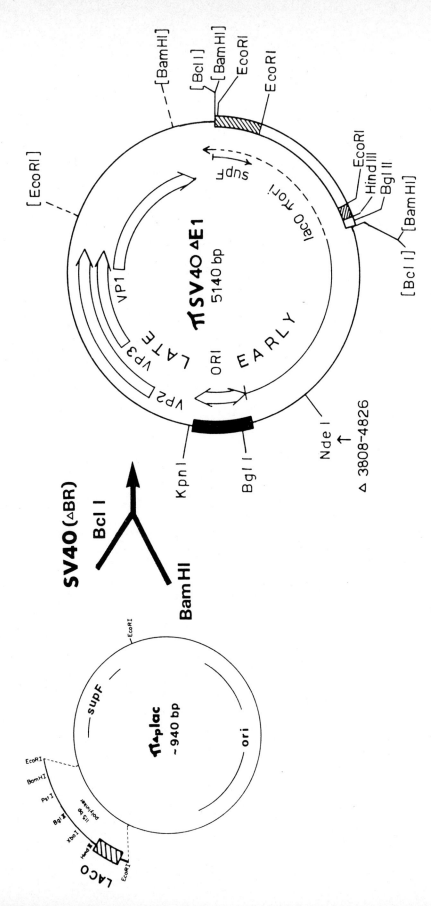

Fig. 2. Scheme for the construction of a shuttle-virus. Divisions within the circles indicate functional components including bacterial-plasmid and SV40 origins, selectable gene (*supF*) and mutation locus (*lacO*). Inner arrows show major transcripts. Restriction enzyme sites indicated in brackets are deleted. Details will be described elsewhere.

course studies and more complex treatment protocols. It remains to be seen if the low copy number of these vectors contributes to their stability and may more closely approximate the host chromosome replication and repair than the high copy number, and rapidly replicating, papovaviruses.

On the other hand the approaches using SV40 as described above retain considerable advantages, namely: (1) high efficiency, approaching 100%, of infection compared to 5–10% transfection of mammalian cells; (2) ideal delivery to cells *via* virus-particle transport to the cell nucleus; (3) efficient virus replication: at least 10- to 100-fold greater than shuttle vectors; (4) efficient recovery of very pure DNA in the form of virus particles. An attractive possibility with these viral systems is the ability to work with untransformed diploid fibroblasts as this would permit studies in all of the human DNA repair deficiency syndromes.

To obtain, for mammalian cells, mutation data at the detailed molecular level comparable to that which exists for bacteria remains a formidable task. Modern experimental tools in biology are, however, very powerful and we are confident that one of the variety of approaches being examined by ourselves and others will succeed eventually in this aim.

C. F. M. Menck holds a postdoctoral fellowship from CNPq, Brazil; M. R. James acknowledges the support of IARC (Lyon, France) during the earliest stages of these projects and is now supported by ARC (Villejuif, France). This work has been supported by grants from ARC (Villejuif, France) and from the Commission of the European Communities (no. B16-163 F, Brussels, Belgium).

REFERENCES

Bourre, F., Gentil, A. & Sarasin, A. (1983). Molecular analysis of ultraviolet induced mutagenesis on simian virus 40 DNA. In *Genetics: New Frontiers* (ed. V. L. Chopra, B. C. Joshi, R. P. Sharma & H. C. Bansal), pp. 385–393. New Delhi: Oxford & I.B.H. Publishing Co.

Bourre, F. & Sarasin, A. (1983). Targeted mutagenesis of SV40 DNA induced by UV-light. *Nature, Lond.* **305**, 68–70.

Calos, M. P., Lebkowski, J. S. & Botchan, M. R. (1983). High mutation frequency in DNA transfected into mammalian cells. *Proc. natn. Acad. Sci. U.S.A.* **80**, 3015–3019.

Cleaver, J. E. & Bootsma, D. (1975). Xeroderma pigmentosum: biochemical and genetic characteristics. *A. Rev. Genet.* **9**, 19–38.

Cooper, G. M. (1984). Activation of transforming genes in neoplasms. *Br. J. Cancer* **50**, 137–142.

Daya-Grosjean, L., James, M. R., Drougard, C. & Sarasin, A. (1987). An immortalized xeroderma pigmentosum, group C, cell line which replicates SV40 shuttle vectors. *Mutat. Res.* (in press).

Gentil, A., Daya-Grosjean, L., Margot, A. & Sarasin, A. (1985). Survival and mutagenesis of ultraviolet irradiated Simian virus 40 in foetal human fibroblasts. *Biochimie* **67**, 393–398.

Gentil, A., Margot, A. & Sarasin, A. (1982). Enhanced reactivation and mutagenesis after transfection of carcinogen-treated monkey cells with UV-irradiated simian virus 40 (SV40) DNA. *Biochimie* **64**, 693–696.

Gentil, A., Margot, A. & Sarasin, A. (1984). Apurinic sites cause mutations in simian virus 40. *Mutat. Res.* **129**, 141–147.

Guerrero, I., Willasante, A., Corces, V. & Pellicer, A. (1984). Activation of a c-K-*ras* oncogene by somatic mutation in mouse lymphomas induced by gamma radiation. *Science* **225**, 1159–1162.

GLUZMAN, Y. (1981). SV40-transformed simian cells support the replication of early SV40 mutants. *Cell* **23**, 175–182.

LEBKOWSKI, J. S., DuBRIDGE, R. B., ANTELLE, E. A., GREISEIN, K. S. & CALOS, M. P. (1984). Transfected DNA is mutated in monkey, mouse and human cells. *Molec. cell. Biol.* **4**, 1951–1960.

LITTLE, P. F. R., TREISMAN, R., BIERUT, L., SEED, B. & MANIATIS, T. (1983). Plasmid vectors for the rapid isolation and transcriptional analysis of human β-globin gene alleles. *Molec. Biol. Med.* **1**, 473–488.

RAZZAQUE, A., MIZUSAWA, H. & SEIDMAN, M. M. (1983). Rearrangement and mutagenesis of a shuttle vector plasmid after passage in mammalian cells. *Proc. natn. Acad. Sci. U.S.A.* **80**, 3010–3014.

SARASIN, A. (1985). SOS response in mammalian cells. *Cancer Invest.* **3**, 163–174.

SARASIN, A. & BENOIT, A. (1986). Error-prone replication of ultraviolet-irradiated simian virus 40 occurs in mitomycin *c*-treated host cells only at low multiplicity of infection. *Molec. cell. Biol.* **6**, 1102–1107.

SARASIN, A. & HANAWALT, P. C. (1978). Carcinogens enhance survival of UV-irradiated simian virus 40 in treated monkey kidney cells: induction of a recovery pathway. *Proc. natn. Acad. Sci. U.S.A.* **75**, 346–350.

SHAAPER, R. M. & LOEB, L. A. (1981). Depurination causes mutations in SOS-induced cells. *Proc. natn. Acad. Sci. U.S.A.* **78**, 1773–1777.

SMITH, K. & SARGENTINI, N. J. (1985). Metabolically-produced "UV-like" DNA damage and its role in spontaneous mutagenesis. *Photochem. Photobiol.* **42**, 801–803.

SUKUMAR, S., NOTARIO, V., MARTIN-ZANCA, O. & BARBACID, M. (1983). Induction of mammary carcinomas in rats by nitroso-methyl-urea involves malignant activation of H-*ras*-1 locus by single point mutations. *Nature, Lond.* **306**, 658–661.

THACKER, J. (1985). The molecular nature of mutations in cultured mammalian cells: a review. *Mutat. Res.* **150**, 431–442.

YATES, J. M., WARREN, N. & SUGDEN, B. (1985). Stable replication of plasmids derived from Epstein-Barr virus in various mammalian cells. *Nature, Lond.* **313**, 812–815.

J. Cell Sci. Suppl. 6, 333–353 (1987)
Printed in Great Britain © The Company of Biologists Limited 1987

THE ROLE OF O^6-METHYLGUANINE IN HUMAN CELL KILLING, SISTER CHROMATID EXCHANGE INDUCTION AND MUTAGENESIS: A REVIEW

RUFUS S. DAY, III

Molecular Genetics and Carcinogenesis Program, Department of Medicine, Cross Cancer Institute, Edmonton, Alberta, Canada T6G 1Z2

MICHAEL A. BABICH

Nucleic Acids Section, Laboratory of Molecular Carcinogenesis, DCE, NCI, NIH, Bethesda, Maryland 20892, USA

DANIEL B. YAROSH

Applied Genetics, Inc., 205 Buffalo Ave, Freeport, NY 11520, USA

AND DOMINIC A. SCUDIERO

Program Resources Incorporated, Frederick Cancer Research Facility, PO Box B, Frederick, MD 21701, USA

SUMMARY

O^6-methylguanine (O^6mG) produced in DNA by such SN1 methylating agents as N-methyl-N-nitrososurea and N-methyl-N'-nitro-N-nitrosoguanidine (MNNG) has been suggested by some to be the lesion that leads to certain biological endpoints in mammalian cells: cell killing, sister chromatid exchange (SCE) production, mutagenesis and cellular transformation. Other evidence is interpreted as inconsistent with this point of view. The finding of Karran & Williams (1985) that O^6mG delivered to cells in culture resulted in the depletion of the activity of the protein responsible for repair of O^6mG in DNA (O^6mG-DNA methyltransferase, O^6MT) provided a tool for the assessment of the role of O^6mG in producing biological endpoints. In this paper we review much of the literature on human cells pertinent to this question. In addition we present our survival data obtained using the depletion technique of Karran & Williams as well as data supporting a model invoking a mismatch and excision response to O^6mG proposed by Sklar & Strauss (1980). Although data linking O^6mG to causation are inconclusive, it is premature to conclude that O^6mG is not a lesion lethal to certain cultured cells.

INTRODUCTION

The ideal system: one base change/one lethal hit

It is important to know the identity of the DNA lesions that produce biological endpoints such as sister chromatid exchange (SCE) induction, mutation and loss of reproductive capacity, because this knowledge will lead to the experimental determination of the molecular mechanism by which these endpoints are caused. Identification of the initiating lesion is merely the first step. The fact that the production of about one pyrimidine dimer per genome correlated with the production of one 'lethal hit' in a population of *uvrA recA Escherichia coli* (Howard-Flanders & Boyce, 1966) demonstrated the possibility of assigning specific DNA lesions to the production of biological endpoints in genomes having of the order of

10^7 nucleotides. Bacteria that are wild-type with respect to repair contained 3700 dimers at one hit lethality (37 % survival). In *uvrA* mutants, unable to repair dimers, a lethal hit correlated with the production of roughly 50 dimers per genome and in *uvrA recA* mutants with 1·5 dimers per genome. It is likely that one to two dimers are lethal to *uvrA recA* mutants, but it is impossible to distinguish without further knowledge whether a dimer or another lesion, possibly a lesion produced 50-fold less frequently but repaired like a dimer, is the lesion lethal to *uvrA* mutants. We believe dimers are lethal to *uvrA* mutants for two reasons. The first is that photoreactivation, which reverses only dimers among known DNA photoproducts, reverses the lethal effects due to much of the ultraviolet light (u.v.) dose to *uvrA* mutants. The second is that restoring to the *uvrA* mutants the ability to remove dimers increases post-u.v. survival. (See Harm (1980) for review.) Eight years ago a spokesman from the DNA-repair community charged it with the responsibility of determining the biological effects of individual *lesions* rather than of DNA damaging *agents* (Cerutti, 1978). This has not proved to be an easy task.

Lesions due to methylating agents: strategies to determine their effects

We are concerned with considering the identity of the lesions that direct the biological changes in human cells treated with the DNA methylating agents MNNG (*N*-methyl-*N'*-nitro-*N*-nitrosoguanidine) and MNU (*N*-methyl-*N*-nitrosourea). The genome size of human cells is about 2 m, 2000 times that of *E. coli*, but the basic considerations are the same as used for *E. coli*. We find mutants that are unable to repair given lesions and determine what differences in methylation-produced biological phenomena occur; or we produce changes in the number of one kind of lesion and observe the corresponding changes in biological effects. If we find cases in which there are fewer than one of a given lesion per genome but more than one biological event per biological unit, that lesion is unlikely to have caused the effect.

MNNG or MNU produce many alterations in DNA components, methylating nitrogen and oxygen atoms (Fig. 1). MMS produces 25-fold less O^6-methylguanine (O^6mG). Comparing biological responses after treatment with MMS with those obtained after treatment with MNNG or MNU can thus give information regarding the relative roles of methylated nitrogens and methylated oxygens in producing the effects.

Recognition of O^6-methylguanine: altered base pairing

The question of the biological effects due to O^6mG begins with the paper of Loveless (1969), who when reporting the discovery of O^6mG in DNA treated with *N*-methyl-*N*-nitrosourea pointed to the expected 'atypical base pairing' properties of O^6mG as a possible explanation of the high mutagenicity and carcinogenicity of compounds like MNU (Fig. 2). Overall, pairing of O^6mG with thymine appears better than pairing of O^6mG with cytosine. The question is whether and in what ways the cell is able to recognize such mispairing in DNA. The presence of misrepaired O^6mG might be monitored during DNA replication, or there might be a mismatch repair system involved in O^6mG recognition. (For a short review, see Discussion.)

Alkylation of DNA sites by MNNG and MMS

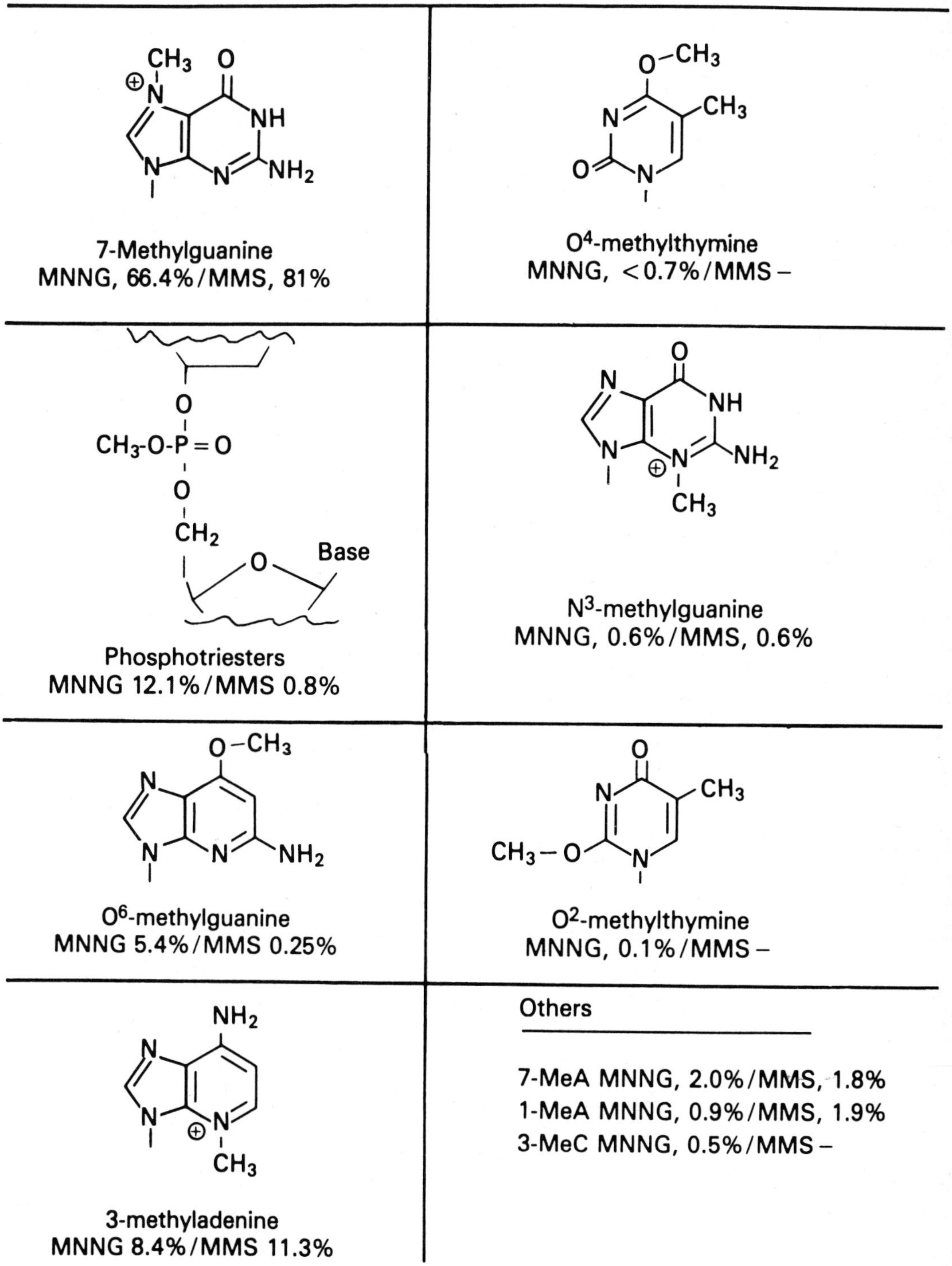

7-Methylguanine
MNNG, 66.4% / MMS, 81%

O^4-methylthymine
MNNG, < 0.7% / MMS −

Phosphotriesters
MNNG 12.1% / MMS 0.8%

N^3-methylguanine
MNNG, 0.6% / MMS, 0.6%

O^6-methylguanine
MNNG 5.4% / MMS 0.25%

O^2-methylthymine
MNNG, 0.1% / MMS −

3-methyladenine
MNNG 8.4% / MMS 11.3%

Others

7-MeA MNNG, 2.0% / MMS, 1.8%
1-MeA MNNG, 0.9% / MMS, 1.9%
3-MeC MNNG, 0.5% / MMS −

Fig. 1. Products of the reaction of MNNG or MMS with DNA. (From Beranek *et al.* 1980; see also Lawley & Thatcher, 1970; Swenson & Lawley, 1978.)

RESULTS

A lesion having a methylated oxygen is lethal to adenovirus when infecting cells deficient in repair of O⁶mG

MNNG-treated adenoviruses show greater survival when infecting cells of some lines (defined as Mer$^+$) than when infecting cells of others (Mer$^-$; and the differential survival correlates with an ability or inability of the cells to repair O^6mG in DNA; such ability or inability is defined as Mex$^+$ or Mex$^-$, respectively) (Day *et al.* 1980*b*; Sklar & Strauss, 1981; Watatani *et al.* 1985). A similar differential inactivation is seen with adenoviruses treated with MNU (Day *et al.* 1980*a*) or

Base-pairing properties of
guanine and *O⁶*-methylguanine

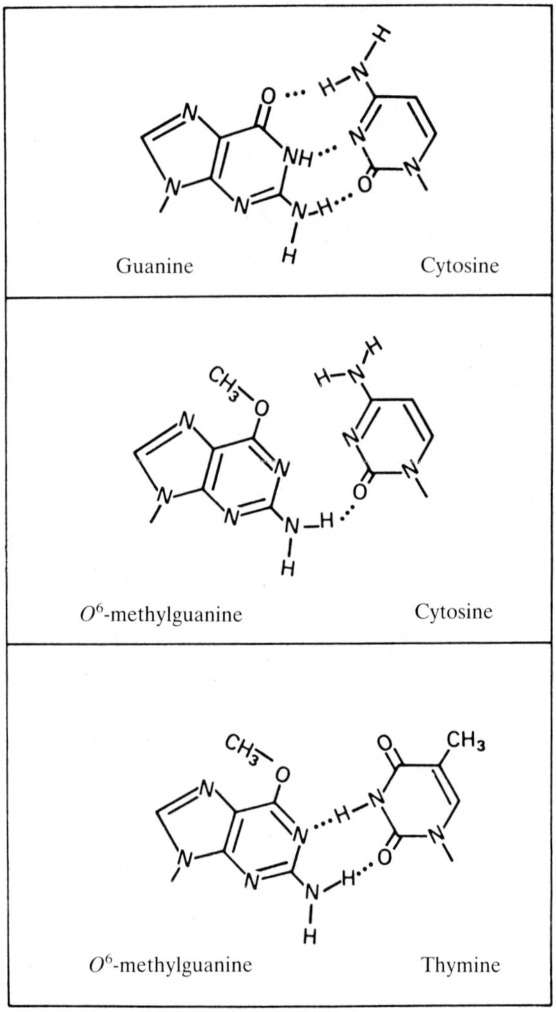

Fig. 2. Base pairing of guanine with cytosine and of O^6-methylguanine with cytosine and thymine. (Based on discussion by Loveless, 1969).

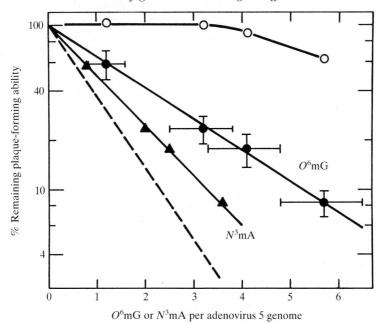

Fig. 3. Survival of [³H]MNNG treated adenovirus 5 as a function of O^6-methylguanines (○, ●) or 3-methyladenines (▲) produced per viral genome. (●) and (○): respectively, survival as measured in strains incapable and capable of repairing O^6mG in their DNA; (–––) the survival expected if one methylated purine per genome were lethal.

MTIC (5-(3′-methyl-1-triazeno)imidazole-4-carboximide (Hayward & Parsons, 1984). By contrast, adenoviruses treated with MMS show a survival independent of the ability of the cells infected to repair O^6mG (Scudiero *et al.* 1984*b*). It would therefore seem likely that a lesion produced by MNNG, but not by MMS, is a lesion lethal to the virus. The lesion would be repaired by a mechanism lacking in Mer⁻ strains, possibly similar to that which repairs O^6mG. It was determined that one lethal hit to the virus population correlates with the production of 2·3 O^6mG, 1·4 3mA, 16 7mG, and about 5 methyl phosphotriesters per viral genome (Fig. 3; and Day *et al.* 1984). All other lesions as O^4mT, O^2mT, 3mG and 7mA are too few to be present at one/genome for one lethal hit per virion. 3mA is repaired both by cells able and by cells unable to repair O^6mG (Day *et al.* 1984). 7mG (Day *et al.* 1980*a*, 1984) and methyl phosphotriesters (Yarosh *et al.* 1985) appear to be repaired slowly or not at all and independently of the ability of the cell to repair O^6mG. Thus, if one were pressed for an answer, one would guess that O^6mG is the lesion lethal to adenovirus infecting cells deficient in ability to repair O^6mG.

Consideration of O^6mG as a lesion lethal to cells

Scudiero *et al.* (1984*a*) studied inactivation by MNNG of 23 human cell strains prepared from normal and tumorous human tissue. Their sensitivities, assayed by cell killing, correlated with their ability to repair O^6mG. Sensitivities fell into one of three groups (Fig. 4). The first group showed proficient repair of MNNG-treated adenovirus (Mer⁺), repaired O^6mG in their DNA (Mex⁺) and had cell killing sensitivities in the range of normal human fibroblasts (Rem$^+$; Scudiero, 1980; Scudiero *et al.* 1981). Strains belonging to the second group were also able to repair MNNG-treated adenoviruses (Mer$^+$), but repaired O^6mG (and so are Mex$^+$) but less than the first, and showed three- to fourfold more sensitivity to MNNG killing (Rem$^-$). The third group (most sensitive to killing by MNNG, Rem$^-$) showed lack of ability to repair MNNG-treated adenoviruses (Mer$^-$) and inability to repair O^6mG (Mex$^-$). Sensitivities ranged from 0·19 lethal hits per μM-MNNG in an osteosarcoma cell line to 18·0 hits per μM-MNNG for an ovarian cancer line, approximately 100-fold more sensitive to killing. As a group, the Mer$^-$ Rem$^-$ strains were 20-fold, and Mer$^+$ Rem$^-$ strains threefold, more sensitive to killing than was the Mer$^+$ Rem$^+$ group. Thus a good correlation between O^6mG repair and sensitivity to MNNG was established. Evidence along similar lines was published by Day *et al.* (1980*b*) and by Domoradski *et al.* (1984).

Scudiero *et al.* (1984*b*) studied many of the same strains in an attempt to understand the mode of cell killing by other chemical agents, methylmethane

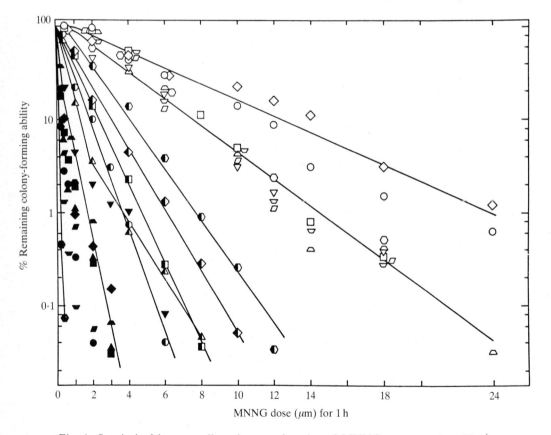

Fig. 4. Survival of human cell strains as a function of MNNG concentration. Mer$^+$ Rem$^+$ strains: (○) KD; (△) HT29; (◇) TE85; (□) HuTu80; (▽) A673; (▽) U138MG; (◑) U373MG; (▱) A427F; (△) CRL 1187. Mer$^+$ Rem$^-$ strains: (◐) A2182; (◆) A704; (◧) A549; (▲) A498; (◓) A388. Mer$^-$ Rem$^-$ strains: (●) A172; (▲) A1235; (▼) U105MG; (◆) U87MG; (■) A2095; (◉) A1336; (◢), A875; (◤) A427; (▰) BE.

sulphonate (MMS), 1,3-bis-(2-chloroethyl)-1-nitrosourea (BCNU), 1-(2-chloro-ethyl)-3-(2-hydroxyethyl)-1-nitrosourea (HECNU) and N-ethyl-N'-nitro-N-nitro-soguanidine (ENNG) (Fig. 5). With MMS, which produces primarily 7mG and 3mA in DNA, there is less of a range of cell killing than with MNNG. On average the strains deficient in O^6mG repair were about two to four times more sensitive to MMS killing than the repair-proficient ones. MMS produces about 25-fold less O^6mG than does MNNG (Lawley *et al.* 1975) or MNU (Beranek *et al.* 1980) relative to total methylated DNA adducts produced. The different sensitivities of the strains to inactivation by MNNG and MMS are therefore consistent with a heightened lethality of O^6mG in Mer$^-$ cells. Sensitivities of the strains to inactivation by MNNG and MMS would be understood.

Events other than DNA methylation in treated cells should be mentioned. We are assuming that it is *DNA* alteration by MNNG, MNU or MMS that produces the lesions lethal to cells. This is a reasonable assumption because in the field of DNA repair, DNA-repair defects, not other defects, have been identified in cells abnormally sensitive to DNA damaging treatments. However, it is known that MNNG and MNU methylate primarily the lysines and arginines of cellular nuclear proteins, whereas MMS methylates cysteine and histidine preferentially (Boffa & Bolognesi, 1985*a,b*), so that methylation of protein could conceivably contribute to the differential lethal effects of MMS and MNNG. Because this would appear to be a less-attractive possibility, very little work has been done in this area. In addition, glutathione depletion due to MNNG-activation (Lawley & Thatcher, 1970; Sedgwick & Robins, 1980) may be important in the cellular response to that agent.

Mer$^-$ Rem$^+$ strains: fly in the 'O^6intment' or proof of the pudding?

It was shown that transformation of apparently normal Mer$^+$ Mex$^+$ fibroblasts by simian virus 40 (SV40) often results in the production of Mer$^-$ Mex$^-$ transformed cell lines (Day *et al.* 1980). Indeed 8 of 12 SV40-transformed cell lines have now been shown to be Mer$^-$ in our laboratory. The response of these Mer$^-$ lines to cell killing by MNNG is greatly *different* from that expected on the basis of the extreme sensitivity shown by Mer$^-$ human tumour lines (Day *et al.* 1980; Scudiero & Day, unpublished results). The Mer$^-$ SV40-transformed lines are as resistant to killing by MNNG as are both Mer$^+$ SV40-transformed lines (Fig. 6) and normal human fibroblasts, and are therefore called Mer$^-$ Rem$^+$. Although these strains are resistant to killing by MNNG, we believe that other assays may reflect their inability to repair methylated-oxygen lesions in DNA: (1) they fail to repair MNNG-damaged adenovirus (Day *et al.* 1980*b*); (2) they show as sensitive induction of SCE due to MNNG treatment as seen in the tumour Mer$^-$ cell lines (Day *et al.* 1980*b*; (3) they are as hypersensitive to killing by HECNU as are the tumour Mer$^-$ lines (Scudiero *et al.* 1984*b*); (4) they are hypermutable by MNNG compared with a Mer$^+$ SV40-transformed line (Baker *et al.* 1980; these authors were using cells differing in repair of O^6mG, see Day *et al.* 1980*b*).

Thus, if O^6mG is a lesion lethal to the tumour Mer$^-$ lines, it is certainly not a lesion lethal to the SV40-derived Mer$^-$ lines. And one could certainly remain within

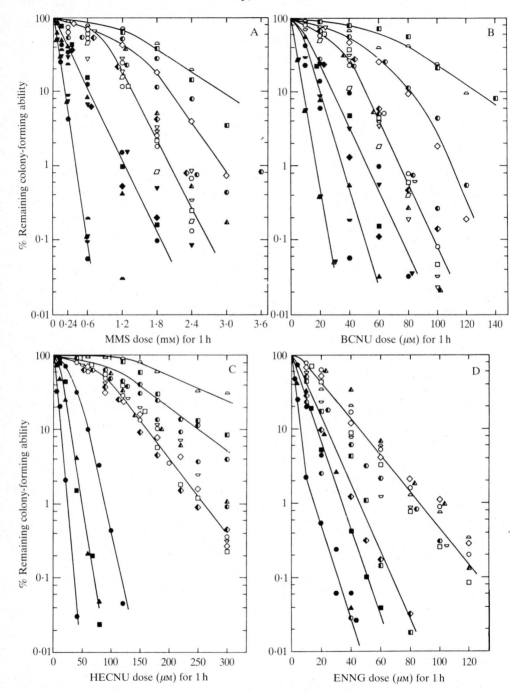

Fig. 5. Survival of human fibroblasts and tumour cell strains after treatment with MMS (A), BCNU (B), HECNU (C), ENNG (D), MNNG (E) or u.v. (F). Cells were treated and assayed for remaining colony-forming ability. Symbols are the same as for Fig. 4.

the guidelines drawn by the data should one propose that O^6mG is not a lethal lesion at all. The most direct rationale for this is that two groups of cell lines (Mer$^-$ Rem$^+$, Mer$^-$ Rem$^-$), showing widely different cellular sensitivities to MNNG killing, both fail to repair O^6mG. Therefore, how could O^6mG be implicated in lethality? It is more difficult to build a good argument against the involvement of an alkylated DNA oxygen in MNNG-produced SCE formation and mutagenesis, and in HECNU-produced cell killing. In these endpoints, lines that fail to repair O^6mG are uniformly hypersensitive, independently of their sensitivity to MNNG-produced cell killing. We know that Mer$^-$ cells lack repair of O^6mG. It is possible that they all lack another repair mechanism, e.g. for 3mG, 3mA or another methylated DNA nitrogen. Were this the case, MNNG and MMS would be expected to cause the same magnitude of differential response in Mer$^+$ and Mer$^-$ cells. For adenovirus inactivation this is not the case (Scudiero *et al.* 1984*b*). MNNG produced many more SCE than did MMS in Mer$^-$ than in Mer$^+$ lines (Wolff *et al.* 1977; the lines used were later identified as Mer$^-$ and Mer$^+$; Day *et al.* 1980). We are not, however, aware of a study comparing MMS and MNNG with regard to mutagenesis of human cells. Certainly, there is among human cells a correlation between ability to repair O^6mG and resistance to MNNG-induced mutagenesis (Baker *et al.* 1979, 1980; the cells used were Mer$^-$ and Mer$^+$; see Day *et al.* 1980*b*; Domoradski *et al.* 1984).

In summary, the very existence of MNNG-resistant lines that lack repair of O^6mG casts considerable doubt as to the role of oxygen-methylated DNA bases in lethality to Mer$^-$ Rem$^+$ cells. On the other hand, these lines have sensitivities much like MNNG-sensitive O^6mG repair-deficient (Mer$^-$ Rem$^-$) lines in terms of repair of

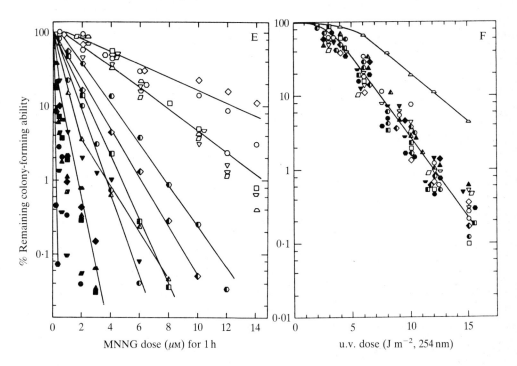

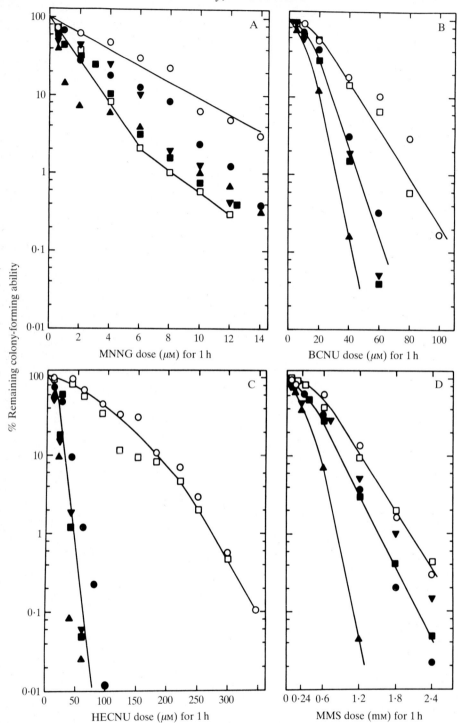

Fig. 6. Survival of SV40-transformed human fibroblast lines after alkylation treatment. Mer⁺ strains: (○) W98VA1; (□) WI26VA4. Mer⁻ strains: (●) W18VA2; (▲) GM638; (▼) IMR90-830; (■) WI38VA13.

methyl-damaged virus, susceptibility to MNNG-produced SCE and mutations, and to killing by HECNU. This latter encourages the idea that O^6mG (or another lesion both repaired by a mechanism lacking in Mer$^-$ cells and produced by agents that produce O^6mG) leads to these endpoints.

Depletion of O^6mG-DNA methyltransferase by free O^6mG: the ultimate test?

If one were able to alter cellular repair of O^6mG in DNA preferentially over other lesions, one would have a very good tool for determining the effects due to O^6mG in DNA. Karran (1985) and Karran & Williams (1985) found that free O^6mG, when delivered in culture to cells proficient in repair of O^6mG, would result in the depletion of O^6MT (O^6mG-DNA methyltransferase), the protein responsible for repairing O^6mG in Mer$^+$ cells and absent from Mer$^-$ cells (Yarosh et al. 1983, 1984). This finding provided a tool for reducing cellular capacity to repair O^6mG in a presumably selective fashion. Karran & Williams (1985) reported that depletion of O^6MT by 0·1 mM free O^6mG failed to sensitize Mex$^+$ Raji cells to inactivation either by MNNG or by CNU (1-(2-chloroethyl)-1-nitrosourea). Were all O^6MT activity fully depleted during the period when DNA lesions produced by MNNG became lethal, then the conclusion of the authors, i.e. that O^6mG in DNA has nothing to do with cell killing by either agent, would be correct. However, Dolan et al. (1985b) showed that a greater dose of O^6mG (0·4 mM) sensitized HeLa cells to killing by CNU in a major way, and to killing by MNNG in a minor way. Mutagenesis due to MNNG treatment of human fibroblasts was enhanced somewhat by a pretreatment with 0·4 mM-O^6mG (Domoradski et al. 1985). Our own results, obtained with a 2 mM-O^6mG pretreatment (Fig. 7) are consistent with those of Dolan et al. (1985b). As a control, we detect little sensitizing effect of the pretreatment on the killing of Mer$^-$ cells by CNU. This would be expected if a lesion not repaired by Mer$^-$ cells were the lesion whose lethality was enhanced by the O^6mG pretreatment. We have found that protein fractions containing O^6MT activity had little if any capacity to repair methylphosphotriesters or O^4mT in DNA (Yarosh et al. 1985) so it is unlikely that depletion of O^6MT alters repair of these lesions. Thus, the O-4 position of Thy and DNA phosphate can in all likelihood be excluded from consideration as target sites for lethality of CNU.

We do not detect a great sensitization by free O^6mG of Mer$^+$ cells to killing by MNNG (Fig. 8). However, treatment of HT29 cells with even 2 mM-O^6mG fails to block completely the repair of O^6mG produced in HT29 DNA by a 1-h treatment of cells with 12·5 µM-MNNG (Fig. 9). Therefore, significant recovery of the cells due to repair of O^6mG in DNA is expected. We agree with the explanation of Dolan et al. (1985a) that accounts for the difference between sensitization to CNU and to MNNG. In the case of CNU, if O^6-choroethylguanine is not repaired rapidly, DNA crosslinks that are not repairable by O^6MT would accumulate within hours (Kohn, 1977) (see Fig. 10; for discussion of repair of O^6-haloethylguanine adducts and the DNA crosslinks they produce, see Scudiero et al. (1984b).) The lethal lesions, the DNA crosslinks (Sasaki (1977) has shown that crosslinking agents are five- to tenfold more lethal than their non-crosslinking congeners), would become fixed. In the case

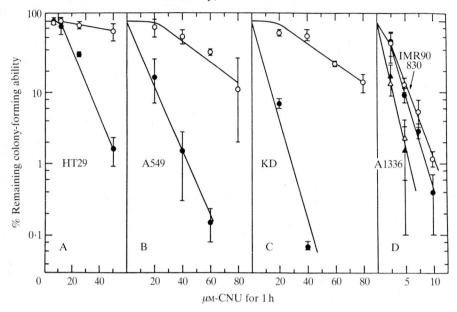

Fig. 7. Survival of Mer⁺ (HT29, A549, KD) and Mer⁻ (A1336, IMR90-830) strains with (filled symbols) and without (open symbols) a 3-h pretreatment with O^6mG just prior to a 1-h treatment with CNU.

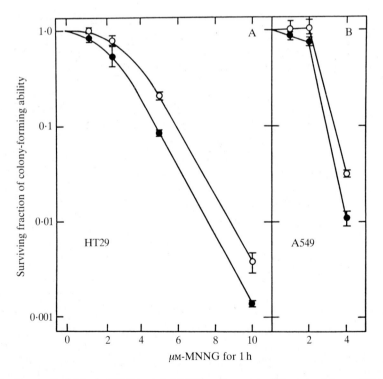

Fig. 8. Survival of Mer⁺ (HT29 and A549) strains with (●) and without (○) a 3-h pretreatment with O^6mG just prior to a 1-h treatment with MNNG.

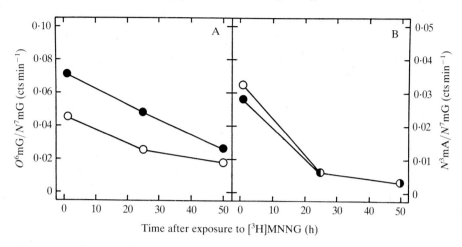

Fig. 9. Persistence of O^6mG and 3mA (relative to 7mG) in HT29 cells that were treated for 1 h with $12\cdot5\,\mu$M-[methyl-^{3}H]MNNG just after a 3-h pretreatment with 2 mM-O^6mG (●) or after a mock pretreatment (○). A, O^6mG; B, 3mA.

Possible reactions of BCNU and HECNU with
DNA and repair of adducts formed

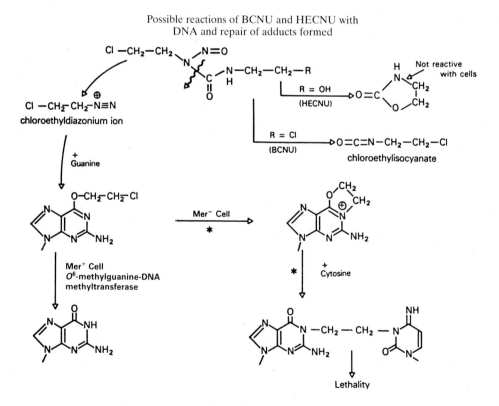

Fig. 10. Reaction of chloroethylating nitrosoureas with guanine in DNA: crosslink formation in Mer⁻ cells; and repair by Mer⁺ cells. For reactivity of chloroethylisocyanate see Kann et al. (1974). For crosslink formation by chloroethylating agents by the pathways marked by the *, see Tong et al. (1982).

of MNNG, where little sensitization due to depletion with O^6mG occurs, DNA lesions relevant to survival would be repairable over a longer time before their lethality becomes fixed. Several experimental results would be expected according to this hypothesis: (1) Mer$^-$ Rem$^+$ strains, to which we do not believe O^6mG should be lethal, should not be sensitized at all to killing by MNNG by the free O^6mG treatment; and (2) cells whose O^6MT is depleted by free O^6mG prior to MNNG treatment, and which are thereby sensitized somewhat to MNNG killing, should be sensitized further by a post-MNNG treatment with free O^6mG. However, O^6mG may not be lethal. O^4mT, O^2mC and O^2mT are repairable lesions (Den Engelse *et al.* 1986), and these are logical candidates for being lesions lethal to Mer$^-$ Rem$^-$ cells. It is conceivable that O^6mG could be excised from DNA. Such removal would not be likely to be blocked by the free base O^6mG so that sensitization of colony-forming ability by free O^6mG would not be observed. If O^6mG were excised from DNA, Mer$^-$ cells would have to lack the excision process as well as O^6MT because there is no loss of O^6mG from MNNG-treated Mer$^-$ cells.

The depletion of O^6MT produced by treating cells with the free base O^6mG sensitizes cells much more to killing by CNU than to killing by MNNG. Although both results can be understood in terms of O^6mG (or related lesion) as lethal, explanations based on the lethality of other lesions are not excluded.

Increased DNA repair synthesis in Mer$^-$ strains: a key to the lethal lesion?

Because of its altered base pairing, it is not difficult to imagine why O^6mG might be mutagenic. It is far more difficult to divine the mechanism by which O^6mG might be lethal. We suspect that a type of mismatch repair operating improperly on the O^6mG:C mismatch may trigger lethality.

Altamirano-Dimas *et al.* (1979), Day *et al.* (1980*a*) and Scudiero *et al.* (1984*a*) have shown that MNNG-treated Mer$^-$ (Mex$^-$) and Mer$^+$ Rem$^-$ strains show more incorporation of [^{3}H]dThd into double-stranded DNA than do MNNG-treated Mex$^+$ strains. Together with the fact that this damage-stimulated incorporation (DNA repair synthesis) was less with MMS (Altamirano-Dimas *et al.* 1979), the evidence points to a DNA lesion methylated at oxygen as causing the increase. Mer$^-$ Mex$^-$ strains show no removal of the O^6mG produced in their DNA. Were O^6mG the lesion triggering increased DNA repair synthesis it would not, therefore, be reasonable to suppose that the increased DNA repair synthesis is associated with removal of the DNA lesion, as in the case of removal of pyrimidine dimers from the DNA of u.v.-irradiated normal fibroblasts (Cleaver, 1968). However, repair may occur in the strand opposite the lesion (Sklar & Strauss, 1980), in which case either dCMP or dTMP might be incorporated opposite O^6mG. Because neither Cyt nor Thy pairs exceptionally well with O^6mG (see Discussion) a recognizable mismatch might still exist. The mismatch would continue to stimulate incorporation of dTMP into the DNA of Mer$^-$ cells (Fig. 11), whereas Mer$^+$ cells would be expected to cease repair DNA synthesis once the lesions were removed by O^6MT. The results of an experiment in which cells were treated with 40 μg ml^{-1} MNNG for 1 h and incubated with [^{3}H]dThd (in the presence of hydroxyurea to block semiconservative DNA synthesis) for 1-h periods are shown in Fig. 12. The A172 and A427 strains (both Mer⁻ Rem⁻) show such an effect as does the A549 strain (Mer⁺ Rem⁻; the O^6MT is severely depleted at this MNNG dose; Scudiero *et al.* 1984*a*). Further experiments need to be done.

DISCUSSION

Lethal lesions: cell and virus

We have seen that the group of MNNG-produced lesions possibly lethal to cells that fail to repair O^6mG is narrowed to those lesions not made in any great quantity by MMS, i.e. almost certainly to lesions containing methylated oxygen. O^6mG is very probably the lesion lethal to MNNG-treated adenovirus infecting cells incapable of repairing O^6mG, encouraging the idea that O^6mG can be lethal. In addition CNU or HECNU, both chloroethylating agents believed to produce crosslinks in DNA through an O^6-chloroethylguanine intermediate, probably produce lethal lesions primarily by attacking the O-6 of guanine.

Methylated DNA components leading to SCE and mutations

The lesion responsible for the production of SCE and mutagenesis is one that is repaired by neither Mer⁻ Rem⁻ nor Mer⁻ Rem⁺ strains. It may be O^6mG or another

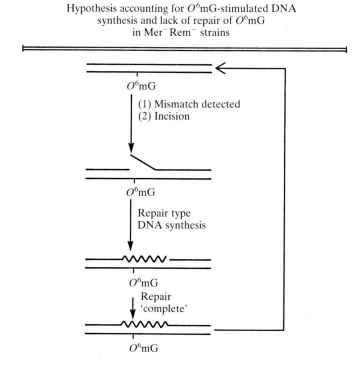

Hypothesis accounting for O^6mG-stimulated DNA
synthesis and lack of repair of O^6mG
in Mer⁻Rem⁻ strains

Fig. 11. Scheme to account for increased MNNG-induced incorporation of [³H]dThd into double-stranded DNA by Mer⁻ compared with Mer⁺ cells after MNNG treatment.

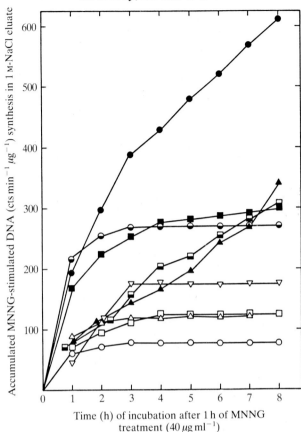

Fig. 12. Accumulated MNNG-stimulated DNA synthesis in double-stranded DNA as a function of post-MNNG incubation time. Cells were blocked in DNA synthesis by 10 mM-hydroxyurea (HU) for 30 min, then treated from 0–1 h with 40 μg ml^{-1} MNNG and 10 mM-HU. At 1 h, the medium was removed and replaced with medium containing 10 mM-HU. During the 1-h prior to a data point the cells were exposed to the same medium, but containing 5 μCi ml^{-1} [^{3}H]dThd in order to label repaired regions of DNA. Separation of double-stranded DNA from DNA with single strands was done by BND-cellulose chromatography. (See Day *et al.* 1980*a*; Scudiero *et al.* 1984*b*, for details.) Cell strains: Mer$^+$ Rem$^+$: (○) KD; (△) CRL 1187; (▽) U138MG; (□) TE85. Mer$^+$ Rem$^-$: (◑) A388; (◨) A549. Mer$^-$ Rem$^-$: (●) A172; (▲) A427N; (■) A1235.

lesion that is not lethal to Mer$^-$ Rem$^-$ strains. In the case of production of SCE, the lesion appears not to be produced by MMS. In the case of mutagenesis of human cells, comparative data obtained with MMS are not available to these authors' knowledge. (They would certainly like to be informed if there is.) Were O^6mG again considered to be the mutagenic lesion, the available data would be accommodated, including the increase in mutability seen after O^6MT depletion (Domoradski *et al.* 1985).

O^6mG in DNA is detected by cells: polymerases and mismatch recognition

In this section we consider the known ways in which *in vitro* or *in vivo* systems are known to respond to O^6mG to provide a basis for the hypothesis in Fig. 11.

Polymerases. Using synthetic templates with DNA polymerase I from bacteriophages T4 and T5, and *E. coli*, Snow *et al*. (1984) found that O^6mG in template DNA directed the *in vitro* incorporation of dTMP in preference to dCMP by ratios of 6 (T4), 10 (T5) and 100 (*E. coli*). O^6mG in the template slowed down but did not terminate incorporation. Stronger preference for TMP incorporation was accompanied by a high turnover ratio (dNMP released per dNMP incorporated). Blocks to DNA synthesis introduced by MNNG into DNA used as an *in vitro* template for primed synthesis by the polymerase I Klenow fragment occurred most frequently before the positions of Ade residues (Larson *et al*. 1985), indicating no particular tendency for O^6mG to cause chain termination. There are conflicting reports concerning the ability of *polA* mutants of *E. coli* (which lack polymerase I) to repair O^6mG in DNA (Warren & Lawley, 1980; Karran *et al*. 1982), but it appears that *polA* mutants do not show the adaptive response (Samson & Cairns, 1977) to the lethal effects of alkylating agents (Jeggo *et al*. 1977, 1978), indicating involvement of polymerase I in this response.

Mismatch repair. One mismatch repair mechanism in *E. coli* is believed to work on newly replicated DNA. Mismatches are detected, and the daughter strand, distinguished from the m6Ade-methylated parental strand by its lack of m6Ade, is repaired. The m6Ade-methylated parental strand is used as a template, and replacement of DNA occurs over a stretch of some 3000 nucleotides (Wagner & Meselson, 1976).

A site-specific mismatch repair mechanism that restores CC(A/C)GG sequences in phage lambda operates over a shorter distance (roughly 5–10 base pairs) and is independent of *dam*-dependent Ade (or *dcm*-dependent Cyt) methylation (Lieb, 1985). A similar but not identical system operates in *Streptococcus pneumoniae* (Lacks *et al*. 1982; Lefevre *et al*. 1984).

On the basis of their data on MNNG-induced multiple site mutations in *E. coli*, Sklar & Strauss (1980) suggested that the *uvrE* product may be involved in correction of a mismatch between an O^6mG (parental strand) paired with a Cyt (daugher strand) near the replication fork. The resolution of the mismatch would, however, not be repair, but error production: the removal of Cyt and replacement with Thy. *E. coli dam* mutants are sensitive to MNNG (but not dimethylsulphate, DMS)-produced killing, and this sensitivity was suppressed by *mutL* or *mutS*, indicating involvement of a mismatch-triggered response in determining resistance to a lesion made by MNNG but not by DMS, presumably a lesion having a methylated oxygen (Karren & Marinus, 1982). Eadie *et al*. (1984) used the polymerase I Klenow fragment to incorporate O^6mG during *in vitro* DNA synthesis across from a single-stranded bacteriophage f1/pBR322 based *Amp*$^+$ vector used as template. *Amp*$^-$ mutants were produced when transfecting the double-stranded product into *E. coli mutH* deficient in mismatch repair, or when the replicated vector was methylated with *dam* methylase (removing the signal triggering mismatch repair) prior to transfection of cells competent to repair mismatches. Such mutants were not observed on transfection of repair-proficient hosts. Solely A·T to G·C transitions were observed as expected if O^6mGMP had been incorporated across from Thy. Apparently mismatch repair processes resulted in the loss of mutant molecules of the vector. In summary, O^6mG in DNA is a lesion that slows but does not block DNA replication. Its presence in DNA is detected by mismatch repair systems in *E. coli*. It would not be surprising if mammalian cells responded similarly because these also may carry mismatch repair systems (Lai & Nathans, 1975; Miller *et al.* 1976; Wake & Wilson, 1980; Folger *et al.* 1985). Hare & Taylor (1985) provided evidence that the strand selection mechanism may be 5mCyt methylation of the parental strand and/or proximity to a nick. The involvement of mismatch recognition in leading to loss of genetic material has been supported in bacterial transformation systems (see Day & Rupert, 1971). Such an event could be lethal.

REFERENCES

ALTAMIRANO-DIMAS, M., SKLAR, R. & STRAUSS, B. (1979). Selectivity of the excision of alkylation products in a xeroderma pigmentosum-derived lymphoblastoid line. *Mutat. Res.* **60**, 197–206.

BAKER, R. M., VAN VOORHIS, W. C. & SPENCER, L. A. (1979). HeLa cell variants that differ in sensitivity to monofunctional alkylating agents, with independence of cytotoxic and mutagenic responses. *Proc. natn. Acad. Sci. U.S.A.* **76**, 5249–5253.

BAKER, R. M., ZUERNODORFER, G. & MANDEL, R. (1980). Enhanced susceptibility of a xeroderma pigmentosum cell line to mutagenesis by MNNG and EMS. *Environ. Mutagen.* **2**, 269–270.

BERANEK, D. T., WEIS, C. C. & SWENSON, D. H. (1980). A comprehensive quantitative analysis of methylated and ethylated DNA using high pressure liquid chromatography. *Carcinogenesis* **1**, 595–606.

BOFFA, L. C. & BOLOGNESI, C. (1985a). Nuclear proteins damaged by alkylating agents wtih different degrees of carcinogenicity. *Chem.-Biol. Interact.* **55**, 235–245.

BOFFA, L. C. & BOLOGNESI, C. (1985b). Methylating agents: their target amino acids in nuclear proteins. *Carcinogenesis* **6**, 1399–1401.

CERUTTI, P. A. (1978). Repairable damage in DNA. In *DNA Repair Mechanisms* (ed. P. C. Hanawalt, E. C. Friedberg & C. F. Fox), pp. 1–14. New York, London: Academic Press.

CLEAVER, J. E. (1968). Defective repair replication of DNA in xeroderma pigmentosum. *Nature, Lond.* **218**, 652–656.

DAY, R. S. III & RUPERT, C. S. (1971). Ultraviolet sensitivity of *Haemophilus influenzae* transforming DNA. I. Effects of genetic mismatch and target size. *Mutat. Res.* **11**, 293–311.

DAY, R. S. III, YAROSH, D. B. & ZIOLKOWSKI, C. H. J. (1984). Relationship of methyl purines produced by MNNG in adenovirus 5 DNA to viral inactivation in repair-deficient (Mer⁻) human tumor cell strains. *Mutat. Res.* **131**, 45–52.

DAY, R. S. III, ZIOLKOWSKI, C. H. J., SCUDIERO, D. A., MEYER, S. A., LUBINIECKI, A. H. J., GIRARDI, A. J., GALLOWAY, S. M. & BYNUM, G. D. (1980a). Defective repair of alkylated DNA by human tumour and SV40-transformed human cell strains. *Nature, Lond.* **288**, 724–727.

DAY, R. S. III, ZIOLKOWSKI, C. H. J., SCUDIERO, D. A., MEYER, S. A. & MATTERN, M. A. (1980b). Human tumor cell strains defective in the repair of alkylation damage. *Carcinogenesis* **1**, 21–32.

DEN ENGELSE, L., MENKVELD, G. J., DE BRIJ, R.-J. & TATES, A. D. (1986). Formation and stability of alkylated pyrimidines and purines (including imidazole ring-opened 7-alkylguanine) and alkylphosphotriesters in liver DNA of adult rats treated with ethylnitrosourea or dimethylnitrosamine. *Carcinogenesis* **7**, 393–403.

DOLAN, M. E., CORSICO, C. D. & PEGG, A. E. (1985b). Exposure of HeLa cells to O(6)-alkylguanines increases sensitivity to the cytotoxic effects of alkylating agents. *Biochem. biophys. Res. Commun.* **132**, 178–185.

DOLAN, M. E., MORIMOTO, K. & PEGG, A. E. (1985a). Reduction of O^6-alkylguanine-DNA alkyltransferase activity in HeLa cells treated with O^6-alkylguanines. *Cancer Res.* **45**, 6413–6417.

DOMORADSKI, J., PEGG, A. E., DOLAN, M. E., MAHER, V. M. & McCORMICK, J. J. (1984). Correlation between O6-methylguanine-DNA-methyltransferase activity and resistance to the cytotoxic and mutagenic effect of N-methyl-N'-nitro-N-nitrosoguanidine. *Carcinogenesis* **5**, 1641–1647.

DOMORADSKI, J., PEGG, A. E., DOLAN, M. E., MAHER, V. M. & McCORMICK, J. J. (1985). Depletion of O^6-methylguanine-DNA-methyltransferase in human fibroblasts increases the mutagenic response to N-methyl-N'-nitro-N-nitrosoguanidine. *Carcinogenesis* **6**, 1823–1826.

EADIE, J. S., CONRAD, M., TOORCHEN, D. & TOPAL, M. D. (1984). Mechanism of mutagenesis by O^6-methylguanine. *Nature, Lond.* **308**, 201–203.

FOLGER, K. R., THOMAS, K. & CAPECCHI, M. R. (1985). Efficient correction of mismatched bases in plasmid heteroduplexes injected into cultured mammalian cells. *Molec. cell. Biol.* **5**, 70–74.

HARE, J. T. & TAYLOR, J. H. (1985). One role for DNA methylation in vertebrate cells is strand discrimination in mismatch repair. *Proc. natn. Acad. Sci. U.S.A.* **82**, 7350–7354.

HARM, W. (1980). *Biological Effects of Ultraviolet Irradiation.* Cambridge, New York: Cambridge University Press.

HAYWARD, I. P. & PARSONS, P. G. (1984). Comparison of virus reactivation, DNA base damage, and cell cycle effects in autologous human melanoma cells resistant to methylating agents. *Cancer Res.* **44**, 55–58.

HOWARD-FLANDERS, P. & BOYCE, R. P. (1966). DNA repair and genetic recombination: studies on mutants of *Escherichia coli* defective in these processes. *Radiat. Res. Suppl.* **8**, 156–184.

JEGGO, P., DEFAIS, M., SAMSON, L. & SCHENDEL, P. (1977). An adaptive response of *E. coli* to low levels of alkylating agent: comparison with previously characterized DNA repair pathways. *Molec. gen. Genet.* **157**, 1–9.

JEGGO, P., DEFAIS, M., SANSOM, L. & SCHENDEL, P. (1978). The adaptive response of *E. coli* to low levels of alkylating agent: the role of *polA* in killing adaptation. *Molec. gen. Genet.* **162**, 299–305.

KANN, H. E., KOHN, K. W. & LYLES, J. M. (1974). Inhibition of DNA repair by the 1,3-bis(2-chloroethyl)-1-nitrosourea breakdown product, 2-chloroethylisocyanate. *Cancer Res.* **34**, 398–402.

KARRAN, P. (1985). Possible depletion of a DNA repair enzyme in human lymphoma cells by subversive repair. *Proc. natn. Acad. Sci. U.S.A.* **82**, 5285–5289.

KARRAN, P. & MARINUS, M. G. (1982). Mismatch correction at O^6-methylguanine residues in *E. coli* DNA. *Nature, Lond.* **296**, 868–869.

KARRAN, P., STEVENS, S. & SEDGWICK, B. (1982). The adaptive response to alkylating agents: the removal of O^6-methylguanine from DNA is not dependent on DNA polymerase I. *Mutat. Res.* **104**, 67–73.

KARRAN, P. & WILLIAMS, S. A. (1985). The cytotoxic and mutagenic effects of alkylating agents on human lymphoid cells are caused by different DNA lesions. *Carcinogenesis* **6**, 789–792.

KOHN, K. W. (1977). Interstrand cross-linking of DNA by 1,3-bis-(2-chloroethyl)-1-nitrosourea and other 1-(2-haloethyl)-1-nitrosoureas. *Cancer Res.* **37**, 1450–1454.

LACKS, S., DUNN, J. J. & GREENBERG, B. (1982). Identification of base mismatches recognized by the heteroduplex-DNA-repair system of *S. pneumoniae*. *Cell* **31**, 327–336.

LAI, C. & NATHANS, D. (1975). A map of temperature-sensitive mutants of simian virus 40. *Virology* **66**, 70–81.

LARSON, K., SAHM, J., SHENKAR, R. & STRAUSS, B. (1985). Methylation-induced blocks to *in vitro* DNA replication. *Mutat. Res.* **150**, 77–84.

LAWLEY, P. D. (1976). Carcinogenesis by alkylating agents. In *Chemical Carcinogens*, ACS Monograph 173 (ed. C. E. Searle), pp. 83–244. Washington, DC: Am. Chem. Soc.

LAWLEY, P. D., ORR, D. J. & JARMAN, M. (1975). Isolation and identification of products from alkylation of nucleic acids: ethyl- and isopropyl-purines. *Biochem. J.* **145**, 73–84.

LAWLEY, P. C. & THATCHER, C. J. (1970). Methylation of deoxyribonucleic acid in cultured mammalian cells by N-methyl-N'-nitro-N-nitrosoguanidine. *Biochem. J.* **116**, 693–707.

LEFEVRE, J. C., GASC, A. M., BURGER, A. C., MOSTACHFI, P. & SICARD, M. (1984). Hyperrecombination at a specific DNA sequence in pneumococcal transformation. *Proc. natn. Acad. Sci. U.S.A.* **81**, 5184–5188.

LIEB, M. (1985). Recombination in the lambda repressor gene: evidence that very short patch (VSP) mismatch correction restores a specific sequence. *Molec. gen. Genet.* **199**, 465–470.

LOVELESS, A. (1969). Possible relevance of O-6 alkylation of deoxyguanosine to the mutagenicity and carcinogenicity of nitrosamines and nitrosamides. *Nature, Lond.* **223**, 206–207.

MILLER, L., COOKE, B. & FRIED, M. (1976). Fate of mismatched base-pair regions in polyoma heteroduplex RNA during infection of mouse cells. *Proc. natn. Acad. Sci. U.S.A.* **73**, 3073–3077.

SAMSON, L. & CAIRNS, J. (1977). A new pathway for RNA repair in *Escherichia coli*. *Nature, Lond.* **267**, 281–282.

SASAKI, M. S. (1977). Role of DNA repair in the susceptibility to chromosome breakage and cell killing in cultured human fibroblasts. In *Biochemistry of Cutaneous Epidermal Differentiation* (ed. M. Seiji & I. A. Bernstein), pp. 167–180. Tokyo: University of Tokyo Press.

SCUDIERO, D. A. (1980). Decreased repair synthesis and colony forming ability of ataxia telangiectasia fibroblast cell strains treated with N-methyl-N'-nitro-N-nitrosoguanidine. *Cancer Res.* **40**, 984–990.

SCUDIERO, D. A., MEYER, S. A., CLATTERBUCK, B. E., MATTERN, M. R., ZIOLKOWSKI, C. H. J. & DAY, R. S. III (1984a). Relationship of DNA repair phenotypes of human fibroblast and tumor strains to killing by N-methyl-N'-nitro-N-nitrosoguanidine. *Cancer Res.* **44**, 961–969.

SCUDIERO, D. A., MEYER, S. A., CLATTERBUCK, B. E., MATTERN, M. R., ZIOLKOWSKI, C. H. J. & DAY, R. S. III (1984b). Sensitivity of human cell strains having different abilities to repair O^6-methylguanine in DNA to inactivation by alkylating agents including chloroethylnitrosoureas. *Cancer Res.* **44**, 2467–2474.

SCUDIERO, D. A., MEYER, S. A., CLATTERBUCK, B. E., TARONE, R. E. & ROBBINS, J. H. (1981). Hypersensitivity to N-methyl-N'-nitro-N-nitrosoguanidine in fibroblasts from patients with Huntington disease, familial dysautonomia, and other primary neurological degenerations. *Proc. natn. Acad. Sci. U.S.A.* **78**, 6451–6455.

SEDGWICK, B. & ROBINS, P. (1980). Isolation of mutants of *Escherichia coli* with increased resistance to alkylating agents: mutants deficient in thiols and mutants constitutive for the adaptive response. *Molec. gen. Genet.* **180**, 85–90.

SKLAR, R. & STRAUSS, B. (1980). Role of the *uvrE* gene product and of inducible O^6-methylguanine removal in the induction of mutations by N-methyl-N'-nitro-N-nitroso-guanidine. *J. molec. Biol.* **143**, 343–362.

SKLAR, R. & STRAUSS, B. (1981). Removal of O^6-methylguanine from DNA of normal and xeroderma pigmentosum-derived lymphoblastoid lines. *Nature, Lond.* **289**, 417–419.

SNOW, E. T., FOOTE, R. S. & MITRA, S. (1984). Base-pairing properties of O6-methylguanine in template DNA during in vitro DNA replication. *J. biol. Chem.* **259**, 8095–8100.

SWENSON, D. H. & LAWLEY, P. D. (1978). Alkylation of deoxyribonucleic acid by carcinogens dimethyl sulfate, ethyl methanesulfonate, N-ethyl-N-nitrosourea and N-methyl-N-nitrosourea. *Biochem. J.* **171**, 575–587.

TONG, W. P., KIRK, M. C. & LUDLUM, D. B. (1982). Formation of the crosslink 1-[N^3-deoxycytidyl],2-[N^1-deoxyguanosinyl]ethane in DNA treated with N,N'-bis(2-chloroethyl)-N-nitrosourea. *Cancer Res.* **42**, 3102–3105.

WAGNER, R. JR & MESELSON, M. (1976). Repair tracts in mismatched DNA heteroduplexes. *Proc. natn. Acad. Sci. U.S.A.* **73**, 4135–4139.

WAKE, C. T. & WILSON, J. H. (1980). Defined oligomeric SV40 DNA: a sensitive probe of general recombination in somatic cells. *Cell* **21**, 141–148.

WARREN, W. & LAWLEY, P. D. (1980). The removal of alkylation products from the DNA of *Escherichia coli* cells treated with the carcinogens N-ethyl-N-nitrosourea and N-methyl-N-nitrosourea: influence of growth conditions and DNA repair defects. *Carcinogenesis* **1**, 24–78.

WATATANI, M., IKENAGA, M., HATANAKA, T., KINUTA, M., TAKAI, S., MORI, T. & KONDO, S. (1985). Analysis of N-methyl-N'-nitro-N-nitrosoguanidine (MNNG)-induced DNA damage in tumor cells strains from Japanese patients and demonstration of MNNG hypersensitivity of Mer$^-$ xenografts in athymic nude mice. *Carcinogenesis* **6**, 549–553.

WOLFF, S., RODIN, B. & CLEAVER, J. E. (1977). Sister chromatid exchanges induced by mutagenic carcinogens in normal and xeroderma pigmentosum cells. *Nature, Lond.* **265**, 347–349.

YAROSH, D. B., FOOTE, R. S., MITRA, S. & DAY, R. S. III (1983). Repair of O^6-methylguanine in DNA by demethylation is lacking in Mer⁻ human tumor cell strains. *Carcinogenesis* **4**, 199–205.

YAROSH, D. B., FORNACE, A. & DAY, R. S. III (1985). Repair of O^4-methylthymine and methyl phosphotriesters in DNA by human O^6-alkylguanine alkyltransferase. *Carcinogenesis* **6**, 949–953.

YAROSH, D. B., RICE, M., DAY, R. S. III, FOOTE, R. S. & MITRA, S. (1984). O^6-methylguanine-DNA methyltransferase in human cells. *Mutat. Res.* **131**, 27–36.

The Company of Biologists Limited is a non-profit-making organization whose directors are active professional biologists. The Company, which was founded in 1925, is the owner and publisher of this and *The Journal of Experimental Biology* and *Development* (formerly *Journal of Embryology and Experimental Morphology*).

Journal of Cell Science is devoted to the study of cell organization. Papers will be published dealing with the structure and function of plant and animal cells and their extracellular products, and with such topics as cell growth and division, cell movements and interactions, and cell genetics. Accounts of advances in the relevant techniques will also be published. Contributions concerned with morphogenesis at the cellular and sub-cellular level will be acceptable, as will studies of micro-organisms and viruses, in so far as they are relevant to an understanding of cell organization. Theoretical articles and occasional review articles will be published.

Subscriptions

Journal of Cell Science will be published 13 times in 1987 in the form of 2 volumes, each of 5 parts, and 3 Supplements. The subscription price of volumes 87–88 plus Supplements 6–8 is £210.00 (USA and Canada, US $525.00; Japan, £235.00) post free. Individual volumes may be purchased at £21.00 (USA and Canada, US $55.00) each, plus postage. Supplements may also be purchased individually – prices on application to the Biochemical Society Book Depot. Orders for 1987 may be sent to any bookseller or subscription agent, or to The Biochemical Society Book Depot, PO Box 32, Commerce Way, Colchester CO2 8HP, UK. Copies of the journal for subscribers in the USA and Canada are sent by air to New York for delivery with the minimum delay. Second class postage paid at Rahway, NJ, and at additional mailing offices. Postmaster, send address corrections to: Journal of Cell Science, c/o Mercury Airfreight International Inc., 10B Englehard Avenue, Avenel, New Jersey 07001, USA.

Back numbers of the *Journal of Cell Science* may be ordered through The Biochemical Society Book Depot. This journal is the successor to the *Quarterly Journal of Microscopical Science*, back numbers of which are obtainable from Messrs William Dawson & Sons.

Copyright and reproduction

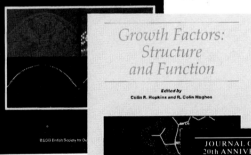